STEEL AWAY

A Guidebook to the
World of Steel Sailboats

LeCain W. Smith / Sheila Moir

Illustrations by Gué Pilon

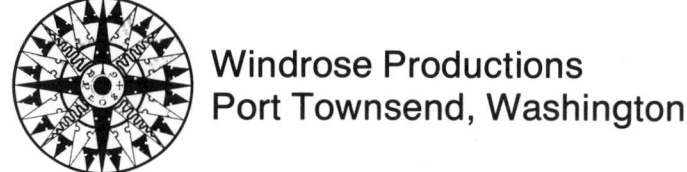

Windrose Productions
Port Townsend, Washington

To those who sail in the spirit of peace

The findings detailed in this book reflect the authors' own opinions and research. The authors take no responsibility for the use or misuse of the information contained herein.

Windrose Productions, P.O. Box 619, Port Townsend, WA 98368

Published 1986. Printed in the United States of America

94   7

ISBN 0-9615508-0-5

Contents

Acknowledgements

Books—at least books the size of *Steel Away*—have a way of turning into something of a community effort. Or perhaps a community grows up around them through the writing, consulting, research, and production that they require. We feel privileged to have been given the opportunity of working with the people that this project attracted.

Right at the very top of our thank-you list are Cindy Wacker, Lee Ehrheart, and Gué Pilon. Cindy, who designed the book and carried the major share of production, taught us how a professional works and became a dear friend in the process. To her credit goes the laying down of a third of a mile of border tape. Lee took valuable time away from his busy Havørn Marine Services to review and comment on the entire manuscript. In creating the wonderful dragon illustrations, Gué helped to provide some much-needed inspiration; her technical illustrations are exactly what we wanted: elegant and informative.

We want to recognize the valiant effort of Helen Byers, our copy editor, as she struggled with the nautical vocabulary, incidentally coming up with a great definition of "athwartship:" "Is that the opposite of courtship?" Our proofreaders, Tom Lemmons, Peter Johnson, and Pam Gaskins, also deserve much thanks for their fine-tooth-comb work. We appreciate Lisa Holloway's jumping in on the computer keyboard when we needed her most. We're very glad that the Port Townsend Library and the Washington State Inter-Library Loan System exist. We were able to get most of the research materials we needed through them without leaving home.

Special thanks must go to George Shearer, Cindy Wolpin, and Lynn Anju at Graphiti both for access to equipment and for their support and advice. We are especially grateful that George is able to sleep through the noise of a typesetter running all night. Thank you also to Roger Hagen and John Newsome at the Word Processor Store for getting us started in the high-tech world of instant corrections, and to Tom Rehder and Max Moon at Advertising Services for helping us to get the cover we wanted.

We greatly appreciate the information provided by all the designers and builders we queried, but the contributions of three people need special words of praise. Not only did designer John Simpson and the partners in Waterline Yachts, Wally Horniak and Ed Rutherford, put up with constant questions and long phone calls, but they also designed and built us the most beautiful hull in the world.

We are particularly grateful to the following people who reviewed materials for technical and nautical accuracy: Stewart Beaubien of New Dungeness Boat Co., Bill Campbell, Sheridan Crooks, David Disney of Solea Marine Enterprises, Dick Forsythe, Lowell Haskins, Carol Hasse and Nora Petrich of Port Townsend Sails, Doug Knight of Sierra Yachtwerks, Peter Langley of Port Townsend Foundry, Bob Maginnis, Joe Pence, Jr. of Pence Marine, Rick Proctor of Cruising Equipment Co., Hal Sweren of American Ocean Services, Hank Tjemsland, Richard Walcome of New Found Metals, Daryl Walker, Declan Wescott, and designer Charles Wittholz.

We also appreciate the support and understanding of our friends, who were always willing to believe us when we refused yet another dinner invitation with the muttered words, "It's almost finished."

And thanks to the members of our families, both those who are with us and those who are sailing through the stars: you gave us life, you gave us support, and you gave us the wide world with its vast and glorious oceans.

—Introduction—

What is a guidebook? It's a volume about the virtues of planning ahead so that you have the time and information to choose correctly. It's a collection of ideas with the final decisions left up to you. It's a list of everything you'll need to create a comfortable home on the high seas.

It's a "what-to" book, rather than a "how-to" book that simply gives you directions. There's a special kind of creativity that flares up when a sailor takes a boat and turns it into a dream boat. But this creativity only seems to be possible when knowledge and understanding are already present.

We have to confess that a little "how-to" snuck in. It's impossible to talk about steel boats, and especially modern steel boats, without delving into the new design and building techniques that are used to turn out the beautiful yachts presently afloat.

Whether you're an armchair dreamer, an intermediate adventurer, or a genuine salty dog, we hope that this guidebook has something for you. The emphasis is on providing information to help anyone organize a logical plan to obtain and outfit a steel boat. Since the internal organization of the book is in approximately the same order in which you'd put a cruising sailboat together, you can pick it up at any stage. If you're building a complete boat yourself, most of the decisions you'll have to make are outlined and discussed. If you're having a boat built, you'll be able to understand what the designer and builder are talking about, so that you can participate more effectively in the process. If you're already designing or building steel boats, there should be some food for thought.

It was the Industrial Revolution that gave us steel, but today's revolution is in marine technology. New formulations of paint offer incredible corrosion resistance for steel hulls. Improved welding techniques and equipment allow lighter scantlings to be used in constructing steel yachts that can outperform and outlast their forerunners. At the same time, interest in the traditional marine trades like foundry work is increasing. Blending technology and the traditional wisdom of the sea is the challenge in outfitting a steel cruiser.

Outfitting a boat involves making a series of decisions about what kinds of materials and joinery to use. These choices are especially important on a steel boat, because many of the traditional materials and installation methods are not compatible with steel's requirements for protection from corrosion. There are so many products available to mariners today that it's important to understand which are appropriate for every system of the boat. In each of the chapters on boat systems, we will be focusing on the pro's and cons of the various materials. The choices are here, but you decide exactly what you need.

Cost is always an issue when a major expenditure is planned. The appendix on Material Costs is an excellent planning and budgeting tool that challenges you to beat the lowest prices listed.

When it comes to outfitting your dream boat, use and lifestyle are what count. And everyone has a different dream. Ours is a center-cockpit ketch with a round hull, which is equipped as a comfortable, but simple, live-aboard home for world cruising. If someone finds water desalination units or electric dishwashers missing from the list of "basics," we're sorry, but that was *our* choice.

Another choice we had to make was what to call this creation of steel and wood and plastic and paint and wire and rope that we're dissecting here. We chose not to decide, since, frankly, we needed as many different words as we could find for the central topic of this book. The term "yacht" has unfortunate connotations of wealthy characters cruising a Sound, sipping a dacquiri delivered by a white-jacketed steward. But "yacht" also means a beautiful, well-cared-for boat with her sails glowing in the reflected sunset. "Cruiser" might make some people think about power boats, but it's a word that encompasses the notion of living and traveling onboard a sailing home. "Boat" is simple and useful, and "vessel" adds a few tons of dignity to any discussion.

We are perhaps proudest of the Directory of Designers and Builders Working in Steel that is part of *Steel Away*. It's the first-ever attempt to provide a list of professionals working in the field. We hope that it serves its dual purpose: to become a resource for sailors who want boats designed and built and to recognize those people who are creating boats that are so beautiful and seaworthy that they shiver your timbers.

This guidebook is not the final word on steel boats. Steel is just now coming of age for the cruising yacht, and the final word is many years away. There are still too many questions to be answered and too much research to be carried out at sea. We'll do our best to further the gathering of knowledge, because we've seen the writing on the wall: STEEL AWAY!

A fine steel hull plowing the seas is a fair sight for any eyes—the Endurance 44, *designed by Peter Ibold.*
Photo by Roger Smith-Cowes, courtesy of the designer

Chapter 1

Why Choose Steel

People own boats for many reasons. Some like to make occasional offshore passages. Others are content with a day sail or an overnight adventure. Racing thrills some sailors. Then there are the cruisers, those people who live and work and travel aboard their boats. We who choose the lifestyle of the sea want boats that can stand up to all the moods of the ocean, from gales to zephyrs. Selecting the right hull material can make a tremendous difference, no matter how the boat will be used.

Many designs have lines and layouts that assure comfortable cruising. But what hull material is right? It's the one that produces the safest, most comfortable boat, a vessel that performs well and is affordable to build and maintain. It's steel. The boat may be finished to yachty standards or may look more like it carries cargo between tropical islands: a steel hull can combine the strength of a work boat with the beauty of a yacht.

Over the years, sailors have come to agree on the qualities that make a hull good for offshore cruising. At the top of the list are strength, safety, and performance. Design plays a major part in determining the boat's ability to cope with the demands placed on it by an active cruising life. But the hull material can work for or against the designer and owner. The material chosen must be accessible, not too expensive, and relatively easily worked without posing excessive health hazards. Construc-

tion costs, including both materials and labor, must be reasonable, whether the yacht is built by a professional or in your own backyard. Proper tooling, building techniques, and skilled workmanship are required to produce a cruising hull. Of course the hull is only part of the whole boat, and the material of which it's constructed must be compatible with the materials used in the other systems and must allow for proper joinery and installation. Finally, the hull must resist corrosion and the stresses imposed on it by wind and sea.

Obviously, hull materials can be compared according to how well they measure up to these criteria. Table 1-1 makes that sort of comparison. Steel, aluminum, fiberglass, wood, and cold-molded wood are rated on their performance in each particular area. These five materials were chosen because they are the most realistic hull choices today. A decade ago, there were many ferrocement hulls being built, but their popularity has waned because of problems with construction and maintenance. Other materials, such as stainless steel, cupronickel, leather, paper, reeds, and hides, have been used but are impractical, due either to high cost or lack of strength.

For much of recorded history, iron has played a role in shipbuilding, from fasteners and fittings to the sheathing of ironclad warships. It was the Industrial Revolution and the introduction of new processes that brought

3

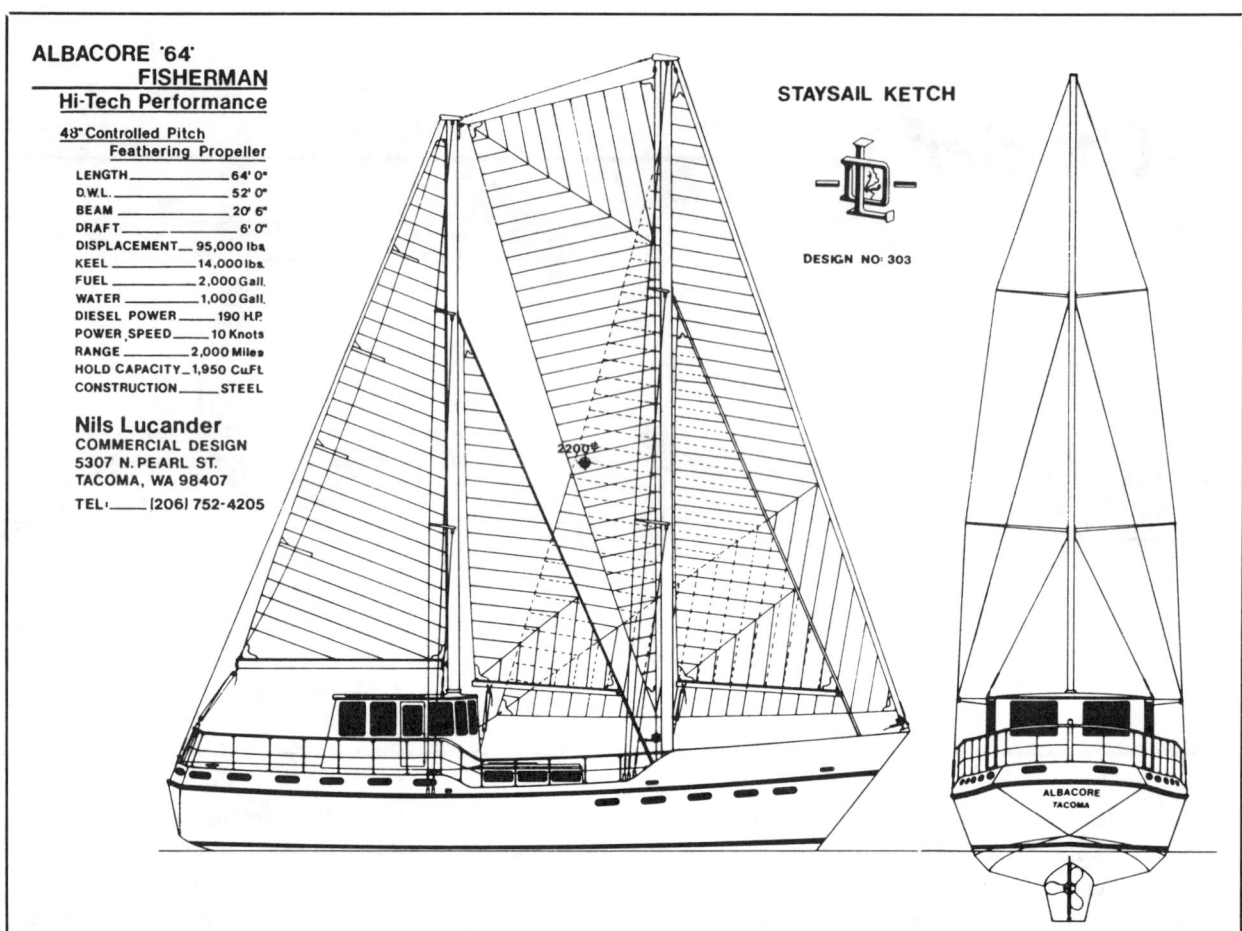

Fig. 1-1. *Steel workboats can be beautiful as well as functional.*

Courtesy of Nils Lucander.

Table 1-1. A COMPARISON OF HULL MATERIALS

Rating Scale: 1 (poor) to 10 (excellent)

	Steel	Aluminum	Fiberglass	Wood	Cold Molding
Design Limits	7	8	9	8	10
Comfort	10	10	10	10	10
Strength	10	7	5	6	6
Weight	6	8 10 (+2)	9	7	10
Watertight and Dry	10	10	9	7	10
Ease of Construction	8	7	8	6	7
Hazards	7	9	6	8	5
Cost	9	6 8 (+2)	10	5	7
Ease of Repair and Alteration	8 9	6 8 (+2)	7	7	6
Life Expectancy	9 8	8 10 (+2)	7	6	9
Safety at Sea	10	7 10 (+3)	5	5	7
TOTALS	94	86	85	75	87

+ 11 97

Note: *These ratings are based on the author's opinions. Builders and designers may disagree on some points, depending on their experiences.*

down the cost of steel plate so that it was economical to build steel-hulled ships for carrying passengers and cargo.

Once long-distance cruising in small boats was popularized by men like Slocum and Herreschoff, different countries began producing different types of cruising yachts. In America, for a while wood was plentiful, and, while steel was used for cargo vessels, the pleasure boat was crafted of wood. However, in Holland and Germany, wood was scarce, and steel was quickly adopted for use in smaller craft. When fiberglass was introduced after World War II, the U.S., with its fondness for new technology and easy profits, began to build its yachting hulls primarily of this material. The Dutch just continued to improve their ability to build small boats of steel. However, in recent years, sparked partly by the work of Thomas E. Colvin and Bruce Roberts, American designers and builders have recognized the potential of small steel ocean cruisers and have refined steel construction techniques.

Aluminum boats, like steel, are becoming more and more popular, especially in the racing world; they are also used as commercial fishing vessels. Aluminum construction has become easier and less expensive in recent years, partly because of improved welding methods. There are many different types of aluminum alloys (see Chapter 2), and the successful use of aluminum for a hull lies mostly in the correct choice of alloys, although construction methods are also important.

The majority of today's small sailing boats are constructed of fiberglass, also referred to as FRP (fiberglass-reinforced plastic) or GRP (glass-reinforced plastic). This construction method combines an adhesive (usually polyester resin) with roving, mat, or cloth of woven fiberglass strands (although stronger polypropylene fibers are sometimes used). The cloth can be laid on a lightweight core material such as honeycomb plastic, foam, balsa wood, or cork. Although the price of petroleum products is rising, it seems that fiberglass hulls are going to be around for a while.

Wood's share of the market may be small, but its resurgence over the last decade seems to be holding strong. Wood is quite different from the other hull materials because it was once alive. Unlike steel and aluminum, whose properties can be tightly controlled in the manufacturing process, many of the qualities of a plank of wood depend on the tree from which it was cut. There are also many types of traditional plank-on-frame wood construction: carvel, lapstrake, strip plank, seam batten, and multiple diagonal.

Cold molding is a building method that seems to be growing in popularity, although its name is not very accurate. A better term would be "epoxy laminate." There are many different lamination methods (the West System is the best known of these), but most types use epoxy glues to laminate thin wood strips into a hull shape. In a sense, a cold-molded hull is high-quality plywood that conforms to a complex hull shape.

The successful use of any hull material depends on the design, the builder's skill, and the construction methods. These three things add many variables to any rating system. For example, fiberglass boats can have vastly different strength characteristics depending on the lay-up and the type of core material used. It's also impossible to predict the kind of use and abuse that a hull will experience over the years. Sound vessels can be built of many materials, but when their qualities are compared side by side, you'll find that steel gets the best rating for overall performance.

DESIGN LIMITS

The extent to which the material can or cannot be molded into complex shapes to produce a fair hull. The shape of a hull depends on whether or not compound curves are contained in its profile and body plan. A round hull contains many of these compound curves, while a chine hull is shaped instead by butting flat sections together at different angles. Some people object to chine hulls as unattractive and think that the turbulence created by the chines affects performance. The beauty of a boat is a matter of personal taste and really can't be argued, although the sweet lines of a round hull are certainly pleasing to the eye and increase the resale value of the boat. The motion of round-hulled sailboats seems more comfortable, so they are are easier to handle. Of course chine hulls can be fine, able performance cruisers, as the many chine-hull designs testify. Although both chine and round hulls can be built of all hull materials, the bending characteristics of each material do influence the shapes that can be constructed easily.

Steel is a stiff material—it bends well, but it is hard to bend. Therefore it is difficult, especially for novices, to fabricate into compound shapes. Most older steel hull designs use chine construction, since these hulls are easier to plate. However, by employing molded-radius sections, conically developed plate, good tooling, and rolling, cold bending, hammering, and heating techniques, the compound shapes contained in a round hull can be fabricated with only a little more effort than a chine hull.

The real building challenge is obtaining a *fair* round hull (or, for that matter, a fair chine hull) that doesn't need any filler to smooth out the plate. A thorough knowledge of steel—how it bends, how it reacts to heat, how much you can ask of it—is only the first requirement. Proper design, framing, and welding sequence are needed to prevent distortion, which can leave a hull looking like an old battleship with wavy, dished plates between each frame. Dutch builders have been turning out beautiful round hulls for many years, and, like the artisans who built the legendary wooden hulls, the new breed of steel boatbuilders are showing that round steel hulls can be as smooth and fair as any fiberglass boat.

Fairness can be hard to achieve with any hull material, and filler or fairing compound is commonly used on both wood and fiberglass boats. If necessary, a steel hull can be faired with good epoxy filler, but its use is best avoided, since the filler can lose adhesion and flake off. Once the filler begins to let go, the only real solu-tion is to sandblast the boat and start over—an expensive proposition.

Aluminum. Since aluminum is neither as stiff nor as heavy as steel, it is more easily bent into compound shapes. Distortion during welding is also less of a problem since aluminum transfers more heat away from the weld zone to the surrounding plate. The special welding required also produces less heat. But, like steel, aluminum will take on a dished look if improperly welded. Most aluminum hulls are built with chine construction, although round bottoms are certainly feasible.

Fiberglass. Because fiberglass hulls are built of very flexible cloth and mat laid over a mold, this material has the fewest design limitations. The mold can be any shape, although excessive curvature may affect the boat's performance or safety. Certain sharp or stressed areas may also eventually delaminate.

Wood. Different types of wood have different bending qualities, and unusual hull shapes can be achieved by using special woods. However, no wood can be bent beyond a certain point, even when steam is used to assist

Fig. 1-2. *This 35-footer shows the level of fairness that can be achieved on a steel hull without using filler.*

Courtesy of W.H. Schwarz

6

Fig. 1–3. *Grahame Shannon's original* Amazon *design combines a radiused upper chine with a hard lower chine to produce a beautiful steel hull.*

the bending, so it has some practical limitations. Many shapes can be formed by joining small pieces of wood, but this means extra work for the builder. Unlike planks, plywood is very difficult to bend in tight or compound curves without cracking, so chine shapes are generally used in plywood construction. Plywood is even more limited than steel in its bending characteristics.

Cold molding. Most complex curves are fairly easy to shape using the cold-molding process, since the thin veneer strips which make up the laminations are light and easy to bend. In fact, these hulls are known for their fair, smooth finishes, as long as the builder takes time to make a fair mold before lamination begins.

COMFORT

How easy the hull is to live in, especially in terms of space, warmth, and acceptable noise levels. Comfort is a personal issue: what's comfortable for one person may be unacceptable to another. In general, though, a long-distance cruising boat should have as much usable space as possible. Easy living depends more on design than on material, and certain designs are easier to live with than others. Comfort must sometimes be compromised a bit for the sake of performance, but in the hands of a good designer, such compromises are rarely noticeable. Insulation is required by all hull materials (with the possible exception of wood) if you want to be comfortable.

Steel is often thought of as a cold, hard, insensitive substance. Well, it is. That's what makes it so suitable as a hull material. The thin steel plate that is used does transmit temperature changes and noise, but when the boat is properly insulated, it's as warm and cozy and quiet as any hull can be. All hulls are noisy as they pound through the seas, the noises are just different. In a steel boat, you may be able to hear the dolphins talking below you. There will generally be plenty of room below on a steel boat because the thin steel plate has very high panel strength, so widely spaced framing stock of small dimensions can be used. An interior that is pleasing to the eye and comfortable for the body is easily obtained in a steel hull, since any type of woodwork can be attached to tabs or studs welded into the hull during construction or to the frames themselves.

Aluminum. Since aluminum is not as stiff as steel, heavier frames spaced more closely are required, so there will be a bit less interior space. Like any metal boat, an aluminum hull has its own distinct noise when running in a seaway, although it does absorb sound better than steel. Insulation will surely be needed if the boat is afloat in cold water.

Fiberglass. Because fiberglass hulls are built on a mold, they are essentially constructed without frames. Instead, the bulkheads are important structural members, and the interior must be designed around them. Some lightly built fiberglass hulls can flex and vibrate heavily when underway, and the deck may give off an irritating squeak where it is joined to the hull. In the northern latitudes, the relatively thin layer of fiberglass will need insulation.

Wood. Wood is well known for its warmth and softness, and wooden hulls are commonly built without insulation, although a ceiling that provides an insulating effect is often fitted in the cabin. However, the large frames and thick planks that must be used for wood hulls often decrease the amount of living space below. The creaks and groans of a wood boat are probably the most romantic of all sea sounds, although if the hull is under stress, the sounds may only make you nervous.

Cold Molding. Cold-molded hulls, like fiberglass ones, are commonly constructed without frames, but the laminations can be made stronger and stiffer than fiberglass, so fewer structural bulkheads are required. This construction method produces the boat with the most interior living space. However, it will also need to be insulated to keep out sound and cold.

STRENGTH

The ability to withstand the various stresses exerted on the hull material. The environment of wind and water in which a cruising boat "lives" exerts physical forces on the hull, and these forces cause stresses. The stresses, in turn, cause strains and deformation in the hull material. (If you're interested in the origin of words and phrases, here's the source of "stresses and strains.") Sometimes the stresses act together to produce different types of strains. It's a chain of events with your boat on the receiving end. The material used for a cruising hull must be strong enough to resist these strains.

The mechanical properties called "strength" are determined by the physical properties of a material—for example, grain structure, direction of fiber, flexibility. Materials are run through a battery of tests to determine their ability to withstand different types of stress. The types of strength that a material demonstrates make it more or less effective for particular uses.

Stresses can cause materials to deform, but the damage may not be permanent. If the material deforms elastically, it will return to its original shape after the stress is removed. Plastic deformation, on the other hand, permanently changes the shape of the material. The modulus of elasticity under a given load shows a material's ability to deform elastically; the higher this figure, the more stress can be applied without permanent deformation. This property is called the material's stiffness.

Of all the hull materials, steel is the stiffest, with a modulus of elasticity of 30×10^6. As steel deforms it becomes even stiffer, a phenomenon known as work-hardening. Different materials can only be as stiff as steel if thicker sections are used. The stiffness of a $1''$

piece of wood, $\frac{5}{8}''$ of ferrocement, and $\frac{1}{2}''$ of fiberglass are all about equal. Aluminum $\frac{3}{16}''$ thick is three times stiffer, while $\frac{5}{32}''$ steel is as much as eight times harder to deflect.

Both yield stress and tensile stress are caused by pulling forces. If the force applied surpasses the yield strength, deformation becomes plastic. If the force exceeds the tensile strength, the material will actually tear apart. A material which has a good spread between yield and tensile strength will warn you by bending before it breaks. The ability of a material to deform without rupturing is called "ductility."

The type of steel plate that would be used on the average 40′ boat has a yield point of 36,000–42,000 psi (pounds per square inch), about half its ultimate tensile strength, which is 60,000–70,000 psi. Therefore, it may dent or deform, but rarely will tear. In fact, you won't often hear of a steel hull breaking up. The weld zone is even stronger than the plate surrounding it. Cast iron, on the other hand, is brittle and fails rapidly. Many grades of stainless steel have higher tensile strength than plain carbon steel, but they also rupture without much yielding, and therefore they may prove to be unsafe. Even so, a few of these expensive hulls have been built.

In December 1982, a number of sailboats were anchored off the beach at Cabo San Lucas on the Baja Peninsula of Mexico. A sudden storm came up, and the high wind and waves piled 26 boats onto the beach. Only a few hulls survived this ordeal, and *Joshua,* Bernard Moitessier's steel ketch, was one. A couple of fiberglass boats were driven up high on the beach and made out okay, but the rest were smashed into toothpicks and splinters, including several that had the misfortune of landing on top of *Joshua. Joshua* was pulled off the beach and is still sailing under new ownership.

A material is tough if it can deform plastically at points of high stress concentration, like those caused by notches. A notch occurs anywhere there is an abrupt change in the section of the material—for example, at the scupper drains or hatches. Notches can also be voids in weld zones, panels, and laminations or sharp rather than rounded corners cut in the material. Very high stresses concentrate at these notches, so that the tensile load is increased locally. Brittle fracture, appearing as cracks, occurs at notches if the material is weak. Notch toughness measures the material's ability to resist brittle fracture; notch sensitivity describes the sensitivity of a material to abrupt changes in section.

Steel rates high in notch toughness and low in notch sensitivity. Thicker plate is more notch-sensitive than thin because different finishing temperatures are used during manufacturing. Incorrect joint design and welding cause the only problems. Notch toughness increases in curved, rolled sections (which is another point in favor of round bilges).

Compression strength refers to the material's ability to withstand crushing forces without buckling. Masts are the most susceptible to deformation by compression stress. Steel rates fairly high in compression tests, with a strength of 60,000 psi. Materials designed to carry loads, like cast iron, generally have high compression strength.

Shear stresses are caused by forces working to pull the material apart in opposite but roughly parallel directions, either vertically or horizontally. Bending stresses occur when these shear stresses place one surface in tension and the other in compression. These are the forces responsible for hogging (upper surface in compression) and sagging (lower surface in compression), especially on large ships. The shear strength of steel, at 23,000 psi, is a little lower than its yield point; however, it is higher than that of any other material and, more importantly, is strong enough.

The hardness of a material determines both its impact resistance and abrasion resistance. Impact resistance depends on surface hardness and describes the material's ability to withstand severe blows without failing. It is also related to ductility. The surface hardness also allows the material to resist abrasion without being scratched. Hardness is commonly judged by comparing the hardness of a material to the standards of Moh's Scale of Hardness. On this scale, fiberglass would be rated 1; diamond, 11; steel, 7. Steel has an impact resistance of 10,000 psi, which is high, and a steel surface can be struck with an axe without any damage. Try that on a fiberglass or wood boat.

Steel is the strongest hull material except for copper-nickel alloys, which are too expensive to be practical. Steel hulls are so strong that they can be trusted to survive against the hazards of the sea—ice jams, logs, freighters, reefs, gales, whales, flotsam, jetsam, a lee shore.

Aluminum. Although aluminum has a yield strength near that of steel, the spread between yield and ultimate tensile strength is not so great. These strengths vary greatly depending on the exact alloy used, and the 5000 and 6000 series are the types generally used for hull plating. Series 5000 can have yield strength ranging from 20,000–37,000 psi and a tensile strength between 23,000 and 47,000 psi. The heat-treated 6000 series is rated at a yield strength of 18,000–40,000 psi and a tensile strength of 33,000–45,000 psi. The round or oval extruded shape used for spars increases the strength of the 6000 series. Unlike steel, the weld zone is the weakest link in an aluminum hull, and it can rupture before the panel. The compression strength of aluminum is ap-

Fig. 1-4. *Rafting does more damage to docks than to hard steel hulls. No problem here for a large schooner designed by George Sutton or the smaller* Gazelle *by Thomas E. Colvin.*

9

proximately 32,000 psi, about three-quarters of its tensile strength. Its shear strength is also less than that of steel.

Aluminum has a lower modulus of elasticity (10×10^6) than steel, so it is not as stiff and is more liable to dent. Because aluminum has better corrosion resistance than steel, theoretically an aluminum hull could be constructed of thinner plate. But, because of its lower stiffness, thicker plate (or heavier framing) is needed. Aluminum is second only to steel in abrasion resistance, but it is common to see scratches and gouges on an aluminum hull.

Aluminum is more notch-sensitive than steel, and its notch toughness is about half that of steel. The designer may have to take special measures to relieve stress at the notches.

Fiberglass. The strength of fiberglass is particularly difficult to analyze because it depends on so many factors. The type of cloth, type of resin, cloth-to-resin ratio, core material, angle and direction of lay-up, lamination schedule, difference between hull and deck make-up, and production standards can all affect strength values. Up-to-date construction methods using good core materials, carbon fibers, high-quality resins, etc., can produce fairly strong hulls that are adequate for all types of cruising.

A higher glass-to-resin ratio increases the strength of fiberglass. A hull made of chopped mat with 25%–30% glass will have a tensile strength of 13,000–18,000 psi; one built with woven roving with 40%–50% glass has a tensile strength of 20,000–30,000 psi. The yield strength of fiberglass is quite close to its tensile strength, which means that fiberglass will rupture soon after it yields. If designed correctly, however, the skin thickness can be varied as needed for strength without abrupt changes that would cause notches. Repeated flexing, however, may cause brittle fractures. The shear strength

of fiberglass is also low. Compression strength is relatively good but inferior to that of steel.

When fiberglass was first being used for hulls, it was thought to have good ductility. Now that these hulls have been around long enough to be tested, problems are surfacing. As the polymer chains in the resins cure and become harder, the fiberglass becomes more brittle. Ultraviolet rays also contribute to increased brittleness. As the fiberglass ages, it slowly becomes more and more prone to brittle failure.

Fiberglass is only as strong as its laminations. Unfortunately, some of the polyester resins used on the early fiberglass boats, and even on recently built light production boats, are now beginning to delaminate, seriously diminishing the structural integrity of the hulls.

Fiberglass is very notch-sensitive, and its notch toughness is also very low. Stress concentrations, especially where bulkheads meet the hull, must be carefully designed out by spreading the stress across a larger area. Reinforcements may also be needed to disperse hard spots and stresses.

Fiberglass's modulus of elasticity is quite low (an average of 2.8×10^6), but fiberglass will readily flex and return to its original position as long as its yield strength is not exceeded. Impact resistance and abrasion resistance can also be low, and may be decreased further as the hull ages and becomes more brittle. A fiberglass hull could never take the beating a steel boat can sail away from.

Wood. The strength of wood varies greatly depending on the kind of wood and the actual construction methods used. In fact, strengths can vary in different parts of the ship and even within the same piece of wood. Wood has a distinct vertical grain produced by its annual rings, and its properties are measured in three different directions to this grain: longitudinal, radial, and tangential. Strength may vary in these three directions,

Table 1-2. COMPARATIVE STRENGTHS OF DIFFERENT MATERIALS

	Steel	Aluminum	Fiberglass	Wood	Cold Molding
Yield Strength (in psi)	36–42,000	18–40,000	10–15,000	12–20,000	12,000
Tensile Strength (in psi)	60–70,000	23–47,000	15–34,000	16–27,000	—
Compression Strength (in psi)	60,000	32,000	fair	2–13,000	good
Shear Strength (in psi)	23,000	17,000±	low	.7–3,000*	good
Modulus of Elasticity ($\times 10^6$)	30	10	2.8	.7–2.3	—
Hardness (Moh's Scale)	7	4	1	1–3	2

*unsupported, dry wood

and proper construction orients the grain in its strongest direction.

When talking about wood, tensile strength is called the modulus of rupture. It varies with different types of wood and describes the maximum load-carrying capacity parallel to the grain. Greenheart, one of the strongest woods, has a modulus of rupture of 9,400–25,500 psi; Douglas fir rates at approximately 8,000–12,000 psi; and oak at 8,300–15,200 psi. With fir planking on oak frames, the composite strength might be somewhere between 16,000–27,000 psi at the frame section. Different species of wood vary in "yield strength," but in most cases it is close to the modulus of rupture. Compared with that of steel, the strength of wood is low, even though other structural members such as deck beams and cabin add support to the hull assembly.

Wood flexes well, and by flexing is able to absorb some stress. Some woods are very resilient and will retain their shape even after repeated stresses—spruce has a high modulus of elasticity and is quite ductile. Other species, like cedar, are not stiff and will rupture more easily. As anyone who has ever tried to bend wood knows, wet wood flexes better than dry, but in a good design, the planks will not work much between the frames.

Compression strength in steel can be compared to the maximum crushing strength of wood parallel to the grain. It is generally about half of the modulus of rupture. When a boat rubs against a dock, not much force is needed to make the wood give a little, but a lot of compression is needed on the surface to crack the wood. Shear strength is measured parallel to the grain and is quite a bit lower than either compression or "tensile" strength. Hardness, which determines the wood's ability to resist local denting, varies greatly, but is generally less than half of compression strength. Impact resistance is also lower than steel.

Cold Molding. Strength figures for cold-molded hulls are even more difficult to find than those for fiberglass. The grain direction is not as critical as with plank-on-frame construction, since laminations with crossing wood grains make a very strong hull. However, the use of less-flexible wood can sometimes lower the breaking point of the lamination. The strength factors are consistent directionally, since the laminating method produces a monolithic hull. A well-constructed epoxy laminate will have better panel strength than a pywood one of the same scantlings. Many cold-molded boats are stiffer than fiberglass hulls of equivalent design, and the epoxy resin used for cold molding is less brittle than the polyester used in fiberglass. A cold-molded hull will also flex more before rupturing than a wooden hull.

WEIGHT

Weight depends on the density of the material in question, and it is usually compared on the basis of pounds per cubic inch or pounds per cubic foot. (In order to convert pounds per cubic inch to pounds per cubic foot, multiply the lbs. by 1748.4.) Most cruisers want either a moderate or a heavy displacement vessel to handle the extra load of gear, stores, etc., and to provide comfortable cruising performance.

Low carbon steel weighs 490 lbs. or 0.283 lbs./cu. in. The weight of steel hulls has long been considered a shortcoming, but this is only an important consideration for hulls under 35'. Some large steel vessels are even lighter than comparable wood hulls. Careful design to reduce plate thickness, scantlings, and the weight of the steel superstructure can produce a 40' cruiser that only weighs 4,000–7,000 pounds more than its fiberglass counterpart. A little extra weight in the keel (which is usually built with thicker plate) may also be considered a bonus, since it reduces the need for expensive ballast. Other factors, like hull shape, sail area, and underwater profile, help to counteract any weight problems in a steel cruising boat.

Fig. 1–5. *The* Snapper 28 *proves that small steel boats can perform well despite their weight.*
Courtesy of Nils Lucander.

The consistency of steel weights is a great help in design work. The only variations are slight and are caused by unevenness in the rolled plate created by the manufacturing process. The designer doesn't have to worry about different lamination methods or species of wood.

The strength-to-weight ratio is another way to compare hulls, and it is especially important for racing boats. Steel vessels have lower strength-to-weight ratios than aluminum or cold-molded boats, so someone interested in a racing hull would probably not be happy with steel.

The strength-to-weight ratio of steel can also be viewed in another way. There is a minimum plate thickness that must be used to produce a fair hull, since thinner plate will distort under the heat of welding. But the strength requirements for a hull under 90′ are actually less than that provided by this minimum plate thickness. Therefore, a small steel hull has a safety margin of strength in each pound of weight. This "extra" plate also helps prevent failure if the plate thickness is reduced by corrosion.

Aluminum. If the five hull materials were listed in order of weight, aluminum would fall in the middle, not far behind fiberglass. The 5000 series used for plating weighs .098 lb./cu. in. or 171 lbs./cu. ft. (about a third that of steel). Its lightness is one of the major assets of

aluminum, and it allows a hull increased speed, carrying capacity, and fuel economy. Aluminum is often used for racing hulls, where light weight is more a concern that it is for displacement ocean cruisers. Its strength-to-weight ratio is the best of all five materials.

Fiberglass is definitely a light hull material; in fact, it weighs less per cubic foot (90–110 lbs./cu. ft.) than any other material except certain cold-molded laminations. This lighter hull allows more weight for stores and ballast, and, like aluminum and cold molding, produces a faster boat that is easier to power through the water. Fiberglass cruisers also have good strength-to-weight ratios.

Wood. The weight of a wooden hull changes with the moisture content of the wood itself, its density, and the type of construction. The average density is about 35 lbs./cu. ft., and the overall range is from 10–65 lbs./cu. ft. Moisture content is generally discussed in terms of specific gravity, which is the average ratio of the density of wood to the density of water at 40°C in dry wood. Fir, a commonly used boat wood, weighs 32 lbs./cu. ft. with a specific gravity of .46 at a water content of 12%. However, the heavy framing and planking of traditional wood construction uses a lot of wood. A wooden hull is somewhat heavier than one of fiberglass or aluminum, but it is not much lighter than a steel hull.

Table 1-3. DISPLACEMENTS OF A RANDOM SELECTION OF CRUISING YACHTS BUILT IN DIFFERENT HULL MATERIALS.

Hull Material	Designer	Design Name	LWL	LOA	Beam	Draft	Displacement in lbs.
F.G.	Perry	*Tayana*	31′	36′8″	11′	5′8″	24,000
F.G.	Mason	*Mason 43*	31′3″	43′10″	12′3″	6′3″	25,000
Steel	Ted Brewer	*Kaiulani*	31′4″	37′	11′	5′0″	20,500
F.G.	Meumer	*Reliance*	31′5″	44′	11′8″	6′2″	28,000
F.G.	—	*Valiant*	31′8″	37′	11′6″	5′10″	17,000
Wood	Roberts	*Spray*	31′11″	40′	14′4″	4′2″	35,840
Wood	Atkin	*Ingrid*	32′	37′8″	11′7″	5′8″	25,000
F.G.	—	*Corbin*	32′	38′6″	12′1″	5′6″	22,800
Steel	Wallstrom	*Goderich*	32′	40′9″	12′7″	5′10″	23,600
Steel	Roberts	*Mauritius*	32′6″	43′3″	13′	5′	27,960
Steel	Ibold	*Endurance*	32′10″	44′	12′1″	6′1″	29,380
Steel	Shannon	*Pearl*	33′	38′	12′	5′6″	24,000
Steel	Colvin	*Gazelle*	33′	42′2″	11′4″	3′10″	18,168
Steel	Hundy	*Tahitian Bay*	33′2″	42′2″	12′6″	5′8″	31,000
F.G.	Crealock	*Westsail*	33′4″	42′	13′	5′8″	31,500
F.G.	—	*Cape Dory Yacht*	33′6″	45′2″	13′	6′3″	24,000
Steel	Brewer	*Verity*	33′8″	40′1″	11′9″	6′0″	22,950
Steel	Knocker	*Joshua*	34′3″	39′9″	12′	5′3″	24,000
F.G.	Huntingford	*Passport 42*	34′10″	41′9″	12′10″	6′4″	25,500
F.G.	Morgan	*Morgan 43*	35′4″	43′	13′6″	6′6″	23,500

Although wood construction does not have a high strength-to-weight ratio, it can be better than that of steel. Some woods like balsa have the best ratio of any material, but balsa is only practical in boatbuilding as core material in fiberglass construction.

Cold Molding. With today's construction techniques, cold-molded hulls can be turned out that are stronger and weigh even less than fiberglass. Use of the lighter softwoods can also decrease weight. One of the weight advantages of cold molding is that a great many frames are not required, since the laminations are inherently strong. The strength-to-weight ratio of cold-molded hulls is similar to but better than that of fiberglass boats, since their construction methods are similar, so these boats are excellent for racing.

WATERTIGHT AND DRY

The ability of a hull to remain watertight is related to three factors: homogeneity, porosity, and monolithic construction. A homogeneous material has the same structure throughout, and a hull which is monolithic is basically seamless. Porosity describes the makeup and mechanical defects, such as voids, pits, pockets, and holes, which allow the material to take in water.

Steel is by nature a homogeneous material, with the same strength and structure throughout. Therefore, there is no cracking or working to open up seams where water can come in. The porosity of steel depends on its internal structure. Mild steel, like most metals, is somewhat porous, but when it is properly coated, it should not absorb any water. A problem can arise, however, when there are large porous areas caused by poor welding techniques or defective steel.

Since the steel hull consists of plates welded together, and since a proper weld is stronger than the steel plate surrounding it, a steel hull is essentially one piece of metal. In other words, it is monolithic. The plate will break before a weld seam opens up, and both of these events are very unlikely.

Since the steel hull is homogeneous, non-porous, and monolithic, it is virtually watertight. Would you believe cobwebs in the bilge?

All hull materials are subject to sweating and condensation. Higher air temperatures allow the air to hold more water vapor before condensing, so condensation is seen more often in northern latitudes. Dryness is mostly controlled by heating from within, good ventilation, and insulating from without, and all three of these

controls are required on any boat. Painting the exterior of the hull a dark color will help prevent condensation because the hull will absorb heat from the sun and help keep the air temperature inside the boat at a higher level.

Aluminum, like steel, is homogeneous and monolithic, and probably matches steel's capacity to stay watertight and dry. Both will condense, given the right conditions, although aluminum sweats more than steel. Aluminum is also basically non-porous and is generally not painted, since a coating is not necessary for corrosion protection.

Fiberglass, like steel, is slightly porous. When determining the watertightness of fiberglass, both the type of resin used and the type of lay-up must be considered. Epoxy resins have superior abrasion resistance and absorb very little water, although polyester resin is less expensive, is easier to apply, and has good chemical and heat resistance. A fiberglass hull is basically homogeneous, although the weave patterns of the cloth can create some minor irregularities.

Wood is not a homogeneous material since it has grain, although plywood has somewhat equal grain in both directions. Since wood construction is not monolithic, it has many seams with a potential for leaking. The moisture in the interior of a wood vessel is higher than in other hulls in the same environment because more moisture (up to 12%) remains in the wood after it is considered "dry."

Cold Molding. Unlike wood boats built with plank-on-frame techniques, cold-molded hulls are monolithic and keep water out. If they are totally sealed, they can be considered non-porous. As mentioned above under *"Fiberglass,"* epoxy resins produce a strong bond and little shrinkage, yielding a higher lamination strength than when polyester resins are used.

EASE OF CONSTRUCTION

You won't find anyone who has built a boat willing to say that it's easy work. But if the hull material itself causes difficulties, it can mean added frustration for the home builder and extra time and expense for a professional yard. But no matter what the material, certain skills are necessary to work it successfully. Anyone starting out to build a boat needs to be able to read plans, do simple lofting, and work with basic hand tools. However, different materials also require other special skills if a quality product is going to be turned out.

How easily a material can be worked is called, not surprisingly, workability. This can be sudivided into machinability (the extent to which the material can be cut, bored, drilled, or shaped with tools) and malleability (the capacity of the material to be shaped by bending, rolling, or hammering). When discussing metals, weldability must also be considered: the ease with which the material can be welded and the effect that heating and cooling during welding will have on the material's internal structure. And, finally, we need to consider how easily the material can be fastened to itself and to other materials.

Steel is very malleable, although not as easily shaped as wood, and machining it is not difficult with the correct tools. Mild steel also displays good welding properties. If the size of the plate sections to be used is matched with the proper lifting tools, the steel bars and plates can be handled fairly easily, although you might want to pump a little iron in a weight room before you pump steel plate. Some newer designs take ease of handling into account and specify smaller plate sections that can be more easily handled.

For steel construction, the builder must know the basics of metallurgy, cutting and fitting techniques, lifting and dogging procedures, and, most important, proper welding sequence. Many schools teach basic welding techniques, and welding is easier to learn than woodworking. Many professional builders have developed tricks and special tools which allow them to produce fair hulls more efficiently; the amateur may have to take the long way around. And some of the work, like plate rolling and sandblasting, can be contracted out.

Aluminum. In the dimensions in which it is used for hull plating, aluminum's weight and flexibility make it fairly easy to handle and cut, and special lifting tools are usually not required. Aluminum can be welded more rapidly than steel, but aluminum welding is more difficult, and the welding preparation (the cleaning and fitting of the weld zone) is much more critical. A variety of shapes can be extruded (masts, for example), but the dies used for this specialized process are expensive. Aluminum and steel require about equal skill in the building process, although because of its difficulty aluminum welding requires more attention.

Fiberglass. Skill is required in building the mold for a fiberglass hull, but actually laying up the hull and grinding it smooth require more tolerance for itching and messes than skill. Because the mat or cloth used to construct fiberglass hulls is lightweight and very flexible, there are few real problems with the workability of the material.

Wood can be cut, drilled, and planed quite easily once the skills are acquired, although the fitting process is more involved than with other materials. Its workability depends on the moisture content: the drier the wood, the easier it is to work with hand tools, except, of course, for bending. It takes time and experience to learn all the ins and outs of wood construction, and the many types of conventional plank-on-frame construction challenge the builder to use the inherent strength of the wood properly.

Fig. 1–6. *The* Prospect of Whitby *prances along.*
Courtesy of Sparkman and Stephens.

Cold molding requires about the same skill level as fiberglass construction, although the lamination process might be considered more difficult. Because thin, light strips of wood are used, the construction materials are easy to work with and to secure in place. This method could become popular in parts of the world where quality plank-on-frame material is scarce.

HAZARDS

All types of construction can be dangerous, and standard safety precautions should always be followed.

However, whenever a construction method uses toxic chemicals, such as resins, glues, and paints, the builder must take extra measures to protect his or her health. It seems that each new "wonder glue" is more toxic than the one it replaces.

When working with steel, there are no toxic glues to deal with, but sparks, hot slag, and fumes are often present. The eyes can also be damaged by the flash of the welding arc. Proper body and eye protection is required: a welding helmet, leather chest protector, welding gloves, goggles for cutting and grinding, and proper footware. Because a welding machine uses high-voltage current, the area should always be kept dry and free of electrical hazards. Lifting the heavy plates and frames can damage your back if tools are not used when they are needed. Grinding produces fine dust particles, and a face mask will help keep them out of your lungs. A good protective suit and respirator are necessary for sandblasting and spray painting, especially epoxies and polyurethanes. When considering the entire process of building a steel boat, few hazards can be found. If you contract the blasting out, the biggest headache (or lung ache?) is eliminated.

Aluminum construction is even less hazardous than working with steel, since the plates are lighter, requiring less heavy lifting. Of course, the same eye and body protection is required, since the construction processes are similar. However, less grinding is needed on aluminum hulls.

Fiberglass. The solvents used in mixing fiberglass resins are usually very toxic. The skin must be protected to prevent rashes, and proper respiratory equipment must be used so that the vapors aren't inhaled. The chemical cleansers used on fiberglass hulls can also introduce toxins into the body. Proper protection is definitely a must during the lay-up and sanding or grinding operations.

Wood is used in the interior of almost every boat, no matter what the hull material. It is basically a nontoxic construction material, although some applied glues may be hazardous. The dangers of wood construction come with the use of large power tools. There are many boatbuilders who have sacrificed fingers to the great god Speed. Some woods also splinter more easily than others, and splinters can cause infections and loss of work time.

Cold molding also involves the use of toxic materials. Proper skin and respiratory protection from the epoxies is important, since they are carcinogenic. The dangers associated with power tools are fewer with cold molding than in conventional wood construction.

COST

It's the rare (and lucky) person who has an unlimited amount of money to spend on a boat. Boats are not cheap—buying one is like buying a house. If by choosing a particular material you can save some money on the hull, so much the better. Unfortunately, cost is one of the most difficult factors to compare, since it varies with hull material, geographic location, the builder's skill (and speed), required tooling, construction time, and wastage. And the hull itself is only a portion of the total cost of the vessel. Although the other parts of the boat will usually cost the same no matter what hull material is used, this is not necessarily true with steel. Parts of other boat systems, such as plumbing, electrics, or safety equipment, can be integrated with the hull to save money. Lifestyle, which dictates what gear is necessary, also has a great effect on the final cost of the boat. There is also the hidden cost of maintenance, which can be reduced by choosing a good design and proper construction methods.

In 1985, steel is the least expensive hull material, available for 16–25 cents per pound in the Pacific Northwest. Enough steel for a 40' hull would therefore cost between $4,000 and $7,000. Of course the cost of welding rod or wire, gas or electricity for the welding machine, and bracing material must be added in, but no nails, screws, glue, or resin are needed in the hull itself. Steel is perfect for one-off construction, since no jigs or molds are needed. Steel is also economical to use because there is only about 5–8% waste (this figure will be a bit higher for round hulls). Many pieces of scrap steel can be transformed into tools and fittings.

The tooling for steel construction does not need to be too elaborate, although the equipment used by professionals (for example, MIG welders and plasma cutters) will often allow them to turn out a better hull. However, the costs of owning and maintaining this equipment may be passed on to you. Basic equipment includes a welding machine, cutting machine, plate-moving and shaping equipment, and a grinder or two.

Professionals are available to do everything from building the hull to designing and installing electrics or plumbing. The availability and cost of professional labor varies greatly depending on location. In the U.S., marine welders charge between $8 and $30 an hour, with an average cost of $15–20 per hour. Although this rate is higher than builders in other materials might charge, a professional should be able to weld up a hull in a relatively short time, so the total labor cost will not be excessive. Sandblasting and painting are areas in which an investment in professional expertise will pay off, since special equipment and protective gear are needed for these operations.

Construction time depends largely on who builds the hull. A professional yard stays sharp by constantly building hulls, and it will obviously beat an amateur's time. A yard employing two or three people could weld up, blast, and prime a steel hull in 2 to 6 months, depending, of course, on how complicated the design is and how many extras are included. Since the construction time is so short, labor costs for steel hull and deck assemblies are lower than for hulls made of other materials, although some fiberglass production boats cost the same or less than steel. Naturally, an amateur doing his or her first boat will take longer to turn out perfect welds and fair plating. But, whether an amateur or professional does it, building quickly and cheaply doesn't always turn out a good hull. To build efficiently is the aim of most builders.

Although the cost of the hull itself can be lower if the boat is made from steel, the total cost of the boat may not be much lower if high-quality materials are used for the boat systems. However, substantial savings on fittings—stanchions, samson posts, deck eyes, bollards, chainplates, throughhulls, mooring gear, deck hardware—can be achieved, since they can be fabricated of scrap steel and welded to the deck or cabin. Of course, stainless fittings and hardware can also be welded to the deck, but the savings won't be as great.

There is one final way to save money if you build a steel boat: a fancy covered shelter is not necessary (although it's certainly a nice option if you can afford it). Weathering will not damage the steel before it is blasted, and, in fact, if the mill scale on the steel rusts loose, it will be easier to remove by sandblasting. However, if MIG welding is used, shelter from the wind will have to be provided.

Aluminum costs more than steel because the manufacturing process is more expensive. The price of aluminum varies in different parts of North America; in 1985, aluminum prices averaged $2.40/lb. in the Southeast, $2.00/lb. in the Northwest, and $1.70/lb. in Canada. The cost is often higher for a home builder since he or she isn't buying enough to get a quantity discount. Like steel, aluminum construction does not require jigs or molds, so building a one-off hull adds no extra expenses. As with steel, there is little waste.

Aluminum must be welded with either MIG or TIG equipment, so tooling up can be more expensive than for steel. Aluminum welding is a very specialized trade, and, if professional labor is used, the cost will be between $15–30 per hour. However, some aluminum boatbuilders have lowered their prices to stimulate the market. Other equipment will probably average out the same. Aluminum does not need to be sandblasted (although some etching is required), so no equipment or labor is required for this. Aluminum has more corrosion resistance than steel, so the paint systems that must be purchased and applied are not as complex or expensive. *← Bull!*

Table 1-4. CONSTRUCTION TIMES FOR DIFFERENT HULL MATERIALS

For the average 40′ yacht being built by two or three professionals, faired and ready for final coating. Lofting time is not included. These figures are only averages; the actual time to build a specific boat can vary immensely.

Aluminum	3–4 months
Steel	3–5 months
Fiberglass	4–6 months, excluding mold
Cold molded	4–8 months, excluding mold
Wood	8–14 months

Aluminum hulls can be built a little more quickly than steel, but the increase in building speed is minimal. MIG welding is quicker than stick welding, but this time savings is offset by lengthy weld preparation and precise cutting and fitting requirements. *← same with steel*

Unfortunately, aluminum is not compatible with galvanized and steel fittings, and the more-expensive stainless and aluminum types must be used. Welding stainless to aluminum may cause problems because the two materials react differently to the heat of welding. Aluminum is much more difficult to fabricate into fittings, and non-aluminum fittings generally must be bolted to the hull.

If a particular design that could be built in either steel or aluminum were built in steel, the hull and deck assembly would probably be 20–30% cheaper than if the same design were built in aluminum.

Fiberglass. Although the cost of fiberglass averages $2 a pound, that pound of fiberglass will cover a large area, making this the least-expensive hull material. However, the constantly rising cost of petroleum products will surely lead to increases in this material cost. Fiberglass hulls must be built over a mold, and the mold accounts for 50% of the price of the hull. Wastage runs between 10% and 15%, since the cutoffs are not reusable. There are no savings on boat systems, since manufactured stainless, galvanized, aluminum, or bronze fittings must be used.

Tooling for fiberglass construction is neither extensive nor expensive. Labor is also fairly inexpensive, since in most yards the low man (or woman) on the totem pole gets stuck with the messy, toxic fiberglass work. Of course, you get what you pay for at $4–8 per hour. Building time is to some extent controlled by the weather, since the resins must be applied within tight temperature and moisture ranges if they are to cure properly.

Fiberglass hulls are quite inexpensive when they are built as production hulls, since once the expensive mold is made, many boats can be laid up on it for only the cost of the materials and labor. Unfortunately, some production boats have gotten a bad name since the builders have skimped on the quality and quantity of materials.

Wood. The scarcity and rising cost of quality boat wood is making this hull material almost too expensive for any but wooden boat enthusiasts. Of course, good scroungers and yards that can buy quantities at a discount can bring down the total price. But wood construction generates a large amount of waste, from 25% to 30% after planing, sawing, and sanding to get correct dimensions and cutting off ends to get correct length. A great many metal fasteners and some jig material will also be needed to complete the hull. The total cost of the hull is highest in conventional wood construction.

Tooling for hull construction can be expensive, since many specialized hand and power tools are needed if the job is to be accomplished in a reasonable amount of time. However, there have been many fine wooden boats built with simple tools. The same tools are also used for interior joinery, so their cost can be spread out over both exterior and interior uses.

Building a wood hull often takes more time than any other method, because it requires drying the wood, lofting, assembling, and fairing. Wood construction is very labor-intensive, since fairness and hull integrity require very careful fitting, fairing, planing, and sanding. The wages of a professional wooden boatbuilder, although only $7–25 per hour, probably comprise a larger percentage of the total cost of the hull than do the wages of builders using other materials, because of the time

involved. For this reason, wood construction is more practical for the amateur builder. And wood is a versatile and enjoyable material with which to work.

Fittings for boat systems are also somewhat expensive since bronze or stainless fasteners and fittings should be used. Galvanized fasteners, though acceptable, have a shorter lifetime and can eventually bleed onto the finished hull, causing unsightly rust streaks.

Cold molding. The cost of cold-molded construction is somewhat less than that of conventional wood methods and often only a little more than that of fiberglass. The required thin strips of wood can be acquired much more easily than good boat wood and can be used with less waste. Fewer fasteners than with wood are needed but this savings is offset by the cost of epoxy. There are no appreciable savings on boats systems, and wastage runs between 10% and 15% (but can be as high as 20% if the strip plank system is used). Most cold-molded boats are built over a male or female mold, so there is that expense to consider too.

Tooling requirements for cold molding are similar to those for wood, but are not quite as extensive. A thickness planer and a good pneumatic staple gun will make the job easier.

Labor is a bit more expensive than for fiberglass, from $8–15 per hour, because a higher skill level is needed for the wood lamination. "Combat pay" may be appropriate for people having to work on a day-to-day basis with the dangerous epoxies.

EASE OF REPAIR AND ALTERATION

If a material is to be used successfully on a cruising vessel, repairs and alterations must be easy to make, and the needed material must be readily accessible in all parts of the world.

Because steel can be fabricated into many shapes by cutting and welding, it is easier to alter the hull, although proper welding sequence must be observed to avoid distortion. If the hull is damaged, it can be repaired simply by hammering out the dent or by welding up the hole or crack, even by inserting a new piece of steel if necessary. In fact, in an emergency, steel can even be welded underwater with special equipment. Repairs to a mild steel hull can be carried out in almost any part of the world because steel is easily accessible for a reasonable price in any fairly civilized country in the world, and welding is a fairly basic skill in any economy. In a pinch, even junkyard raids can turn up usable steel.

Aluminum. Hull-grade aluminum, on the other hand, may be difficult to find in out-of-the-way places. Even in the U.S., it is not always available in certain shapes. Although aluminum is easy to cut and fast to weld, a MIG or TIG welding unit and portable tent or tarp to shelter it from the wind will have to be carried along. If a professional is needed to do the repair welding, he or she may be difficult to locate. Anyone who owns an aluminum boat should be prepared to do some aluminum welding.

Fig. 1-7. *It's possible to do things with steel that you wouldn't dream of doing with another hull material. These flush steps are ingenious, but may lead to corrosion problems.*

Fiberglass and resins are generally accessible, but they are not found lying around foreign ports like steel. Claims for ease of repair and alteration have been somewhat exaggerated, but fiberglass is a fairly easy material to work with. However, in wet or emergency conditions, the temperature or moisture level may not allow resins to cure and may prevent repair.

Wood. The accessibility of wood, of course, varies depending on location. In many areas, with a little searching, almost any kind of wood can be found. Repairs and alterations aren't too difficult for a good woodworker, but a fair number of hand tools and fasteners must be carried on board. Emergency patching can also be done easily, although it may be difficult to get to the spot that needs repair without removing other pieces of wood that are in the way.

Cold molding is often used because good wood is not available. Preparing strips for the laminations is easily done, and repair stock that is carried on board takes up less room than plank-and-frame material. The required epoxy resins are becoming more available around the world. Cold-molded hulls are a bit tricky to repair, but not as difficult as people are led to believe.

LIFE EXPECTANCY

Any hull material that is exposed to the harsh marine environment will undergo some form of deterioration that makes it less able to withstand the stresses placed on it. Wear and tear caused by repeated use may affect some parts of the boat more than others. Different hull materials are subject to different types of deterioration, and periodic maintenance is necessary to prevent damage to the hull. The ideal hull material is one whose deterioration can be controlled with a limited amount of maintenance.

Worms, rot, moisture, resin decay, and ultraviolet light are all organic causes of deterioration. Corrosion is a specific type of deterioration that is caused by chemical reactions in metals, and in steel its product is the old boogey-man, rust. There are many different types of corrosion associated with metals (see Chapter 3). Corrosion occurs in all metal, whether it's a steel hull, the fasteners in a wooden hull, or the zerk fittings in throughhulls of a fiberglass boat.

Like any metal, steel is subject to corrosion, although different elements added to alloy steels help to increase their corrosion resistance. Corrosion can be designed out of a hull by a knowledgeable designer, and modern coatings systems can prevent the corrosion reaction. Insulation and gaskets protect the steel when dissimilar metals are used. Electrical systems can be designed to keep the current where it belongs. In other words, corrosion can be controlled. Organic deterioration is not a problem with steel, although some organisms like barnacles can enhance corrosion on the ship's bottom.

Hull materials are also subject to fatigue, which causes the material to fail under repeated cycles of relatively low stress. A fatigue fracture generally begins as a small crack which successive stresses lengthen. Some materials fail due to fatigue after long-repeated low stresses, while others fail due to one heavy load. Corrosion fatigue is generally a problem with the more noble and brittle metals like stainless steel.

Steel has high fatigue resistance and can withstand many bouts of repeated low stresses, an important factor when considering the way a hull is stressed by the sea. Because the steel hull can handle this cyclic loading, rigging can be set tauter and therefore will hold up better since it will flex less.

Many professional builders will guarantee their steel hulls for up to 15 years, as long as the boats are properly maintained. These builders know that their construction methods will stand up structurally. They also know that proper coating and regular maintenance are the keys.

Because a steel hull does not have any seams or joints to work, causing the paint to lose adhesion, maintenance is generally limited to renewing anti-fouling paints and touching up nicks in the coating system. The boat can be hauled out for winter storage without the problems associated with wood hulls, whose planks dry up and shrink, requiring additional work in the spring. Steel boats can actually ride out the winter in a frozen harbor, although some paint may be scraped away at the waterline by ice.

Aluminum has fewer corrosion problems than steel because it is covered with a protective oxide film, but aluminum corrodes much more quickly than steel once the action is started. Like steel, aluminum hulls must be protected from dissimilar metals. A copper penny lost in the bilge can hole an aluminum boat more quickly than most people would believe. Choosing the correct aluminum alloy will help prevent such disasters. Some high-alloy aluminums are less susceptible to corrosion, but these aircraft grades are even more expensive. Electrolysis is more a problem for aluminum boats than for steel. A good coating system will help prevent corrosion, even though it isn't absolutely necessary. Aluminum is not subject to either organic deterioration or corrosion fatigue.

Because there is no coating system to worry about, aluminum requires less maintenance than steel. Aluminum designs must allow oxygen to reach the aluminum at all times, so that the protective oxide layer is not lost.

Fiberglass. Although fiberglass is immune to chemical corrosion, it is subject to other kinds of deterioration. Delamination is a major problem in older or poorly constructed fiberglass hulls and can be seen at termination points, like the top of the sheer, where stresses are high and water can seep in and dissolve the resin. Fastenings going through fiberglass must be well bedded to prevent seepage from causing delamination. Fiberglass resins are sensitive to ultraviolet rays, which break down the resins and eventually threaten the integrity of the hull. Special paints that block these UV rays are necessary.

Fiberglass is also subject to creep, the tendency of a material to change shape slowly under sustained load in stress areas. Vibrations can also cause embrittlement and fatigue in certain areas such as the propeller shaft and engine mounts if they are not properly designed and reinforced.

Although fiberglass has been applauded for ease of maintenance, older boats are beginning to show problems with gel coats—problems like blistering, crazing, and hairline cracking. Proper waxing and maintenance of these gel coats is necessary for control of deterioration.

Wood is most subject to organic types of deterioration. Worms, fungus, moisture, and rot will severely weaken wood. Fasteners and dissimilar metals in contact with wet wood can corrode, often staining the wood and weakening its grain structure. Wood is strong, but it can fatigue and crack under cyclic stress, which also weakens and loosens the fastenings. The effects of sunlight on wood are minimal, but in tropical areas they can include checking, cracking, and warping. In time, even teak decks can end up looking pretty bad.

Wooden hulls will only last if plenty of time and effort are given to maintenance. The wood must be protected from the elements by paint or oil, but the movement of planks and the constant change in moisture content cause paint to lose adhesion fairly rapidly. Interior moisture traps must also be avoided. Conscientious attention must be given to the bottom, especially when cruising in the tropics, so that worms and other creatures don't destroy the wood.

Cold molding. Cold-molded vessels are less likely to deteriorate than conventionally planked boats because the epoxy resin, which is very nonporous, seals out the elements. Creep, corrosion, and fatigue are unlikely, although dissimilar metals must be properly bonded to the hull, and uncovered epoxy is more resistant to UV rays than polyester resins. If the laminations are properly constructed and saturated with resin, a cold-molded hull is quite stable and requires only minimal maintenance.

SAFETY AT SEA

You'd be crazy to set sail in a boat that is not safe. Dangers can come from within in the form of fire or explosion and from without in the form of the lightning, logs, reefs, and rocks. If you don't have confidence in the ability of the hull material to stand up to all these potential dangers, you're never going to feel quite safe at sea.

Steel boats basically do not burn, a fact which insurance companies should recognize. The melting point of steel is over 1700°F, and it resists changes in temperature. Because a steel hull does not transmit high temperatures as quickly as aluminum and other materials, the wood or insulation around the steel will take longer to catch fire. However, if the insulation does burn, the fumes can be very toxic. Therefore, it's important to have fire extinguishers and safety equipment accessible onboard.

A steel hull is the best protection against the tangle of deadheads, freighters, and whales at sea, since, even if the boat hits one of these, steel's high tensile strength and ductility mean it will only be dented, not holed. Watertight bulkheads can easily be designed and welded into a steel hull, so that, in the unlikely case of the boat being holed, it will still float. If the hull has been protected from corrosion, steel's durability is unmatchable.

David Lewis, aboard his steel sloop *Ice Bird,* rolled over three times while sailing off Antarctica without any damage to the hull. Hitting the ice didn't hole the hull. Steel boats have fallen from cranes, landing on cement docks 20 feet below, with no more damage than a few scratches (you should have seen the cement dock, though!).

Lightning will strike almost anything, and some people fear that steel hulls may attract it. Actually, steel hulls are extremely safe when struck because the entire hull and everything attached to it is grounded, so the current will flow right through the hull without short-circuiting through someone's body.

The only problem you might have with a steel hull is magnetic interference with the compass. This can easily be prevented by proper compass placement, the use of compensators, and by insulating the compass from the hull. You won't get lost.

Aluminum, like steel, is very fire resistant, although it does have a lower melting point (1217°F) than steel, and the heat of a fire could anneal the aluminum, weakening it somewhat. Aluminum has higher internal thermal conductivity and heats up more quickly than steel. An aluminum hull can handle most disasters fairly well, but it will rupture more readily than steel because its tensile strength is less. Since aluminum is nonferrous

and therefore nonmagnetic, there will be no problems with the compass and compass placement.

Fiberglass is vulnerable to fire since it has good thermal conductivity. Fiberglass made with cloth mat and 25% glass melts at 400–500°F, and roving distorts badly when heated. Fire-retardant resins can hold down the rate of spread of a fire, but the smoke from these resins is very toxic. When run aground, fiberglass boats do poorly and tend to turn into matchsticks. Sometimes, though, when light fiberglass boats are beached they are pushed up high enough to survive.

Wood, like fiberglass is not fireproof. It absorbs heat more quickly than most materials, but it also will lose that heat more rapidly. The abrasion resistance of thick wood hulls will prevent some holing, but not as well as steel. If a wooden boat should be struck by lightning, structural damage, fried electrics, or lost masts can result when grounding isn't adequate.

Cold molding, like fiberglass, has good thermal conductivity and will burn fairly easily. Burning resins are a major health hazard when fighting a fire onboard, and firefighters should always stay upwind of the boat. Although cold-molded hulls generally rank better than fiberglass hulls in resisting punctures, they may not be better than heavy-displacement conventional wood cruisers.

CONCLUSION

All materials have their own strengths and weaknesses, and, in the hands of an experienced builder, each can make a good hull. However, steel is the strongest and the safest. The cost of a steel hull is reasonable, and maintenance and repair are easy and inexpensive. Steel hulls aren't meant for everyone, but for the ocean voyager they can make a fine home—one you can bet your life on.

—Chapter 2———————————————

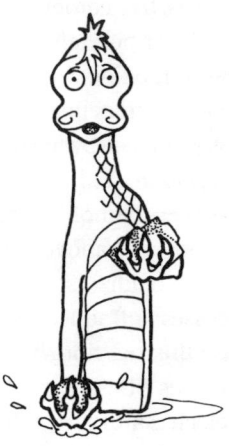

Talking About Metals

Wooden boatbuilders pride themselves on knowing their woods—grain, bending qualities, planing characteristics, strength, rot resistance. With this information, they know exactly how a piece of wood can be used. If you plan to build or own a boat of steel, it is equally satisfying to understand the structure of steel, to know why it behaves in ways that make it so suitable as a hull material. The field of metallurgy, which explains the formation and behavior of steel and other alloys, is fascinating but incredibly complex. You certainly won't be a metallurgist after reading this chapter, but you will understand why steel is as "alive" as wood.

Structure and mechanical properties depend on the elements that are mixed to produce the alloy or homogeneous mixture that we call steel. Although iron and carbon are the primary constituents of this alloy, many other elements can be included in small amounts to enhance performance. Steel and cast iron are both iron-carbon alloys with different carbon contents: steel has a carbon content below 2.2% (generally less than 1.5%), while cast irons contain more than 2.2% carbon. These different carbon contents determine the structure that is formed during manufacturing as the molten metal cools to a solid, and the structure produces the mechanical properties of the alloy. These properties can be enhanced or degraded by techniques used during manufacturing, fabricating, and heat treating.

Plain carbon steel is the type most often used for hulls. It is strong and stable, doesn't lose its toughness with extreme temperature changes, and is resistant to fatigue and stresses. This steel is ductile enough to be easily shaped but stiff enough to withstand the forces of the sea. Easily welded and machined, it doesn't harden or become brittle locally when cut, and it can be heated red hot for shaping without much alteration in its properties.

Other metals are used in a variety of ways onboard a steel boat: fittings, shafts, spars, propellers, winches, windlasses, deck hardware. Most are used in an alloy form, and each has properties that make it particularly suited to its uses.

THE MANUFACTURING OF STEEL

Most metals have a mineral form, generally combined with oxygen or sulfur (for example, aluminum oxide, zinc sulfate, or chromium oxide). The manufacturing of steel begins with iron ore, which is earth or rock containing chemically bonded iron and oxygen as the mineral iron oxide.

In order to remove the iron from iron oxide, the ore is dressed (crushed and then ground to a fine powder), and the iron oxide is separated magnetically or mechanically (by processes like flotation and sieving). The purified oxide is then agglomerated into heat-hardened pellets. These pellets are loaded into a coke-burning blast furnace, where the chemical bond between the iron and oxygen is broken by a process called reduction. As the coke burns, free carbon, carbon monoxide, and water vapor are formed, all of which react with the oxygen in the iron oxide, freeing the iron. The other metals are separated from their ores by similar methods.

The pig iron produced by the reduction process must next be converted to steel. It is mixed with scrap iron and then the excess carbon, manganese, phosphorus, sulfur and silicon, are removed by oxidation. All of the major impurities oxidize sooner than iron, so steel-making processes introduce oxygen into the liquid metal to cause this reaction. The four common steel-making processes (Bessemer, basic oxygen, open-hearth, and electric arc) vary in the way in which heat is generated and whether air or oxygen is blown in. The end products of each, however, are steel and slag (containing the impurities). None of the processes are perfect, and small amounts of some materials, especially carbon and gases, remain in the steel. If other elements are to be combined with the steel to form a specific alloy, they are often added at the end of the reduction process.

Next the liquid steel is poured into molds where it cools into ingots. Since steel solidifies or "freezes" from the outside in, gases dissolved in the molten steel can become trapped in the interior of the ingot. Dissolved oxygen is usually present after the reduction process and is particularly harmful because it is chemically very active. It can combine with free carbon to produce carbon monoxide in a reaction that produces blowholes, which are small cavities either near the surface of the ingot or in its interior that may cause seams in the finished product if the cavities do not weld together under the pressure of rolling. Gas entrapments can also cause shrinkage cavities called pipes in the ends of the ingot. If the oxygen reacts with other elements, these oxides may be trapped in the steel as inclusions. In order to control these defects, steel is generally deoxidized with aluminum or silicon to allow it to solidify quietly in the mold. However, there is a chance that these de-oxidizing agents will also react to form inclusions.

There are four types of steel, each named according to the way it is deoxidized. Semi-killed steel is the one commonly used for the structural shapes, bars, and plates employed in shipbuilding. It is only partially deoxidized, and the oxygen that is left can cause some defects. Killed steel is more expensive than semi-killed

and has been so deoxidized that no gases have formed in the mold: this is steel with a homogeneous, sound structure. Steels with carbon contents over 0.30% are generally killed, as are alloy steels and forging steels. Rimmed steel is not deoxidized at all, and the gases come boiling out of the cooling steel. The ingots have a thick, pure outer skin, and they are excellent for pressing applications. Capped steel is produced by allowing the rimming action to take place in a mold that is sealed with a cast-iron cap.

While ingot pouring is still widely employed, many modern steel plants bypass this step and produce material ready for forming by pouring the molten steel through a continuous casting machine.

No matter what process is used to manufacture the steel or how pure and free of gas it is, as it cools and solidifies a series of changes takes place that determines its final structure and properties.

THE MICROSTRUCTURE OF STEEL

Steels with different carbon contents and different percentages of alloy elements show great variations in mechanical properties such as hardness, ductility, yield strength, and tensile strength. These differences are due to the microstructure of the particular steel, which in turn depends on the carbon content and the manufacturing practices.

In nature there are three groups of elements: metals, metalloids, and nonmetals. All true metals are crystalline in the solid state; that is, their atoms form a specific three-dimensional pattern. The most common patterns are: 1) cubes (iron, aluminum, copper, nickel, lead, chromium, tungsten, manganese); 2) closed-packed hexagons (magnesium, zinc); and 3) tetragons (tin). Part of the science of alloys is determining the effects of combining different crystalline structures.

Crystallization occurs as a metal cools from liquid to solid form. At a certain temperature (different for each metal), small crystal centers or nuclei begin to form randomly throughout the liquid. Atoms are attracted to these nuclei, and a crystal begins to grow. The size of the crystal depends on the rate of cooling. Fast cooling yields small crystals, since many nuclei are formed very quickly, while slow cooling produces larger grains. Fine-grained steels are stronger and tougher than those with large, coarse grains, but are more difficult to form.

As cooling proceeds, the individual crystals grow and coalesce until they touch other crystals and distinct grain boundaries are formed. In pure metals, this grain boundary is very strong, and fractures generally occur along cleavage planes (parallel planes along which atoms are situated in the crystal), rather than along grain boundaries. In less-pure metals, however, impurities and inclusions tend to precipitate out at the grain boundaries, weakening the bonds. Most fractures in steel and also in other alloys occur along these grain boundaries.

Most cast metals are equally strong in all directions, a property called "isotropy." However, during mechanical working (for example, during rolling), the crystals orient in the direction of the work and the metal becomes stronger in that direction.

Mechanical properties also depend on the way that the iron and carbon combine physically and chemically—on the microstructure. Steel has a high melting point (up to 2700°F, depending on the type of alloy), and it is solid for a long time before it reaches room temperature. As it cools, the steel passes through different physical forms or phases, even though it seems to be solid and quiet. These changes occur because iron is allotropic: the arrangement of atoms making up its cubic crystals is different at different temperatures.

The two different types of cubic crystals that iron can form are called "body-centered" and "face-centered." Face-centered cubic crystals contain more atoms than body-centered ones, while body-centered cubes have more slip planes along which the metal can deform, and these produce a more ductile metal.

The allotropic form of iron present in the steel determines the way in which iron and carbon combine. Face-centered (and, to a limited extent, body-centered) cubes allow carbon atoms to occupy spaces between the iron atoms that form the iron crystal, creating a solid solution. (Although "solid solution" sounds like a contradiction in terms, the chemistry is the same as that of a liquid solution.) The carbon atoms distort the iron crystal, yielding a metal with greater mechanical strength.

The carbon content of the steel determines how it will change as it cools. Rather than talk generally, let's look at low-carbon steel, the type most often used for steel boatbuilding. This steel has a carbon content between 0.15% and 0.25%. Other types of steels and cast irons change similarly, but with slightly different end products.

As the steel begins to cool, the iron in it exists in a body-centered form called delta iron. At a temperature determined by its exact carbon content, it begins to change to face-centered gamma iron, and at an even lower temperature, to body-centered alpha iron.

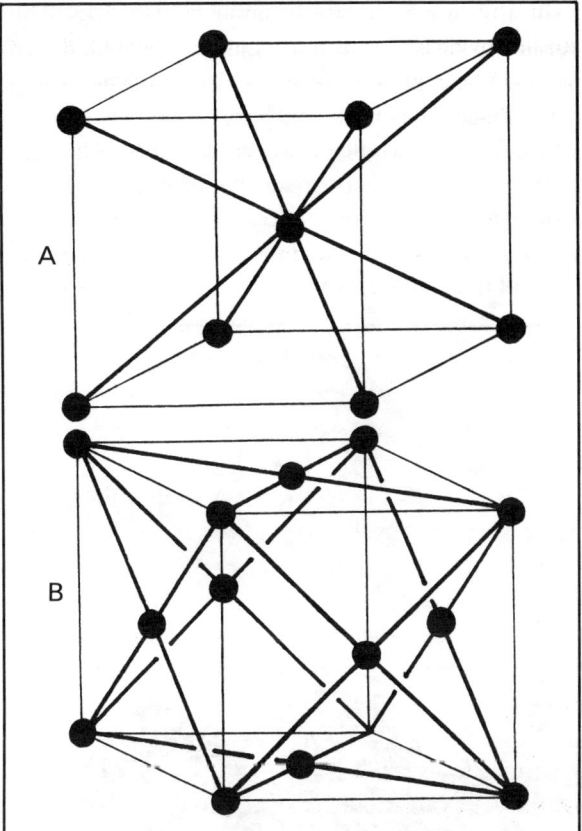

Fig. 2-1. *A. Face-centered cubic crystal. B. Body-centered cubic crystal.*

When the body-centered delta iron changes to face-centered gamma iron, a phase called austenite is produced. Austenite is an interstitial solution of iron and carbon characterized by fine grains and high tensile strength. It is not normally stable at room temperature, but heat treatments can be used to stabilize the steel in the austenite phase in order to take advantage of its greater mechanical strength. The gamma iron in it is nonmagnetic, a feature that can be used to determine whether the steel has reached the austenite phase.

As the temperature continues to fall, the austenite begins to change to ferrite, which is pure body-centered alpha iron with just a little carbon dissolved in it. This ferrite precipitates out of the austenite solution. The alpha iron of which ferrite is composed is soft, ductile, and magnetic, but the ferrite is not as strong as austenite. As the change from austenite to ferrite occurs, any carbon that can no longer be dissolved in iron instead combines *chemically* with the iron to produce cementite (Fe_3C), which is a hard, brittle, cement-like structure. (Iron-carbon alloys with higher carbon contents also have free carbon or graphite [a crystalline form of carbon]).

At a certain temperature, suddenly carbon can no longer be dissolved in ferrite; in other words, a solid solution can no longer exist. Another phase change takes place. The remaining ferrite and cementite are precipitated out at once and together, forming pearlite, which is a mechanical mixture of the two laid down in a lamellar (plate-like) pattern. The ferrite that has already precipitated out is deposited at the grain boundaries of the pearlite.

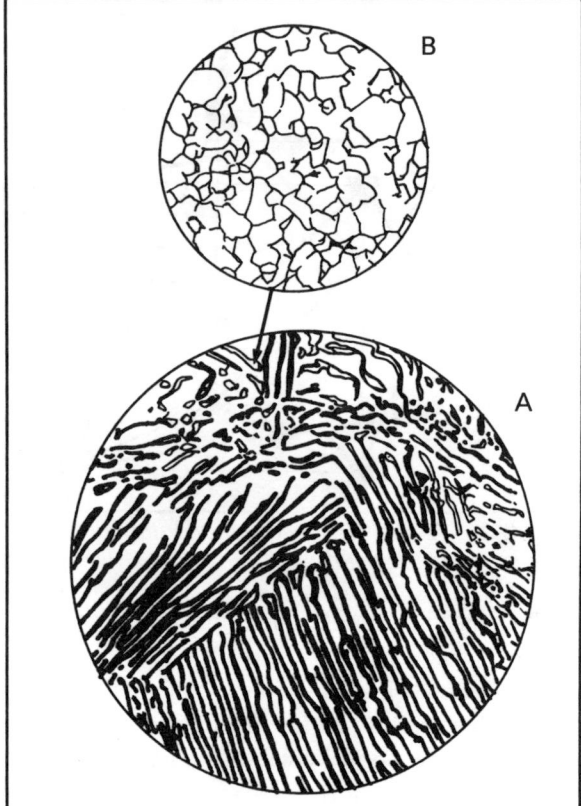

Fig. 2-2. *The microstructure of low-carbon steel. A. Pearlite B. Ferrite*

So, the final microstructure of low-carbon steel is a mechanical mixture of ferrite and pearlite (which itself is a mechanical mixture of ferrite and cementite). The ferrite contributes strength and ductility, and the pearlite adds hardness. The grain size, which also helps to determine the strength of the steel, depends on how quickly or slowly the steel has been cooled.

The temperatures at which the iron changes phase are called "arrest points" or "critical points," and they vary depending on the carbon content and the percentage of other elements that have been added to the alloy. These transformation temperatures are important during heat treatment, when the steel is heated back up to the austenite phase.

The rate of cooling affects the microstructure in several ways. As noted above, faster cooling yields a steel with smaller grain size. The speed of cooling also changes the transformation temperatures. The faster austenite is cooled, the lower is the temperature at which pearlite is formed. And the lower this temperature, the more closely spaced are the plates that make up the pearlitic structure. The closer the plates are, the harder the steel. However, if the steel is cooled too quickly, it also becomes brittle, and can even crack during the cooling. The art is to find the correct balance.

The phase transformations and the speed with which they occur set up internal stresses in the steel. Because austenite has a face-centered cubic structure with more atoms per cube, when it changes to ferrite the steel actually must expand since there are more crystals with fewer atoms each in the structure. The opposite occurs in heating, when the steel contracts during the formation of austenite.

There are other microstructures of iron-carbon alloys, such as martensite, bainite, or ledeburite. Their formation is also related to phase changes, but none is appropriate as a boatbuilding material.

HEAT TREATMENT OF STEELS

Heat treatment of metals includes a number of processes whose purpose is to improve mechanical properties such as hardness, toughness or resistance to shock. Other types of heat treatment soften the metal, allowing it to be shaped more easily into complex curves.

Heat is also used to relieve stresses within the steel, stresses created during phase transformation and fabrication. Both hot and cold working methods produce certain stresses that may cause distortion, cracking, or failure below the loads the steel should be able to handle. Heat treatment may be carried out by the manufacturer or in the field after the metal has been worked.

In all of the processes, steel is heated either above or just below the critical temperature for austenite transformation (1000–1250°F). From here, changes can occur in the phase, the grain size, or the microstructure. The holding time at that temperature and the rate of cooling are also parts of the heat treatment.

When steel is heated above the transformation temperature, the pearlite and ferrite (or pearlite and cementite, or ferrite and graphite, or whatever other combination is present) changes back to austenite. This austenite has the potential to crystallize in small grains if cooled immediately. The longer steel is held above the critical temperature, the larger the austenite grains will be. The grain size of the ferrite and pearlite at room temperature is determined by the grain size of the austenite. Many heat treatments are used to refine the grain size of the metal, because steels with coarser grains are generally less strong.

If the steel is heated to just below the critical point, the ferrite is able to dissolve more carbon. It must then be quickly cooled to freeze the carbon in the ferrite, since with slow cooling the original transformation from ferrite to pearlite would occur again. The additional carbon makes the steel stronger and harder, but a little more brittle.

Steel can be cooled in a furnace, in air, or by using various quenching media. When quenching is used, the cooling rates differ depending on the type of quenching. Quenching media can be divided into those that hold some heat and allow the steel to cool more slowly (oil) and those that transmit heat to permit faster cooling (water, brine). Fast cooling will develop hardness; slow cooling will soften and increase ductility.

When other elements are added to the iron-carbon alloy, the phase transformations are affected. Some (manganese, nickel, cobalt, copper, carbon, nitrogen) allow austenite to remain stable at a lower temperature, while others (chromium, silicon, molybdenum, tungsten, vanadium, tin, phosphorus, aluminum, titanium) cause ferrite to be formed at a higher temperature. Manganese and nickel also lower the temperature of pearlite transition, so that the plates are laid down closer together and the steel is harder.

Nonferrous metals generally don't respond to heat treatment, although some types of aluminum and some nickel alloys can be heat-treated. Aluminum bronze is most like steel in its capacity to respond to heat treatment.

Annealing

Annealing is one of the most common forms of heat treatment. It is primarily used to relieve stresses caused by hot or cold working, making the steel more ductile and easier to machine or form. Full annealing, which is carried out at relatively high temperatures, yields coarse pearlite, which has good machinability. A finer-grained, harder pearlite can be obtained by changing the annealing temperature. Cooling after annealing is generally carried out in the furnace to preserve ductility.

Spheroidize annealing or spheroidizing changes the plate-like pearlite into globes of cementite in a ferrite matrix. This softens coarse pearlite and improves its machinability and shock resistance, especially in low and medium carbon steels that have been cold worked. Spheroidizing is carried out at a temperature lower than the critical transformation temperature.

Process annealing involves heating especially cold-worked metals to subcritical temperatures in order to recrystallize the grains, soften the steel, and relieve stress.

Normalizing

Normalizing is a type of annealing that is preferred for steels with relatively low carbon contents. It refines the grain sizes and helps to distribute carbides more uniformly, making the steel more amenable to further heat treatment. The steel is heated slowly above the critical temperature and is then allowed to cool in the air.

Tempering

Tempering is probably the best-known type of heat treatment. Many hand tools and knives are advertised as made of tempered steel. This is actually a type of an-

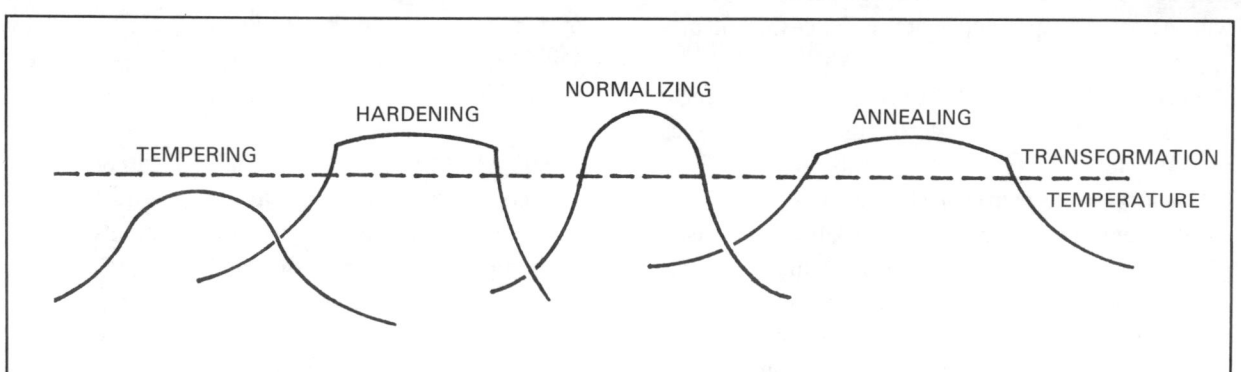

Fig 2-3.   *The heating, holding and cooling curves for the different types of heat treatments.*

nealing which is done at very low temperatures (200–600°F). Only a slight transformation occurs at this low temperature, but the steel is softened and any residual stresses are relieved. Tempering low-carbon steel also affects notch toughness; the notch toughness increases up to 400°F, decreases between 400° and 600°F, and increases rapidly above 800°F.

Quenching or Hardening

Quenching is used to harden steel by cooling it so quickly that neither ferrite nor cementite is formed. The austenite transforms into another structure called martensite. Martensite is very hard, but extremely brittle, and steels that have been hardened by quenching are usually tempered to make it possible to work with them. Too-rapid quenching may cause cracking or distortion due to thermal and transformation stresses.

Case Hardening

Case hardening is used to increase wear resistance, especially in tools and moving parts. This form of heat treatment produces a hard outer shell without affecting the ductility of the interior of the steel piece. There are two methods commonly used. Carburizing involves heating the steel in the presence of carbonaceous material. A high-carbon surface layer is thus imparted to the steel. Nitriding produces the hardest surface and is carried out by heating the steel in the presence of nitrogen.

FORMING THE STEEL

The average steel boat builder never encounters steel in the form of ingots. It has already been further processed into plates, bars, tubes, or other structural shapes. And during construction of a steel boat, the steel will be further shaped and bent to produce the hull and appendages.

Steel can deform without fracturing (a mechanical property called toughness) because there are slip planes in its structure along which the crystals can move. Each crystal form has its own characteristic slip structure, and the greater the number of slip planes, the more easily plastic deformation will occur. Coarse-grained steels have the most slip planes and are easiest to form. Working against this slipping motion are imperfections in the structure, called "dislocations," which are caused by internal stresses. These stresses increase as the steel is deformed. The more dislocations there are, the harder the steel is and the more difficult it is to deform further. This is the phenomenon known as strain or work hardening. Stainless steel and other high-tensile strength alloys are more susceptible to work hardening than is mild steel.

Plastic deformation generally occurs through either hot or cold working. Hot working includes the hammering and pressing that are part of forging operations, rolling, and extrusion. Cold working consists of cold rolling, cold drawing, and cold extrusion. Steel is easier to deform when it is hot because the crystals can recover from the dislocations caused by deformation. In cold working, there is a greater chance of work hardening, although some work hardening enhances the stiffness of the material.

Steel plate is produced by hot rolling either from reheated slabs of steel or directly from ingots. The plate is described by the type of mill used in its production. Sheared plate is rolled between horizontal rollers and trimmed on all edges. Mill-edge plate is also rolled between horizontal rollers, but only two edges are trimmed, while the other two have the as-rolled edge. Universal mill plate is rolled simultaneously between horizontal and vertical rollers and is trimmed only at the ends. Rolling in both directions yields plate with good notch toughness and ductility in both directions.

The steel plate used in shipbuilding is generally furnished in an as-rolled condition. However, normalizing can be carried out to reduce any stresses caused during the rolling. Lloyd's rules do not require normalizing for plate thicknesses that would be used on a steel sailboat hull, although it is mentioned as a possible heat treatment.

The surface of steel plates formed by hot rolling is covered with a hard, black oxide called "mill scale." It is acceptable practice to let mill scale rust away before final sandblasting, but it can also be removed at the mill by a process called "pickling." Pickling is carried out by submerging the steel in a dilute muriatic (hydrochloric) or sulfuric acid bath which is held at a particular temperature.

Bar stock (angle, T, flat, or channel) can be formed either by hot rolling or cold extrusion. The cold-worked types are generally used as structural elements for steel hulls, and have higher tensile and yield strengths than their hot-worked counterparts.

Cast or forged steels are not favored for hull construction, although they are certainly used for marine equipment such as anchor chain, shafts, rudder stocks, and anchors. Forged steel is more acceptable than cast, and forged fittings that have been normalized are best.

DEFECTS IN STEEL

Steel is subject to a variety of defects, many of them caused by the manufacturing process and others by forming processes or improper handling. It's wise to examine steel for a hull with these defects in mind.

The actual thickness of the plate may vary from that specified by as much as $\frac{1}{32}$ inch, due to variations in tolerance during the rolling process. This is not really a defect, but it may cause a slight increase in the overall weight of the boat under construction.

These defects are not common, since inspection is carried out at the mill, and any ethical dealer should be willing to replace defective material. Buying *certified* (inspected) steel is the best way to go.

Table 2-1. COMMON DEFECTS IN STEEL

1) *Sheet with wavy configuration (small areas out of flat)* — Caused by inadequate or uneven cooling at the mill.

2) *Pipe* — Cavity in center of end surface caused by shrinkage cavity in ingot.

3) *Fins and overfills* — Caused by trying to extrude a section too large to pass through the mill.

4) *Underfills* — The opposite of overfills. Most common in round bar and channel.

5) *Laps* — A protrusion that has been rolled over into the surface.

6) *Seams* — Crevices that are closed but not welded together. Caused by blowholes or cracks in the original ingot that occurred because of gas entrapment.

7) *Rolled-in scale* — One of the most prevalent defects, caused by scale formed during earlier heat treatment that has not been eliminated during rolling.

8) *Buckle (up and down) and kink (side to side)* — Corrugated or wrinkled surface; caused by improper handling.

THE CLASSIFICATION OF STEEL

Steel and other metals are classified according to composition, finishing methods, and finished shapes. There are several groups in the U.S. that write both designations and specifications for various metals.

The designations written by the American Iron and Steel Institute (AISI) and the Society of Automotive Engineers (SAE) are the ones commonly used to describe the chemical composition of the material. For example: 10xx is plain carbon steel; 13xx is manganese steel; 3xxx designates nickel-chromium steel; and 5xxx is used for chromium steels. The first two X's show the principal alloying elements, and the last two indicate the carbon content in hundredths of a percent.

Specifications describe the attributes that the metal must have and can also include the designation of chemical composition. The most commonly used specifications are those of the American Society for Testing and Material (ASTM). Some are generic; for example, general-purpose carbon steel plates, bars, and shapes are classified as A36. (The prefix A is used for all ferrous materials.) The American Society of Mechanical Engineers uses a similar specification system, but adds an S to the ASTM specification number—SA36.) Most specifications indicate the performance that is required from the steel: A529 is structural carbon steel, A441 and A572 are high-strength, low-alloy steels, and A242 and A588 are corrosion-resistant alloys used for structural plate.

TYPES OF STEEL

Plain Carbon Steels

Plain carbon steel is the type most often used to build steel hulls. Carbon is the principal alloying element, but the steel may contain up to 1.65% manganese, 0.60% copper, 0.60% silicon, and much smaller amounts of other elements. If greater amounts of other elements are present, the steel is called "alloy steel."

The exact carbon content is important since hardness, tensile strength, and yield strength increase with increasing carbon content, but ductility decreases, causing brittleness in high-carbon steels. Also, the higher the carbon content, the more difficult the steel is to weld, and special low-hydrogen electrodes may be necessary.

The structure of carbon steel is predominantly pearlite, and hardness and ductility increase as the lamellar spacing of the pearlite and the grain size decrease. Most plain carbon steels are used without heat treatment, and the temperature of the hot-rolling process and the cooling rate determine the nature of the pearlite.

Low-carbon steel (mild steel) contains between 0.15–0.25% carbon. It is easily welded, but its hardness doesn't increase much when it is heat treated. It can, however, be case hardened. The tensile strength of low-carbon steel is 60,000–70,000 psi, and it is very tough, ductile, and easily formed, welded, and machined. This is the type generally used in steel boatbuilding. Steel plate for general use contains 0.15–0.2% carbon, while steel bar used for machining, studs, and bolts contains 0.2–0.25% carbon, with the additional carbon adding strength.

Medium-carbon steel contains .30–.50% carbon. It can't be worked as easily as low-carbon steel, and must be welded with special electrodes. However, medium-carbon steel responds to heat treatment better. It is generally used for hammerheads and tool parts, high-strength studs and bolts, axles, shafts, and gears.

High-carbon steels contain .60–1.5% carbon. They are used for products which must be heat treated, and are strong enough to withstand high-speed applications. Although not appropriate as hull materials, high-carbon steels are used for drills, saws, hammers, shear blades, forging dies, chisels, gouges, reamers, and other woodworking tools.

Alloy Steels

There are over 600 alloy steels in use today, all of whose principal properties are obtained from elements other than carbon. Up to 50% of these alloying elements can be added to improve the mechanical properties of the steel, and they are chosen for very specific reasons.

The alloying elements can be divided into two groups: those that combine with carbon to produce carbides and those that actually dissolve in the ferrite. Carbide formers, which help to increase abrasion resistance, include chromium, manganese, molybdenum, titanium, tungsten, and vanadium. Aluminum, copper, nickel and silicon all dissolve in ferrite, although all elements dissolve in it to some extent. Some help to strengthen the ferrite.

These elements are also used as the primary or secondary components in nonferrous alloys. There are probably an infinite number of combinations, each with unique properties.

Chromium (Cr) is the primary additive in stainless steel alloys, but it is also used as an alloying element in other steels. Small amounts of this hard, lustrous element increase the wear resistance, tensile strength, and hardness of the steel without lowering ductility. Density: .2451 lb./in.^{3}; melting point: 2750°F.

Cobalt (Co) is a hard, brittle metallic element that is added to steel to strengthen it. Its high temperature resistance helps the steel to remain hard even when red hot. Cobalt is used as an alloying element in the manufacture of very hard alloy equipment. Density: .307 lb./in.^{3}; melting point: 2714°F.

Copper (Cu) increases corrosion resistance and improves machinability. A small amount of copper is allowed even in plain carbon steel. Higher strength steels like Corten, used on some boat hulls, contain small amounts of copper. Density: .332 lb./in.^{3}; melting point: 1981°F.

Table 2-2. THE EFFECTS OF ALLOYING ELEMENTS ON STEEL

		Increases hardness	Increases ductility	Increases wear resistance	Increases toughness	Increases strength	Increases corrosion resistance	Increases machinability	Increases high temperature resistance	Increases notch toughness	Increases elasticity	Increases hardenability
Carbide Formers	Chromium	X		X	X		X					
	Manganese	X	X							X		
	Molybdenum	X			X							X
	Titanium			X		X						X
	Tungsten	X		X					X			
	Vanadium			X		X						X
Dissolve in Ferrite	Aluminum			deoxidizes steel								
	Cobalt	X				X			X			
	Copper						X	X				
	Magnesium							X				
	Nickel					X	X					X
	Silicon					X					X	

Magnesium (M) is the lightest metal and the least noble. It is rarely used in the marine environment because its low nobility causes it to pit rapidly. Its use in alloys is mainly to enhance machinability and to help produce high strength-to-weight ratios. Density: .064 lb./in.³; melting point: 1204°F.

Manganese (Mn) dissolves in ferrite or austenite, producing a fine grain structure with great notch toughness, hardness, ductility, and elasticity. It is the main additive in austenitic manganese steel (12–14% Mn), which is very wear resistant, and plain carbon steels generally contain small amounts of manganese. However, too much manganese makes steel hard to machine. Density: .289 lb./in.³; melting point: 2237°F.

Molybdenum (Mo) produces the greatest hardening effect, yielding a strong, tough but machinable steel. It increases heat resistance, inhibits temper brittleness, improves the creep resistance of carbon steels, and helps prevent corrosion cracking and weld decay in some stainless steels. Density: .368 lb./in.³; melting point: 4748°F.

Nickel (Ni) is added to improve corrosion resistance, impact strength, and toughness without decreasing ductility. Nickel steels are among the oldest alloys. Nickel slows down grain growth at high temperatures, but it also promotes the formation of graphite. A small amount of manganese is always added to nickel steels to stabilize the carbides and prevent this reaction. Nickel is used in special electrodes for welding brittle metals like cast iron. Nickel steels are also used to electroplate corrosion-resistant alloys and batteries. Density: .319 lb./in.³; melting point: 2650°F.

Silicon (Si) is a very light element used to improve strength and elasticity in bending. Silicon steel is tough and resists fatigue, but the grain size tends to be large unless the steel is properly heat treated. Surface impregnation with silicon gives a hard, oxidation-resistant surface. Density: .087 lb./in.³; melting point, 2600°F.

Titanium (Ti) improves strength, hardenability, and wear resistance. Like chromium, titanium also forms a protective oxide film on the surface of the metal. Titanium-tungsten carbon steel is used in bit tips to which the cutting chips will not adhere. Density: .163 lb./in³; melting point: 3270°F.

Tungsten (W) is a hard, brittle, corrosion-resistant metal whose high melting point makes it useful in alloys to be used at high temperatures. It makes the steel very hard and resistant to wear, and when added in the proper amount also makes the steel self-hardening and heat-resistant. Tungsten steels are used primarily for tools and high-speed cutting tips, as well as in ball bearings. Density: .690 lb./in.³; melting point, 6170°F.

Vanadium (V) is a soft, ductile element found in several mineral forms. It improves strength, hardenability, and wear resistance, as well as inhibiting grain growth when steel is heated above the critical range. Vanadium is used in strong, rust-resistant, high-speed steel tools. Density: .1987 lb./in.³; melting point, 3146°F.

There are many other elements that are used in very specialized alloys. These include: antimony, arsenic, beryllium, boron, cadmium, gallium, platinum, rhodium, and uranium. Interestingly, uranium has occasionally been used for yacht keels, but unless you own a mine it's far too expensive for practical use.

HIGH-STRENGTH LOW-ALLOY (HSLA) STEELS

There is a special class of alloy steels, called high-strength, low-alloy, in which only small quantities of alloying elements are added. The hull plates of the *S.S. Mauretania*, built in 1907, were made of steel containing 1.00% silicon and 0.25% carbon. The most well-known brand is Corten, which was introduced in 1933 as a low-maintenance steel for use in bridges. Recently, the brand Mayari R50 was used for 75' commuter ferries built by Blount Marine.

HSLA steels are known for their high strength (1.4 times that of plain carbon steel), good atmospheric corrosion resistance, formability, toughness, and fatigue resistance, as well as their easy weldability. The reason for their increased strength is that the alloy additions allow microstructural improvements that are difficult if not impossible to obtain in carbon steel.

This high corrosion resistance means that a boatbuilder can use thinner plates with less chance of distortion during welding, since the thinner plates absorb less heat during the process. However, its hardness makes the steel more difficult to bend and form. Its corrosion resistance in seawater is questionable, and the steel still must be protected.

Carbon, manganese, silicon, and copper are the major alloying elements, but HSLA steels also may contain phosphorus, nickel, chromium, vanadium, zirconium, or molybdenum. For example, Corten A contains a maximum of 0.12% carbon, 0.20–0.50% manganese, 0.25–0.75% silicon, 0.25–0.55% copper, 0.07–0.15% phosphorus, a maximum of 0.65% nickel, and 0.30–1.25% chromium. Its yield point is 90,000 psi, and its tensile strength is 100,000–130,000 psi. It is 2–6 times more corrosion resistant than plain carbon steel in atmospheric conditions.

With these attributes, it's no wonder that Corten is constantly discussed as a hull material. Many boats have been plated with Corten, but it has several shortcomings. It is more subject to electrolysis underwater (probably because of its high copper content), takes longer to blast, and costs about 15–30% more than mild steel. It is difficult to cut with a nibbler and requires MIG welding. And the difficulty in shaping Corten makes it less practical to use for round hulls, especially for the amateur. It's probably best reserved for its intended use—bridges.

High-Alloy, High-Strength Steel

These steels contain great quantities of alloying elements and can be made up to ten times stronger than carbon steel. Their high cost is not offset by increased corrosion resistance, so they are rarely used in steel hull construction, although they could be used in chafe areas or for fittings.

Stellite is the trade name for a group of complex alloys used at high temperatures. They contain 2–25% tungsten, 20–65% cobalt, 11–32% chromium, and 0.5–2.5% carbon, as well as some nickel, molybdenum, vanadium, manganese, and/or silicon.

Stainless Steel

Stainless steels are perhaps the most well-known of the alloy steels. Stainless has been lauded as one of the best metals for use in a marine environment because of the high corrosion resistance promoted by high percentages of chromium, and some hulls have been built of stainless steel. It is an excellent marine metal, but its drawbacks and limitations must be properly understood so that it can be used correctly.

Stainless fittings, in general, withstand chafe and friction better than plain or galvanized steel fittings, although they are more expensive. Stainless is especially good for items such as fairleads, chocks, and hatch slides, while galvanized is more practical for bollards, cleats, and handrails, which are not chafed as frequently. (Contrary to popular belief, a properly served galvanized wire rigging system will last longer than a stainless one for a much lower cost.) Fittings like winches, sheet tracks, mast fittings, and other items not secured directly to the hull are also commonly made of stainless steel.

Stainless steels have a high chromium content, 12% or more. The chromium content must be at least 13–14% in order to prevent corrosion, and the more there is, the better the corrosion resistance. Silicon, nickel, molybdenum, titanium, tungsten, and niobium can be included to enhance this effect of the chromium.

Stainless owes its high corrosion resistance to the formation of a thin chromium oxide film on its surface. The presence of oxygen is required in order to maintain this film, and, when the oxide film is destroyed, a type of corrosion called "pitting" occurs. Therefore, stainless should not be submerged, but should be used only above the waterline, except for type 316. Some precipitation-hardened types (grade 630) like 17–4PH or 17–7PH with high strength and corrosion resistance can also be used underwater and for propellers and shafts. Nitronic 50 is used for rod rigging as well as shafting. Other underwater uses might include seacocks, rudder shoes, bolts or studs for zincs, bobstay eyes, and the rudder stock.

Stainless is difficult to form since it transmits heat poorly and is prone to warp during welding. Use of the correct electrodes, such as 308, 309, and 316 for arc welding, make the job easier. Improper welding may cause impoverishment of the chromium, which can lead to a complete loss of corrosion resistance. Cleats or other items that must be attached to a steel hull are better bolted down with stainless steel bolts, after insulating them from the less-noble steel below, to prevent galvanic corrosion.

However, it is easy to bend stainless with a jig. Pulpits, pedestals, and guards can be fashioned without too much effort, (although this depends on the wall thickness of the tubing), and the cold working even hardens the steel.

Heat treatment, especially annealing, may be used to relieve stresses, but grain size cannot be refined with heat. Once a large grain size is established, it cannot be changed. But cold-worked stainless is stronger than that which is heat treated. Stainless that is going to be used underwater can benefit from being annealed after welding.

Stainless steels are subject to stress corrosion and cracking caused by continual tensile stresses. Under these conditions, stainless rigging and fittings have been known to break in two, so proper design of fittings to relieve stress raisers is important.

Austenitic stainless steels (200 and 300 series) are the type most often used on boats, although ferritic and martensitic stainless are also available. When you hear sailors talk about stainless, the chances are good they mean austenitic stainless. It is an iron-chromium-nickel alloy in which the nickel allows a fine-grained austenite structure to exist at room temperature, so that the metal is extremely tough and ductile. The iron is in its face-centered gamma phase, and is nonmagnetic. Austenitic stainless cannot be hardened by heat treatment, but cold working does harden the steel through the mechanism of strain or work hardening, yielding exceptionally high tensile and yield strengths. Since heating (for example, by welding) destroys these properties, specially designed joints are required. Austenitic stainless does not need to be annealed after welding unless it is to be used underwater.

The most common austenitic stainless is No. 302, or 18–8 stainless, which contains 18% chromium, 8% nickel, and about 0.05% carbon. It has a yield strength of 36,000–75,000 psi and a tensile strength of 90,000–110,000 psi. Nos. 302 or 304 are commonly used for rigging wires. Some fittings may be made with Nos. 201 or 202 stainless, but they are at the bottom line of acceptability for marine use. No. 316 contains small amounts of manganese and molybdenum. It is more difficult to weld, but has better resistance to cavitation and lower oxygen requirements for maintaining its protective film. Most marine fasteners, slide tracks, cleats, and chocks are made of No. 316 stainless.

Ferritic stainless is a chromium-iron alloy with a coarse grain structure, making it difficult to weld and more prone to rupture. Its yield (35,000–80,000 psi) and tensile (65,000–90,000 psi) strengths are a bit higher than those of plain carbon steel, but its ductility is lower. It becomes quite brittle when welded, but can be made more ductile if annealed. Ferritic stainless is used in automotive trim and in trailers and railway cars. It is less expensive than austenitic stainless because the expensive nickel is not included in its makeup.

The third type of stainless steel is called martensitic, and it is the high-chromium equivalent of quenched and tempered martensitic carbon steel. Its yield and tensile strengths are higher than those of plain carbon and alloy steels of the same carbon content, and it is very hard. It can be hardened further by heat treatment, and is brittle after rolling. Martensitic stainless is used for aircraft fittings, bolts, cutlery, forged and machined parts, and other fasteners.

A nitric acid solution and a wire brush will clean stains off of stainless steel. Zinc oxide grease also helps to keep certain stainless items free from foreign particles so that the oxygen supply to the surface is not in-terrupted. Underwater parts should also be regularly cleared of barnacles and other growth to avoid pitting corrosion. Stainless above the waterline should be washed with fresh water to clean off salt deposits.

OTHER METALS

There are many other metals that have been used over the years in boatbuilding. Some are not very practical, and some are not compatible with a steel hull since corrosion can occur when dissimilar metals contact each other. But some of these metals and alloys have special properties that are useful in the systems of a steel vessel, for example, ballast, plumbing, deck gear, engine, etc. Since only small amounts of stainless or bronze are secured to a steel hull below the waterline, the larger area of the steel will limit the extent of any corrosion.

Iron

Iron, of course, is one of the elements alloyed in steel. But pure iron is occasionally used on boats, and the first metal ships were made of iron, although the lighter weight of steel makes iron impractical these days. The tall ship, *Star of India*, built in 1863, though heavy, is still afloat in San Diego. Pure iron, which contains a very small number of impurities and little carbon, is most commonly found in boat systems rather than in hulls (for example, as ballast).

Wrought iron (also called "black iron") is the oldest form of iron. It contains about 0.2% carbon and less than 0.5% impurities, and is made by mixing pure iron with slag. Wrought iron is quite corrosion resistant, even without coatings, and has a tensile strength of 42,000 psi. It is tough and resists fatigue and shock. The iron bends easily and slowly, and is therefore easily welded and forged. Drop forging is often used to make ships' fittings these days, which is where most wrought iron will be found, although wrought steel is also used for this purpose; chain is often made of wrought iron. Iron fittings can only be welded to the hull if the correct electrodes are used.

CAST IRON

Cast iron is an iron-carbon alloy with a carbon content greater than 2.2%. Its microstructure shows fine, soft graphite in a ferrite matrix. Cast iron is not as strong

Fig. 2-4.   *A rare example of a black iron boat. This riveted round hull was built in Holland in the 1950's. A home-built chine hull rests alongside.*

as wrought or rolled iron or steel, and it must be welded carefully. Although cast iron has a reputation for extreme brittleness because of its high carbon content, modern technology has succeeded in producing more ductile cast irons.

Gray cast iron gets its name from the color produced by the graphite in its microstructure. It is the most popular form of cast iron used today, and it has a little more corrosion resistance than plain carbon steel because of the copper, chromium, and nickel included in the alloy. Most gray cast iron contains between 2.5% and 4% carbon. Strength and hardness depend on a slow cooling rate which yields a graphite-ferrite mixture, but it is always somewhat soft and brittle. The tensile strength of gray cast iron is a low 20,000–27,000 psi, and it has a melting point of 2802°F. Its density is .260 lb./in.^{3}. Gray cast iron is commonly used for ships stoves, as well as automobile and tractor engine blocks, crankshafts, gears, pipelines, and other industrial applications.

In white cast iron, which contains more then 1.7% but less than 4.27% carbon, the carbon is chemically combined with the iron as cementite. It is produced by slow cooling of gray cast iron so that enough time is allowed for the cementite to form. The typical structure is pearlite in large areas of cementite. This high cementite concentration means that white cast iron is brittle, hard, and wear resistant, although ductility is low. It has poor resistance to shock, and will fracture easily. White cast iron is primarily used for machine parts and casting.

Malleable cast irons are made by heating white cast iron above the critical point to form austenite. As it cools, the carbon forms irregular blobs in a ferrite matrix. Because of this microstructure, it is easily machined, and is used to make oddly shaped castings. It has a tensile strength of 50,000–95,000 psi and a yield strength of 32,000–80,000 psi. Malleable cast iron can be welded as long as the welding process does not heat it above the critical temperature.

Nodular cast iron, which has the same carbon content as gray cast iron, has its graphite present in tiny nodules whose formation during the casting process is assisted by either magnesium or cesium. Normalizing yields a cast iron with a tensile strength of 60,000–175,000 psi and a yield strength of 40,000–150,000 psi. A hardened martensitic structure can be obtained by quenching and tempering. It is ductile, easily machined, and easily cast, but it corrodes rapidly.

Elements such as nickel, chromium, or silicon are used in alloy cast iron and add special properties to the finished product.

Brass (Copper-Zinc Alloy)

Brass is commonly found in nautical decorative items and in fastenings for nonstructural applications. However, a lightship formerly in service off the Columbia River bar was built with an all-brass superstructure, since brass is nonmagnetic and would not interfere with radio beacon signals. The crystal structure and properties of brass change with the amount of zinc that is added. A soft ductile alpha phase, also called yellow brass, is formed with zinc contents of between 20% and 36%. The harder, stronger, more brittle beta phase is formed with higher zinc contents.

The brasses are all prone to stress corrosion cracking and pitting caused by de-zincification, when zinc dissolves out of the alloy. De-zincification occurs more rapidly underwater, so in the marine environment these metals should be used above the waterline and preferably out of the weather altogether.

Table 2-3. SYMBOLS FOR THE CHEMICAL ELEMENTS	
Aluminum	Al
Carbon	C
Chromium	Cr
Cobalt	Co
Copper	Cu
Hydrogen	H
Iron	Fe
Lead	Pb
Magnesium	Mg
Manganese	Mn
Molybdenum	Mo
Nickel	Ni
Oxygen	O
Phosphorus	P
Silicon	Si
Sodium	Na
Sulfur	S
Tin	Sn
Titanium	Ti
Tungsten	W
Vanadium	V
Zinc	Zn

Alpha brasses include cartridge brass, admiralty brass, and aluminum brass. Cartridge brass is ductile and stretches easily. Admiralty brass contains a little tin for added strength and corrosion resistance, and is considered a good-quality brass. Aluminum brass has the highest tensile strength of all brasses, and forms a self-healing oxide film for protection from cavitation. The alpha brasses need to be annealed after cold working to prevent cracking.

Muntz metal, with a zinc content of 40%, contains a combination of the alpha and beta phases, and it is much stronger than alpha brass. It is used commercially for large nuts and bolts and valve stems, as well as for ship sheathing.

Red brass contains less zinc (up to 20%) than alpha brasses, which makes it less prone to de-zincification. It is used for fasteners and as red brass wire.

Naval brass, also called Tobin bronze, contains 39% zinc with small amounts of tin and lead to improve machinability. It is used for some propeller shafting, turnbuckles, valve stems, nuts, and other hardware.

Manganese bronze is actually a high-tensile-strength brass with 39% zinc and small amounts of aluminum, manganese, iron, and tin. Manganese bronze propellers, although they may de-zincify, can be used on a steel boat because, like stainless, they are more noble than the steel and the chances of corrosion leading to de-zincification are reduced. Manganese bronze is fine for wooden mast or deck fittings when it is well insulated from the steel. Although most propellers are fabricated of manganese bronze, nickel manganese bronze is better, since the addition of nickel increases resistance to high-velocity attack. However, it is more expensive.

Gunmetal, with 10% tin and 2% zinc, is a good casting metal which can be used underwater, though it has low strength. It has been cast for seacocks, rudder tubes, fairleads, bollards, and, as the name suggests, guns. Many old marine fittings are made of gunmetal.

Bronzes (Zinc-Free Copper Alloys)

Bronze has always been considered one of the superior metals in the marine environment. It is definitely superior to the brasses in terms of corrosion resistance since there is no chance of de-zincification and it is easily cast. As in all alloys, addition of other elements increases certain strengths. Its use on steel boats is generally limited to propellers and seacocks because of the risk of galvanic corrosion.

Basic bronze, also known as tin bronze, has no zinc and 5–10% tin, and may contain lead to improve machinability. It is the earliest type of bronze developed by man, but there is little use for it on a steel vessel except for seacocks, which should be well insulated from the steel with non-conductive gaskets.

Aluminum bronzes contain from 4 to 11% aluminum and other elements, such as iron, manganese, nickel, and silicon. They have good wear and fatigue resistance, and can be used underwater, even though they may suffer from de-aluminification. Heat treatment and a water quenching cause an increase in strength and hardness. Aluminum bronze is well suited for use in propellers since it resists pitting, crevice and stress corrosion, and cavitation. Nickel aluminum manganese bronze con-

Table 2-4. A COMPARISON OF METALS

Metal	Specific Gravity	Principal Alloying Elements	Density in lbs./cu. in.	Melting Point (°F)	Modulus of Elasticity × 10⁶	Yield Strength in psi	Tensile Strength in psi	Comments
Wrought (Black) Iron	7.70		.278	2750	28	27,000	42,000	Used for hull plate on riveted hulls. Occasionally found as fuel tanks. Limited use on steel boats today.
Gray Cast Iron	7.13		.260	2800	25	25,000	27,000	Used for ballast, engine blocks, stoves, exhaust manifolds, rails and some fittings like portholes.
Low-Carbon Mild Steel (A36)		under 1.5%C	.284	2700	30	36–42,000	60–70,000	Used for steel hulls and appendages. Forged steel has similar qualities.
Soft Cast Steel	7.83		.284		30.1	35,000	63,000	Good shock resistance. Used for engine beds, stern tubes, spar fittings, and wire.
Hard Cast Steel	7.82		.284		30	42,000	75,000	Good resistance to wear and crushing; easily galvanized. Used for deck fittings, windlasses, portholes, chain pipe, slides, and anchors.
HSLA Steel		varies greatly	.284	2600	29	45–90,000	65–130,000	Hard, strong alloys like Corten. Used for hulls and structural members.
302 Stainless Steel		18% Cr 9% Ni .15% C 2% Mn	.286	2550	29	37–150,000 (35,000 cast)	90–180,000 (77,000 cast)	Used for nuts, bolts, rigging wire, ladders, rails, trim pieces, stanchions. As corrosion resistance increases, strength decreases.
304 Stainless Steel		18% Cr 9% Ni 1%Si 2% Mn	.286	2550	29	35–150,000 (37,000 cast)	85–180,000 (76,000 cast)	Used for studs, galley gear, rigging wire, railings, and tube. (Types 303 and 305 used for fasteners.) Lower strengths are in annealed condition.
316 Stainless Steel		17% Cr 12% Ni 2.5% Mo 2% Mn	.286	2550	29	35–125,000 (42,000 cast)	85–150,000 (80,000 cast)	Used for spar fittings, wire, fasteners, fittings pins, eyes, tracks, stanchions, shafts, studs, seacocks, deck hardware. Tempering increases strength; best for chafe areas
317 Stainless Steel		19% Cr 14% Ni 3.5% Mo 2% Mn	.286	2550	29	40–95,000 (40,000 cast)	90–120,000 (82,000 cast)	Used for propellers, engine shafts, winch parts, rudder posts. Substitute for 316. All types are austenitic.
Zinc	7.02		.257	788	12.4			Used for anodes and isolator pads, and in coatings and socket terminals.

Table 2-4 (cont.). A COMPARISON OF METALS

Metal	Specific Gravity	Principal Alloying Elements	Density in lbs./cu. in.	Melting Point × 10⁶	Modulus of Elasticity in psi	Yield Strength in psi	Tensile Strength	Comments
Series 5000 Aluminum	2.67	4.5 Mg .8 Mn	.098	1208	10.5	20–37,000	23–47,000	Used for hull plate (5083, 5086, 5454, 5456), cabin tops, panels, stanchions, rivets (5056), and railings. Not heat treatable. Strength varies with tempering.
Series 6000 Aluminum	2.67	.9% Mg .6% Si .25% Cr .28% Cu	.098	1205	10.5	18–40,000	35–45,000	Used for spar extrusions (6010, 6061, 6063, 6070). Heat treatable. Strongest type.
Cast Aluminum	2.56		.097		10.5	15–43,000	24–47,000	Used for deck hardware, portholes, travelers, hatch slides, cleats, winches, and some spar fittings.
Manganese Bronze	8.39	58% Cu 39% Zn 1% Sn 1% Fe .3% Mn	.302	1600±	9.2	30–70,000	71–115,000	Used for spar fittings, quadrants, propellers, winch handles, and miscellaneous hardware. Easily worked cold; good casting qualities. Very strong.
Aluminum Bronze	8.22	7% Al 9% Cu 2% Fe	.274	1950	17.5	28–65,000	60–105,000	Used for seacocks, some fittings, and propellers (nickel-aluminum bronze is better for propellers).
Silicon Bronze		9% Cu 2% Ni 3.6% Si	.308	1800	18	16–39,000 (25,000 for fasteners)	40–90,000 (55,000 for fasteners)	Used for seacocks, fasteners, portholes, turnbuckles. All-purpose alloys.
Phosphor Bronze		90% Cu 10% Pb .2% Sn	.318	1830	18	20–30,000	40–62,000	Used for bearings, gears, and propellers. Very tough and elastic.
Copper-Nickel	7.80	55–88% Cu 4–30% Ni 2–4% Fe	.322	2140	22	27–55,000	44–78,000	Used for exhaust plates, tubing, guardrails, fittings, shafts, tanks, anti-foulant sheathings and very expensive hull plate. Very resistant to velocity effects.
Lead	11.55	.1–11% Al 1% Mn	.406	621	2		2,500	Used for ballast and soundproof sheathing.
Monel 400		67% Ni 31% Cu 1.2% Fe 1% Mn	.319	2400	33	25–100,000	70–120,000	Used for propeller shafts, propellers, wire, and special fittings. Very corrosion resistant in moving sea water.

35

tains 2% nickel, 8% aluminum, and 12% manganese. This is a superior propeller material because of its resistance to pitting, crevice and stress corrosion, and water velocity effect. However, it is not as available as manganese bronze (brass), and is very expensive.

Silicon bronzes with less than 5% silicon are the strongest work-hardened copper alloys. They can generally be used with confidence underwater, but need to be well-insulated on steel vessels. Silicon bronze is used in ring barb nails, which are good for interior plywood joinery and are cheaper than stainless screws, and it makes great fastenings for wooden boats. On steel boats, its use is generally limited to well-bedded and insulated seacocks and deck fittings and to spar fittings and fasteners.

Phosphor bronze is deoxidized with 0.01–0.5% phosphorus. Containing 1–11% tin, it has high strength and toughness as well as high corrosion resistance. It is widely used for springs and snap shackles since it has a low friction coefficient. It is easily cast, but it should be welded by the TIG method.

Copper-Nickel Alloys

Copper-nickel alloys are the Cadillacs of the boat metals. They contain up to 30% nickel, and are very strong and highly corrosion resistant. Unfortunately, they are also very, very expensive, which has limited their use in boatbuilding. Cupronickel alloys are available as thin pressurized adhesive coatings which are applied to the hull underbody for antifouling protection. 90–10 copper-nickel, with 1.5% iron, provides the most corrosion-resistant hull a boat owner could want. 70–30 copper-nickel contains a smaller percentage of iron and is even more corrosion-resistant and stronger than 90–10 copper-nickel. Nickel bronze is another type of cupronickel alloy.

Cupronickel hulls with extremely good antifouling properties have been built for those who could afford them. They have been known to last indefinitely without even being painted since no cathodic protection is needed. This alloy is sometimes seen in exhaust pipes or guardrails, but the expense doesn't often seem warranted.

Nickel Alloys

Nickel alloys are those in which nickel is the predominant element (greater than 63%), and the most well-known is monel. Nickel is very corrosion resistant, although it can suffer from pitting like stainless steel.

These alloys are very resistant to high water velocity attack, and are excellent shaft materials, though very expensive. Monels can be welded or brazed, but a special flux is needed.

Monel series 400 alloys contain 66% nickel, 32% copper and small amounts of iron, manganese, silicon, carbon, and sulfur. This is the commonest type of monel, used for shafts and various marine fittings. It can be used on a steel hull as long as the steel is protected from corrosion by zinc anodes. Monel series 500 (K monel) is similar to series 400, but tin and aluminum have also been added. It is even stronger than series 400.

Although monel is one of the best metals for underwater use, its nobility can cause corrosion problems when it is used on a steel hull. The chance of corrosion is high enough that a 316 stainless propeller shaft might be safer, since stainless is less apt to promote corrosion of any bare steel than is monel.

There are other, very expensive high-strength nickel alloys that contain hardly any copper, but 15–22% chromium, up to 8% molybdenum, and iron. They are very strong and virtually inert in seawater. These alloys are used in making wire rope, water injection exhaust piping, and super cavitating propellers. Look for them under the trade names Inconel, Incoloy, or Hastelloy.

Aluminum

Aluminum is a very light nonferrous metal that alone is very soft and therefore not used for much except forming or pressing. Marine-grade aluminum is an alloy containing up to 15% silicon, iron, copper, magnesium, manganese, chromium, zinc, or titanium. Aluminum alloys have a very high strength-to-weight ratio, and are generally very corrosion resistant because they form protective oxide films similar to stainless steel. However, those alloys that have this superior corrosion resistance are not as strong as plain carbon steel. For this reason frame scantlings for aluminum boats are larger than for an equivalent steel hull.

Aluminum, like most other metals, is either wrought or cast. Wrought aluminum is shaped during the manufacturing process either by rolling or extrusion through a die (for spars). Most wrought aluminums cannot be heat treated, but develop strength through strain hardening. The grades containing magnesium (5000 and 6000 series) are very strong, ductile, and corrosion resistant. Cast aluminum, the material of which most fittings are made, is poured into a mold; some cast aluminum can be heat treated. The addition of silicon or copper improves casting characteristics, but may lower corrosion resistance.

Aluminum can't be flame cut or arc welded efficiently, and TIG or MIG welding processes must be used to assure a correct bond. Since aluminum is not very stiff, it is more easily deflected than steel. It is also more notch sensitive than steel, and can fracture.

Galvanic corrosion is not generally a critical problem on aluminum hulls, but it can be quite serious once it starts since aluminum is low on the galvanic scale. It should be insulated even from metals of similar galvanic position, especially below the waterline. There is no reason to use aluminum underwater on a steel boat. Contact between aluminum and stainless steel, mild steel, or monel above the waterline is usually harmless, but some bedding between the two is still recommended. The use of copper, brass, or bronze near aluminum should be avoided; aluminum is usually fastened with stainless fasteners or aluminum rivets. When an aluminum mast is used on a steel boat, proper insulation at the mast step and the point where the mast passes through the cabin is required.

Some aluminum is anodized, that is, made the anode in an electrical treatment, to thicken its protective oxide film. As it builds up, the protective oxide layer gets flaky white and powdery if not painted, which affects its appearance. Although pitting occurs in aluminum, it is mild and not serious. Poultice corrosion, the formation of a sticky white hydroxide on the surface of aluminum, is caused by high moisture levels and, while not a critical type of corrosion, detracts from its appearance. Chromate paints are recommended for aluminum, and paints with lead, mercury, or copper should never be used since they are more noble and will lead to galvanic corrosion.

Like steel, the different types of aluminum are divided into various series depending on the principal alloying element. However, only two are generally used for marine applications.

The 5000 series is made up of alloys that variously combine aluminum and magnesium with traces of chromium and manganese. These alloys are noted for good weldability, corrosion resistance in seawater, high tensile strength and hardness. The 5000 series is available in many forms, including rod, pipe, bar, and extrusions. Most aluminum hulls are made from this type of aluminum, as are rivets and fittings. The 5086 aluminum commonly used for hull construction has a yield strength of 37,000 psi and a tensile strength of 47,000 psi; 5154 and 5454 have also been used for hulls. Type 5056 is used for rivets, and it has a yield strength of 50,000 psi and a tensile strength of 60,000 psi.

The 6000 series adds silicon and traces of titanium and copper to the elements used for the 5000 series in order to produce high corrosion resistance and high strength. Masts and other spars are manufactured from 6000-series aluminum, since it is easily shaped and welded. Nos. 6009, 6010, and 6061 are also made into sheets and forgings. No. 6061 is used for spars or hull plating; it has a yield strength of 40,000 psi and a tensile strength of 45,000 psi. Spars are also fabricated of Nos. 6063, 6066, and 6070. 6000-series aluminum can be heat treated.

The 7000 series is not corrosion resistant enough to survive for long in the marine environment.

Aluminum is not generally used on steel vessels except for spars, hatches, winches, and a few other deck fittings. Aluminum, though cheaper than bronze, is generally more expensive and less durable than galvanized or stainless steel. It is also very difficult to weld aluminum to steel unless transition blocks are used.

Aluminum is occasionally used for the deck or cabin of a steel boat in order to keep the topsides weight lower. Aluminum decks are occasionally riveted to the hull, but this method is not recommended even if the aluminum is well bedded. Special transition blocks, which are aluminum on one side and steel on the other and are formed by fusion welding, can be placed between a steel deck and an aluminum cabin so that each can be welded to the other. These blocks are very expensive and are only used by a few shipyards. The aluminum cabin can more easily be bedded and bolted onto a steel flange.

One of the most important uses for aluminum on a steel hull is in metallizing (see Chapter 10).

Zinc

Pure zinc is most commonly used in anodes to protect the hull from galvanic corrosion. However, zinc is an important element in many alloys. It is also used in coatings, especially flame-sprayed primers and zinc chromate primer coats. Gar alloy (zinc with copper and silicon) may sometimes be found on board in galley utensils. It is less expensive than pewter, for which it is often used as a substitute.

Tin

Tin, like zinc, is more often seen as an alloying element rather than as the principal element of an alloy system. However, tin coating of water tanks is very common. Pewter, which is a tin-antimony-copper alloy, might be found in fancy serving dishes in the galley. However, old pewter contains lead and should not be used for serving food.

Lead

Lead is a very dense metal with a low melting point that is extremely valuable in alloys, although it is too soft to have any structural applications. It has good corrosion resistance and is easily shaped, but it will creep. Antimony or tin can be added to harden the lead. Its primary marine use is as ballast, but it is also combined with other materials as sound insulation, particularly over the engine room. By itself, lead is virtually noncorroding in seawater.

Lead solder is an alloy of lead and tin and should not be used on a steel boat. The joint will have problems because of galvanic corrosion in seawater, and may leak during a fire. Silver solder, containing 7.5% copper, is better for brazing and is easily worked. Solder's only real use aboard a steel ship is in the installation of the electrical system.

Titanium

Titanium is an unusual and expensive metal that may have a good future in steel boatbuilding because it is very strong, light, and inert. It is already a common addition to alloys. It is very noble and inert. A hull built of titanium-clad steel would probably last forever, but you also might be paying for it forever.

CONCLUSION

Most of the metals discussed here can be excluded from use on a steel vessel. The fewer the different metals that are used, the better. Stainless should be limited to above-water use, except that 316 can be used for propellers and shafts.It will probably be used mostly for items like the bow roller assembly, the chainplates, nonintegral water tanks, travelers, slides, and rigging; to strengthen chafe points; and for interior woodwork fasteners. Manganese bronze might be used for propellers, seacocks, and mast fittings, while coppers are limited to heat exchangers, tubing, and electrical wire. Aluminum can be used for portholes and deck fittings, but is better limited to spars and metallizing. Nickel alloys, like monel, are acceptable as propeller shafts if you can afford them. Zinc is best for anodes and primer coatings, while lead or iron is still the standby for ballast. There is really no need for the brasses (other than manganese bronze) except as interior decoration or the ship's bell.

—Chapter 3——————————————————————

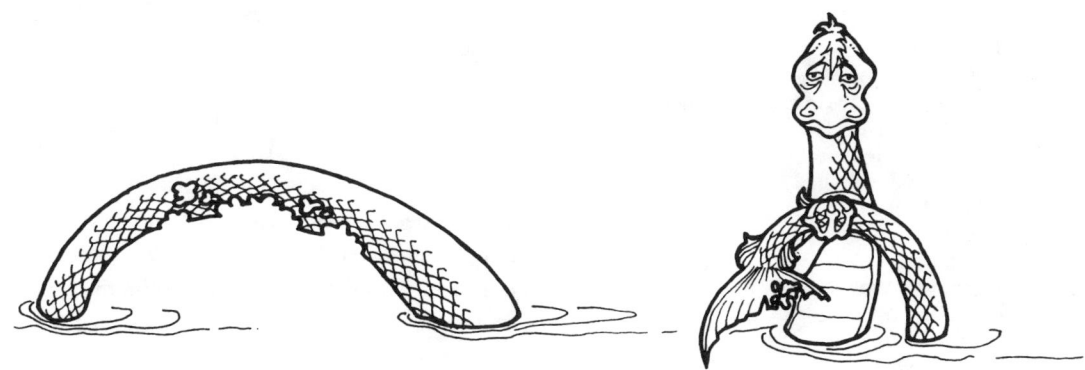

Preventing Corrosion

Most of the horror stories about steel hulls (and every hull material has its share of stories) are inspired by corrosion. But a proper understanding of the corrosion processes and how to prevent them will take the horror out of any steel boat story. That old saying about an ounce of prevention proves true once again for boats made of steel.

Nature seems to have a way of reducing things to their most stable forms: rock erodes, wood rots, and steel rusts. Corrosion is the natural process by which metal alters and deteriorates through chemical or electrochemical reactions. Different metals corrode differently, and the marine environment influences the way in which this process occurs.

The dreaded rust is simply the byproduct of a chemical reaction in which free oxygen (either in the water or the air) combines with iron ions from the steel to form iron oxide. The simple chemical breakdown of steel actually occurs fairly slowly when the process is left to progress at its own rate, even if the bare steel is submerged in sea water. The layer of rust that develops insulates the steel beneath it to some extent, since rusting will not begin unless bare steel is in contact with oxygen. Mill scale on a steel hull under construction actually protects the steel until the rust is blasted off. However, in a saltwater environment, this simple chemical reaction can be transformed into an electrochemical

process that can destroy bare steel in a very short time. Other types of corrosion are caused by stresses acting on metals when the boat is in motion. But all kinds of corrosion can be prevented by proper design, construction, coating, and maintenance. If the first three actions are executed well, the time needed for maintenance will be greatly reduced.

ELECTROCHEMICAL CORROSION

While simple corrosion requires only iron and oxygen for the reaction to occur, electrochemical corrosion is more complex. Metals with different electrical potentials must be placed in an electrolyte, and an electric current must then pass through the electrolyte. Galvanic corrosion and electrolysis are both produced by electrochemical reactions and are differentiated by the way in which the current is generated.

Every metal has a particular electrical potential—the tendency to attract or lose electrons and thereby generate an electric current—determined by the atomic structure of the metal. This potential is expressed in terms of voltage. The galvanic series, which lists metals in order of their increasing tendency to lose electrons, is a quick way to see how metals will interact, which will gain and which will lose electrons. The greater the dif-

Table 3-1 THE GALVANIC SERIES OF METALS IN SEAWATER

Cathodic or noble (−)	Platinum
	Gold
	Graphite
	Silver
	Titanium
	Hastelloy C
	Stainless steel (types 304 & 316, passive)
	Iconel (passive)
	Nickel (passive)
	Monel (400, K-500)
	Silicon bronze
	Copper
	Red brass
	Aluminum bronze
	Admiralty brass
	Yellow brass
	Iconel (active)
	Nickel (active)
	Naval brass
	Manganese bronze
	Muntz metal
	Tin
	Lead
	Stainless steel (types 304 & 316, active)
	50-50 lead-tin solder
	Cast iron
	Wrought iron
	Mild steel
	Cadmium
	Aluminum alloys
Anodic or base (+)	Galvanized steel
	Zinc
	Magnesium

Note: *The position of metals in the galvanic series can vary depending on their exact compositions and the methods used to determine their electrical potentials.*

Although an electric current will flow under many conditions, it flows best through an electrolyte. An electrolyte is a solution of water and different salts containing positively and negatively charged ions (atoms or molecules that have acquired an electric charge by gaining or losing electrons), which help the current move along. Sea water contains up to 3.5% sodium chloride and traces of calcium carbonate and magnesium sulfate. All of these salts ionize easily, so salt water is readily transformed into an electrolyte.

The corrosion rate depends on the current flow, which in turn is affected by the distance between the dissimilar metals, their positions on the galvanic scale, the relative surface area involved, oxide films on either of the metals, and the particular conductivity of the electrolyte. For example, the smaller the surface of the noble metal and the larger the surface of the base metal, the less severe the corrosion of the base metal will be. On a steel boat with a bronze seacock, the steel will corrode slowly because the hull has a much greater surface area than the more-noble seacock. The rate of corrosion is also increased in areas where extra oxygen is present (for example, in the splash zone).

Environmental conditions can also influence the rate at which corrosion will occur. The warmer the water, the more rapid the corrosion, since higher water temperatures increase the conductivity of the electrolyte as well as its ability to dissolve salts. Acid-polluted water, which usually contains hydrogen sulfide, accelerates corrosion, while alkaline conditions like those produced in the presence of cement retard corrosive attack. Certain sulfate-reducing bacteria, found in some muds, also increase the rate of attack. Water moving past the hull washes away any protective film and provides extra oxygen to the metal, accelerating corrosion.

Galvanic Corrosion

Galvanic corrosion is caused by a current which is generated because of the difference in electrical potentials of dissimilar metals that are electrically connected. As the metals gain or lose electrons to ions in the electrolyte, they become charged (either positively or negatively), and an electric current begins to flow between them, creating a galvanic cell. The less-noble material becomes the negative anode and loses electrons into the electrolyte solution, while the more-noble metal becomes the cathode, acquires a positive charge, and attracts free electrons. As a result, the less-noble metal loses mass.

ference in voltage between two metals, the more intense the activity will be. Those metals high on the galvanic series are called "noble"; those lower down are "base." The noble metals are more active and tend to gain electrons, while the base metals, which have a higher electrical potential, tend to lose electrons. As a metal loses electrons, it corrodes and loses mass. Each metal's electrical potential and place on the galvanic scale can vary depending on the exact alloy composition and the immediate environment.

In order for a current to flow between two metals, they must be electrically connected; in other words, there must be a path along which the current can flow. When two bare dissimilar metals touch each other, they are electrically connected. Metals can also be connected by a wire running between them.

Fig. 3-1. *Unchecked corrosion can really damage a hull. But restoration projects can still be successful.*

Galvanic corrosion occurs fairly slowly because the current involved is quite low. As the reaction continues, the cathode becomes coated with a film of the anodic metal, and the current is reduced even more. (However, this film can easily be washed away when a boat is in motion.) The protection that metallizing provides to a steel hull is actually a useful form of galvanic corrosion. If the hull is scratched to bare steel, the layer of less-noble zinc or aluminum deposited during metallizing becomes the anode, and the bare steel cathode is coated with a protective blanket of zinc or aluminum.

However, with anti-fouling paints containing copper, the same reaction can lead to hull corrosion. If the hull

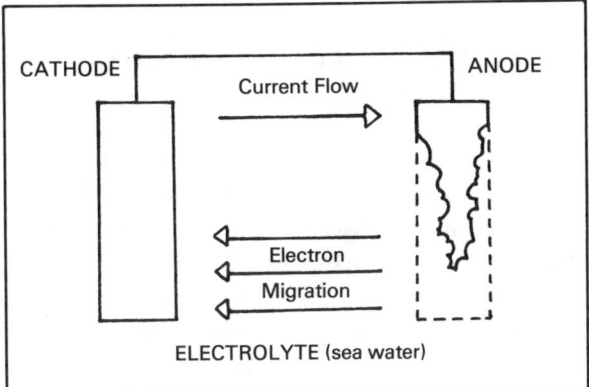

Fig. 3-2. *A galvanic cell. The anode might be bare steel or a zinc; the cathode, a bronze or stainless fitting.*

is scratched down to bare metal, the copper anti-foulant becomes cathodic and the steel corrodes. Special barrier coats or high-build primers are required between the hull and copper anti-foulants to prevent this reaction. The best prevention, however, would be to choose a non-copper bottom paint.

Since steel is so low on the galvanic scale, any time a dissimilar metal is used on a steel hull, there is a chance that galvanic corrosion will occur. The risk of corrosion is even greater below the waterline. The ideal hull would have all fittings and attachments fabricated of steel, welded directly onto the hull, and treated with the hull in the coating process. In practice, though, other metals will be used. Stainless steel propellers, bronze seacocks, lead ballast, monel shafts, aluminum spars, and copper wire have all been used successfully on steel hulls. But success is only possible if the bare metals are prevented from touching each other and if sacrificial zinc anodes are used for protection.

Galvanic corrosion is also seen in wooden boats in the form of "nail sickness." The current generated between metal fasteners and, for example, an iron keel or a bronze seacock, can cause the fasteners to deteriorate. If steel fasteners are used, even galvanizing doesn't prevent this reaction, since galvanized coatings tend to lose adhesion, especially when the fasteners are used in wood. Silicon bronze nails are subject to de-zincification (which will be discussed later). Galvanic corrosion near

Fig. 3-3. *A water trap caused by poor deck camber. Fortunately, if rust begins in this spot, it will be seen.*

wood in some cases can cause the wood to decay if it is not kept dry and painted. For example, if stainless steel is secured in wet mahogany, the mahogany will turn black.

Electrolytic Corrosion

Electrolytic corrosion (commonly called "electrolysis") is much more destructive than galvanic. The corrosion is caused by a current coming from an internal or external source (the equally-dreaded stray current)—a shore power cord drooping into the water, an improperly grounded battery, a break in the insulation around wires, failure to isolate an AC power hook-up. In galvanic corrosion, the current voltage is quite low, but stray current can range from a trickle to the hefty current discharged into the water by a short circuit in a shore power cord. This high current causes bare metal to corrode at an alarming rate.

Although steel is basically a homogeneous material, there are small differences in electrical potential not only among different pieces of steel but also within a single piece. This small difference is not enough to generate a current, but if an external current is present, even these similar metals can become the anode and cathode in a galvanic cell. If stray current is present in the hull itself due to an improperly grounded electrical system, a bit of surface dampness or a small puddle of salt water on the deck or cabin is enough to start the reaction.

Although electrolytic corrosion due to external currents is rare at sea, trouble may be waiting back in port.

A corrosion meter can be set up onboard to pick up signs of trouble. There are several variations, some that simply monitor current and some that control the level of protection provided by the zincs. In monitoring systems, stray current shows up as an increase in the base reading of the normal current flowing between metals and the sacrificial zinc anodes. An increase in voltage also can indicate that the zinc is being called on to provide extra protection (for example, if the steel hull is scratched to bare metal). Systems which can also control the zinc output voltage allow precise monitoring and adjustments to the corrosion protection system so that zincs are conserved and the metal is not overprotected. Radio grounding and lightning protection are also reportedly improved. Both portable and throughhull meters are available for both types of systems.

PREVENTING ELECTROCHEMICAL CORROSION

Since electrochemical corrosion attacks only bare steel, the best way to prevent it is to make sure that the metal is always protected by paint, bedding, or insulating gaskets (or all three). However, chances are good that sometime on an active ocean voyage bare metal will be exposed. So prevention must take several different forms. A well-designed steel hull will not corrode if it has an intact coating system, properly attached and insulated fittings, a negative-ground electrical system, and cathodic protection with zincs or metallizing.

Corrosion prevention must be considered even at the design stage. Designing out corrosion includes making sure that all areas of the boat are accessible for inspection and painting, that all sharp steel edges are beveled or rounded so that the paint can adhere well, that the use of dissimilar metals is limited, and that stresses are not allowed to concentrate in any one area of the hull. All areas must be properly drained so that there are no water traps present.

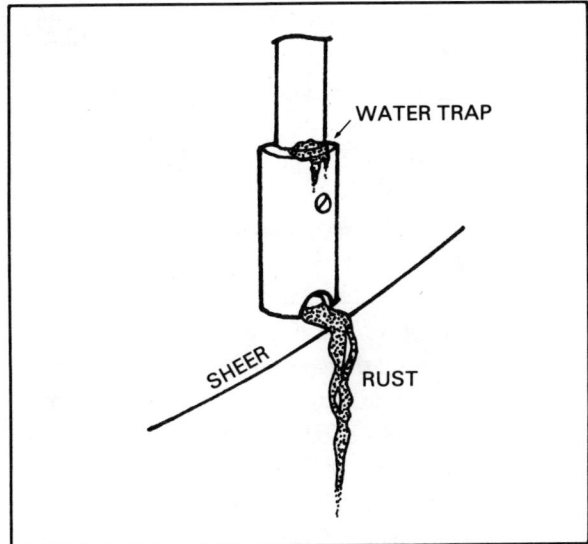

Fig 3-5. *Water traps in this poorly designed steel stanchion are also responsible for rust streaks.*

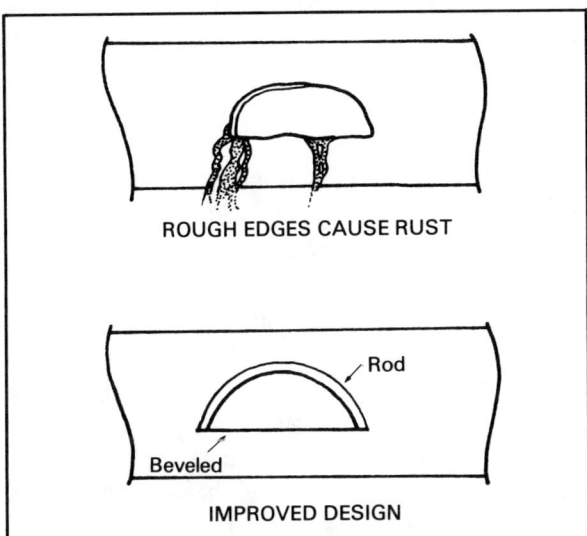

ROUGH EDGES CAUSE RUST

IMPROVED DESIGN

Fig. 3-4. *The sign of a corrosion-free boat is that small details, like the correct finishing of scupper drains, get careful attention.*

In the last few years, advances in paint chemistry have created coatings that offer incredible (though not guaranteed) corrosion resistance. Since the coating system (possibly including metallizing) is so vital to the health of a steel hull, the largest chapter in this book is devoted to discussion of the different kinds that can be used. As on any boat, conscientious maintenance and regular haul-outs will be necessary to keep the coating system intact.

As mentioned above, the best fittings for a steel boat are of mild steel, since the traditional metals used for marine fittings (stainless steel, bronze, and brass), as well as the more exotic but useful metals (cupronickels, aluminum bronzes, monels, etc.), are more noble than the hull. Often these dissimilar metals have properties that make them more apppropriate than steel for other boat systems, and they can be used if they are totally insulated from the steel by non-conductive gaskets or bedding so that no current can flow. Bedding also helps keep salt water from getting trapped between metals where, as an electrolyte, it will enhance corrosion. Most of the best choices for gaskets and bedding are the new high-tech plastics and compounds (see Chapter 12).

Steel should never be joined directly to any other metal except by welding, and, with other metals like stainless steel, this should only be done above the waterline. Nickel, tin, lead, or soft solders in contact with steel will almost guarantee corrosion. If more noble metals that can't be welded to steel (like bronze) are used, they must be fastened mechanically with bolts or studs that have been properly insulated.

The other way in which dissimilar metals can be a problem is if loose metal objects, such as coins (especially nickels), gold, silver, or platinum jewelry, or pencils with graphite leads slide out of sight in the bilge. If any bare steel is exposed down there, corrosion can result. This is much more of a problem with aluminum boats, since the metal is often left uncoated.

Although electrolytic corrosion can be a real headache in crowded harbors, there's no need for it to exist within your own hull. Grounding the electrical system on a steel hull is very simple, but the method is different from that used on other hulls. All the wiring should have a two-wire insulated return in which one wire (the negative) completes the circuit and the other grounds the circuit to the hull at a single point, often the engine bed. The hull should never be used to complete the circuit; in other words, current should never be running through the hull. A copper bonding strap, like that used on wood or fiberglass hulls, is not required. If the electrical system is going to be plugged into AC dockside current, an isolation transformer should be fitted between the AC plug-in and the boat's electrics. (See Chapter 16 for other ways to prevent stray current from occurring within the hull, including using proper wire size and protecting circuits.)

No matter how careful you are with *your* boat, you have to protect it from stray current generated by careless folks and overlooked situations. You also have to deal with the fact that there may be small galvanic cells set up within the hull because of variations in purity within the hull plate. The zinc anodes used on almost every boat are even more useful on a steel hull. Since it is less noble than steel, the zinc, rather than any bare steel, will become the anode if a galvanic cell is created and will sacrifice itself and protect the steel. Magnesium, like zinc, is low on the galvanic scale and could be used as an anode. In practice, however, it is difficult to shape and more expensive than zinc.

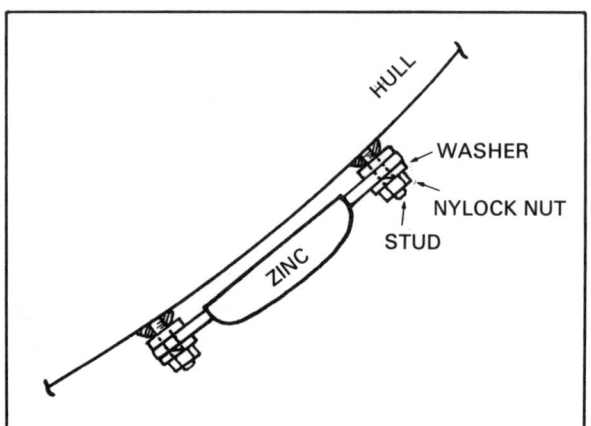

Fig. 3-6. *A zinc anode correctly mounted on studs.*

The effectiveness of a zinc anode depends on two factors: proper placement of the anode and proper electrical connection to the hull. The purity of the zinc is also important, and special grades, like US Military Specification 18001H, should be used rather than commercial zinc. A zinc anode must be placed fairly close to the concentration of dissimilar metals, such as near the propeller, transducer, or throughhulls; although, because sea water is such a good electrolyte, the zinc can protect areas at a little distance from it. (For the sake of performance, zincs should not be placed in areas of unusual turbulence, since they will further interrupt the flow of water past the hull.) The zinc anodes must be electrically connected to the steel in order to protect it, so they are best bolted directly onto steel studs that have been welded to the hull. Of course, theoretically, the zincs could be welded to the hull by their steel straps, but this method is impractical since they need to be replaced fairly

often if they are doing their job. Since they are in direct contact with the hull through the studs, the zincs do not require additional bonding to the hull and dissimilar metals, as must be done on non-metal hulls. The steel hull itself provides the bond. Does it need to be mentioned that zincs should never be painted over?

Impressed-current systems protect the hull by using an externally generated current that simulates the voltage of zinc. The current flow is adjusted so that the hull is made the cathode in a galvanic cell whose anode is a non-corroding material (often platinum). These systems are really only practical for use with shore power or for big fancy yachts with large generating plants, because of the high power requirements involved; they also tend to cause the paint to lift off the hull. Occasionally, impressed-current systems will be found in sophisticated marinas, but there is always a danger that the system will fail and current will short-circuit through the hull and cause rapid corrosion.

Cathodic protection with zinc anodes can also be used to prevent corrosion of underwater fittings such as those made of stainless, manganese bronze, aluminum bronze, or monel. These are all more noble than zinc, and so become the cathode in any galvanic cell. In this case, the zinc must be electrically connected to the item to be protected. Perhaps the best example is zincs attached to stainless or bronze propellers and shafts.

CORROSION IN ALUMINUM AND STAINLESS STEEL

Two of the most common other metals that will be used on a steel hull are aluminum and stainless steel. Both of these metals have similar corrosion problems because each derives its protection from an oxide layer that develops on the surface of the metal. If the oxide layer is deprived of oxygen so that it cannot renew itself, certain types of corrosion will develop.

Crevice corrosion is the chemical reaction in which the protective oxide film is broken down. It commonly occurs in stainless and some aluminum fittings that are either submerged or contain voids that are not sealed or covered.

Proper design of fittings and appropriate use of materials can help to prevent crevice corrosion. Stainless stanchions and rigging terminals or aluminum masts that allow sea water to collect inside them will fall prey to this type of corrosive attack. Type 316 stainless is really the only kind that can be used underwater with some degree of assurance that crevice corrosion will not occur. Aluminum can be anodized to thicken its oxide layer.

Once the protective oxide film has been broken down, *pitting* can occur. The unprotected area becomes anodic to the surrounding surface, setting up a galvanic cell. (Carbon steel will also pit if a very small area of steel becomes anodic to the rest of the hull.) The pitting can be quite deep because of the small area of the anode in relation to the large cathodic area. Pitting is especially prevalent in submerged metal because salt water is such a good electrolyte, but even the constant washing of fittings or rigging wire by salt spray can lead to this type of corrosion. Stainless steel shafts are particularly prone to pitting near and under the shaft bearing, and this area should be checked as often as possible, especially if an inspection shows that the zinc has totally deterioriated.

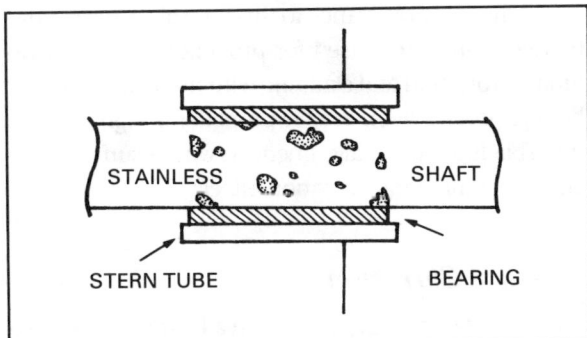

Fig. 3-7. *The pitting in a stainless steel shaft.*

Of course, both stainless and aluminum are also subject to electrochemical corrosion, although aluminum presents more of a problem in this area because it is low on the galvanic scale and tends to corrode rapidly once the process has started. Especially with aluminum masts, fittings must be chosen with care and properly insulated from the spar. The best choices are aluminum, stainless steel, and monel, although galvanized steel can be used successfully. If an aluminum mast is stepped directly on the steel deck or hull, an insulating gasket must be fitted.

Stainless steel is subject to another type of corrosion called *weld decay.* This generally occurs in austenitic stainless that has been reheated to between 600 and 900°C during welding. Weld decay describes an intercrystalline attack of corrosive liquids that causes chromium carbide to precipitate from the stainless, thus affecting its inherent corrosion protection. The corrosion is not limited to the weld itself but to the whole area that has been reheated. It can be prevented by using stainless with a low carbon content and by proper welding techniques.

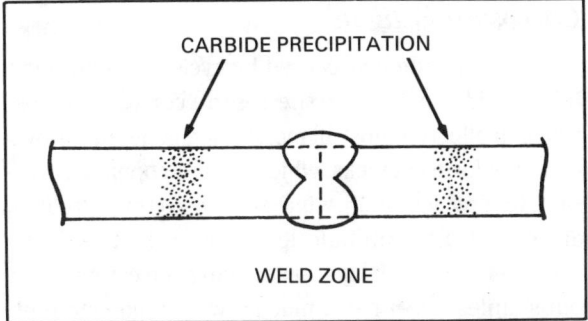

Fig. 3-8. *Weld decay.*

There is one more type of corrosion, *stress corrosion,* which particularly affects stainless steel and other brittle metals with high notch sensitivity. It is caused by steady tensile stress in wet, corrosive conditions, exactly the stresses acting on rigging wire, spar tangs, and fittings. Internal stresses produced during fabrication can also cause stress corrosion. The constant tensile loading causes tiny cracks in the metal that then corrode rapidly. It most often shows up in the form of cracks, and, although they may be slow to develop, rigging failure stemming from this type of corrosion can be quite abrupt and life-threatening. Stress corrosion is affected by the concentration of salts in sea water, high temperatures, rough edges, and poor weld beads, so proper design and fabrication can help to prevent it. Carbon steel is generally not subject to stress corrosion, although stress concentrations can have other effects.

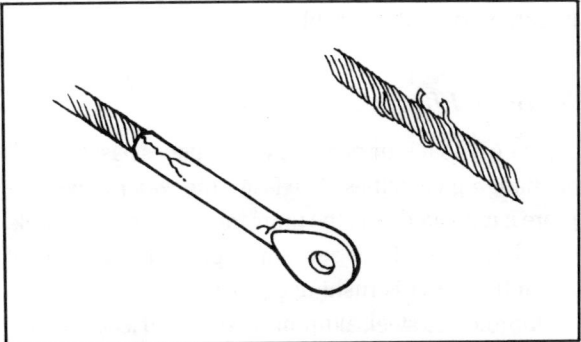

Fig. 3-9. *The signs of corrosion fatigue in stainless terminals and wire.*

OTHER TYPES OF CORROSION

There are a number of other types of corrosion which can cause the failure of metal parts of a boat. Some are due to poor fabricating techniques, some to the nature of the metal, and some to stresses acting on the hull.

Corrosion Fatigue

Corrosion fatigue is caused by cycles of alternating tensile and compression stresses in a corrosive atmosphere. It affects almost all metals, and generally shows up in the form of cracks, which are then open to corrosion. Rolling, vibration, wind, and stress concentrations at notches all contribute to corrosion fatigue. Zinc-coated steel resists fatigue better than plain carbon steel, but stainless steel has a much lower fatigue strength than carbon steel. This type of corrosion is more likely to show up in deck fittings, rigging, or masts, although if the steel hull is not properly stiffened in, for example, the area near the propeller, fatigue can show up in the hull.

Corrosion fatigue (and, for that matter, stress corrosion) can also occur in extremely cold weather. When the steel is very cold, rather than deforming plastically, it can become brittle and crack. When a metal is subject to brittle failure, any stresses, for example rolling seas, can cause cracking.

Hydrogen Embrittlement

Hydrogen embrittlement is a type of stress corrosion that occurs in steel and stainless steel when improper welding electrodes are used. Lower grades of stainless steel can absorb hydrogen, making the metal more brittle and subject to cracking. Mild steel is not usually subject to hydrogen embrittlement except in the weld zone, and the use of series-7000 low-hydrogen electrodes will help to prevent this problem.

Velocity Effects

When a boat is underway, water rushes past the hull at changing velocities. The faster the water flows, the more it is aerated, and the more free oxygen is available in it. The effect of this aeration depends on the type of metal the water is rushing against.

Unprotected steel, aluminum, zinc, and lead are subject to a type of corrosion called *impingement*, which progresses rapidly. More noble metals, like stainless steel or monel, have good resistance to impingement. The fast-flowing water washes away any fouling organisms that can increase corrosion, and the tendency of the oxide layer on stainless to break down underwater is counterbalanced by the availability of extra oxygen. Manganese bronze and copper erode more easily, although copper performs better in fresh than in salt water. The design of the hull profile, throughhulls, and other protruding objects should ensure that there are no high-turbulence areas that will add to this velocity effect. Throughhulls, like transducers for depth sounders, can be recessed or mounted in a heavy-duty plastic casing to preclude both turbulence and corrosion.

The second type of corrosion caused by water velocity is called *cavitation*. It occurs especially on propellers when the back-eddy effect of the blades' motion causes a decrease in water pressure around the blades. Tiny airless bubbles are formed, and as they collapse on the surface of the metal, they actually pull off little chunks of it, causing pitting. Cavitation causes loss of speed, vibration, and noise. The more noble the metal, the better resistance it will have to cavitation. Of the common propeller materials, monel and stainless steel perform the best, followed by manganese bronze. Steel and aluminum have poor resistance to this type of corrosion and therefore are rarely used for propellers, although cathodic protection and cladding with more noble metals help to protect steel. Proper propeller design (mainly more blade area) and alignment, as well as surface hardening, can prevent cavitation effects.

Selective Corrosion

Pure metals are rarely used on a boat (the main exceptions, of course, are lead ballast and zinc anodes). Whenever an alloy is used, it may be subject to selective corrosion, in which the less noble element in the alloy is eaten away due to electrochemical reactions. This is particularly prevalent with the brasses (including manganese bronze), and is one reason that the use of brass underwater is not recommended. Brasses contain zinc and copper, and de-zincification, in which the zinc is dissolved away, leaving a soft mass of copper, occurs easily underwater. Alloys containing aluminum are subject to de-aluminification, and cast iron may fall prey to graphitization, in which the ferrite is removed, leaving only weak graphite. De-alloying is often seen in brass or silicon bronze seacocks. The last thing you want to worry about is your seacocks dissolving away, but some of the more noble metals may cause corrosion problems with a steel hull. (The topic of correct materials for seacocks is discussed in Chapter 13.)

Atmospheric Corrosion

This type of corrosion generally occurs above the waterline, and is caused by corrosive agents such as pollution, sulfur, chlorine, oxygen, water vapor, or carbon

Fig. 3-10. *Although the easiest way to attach wood to steel is with studs welded to the hull, if the bedding fails, corrosion can begin.*

Fig. 3-11. *The owner of this boat plans to completely replace the rusted deck plate and then have the hull metallized.*

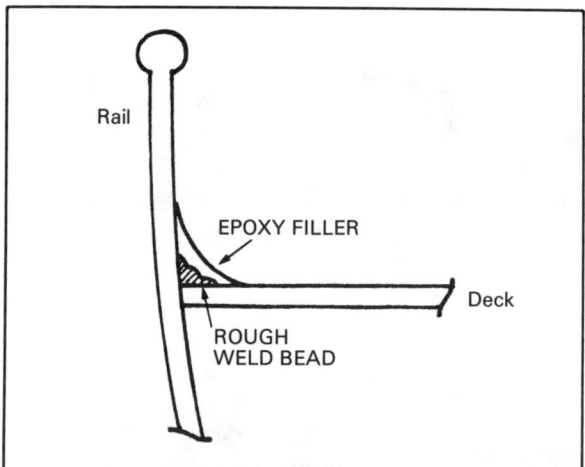

Fig. 3-12. *The rough fillet weld is smoothed with epoxy filler so that paint will adhere and protect it from corrosion.*

dioxide. All metals are affected to some degree by contaminants in the atmosphere. Both aluminum and stainless steel have a natural resistance to atmospheric corrosion because of their oxide films, so no coating is necessary or recommended for them. Other metals will hold up better if they are coated or sheathed.

Breakdown by Mechanical or Physical Means

Wearing, galling, erosion, or static electric corrosion (such as nylon friction) are not major problems in themselves, but can increase in importance when combined with other types of corrosion. They are mostly caused by chafing, so the obvious solution is either to protect the metal or to reduce the chafe.

WOOD DECKS ON STEEL HULLS

Everyone loves a nice wood deck, and it certainly goes a long way to increasing the esthetic appeal of a boat. However, wood decks laid over steel using traditional construction methods almost certainly guarantee corrosion.

It is impossible to totally seal a wood deck. No matter how much polysulfide bedding or other goop is spread between teak boards, the wood will expand and contract, and sooner or later water will become trapped between the wood and the steel. (A possible exception is one of the methods using epoxy adhesives.) As the wood works, it begins to wear away the coating on the

steel, and at some point bare steel will be exposed. The perfect conditions for electrochemical corrosion—bare steel and an electrolyte—are now present, and all you have to do is wait for the rust streaks to appear.

Many different methods have been tried to outwit this fate, including laying plywood down first, holding the wood off the steel by using straps or cleats, securing the wood to steel beams rather than constructing a full steel deck, and so on and so on (see Chapter 15 for more details.) These methods don't always solve the problem, and they add unnecessarily to the work. Steel decking alone is much easier to build and maintain. It comes down to a choice: risk corrosion with wood decks or cover the steel with a product like Vetus or Treadmaster, making the deck more comfortable to walk or lie on.

On small areas like rub rails or bulwarks, wood can be used successfully as long as a good bedding compound is used between the wood and the steel.

CONCLUSION

Although steel does rust, and rusts rapidly under adverse conditions, corrosion can be prevented. A corrosion-free design has soft corners, good clean welds, no irregular surfaces, simple clean metal joinery, proper insulation between metals, a good paint anchor surface, a proper coating system, and some way of draining condensation.

You will sometimes hear that steel boats rust from the inside out. This is only true if the inside is not properly designed and coated, if the electrics are not insulated properly, and if the hull is not surveyed periodically. Bottoms are always inspected at haul-outs, and the beginnings of corrosion are noted and cured. So should the interior of the hull be inspected on an annual basis, and any repairs made promptly. This means that in designing the interior woodwork, you will have to allow for access to potential problem areas. Old steel designs left much to be desired in terms of water traps and framing systems that left crevices. Many older steel boats were not blasted inside, so coating failures were more common.

With a better understanding of metals and the factors that cause their deterioration, designers and builders can make better decisions before the building process begins. And the owner can make better preparations for the maintenance and repair required to keep a fine steel yacht healthy and beautiful.

—Chapter 4————————————

Plans in Steel

Most sailors will argue that the perfect cruising yacht does not exist. And, indeed, it's even hard to define what that ideal might be. Some people like to cruise along slowly, while for others getting there fast is the most important part of a voyage. Different experiences at sea create different opinions about the safest vessel. Although long-distance cruises have been made with varying success on many types of boats, each skipper has had complaints and seen room for improvement. Many compromises must be made to arrive at improvements, but, with the proper design and choice of material, you can come very close to realizing your ideal.

Each new cruising design should be a step toward creating that perfect cruiser: a boat that is completely seaworthy, performs well under all conditions, and is esthetically pleasing. Theoretically, a boat of any shape can be designed, but whether it can be built and, once built, perform as desired, is the true test of a good design.

Of course any owner will be understandably anxious about cost. The final price tag (both design and construction costs) depends largely on the length, beam, and volume of the boat, but also on the ease with which the design can be built. The simpler and cleaner the design, the better are the chances that the cost will be reasonable. Theoretically, again, a steel hull of any shape can be constructed, but the cost and building time required for added complexity may be unnecessary.

Design itself is an extremely complex topic, and we can't cover all its aspects. There are many excellent books devoted to the subject, notably *Sailing Yacht Design, Skene's Elements of Yacht Design,* or *Understanding Boat Design,* listed in the recommended reading section in the stern of this book. All we can hope to do in this chapter is suggest some of the things that must be considered in designing an ocean cruiser, review some of the compromises that can be made, and see how steel fits into the picture.

THE VOCABULARY OF DESIGN

Like any specialized field, yacht design has its own vocabulary. When the designer starts talking about DWL and CLP, you can translate using the following glossary.

Area of wetted surface (Aws) is the area of the underwater surface of the hull, including the keel and rudder, expressed in square feet.

Aspect ratio refers to the height of the sail rig. Split rigs generally have lower aspect ratios than single mast rigs such as sloops or cutters. Higher aspect ratio vessels often have deeper drafts.

Balance refers to a well-designed boat that has just the right amount of weather helm (proper amount of lead between CE and CLP). Proper balance enables a boat to track and handle well.

Beam is the maximum width of the vessel, usually located near amidships above the waterline.

Beam/LWL ratio affects initial and reserve stability. It is often greatest at the deck or waterline. Hulls of different lengths have different optimum figures.

Center of buoyancy (CB) is determined by the underbody shape and is the center of the volume of the boat's displacement. It is usually calculated fore and aft and expressed in feet abaft the bow or percentage of length at waterline (LWL) aft of the amidships position of the design waterline (DWL). The location of the CB changes as the boat heels, and its relationship to the center of gravity (CG) during heeling determines the vessel's stability.

Center of effort (CE) describes the center of the area of the sails with a 100% foretriangle. It is the centroid of the sail area fore and aft and the total of all sail areas. To find the center of effort of a rig with two sails, multiply the area of sail A by the distance between sails A and B and divide this product by the total sail area. This

figure is the distance between the center of sail B and the CE. The CE should be ahead of the center of lateral plane (CLP) to avoid a heavy weather helm.

Center of flotation (CF) is the center of the area of waterplane and the point at which a vessel trims fore and aft.

Center of gravity (CG) is the center of the vessel's weight.

Center of lateral plane (CLP) is the center of the area of the boat's underwater profile, often calculated without including the rudder. Hypothetically, if a boat is pushed sideways at this point, it should not swing toward either end, providing resistance to slipping to leeward. Also called center of lateral resistance (CLR).

Design waterline (DWL) is the waterline length as the designer drew it on paper, not necessarily as it actually sits on the water. The actual waterline may be slightly different depending on loading, although the two should be fairly close for good performance.

Displacement is the weight of the boat expressed in pounds, tons or cubic feet. It refers to the amount of water the boat will displace at rest. The actual displacement specified by a designer should also include all basic equipment and stores onboard. On a new custom

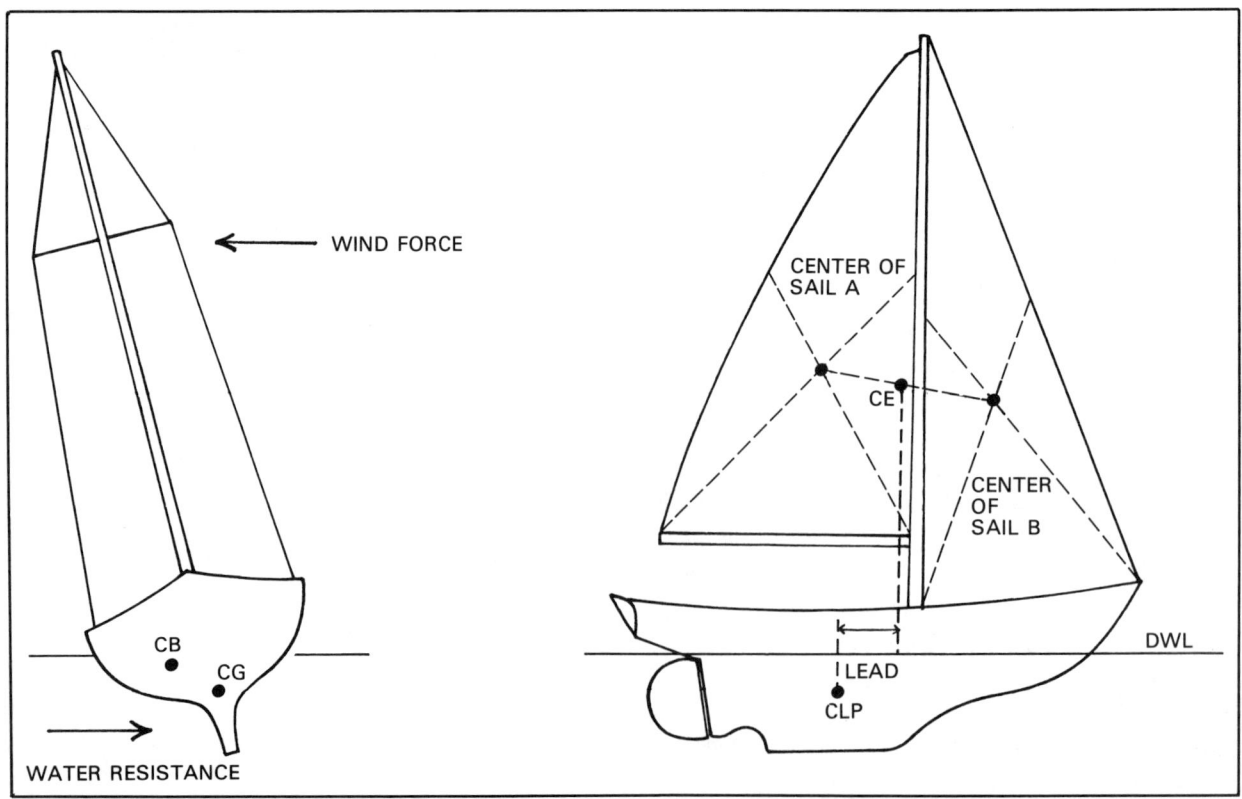

Fig. 4-1. *(right) Finding the center of effort of a rig. (left) The relationship between the center of buoyancy and the center of gravity changes as the boat heels.*

design, the owner should clarify with the designer exactly what was used to arrive at the displacement figure (tanks full or empty, anchor, books and personal gear, etc.).

Displacement-to-ballast ratio (D/B) usually describes the percentage of ballast in relation to the total displacement of the vessel. Most cruisers have about 30–40% of their weight in ballast. The amount of ballast is critical to dynamic stability.

Displacement-to-length ratio (D/L) allows comparison among hulls, and is usually a nondimensional figure. A lower D/L means reduced resistance since there is less form friction. A boat with the same displacement but more length than another will be faster. These figures depend a great deal on the size of the boat, but some common D/L ratios are as follows: racers, under 160; racing cruisers, 160–200; medium offshore, 200–250; medium-heavy cruisers, 250–300; 350 and over, heavy displacement. Smaller boats may have higher ratios. The formula for D/L is:

$$\frac{\text{Displacement (in tons)}}{(.01 \text{ DWL})^3}$$

Draft is the distance from the waterline to the deepest point of the hull, and determines the depth of water needed to prevent grounding.

Hull curve of areas, usually included in lines drawings, represents the longitudinal distribution of the hull volume. This curve gives some indication of the hull resistance, and should be a fair, curved line to reduce resistance.

Lead is the theoretical percentage that the CE is ahead of the CLP at the DWL, found by dividing the distance from the longitudinal CLR to CE of sails by the LWL. The exact amount of lead is measured in percentages, and the optimum varies with the type of rig and use of a centerboard. When underway it is also affected by the beam and type of hull, the sheeting of the sails, the curve of the sails, and the leading edge of the hull.

Length overall (LOA) is the length of the boat from stem to stern and usually includes the bowsprit and boomkin, especially when you're boasting to friends about your boat.

Length on deck (LOD) is the actual hull length and excludes all appendages. This figure is used when you're negotiating moorage fees.

Length at waterline (LWL) is the length of the boat measured in a straight line between perpendiculars fore and aft, from the points at which the bow and stern meet the water. The actual LWL will increase as the boat is loaded or heels over.

Lines drawings show a boat from three different views: side or profile, plane or top, and section or end view (sometimes called the body plan). These are usually the first drawings done by the designer after a preliminary layout is agreed upon.

Moments are used to locate various centers, and are calculated by multiplying weight times distance. The product is expressed in foot pounds. They should not be confused with the moments of inertia used to calculate the stability of a boat.

Moment to change trim one inch (MCT1") is the moment (in foot pounds) to change the trim one inch, that is, ½" down at the stern. Since the balance point (the longitudinal center of flotation) is usually aft of amidships, change at the bow will exceed change at the stern.

Prismatic coefficient (PC or CP) (sometimes called the coefficient of fineness) is the ratio of the volume of displacement to a circumscribing volume equal to the area of the maximum section times the LWL. In simpler terms, it indicates the fineness or fullness of the ends of the boat. The average cruiser has a PC of about .54. A higher PC shows a boat with fuller ends, like a motorsailor, whereas a lower PC would show a boat with finer ends, like a racer.

Table 4-1. SYMBOLS USED IN CONSTRUCTION DRAWINGS	
⋈	Midsection (amidships) of DWL
△	Displacement in pounds (saltwater) or long tons (fresh water)
△T	Displacement in tons
▽	Displacement in cubic feet (volume)
⌀	Diameter
₵	Centerline
⊙	Vertical center of gravity
WF	Wide flange
℞	Plate
[	Channel
F.B.	Flat bar

Sail area (SA) can be found by multiplying the base of the sail by the height and dividing by 2. The formula for determining the best working SA is WL beam × LWL × 2.5.

Sail area/displacement ratio (SA/D) is used to compare different boats. The formula is:

$$\frac{\text{Sail area}}{\text{Displacement (in cu. ft.)}^{2/3}}$$

Displacement in tons can be converted to cubic feet by dividing by 64. This figure is then raised to the 2/3 power (.667) and divided by the sail area. A lower SA/D ratio shows good speed potential. The usual range is between 12 and 24, with 16 about average for a good cruiser. Longer boats tend to have a higher SA/D ratio.

Sail area/wetted surface ratio shows the boat's potential for speed by relating the power of the sails to the resistance of the hull. It also pertains to stability. The figures range from 1.9 (slow) to 3.0 (fast), and boats with long waterlines tend to be fastest.

Scantlings are the basic sizes (dimensions and spacing) of the various structural parts of a hull, deck, and cabin. They govern the strength and integrity of a hull and are often calculated to comply with American Bureau of Shipping or Lloyd's Rules.

Section modulus is a ratio that aids a designer in choosing correct scantlings for frame sizes in the boat. It is related to hull panel length and width and indicates the strength and stiffness of a hull.

Speed/length ratio (V/L) relates the speed of the boat to its LWL. The formula is:

$$\frac{\text{Speed (in knots)}}{\sqrt{\text{LWL (in ft.)}}}$$

A V/L ratio of 1.34 is the limiting factor for a displacement hull, since over this speed the hull will try to climb over its own bow wave and will lose buoyancy in the stern. This drag will lower the boat's speed.

Stability curve, often called intact stability, is a graph showing the hull's stability at increased angles of heel.

Stations are vertical lines dividing a boat into an even number of equal parts which are used as reference points for lines, drawings, and offsets. Framing is sometimes in the same position.

Table of offsets is a series of measurements put in the plans that define hull shape according to distance from the centerline and height from baseline or the ship's waterline. They are usually expressed down to eighths of an inch and occasionally to $\frac{1}{16}$ ±.

THE IDEAL CRUISING VESSEL

The best performance cruiser is really a blend of the traditional cruising yacht and the ocean racer. In the early days of long-distance cruising, many slow but beautiful sailboats like John Hanna's Tahiti ketch crossed the oceans. Then designers like John Atkin took traditional European styles and developed them into more streamlined, heavy-displacement vessels. Today this streamlining continues more intensively than ever, especially in the high-priced world of racing yachts. High-aspect ratio sloops with deep fin keels, small mainsails and large foretriangles, reverse transoms, and balanced spade rudders are the new look. Although racing rules have definitely affected cruising design, the quest for high speed can often compromise seaworthiness and handling in all conditions, and the true cruiser is apt to be skeptical of a change until it is well-proven. However, these design advancements and owners' experiences have inspired designers to create vessels with both the traditional qualities of a good cruiser and the improved performance provided by a modern underbody.

The most important requirements for a cruising yacht are seaworthiness and performance. A seaworthy vessel should be safe and stable and ride the waves comfortably with a seakindly motion. A good performer must have fine weatherly ability, tracking ability, and speed. Traditional heavy-displacement vessels were known for their seaworthiness, but also for their poor performance due to excessive weight and a long and sometimes blunt underbody. Today's seaworthy vessel doesn't have to be slow. In addition, a good cruising vessel should have ample displacement and volume to carry goods and crew, have a proper sail rig, and be designed in a material that is practical for general operation as well as hazards, haul-outs, maintenance, and cost.

Seaworthiness

A good cruising yacht neither heels excessively in moderate conditions nor capsizes when being driven under more severe conditions. Its stability is divided into two components: initial or form stability and reserve or dynamic stability. Form stability (multi-hulls rely almost 100% on this) is responsible for keeping the boat upright at angles of heel up to 40° and is derived from the shape of the hull and the location of the center of buoyacy. Dynamic stability, which keeps the hull from

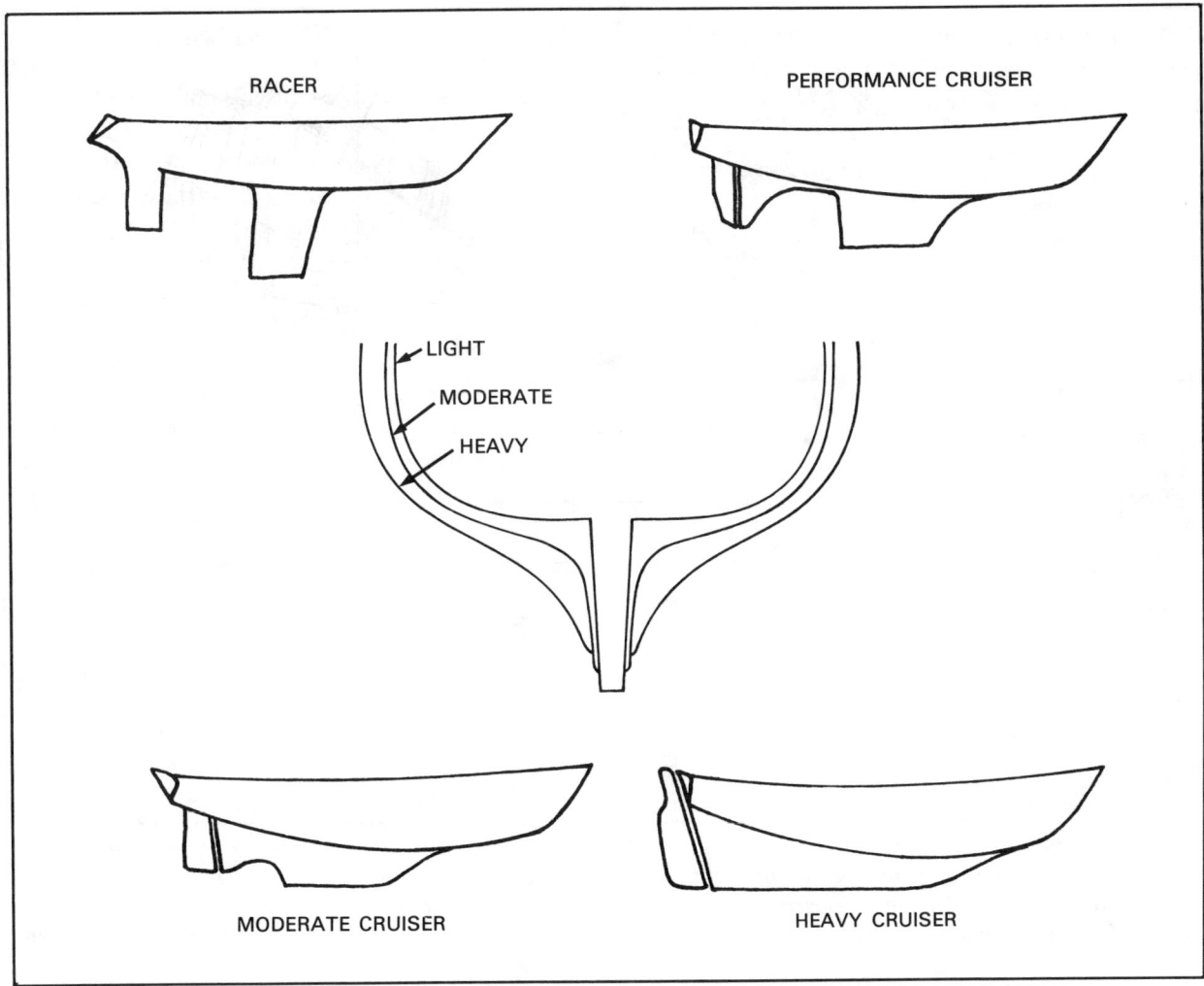

Fig. 4-2: *Sailboats are classified by their hull shapes and lines.*

capsizing, depends on the location of the center of gravity. The two are closely interrelated, and excessive initial stability can sometimes affect reserve stability. Traditional lifeboats, which must be extremely stable to serve their purpose, are very tender until loaded, but once the center of gravity is lowered by the weight of the survivors, these boats rarely capsize. A third, and equally important, consideration is inverse stability, the tendency of a hull not to return to the upright position after a roll of over 180°. This is a problem of boats with shallow underbodies and little ballast, like multi-hulls.

Form stability depends primarily on the vessel's shape. A hard chine at the bilge and a flat bottom increase initial stability, while a softer, curved hull decreases it. The amount of deadrise in the underbody and the distribution of volume fore and aft also influence a vessel's stability. However, too much beam can sometimes adversely affect the range of stability and also create resistance. Moderately full ends add reserve buoyancy, and moderate overhangs prevent pounding and being pooped or pitchpoled.

More important, however, is the location of the center of gravity and its relationship to the center of buoyancy and the aspect ratio of the rig. A good cruiser will generally have ample beam and draft and be properly ballasted to counteract the force of the wind on the sails. The center of gravity, and therefore the weight, should be kept as low as possible. Extreme freeboard or a large superstructure increase windage and weight topsides, raising the center of gravity and requiring more ballast to maintain dynamic stability. The proper displacement-to-ballast ratio is critical for reducing excessive heeling and preventing inverse stability.

A high-aspect ratio rig with a large sail area needs a deeper, heavier keel to provide stability, especially when the wind gusts, but this deeper draft may limit en-

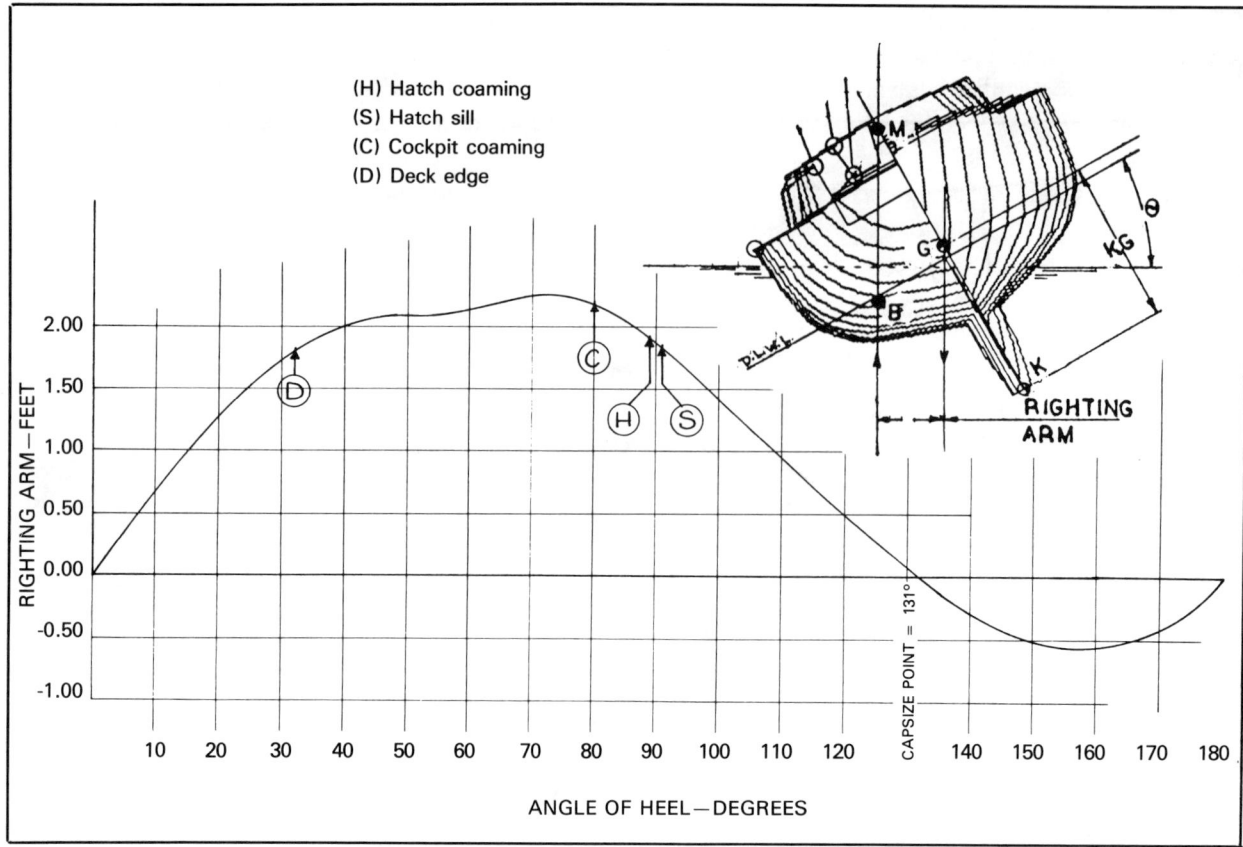

Fig. 4-3. *The intact stability curve for* Perelandra *shows the angles of heel at which the various parts of the boat are underwater. The curve and other particulars are for worst condition (overloaded with fluids at 100% but with all hatches and openings closed with watertight doors. The distance of the curve between C and D shows good prolonged stability.*

Courtesy of John Simpson

trance into shallow harbors and, more importantly, may cause the boat to trip over the keel in a rolling seaway. On the other hand, too small a keel hurts stability as well as performance. Centerboards and twin keels have their places, as long as they do not affect stability.

While some may feel that comfort is not as important to safety as stability, it's a wet, tired sailor who makes the most mistakes. The hull's stability and its ability to keep water out are important to crew comfort. A comfortable boat handles the sea without undue bouncing, pitching, yawing, or hobbyhorsing, all of which are fatiguing to the crew. Of course in a gale there will be some wild motion even on a good cruiser. But then the crew will be using gale tactics and will be prepared to handle the additional stress.

A dry interior depends on the hull's ability to keep water out, while dryness topsides is affected by the amount of freeboard and overhang. Not enough overhang can make the boat uncomfortably wet, but too much overhang or extreme bow flare can created excessive pounding in head seas. The shape of the stern topsides determines if the person at the helm stays dry when running downwind or meeting quartering seas. Although the old-style double-enders part the seas with minimum wake, a larger transom tends to rise above the waves and prevent them from crashing over the stern. On the other hand, too large a transom (like that found on some motorsailers), especially when combined with poor seamanship, tends to increase the chance of broaching when running before heavy seas.

Although safety depends very much on the vessel's stability, performance is also important. A safe hull will heave-to properly in a storm and will not tend to pitch-pole, broach, or capsize, although these misfortunes can hit any boat in extreme situations, especially if she's not properly handled.

Performance

Speed is not the only kind of performance required of a good cruiser. She must also be able to point to windward well and have good tracking ability. Each of these depends largely on the underbody profile, although other factors contribute to performance, so it is there that the most compromises need to be made to achieve a proper shape.

How well a vessel tracks or holds a steady course is due to her ability to resist turning. The keel and underbody area provided directional stability and resist the forces of wind and water, keeping the vessel from drifting to leeward. A vessel that tracks well holds her course without unnecessary helm adjustment or use of an autopilot, an especially important characteristic when cruising with the trade winds. Crew members will be rested and safer thinkers if they are not fighting to hold a restless boat on course.

Of course the vessel must do well on all points of the wind, since the ability to go to windward in critical times can be a life-or-death matter. Windward performance is closely related to general performance: the vessel should have minimal underbody resistance (for example, a canoe shape); a low center of gravity so that she will not heel excessively, since an upright position allows more efficient use of sails; and a tall rig with a 100% foretriangle and a good sail profile. The balance between the low center of gravity provided by ballast and the weight and sail area aloft is also important. Large headsails give the boat drive but may be impractical for cruising, since a very tall rig often requires a deeper draft. The worst performance would come from a turbulent hull with a low aspect ratio rig; a moderate-to-high aspect ratio with a moderate keel depth is best for a cruising sailboat.

Speed describes the forward motion of a vessel and depends on how much resistance the hull offers to the water. Resistance is caused by the shape and amount of wetted surface; in other words, by the underbody and keel. The displacement-to-length ratio, the sail area-to-displacement ratio, and the sail area-to-wetted surface ratio are all helpful in estimating the capacity for speed. Increased waterline length, lighter displacement, and smooth hull shape contribute positively to speed. The vessel's stability is also important, since reduced heel angles give improved driving force to the sails.

So, for the best overall performance, a compromise must be found in an underbody which resists lateral motion but has its wetted surface reduced sufficiently to increase speed. Fortunately, the ability to track and hold course is based on proper balance among the underbody area profile, the center of lateral plane, and the sail area of effort rather than on the lateral volume of the underbody. As long as this balance is maintained, wetted surface can be reduced. Tank tests have shown that great wetted surface area is not necessary for tracking and that the deadwood area and forefoot contribute more to lateral plane than is necessary. The deep fin keel and high aspect ratio rig like that of ocean racers is the ultimate attempt to reduced wetted surface while maintaining stability.

Performance cruisers, on the other hand, do not want to limit entrance to harbors by deep drafts, and so must strike a compromise between keel depth and wetted surface. Therefore, their keels commonly have a cutaway forefoot, reduced deadwood area, and a gentle slope to the leading edge of the keel to prevent any tripping and allow the hull to ride over submerged objects at the aft end of the keel. These cutaways also help the vessel to round up more quickly, be more responsive when coming about, and get free from a grounding. (Some critics say that with this underbody the vessel will sail more at anchor, but actually the boat will "turn to" rather than charge off too far one way and then back. A small steadying sail can reduce this action if necessary.) This type of keel might be described as a three-quarter keel or a long (rather than deep) fin with moderate draft and the rudder mounted on a skeg. Designer Ted Brewer has also developed "the bite," a cutaway in the deadwood area of a full-keel design as a compromise for tradition-oriented customers who don't want a separate skeg-rudder arrangement.

Rudder design and placement must be considered along with the keel shape, since the two work together to steer the boat. Separately mounted spade rudders are often used with deep fin keels and do provide quick control, especially when backing down. However, these sensitive rudders are often weak and vulnerable, and they have a low stall angle, making them impractical for cruisers. Skeg-mounted rudders have proven the best because, due to the fixed leading edge of the skeg, rudder stalling occurs much later. In other words, the skeg and rudder work together as a complete foil unit, and the skeg also protects the rudder when going over a submerged object.

When a skeg rudder with either reduced deadwood or a bite is used, the propeller aperture (for those vessels with engines) can be located forward of the skeg, where it will not cause turbulence around the rudder. This propeller location also gives the helmsperson better steering control and helm responsiveness. The only draw-

Fig. 4-4. *The 34-foot* Turtle *of the Crusader Class shows the meaning of the word "fairness."*

Courtesy of Sparkman and Stephens

back is that the exposed prop might snag a submerged object, but this is unlikely and can be anticipated by fitting a guard around or below the propeller. The keel also protects the propeller by deflecting the object as it passes under the boat.

Performance is also affected by the lines of the hull, especially at the waterline. A cruiser must have ample beam in order to let the crew live comfortably, but combining this beam with the narrow ends that promote speed will cause the boat to turn, reducing its tracking ability. So increased beam at the waterline demands full ends. Although moderately increased beam could mean increased resistance and lower speed, combining it with sufficient draft reduces the angle of heel so that the hull and keel work more efficiently to keep the vessel upright, and speed and windward performance are improved.

Traditional heavy-displacement cruising boats are often faulted for lack of speed. Although a lighter-displacement hull might handle more responsively and maneuver better in tight corners, heavy displacement is no longer an excuse for poor performance if a modern underbody is matched with optimum sail area. In other words, a moderate-to-heavy displacement cruiser made of *steel* can be fast and able when she carries sufficient sail and has a good hull shape with reduced wetted surface and a long waterline.

Other Factors

The rig chosen for a vessel will determine its ability to "carry sufficient sail." Like many other decisions, this one is governed by personal preference based on past experience. In general, marconi cutter or sloop rigs are appropriate for boats under 40', ketch or yawl for vessels 35–50', and schooner rigs for boats over 50'. As always, there are many exceptions—pocket schooners or large, cutter-rigged ocean racers—which are specialized craft and do not always work well in all situations. Increasing the number of masts and sails adds to cost, but using the best rig is more important than cost.

The main decision for the cruising sailor is whether or not to use a split rig. In this age of racy sloops, one of the main arguments against split rigs is their lack of windward performance. It's true that cutters generally perform better to windward than ketches, but they must have high aspect ratio rigs (and therefore usually deeper drafts) in order to carry enough sail for good speed. Split rigs have many other advantages that may be more important to a cruiser.

When sailing with two sticks, no one sail will be so large that it cannot be handled safely by the average crew or even singlehandedly, if necessary, without relying on roller furling. Two separately stayed masts also increase safety, since if one mast is broken sufficient sail

Fig. 4-5. *This Merritt Walter* Rover *has traditional looks with her clipper bow and figurehead, but she's built with a strong, steel hull.*

can be jury-rigged on the other to bring the vessel safely home. Although the masts for split rigs need to be high enough to carry the correct amount of sail, a bowsprit can be used to allow more sail to be carried forward. Then the aspect ratio of the rig can be lowered, which allows the shallower keel necessary for entrance into many tropical harbors. The many possible combinations of sails also allow the skipper to set those sails which provide the most comfortable motion, and to adapt to changing wind conditions without early reefing.

Of course there are many other sailing rigs that have their devotees—Chinese junk, lateen, staysail, lug, galleon, wishbone—and many perform quite well. Some boats use wings rather than sails. Jacques Cousteau is even experimenting with a "sailboat" powered by a Flettner rotor (a special rotary sail).

Even more important than the number of masts is a sail plan that is well designed, so that each sail is able to work efficiently as often as possible. For performance cruising, the best choice is a ketch with a fairly small, yawlish mizzen that will not interfere as much with the main when going downwind. The sails can be used to go jib and jigger downwind, but still will perform well on the wind, giving you a very flexible rig that approaches the performance of a cutter.

Once those sails are driving the boat to distant islands, the crew needs to be able to dip into the goods and stores carried onboard. Each person onboard will add about 700 pounds to the displacement, if his or her body weight, food, clothing, and equipment are taken into account. In addition, a gallon of water per person per day must also be loaded on board. If any trading is planned, even more storage space will be needed. Volume, rather than displacement, is the factor that decides the boat's capacity to carry goods, although it must be designed to handle the displacement caused by the weight of these goods, since overloading will hurt performance. A light vessel with good volume will allow more to be carried. Volume can be estimated by looking at the length and beam of the vessel (but it can only be estimated, since the beam changes below the waterline).

The ideal cruiser will bring all these features together into a homogeneous unit in which each part works with rather than hinders the others. This boat will probably be described as moderate: fairly wide beam, fairly full bow, not too much overhang at the ends, some cutaways in the keel. Moderation is a good attitude for someone whose life may depend on a hull. But it's only through evolution that an ideal can be achieved. It can be quite an adventure, too!

STEEL DESIGNS

How well does steel meet the requirements for a perfect cruiser? Steel hulls are the safest and most comfortable afloat, and, although they probably won't win many races, their performance is all that a cruising sailor could hope for. But nothing can replace good seamanship when it comes to safety.

The weight of steel is sometimes called an obstacle to good performance, but as we've seen, performance doesn't depend on displacement alone. As long as steel can be shaped to lines promoting good performance characteristics (which it can, especially with round hulls), its weight will not be detrimental, especially in hulls over 30'. It is the design that is critical. Steel designs are becoming lighter as designers recognize the strength of steel and reduce the scantlings of plate and framing accordingly. Much of the stability and comfort demanded by full-time cruisers is easily found in heavy-displacement steel boats that ride the waves with a sea-kindly motion.

Its strength and toughness make steel very attractive to a sailor. You can do things with steel that may cause difficulties when another hull material is used. For example, a steel skeg provides excellent support for the rudder, so that the designer can cut away some of the deadwood without creating problems. And it's worth mentioning again that the strength of steel helps the boat to survive groundings or encounters with rocks, reefs, and floating obstacles like whales, ice, or freighters. Even the best sailors go aground or hit submerged objects. It's reassuring to know ahead of time that you and your boat will survive.

Bodily comfort demands a dry interior, and a steel hull with the deck and cabin welded in place will not leak or work loose, causing the headaches and wet bunks found especially in some wooden boats. There will be no separation or delamination where the hull meets the deck, as in some fiberglass boats. The seas will stay outside where they belong.

Many people, when they hear "steel boat," immediately envision a chine hull. There certainly are more chine hulls afloat than round ones, but round-hull champions (like us) argue that a round canoe underbody gives better fuel efficiency, greater stability, and a kindly motion in various sea conditions: in other words, a 5–10% higher comfort and performance rating. After all, dolphins weren't made with chine bodies. Still, chine proponents would counter that performance is better with a chine hull. (In most cases, they are refer-

Design Name	Designer	LOA	DWL	Beam	Draft	Displace-ment	Ballast	Sail Area	D/L	SA/D
Waterline 333	Waterline	33.25	27.08	11.16	5	14,500	5000	578	325	15.5
Departure 35	Wittholz	35	27.8	10.4	4.25	15,300	5500	600	318	15.5
Goderich 35	Brewer/Wallstrom	35.6	28.3	11	4.75	17,000	5700	644	335	15.6
Pheon	Harris	38	30	11.9	5.5	24,389	—	800	403	15.18
Goderich	Wallstrom	40.9	32	12.7	5.83	23,600	8000	907	322	17.6
Amazon	Shannon	37	32.2	12	5.6	18,900	7000	683	253	15.37
Mauritius	Roberts	43.3	32.6	13	5	26,880	8840	752	346	13.38
#15	Haag	39	32.8	12.33	—	24,000	—	734	304	14.09
Endurance	Ibold	44	32.83	13.08	6.08	29,500	1100	910	398	15.22
	Hartog	39.83	32.83	11.83	5.5	30,000	—	865	405	14.31
Gazelle	Colvin	42.2	33	11.14	3.83	18,168	—	854	226	19.73
	Pape	45	33	12.9	6.5	34,000	1000	888	422	13.51
Tahitian Bay	Hundy	42.2	33.2	12.5	5.67	31,000	—	962	378	15.57
#323	Brandlmayr	41	33.4	12	6	28,774	8000	755	345	12.8
Corten	Brewer	40.3	33.4	12.4	5.5	29,000	—	1002	347	16.95
Horizon	Carius	44.9	33.6	12	6	29,800	8800	833	351	13.84
Verity	Brewer	40.1	33.8	11.9	6	22,950	8250	836	265	16.53
Oceans 44	Beckmann	40.95	33.83	13	5.9	34,000	—	850	419	12.93
	Lucander	41	33.9	12.3	4.6	20,000	5000	727	229	15.76
Joshua	META	39.9	34.3	12	5.3	24,000	8818	900	266	17.27
Navigator	Lucander	45	35	13.6	4.9	33,000	8000	800	344	12.43
	Perry	41.11	36	12.5	7.2	24,000	8400	—	296	16.60
Ocean Rover	Walter	45.8	36	13.5	5.2	39,000	—	906	373	12.58
	Wittholz	45	36.7	13.3	5.9	32,370	1200	1070	292	16.82
Miami	Brewer	44.11	36.8	13.11	6	36,000	1350	1157	322	16.94
	Sutton	42	37	12	4.8	—	—	1000	—	—
Perelandra	Simpson	43.11	37.1	13.8	5.83	34,000	1050	1042	297	15.85
Cruiser	Warwick	47	39	13.7	6.7	32,000	1100	1380	241	21.86
Roberts 40	Roberts	50	39.2	14	6.5	41,000	—	1077	303	14.50

Table 4-2.   A COMPARISON OF STEEL CRUISING YACHTS

ring to planing and speed capabilities.) Indeed, some multi-chine hulls have a shape so close to round that the difference in overall performance is negligible. Chine hulls are almost always easier to build than round, a significant factor for home builders. Whether the hull is to be round or chine is an important decision (see Chapter 5).

Combination Hulls

Steel boats can be designed that use different materials for major sections of the vessel, especially for the cabin or cabin and deck assembly. Lighter-weight aluminum, fiberglass, and wood are the materials most often used with steel to reduce weight topsides and keep the center of gravity low. These combination hulls are not difficult to construct and, in some cases, have other benefits besides lower weight and center of gravity, such as decreased maintenance or a softer appearance. The ratio of steel to nonsteel materials varies in a composite,

but the usual joining points are either cabin-to-deck or deck-to-hull.

Joining an aluminum cabin to a steel deck is fairly easy. The proper gasket (usually neoprene) is laid down, and then the aluminum is secured with stainless steel bolts. Insulated collars around these bolts also help to isolate the metals to prevent corrosion. However, a more expensive method seen in large shipyards uses "transition blocks": imploded aluminum-steel strips in which a piece of steel is fused to aluminum through an explosive method. These blocks are first welded to the deck, and then the aluminum cabin is welded to the aluminum side of the block. Unfortunately, its cost can make this method impractical for most builders, although when used on a large-scale production basis this system is cost-efficient and less prone to galvanic corrosion.

Wood or fiberglass, in the same way as aluminum, can also be used for superstructure construction. If wood is used, a cold-molded epoxy-laminate method, rather than conventional plank-on-frame, would be best both to keep weight down and to prevent flexing, rot, and possible leaking at the joints. Wood or fiberglass can be joined to the "covering board" of a steel deck or a "carlin" flange by proper bolting and bedding. If done properly, the results can be very pleasing.

Other combinations of materials or points at which the steel-material joint is made are possible, but limited, and proper joinery and insulation are important in all cases. For example, an aluminum boat with steel frames would guarantee corrosion problems even with proper bedding. Materials should not be combined without good reason (for example, weight reduction or ease of construction). There are many corrosion problems associated with wood decks laid over steel beams, and the joinery and bedding should be carefully planned and executed.

Although using a combination of steel and lightweight material makes sense, in many cases the cost and labor time will be higher. The idea of a fully welded, monolithic steel structure is more appealing.

Frameless Construction

Some designers are so convinced of the appropriateness of steel for hulls that they have been working to develop lighter displacement designs to be used especially for racing yachts. The result is a hull built with frameless construction. The floors and deck beams, rather than frames, keep the assembled hull rigid. During construction, an external jig built of angle bar supports the plate, which is laid on in long strips. Sometimes a single strip is used from bow to stern, but there can be problems in handling a piece of steel this long. The plate is tacked to a deck stringer bar and braced before final welding. The fair and harmonious curvature of the hull plate gives the hull the required stiffness.

A hull built by the frameless method will not be as stiff as one built with conventional framing. However, frameless construction is particularly suited to multi-chine designs, since the chines increase stiffness, as long as the enclosed angle is less than 150°. The long strip used to plate the hull can be narrower and therefore lighter and easier to handle. Frameless designs commonly use thicker plate to create the correct section modulus, and longitudinal frames are usually included. These hulls also rely more on bulkheads for structural strength.

The hull is usually built rightside up, and although the building sequence can vary, fairness depends on the proper joining sequence and the fairness of the jig. Proper fitting with clean plate edges and good welds is most important, and all tacked plates must be fair before final welding.

This construction method is generally applicable only to hulls under 40' long, since fairness and a proper section modulus are difficult to obtain in larger sizes. Designers like Van de Stadt of Holland have frameless designs available, and Mr. Van de Stadt also has a building manual explaining the system.

SCANTLINGS AND SECTION MODULUS

An owner counts on the designer to produce a hull that meets recognized standards for strength and stiffness. Scantlings for steel vessels have been specified by many groups, including the American Bureau of Shipping (ABS), Lloyd's Rules for Shipping, US Coast Guard, US Navy and others. The designer can judge his or her scantlings against those published by these rulemaking groups. These rules have usually been written for large ship construction, and revisions for construction of small craft have been slow to occur.

In the last few years, designers have recognized the possibilities of creating lighter steel vessels, and are attempting to reduce the scantlings while still maintaining strength. Technological advances in coatings which reduce corrosion also allow lighter plate to be used. The older rules specify heavier plating to give a safety margin for corrosion of the plate, adding unnecessary weight. New types of equipment (for example, MIG welders, nibblers, and plasma cutters), which cause less distortion during the construction process, have also helped reduce scantlings, as have improvements in building techniques, (such as the use of longitudinal rather than transverse framing and cold bending).

Both ABS and Lloyd's are continually re-evaluating small yacht standards, and their rules are used by some designers, but even the updated rules incorporate numerous steel sections which are not necessary for strength and only increase weight. ABS does publish a manual titled *Steel Vessels Under 60 Meters*, but Lloyd's rules are more detailed. If the vessel is to be used commercially, the design scantlings should be compared to the ABS rules, since the Coast Guard requirements for commercial use follow ABS scantlings closely. The Navy has its own ratings and procedures.

Reduced scantlings produce a more logical weight for a small steel cruising yacht. Of course, to produce a

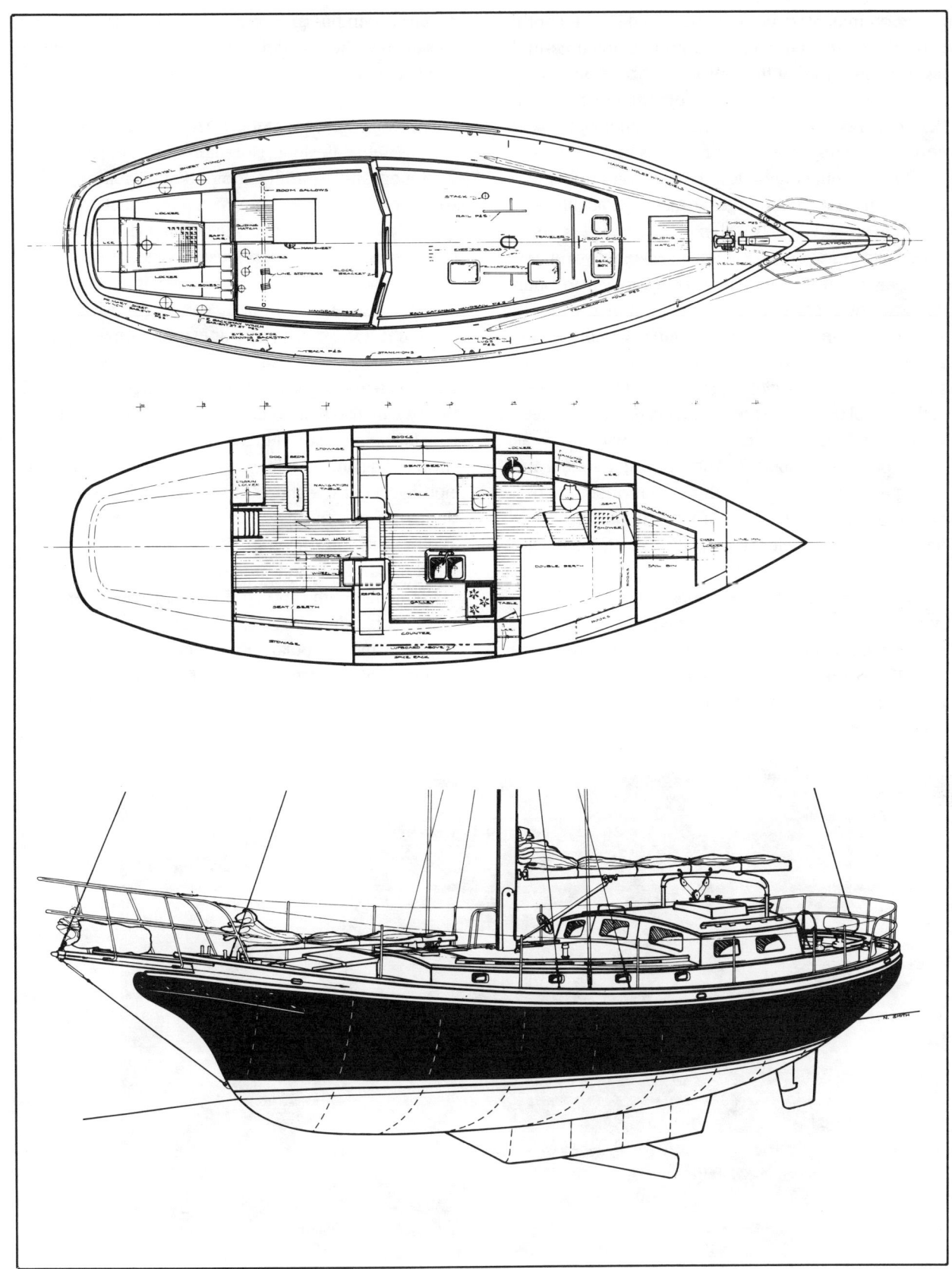

Fig. 4-7. *This traditional boat with a modern underbody was designed by Nathan Smith.*

Courtesy of the designer

distortion-free, weldable hull, the thickness of the plate can only be reduced so much. But today designers and builders are proving that fair hulls can be built from thicknesses just over ⅛″ (9-10 gauge) plate rather than the ³⁄₁₆″ (7 gauge) or even ¼″ plate of which older steel cruising designs were built. Frameless vessels use ³⁄₁₆″ plating and come out quite fair. Steel boats under 80′ can use either 10, 9, 8, or 7 gauge plate for the hull, with 12 gauge possible for the cabin tops, although 8 and 9 gauge plate may be difficult to find. Vessels over 80′ generally require ¼″ hull plate (7 or 6 gauge) to maintain minimum panel stiffness.

The key to preserving strength with lighter plate is the proper balance between the dimensions (weight and strength) and spacing of the frames and the thickness of the hull plate. Thus a proper section modulus is created, and stiffness is distributed evenly with no weak panels or real hard spots. The desired displacement and strength factors determine the section modulus of a design. Generally, boats built with thinner plate use heavier framing, while thicker plating allows for smaller frame scantlings.

A good designer who has proposed a certain framing system to create a certain section modulus can easily adjust the type of framing, plate thickness, and dimensions to fit the preference of a builder. However, the builder's framing system must result in a similar section modulus.

If the chosen builder can't construct the vessel to the designed section modulus, then the boat will be either too heavy or too weak and liable to distort.

COMPUTERS IN DESIGN

The expanding use of computers in marine design work primarily saves time. With the correct programs, many designers use them to calculate optimum loading, statistical stability curves, weight calculations, hydrostatics, performance predictions based on calm seas condition, volume distribution, center of gravity, ABS scantling comparisons, and final lines drawings to any scale. Some yacht designers like Grahame Shannon have even developed their own software systems. Computers can also help in fairing the hull lines, although true fairness must be judged by a designer and during the building process. However, computer programs cannot figure out the shape of round plate; this must be done by a marine engineer, possibly with the aid of a shell expansion drawing. The computer can only do what the designer tells it to do.

Computers with very sophisticated programs are used in the large ship yards; the CAD/CAM design system is one of the more popular. During construction, advanced programs allow computers to control robot plasma arc cutting or welding. In the future braking machines and

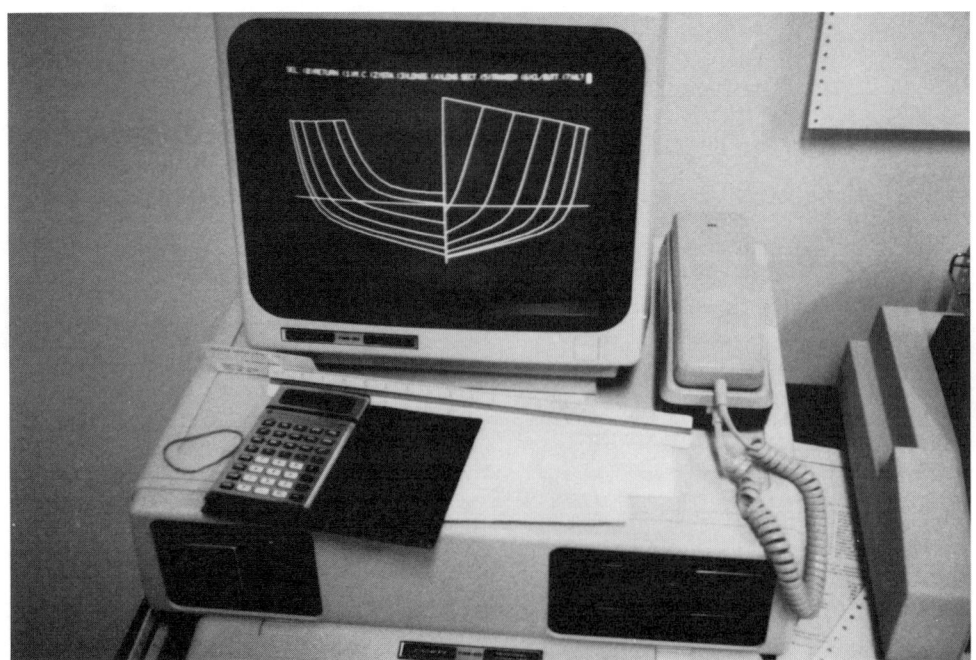

Fig. 4-8. *Computers do work some magic. Press a few buttons and—presto! The body plan appears.*

rollers may also be computer-controlled. But even in designers' offices, computers connected to plotters are already being used to print out full-scale mylar templates. A small plotter prints out the template in sections which are then glued together.

CHOOSING A DESIGN

The Plans

At some point, all the ideas and dreams of a prospective steel boat owner have to come true. The plans for the design are the blueprint for the creation of a dreamboat. Unless you are going to purchase an existing hull, you will have to choose a particular design and decide how to get the rights to build a hull from it. There are several options, including purchasing stock plans, altering stock plans (semi-custom), or contracting with a designer to produce a new custom design.

If both U.S. and foreign designers are included, there are a fair number of stock plans available, some more popular or more suited to home building than others. Colvin's *Gazelle,* Wittholz's *Departure 35,* and Roberts' versions of the *Spray* have been built many times by both professionals and amateurs. The right to build one of these hulls is obtained by purchasing stock plans. But if a boatbuilding yard has an exclusive on a design, the only way to get a boat is to purchase it from that yard.

Stock plans are usually the least expensive, since the designer is providing only copies of his or her original drawings. If a boat has been built from these plans, the designer already may have corrected problems discovered during the lofting and building processes. Different rig options and interior layouts are commonly available. But you often get what you pay for. The designer is only selling plans, not any backup, and such plans can be like a complicated tool without instructions.

The completeness of plans varies dramatically among designers. If an amateur builder is considering a stock design, it would be helpful to find out if a hull has been built from the design and talk to the builder about any peculiarities in it.

The cost of stock plans depends on the number of drawings, which in turn usually depends on the complexity of the design. Basic plans usually have six to eight sheets, but the page count can run as high as 20 sheets. The price of stock plans varies between $200 and $10,000, depending on the size of the boat, and the price is usually a percentage of the original cost of drawing up the plans (sometimes about one-fifth). However, the cost is up to the designer, and may be higher or lower.

You may find a stock plan that needs only a few changes to fit your dream. For example, the hull shape may be fine, but the rig or layout may not. Consulting the designer to make changes in the stock plans is possible for an additional charge, with the charge dependent on the number of changes. Because steel is framed longitudinally, changes in interior layouts can usually be made without changing either the lines or construction plans, and tabs can easily be added for new bulkheads. If the changes are extensive, changing one or two sheets may cost as much as the whole set of stock plans. And if the hull lines need to be adjusted, a custom design might be a better solution.

The experienced cruiser who knows exactly what he or she wants may have to have a new custom design drawn up by an experienced steel boat designer. This is especially true for round hulls, since there are few stock round designs compared to the number available for chine construction. However, that situation is changing. Even now, designers like Brewer, Sutton, Hundy, Shannon, Simpson, Wittholz, and Lucander, to name only a few, realize that round-hulled steel vessels have an important place in the future for both professional yards and amateurs who have the skill to turn out a fair round hull.

The charge for custom plans can be up to 10% of the value of the complete vessel. These plans will cost from $2,000 to $12,000 depending on the complexity and number of drawings, but the end product may be well worth it. In this case the owner is also paying for the designer's services, and should be prepared to spend time consulting with the designer in developing the plans, and possibly later, once building has begun. Compromises in the original dream may be necessary when considering the design realistically, and the designer may understand better than the owner where these compromises should occur. However, the designer's time must be respected, and he or she should not be pestered or rushed. Decisions about arrangement, location and details of joinery, tankage, accommodations, etc. should be made at the preliminary design stage so that they can be incorporated into the construction plans, avoiding changes after the hull has been built. Exact specifications for items such as hatches, tankage, windlass, fairleads, or travelers that must be mounted or welded to precise locations also need to be determined before the welding is completed. Changes to the plans, whether they are stock or custom, may be

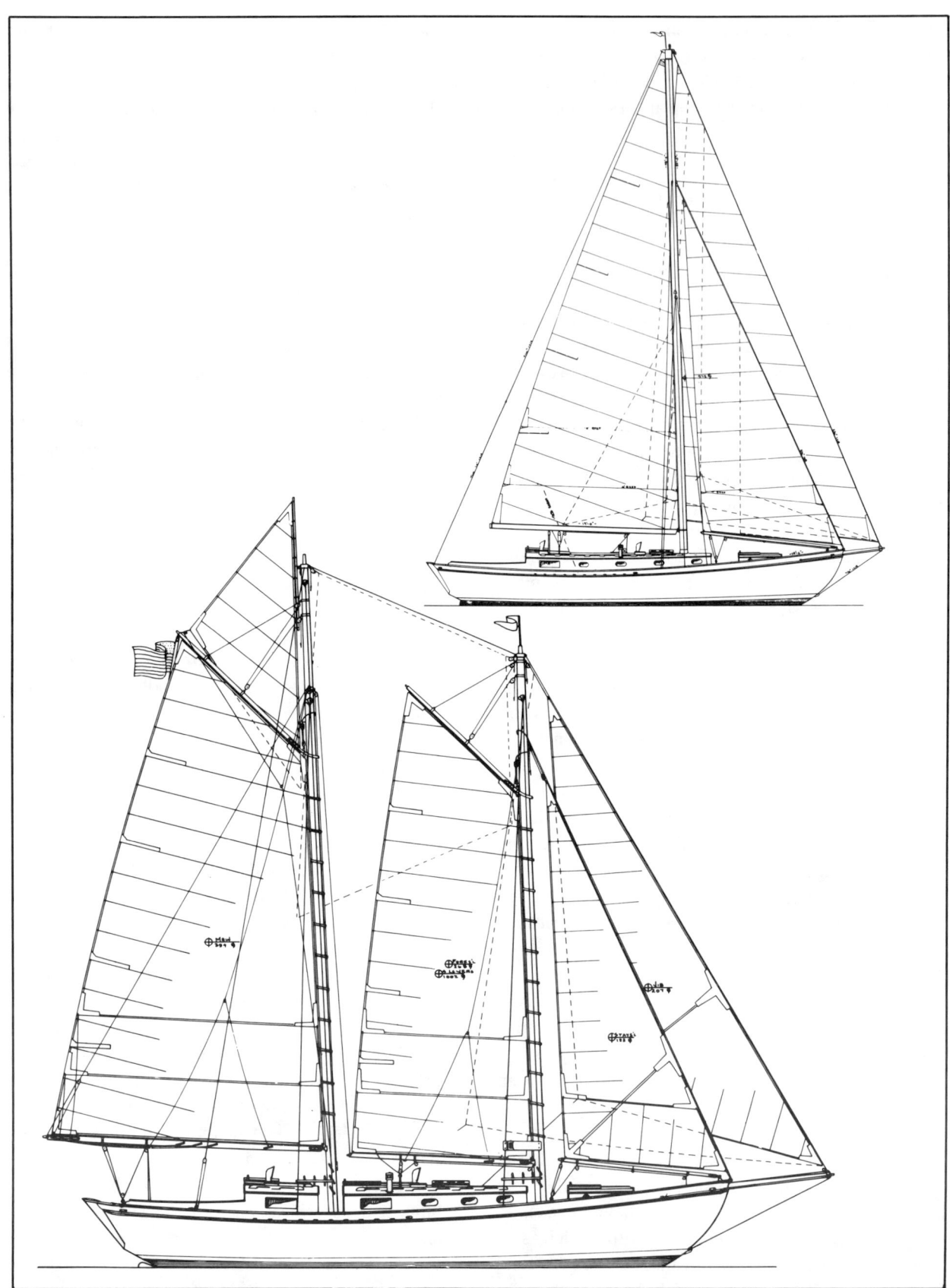

Fig. 4-9. *Like many other boats, Ted Brewer's* Corten *is available with different rigs.*   Courtesy of Jefferson Marine

NAME	M.P.H.	W.T.	FOOT	LUFF	AREA	REMARKS
MAIN SAIL		7.7	SEE	SAIL PLAN		ROLLER REEF., 2 ZIPPERS, CUNNINGHAM GROMMET
MIZZEN		7.7	SEE	SAIL PLAN		
STORM TRYSAIL	50-60	8.5	19.0	26.0	247	ROPE TACK PENNANT
STORM STAYSAIL	45-50	8.5	12.5	30.0	138	17'HD. PEN., 2' TACK PEN.
FORE STAYSAIL	40-45	8.0	16.75	47.0	343	STRETCHY LUFF, NON FOULING HANKS
#3 JIB TOPSAIL	30-40	8.0	21.5	50.0	430	19'HD. PEN., 1' TACK PEN.
28' GENOA	30-35	8.0	28.0	55.0	720	15'HD. PEN., TACKING LINE GROMMET
32' GENOA	25-30	7.0	32.0	60.0	900	9'HD. PEN.
35.5' HEAVY GENOA	15-25	7.0	35.5	65.7	1100	"
38' GENOA REG.	3-15	3.5	38	69.0	1242	CUN. GROMMET
40.5' REACHER	-	3.8	40.5'	69.0	1242	WIRE LUFF
39' DRIFTER	0-3	0.75N	39	69.0	1242	WIRE LUFF, SETS FLYING
MIZZEN STAYSAIL		1.5N	26.0	41.0	443	
TALL SPIN. STAYSA.		2.2	120	56.0	328	TACK BRIDLE LINES
SPINNAKER		1.5N	I.O.R	RULE	MAX.	REACHER
LIGHT SPINNAKER		0.75N	"	"	"	RUNNING
FLOATER SPINNAKER		0.5N	"	"	"	ALL AROUND
SPANKER (STORM SPIN.)		2.2	HOOD	DIM'S.		
MIZ. SPINN.		0.75	-		443	MAX WITHOUT PENALTY
MIZ. GENOA		4.1	13.0	36.2	227	SHEETS TO QUARTER

* 3.0 oz. GENOA SETS FLYING, NO SEASTAY BOLT ROPE.

DESIGN Nº 2055
SAIL PLAN
42'-6" DWL AUX. YAWL

SCALE: ¼"=1'-0"
SPARKMAN & STEPHENS, INC.
79 MADISON AVE., N.Y., N.Y.
20 JULY '71 MT/KIP DWG. Nº 2055-11-T
ALT.:

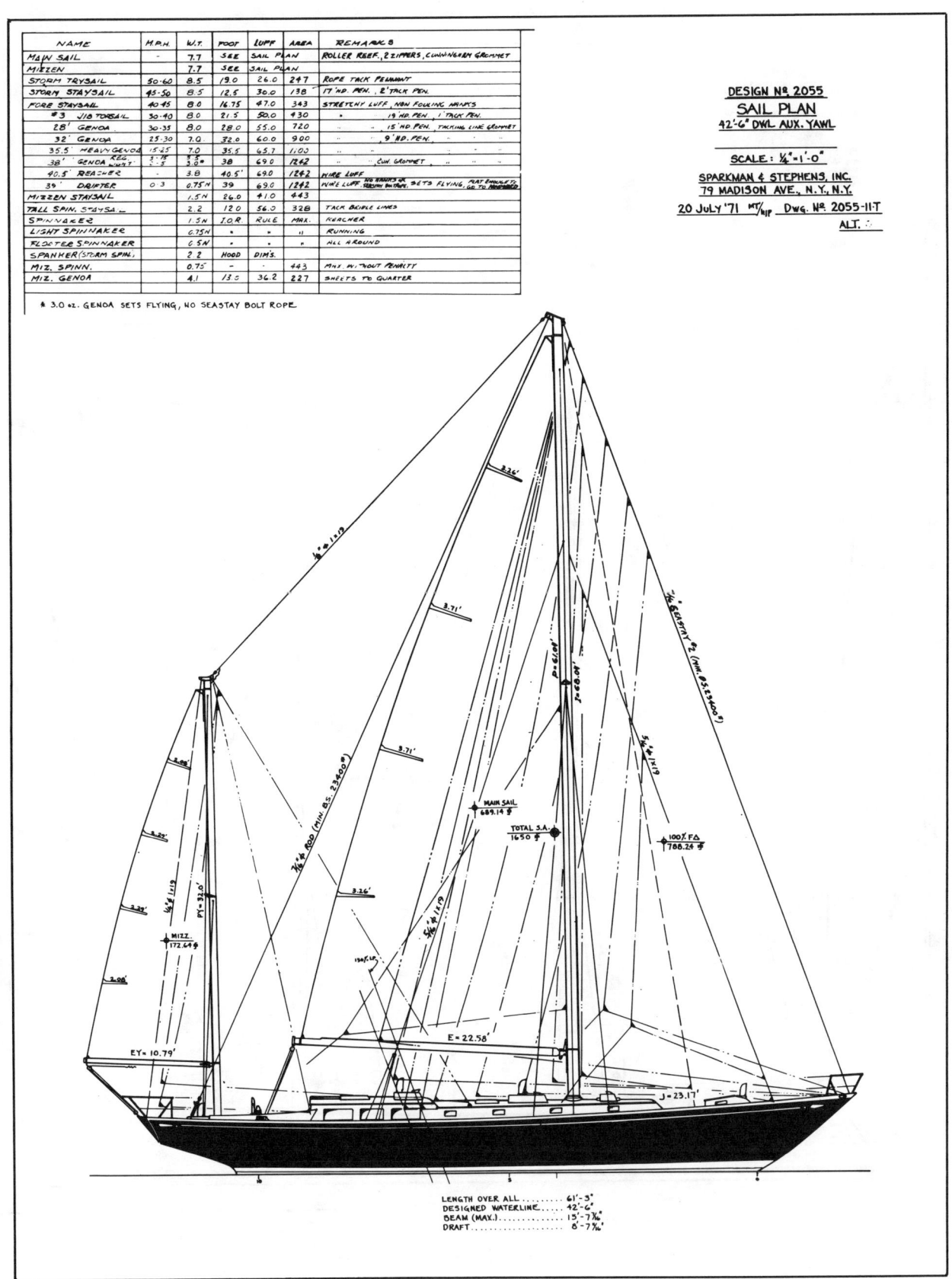

LENGTH OVER ALL .... 61'-3"
DESIGNED WATERLINE ...... 42'-6"
BEAM (MAX.) .... 15'-7 7/16"
DRAFT .... 8'-7 7/16"

Fig. 4-10. *The stock plans for this handsome yawl are available from Sparkman and Stephens.*

Courtesy of the designer

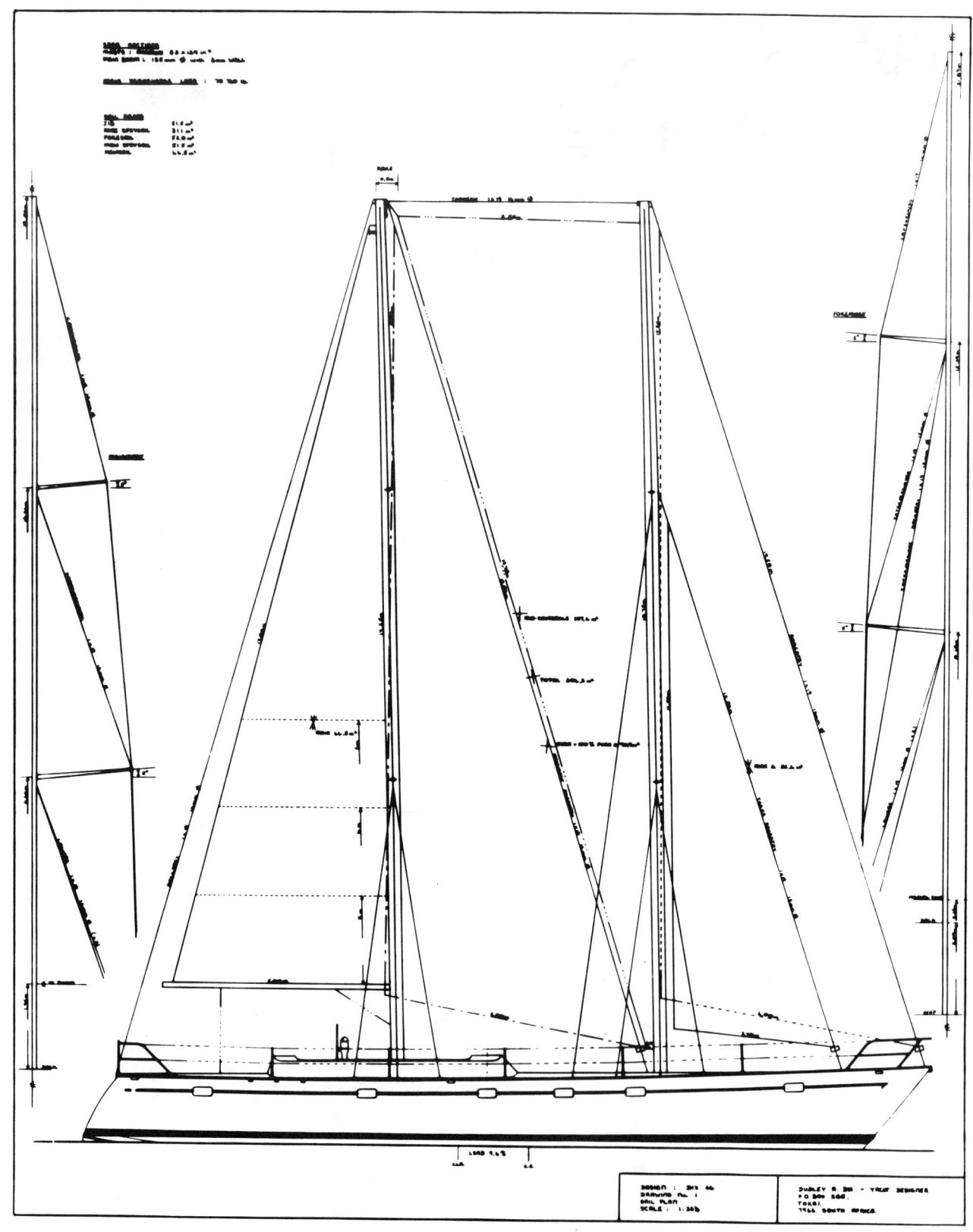

Fig. 4-11. *Dudley Dix recently completed this custom design for the eager owners.* Courtesy of the designer

suggested by the builder, particularly with regard to framing methods. Although minor changes may be successfully incorporated, any deviations from the original plan should be discussed with the designer.

If the design has been done outside the U.S., the designer may be using the metric system for his or her calculations. The cost of the design will also need to be converted to U.S. dollars.

The Designer

A good steel boat designer is someone who understands steel. Some fiberglass and wood designers may argue that designing a steel hull is not that different, since weight and material allowances can be easily calculated from tables, and their knowledge of hull forms and shapes will take care of the rest. This is true to some extent, especially for chine hulls. There is, however, much more to be considered.

Designing a steel hull, whether round or chine, demands that the designer understand steel construction methods and the kinds of curves and shapes that can be formed with a reasonable amount of tooling and a reasonable amount of "persuasion." His or her lines will reflect this knowledge, since ease of plating makes all the difference in saving time and money. For example, some designers have created hull lines with a constant radius fore and aft at the turn of the bilge so that plate rolling is easier.

Everyone—owner, designer, and builder—wants a fair hull. But even some designers who have worked in steel produce lines drawings that are not properly developed for ease of construction and fairness. Adjustments for the material must be considered if unusual shapes are used (for example, extreme twists or wineglass shapes), or the builder may have a good laugh at the designer's expense or, worse, turn out a poor hull.

Table 4-3. SOME HANDY CONVERSION UNITS

MULTIPLY	BY	TO OBTAIN	MULTIPLY	BY	TO OBTAIN
Centimeters	0.3937	Inches	Cubic feet	28.32	Liters
Centimeters	0.03280	Feet	Cubic feet	59.84	Pints
Centimeter	0.01	Meters	Cubic feet	29.92	Quarts
Centimeters	10	Millimeters			
			Gallons, U.S.	3785	Cubic centimeters
Inches	2.540	Centimeters	Gallons, U.S.	0.1337	Cubic feet
Inches	25.4	Millimeters	Gallons, U.S.	231	Cubic inches
Inches	.0254	Meters	Gallons, U.S.	3.785×10^{-3}	Cubic meters
Inches	.0833	Foot	Gallons, U.S.	4.951×10^{-3}	Cubic yards
			Gallons, U.S.	128	Fluid ounces
Feet	30.48	Centimeters	Gallons, U.S.	3.785	Liters
Feet	12	Inches	Gallons, U.S.	8	Pints
Feet	0.3048	Meters	Gallons, U.S.	4	Quarts
Feet	1/3	Yards	Gallons, Imperial	1.20095	U.S. gallons
			Gallons, U.S.	0.83267	Imperial gallons
Meters	100	Centimeters	Gallons water (US)	8.3453	Pounds of water
Meters	3.281	Feet	Gallons water (US)	3.785	Kilograms
Meters	39.37	Feet			
Meters	10^{-3}	Kilometers	Square feet	144	Square inches
Meters	10^3	Millimeters	Square feet	.0929	Square meters
Meters	1.093	Yards			
			Pounds (avoir.)	.0005	Short tons
Millimeters	0.1	Centimeters	Pounds (avoir.)	.0454	Kilograms
Millimeters	0.03937	Inches	Kilograms	2.205	Pounds
			Kilograms	1.102×10^{-3}	Short tons
Cubic feet	2.832×10^4	Cubic centimeters			
Cubic feet	1728	Cubic inches	Pounds of water	0.01602	Cubic feet
Cubic feet	0.02832	Cubic meters	Pounds of water	27.68	Cubic inches
Cubic feet	0.03704	Cubic yards	Pounds of water	0.1198	Gallons
Cubic feet	7.48052	Gallons, U.S.	Pounds of water	0.10	Imperial gallons
Cubic feet	6.23	Gallons, Imperial			

Fig. 4-12. *This vessel illustrates the Dutch style of design: a beamy, shoal-draft boat that has ample room below and can navigate in shallow waters.*

Occasionally the designer will propose a construction detail that could jeopardize hull fairness. A good builder will know practically, rather than theoretically, what he or she can ask of the steel, and will question the designer about such a detail. One of the best "tests" of a designer is whether his or her steel hulls have been built, by whom, and how fair they are. Of course choosing the wrong builder can also ruin a good design.

The owner naturally wants to pay the least possible amount of money for the boat. If the designer is familiar with the sizes, shapes and accessibility of the various metal parts to be used, special machining and complicated joinery can be avoided, saving the owner money. Of course, in certain areas of a larger boat, special machining can't be avoided. Some designers make things too complex, while others don't include enough. Although simplicity is preferable, plans for an amateur builder should include sufficient detail to answer most questions. Professional builders can do with less detail as long as the pertinent details are specified.

Since the reasonable limits of steel yacht construction have not yet been clearly defined, most steel designers create a shape that can be rolled and fabricated without resorting to extreme measures. This approach produces a good, moderate cruising hull shape. However, if the designer knows the material and understands construction techniques used by experienced builders, he or she is free to design a hull that is closer to the ideal cruiser. Thus the designer is helping expand and define the limits.

On the other hand, designers realize that skill levels vary immensely among builders, from the Dutch-trained craftsperson to the amateur constructing his or her first hull. Expertise also varies among professional yards, and few yards have enough demand for "production" boats to become expert with a particular design. However, since there is no limit to what can be done with proper skill and tools, an experienced builder might take on the challenge of an intricate hull shape (and charge accordingly). And some owner-builders are more conscientious than any professional and take time to do a good job. It helps if the designer knows ahead of time who is going to build the hull.

Designers are often particular about which yard builds their hulls, knowing that a complicated design in the hands of an unskilled builder will yield a distorted hull and a distorted reputation for the designer. Poor designs, as well as poor construction, are detrimental not only to one hull but to the reputation of steel (or anything else) as a hull material.

Some designers specialize in plans for home builders, and their drawings may specify more details than a professional yard would need. An amateur would be wise to consider those designs already successfully built by someone of his or her skill level. Full-scale plans on mylar (not paper, which can change dimensions by swelling in high humidity or by bending) may be available for a design, and can save lofting time and expense.

A good steel designer will design corrosion out of the hull, and will make sure that all areas are accessible for inspection and maintenance. Particular attention will be paid to eliminating stress concentrations. He or she will also make sure that the hull can be welded correctly with proper joint placement and shapes that will hold paint well, and that dissimilar metals are well insulated and properly used.

It's best to beware of those designers who say that a particular hull is designed for construction in all materials. The weights change with a change in materials, and the lines that define the shape may need some adjustment. You'll end up with a better hull if you start with a shape you like and then have it adjusted to the building material.

Working with the Designer

Designer Charles Wittholz has kindly given permission to reprint his guide for owners beginning to work with a designer on custom plans, which includes a good description of the drawings included in a plan. Our additional comments are included in italics. Most designers work on this format, but there may be differences in minor details or procedures.

How We Design a New Boat

While there are many variations in boat design procedures, the following steps cover the major items of the design process in their usual sequence:

1. Material is gathered by the Owner, including photos, sketches, magazine articles, etc. to show examples of design style, unique features, and general concepts for the new design. Along with this are the initial concept of basic dimensions, construction material preferences, power, speed, fuel and water requirements and an idea of the general arrangement. Ideas as to design of the masts and rigging are also important in the case of a sailboat. *If the client has little idea of particulars, the designer can help, but cannot be responsible for the client's final decision.*

2. The Architect proposes a Preliminary Study Plan, usually on one large sheet, showing the Preliminary Lines, Body Plan, an Inboard Profile, Outboard Profile or Sail Plan, Arrangement Plan and Particulars *(principal dimensions)*. The Study Plan is made to a small scale, and is not detailed, but is a capsule design which shows the proper relation of the hull form to the accommodations and the rig, power, and speed to make a successful vessel.

3. At this point the Owner is asked to review and comment on the Preliminary Study Plan which is the Archi-

tect's concept of all the Owner's requirements. The Owner's review is a critical phase of the new design since it is relatively easy to revise or change the Preliminary Study Plan one or more times as necessary to get all the Owner's ideas in proper perspective. Changes later on after the final working drawings are begun are very expensive.

The completed preliminary study plans are generally adequate for use in getting preliminary bids from builders, although certain additional construction and framing details may be necessary before a building contract is signed.

4. When the Preliminary Study is accepted by the Owner, larger scale working plans are developed including:

> Lines and Offsets, with detail dimensions, calculation of displacement and design coefficients for proper performance, speed and power. *Designers often do the lines drawings first and send them on to the customer before continuing.*

> Calculation of Scantlings or adequate strength of steel, frames, beams, etc. *They are usually done at an amidships station. If a client has chosen the builder, it is most helpful for the builder to consult with the designer on the framing system particulars and construction details.*

> Construction Plans (consisting of scantlings, plan profile, sections, etc.) showing inboard profile with keel, floors, frames, tankage, engine installation, shaft, prop, spars and ballast; bottom framing plan; deck framing plan; construction sections; and all scantling specifications. *Plumbing, wiring, and rudder arrangements may also be included. The construction plan may involve more than one drawing if the design is complex. These are the basic drawings needed by a builder to give a correct final bid because the extent of extras can change the amount of building time and the charge. The amount of steel needed can be calculated from these drawings.*

> Weight and Trim Calculations, involving the exact calculated weight of all items of construction, mechanical equipment, tankage, interior and exterior finish, accommodations, ballast, rig, fittings, stores, and crew and passengers. The weight total and center of buoyancy to be adjusted as necessary in the calculations and on the plans for the boat to float on her designed waterline.

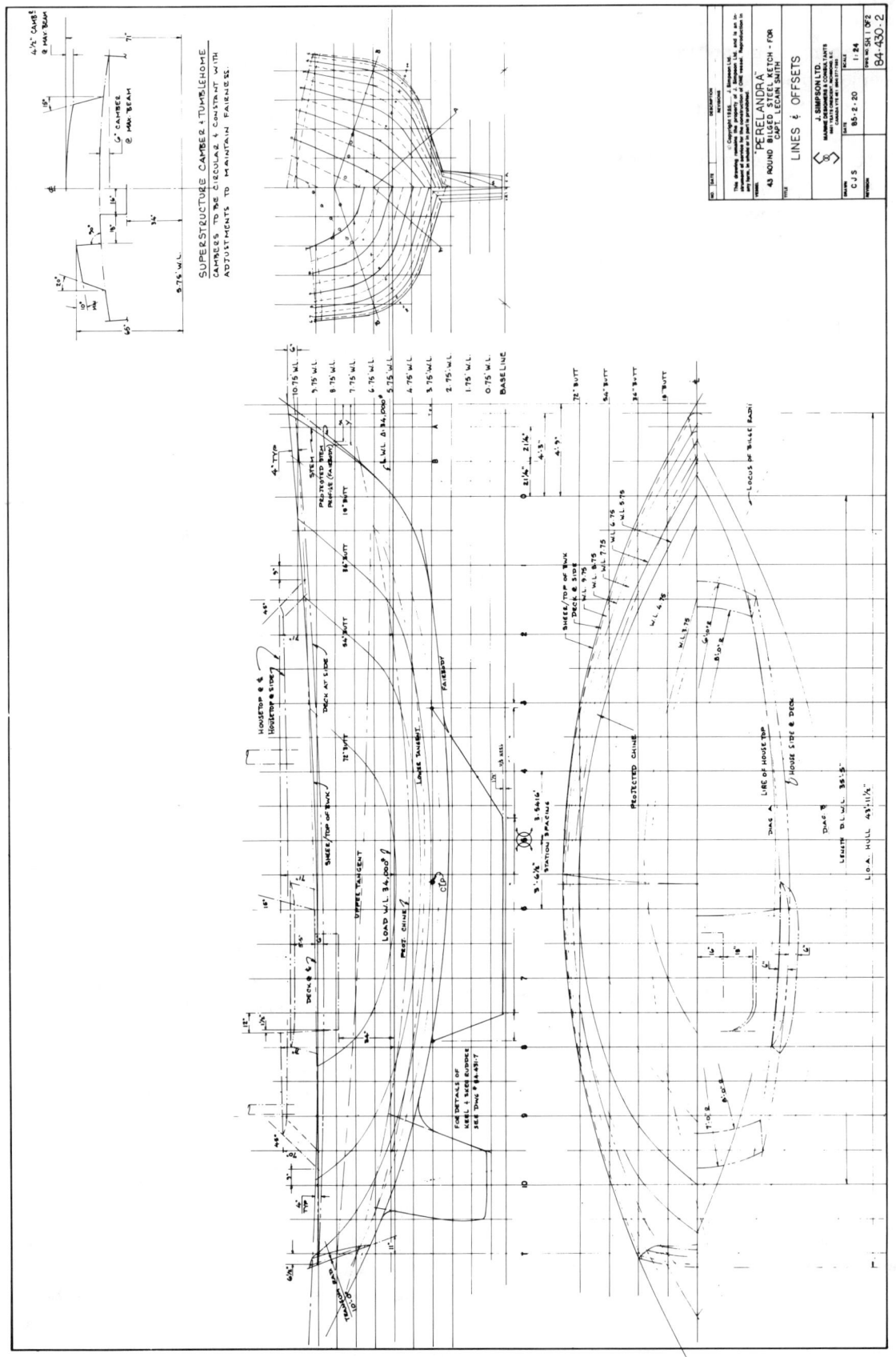

Fig. 4-13. *The lines drawings for John Simpson's Perelandra.*

Courtesy of the designer

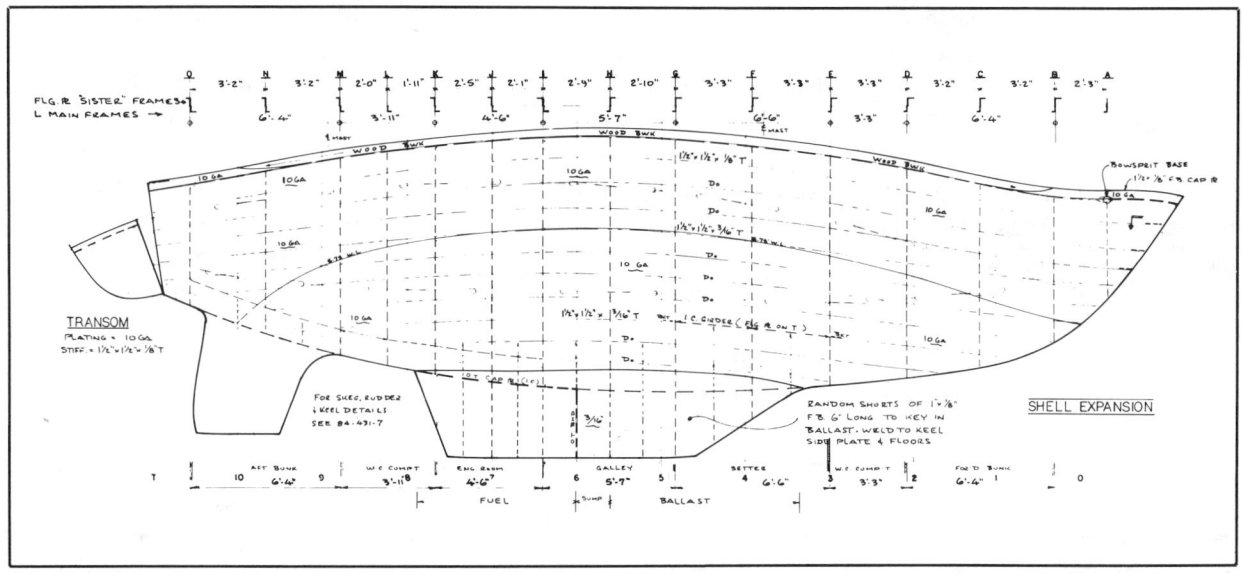

Fig. 4-14. *An example of the shell expansion that is sometimes included in construction plans.*

Courtesy of John Simpson

Arrangement Plan to show the detailed layout of the cabins, main deck and upper decks as necessary, with dimensions and details of special features.

Outboard Profile or Sail, Spar and Rigging Plan shows the final appearance of the boat in the water. For sailboats, this drawing includes spar strength calculations, spar dimensions and specifications, standing rigging specifications, rope list, block list and sail specifications.

Shell expansion drawing showing the hull in profile, stretched out flat (like a Mercator projection chart). Its purpose is to show the position of longitudinals and transverse frames on any type of hull and the tangents of radius sections on a round hull in relation to the framing. It acts as a guide for the builder in planning plating position and seams.

The cost of the above service depends upon the amount of time involved, and the degree of plan work required by the Owner and Builder.

PERELANDRA

What does all this consulting and drawing and defining and redefining lead to? For the authors, it pointed to *Perelandra*, a 44′ foot steel cruising ketch designed by John Simpson; her hull-deck assembly was built by Waterline Yachts. As far as we're concerned, this design is definitely that step toward realizing the ideal we spoke of earlier. Here's something about her.

Length (hull)	43′ 11″
Length O.A. (boom-sprit)	50′ 10″
Length LWL	37′ 1″
Beam (MLD)	13′ 8″
Draft	5′ 10″
Displacement	34,000 lbs.
Ballast	10,500 lbs.
Sail area (100% foretriangle)	1042 sq. ft.
Power	61 S.H.P.
Fuel (U.S. gallons)	200
Water - fresh	205
Water - gray (holding tanks)	35
D/L ratio	297
SA/D ratio	15.9
SA/WS ratio	2.10
Aws	495 sq. ft.

Perelandra is a new custom design created for performance ocean cruising. She has a round steel hull with a center cockpit and a ketch rig, and is intended to be used as a home for world voyaging with potential for chartering.

The hull is of moderate displacement with a three-quarter full keel (large fin) with the forefoot and deadwood cut away to reduce wetted surface, giving responsiveness to windward. The entrance is somewhat fine, yet she is still quite full at her ends, with only moderate overhangs. With her ample beam (13′ 8″) and moderate draft (5′ 9″), she can cruise near the one-fathom line yet stand up well and return nicely from a roll.

The steel hull is fully developed with a somewhat constant and large radius at the turn of the bilge throughout its midsection, and conically developed in the topsides and underbody, making it an easy hull to plate as well as a less turbulent shape. The rudder is hung far enough aft to give good turning ability, and is also low enough to be useful in deep, rolling seas. The rudder tube can be extended to use for emergency tiller steering from either the aft stateroom or on deck.

Perelandra sails well in all kinds of weather. She has good speed and maneuverability because of hull shape, reduced wetted surface and the ample sail area (including 100% foretriangle coverage) in relation to her displacement. So she is very responsive in clawing away from a lee shore in a blow or tacking up a channel with the current against her. The rig is tall enough to help her perform well in light airs, yet low enough to prevent excessive heeling and early reefing. She is very stiff and will stand up well when necessary, as comfortable in a gale as on a sparkling day. Her 61-hp Perkins 4-cylinder diesel engine gives her plenty of power to cruise over 7 knots in moderate seas. With 200 gallons of fuel, she has a cruising range of over 1000 miles, and the engine is linked by a short shaft to a propeller located close to the fore-and-aft center for good control.

Her well-balanced rig and fullish lateral plane add good self-steering qualities, enabling her to hold course and track well, as well as sit aground or be hauled out easily. *Perelandra* can be handled by one experienced person quite easily with the help of self-steering devices. Handling her mizzen is easy, since the boom hangs over the deck rather than overboard. Jiffy reefing allows the sail to be reduced from the cockpit in heavy seas. These qualities are naturally important to a real ocean cruiser.

Perelandra has a somewhat traditional look with her sweeping sheer and short bowsprit. The cockpit coaming and dodger are low and streamlined, lending an attractive appearance and reducing windage up high.

The moderate-sized, shallow cockpit with a convertible dodger protects its occupants from the elements, yet allows them to climb in and out without obstruction. A center-cockpit arrangement allows good self-tending and easy singlehanding. There is ample room on the aft deck for a small dinghy, and the foredeck is clear of clutter for ease of handling sails. The cockpit has a binnacle with wheel steering, and, though shallow, is large enough to easily seat six people or sleep two. Underneath the cockpit coaming on the starboard side is a self-bailing storage bin, accessible from above; a self-draining propane locker is also located within the coaming. The cockpit sole has a removal panel for engine installation.

Since she's built of steel, she is safe from most ocean disasters. Her good insulation and proper coating system mean a comfortable, low-maintenance lifestyle for her owners.

Accommodations aboard *Perelandra* include a master stateroom in the aft cabin with lockers and a head (shower optional). Additional storage is provided in the accessible stern lazarette locker. There are two companionways leading from the cockpit: one to the aft cabin and the other to the main cabin, both just off center to port. Also to port is a walk-through from the aft section to the main cabin, which incorporates a storage area with a built-in tool bench, convertible to a small pilot berth. The walk-through also provides access to the engine room, located under the cockpit. The engine room has ample room for other equipment and good access to the engine for maintenance. As you enter the main cabin either down the companionway or by the walk-through, the first area to port is a navigation station with good chart storage. Opposite it on the starboard side is a nice galley, and a wet locker is near the cockpit companionway. Forward of this is the salon area. The port side of the salon includes a settee with a quarter berth behind it; the starboard side has another settee with storage lockers behind it. A dining table stands between these two settees. Forward of the salon is a head with a locker opposite it to starboard. The fo'c's'le is conventional, although there can be either one double or two single berths. Forward of the fo'c's'le is the fair-sized forepeak for stowage of anchor chain and line.

The yacht is most comfortable for two couples, but could easily handle six on long cruises or charters. If necessary, on short trips eight people can sleep comfortably: two in the aft cabin, one on the pilot berth in the walk-through, three in the salon area, and two in the fo'c's'le.

Perelandra carries over 200 gallons of water and with ample storage can carry supplies enough to visit many deserted islands before returning to civilization. There is also room for extra large equipment in the engine room, as well as small cargo in numerous storage areas.

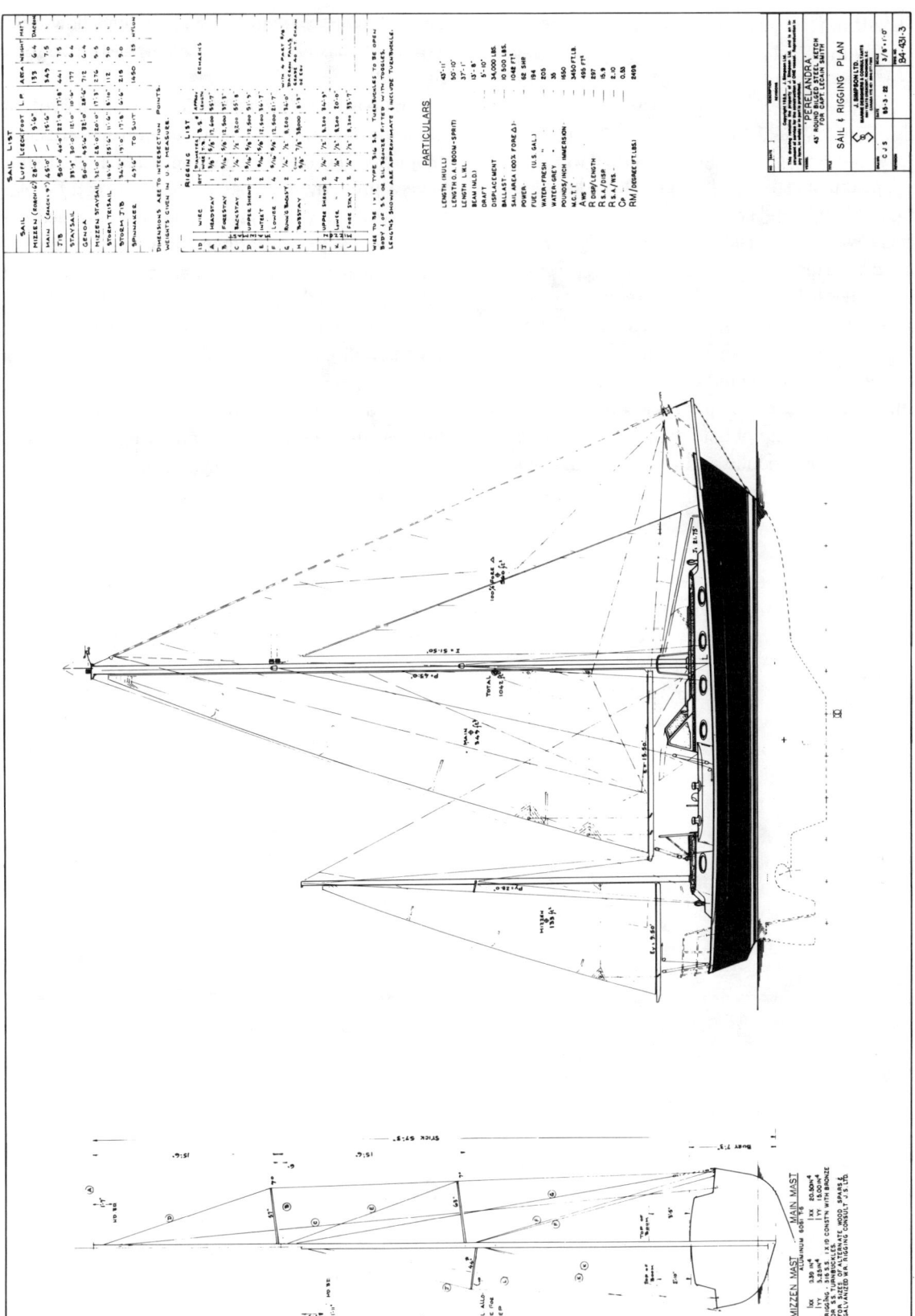

Fig. 4-15. Perelandra *was designed by John Simpson for the authors.* Courtesy of the designer

73

CONCLUSION

Unfortunately, we've only been able to touch the surface of the various design aspects of steel cruising vessels. As you can see, steel has great potential as a hull material for a cruising design. It just has to be handled like steel, not like fiberglass or wood.

Designers who are considering steel design work should familiarize themselves with the building process. A steel hull needs to be designed with stresses that flow smoothly, smooth surfaces that are conducive to coating adhesion, and proper attention to detail to prevent corrosion problems. There should be no extreme curves or flare and no crevices or sharp corners which will act as stress points and will not hold paint. As with other materials, the section modulus and stability calculations must be well-executed. The design scantlings should be as light as possible, yet strong enough to withstand the rigors of service.

In working out the construction drawings, the designer should always consider cost, amount of welding, and simplicity and ease of construction. The hull should have a properly developed shape that can be plated without difficulty by a qualified builder. If you see an ugly boat that has been designed by a reputable designer, don't necessarily blame the designer. Both professional and amateur builders can ruin a good design.

There are a growing number of reputable steel designs, and for the sailor with particular needs, the process of acquiring a custom round-hulled performance cruiser can be an enjoyable learning experience. Steel designs are getting lighter and will always be the strongest and safest choice you can make.

—Chapter 5

Steel Hull Shapes

With modern tooling and techniques, steel can be formed (or, more correctly, deformed) into practically any hull shape. This was not always so. Some skeptics think that steel hulls are limited to chine construction and that it's impossible to build a fair steel hull. Do they believe that beautiful round steel hull anchored next to them is made of fiberglass?

In the early days of steel yacht construction, most building methods were carry-overs from wood construction. Plating was commonly welded directly to transverse frames, as a plank would be attached to a frame, resulting in wavy, distorted hulls. Builder W.H. Schwarz of Two Rivers, Wisconsin, relates a construction story dating back to World War II:

> On an 81-foot ketch, built with a rounded stern, they had to fill in with hull cement between transverse frames as much as ⅝". To hold the transverse frames in place scrap steel bars were welded to the inside of frames. On the mid-section area, it was not a problem but [in] the bow and stern sections with the plating it was a problem to keep the fairing bars from breaking loose due to the excessive force which had to be used to make the compound curve in the plating.

Since that time, Mr. Schwarz and his colleagues have changed to new yacht-framing systems, especially those based on longitudinal framing. Today, transverse frames are used to support these longitudinals and give proper hull stiffness, but are rarely welded directly to the plating. Transverse framing is more common in Europe, but, even there, longitudinal framing is becoming the norm.

Steel is a stiff panel material that is difficult to bend, so nearly all the early steel designs were created for chine construction. This easy, low-cost method was especially suited to amateurs, and even many professionals felt that the more complex twists and turns of a round hull were too demanding and required too much time in fitting and welding. They wanted to keep their prices low enough so that they could sell hulls. Of course, they didn't develop the experience in building round hulls that makes construction quicker and easier. Many fine and able chine hulls have been built, and they have contributed to the interest in steel hulls. In the last few decades, when steel became popular with amateur builders, designers promoted mostly chine hulls for this market.

Chine hulls are neither bad nor necessarily ugly. They may not be as comfortable in a seaway or perform as well as round hulls because the chine causes turbulence. Many chine hulls also tend to heel excessively in high winds. A great deal depends on the location of the chine and the amount of deadrise. Chines are preferable for power boats because the chine enhances the planing characteristics that help the boat to go faster.

There have always been round steel hulls, especially in Europe. Most designers in the 1940's and '50's didn't worry about the difficulty of construction. They designed what the customer wanted, with performance in mind, and depended on big yards with expensive tooling to build a truly round hull with a truly huge price tag. But many people who couldn't afford the bill were still interested in round hulls.

Fig. 5-1. *A rare thing and a thing of beauty—a true round hull, built by W.H. Schwarz.*

Courtesy of the builder

Designers and builders kept working to develop reasonably priced round hulls. They were aided in this effort by research on aircraft plating. Aerodynamics require a smooth curve unbroken by any turbulence where plates meet. Sam Rabl, Ulmann Kilgore, and Kaiser Aluminum all devised formulas that allow lines to be conically developed so that flat plate will lie smoothly on a curved frame. Yacht designers learned to insert a rolled, constant-radius section between two sections of conically developed plate to create a shape called a "fully-developed molded radius," which is easier to build than a true-round hull, but which, when well built, looks and performs like one.

CHINE HULLS

Chine hulls will always be popular when a hull is being built in a panel material like steel, aluminum, or plywood. If the hull is properly designed and the lines conically developed, turbulence at the chine lines will be kept to a minimum while ease of construction is retained.

Chine hulls can be called either "hard" or "soft" depending on the type of joint at the chine line. In hard-chine hulls, the plating of the underbody and topsides meets directly, creating a sharp edge. Rod, flat bar, or even pipe (the latter is not recommended) are used as longitudinal stiffeners where the plating meets at the chine. Some chine hulls, including the lightweight frameless designs, may have no chine bars, but careful plate fitting is necessary in these cases.

In soft-chine hulls, the plating does not butt directly with an abrupt change in direction, but is welded to split pipe, T-bar, flat bar, or a narrow strip of plate to "soften" the look. These softer edges also help to reduce turbulence. The section inserted at the chine is usually under 1 foot wide. Soft-chine hulls are occasionally referred to as "radius chines" or even "molded-radius chines," both of which are incorrect terms. The word "radius" in a description means that a rolled section has been used, and chine strakes are never rolled. "Molded-radius chine" more correctly designates a hull that uses small radius sections, and often refers to a chine-to-round conversion in which a narrow rolled section is used in place of a flat chine strake. (This hull shape will be considered under *molded-radius hulls.*)

Single-chine hulls are the simplest to build, and generally cost the least, since fewer tools are needed and construction goes quickly. Some single-chine production hulls have been built in as little as three weeks. Simple V-bottom single-chine hulls can also be built rapidly. If the plating is developed, a smooth transition at the chine line is possible, and, depending on its location, the chine may be hardly visible. Colvin's *Gazelle* and Wittholz's *Departure 35* are very popular and proven single-chine designs.

Strip chine is a soft variation of single chine in which a narrow plate of constant width is welded between the underbody and topside plating. Many European designers use this method.

Double-chine shapes have handling characteristics closer to round hulls, although there is still some turbulence as in all chine hulls. This type of construction requires more welding, and fitting problems can arise where the chines meet at the stem and stern. Builders have developed many unique ways of solving these problems. The upper chine is usually visible on the topsides, but its appearance can be softened using strip- or soft-chine methods. Double-chine construction makes a great deal of sense for large working sailboats because

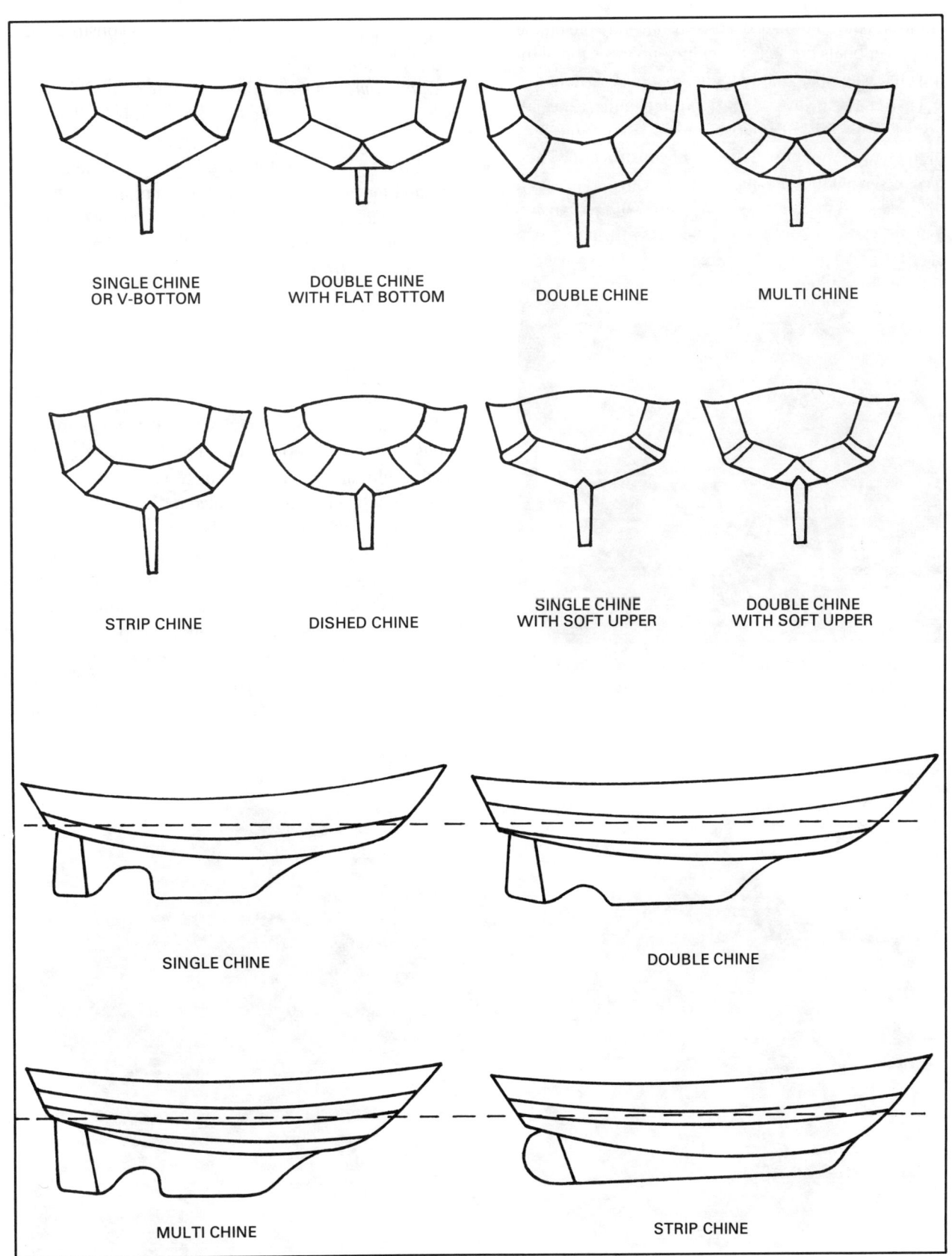

SINGLE CHINE
OR V-BOTTOM

DOUBLE CHINE
WITH FLAT BOTTOM

DOUBLE CHINE

MULTI CHINE

STRIP CHINE

DISHED CHINE

SINGLE CHINE
WITH SOFT UPPER

DOUBLE CHINE
WITH SOFT UPPER

SINGLE CHINE

DOUBLE CHINE

MULTI CHINE

STRIP CHINE

Fig. 5-2.   *Chine hull shapes.*

deadrise in the underbody can be decreased, allowing more volume for storage.

Multi-chine hulls with three or more chines are fairly rare and often can't be distinguished from double-chine construction. These hulls require about the same amount of welding as for round ones. In some cases, multi-chine hulls are almost round, especially when the plate is intentionally dished out and wrapped around deeper longitudinals, producing a "belly" shape. Weston Farmer's *Tahitiana* is a good example of the use of this technique.

ROUND HULLS

Since chine hulls were originally the predominant designs in steel, the early rounded hulls were variations on the chine shape. The thinking was: since flat plating is easier, why not just put a rolled radius section in between relatively flat sides and bottoms to make an easily-constructed round hull without much increase in welding time? Unfortunately, this doesn't really work, and you should be wary of any chine-to-round conversion designs unless they are well developed.

Two methods can be used to produce a fair round hull: true round, in which the steel must be deformed into shape, and fully-developed molded-radius, in

Fig. 5-3. *This unique Danny Greene design combines a double chine with a flat bottom.*

Courtesy of the designer

Fig. 5-4. *The way that Nils Lucander has ended the chines on his* Albacore 64 *produces a fine entry and a soft run aft.*

Courtesy of the designer

Fig. 5-5. *A home builder turned out a beautiful hull using the lapstrake construction method.*

which the plate lies in place with only a small amount of coaxing.

True-round hulls have been built by the Dutch and Germans for years to varying degrees of fairness. However, some of these boats had to be faired with large amounts of filler. They are designed solely for seaworthiness and performance, and the shape is hardly adjusted even though steel is to be used (although some designers do develop the lines). These hulls may have tumblehome, extreme twists, and wineglass or double-ended shapes that require expert construction techniques and specialized tools—rollers, brakes, dies, heat processes, furnace forming, and bizarre plate shapes and plating sequences. True-round hulls are the hardest to build.

There are some alternative plating methods that can be used to lessen the struggle of building a true-round hull. Lapstrake construction can produce very fine results, even for amateurs. (Bernard Moitessier's famous *Joshua* was built with lap seams.) Accurate fitting and butt welds are not necessary, but corrosion may be a problem since there is, in effect, a double seam. The best lap seams are only slightly doubled and fully welded, and the edges of each lap are ground down to promote good paint adhesion. This method does produce a strong hull that doesn't require as many longitudinals, but more welding is needed, especially if each lap plate is very narrow, following the traditional wooden lapstrake method.

Fully-developed molded-radius hulls are the best and most practical alternative. At the turn of the bilge, these hulls have a rolled section welded between two conically developed plates that make up the underbody and topsides. The radius of the rolled section is usually a minimum of 2 feet. The larger the radius of the rolled section, the more round the hull will be. However, larger radii increase the amount of welding, because the butt seams are longer and the radius plate sections generally shorter. Early molded-radius designs used smaller radii to minimize the increase in welding.

The radius is created by first drawing a single-chine hull with its chine located at a vertex point located far down and outboard of the normal turn of the bilge. Then the designer decides on the radius of the rolled plate that will be inserted along this curve, basing his or her decision on the size of the boat. (Larger vessels generally have larger radii and gentler curves to make plating easier.) Tangent points are picked off above and below the vertex and connected with a smooth curve. These tangent lines thus form the boundaries of the rolled plate, and can either be carried out all the way from stem to stern or can end short of the stem. The exact length depends on the hull shape. There is usually no wineglass shape where the hull meets the keel; some designers place a reverse chine plate or reverse rolled section here, but the work seems unnecessary. The smooth curve achieved with this method gives the look, shape, and performance of a round hull.

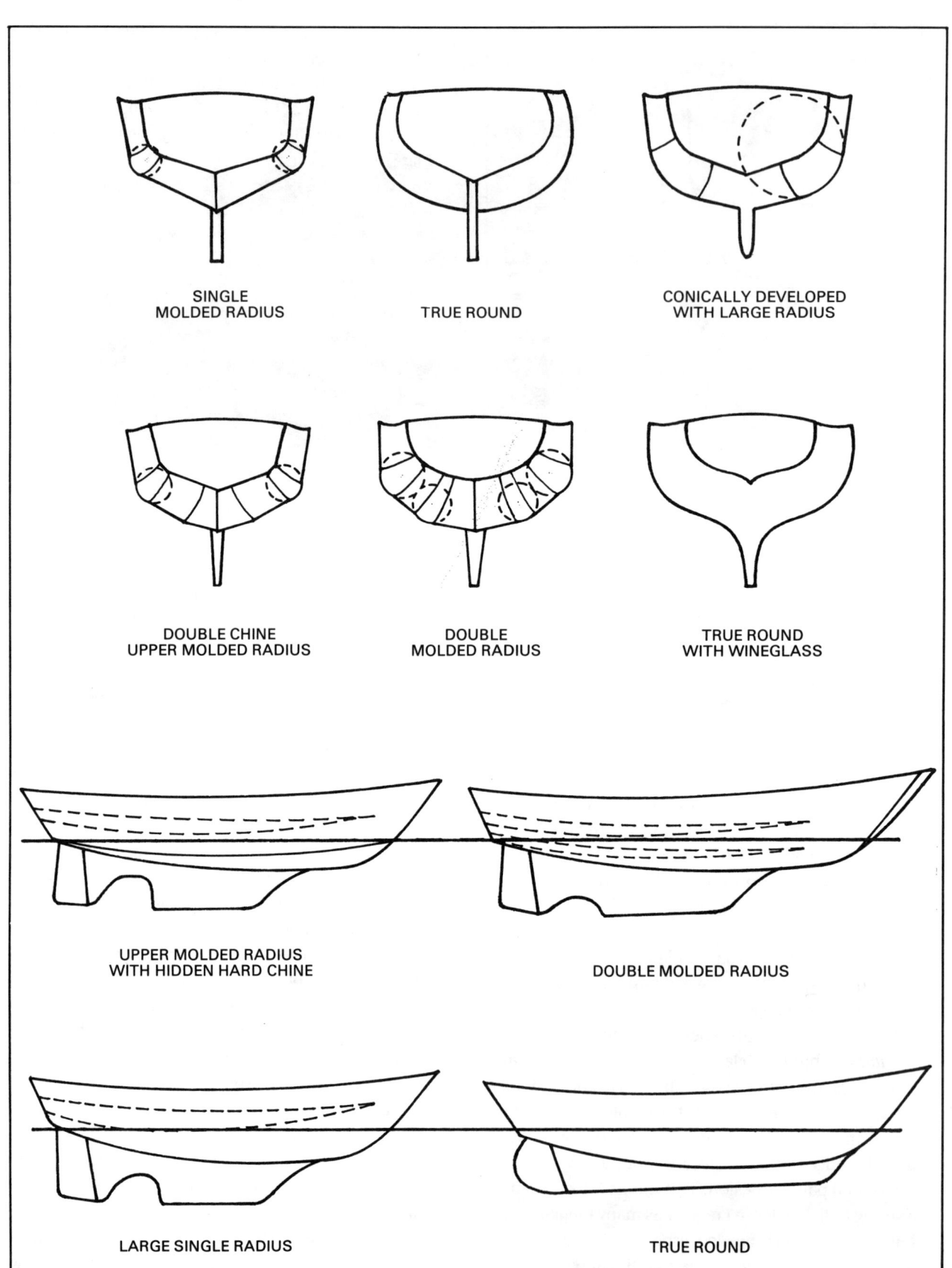

SINGLE
MOLDED RADIUS

TRUE ROUND

CONICALLY DEVELOPED
WITH LARGE RADIUS

DOUBLE CHINE
UPPER MOLDED RADIUS

DOUBLE
MOLDED RADIUS

TRUE ROUND
WITH WINEGLASS

UPPER MOLDED RADIUS
WITH HIDDEN HARD CHINE

DOUBLE MOLDED RADIUS

LARGE SINGLE RADIUS

TRUE ROUND

Fig. 5-6. *Round hull shapes.*

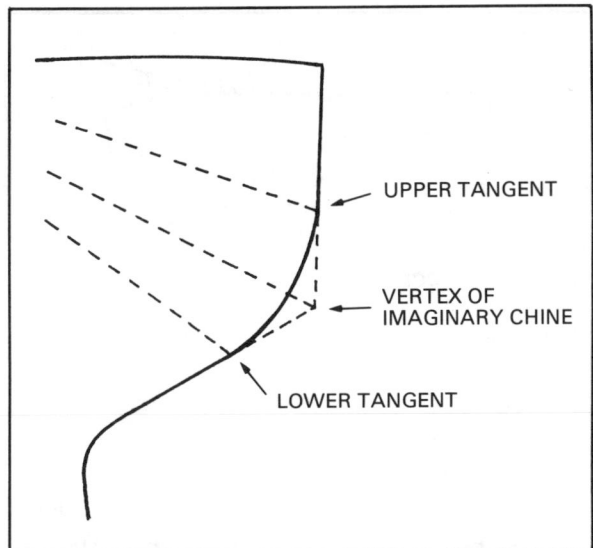

Fig. 5-7. *Creating the radius section.*

Since the radius section must be rolled, a constant radius fore and aft between the upper and lower tangents is preferable to a changing radius, although a slight change in radius can be handled by a builder by using a bit more mechanical encouragement. A taper in the rolled section is no problem, but if the radius itself changes, the plate may have to be formed by special rollers, dies, or heat processes. A separate piece of plate can also be rolled to a slightly different radius that will be a better fit in a particular section. A typical 40′ molded-

radius hull may have three slightly different radii at the bow, amidship, and at the stern.

Some designers stop right there. But the real key to a fair round hull is to conically develop the hull lines so that the flat plate curves to meet the radius section. Plate that is laid on the frames of a conically developed hull wraps into place as if it had always wanted to be there—no buckling, twisting, overlapping, or stress. Conic development is based on geometric formulas that consider planes, origins, and an apex point at the top of a cone. The designer first makes sure that the hull shape is designed with steel construction in mind, avoiding the extra flare, tumblehome, and extreme twists that aren't critical to performance. Then he or she applies the formulas to make small adjustments in the lines, creating a new plate shape with coordinated shifts in curvature at each station fore and aft. Where twists cannot be avoided (for example, with some clipper bows), conic development will lessen the amount of persuasion necessary to move the steel into place.

Some double-chine hulls have been converted either to double molded-radius or to an arrangement in which

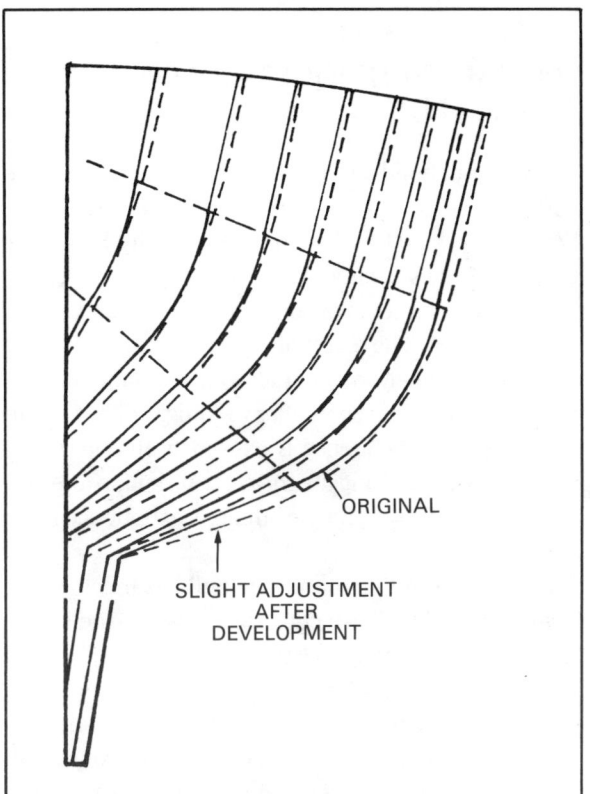

Fig. 5-9. *An exaggerated example of how conic development changes the shape of the plate. The solid lines show the original shape; the dashed line, the shape of the developed plate.*

Fig. 5-8. *A tapered bow cone continues the curve of the hull. The boat was designed and built by Waterline Yachts.*

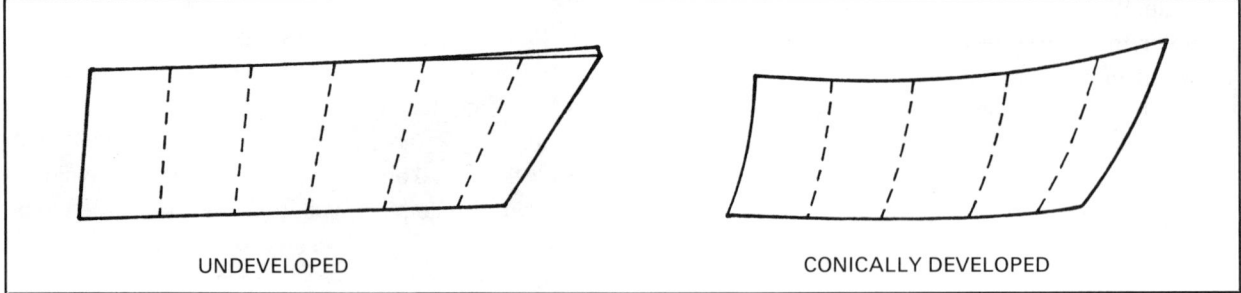

UNDEVELOPED

CONICALLY DEVELOPED

Fig. 5-10.   *The plate on undeveloped hulls tends to twist unevenly* (left), *while conic development creates even twists* (right). *(The drawing is exaggerated to clarify the concept).*

the upper chine is a molded radius and the lower chine, underwater and not visible, is hard. (In the former method, from sheer to keel, the plating sections are flat, rolled, flat, rolled, flat.) The width of the radius section on a double molded-radius hull is quite small, under 30″. Upper radius sections generally end before the bow, where the topsides are flatter. Although the smaller plates used on a double molded-radius hull are easier to fit and handle, this advantage is outweighed by the extra welding required.

SPECIAL TECHNIQUES FOR BUILDING A ROUND HULL

In order to build a round hull, the steel—both plate and frames—must be bent or cut into a round shape. With a developed hull shape the difficulty is neither bending frames to support the plating nor rolling the plate to the correct radius, since bending jigs and rollers do the job well. The real challenge is cutting and fitting the plate accurately, making allowances for the contraction of the steel as it cools after welding. Following the proper welding sequence is extremely important for round hulls, as is using the correct plate length fore and aft. Both the design and the builder's experience must be the guides.

If you hang around round-hull builders much, you'll hear phrases like "dish cupping," "dished-shell technique," "cramping," "floating longitudinals," "compounding," and "multiple rolls." Some builders are as reluctant to divulge their definitions of these terms as early sea captains were to share celestial navigation secrets. Preference in technique often reflects preference in tools and experience. As in any other trade, there are different ways to complete the job successfully, and the actual design will strongly influence building methods.

Shaping Steel

Because steel resists bending, a fair amount of force is needed to change its shape—more force than normal humans can apply. But steel can be deformed fairly easily using either cold or hot methods. Cold forming, especially with rollers and braking machines, is more common, but heat may be needed to help even rolled plate assume the proper shape. However, heat-shrinking metals to create a curve is tricky, and the results can be disastrous if it is poorly done.

Cold-forming methods can damage steel slightly by creating some additional stresses in the material that can eventually reduce notch toughness and ductility, which can cause cracking. However, while it is deforming, the steel also becomes stiffer due to work hardening, thus lowering the chances of denting or distortion. Stresses in mild steel are relieved very easily by the heat of welding, local annealing, or peening.

Although cold-forming methods also include the use of presses, bending jigs, and dies, the most commonly used pieces of equipment are rollers and braking machines. Radius sections of steel plate are generally shaped with rollers, while braking machines are used for small radii, bar stock, and for fabricating flange plate. In big yards these operations can be controlled by computers.

In order to bend steel permanently, the machine must deliver a force greater than the metal's yield strength but short of its ultimate tensile strength. Some "springback" must be allowed, since steel has a memory and will move slightly back to its original flat position. The more force that is applied, the less tendency there is for the steel to spring back. Practice and accurate calculation of the modulus of elasticity are needed to obtain plate rolled to a specific radius.

The machines used to shape plate are made up of either three or four rollers, which bend, clamp, or move the plate. With most rollers, the larger the diameter of the roller, the thicker the plate that can be run through. The width of the roller only limits the width of the plate that can be fed to the roller. A 6' roller could easily handle the radius section for a 40' boat. The best machines are driven by hydraulics and have all-steel rather than cast frames.

Manually-operated rollers can only handle 14- to 16-gauge plate, so their use is limited to sheet metal fabrication. The larger power rollers that can handle 10- to 12-gauge plate are very expensive, ranging from $5,000 to $25,000, when purchased new. Sometimes used equipment can be found second-hand (in machine warehouses or boilerworks), and many boatbuilders have constructed their own rolling machines (for example, using a converted printing press roller).

Most steel boatbuilding yards don't do enough plate rolling to justify owning rollers. In many areas there are metal fabrication shops that have the rollers to do the job, which is often contracted out to them. Many builders like to supervise the rolling process, since the fit of the rolled plate will make their jobs easy or difficult.

If you are building a boat far away from a city, it may be more practical to build your own roller than to transport the plate to be rolled. Since there is not yet enough demand to warrant production of economical rollers for home builders, you will have to design and build the roller yourself. If your engineering design skills are not particularly good, you may want to check out a roll-

Fig. 5-11. *This roller, fabricated by a home builder, rolled all the plate for the round hull sitting behind it. The upper roller can be adjusted to form a changing radius.*

Fig. 5-12. *This homemade plate roller is powered by a tractor, leaving the builder free to guide the plate through.*   Courtesy of Skip Figg

er design developed by Skip Figg, who recently rolled the plate for his own round hull. This ingenious roller stretches the center of the plate more than the edges, thus forming a compound curve. With multiple passes it will handle 10-gauge plate, and can be used to bend frames as well as to fabricate equipment like anchors. The cost of parts and materials for this roller is under $200, and Mr. Figg will sell you a complete set of plans for the rolling machine for $38. If you're interested, contact: Skig Figg, Rt. 1, Box 46, Reardan, WA 99029, 509-796-4591.

When the rolling is done in a machine shop, one of four types of rolling machines will generally be used. Boatbuilders in Holland use a fifth type that has only two adjustable rollers and requires many passes to get the correct radius. Because of the variations in the finished product, it may be wise to find out the type of roller used by the shop hired to do the rolling.

Pyramid rollers, which have three rollers, have been around the longest. The top roller adjusts to change the bending radius, and the bottom two drive the plate through. The machine leaves long, unusable flat spots at the ends of the plate, increasing waste. Pyramid rollers are limited to thicker material and larger radii.

Initial or pinch rollers also have three rollers, of which one is adjustable. This machine pre-bends the plate to avoid producing the long flat ends that are a disadvantage with pyramid rollers. However, it can only pre-bend one edge at a time, so if both edges are to be pre-bent, the plate must be turned, and the handling is doubled. Initial rollers only roll plate of a limited thickness, and cannot do good cone rolling.

A machine with four rollers overcomes most of the shortcomings of the pyramid and initial rollers. This piece of equipment pre-bends both edges, and can roll thicker plate and good cones. The only real drawback is its higher cost.

A three-roller double-pinch pyramid-type roller is not as common but is the most efficient, as well as being more economical than the four-roller machines. In these units, the two bottom rollers are adjustable, and three rollers are powered to drive the plate through. This system leaves no flat spots on the ends of the plate. Thick plate can be rolled, and the rollers can be tilted to roll cone-shaped pieces with changing radii.

These last two types are especially useful in rolling cones. Both symmetrical and asymmetrical bending can be done, and the rollers can be adjusted to complex ellipses and changing radii.

There are also other types of rollers that can be used to bend angle bar. Their use is limited, since simple hydraulic bending jigs or hydraulic frame benders can shape the transverse framing, and longitudinals on yachts are usually bent in place rather than rolled.

Frame-bending machines are the type of cold-forming equipment most often seen in boatbuilding yards. They are used to bend slab material, and can handle deck beams or transverse frames. Various designs are commonly used and commonly fabricated by boatbuilders.

Braking machines are second only to rollers in their use in the steel fabrication industry. They are used to bend large T-bar frames and stock and pipe for stems, guard rails, and cabin edges. Flange plate is usually

Fig. 5-13. *This plate was rolled on the roller pictured in Fig. 5-12.*

Courtesy of Skip Figg

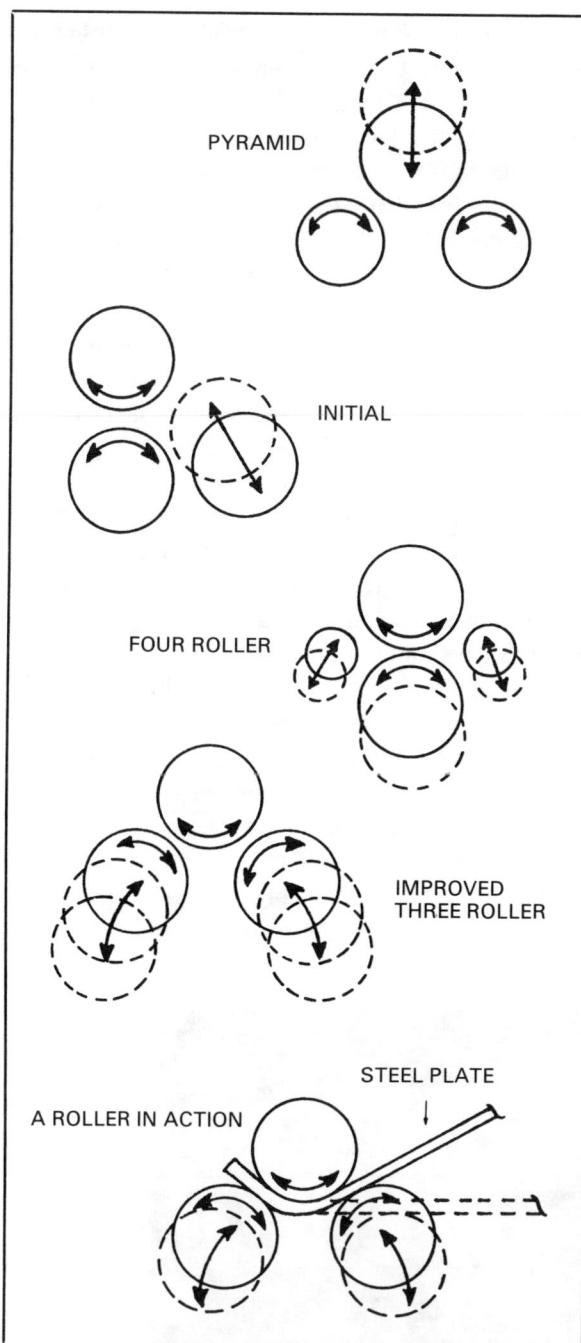

Fig. 5-14. *The different types of rollers.*

created with a brake. Some braking machines are also used to roll plate with a very tight radius, such as bow cones. However, small ridges are often left in the plate.

Most of the other cold-forming machines are not used for the plate thickness and shapes needed in steel yacht construction, especially since rollers and brakes do the job so well. Hydraulic presses or plate-bender presses are used to bend flat bar, brackets, and other components for use on large ships. Metal fabricators will occasionally use this equipment for a particular contract job. Machine presses with female dies or molds, as well as acro jacks, are used to shape hull plate for large ships. These pre-molded dies are very expensive and elaborate tools, but some boatbuilding yards use them. Hydraulic rams are used for molding shapes in the auto industry and are, as yet, impractical for most yacht work.

Before some of today's heavy industrial machinery was available, old-time steel boatbuilders developed and used a method of fabricating compound curves called "plate knocking" or "hammering," a technique that is still in use today. Flat plate is laid against a jig and beaten with large block hammers in a particular sequence until the proper shape is achieved. Many successive hammerings are needed, moving in a pattern designed to take advantage of the plate's bending characteristics. The hammers leave small marks in the plate, which is also slightly work hardened. With the advent of better-suited designs, this method is basically outdated.

Plating a Round Hull

Every hull, whether round or chine, has fore-and-aft curvature, and, on a molded-radius hull, the flat plate sections also must curve from the sheer to the keel to provide a smooth transition between the rolled and flat sections. The plate will have to be bent down flush with the longitudinals and transverses, and a certain amount of force will be needed to achieve the desired shape. During this bending, the object is to avoid locking in

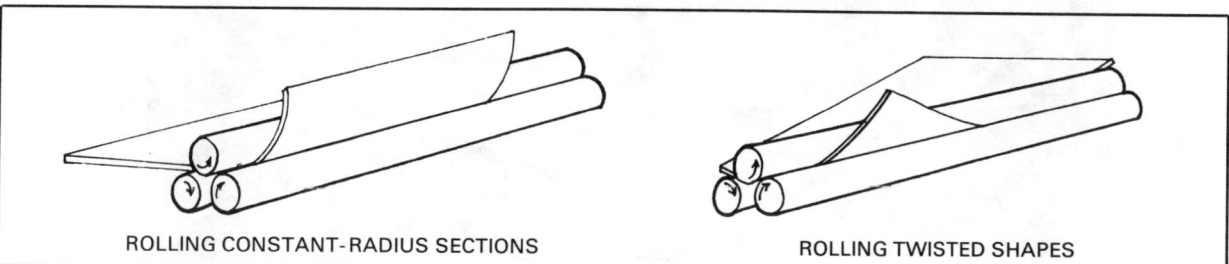

Fig. 5-15. *Plate can be fed into the rollers at different angles to produce different shapes. The top roller can also be adjusted for a changing radius, and the diameter of the roller itself can vary in some machines.*

stresses that will cause the plate to distort during welding. Many of the techniques for preventing distortion, discussed below, apply equally well to chine- or round-hull construction.

Plate thickness is an important variable in preventing distortion. 7- and 10-gauge plate are the most common thicknesses used in yacht hull construction. The thinner 10-gauge bends more easily, reducing the chance of stressed areas. However, thinner plate is more prone to distortion during both cutting and welding. Nibblers or plasma arc cutters (neither of which generate heat) and MIG welding machines (which are faster and produce less heat) are the preferred tooling for creating a fair hull of 10-gauge plate. Thinner plate is lighter and easier to handle, so larger pieces can be used on the relatively flat sections, and less welding will be needed. It's a question of balance and, to some extent, the builder's preference.

In a round-hull design, framing and plating work together to produce the curves. The transverse frames are bent to conform to the developed lines of the hull. Longitudinals are then bent around these transverse frames and either tacked to them or inserted into slots. The final fairness of the hull plate is established as the sections of plate are tack-welded to each other and to the longitudinals. There is very little room for error in bending, cutting, and fitting the frames and plate, since a small error (for example, in the frames) will change the curve of the longitudinals, and when the butt seams of the plate are fully welded and skip-welded to the longitudinals, the plate may distort.

In chine construction, the frame stock is cut to the correct lengths for each plate section, and the pieces are butt-welded to form the shape of the frame. For round hulls, the frames must be bent into a smooth curve by one of several methods. The frames can be constructed of plate cut to shape and, if necessary, the pieces welded together, but this method entails extra work and waste and is not as clean as using angle bar or flange plate. A curve can easily be put into frame stock by special rolling machines (this job will undoubtedly be contracted out) or by hot bending in a furnace. Both of these methods will add to the cost of construction and are rarely used. In almost all situations, both professionals and amateurs will do better to bend the frame stock to the correct shape using a hydraulic jig or simple frame-bending jig. If flange plate is used for frames, a braking machine will be needed to bend a flange in the plate, after which the plate can be cut in sections and installed. The foot of the flange plate is left oversized and cut to the curve of the hull, except where extreme curvature may require machine rolling.

Whether the hull is round or chine, developed lines will make the plating process easier. When a constant

Fig. 5-16. *This interior shot clearly shows the difference in the shape of the frames of a molded radius (upper) and a hard chine (lower).*

radius section must be joined to a flat plate, a plate with a developed surface always has a better chance of good fit, since the plates butt more easily. The curvature in the frames of a developed shape will also encourage the flat plate to lie against the frames where it meets the rolled section. Developed lines are even more critical when thinner plate is used, because the thinner plate has a lower tolerance for distortion.

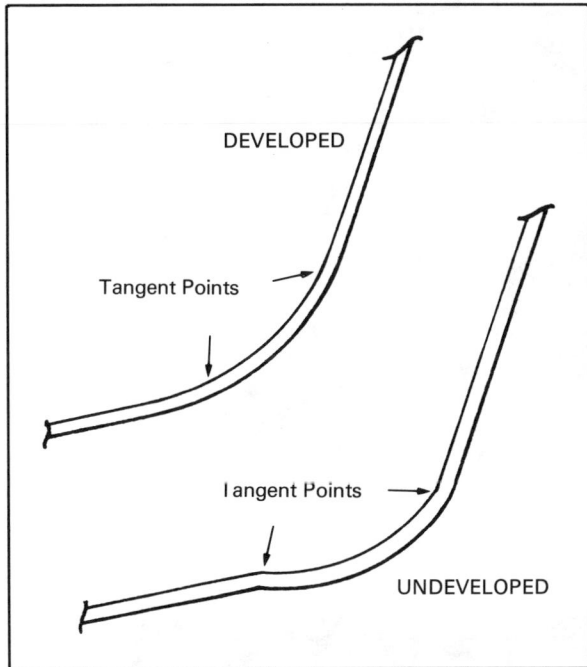

Fig. 5-17.   When the lines are conically developed, the upper and lower sections flow smoothly into the rolled section at the tangent points.

Since the hull plate is all fully welded together before it is welded intermittently to the longitudinals, the shape of each section of plate is critical to the final hull shape. Even with the most precise cutting and fitting, the final fractions of an inch are always the hardest. If the plate is pulled down to meet a longitudinal that has a slightly different shape, the plate (especially 10-gauge plate) may distort. Therefore, several special techniques have been developed for plating round hulls that allow the plate to move freely so that the shape is not distorted by hard spots. (A hard spot is an area of the framing that won't yield to pressure exerted on it by the plate. A heavy transverse against which plate is laid can create a hard spot. So can the points where longitudinals and transverses cross.)

One of these methods is called the "floating longitudinal technique." In this framing system, the longitudinals are not attached to the transverses so that the lon-

gitudinals can float freely and adjust to support the shape of the plate. After all the plate has been tacked to the longitudinals, the longitudinals are adjusted and welded to the transverse frames, and then the hull plate is welded together. Many builders execute variations on this technique.

Another method that allows movement of the frames is tacking the longitudinals to lightweight transverse frames. These frames can adjust slightly as the plate is tacked to the longitudinals, thus preventing hard spots. After the plating is in place, completely welded together and skip-welded to the longitudinals, additional framing is backed to the light primary frames to provide the proper panel strength and stiffness. These sister frames may only be needed at every other frame, and can be placed at stations where bulkheads are to be attached. Although flat bar and angle bar can also be used, flange plate is the best for these sister frames, since it is the deepest and therefore stiffens the frames the most. It also can easily be cut to fit and welded up in sections as it is being installed.

A third method is called the "floating shell technique." In this case, the hull plate is not deformed and pulled into place against frames; instead, all the plate edges are welded together, and the heat of welding dishes the plate into a compound curve. The longitudinals are then pre-bent to meet the plate, reducing the amount of locked-in stress. Although this method is good for hulls that aren't conically developed, it's difficult to use dishing to shape the plate. The actual hull shape may be slightly different than designed.

The order in which the various plate sections of a molded-radius hull are tacked together varies with the preferences of each builder, although this also depends on the size and shape of the rolled section. If the rolled section is small, it is easier to fit than if it is a large radius piece. When the hull lines are developed, the largest size plate possible to lift can be used for the flat sections. This helps to standardize plate sizes and plating schedule.

Some builders plate the underbody and topsides before the rolled section. They claim that the hull holds its shape better since the frames can be pulled out of alignment by the stress exerted by the rolled sections. The edge of the flat plate also forms a nice, fair tangent to which the rolled plate can be fitted. However, the proper fit of the rolled section in between the other plates may be more difficult with this method if large rolled plate sections are used. With smaller sections, especially if the builder can cut the plate in place, inserting the rolled plate is not that difficult. Other builders

Fig. 5-18.   *The reverse-chine garboard on the boat under construction at Schreiber Boats give more room below the shaft.*

Fig. 5-19.   *Plate that has been rolled to a constant radius waits its turn to be cut and fit to the hull being built at SP Metal Craft.*

do the rolled section first, feeling that if the frames are properly braced no movement should occur. The flat plate sections are then installed, and any overhang at the sheer is trimmed off in place. It is harder to get a good fit when large flat plates must be placed flush with a smaller rolled section. Some builders tack the deck on first to keep the frames aligned and stiffen the structure, while others weld on the hull plate first. No matter what method is used, both sides should be plated simultaneously to keep the frame alignment correct.

The size of the plate sections depends on whether or not the plate has been rolled. With any flat plate, developed or not, the longest section that it is physically possible to handle should be used to minimize welding. If it were available, one long piece of steel per side would be best. However, unless the design is good and the plate shapes well planned, using these long pieces may cause a great deal of waste because of the run-off of the sheer. So, practically speaking, several pieces of plate are commonly welded together in the flat sections. Run-off is also the limiting factor for the size of the rolled sections, especially when the radius section is large. Because the hull is curving fore and aft, rolled sections that are too long will not lie flat against the frames. The size of the section can be estimated, but the builder must be prepared to shorten the piece if it does not fit in properly. With small radius sections, longer, narrower plate can be used, although it may be tricky to keep the plate fair.

When the builder is choosing the piece of plate to use for a particular area, he or she may be able to take advantage of the natural inclination of the plate to curl one way or another. All plate is rolled at the manufacturer's and, in the case of thin plate, is shipped rolled in coils. Steel has some residual memory, and the plate will tend to curve in the way it was previously coiled. Surface marks or the way a plate lies down sometimes gives a clue and, when it is cut, nine times out of ten the plate will curl in the direction in which it was coiled. This built-in curve can be used to convince relatively flat plate to lie down properly, as long as the correct side of the plate is on the inside. In areas with extreme flare, plate is commonly turned diagonally so that the roll falls into the flare. This curve in the plate is also placed vertical to the waterline at the stem of a double-ender. If a plate section is to be rolled, the procedure is easier if the coiling direction is used as the basis for rolling. However, as predictable and uniform as steel is, each piece will behave differently due to minute differences in its microstructure.

Fig. 5-20. *A traditional rounded stern can be incorporated into even a chine hull, as the Merritt Walter design demonstrates.*

Builders have developed many other techniques for forcing steel into compound curves. Many of these are especially useful if a true-round hull is being built. But even with a molded-radius hull, the twists and curves of the hull shape may demand special treatment. In difficult areas, the plate can be shaped in a number of different ways:

1) Slitting the plate in certain locations to assist local bending. The places where this technique is most commonly used include: flat plate sections forward or aft of rolled sections; the stern of a double-ender; in the side of a rolled bow cone. In the case of the bow cone, slitting the edges allows the cone to be pulled into place against a curved stem. This method is not generally recommended, since extra welding is necessary to close the slits and unfairness is a common result.

2) Cutting the plate into triangular or odd shapes so that bending is easier and any dishing in the plate will fall in the correct place. This method is also subject to unfairness and requires a great deal of knowledge about the working characteristics of steel. It may require additional heating to dish the plate, which can be tricky.

3) Using long, thin plate sections, even if the plate has been rolled to a specific radius. When the radius section is thinner, the plate will wrap around the frames more easily. This method doesn't require much extra welding,

Fig. 5-21.   *Odd-shaped plates can be used to build fully rounded hulls, as Frank Kelly did when constructing Ted Brewer's* Verity.

Fig. 5-22.   *A narrow molded-radius section that blinds out before it reaches the stem is used in Grahame Shannon's* Amazon. *The boat is ready for blasting.*

but very wide rollers are needed to produce the long strips. It works best in areas where the radius is constant fore and aft.

4) Using narrow vertical plates running fore and aft. Large radius sections are commonly plated with narrow strips to compensate for plate run-off. This method also lessens the chance of poor fitting if the radius changes, so it is commonly used for rolled sections. Although there is more welding involved, a good fit is more easily obtained.

5) Rolling plate to slightly different radii. If this method is used, three radii are generally rolled: one for the stern, one for amidships, and one for the bow. The adjoining plate sections are shaped using a roller that can form a changing radius within a single plate. Special cone rolling for bow cones is also done with braking machines.

Although most of the bending needed for a molded-radius hull can be achieved with cold methods, there are times when a little heat may be needed to persuade the flat plate sections to curve or twist. Heat forming by either rosebud or strip heating can create a dish or cup in the plate. The metal is heated to between 1475 and 2200°F, pulled into place with tackle or hammered to

shape, and then allowed to cool at room temperature. Cutting thin plate with a torch may also cause some dishing, and these slightly developed pieces of plate can be used for special areas of the boat. True-round hulls are often plated with the use of heat.

Heat can also be used to relieve residual stresses in the steel and, to a limited extent, to correct local distortion caused by welding. The steel is heated to 1100–1200°F (that is, below the transformation temperature) to relieve residual stresses in the steel. This method is rarely used, since local annealing is difficult to do properly. But properly carried out, stress is distributed almost uniformly and tensile strength is increased. Slow cooling is important since rapid cooling would cause stress and brittleness in the heat zone. One builder says that a lighter, stronger boat could be built by using light-gauge steel and then annealing it in a furnace to increase tensile strength and relieve stresses. However, he admits that there is a chance of the hull becoming more brittle since the cooling might be hard to control. So far, it hasn't been done.

Building a well-developed molded-radius hull is not beyond the reach of a skilled amateur, but a true-round

Fig. 5-23. *The authors' pride and joy*—Perelandra. *The large radius section is plated with narrow vertical strips of rolled plate. Much larger sections are used for the conically developed underbody and topside plates.*

hull is the most difficult to plate without heavy-duty tooling. Plating often involves using various sizes and shapes arranged in a careful, scientifically determined method with careful consideration for correct size sections. Slitting, diagonal plating, and using odd shapes to create a "patchwork quilt" are not the best ways to deal with plate butts, but they may be necessary here, although they can lead to a lack of fairness. A professional yard, with experience and tooling, will be more apt to turn out a fair, true-round hull. But the chances of needing filler are still very high for the true-round shape. Until new techniques (such as special molds for specific popular stock plans) are developed, true-round hulls will be beyond most people's abilities and pocketbooks. Maybe General Motors could produce hulls with special press molds for each half of a hull and then have them computer robot-welded together in a very short time.

Fig. 5-24.   Pandora IV, *a 69' centerboard ketch, is ready for her first taste of salt water.*

Courtesy of Sparkman and Stephens

—Chapter 6

How to Get a Hull

Although you can build a steel boat inexpensively in your own backyard, don't choose steel as a hull material just because it's cheap. It's not easy to build a fair, high-quality steel yacht that will be a good investment as well as a pleasure. Especially for round shapes, a professionally built hull finished out nicely at home may be the best of both worlds: not too expensive, with the metal work skillfully done. Plus you get to start at a more enjoyable stage of the building process. Professional yards will build a hull to almost any stage of completion—from a bare-hull assembly (also known as a "hull-deck shell" or a "hull kit") to a finished yacht. You can also consider buying a good, second-hand boat. Your choice will probably be based on your skill level, the available funds, and the quality that your dream demands.

If possible, the decision about who will build the hull should be made before the design stage is completed, so that the design can be tailored to the experience and preferred construction methods of the builder. This isn't always possible, especially when stock plans are used. Whether the hull is to be built from existing plans or from a new custom design, careful study of the complexity of construction will help you to decide on the best approach to construction.

Building a steel hull from scratch requires a variety of skills, but welding proficiency is the most important, since the hull will be only as good as the welds. If you're an experienced welder who wants to have total control over quality, you will probably be happier building your own hull. If money is tight, but you have decent welding skills, you'll also probably decide to build the boat yourself. In either case, as a somewhat unskilled amateur boatbuilder, be prepared for the inevitable struggle with new problems, since fitting and plating a hull is different from most other welding applications. You also risk lower-quality work while you're polishing skills. It may take a while to complete the vessel, especially if you have to take time off to work elsewhere to finance the construction. But a good horsetrader and bargain hunter will probably be able to build a fairly inexpensive hull, especially if the use of stainless steel and other expensive alloys is limited. If you can't weld, practice on something else first.

If you are building your own boat, it may help to hire someone else to assist you in the construction. If you're not a good welder, make sure that this person is. Steel plate is easier to handle if there are two people around, and the companionship makes the work seem easier. Apprentices can learn with hands-on work and be inspired to build their own dreamboats. They can then pass the inspiration along to another. After all, that's how the boatbuilding knowledge of our grandparents was handed down.

Many non-welders who have spent some time on boats have quite a bit of experience with woodworking, plumbing, electrics, rigging, and other boat systems. If you are one of these people, you may choose to save enough money to hire a professional yard to weld up a bare-hull assembly. Then you can finish the boat off, calling on a few experts (for example, a sandblaster or engine mechanic) for areas requiring special skills or equipment. Depending on the design and whether the hull is round or chine, a professionally built bare-hull assembly for the average 40' boat can cost $10,000–$15,000 more than the one you build yourself, but that expense is easier to bear if you know that the critical metal work has been done by experts. It's still considerably less than buying a completely finished yacht.

Of course, you can take delivery of a new boat at various stages of completion beyond the basic hull. There are those lucky people who can simply buy a completed boat. They get to sail away without any sweat, an attractive option if it's affordable. And it can be affordable if you buy a good used hull.

PURCHASING A NEW HULL

The most common stages of completion at which yachts are available are: the primer stage, also known as the bare-hull assembly; the motor-away stage; and the complete hull or sail-away stage. Each stage is defined slightly differently by different builders, but there are many similarities.

The bare-hull assembly usually includes the hull, deck, cabin, and basic appendages (rudder, engine beds, bowsprit, stern tube, and others discussed in Chapter 9) that are welded integrally to the hull. All of the metal work is complete, including cutouts and tabs or holes for interior joinery, and an amateur builder with few welding skills can take over and complete the vessel. But here's where the different definitions begin. Some builders blast the interior and exterior, some only the interior, and some neither. If the hull is blasted, it is also primed, and, if required, further coatings can be applied at the yard in a controlled atmosphere. Different amounts of stainless are included in bare-hull assemblies, and some include tankage and ballast. It is obviously important to clarify the builder's definition.

You may want to have fittings or appendages that are not included in the builder's definition welded in place. Or you may want stainless used at chafe points instead of mild steel. Many yards are fairly flexible and will do this additional metal work for an additional charge. Other yards may have schedules to meet that don't allow them to spend any extra time. Try to be as explicit as possible about extra work when you sign the contract, so that the yard can calculate the time needed to complete the whole project.

Some hull kits really *are* kits, in which pre-cut plates or patterns are supplied ready to fit in place. In some of these kits all of the pieces are tacked together, and then you finish the welding. In others, the steel parts are only cut out, and the builder must take it from there. What you are buying is the lofting and layout skills of the company.

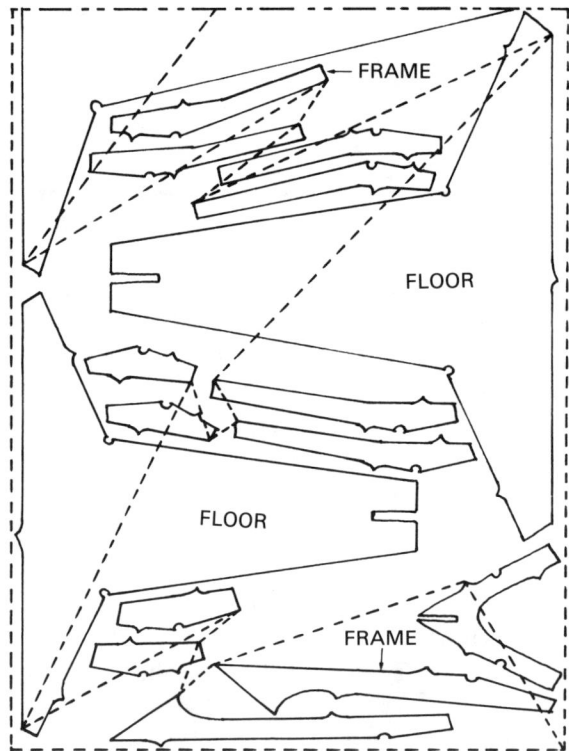

Fig. 6-1. *An example of the layout used to produce the pre-cut plate included as part of a STEEL-KITS package. A plasma cutter is used to cut a number of frames and floors from each plate.*

Courtesy of Jefferson Marine

Professional yards also work to the motor-away stage, in which the hull is blasted, completely painted, and the engine, plumbing, tankage, and prop assembly are completed. Only the interior, finishing, deck gear, spars, and rigging are left up to the owner. The actual extent of work is very negotiable in this stage.

The final stage is a completed vessel, ready to sail after minor alterations and adjustments by the owner. Some builders will also carry this a step further and commission the boat for you.

Of course the outlay of cold, hard cash increases with the amount of work the professional yard does. A professionally built bare-hull assembly finished out by an amateur costs only a third more than an owner-built boat, but a boat completed in a professional yard will run twice (or more) the cost of a bare-hull assembly that has been finished out at home. The cost of labor is the main factor responsible for this increase. There may be ways of working with the builder to save cash (for example, priming the boat yourself after it has been blasted.) However, most professional yards will want to do critical work themselves to protect their reputation for quality and for insurance reasons. Some specify a minimum amount of work they must do before the boat leaves their yard.

Much of the total cost of the boat is determined in the last stage when all of the accommodations, finish work, and cruising equipment are added. Professional builders may be able to get equipment at reasonable discounts and will pass some of the savings on to you, but if you have access to a good discount and, even more important, are a good scrounger, your costs can be lower than the professional's. Unless, of course, the builder is a good scrounger, too.

No matter how much work the professional yard does initially, future changes and additions to the metal work will be costly. Your close attention to detail before construction begins will help to prevent errors.

Choosing a Builder

Choosing a builder is like choosing a crew member, and it's worth taking the time and care to pick someone in whom you have total confidence. Depending on the complexity of the design, the builder's experience may be more important than the price. And although there are many good welders in professional yards, not all of them have lofting and fitting skills or the tooling necessary for round-hull work.

Construction methods can vary among yards without affecting the final quality. Although the builder is primarily responsible to the owner, any major changes should be approved by the designer. If, for example, the builder wants to change the framing system because the framing stock specified is not available, the designer should be consulted on this change. In this case, as long as the hull stiffness and section modulus are not altered, the variation should not cause any problems. Some builders prefer a certain plating sequence or like to build the hull upside-down. Such changes do not affect the design elements, so the designer need not be consulted.

On the other hand, builders have a responsibility to conform to the design, especially if alterations would make the boat unsafe. There is a story about an owner who wanted a professional builder to make changes in plate thickness and welding procedure without consulting the designer, who had already pointed out the disastrous consequence of this change. The builder couldn't change the owner's mind either, and so declined to build the hull.

A builder may suggest alternations in the design if he or she feels that some part of the boat is impractical or too expensive to build. On custom boats, designers will often make modifications for these reasons, especially if they know and respect the builder. There might be a problem if the reason the plans need to be changed is that the designer didn't do a good job. The owner then must let the builder know what to do.

Some builders work only with plans drawn up by a particular designer. If such a builder agrees to construct a hull from plans drawn up by a different designer, he or she may want the lines or other construction details checked by the "in-house" designer. Major changes should still not be made without consulting the original designer.

A builder may have exclusive rights to build a certain design. If you want that design, you'll have to get it from that yard. However, with the continual construction of the same boat, the builder gains experience with that specific hull shape and may have developed some techniques to save time and save you money. Many yards specialize in building certain hulls, even though they don't have exclusives. If you've chosen one of these designs, you may want to have yours built by a yard that has already built several.

Builders who work closely with designers or builders who are also designers can be a good choice, because the design knowledge can help them to see flaws in the design that will prevent a builder from turning out a fair hull. Of course, many builders pick up knowledge about design from the building process, but, if he or she is basing designs only on practical knowledge, with no theory thrown in, you would be wise to be cautious of the designs.

After you've considered the complexity of your design and researched builders who have built the same or

Fig. 6-2. *This well-designed "assembly line" at the Barnes yard includes a special area for turning over the hull. Once finished, the boat moves out of the shop on its own trailer. (Notice the split pipe used to soften the chine.)*

similar boats, you will be able to make a list of builders you would consider hiring to construct your hull. Designers will also often recommend builders who have done quality work on their designs in the past. Having two or three yards bid on the construction will allow you to compare prices.

Before you make your final decision, try to see and, if possible, sail on boats the yard has built. It's definitely worth visiting the building site to see the facilities and equipment and to view hulls under construction. This also allows you to have a personal interview with the builder, so that you can understand his or her construction "philosophy." Enough welding and fitting equipment to do the job (and the skills to use them) should be your primary concern. Many yards also have capabilities for drafting, casting, blasting, metallizing, plumbing, carpentry, or finishing. Doing the work in-house can save you money, but many big yards with lots of equipment have high overheads that are usually passed along to the customer. The best bet may be an efficient, medium-sized shop with a fair amount of tooling.

Many yards stick to the fitting and welding they know best and contract out to other professionals certain jobs such as plate rolling, blasting, or painting. This is fine as long as the yard is straightforward and tells you what you're paying for. You may want to find out if these other marine professionals are located nearby or if you must pay travel expenses. The builder may want some say in the selection of the subcontractor, since he or she is the one who will have to deal with plate that has not been rolled properly, or listen to the owner complain about the lousy paint job. If the builder is expected to oversee the subcontracted work, a small percentage charge tacked on for this extra work is only fair. If the hull must be moved to a different location for blasting and painting, the owner will deal separately with the blaster and painter under a separate contract.

You also should look at the location of the yard to make plans for launching or transporting the finished hull from the building site. Some yards have areas where you can work on finishing out the boat. Others may want you to transport the boat elsewhere to complete it.

Unless you are having an exclusive design built, the builder will need to see and review the final construction plans in order to discuss any changes and to give an accurate estimate of cost. Study plans will not do, but bids based on preliminary drawings are generally fairly close. The more details that are included, the closer the estimate will be. Find out from the builder exactly what plans are needed for bids, package them carefully, and send them off by registered mail.

Fig. 6-3. *This spacious professional shop has room to build two boats at once.*
Courtesy of Millerick Bros.

Once the bids are returned, the quotes must be compared. You must be certain what is included in each quote. One yard may have a lower price but doesn't include blasting and priming, while another blasts and primes for a marginally higher cost. Beware of builders who give low bids to keep the customer interested and then raise the price with add-on extras.

The payment schedule must be settled with the builder before the contract is drawn up. This schedule varies with each builder, but many professional yards will not consider accepting a contract without a deposit to hold a starting date, usually paid at the signing of the contract. After the hull is welded, another sum may be due. The final payment is often made before delivery. A friendly agreement is essential, and the best ones are those in which the details and payments are made clear, so that each party knows where he or she stands. After the original contract is signed, any additions can be treated as addenda to the original contract with their own payment schedules.

After reviewing the plans, the builder should be able to provide a fairly accurate estimate of how long it will take to build the boat, so that the owner can make sure that cash is available at the proper payment times and know when to expect delivery.

The contract should clearly specify that the vessel and all materials and equipment intended for the vessel are the property of the owner as paid for, so that in the event of the builder's death or failure of the business, the vessel and equipment can rightfully be claimed by the owner. And as long as the owner has made proper payments, the builder should not permit any liens, encumbrances, or claims on the vessel.

The builder should carry builder's all-risk insurance, which will protect the owner against damage, loss, fire, casualty, or other damage during construction. As another kind of insurance, a good yard will guarantee the quality of its construction for a specified period of time, varying between 1 and 10 years. The cost of repairs due to integral hull failures during that time should not be charged to the owner. However, most contracts also specify that repair work must be done on the builder's premises.

After construction is underway, it's hard for any owner to stay away. Although it's wise to visit the builder on a fairly regular basis to check on any problems, changes, or adjustments, you shouldn't harrass your builder. It's a cooperative relationship, even though you're paying the bill.

PURCHASING A SECOND-HAND HULL

Before you can buy an existing steel hull, you have to find a good one. You can either do the detective work yourself or go through a broker, who nowadays may have access to computerized listings of boats all over the world. (The Yacht Exchange in Fort Lauderdale, Florida, is one such source, as is Boat Search in Seattle, Washington.) New computer technology allows specialized searches of all listings according to your requirements. If you're trying to find the hull yourself, the process is the same as for any boat: check newspapers, boating magazines, bulletin boards, or go to those areas of the country where boats are abandoned by disenchanted sailors—Florida or Hawaii, for example. You may have better success in Europe, as did a friend who recently went over to France with money in his pocket and found exactly what he wanted at a price he could afford. Considering the favorable exchange rates in 1985, the cost of a used foreign-built hull can be equal to or less than that of a hull kit and do-it-yourself finishing. But finding exactly the right boat in good condition may be difficult.

Once you have found a used hull, it is very important to have it surveyed properly. While a standard marine survey will do for the boat systems, specialized testing should be done to make sure of the integrity of the hull itself. In other words, find a surveyor with experience in steel. Check with brokers, insurance companies, banks, or even naval shipyards. If the boat has been surveyed recently, try to meet with the surveyor to find out what kind of testing was done on the steel. If the existing survey is questionable, try to get the owner's permission for a new one, although it's likely to be at your expense.

Testing Steel

Used hulls are exactly that, and some may have been abused or neglected by previous owners. A survey tests the hull's integrity: will it fail under the stresses that can be expected to act on it? Failure can result from defects in the steel itself, defects caused by the methods by which the steel was worked, or defects caused by corrosion. A single crack or area of porosity is not going to sink a ship, but a combination of weaknesses in a critical area might.

Both nondestructive (NDT) and destructive tests can be used to find these problem areas. Most surveys will start with NDT methods, using destructive methods only if a questionable area is found. NDT can be used to examine either the surface or the interior of the metal, depending on the method. A good surveyor and even some professional builders should know most of these tests, as well as the standards which the steel must meet.

NDT testing on a new hull is not a bad idea, and is performed by some professional yards (although this is rare since these yards already know how well the boat has been welded and realize that their reputations depend on good welding). The home builder working on his or her first and only boat may want to have at least the weld zones tested to make sure they are without defects. Hull plate itself, if new and certified, should not need testing. Most professionals will return any defective plating before the delivery is completed, and regular steel suppliers for such yards usually know their standards and inspect the plate before delivery. The home builder should also be prepared to return defective plate.

The overall condition of the hull (whether it has dents, buckles, or unfairness) can say a lot about its original design and construction, its history, and any abuse by former owners. A great deal can also be learned by visual inspection of the steel. A 1½-to-3 lb. shot-filled hammer, a flashlight or miner's light, calipers, and a felt-tip marker can be used to make this inspection. A boroscope (a precision optical instrument with a built-in light source) is handy for hard-to-see places.

Hammering can reveal weak spots and loose rust in a second-hand vessel. But some chipping may be necessary to discover the extent of any corrosion or the amount of filler used. Possible water traps around coamings, lips, bulkheads, and bulwarks, common in many older designs, should be examined for rust. If the decks are wood over steel and any rust streaks are seen on the covering board area, a sample removal of some decking would be wise. Other critical areas on the exterior of the hull include around the rudder stock, shaft, seacocks, exterior waterline, chafe areas near anchors, the heel of the keel, vents, loose filler areas, any rivets, and areas near dissimilar metals.

A good look in the bilge is recommended, although access is sometimes a problem and can hinder a good survey. A puddle found along a longitudinal may be a sign of leakage or the absence of drain holes. If foam insulation hides the interior, removal of a test section in an area that may be a water trap would be wise.

Weld zones should have a proper bead attached, and the welds should not have craters at their ends. Grooved butt welds and plates should have smooth edges and be clean and properly aligned. Fillet welds should have a smooth surface and proper shape with no undercuts. Welds can be ground, filed, or sanded to bare metal in several spots to inspect for black dots, dead spots, pinholes, or slag inclusions.

If the hull is old, visual inspection is less satisfactory than other NDT methods. There is more chance of stress-induced cracking in an older hull, since it has been in service longer. Plate thickness may also be a concern if improper maintenance in the past has allowed corrosion to develop.

Fig. 6-4.   *If there's any rust on the deck or cabin, eventually it will be washed out the scupper drains and leave unsightly stains.*

99

A digital gauge available from Automation/Sperry can be used to test hull plate thickness, although the equipment cost is high. These gauges run either on AC current or low-voltage DC and are accurate to 1/1000. The Nova-100-D and the UTM110 are very handy portable units that are powered by 1.5-volt batteries, and each costs between $1700 and $2000. The painted surface to be tested must have good adhesion, since a loose coating will give an inaccurate reading, and corroded surfaces may also read as thicker plate.

The simplest and least expensive NDT method is *dye penetrant inspection,* which can only detect surface defects. It is particularly useful to check for hairline cracks in stainless steel. The surface must be carefully prepared and free of oil, grease, oxides, rust, and other contaminants, all of which may block penetration of the dye into the defect. After cleaning, dye is applied to the metal and allowed to penetrate the defect for a few minutes. Excess dye is removed from the surface, and a developer is applied so that dye from the defect is drawn toward the surface. Then the metal is examined using either special lighting or sunlight, depending on the type of dye used. A number of dye penetrant kits are available for prices ranging from $40 to $3000 from companies including the Magnaflux Corporation and Automation/Sperry.

Magnetic particle testing is a more sophisticated method for inspecting heavy outside welds, gouges, and joint preparation of steel. Under good conditions, some subsurface defects may also be found. After the metal is thoroughly cleaned, the part to be tested is magnetized, and then a stream of magnetic particles is passed over it. Particles collect around defects because of the magnetic lines of force concentrating there, showing them up to the trained eye.

In order to find the more serious subsurface defects, such as slag inclusions, porosity, incomplete fusion of metals, inadequate penetration of the root pass, and undercutting, more advanced and expensive NDT methods must be used. Their expense is justified by the knowledge that a more sophisticated test has been used in areas of high stress concentration, especially for heavily loaded deck and hull areas, butts, and seams at the gunwale, bilge, and hatch corners. There are three types commonly used.

In *radiography,* either x- or gamma rays are passed through the metal and record a picture on special film, which is then interpreted by highly trained personnel. It primarily shows areas of different densities within the metal, and therefore can pick up areas of porosity and inclusions. This method cannot be used on butt or T-joints, and cannot detect failures in plate lamination or very thin cracks.

In *ultrasonic testing,* the principle is the same as that used in sonar. High-frequency sound is beamed through the test metal, and defects within the metal reflect the sound waves back to the surface. This method is commonly used to check laminar defects in plate, but it can also pick up excessive nonmetallic inclusions, seams, slivers, pits, and weld defects. Ultrasonic testing effectively shows the depth of the defect, and can also be used to register metal thickness, since the back surface of the metal also deflects the sound waves.

Eddy current analysis is an electromagnetic method of detecting surface discontinuities such as open welds, seams, etc. A test coil, contained in a probe that is passed over the surface or inserted into apertures, carries an alternating current that induces a magnetic field in the metal. Variations in the magnitude of electrical loading caused by structural changes or defects are recorded on a meter. Immediate results are possible, although it takes time to cover large areas. Some instruments are portable, and their cost is moderate.

Destructive testing is a last resort, but may be necessary. It is not as bad as it sounds, since the destruction is controlled, and the areas that have been tested by drilling or cutting can be welded up again. Although destructive methods generally are used only on very old hulls, some surveyors who are not familiar with the more sophisticated tests may use them on any boat. Sample bending and plug cutting are used most frequently; a right-angle drill can obtain a sample from areas that are hard to reach. Plate thickness can be determined and an analysis of the metal's structure made from a plug. Oxygen embrittlement can also be detected in the metal. Ian Nicholson's book, *Surveying Small Craft,* outlines these testing methods.

If a used hull comes up with a clean survey, you can purchase it with confidence as long as you are sure that the money you've paid a surveyor has bought the right kind of experience and testing equipment. If defects are detected in the hull but you are willing to correct them, you have some leverage in negotiating the final price. In any case, if the hull has been tested, you know what you're getting.

BUILDING THE HULL YOURSELF

Building a steel sailboat from scratch by yourself can be rewarding and save many dollars. But your labor and its worth should be taken into account, since the time you spend on the boat could be spent elsewhere.

You might suppose that anyone who can produce a good weld can build a steel hull. That's partly true, since welding is critical to a good hull. But there are many other skills specific to yacht construction, such as lofting or plate fitting, that are also needed. And if you've chosen to build a round hull, you may need to learn about the special rolling and heat treatment techniques that will help you fabricate a fair hull.

An understanding of design is also important in the building process. An informed builder appreciates what is happening when plate curves and, if a problem arises, can judge if the fault is in the plate or in the framing. A common error among amateurs is trying to force the plate into the frames, especially at the bow, which results in distortion. They may not recognize that faulty design of the frames is the cause of the unfairness.

A professional builder doesn't only build the hull. He or she takes care of many other things, like determining the plate sizes, ordering steel, and providing a building site. A home builder first needs to sit down with the construction plans and decide exactly how to build the vessel, carefully studying the construction details. Like a professional, an amateur builder should not make major design changes without consulting the designer. Don't arbitrarily move tankage or change the position of the mast step to make it easier to build. Resist the temptation to beef up the framing, compression rods, bowsprit, engine beds, or plywood sole "for extra strength"; you'll increase the weight so that the boat does not ride on her waterline.

When planning the construction, you must also be aware of the availability of certain shapes and sizes of steel. Today, T-bar in certain sizes is sometimes difficult to find. 8- or 9-gauge plate is also rare, so most yachts are built with either 7-gauge (close to and also called $\frac{3}{16}''$ plate) or 10-gauge (a bit over $\frac{1}{8}''$).

Once any design changes are finalized and the construction plan is thoroughly understood, you will need to figure out how much metal to buy and where to get it. Some designers, especially those designing primarily for home builders, will include a materials list, but these lists are notoriously poor. Materials are the builder's responsibility. You will also need to order stainless steel for chafe areas, chainplates or eyes, where specified. You can save money by very carefully calculating the amount that you will need of this expensive alloy.

The designer will specify plate thickness and the type of material to be used for frames and longitudinals, since

Table 6-1. STEEL SHAPES

Shape	Major Uses on a Steel Boat
Sheet Metal (under 12 gauge)	Tanks, metal boxes, insulation around stoves
Plate	Hull skin, keel, skeg, floors, deck, cockpit, cabin, gussets, bulkheads, doublers, engine bearers, tangs, webs
Flat Bar	Frames, longitudinals, stem, deck beams, tabs
Angle Bar	Staging, frames, longitudinals, deck beams, girders, porthole frames
T-Bar	Longitudinals, deck beams, travelers
Flange Bar	Frames, stringers, girders, stiffeners, engine bearers, brackets, hatch lips, doublers
Bulb Bar (European)	Frames, longitudinals
Channel	Longitudinals, rub rails, stiffeners
Rod	Chine bars, travelers, eyes, studs
Tube	Railings, stanchions, pulpits
Pipe (whole or split)	Stem, chine bars, guard rails, cabin edges, throughhulls, sea chest, nipples, pedestal
Pipe bends	Bowsprit, breather vents, railings
Tube turns	Bowsprit, railings

their total weights have been calculated in the design process. But the plate itself is available in different standard sizes, and you will need to decide what size plates will work best for you, considering your experience and lifting and cutting tools. Design is a factor here, since you can generally use larger plates for chine boats than for round hulls.

Steel is usually sold by the pound, but to find out the weight you will need, you'll first have to determine the square footage of the surface to be covered. A simple method for estimating plate is to multiply girth × depth × length and then add 10%. A more precise method is first to break up the major hull plates into the actual plate sections you will use, minimizing butt welds wherever possible, then to take graph paper marked to scale for the commercially available plate sizes and fit your plate sections on this model. For cabins and cockpits, patterns drawn to scale can be used in the same way. Once you have your final figure, again add 10%. You'll undoubted-

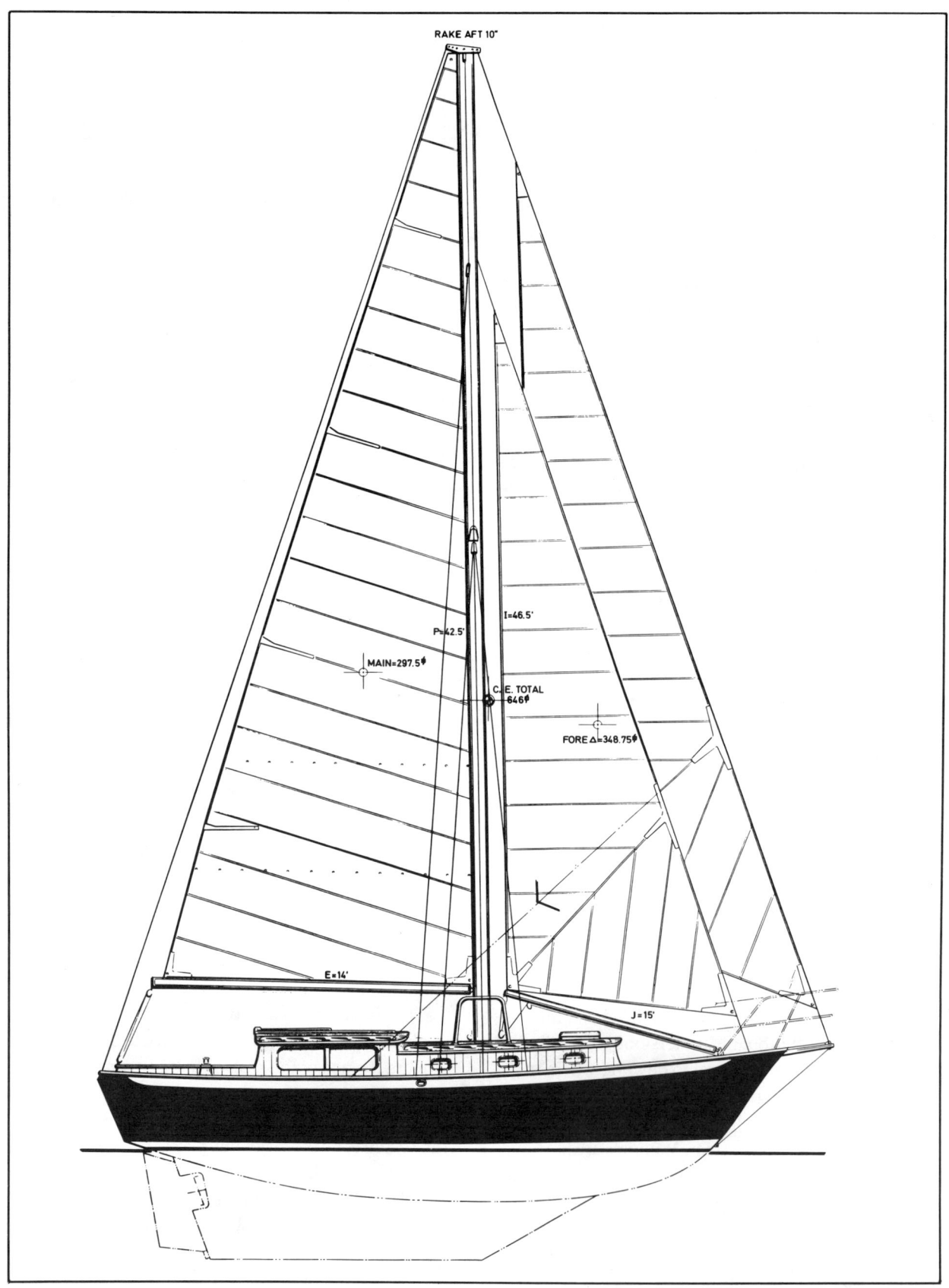

Fig. 6-5. *The* Aurora *was designed by Glen-L Marine specifically for the home builder.* Courtesy of the designer.

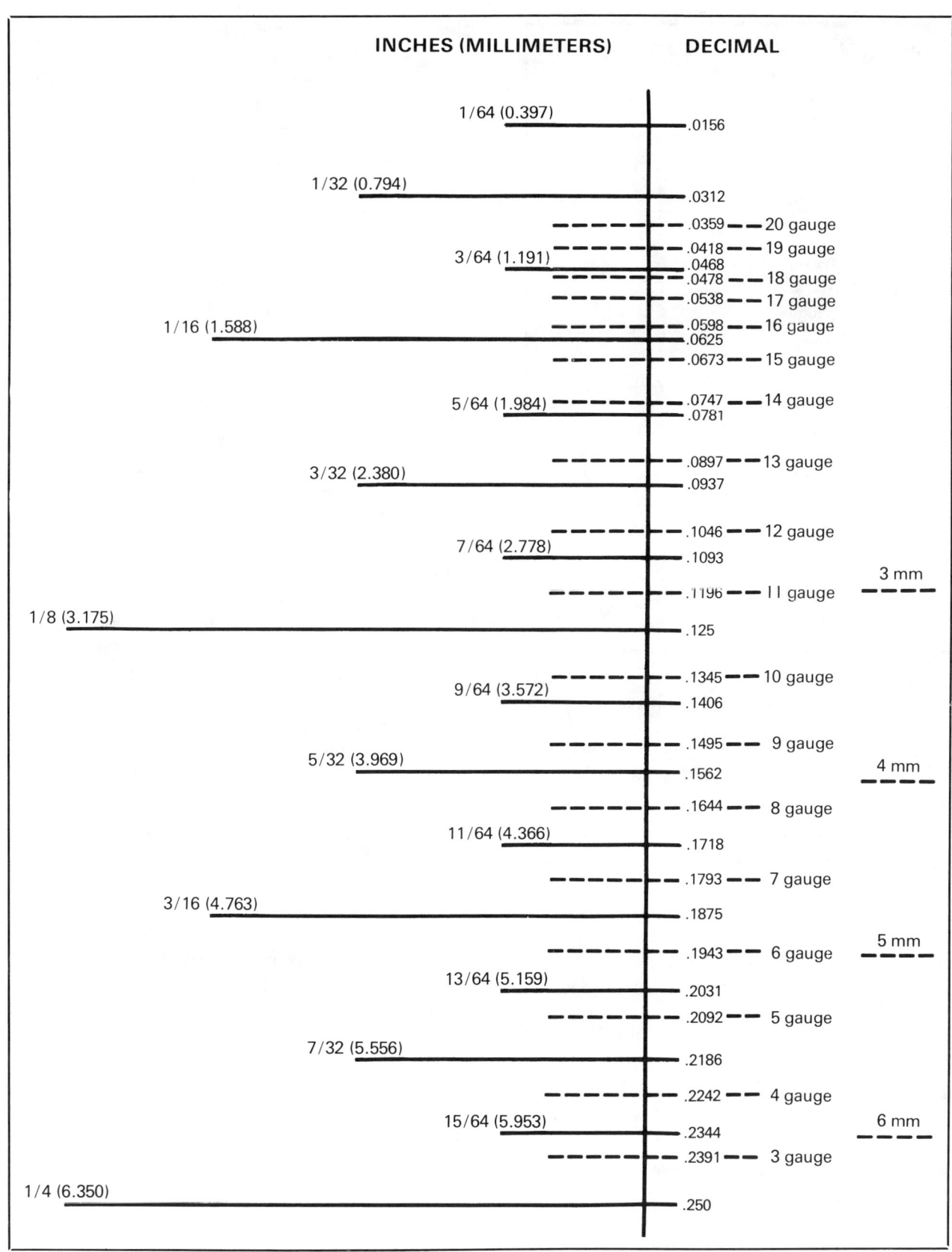

Fig. 6-6. *In the U.S., plate is sized in both inches and gauges. The thickness of metric plate, used in many parts of the world, is slightly different.*

103

Table 6-2. WEIGHTS OF MILD STEEL PLATE

Thickness	Weight in lb./sq. ft.
12 gauge	4.03
7/64″	4.46
11 gauge	4.99
1/8″	5.10
10 gauge	5.52
9/64″	5.74
9 gauge	6.10
5/32″	6.37
8 gauge	6.75
11/64″	7.01
7 gauge	7.30
3/16″	7.65
6 gauge	7.97
13/64″	8.29
5 gauge	8.70
7/32″	8.92
4 gauge	9.14
15/64″	9.56
3 gauge	9.77
1/4″	10.20

abrading machine, but plate lighter than $3/16$″ can easily be distorted by the heat generated during this process. Although companies that do pre-priming often won't guarantee the fairness of 7-gauge or lighter plate, 10-gauge has been successfully wheel-abraded. Regular sandblasting before pre-priming can also be used in the field without as much risk of distortion. Since the builder doesn't always know which side of the plate will be inside until it is assembled, both sides should be pre-primed. But, if it is desired, one-sided pre-priming should only be done when the plate is wheel-abraded, since sandblasting and priming only one side tends to distort plate.

Pre-primed plate is not always suitable, however. If the hull is to be metallized inside, the hull must be completely shot-blasted before metallizing, which will remove all the pre-priming. If you plan to use a coating system manufactured by a different company than the one that produced the primer, you may have to sandblast the hull anyway to get the surface profile specified by the manufacturer for good adhesion.

Even if you decide against pre-primed plate, you'll still probably need to do a fair amount of searching for metal sources in nearby cities. Mild steel distribution is very mixed, and the logical source may not carry what you need. If you are looking for a special kind of steel (like Corten or the newly available, less-expensive Japanese plate), your searching may need to be more extensive. It's important to get plate that is fair, without buckles or defects caused by poor handling. It's wise to buy certified plate and to inspect it carefully before accepting delivery. Your local library may be able to help out with books listing suppliers. The Yellow Pages can also give you a place to start. Scrapyards, metal dealers, and surplus yards can be excellent sources for small quantities of metals like stainless steel and other alloys.

Whether you're building from scratch or finishing out a bare-hull assembly, before construciton begins, sources should be located for the marine equipment needed for each boat system. The first step is to decide on the type of product you want and then on the brand names that provide the quality you require. Then start collecting buyers' guides and getting familiar with the current costs of marine products. Some home builders work on one system at a time, but planning ahead can save time and allow you to take advantage of sales. And with large orders you may be able to get quantity discounts (just remember to plan for the large amount of sales tax tacked onto big orders). (The appendix on ma-

ly find a use for the extra plate, if only to make up for mistakes.

Before ordering, you'll have to know exactly what kind of steel you will need: plain mild steel or an alloy, such as Corten. The designer will have specified the type of steel and used its characteristics in designing the scantlings. However, you have to decide whether or not to buy pre-primed plate.

Pre-primed plate is used to prevent corrosion in areas that are difficult to blast and prime after construction (for example, the backs of T-bar or angle frames). The interior of a hull built with pre-primed plate also does not have to be heavily sandblasted—a nasty and expensive job. The plate can usually be found for a slight additional cost (4–10 cents per pound) in urban areas, but in some parts of the country it is scarce and expensive. The primer used should be the thin, weldable type and must be compatible with the paints that will follow it. If it is not weldable, the weld zones should either be left unprimed or ground clean before welding.

Proper mechanical cleaning and handling are important to pre ent distortion both before and during the priming. Flat plate is usually cleaned by a large wheel-

terial costs provides an example of how to plan for purchasing equipment.)

There are many discount catalogs, mail-order distributors, buyers' co-ops, national boating clubs with discount purchasing, and factory-authorized dealer discounts. Some marine supply stores will give homebuilder discounts, and a professional boatbuilding friend may help you to save by putting your orders through for a small handling fee. It's a good idea to keep a record of sources and costs. That way you won't have to try to remember where you got that great deal on stainless tubing.

The Building Site

Another piece of advance work is to choose and secure a building site. The location should be one where the neighbors, if close by, are friendly and know what you're doing. The ground must be solid enough to support the weight of a completed steel boat, but a cement foundation is not really necessary if a hard dirt or gravel surface is well packed. The surface must be nearly level so that the boat can be easily blocked up level. The site should be convenient to your home, accessible to a road so that the boat can be moved, and not too far from the launching site, unless you like paying trailer fees or have

Fig. 6-7. *A simple European-style cradle, using wooden poles and pipe sections welded to the hull, works well for this home builder.*

no choice in the matter. The best site can range from an industrial area to the woods near a town, but low overhead is probably the most important factor, since building time often seems to be initially underestimated. Access to electric power is mandatory, while running water, though certainly convenient, isn't critical. A friend recently restored a steel lifeboat in a junkyard, where all these criteria were satisfied, with the added bonus of a metal shop just yards away.

One of the nice things about steel hull construction is that you can do without much shelter, except during the coating process. Weathering actually helps to remove mill scale from the steel. However, it may be more practical to plan for a simple post-and-beam shelter or quonset hut, perhaps covered with wood, metal, or heavy plastic tarps. Otherwise, you may have delays when it's pouring rain or too hot to work without shade. In the south, where heat is abominable, screening, mesh, or a tarp roof is a necessity if the site is not shaded by trees. If you're using a MIG welder, you will need shelter from the wind. But you can build right out in the open if you must save costs wherever possible.

Even if the boat itself is not sheltered, a small shed or shop will be needed for storing tools and welding equipment. An old refrigerator with a heat bulb can be put there to provide warm, dry storage for welding electrodes. If the construction drawings did not include full-scale plans (or if you don't trust them), space for lofting and drawing the steel master plate and an area for making patterns or templates and cutting out plate will also be needed.

Fig. 6-8. *Movable staging made of pipe.*

The hull can be constructed on a trailer, cradle, H-beams, railroad ties, or level blocks and hardwood cross beams. The type of grid can vary from simple to complex, and it depends on whether the boat is built right-side-up or upside-down. Staging and bracing made of extra steel or angle bar will also be needed. Some type of crane or hoist system should be on hand for lifting plate and erecting frames.

Building the boat on a trailer, which acts as a level work base and automatically becomes the cradle once the boat is complete, makes some sense since it saves the ordeal of jacking the boat onto a trailer. The trailer must be strong enough to support the finished weight, and its frame should be blocked up so the tires aren't supporting the boat's weight during construction. The trailer can also act as the staging for setting up center-lines, and the hull supports can be welded to it.

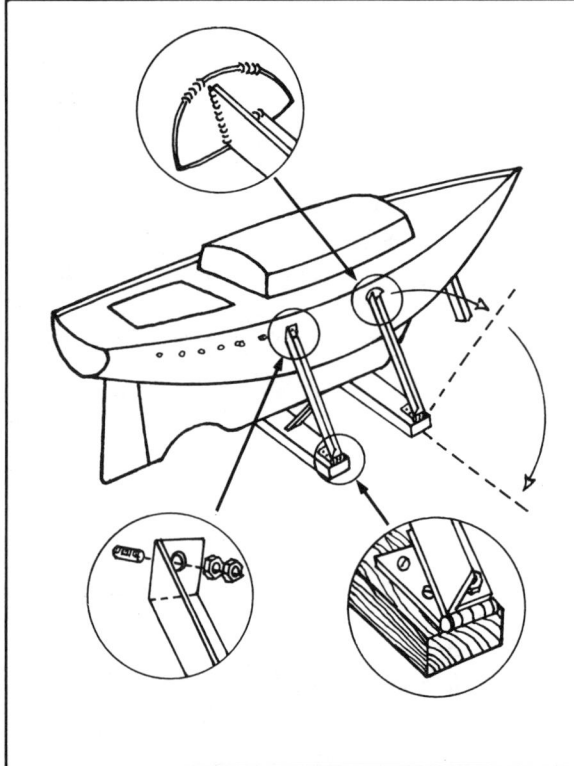

Fig. 6-9. *This cradle holds the boat securely be-cause it is fastened to the rub rail studs or to tabs or scupper inserts that have been temporarily welded to the sides of the hull.*

Although the extra cost of a trailer might be consid-ered unnecessary, it would be a good refresher project in welding before starting the hull. You will also have a trailer to use for other projects or to store your hull on without having to rely on today's overcrowded yards. But if the boat is to be moved a long distance on free-ways, forgetting about the trailer and hiring a profes-sional mover may be the wiser course of action.

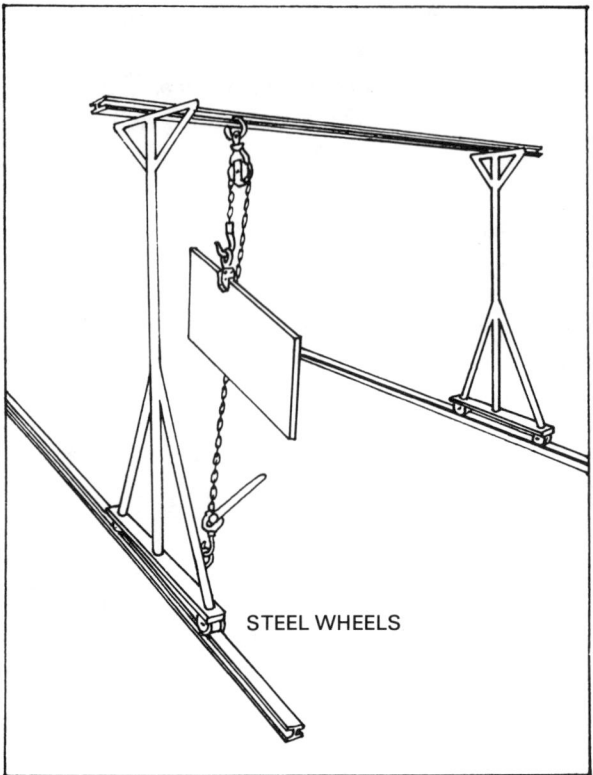

STEEL WHEELS

Fig. 6-10. *Plate moving is easy with this chain hoist assembly that runs on railroad ties.*

Building Position

The final decision to be made before beginning actual construction is whether you will build the boat upside-down or rightside-up. Probably half of all steel boats are built one way and half the other, with a few more pro-fessionals building upside-down.

When the hull is upside-down, assembly of the plate is easier and all of the welding can be done downhand; that is, the welder is on top of or beside the work, which makes it easier to weld (although certain expert welders say that good uphand welding is easier). Some inside tacks and welding will still be needed. Of course, when the hull plate is on, the boat must be turned rightside-up to put on the deck and cabin and to finish the plate welding. Even with a large hull, this operation can be carried out with a simple overhead hoist system, a crane, or a heavy-duty block and tackle. Some profes-sionals use a more advanced and costly drum structure that encircles the hull and can be turned to any position.

If you decide to build the hull upright, you will have to do a lot of overhead welding, so be sure that you can weld overhead with control. You should make the job

Fig. 6-11. *This welded trailer complements the 13-meter staysail schooner it carries.* — Courtesy of Lunstroo Custom

as safe as possible by making sure that no loose slag or hot metal "marbles" will fall inside your clothing. When the hull is built this way, a section of the underbody plating can be left out so that access from the ground to the interior is easier and the grit or sand used in blasting can be shoveled out. This separate piece of plate will have to be blasted and primed and the priming ground away from the weld zones before it is installed. But this sure beats hauling sand up from the bilge.

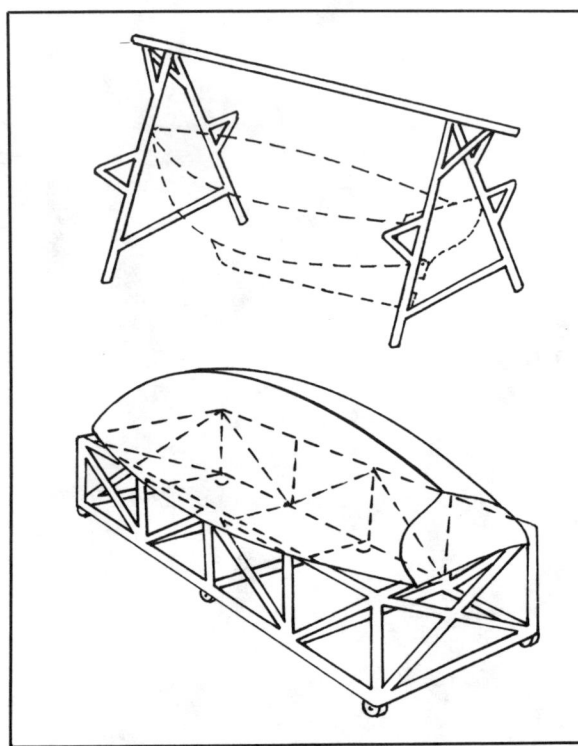

Fig. 6-12. *The building position determines the type of staging that can be used. Although the boat on the bottom could simply be braced on the floor, the movable staging allows the builder to adjust its position. Neither of these examples shows the additional hull bracing that will be required.*

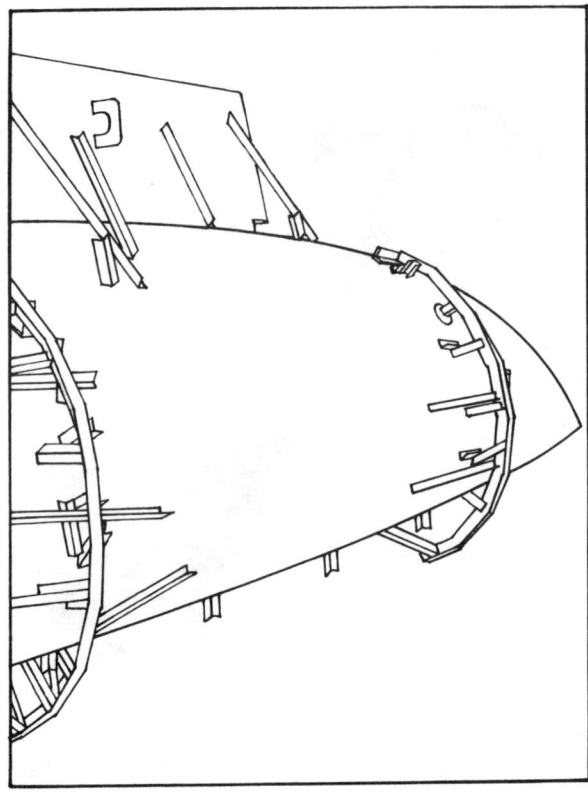

Fig. 6-13. *When a boat is being turned over, a rocker assembly welded to its side will keep the hull from banging against the floor and will help to control the rolling process.*

SOURCES OF NDT GEAR

Magnaflux Corporation
7300 West Lawrence Ave.
Chicago, IL 60656

Automation/Sperry
Shelter Rock Rd.
Danbury, CT 06810-7095
Tel. (203) 796-5000

—Chapter 7

Working with Metals

Naturally, building a steel hull involves lots of work with metals. The plate and frames must be cut and joined; fittings must be cast or fabricated and fastened to the hull; and stresses produced during the construction process may need to be relieved. Metals have been formed and joined for centuries, and many of the methods used in foundries and blacksmith shops haven't changed much, although some have been replaced by more effective procedures. Of course, there are new ways of doing things that are on the leading edge of technology.

Metal work can be divided into cold and hot processes. Cold working includes drilling, cutting, grinding, fastening, and bending. Forging, casting, soldering, brazing, and welding are all hot methods. Heat can also be used to treat the metal after forming and joining by annealing to relieve stresses, hardening, and tempering. Because of the chance of distortion of the metal, hot-working methods are not used unless cold methods cannot do the job.

METAL-WORKING TOOLS

Metal-working tools are used primarily during construction of the bare-hull assembly, but even if you are planning to have the hull built by someone else, a good collection will be handy for repair and maintenance. Many of the tools required to build a hull (for example, benders and jigs) can be fabricated in the home workshop. However, the right, professional-quality tools make the work much easier, so spending some extra money here makes sense. Second-hand equipment can sometimes be found in old warehouses or at auctions, and the price is often much less than for new.

Of course, the number of tools a boatbuilder would like to have is infinite, but some are more essential than others. The job can be done with just a few basic pieces of equipment. Hand tools and those powered by electricity, gas, air pressure, or hydraulics can all be used to shape and join metals. Most electric tools need single-phase 120-amp service, although some heavier equipment requires 220 amps. In most cases, three-phase power isn't really necessary. Each person seems to have his or her favorite brand names, and any comparisons tend to reflect the bias of the builder.

Safety equipment is at the top of any tool list. Chunks of metal and molten slag can do serious damage to eyes and skin. Safety glasses used for metal work should have edge guards to prevent any particles from rebounding behind the front lenses. Safety also includes having a clean work area, with nothing to trip over or slip on. Neither welding nor other metal work is hazardous if the proper precautions are taken.

Table 7-1. SAFETY EQUIPMENT

BASIC
Steel-toed shoes
Coveralls
Leather apron
Leather gloves with cuffs
Ear protectors
Face shield
Goggles with edge guards
Welding hood with various lenses
Respirator
First aid kit with eye wash
Protective hand cream
Fire extinguisher
Industrial vacuum cleaner with extra filters

OPTIONAL
Waxed paper for protecting face shield or
goggles while sandblasting

SHAPING METALS

Forging and Casting

Forging and casting are the principal methods used to make fittings. Both involve heating the metal: in forging the metal is heated red hot so that it becomes soft; casting uses molten metal. Steel fittings are generally forged, while iron, brass, and bronze are commonly cast. Both forging and casting are usually done by professional foundries, but it is possible for an amateur to set up a small foundry at the building site to fabricate fittings.

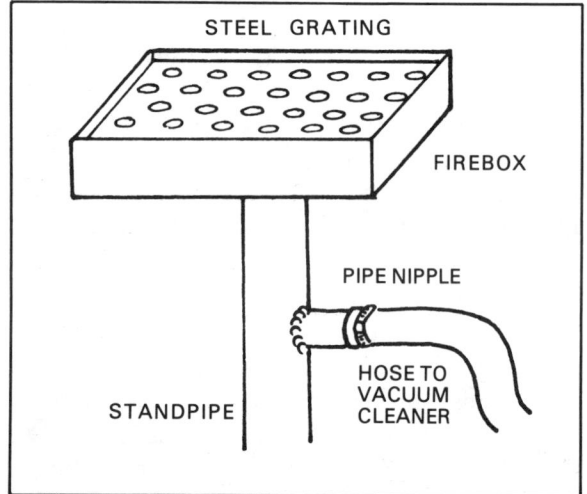

Fig. 7-1. *A vacuum cleaner is used to blow air into this propane-fired, homemade cooker forge.*

In forging, both heat and pressure are used to shape metal. The metal is first heated in the hearth to a red-hot condition so that it will deform plastically. Then it is carried to an anvil, and various hammers—swages, punches, flatters, pullers, hearties—are used to set the metal into a new shape. The hammering work-hardens the steel, making it stronger but more brittle. In drop forging, metal is compressed by impact into a die to produce desired shapes.

In casting, the metal is first heated past its melting point and then poured into a mold. The many different casting processes vary mainly according to the kind of mold to be used. The most common type, often found at small foundries, is sand casting, in which sand is used to line and protect a pattern made of a soft, close-grained wood. Plaster molds make it possible to cast more intricate designs, as does investment casting (also known as the lost-wax method). In die casting, nonferrous metals such as zinc, aluminum, or copper alloys are forced under pressure into polished and hardened steel dies. The finished piece is very smooth and accurate and requires little finish machining. Shell molding is a foundry process in which the molds are made in the form of thin shells.

Although iron is easily forged and cast, it can only be welded to steel by using special nickel electrodes and special techniques. Therefore, its use is generally limited to fittings that can be mechanically fastened (the best example is a cast iron porthole that is bolted through the side of a steel cabin).

Steel can be both forged and cast, although some cast fittings may exhibit brittleness. Most steel fittings used onboard (for example, cleats or blocks) are drop-forged and then welded to the deck, although they can also be secured mechanically. Forged steel fittings are commonly normalized, quenched and tempered after drop-forging, and are often galvanized. Most anchors are also drop-forged, although CQR's are commonly cast.

Production cast-steel fittings are not widely available because stainless seems to have cornered the market. However, steel is easily cast because it melts at a relatively low temperature. Cast steel is graded as hard, soft, common, medium, or special. Hard cast steel is commonly used for hawse pipes, chain pipes, rollers, and cast anchors, all of which are subject to wear. Soft cast steel holds up well against shock and vibration. Common and medium cast steels are stronger than soft cast, and are used for fittings and brackets. Slides, deck lugs, and carriages are usually made of special cast alloy steel, and some special types used in valve parts and pump rotors have high corrosion resistance and can be nonmagnetic.

Stainless steel is much more difficult to form with hot methods like casting and forging. The work hardening caused by forging makes the stainless brittle and liable to crack when bent; cold bending can have a similar effect. Its higher melting point and special cooling requirements can make stainless casting difficult. Hot-forming stainless is best carried out in those industrial foundries that can provide the necessary controlled environment, and most stainless fittings are manufactured this way. However, some stainless shapes can be formed fairly easily by cold-bending techniques, and the fitting produced can then be welded to a steel hull. Depending on the size of the stainless rod or tube and the severity of the bend, heat may be required to ease the bending process. The need for hot-bending methods is determined by the raw shape and the intended design of the end product.

Brasses, bronzes, and aluminum are so easily cast that they are rarely shaped by forging. Cast aluminum is commonly used for gears, worms, wheels, valve seats, bearings, hatch frames, impellers, and portholes. High-quality spar fittings often are cast from manganese bronze. Other brasses are cast as pipe, seen on ferry boat railings, and ship's bells; gunmetal was once very common in all sorts of fittings. Bronze castings are used for mast fittings, deck hardware, couplings, propellers, steering gears, manifolds, hinges, bushings, fittings, and belaying pins. Parts of the new high-tech winches are cast barium. Copper-nickel and monel fittings, such as propellers with high strength and corrosion resistance, are also cast. If any of these dissimilar-metal fittings are used on a steel hull, they must be mechanically fastened with proper insulation and bedding between the metal and the steel.

Cutting

Whenever metal is to be cut, cold methods are preferable to hot because with the former the chance of distortion is lessened. But the choice of cutting method for steel also must take into account the specific alloy and the thickness of the material. As a rule, the thinner the steel, the more it will distort if heat is used during the cutting process. Thin sheet metal can be cut easily with snips or power shears, and some builders use a bandsaw to cut structural steel pieces from plate or flat bar and to notch frames. Thicker plate is harder to cut with a bandsaw, but since thickness reduces the risk of distor-

Table 7-2. TOOLS FOR CUTTING
BASIC
Magnetic straight edge
Hacksaw
Jig saw
Tin snips
Crimper
Bolt/rod cutter
Sheet metal slitter
Metal chop saw
Oxyacetylene torch
Nibbler
Plasma arc cutter
OPTIONAL
Hand seamer
Notcher, hand or power
Rotary cutter
Large-capacity machine shears
Chipper (also called cape chisel, chip hammer, rivet buster)
Metal band saw
Power hack saw
Portable shears, hand or power
Pipe cutter
Parter, hand or power

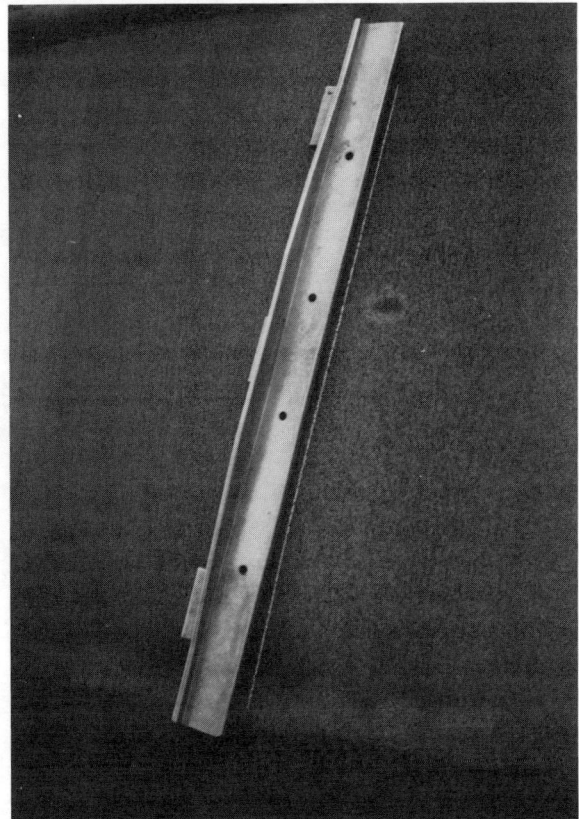

Fig. 7-2. *A magnetic straight edge makes it easy to mark steel plate.*

tion, a torch can be used successfully. Many builders are switching to nibblers or plasma arc cutters to control heat-produced distortion during cutting.

The oxyacetylene torch has been the steel-cutting standby for many years, but the heat produced by the torch may cause the plate to dish or curl. (This effect can be corrected by tapping the edges of the plate after cutting). Torch-cutting can yield quite smooth holes and lines, especially if a jig or straight edge is used, but usually some slag is left, and it must be chipped or ground off. Curved cuts can be trickier, but a skilled builder with experience should be able to turn out a smooth curve.

A nibbler, which cuts mechanically rather than with heat, works well on plate up to $\frac{3}{16}$" thick. It is noisy, but makes a nice crisp cut with no slag to clean up. A nibbler cannot, however, be used to cut steel in place.

A plasma arc cutter is the best of both worlds: it cuts without distortion and can be used to trim plates in place. Ionized gas (nitrogen is commonly used) slices through the metal, producing a dense brown smoke. In the hands of an experienced operator, the cut is very sharp and clean, and the process is incredibly fast and distortion-free. Plasma cutters can handle mild steel plate as thick as $\frac{5}{16}$" and can be used on many different kinds of metals, especially brass, aluminum, and stain-

Table 7-3. TORCH CUTTING EQUIPMENT

BASIC
Torch
Tanks: oxygen, minimum 90 cu. ft.
   and
   acetelyene, minimum 60 cu. ft.
   or
   propane (cheaper but requires special tips)
Tank carrier cart on wheels with safety chain for securing tanks
Tank regulator
Hoses (100 ft. or more)
Tips (Nos. 1–5 plus rosebud for heating large areas)
Tip cleaner
Flint lighter
Spray bottle with soapy water to check for tank leaks

OPTIONAL
Drag tip
Hole shooter assembly
Torch with wheel guide
Jet torch
Portable tank kit to carry onboard

Fig. 7-3. *A plasma arc cutter speeds up the work of cutting plate at Waterline Yachts.*

less. The width of the cut is only ⅛″, and, if necessary, the slit can be welded up in a single pass. Of course, no tool is without its bad points. Plasma cutters have fairly high operating costs, both in terms of electricity used and the fairly frequent replacement of the cutting tips. It is difficult to cut angle and T bar with this tool, and a torch may have to be substituted in areas where access is difficult. But the speed and efficiency of the plasma cutter guarantees it a place on any professional's wish list of tools.

Aluminum cannot be cut with a torch because it oxidizes too quickly. A plasma arc cutter is the best choice, although aluminum can also be cut with a metal bandsaw fitted with the correct blade.

A flame-planing machine can be used to cut plate with curved edges to size. It will also cut a weld-edge preparation with many bevels in one pass. These machines are very expensive and are only found in highly industrialized fabrication shops.

COLD FORMING

As we discussed in Chapter 5, steel flat bar and plate can be easily bent using cold-method tools such as rollers, hydraulic jigs, or homemade frame benders. Fittings can also be fabricated by cold-forming methods, if necessary in pieces that are then welded together.

Steel and other malleable metals like aluminum can be clamped down and hammered into the correct shape. This method is particularly useful for stainless steel, since it cannot be cast, but must be fabricated into shapes by cold methods. A conduit bender will help put a fair curve in tubing and conduit, and a bench scroll-bending jig is handy for bending metal bar stock.

Table 7-4. TOOLS FOR SHAPING, BENDING, AND FORMING
BASIC
Metal work table (or saw horses)
Hammers (heavy metal, soft head, ball peen; different weights)
Block hammer (also called engineering hammer)
Sledge hammer
Cold chisels
Metal punches
Metal files
Metal file tips for drill
Grinders (bench, portable, peanut)
Bender or scroll-bending jig (hand, power, or hydraulic)
Pipe bender (manual)
OPTIONAL
Sheet metal former
Pneumatic chipper
Rollers
Braking machine (hand or power)
Heavy machine brake
Press brake
Metal lathe with surface gauge, vernier protractor, calipers, and micrometer
Foundry equipment (anvil, small furnace, hammers, etc.)
Hydraulic machine press

Grinding is one of the most common ways of mechanically shaping a metal object. Every steel boatbuilder will get his or her fill of grinding, both in preparing and finishing welds and in beveling edges to accept paint. Small fittings can also be shaped with a grinder. Proper fitting and welding reduces the amount of grinding that will be needed. One homebuilder made the mistake of not recessing his chine rod far enough into the frames

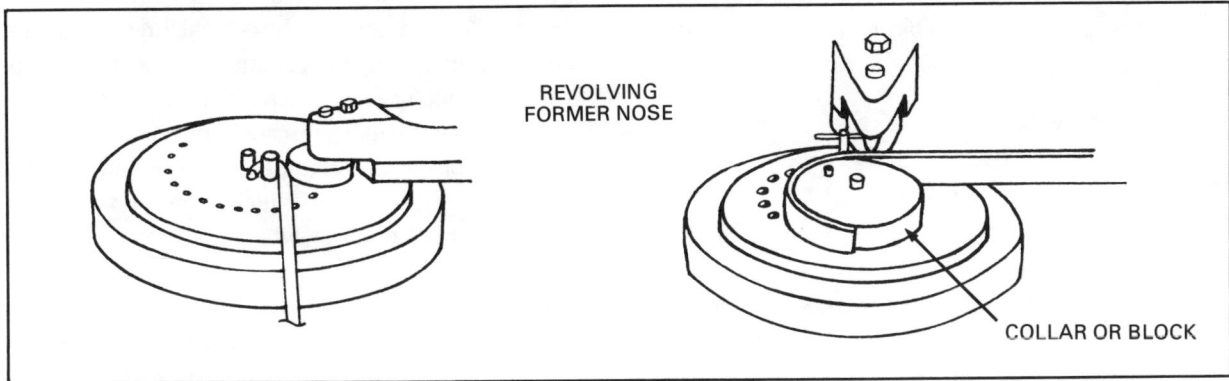

REVOLVING FORMER NOSE

COLLAR OR BLOCK

Fig. 7-4. *Scroll benders can be used to make eyes out of round bar (left) or, with the addition of a collar or block, to bend flat bar, channel bar, angle iron, or tubing (right). Different former noses and collars or block are used to create different shapes.*

Fig. 7-5. *This unique bender is used at the T.D. Vinette yard.*

with the result that when the plate was installed, the bars protruded too much from the hull. He had to weld in extra metal and then grind it all down to get it fair. The hours of extra grinding were only topped by the extra cursing he did.

Power hand grinders are the most common type of grinding tool. They come in different sizes, and different disks can be attached to increase their usefulness. Once a disk is worn down too far to be used on a large grinder, it can be passed down to a "peanut" grinder, which is easier to use in tight areas. A bench grinder is especially useful for shaping fittings, and files also come in handy for places impossible to reach with a grinder.

Grinding stainless steel is not recommended, since it tends to work-harden the stainless and make it more brittle. However, there will be times when some grinding is necessary, and it is possible, though more difficult.

METAL JOINERY

Mechanical Methods

Drilling holes in mild steel can be an arduous task. Although there are special hole shooters that can be used with a cutting torch, for accuracy and cleaner results most holes in frames for interior joinery will be made with hand-held power drills. Good, sharp, high-quality, high-speed bits are the basic tools, along with a powerful drill. Cutting mild steel requires about 1500 rpm, while stainless can be cut at lower rpms. Alumi-

num needs approximately 3500 rpm, and the brasses vary from 1000–2300 rpm. Carbide or tungsten bits, though expensive, do a better job and last longer than carbon steel, and they don't need to be resharpened as often. Drill bits also last far longer if oil is used when drilling, especially when putting holes in stainless. Cutting holes for larger fasteners may require using progressively larger bits in stages to produce the final size hole. Tabs and removable items can be drilled on a drill press before assembly, and center punches, clamping devices, and cutting fluid also make the process easier.

Tap-and-die sets are a must for any builder. The taps are used to thread the many holes drilled in the steel for fastening woodwork, handrails, stanchions, and other fittings, especially if extra holding power is needed or if a nut cannot be used behind the bolt. Spiral-point taps, with two flutes rather than the normal three or four, are stronger and hold up better if many holes must be tapped (for example, when fastening a teak deck). Taps are also needed to clean the threads of nuts that have been welded in place (as in tank access lids). The dies are used for threading rod on which to mount various fittings and are also handy when the threads on a bolt must be extended.

Screws, nuts and bolts, and studs are the standard fasteners for attaching both metal and wood fittings to a steel boat. Although rivets have been replaced by welding for plate joinery, they may still be required for particular items like mast fittings and some deck fittings. A pinner's rivet, like that used for copper rivets on

Table 7-5. TOOLS FOR DRILLING AND FASTENING

BASIC
  Drill (electric or pneumatic)
  Complete set of drill bits (cobalt or tungsten)
  Drill bit gauge
  Point gauge (to check tip angles)
  Tap-and-die set
  Metal punch (hand, electric, hydraulic)
  Drill press
 	
OPTIONAL
  Variable speed drill
  Right-angle drill
  Pipe threader
  Hole punch machine
  Reamer
  Stud gun
  Riveter (for aluminum spar work)

lapstrake wood boats, can be used for thin sheet metal. A good pop rivet gun (the price of which varies greatly depending on the model) will be needed for fastening tangs to aluminum masts and for attaching heavy items like winches.

The fasteners used on a steel boat should generally be made of stainless steel. Galvanized fasteners can be used in various areas, but they could have a shorter lifetime. Bronze should be avoided if it must pass through steel, although it is quite useful for wood-to-wood joinery.

Bolts are commonly used to fasten dissimilar metal fittings as well as woodwork. If a major steel appendage (for example, a lower rudder bearing) must be made removable, it will be bolted to the hull rather than welded integrally. Bolt holes must be pre-drilled, and both the fitting and the bolt must be bedded or sealed before the bolt is tightened. High-quality machine screws (which are actually bolts) are recommended for use with steel. Nylock nuts, which do not loosen, are useful in areas where vibration may loosen the nut. Press fits, set screws, and clamps are other devices to prevent loose fittings. Stanchions or press-fit plastic rudder shaft bearings are often locked in placed with stainless set screws. Stainless machine screws are most often used with thin sheet metals, like those found in nonstructural interior joinery.

On a steel hull, studs (threaded, headless bolts) can be used to good advantage, especially for securing larger items, although bolts are faster, easier, and cheaper. Steel or stainless studs are commonly welded to the hull for attaching the zincs, rub rails, windlasses, and spray shields. The easiest way to make a stud is to pass a bolt through a hole in the steel and then to weld the head of the bolt under the steel. Long sections of metal rod can also be purchased, cut to length with a chop saw, and then threaded on one end before being welded in place. When many studs must be secured, as when laying wood decks over steel, welding them in place with a special stud gun will save time.

Soldering and Brazing

Although the steel boatbuilder will not use any soldering or brazing on the hull itself, the processes may be needed both for wiring and plumbing installation and for fabrication or repair of fittings.

Soft soldering is used to join metals like brass and copper with lead or tin solder at temperatures lower than 800°F. A soldering gun or propane torch is used to heat the adjoining metal, and the solder melts when it is held against the heated surface. Unlike welding, the base metal and the solder do not fuse together, so a soldered joint is not particularly strong. Resin-core solder is the best type to use for wiring, and acid-core solder should not be used for anything other than sheet metal work, since the acid will eventually eat away the electrical connection. A chemical flux is applied to the joint to prepare the clean base metal for accepting the solder.

Brazing, or hard soldering, is carried out at temperatures between 800 and 1400°F. Brass and bronze are commonly joined or repaired by brazing, but it is also very efficient for repairing items made of thin-gauge steel (such as diesel tanks). Silver solder is the best for all applications and is commonly used on diesel fuel fittings. However, it is very expensive, so bronze rods are often used instead. Brass brazing rods are also available. An oxyacetylene torch is usually used for brazing, since a soldering gun doesn't produce enough heat.

Welding

Welding is the single most important skill a steel boatbuilder needs. It's not difficult to learn basic welding—many community colleges and voc-tech schools offer classes—but polishing the skill may take a lot of practice. In order to build a fair hull, though, the builder also must be familiar with the effects of heat on the structure of metal, so that strength is not lowered or the steel distorted by the welding.

The expansion and contraction of metals during the welding process can set up stresses that may result in

Fig. 7-6. *All suited up and ready to weld.*

amateur builders. The welding machine creates a heavy adjustable electric current. Whenever the rod is struck against the steel (which is connected to the machine's ground clamp), a short circuit is established. The electrode is designed to be the weak link in this chain, and it melts and can be deposited at a controlled rate. The electrode is heavily coated with a shielding material such as cellulose sodium or cellulose potassium. As this material burns, it gives off gas that protects the molten weld zone. Shielded metal arc welding can produce sound welds when the joints are well-designed, accessible, properly prepared, and when the equipment is powerful enough to produce the correct current.

A good arc welder provides a minimum of 200 amps of power, and a common example is one with 230 amps

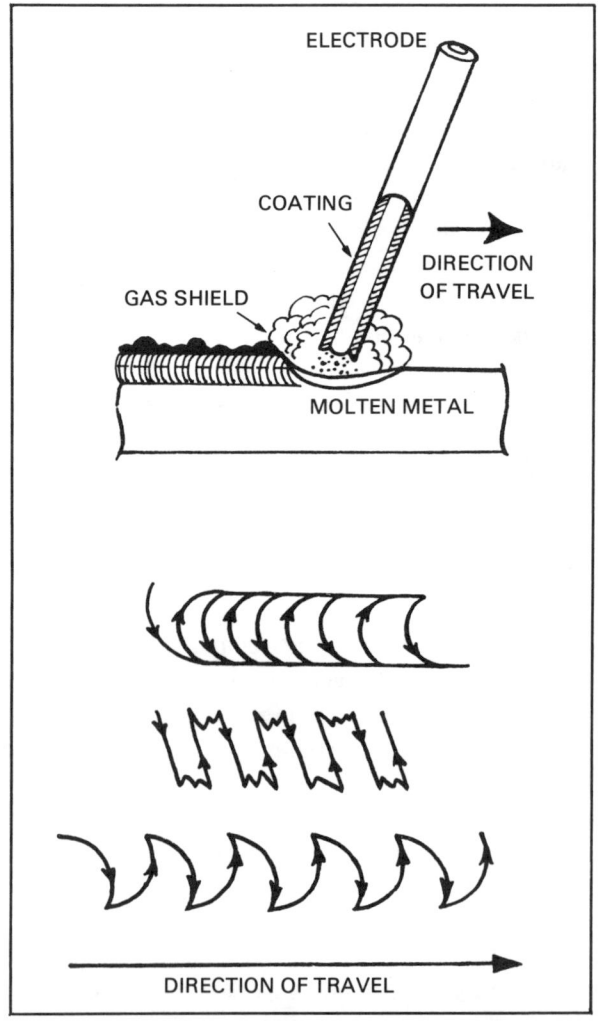

Fig. 7-7. *(above) The stick welding process. (below) The different types of hand movements used during stick welding.*

severe distortion. Temperature variations in the plate when the edge is heated and cooled can produce stress. The changes in crystalline structure in an area that has been heated can cause non-uniform grain structure in the plate, which increases internal stresses. If weld zones cool too rapidly, the steel may become brittle and subject to cracks in the weld zone. (Distortion and how to prevent it are covered in Chapter 8.)

Although there are many different kinds of welding equipment, shielded metal arc (also known as stick or manual electric arc) and gas metal arc (MIG) are most commonly used in steel boatbuilding. Other welding methods include gas tungsten arc (TIG or heli-arc), submerged arc, plasma arc, carbon arc, stud, roller, project, forged, flash, plastic, electron beam, laser, thermal arc, ultrasonic, electric slag, submerged arc, flux cord arc, or electric gas welding. (Whew!) Descriptive material on these different methods can be found in literature distributed by welding machine producers like Hobart, Airco, Linde, and Lincoln.

Stick welding with a rod electrode is the cheapest, most common type of welding, and is often used by

and 50-60 cycles. (The North American standard is 60, while Europeans use 50-cycle service). This machine can be used with a gas, diesel, or electric generator. Rectifier welders, which run on DC power, are another, though more expensive, option. The controlled output of DC machines is better for welding thinner metals, and some electrodes can only be used with DC equipment. AC "buzz boxes" can be purchased for about $250, while a small rectifier welder will cost $500. No matter what the machine, the carrier should ride on wheels so that the machine can be moved easily around the construction area.

The choice of the proper stick electrode will be determined by the builder's welding position, the sequence of the work, and the equipment and material to be welded. Many types of electrodes are used to join mild steel, and there are many other applications for mild steel than in boatbuilding.

Electrodes must be compatible with and have similar properties to the base metal. The 6000 series (6011, 6012, 6013 or 6014) is commonly used by amateurs for yacht construction. However, a better-quality, stronger weld is obtained by using the 7000 series of low-hydrogen electrodes (usually 7018), which reduces porosity and prevents hydrogen embrittlement, the defect responsible for reduced ductility and hairline cracks. A little more skill is needed to use these "low-hy" electrodes than the high-penetration E6000 series. Certain electrodes used for high-speed, single-pass welding (E7024) have relatively low ductility and really should not be

Fig. 7-8. *Oxyacetylene tanks can be mounted close to the work area. Note also the stove stack mounted on a hot water reservoir.*

used for welding main members, although some builders like this "jet rod," sacrificing fairness for increased welding speed. If the hull must pass Coast Guard inspection for commercial use, certain electrodes may be required. It is very important to keep the electrodes dry and sealed before use. Holding ovens or a good refrigerator with a heat light inside can be used for this purpose.

Gas metal arc welding (commonly referred to as MIG) is becoming more popular for yacht construction because it does the job faster with less chance of distortion

---

Table 7-6. A COMPARISON OF AC AND DC WELDING MACHINES

AC	DC
► Uses electricity with transformer. With rectifier can create DC current.	► Powered by gas, diesel, or propane generator with rectifier.
► Constant current, voltage, and polarity.	► Either reverse (DCR) or straight (DGS) polarity. Reverse is more efficient and gives deep, high-quality penetration. Can have constant current.
► Less expensive to buy and operate.	► More expensive.
► Limited flexibility and penetration.	► Good penetration.
► Light, small machine.	► Large, heavy machine.
► Limited stick welding range.	► Allows widest usage of stick welding.
► Quiet.	► Noisy.
► Easy arc starting.	► Arc can wander and create excessive splatter. Craters are more common.
► Free of magnetic arc blows.	► Metal is magnetized and can deflect arc.

Table 7-7. SOME USEFUL ELECTRODES FOR STICK WELDING

Using American Welding Society (AWS) standardized numbering system

MILD STEEL	E 6010	General applications in all positions. Good for tacks and maintenance welds. Deep penetration. Easy to burn. Flat beads. Light slag. Good for beginners.
	E 6011	All positions. Light slag. Can be used on galvanized steel. Good for beginners.
	E 6012	General purpose in all positions. Moderate penetration. Medium slag. Good for poor fit-up work.
	E 6013	All positions. Moderate penetration. Medium to heavy slag. Minimum splatter. Good for poor fit-ups.
	E 6020 and E 6024	Flat and horizontal positions. For single-pass, deep groove welds.
LOW HYDROGEN MILD STEEL	E 7014	All positions. Medium-heavy slag. For high-speed work.
	E 7024	High-speed "jet rod." Very heavy slag. Good for fillet welds. Especially good for downhand weld joints.
	E 7018 AC	AC electrode. Low slag. Can be used on low, medium, or high carbon steels and some HSLA steels.
	E 7028	Flat and horizontal fillet positions. X-ray quality welds. Fast. Preferred for welding heavy sections.
	E 7010-G	Out-of-position welds. Good, deep penetration. Used for downhill pipe welding.
SPECIAL PURPOSE	E 8018's	For nickle-bearing and high-strength steels. Low hydrogen. Low slag. Medium penetration.
	E 9018's	For high-tensile steels. Medium penetration. Low hydrogen. Low porosity. Used for welding pipes, castings, and fittings.
	E 308, 309, 310 312, 316, 317, 320, 330, 347, 410	For stainless steels.
	Nickel alloy	For welding cast iron.

Note: *All E 6XXX series electrodes are subject to hydrogen embrittlement.*

than stick welding. The electrode used in MIG welding is a thin, bare wire that is fed from a spool. A shielding gas, either argon, oxygen, or carbon dioxide, is blown over the surface during welding to prevent oxidation. Carbon dioxide lasts longest, is cheapest, and gives good protection. The gap between the wire and the base metal is less critical than with stick welding, so MIG is easier to learn and to use for tack-welding.

MIG welding machines run on DC current, and can even be adapted for underwater use. They produce 150–200 amps of power (higher amperage is unnecessary) with 60-cycle service. The gun trigger turns the welder on and starts the wire feed motor. Voltage and current (wire speed) are set by dials on the machine.

MIG welding produces good-quality welds at a fast rate (18 pounds of metal per hour) with good penetra-

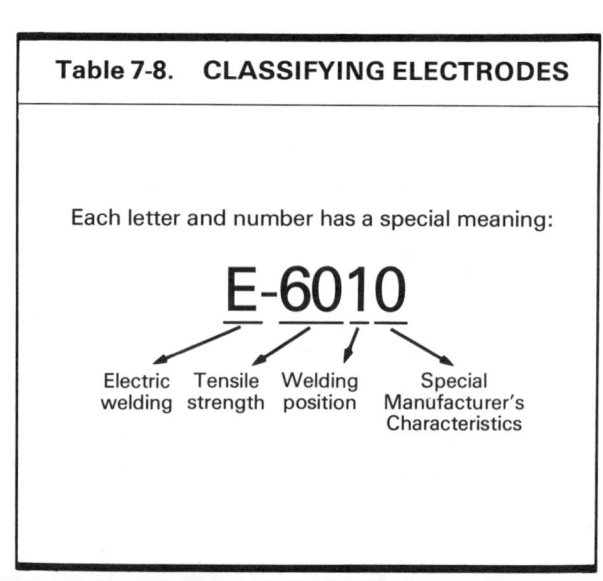

Table 7-8. CLASSIFYING ELECTRODES

Each letter and number has a special meaning:

E-6010

Electric welding | Tensile strength | Welding position | Special Manufacturer's Characteristics

tion. Because you are welding with .035" wire rather than a ⅛" electrode, the weld puddle is far smaller for the same current, giving good penetration and low heat in a small weld zone. Therefore there is less chance of distortion due to welding. The finished weld is clean, with no slag, and fitting and proper bevels are not as important as with stick welding.

The main drawback to MIG welding is its higher initial cost, although used 150-amp MIG's are beginning to show up on the market for as little as $900. You can pay up to $2000 for a machine, some of which may be recouped because of its high resale value. MIG units are not very portable, since the main lead to the gun is only 12 feet. But the machine can be hoisted onto scaffolding and moved around the hull as needed. If the wire-feed motor and spool are moved to a separate housing and the welding cable, gas hose, and motor control wiring extended, the machine can be set as much as 50 feet away from the main power source. During welding, the work area must be protected from wind and the elements, so a screen will be needed if the hull is being constructed outside.

Gas tungsten (TIG or heli-arc) welding is used in boatbuilding, but only in applications where stick or MIG can't do the job. TIG is also good for piecework on stainless tubing or thin-gauge tanks. The welding machine produces a small, high-temperature arc that welds two pieces of metal together by fusion. The process requires an extremely good fit. If that is not possible, a special,

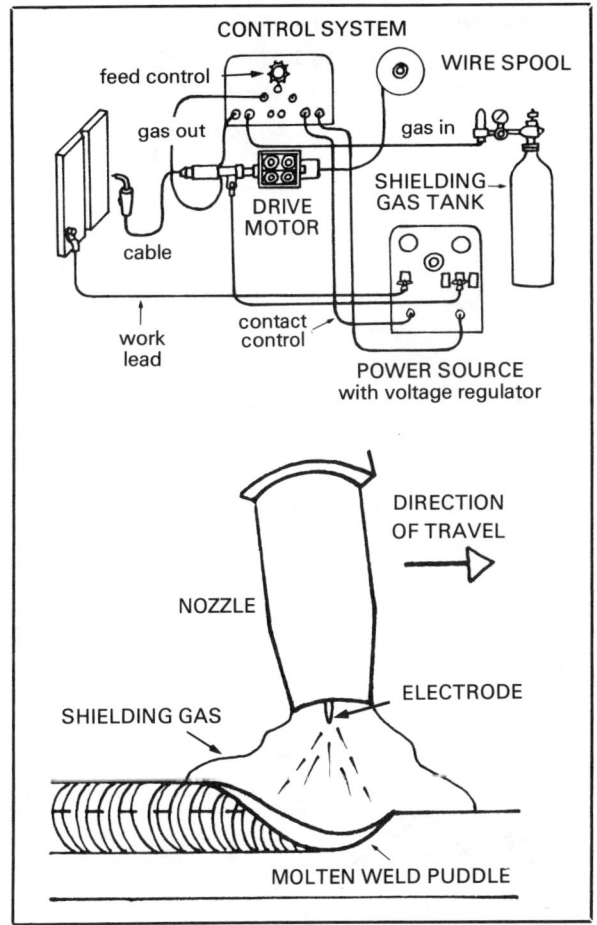

Fig. 7-9. *(above) MIG welding equipment. (below) The MIG welding process.*

Fig. 7-10. *The wire feed for this MIG welder has been mounted in a separate housing so that it can be placed on the deck of this* Verity 40.

deoxidized filler rod is manually introduced into the arc and deposited into the weld puddle. These rods are very expensive, and the work surface and welding tip must be very clean.

Aluminum can only be welded with MIG or TIG methods, and argon or oxygen rather than carbon dioxide must be used for the shield in MIG welding. Most MIG welders require a separate wire-feed gun for the aluminum wire. This piece of equipment is often available only for the higher-priced machines, but the option of branching out into aluminum welding is something to consider if you're buying a MIG welder. MIG machines can also be used to weld stainless steel to mild steel. The electrode wire is the same as that used for welding steel, so the weld zones should be blasted before painting. This is not the case when stick-welding with a low-hydrogen stainless steel electrode.

Many professional boatbuilders are converting to MIG, and it might be a worthwhile investment for the home builder. Practically the whole boat can be weld-ed with MIG equipment, although there are a few places where stick welding will be needed. At any rate, you can rest confident if you find out that the person building your boat is using this method.

No matter what type of welding machine you are using, good welding depends on the same things: proper weld joints, correct weld profile, thoughtful use of the various welding positions, and the size and root of the weld.

One of the best things about welding is that the weld joint is actually stronger than the base metal that it joins, because the alloy content of the electrode is higher. However, this is only true if the weld is free of defects. The most common welding defects are inadequate root penetration, undercutting, slag inclusion, porosity, and cracking. Stick welding is more susceptible to these defects than is MIG welding, because the shielding gas used in MIG welding produces a cleaner weld.

Inadequate root penetration is caused when the root face is too large or the opening too small, when the angle

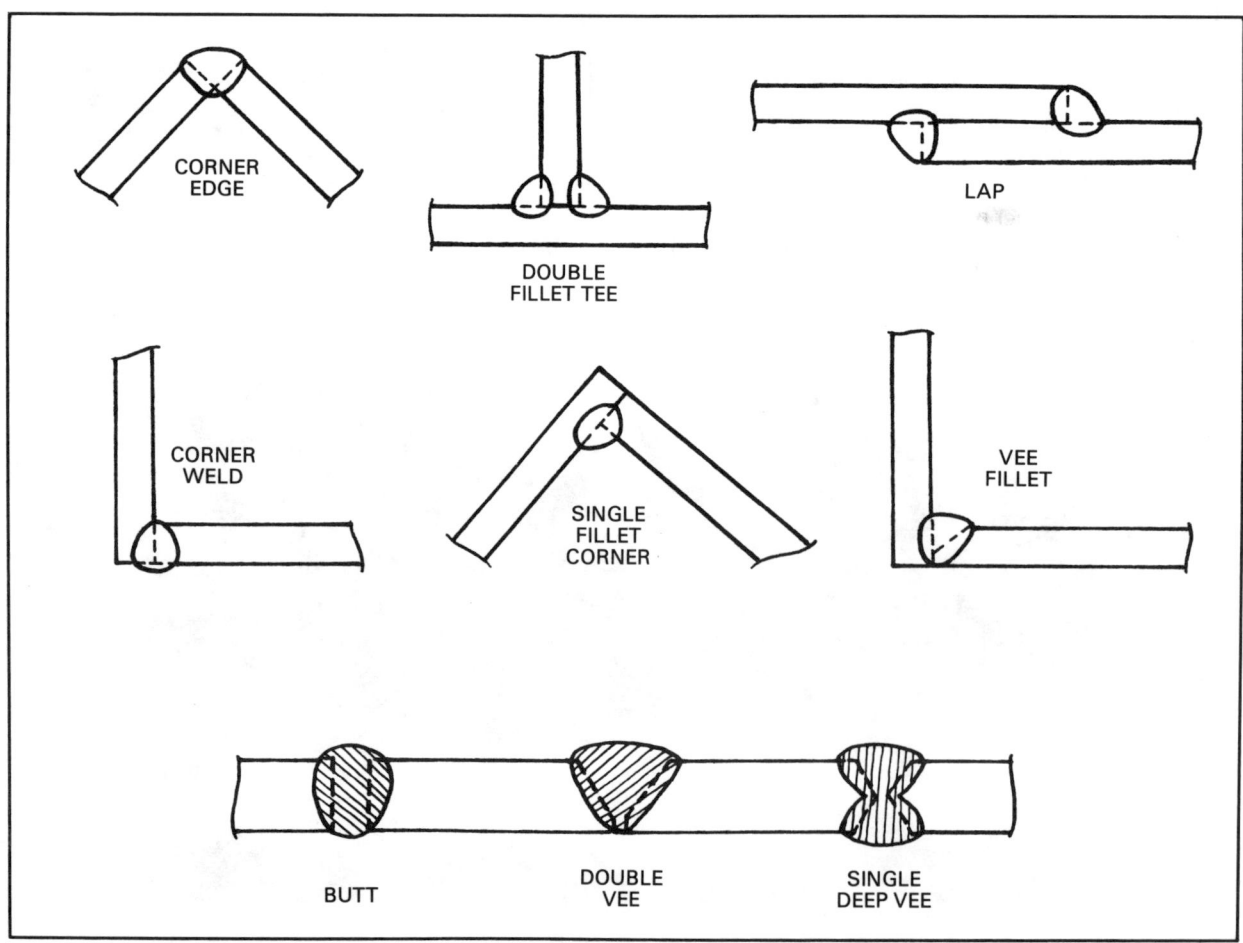

Fig. 7-11. *Different types of weld joints.*

of the groove is too small, if the wrong electrode is used, if there is not enough weld current, or if the groove is not gouged out enough. Obviously, all these problems can be prevented by using the correct procedures.

When the current is too low or the arc too high (both of which depend on the type of electrode), undercutting can result. More metal may need to be deposited. Some slight undercutting is usually all right.

Slag inclusion is the entrapment of nonmetallic material between the weld metal and the base metal. Small amounts of slag inclusion are not considered detrimental. It is caused by improper placement of the weld pass and inadequate cleaning or chipping of slag from previous passes.

Small amounts of fine, widely dispersed porosity do not have a serious effect on the mechanical properties of the weld joints. Porosity is caused by improper welding current and arc length. When low-hydrogen electrodes are used, the welder should use relatively high welding current and short arc lengths. Porosity is also found as a defect in the steel itself in the forms of blow holes, voids, or gas pockets.

Cracking results from high local stress caused by various welding conditions such as improper shrinkage allowance, voids, too-rapid cooling, or poor back-gouging. It occurs most often in cold weather. Cracking can be prevented by using low-hydrogen electrodes, back-step welding, and sometimes preheating to slow down the cooling rate.

STRESS-RELIEVING TREATMENTS

Heat treatments carried out during the building process are generally limited to those that improve ductility and relieve stress: annealing or normalizing. These kinds of heat treatment will not increase stiffness, but they will improve strength. Methods used to harden the steel, such as case-hardening and tempering and quenching, may also be employed if tools are being fabricated.

The internal stresses that develop within the steel due to cold working, machining, or welding can cause the metal to become brittle. These stresses can be relieved using both hot and cold methods. The carbon content of the steel is crucial in determining what can be done to and with the metal.

Stress-relieving using heat should be done as a last resort, only if there is a possibility that the structure will crack. Every attempt should first be made to prevent stress build-up. Making sure that notches have not been produced by improper design, cutting, or fitting is the first step. Preheating an area before welding helps to slow down the cooling rate, thus reducing shrinkage and stress. It can be helpful when creating compound hull shapes. Use of MIG welding in the proper welding sequence also reduces stress build-up, since the welding is done at a lower temperature.

Proper temperature control is the key to any heat treatment process. In some cases the metal is heated above the transition temperature to actually change the grain structure, while in other cases this change is not desired. The temperatures of the steel can be gauged by the color of the metal, and special crayons can be used to check for overheating. The rate of cooling after heating is also important to avoid brittleness, and depends on the metal being treated. Slow cooling is best for a steel hull, since rapid quenching may cause the steel to crack.

In annealing, the steel is heated to a specific temperature below the critical transition temperature and is held at that temperature for a specific period of time in order to allow the carbides to be evenly distributed. The steel is then cooled slowly, either in a furnace or buried in an insulating material such as ash or lime. Normalizing is a variation of annealing in which the steel is held above the transition temperature for a shorter period of time and then cooled slowly in air. Tempering is also used as a low-temperature annealing process. These treatments soften the metal and increase its ductility, making it less brittle and more easily machined, bent, or twisted. They are also used to relieve stress in the metal after it has been welded. Small fittings are easily annealed after they've been forged, thus relieving stress and preventing cracking.

Actually, heating steel plate after it has been welded into a hull is rarely done, because the cooling rate is uneven and hard to regulate. Local heating may be necessary to help improve a fit, but the result can be a non-uniform surface. Although proper heating creates the dishing or cupping effect that can be used to form a rounder shape, it is tricky, and care must be taken not to change the crystalline structure of the metal, making it harder and brittle.

Cold methods can also be used to relieve stress. The most widely-practiced method is careful peening or hammering, either in combination with heat (as the Dutch do) or alone. The weld zone can be hammered as it is cooling. When these cold methods are used, care must be taken not to work-harden the metal, which will increase its brittleness as much as stressed areas will.

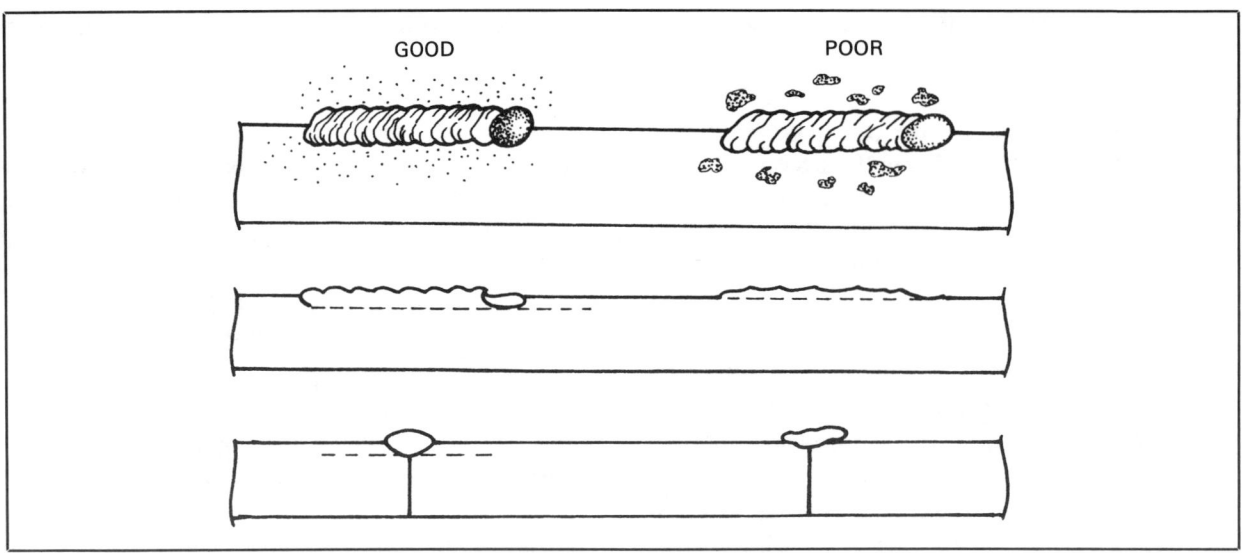

Fig. 7-12. *Different views of a proper weld bead.*

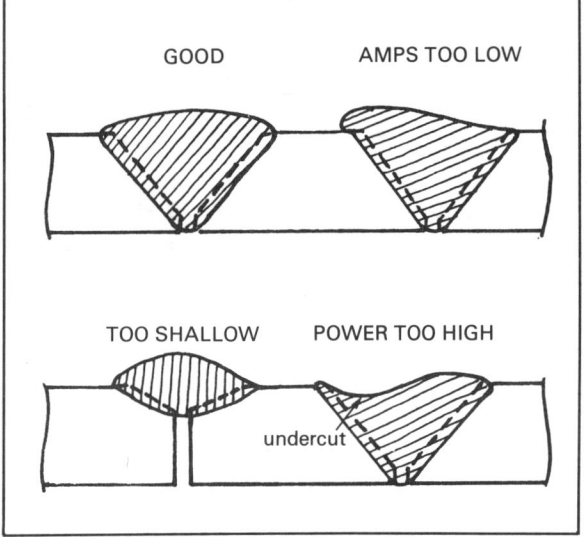

Fig. 7-13. *Penetration on a butt weld is influenced by the current and the voltage delivered by the welding machines.*

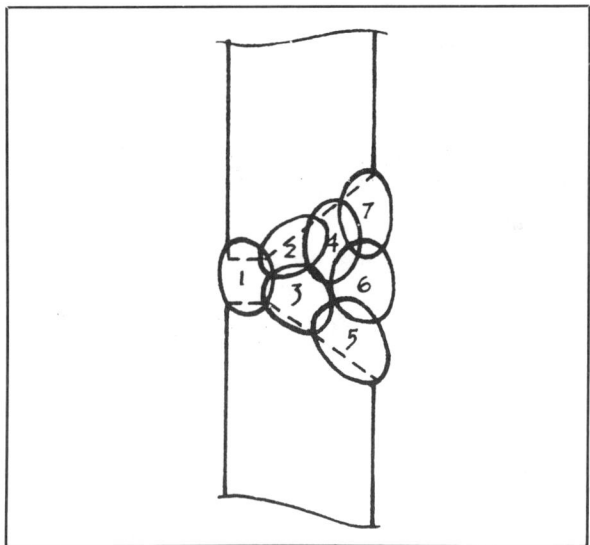

Fig. 7-14. *It may take a number of passes to fill a joint in thick metal.*

—Chapter 8

Hull Construction

Building your own boat is quite a challenge, and the pride and sense of accomplishment gained from this undertaking can be quite rewarding. It's also true that there can be many delays and frustrations during the process, but it's the same with anything worthwhile. A good attitude and the support of other boatbuilders always helps, but the real test of endurance comes from within. The following piece of wisdom from the desk of the late Weston Farmer speaks to this:

> *Press on...Nothing in the world can take the place of persistence. Talent will not; nothing is more common than unsuccessful men with talent. Genius will not; unrewarded genius is almost a proverb. Education alone will not. The world is full of educated derelicts. Persistence and determination alone are omnipotent.*

The people who build their own dreamboats are a unique breed; many might even be considered fanatics. The decision to start from scratch should not be made lightly. It's an incredible commitment of time and money, especially when a steel hull-deck assembly can be bought at a fairly reasonable price. But these people know their boats when they put to sea—how they're put together, how to maintain and repair them. This is knowledge that all real cruisers should have anyway.

This chapter is not going to teach you how to build a boat, but it should help to put the job in perspective.

Reviewing the stages of work and particular construction details may help you to think things out more thoroughly and save time during construction. There's always a chance of unforeseen complications, and planning ahead for the known problems may give you some insight on how to handle the unknowns. Planning also will assist you in determining how much time it will take to build the hull, although this also depends on things like your skill, the tooling at hand, and the complexity of the design. Things always seem to take longer than expected.

The sequence of tasks discussed here may vary somewhat with design and building position. But each will have to be covered at some point during the hull construction.

LOFTING

Because the designer draws the plans of a boat on a very small scale, the measurements contained in the table of offsets often must be corrected by lofting the hull shape out on a larger scale. "Correct" in this case means that smooth curves are produced. A master plate of the body plan is then made from the corrected table of offsets, and frames are built directly from the master plate. Some designers provide full-scale or half-scale paper or

Table 8-1. CONSTRUCTION SEQUENCE

1. Loft to ¼, ½, or full scale and make full-scale master plate of body plan.
2. Set up strongback grid.
3. Build keel (set aside to be added later if hull is built upside-down.
4. Mark centerline and stations for frame positions.
5. Build frame hoops from master plate.
6. Assemble and align hoops.
7. Assemble and align stem and transom.
8. Fair with battens while installing longitudinals.
9. Install longitudinals and stringers (minimal tacking).
10. Cut and fit plates in sequence.
11. Tack each plate in place to each other and to longitudinals.
12. Make final adjustment of plate for fairness.
13. Weld up all plate seams and plates to longitudinals.
14. Weld longitudinals to transverse frames.
15. Turn over; put on keel.
16. Complete deck, cabin, and cockpit framing and small parts.
17. Tack all deck, cabin, and cockpit plates and adjust for fairness.
18. Weld up deck, cabin, and cockpit plate.
19. Check over all for fairness.
20. Put in tanks, engine beds, stern tube, and other integrals (actual timing depends on location).
21. Install ballast.

and transom will also have to be laid out to full scale. Lofting can be done on a wall if this is the only space available, and some builders think it gives a better sense of fairness. But doing the job on the floor is physically easier, although a set of kneepads will be a welcome addition to your work wardrobe.

If there is any rule for lofting, it's "measure twice, but mark only once." The results will be accurate when the table of offsets is read correctly and these figures are carefully transferred to the loft floor, as long as the lofter pays attention to which baseline or reference point is being used for each measurement. For example, fairing stations are intended for fairing the lines during lofting, while bulkhead stations are structural reference points. The two are not necessarily the same. When lofting a steel hull, it's also important to know if the measurements are made to the inside or outside of the plating. If they are to the outside, then the plate thickness must be deducted from any patterns for proper fit.

Table 8-2. TOOLS FOR LOFTING, LAYOUT, AND MEASURING

Lofting floor of plywood, pressboard, masonite, or hardboard painted light gray
Straight edges
Measuring tapes
Fairing battens
Trammels
Piano wire and chalk line
Large right-angle square
Finishing nail, dogs, or U-clamps to hold battens
Steel master plate
Tick stick and punches
Metal fingers
Metal bevel gauge
Carbide-tipped scriber
Steel ballpoint marker
Latex paint crayon
Center punch
Scratch awl
Template and pattern material
Spiling stick or large dividers and compass
Spiling boards

Materials for making a strongback:

Plumb bob and wire
Recess template (guide for various weld joints)
Scribes
Hardwood strips or battens to check frame fairness
Steel assembly aids like angle braces, clips, jigs, jacking points, stiffeners, eyes, cheeks

mylar patterns for a design that has already been lofted. Unfortunately, the paper plans are frequently faulty because they are affected by moisture in the air; mylar patterns are more trustworthy. Careful builders often loft the hull themselves even if patterns are supplied. Seeing is believing, after all.

The lofting process is the same for any hull material, although with steel it is a bit easier, since there are fewer lines than for traditional wood construction, which uses rabbets, bearding lines, and bevels. Accuracy is the key, since the fit of the joints and the actual plate shape depend on fair lines and correct frame shape. Accurate lofting also saves extra labor later to correct mistakes.

Proper lofting requires a flat, dry, painted surface of plywood, hardboard or masonite. If there is only a limited amount of space available, the profile and half-breadth can be drawn longitudinally to half or quarter scale if necessary, although the body plans for the transverse frames must be lofted full scale. The keel, stem,

If the lofting is to be successful, the station lines that are marked on the lofting floor must be truly vertical to the baselines. Flexible fairing battens made of straight-grained wood, plastic, or aluminum rod are then used to fair the lines. All of the lines should end up with nice easy sweeps and no irregularities. If your eye tells you that the line is not fair because of a certain reference point, move that point to its proper position and make the correction in the table of offsets.

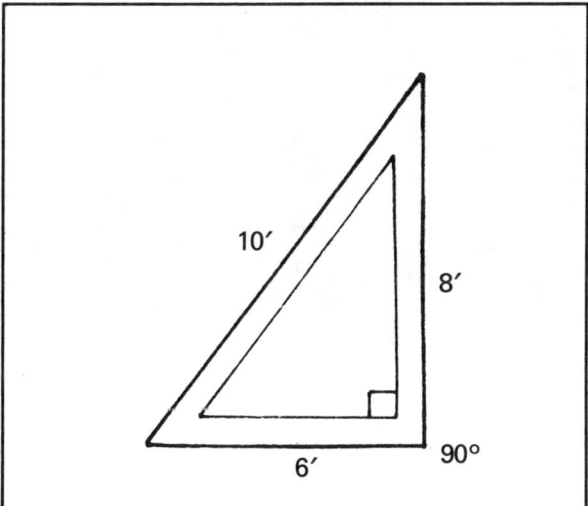

Fig. 8-1. *A large right-angle triangle helps to keep station lines truly vertical to the baseline.*

Once the table of offsets has been corrected, the body plan reference points are punched directly onto a steel master plate at the baseline and waterlines, and the lines at the fairing stations are drawn in with either a batten or a straight edge, depending on whether the hull is round or chine. The body plan can also be lofted elsewhere and then traced on the steel master plate. Patterns for the basic frames, keel, deck beams, and cabin frames are then made from the master plate. Steel can also be laid on the master plate and marked directly. The waterlines, longitudinals, gussets, and other reference points should be marked on the frame assembly as it is put together on the master plate, and their positions should be checked before welding. The patterns can be saved so that the same hull can be built again. The keel and stem can be lofted on a different plate, or the master plate can be used for this after the frames are assembled.

It takes time and patience to loft a hull, but the process can also be enjoyable. If you are not an experienced lofter, you may want to investigate the many books and classes that teach the basics of lofting.

THE KEEL

Keels on steel boats are much stronger than on any other hull. They aren't held on with bolts and bedding, but are continuously welded to the hull, making the keel part of the monolithic structure. Keels are always made of heavier plate than the hull since they form the backbone of the boat and must hold the heavy ballast without distorting. Often the weight of the keel box itself reduces the required amount of ballast.

The keel is commonly built separately from the hull, especially if the boat is built upside-down. The keel is then welded in place before the hull is turned. Sometimes the floors are extended into the keel, and then the heavier shoe and side plate are added. If the hull is built rightside-up, the keel is usually tacked together first, and then the plate is welded up to the correct shape. This gives a nice foundation on which to build.

Although bar keels and wide flange keels made from I-beams and railroad ties are used for power boats, the best keel for a sailboat is a heavy box keel, curved fore and aft to form a good foil shape. The keel is plated with heavy $\frac{1}{4}''$ plate, and its bottom is fitted with a thick, heavy shoe of $\frac{1}{2}''$ plate. Some keels have split pipe or round bar sections inserted at the leading or lower edges to improve the water flow around the keel, lessening turbulence. Flat bar can be used to stiffen the plates where they meet at sharp leading or trailing edges.

Longitudinal stiffeners and intermediate floors are sometimes installed in the keel to hold ballast in place and to prevent distortion when hot lead is poured into the keel for ballast. Steel brackets (also called "random shorts"), which are pieces of flat bar welded to the sides of the keel at various locations, can also be used to keep ballast in place.

It can be hard to weld the floors to the inside of the last piece of keel plate (or, for that matter, to make the final welds inside the rudder or skeg). The welder cannot reach inside from above or see the weld zone clearly. A plug weld, in which a piece of plate is cut away and then welded up, can be used to gain access to this area. A flat backing bar may be needed to secure the last piece of plating during the blind weld. Limber holes also can be cut in the floors to allow the welder to reach through the floors. The limber holes will then allow lead to flow between each bay as the ballast is poured.

Skegs and rudders are best designed with a proper foil shape and, like the keel, are constructed of thicker plate than the hull. They can be left empty, filled with

Fig. 8-2. *This separate keel will be welded on just before the boat is turned rightside-up.*

Fig. 8-3. *The hull plating was extended down to form the keel of this wineglass hull. The ground underneath has been dug out to allow access for painting.*

oil, foam, or tar, or treated with a float coat. (For more details, see Chapter 9.)

FRAMES

Although it wasn't always so, today most framing systems for small steel boats use both transverse and longitudinal frames, as well as cross members that hold the transverses in position during construction. If the boat is built upside-down, the cross members are called "headstock" or "spawls" (the term is a carry-over from the cross spawls used in wooden boats), and they are removed after the deck beams are inserted. The actual deck beams usually replace the headstock if the boat is built upright. Steel bulkheads and the stem and transom also tie the frames together and keep them in alignment during plating.

Many different ways of attaching the longitudinal frames to the transverses have been tried, but only a few are really practical. The two most common methods are: 1) notching the transverses and then slipping the longitudinals into these slots (the notching method); or 2) butting the longitudinals to the back edges of the transverse frames (the backing method). The backing method minimizes hard spots and crevices where the transverse frames would otherwise touch the hull plate. There is also less work in this method, since notches do not have to be cut or welded up later. The notches also

126

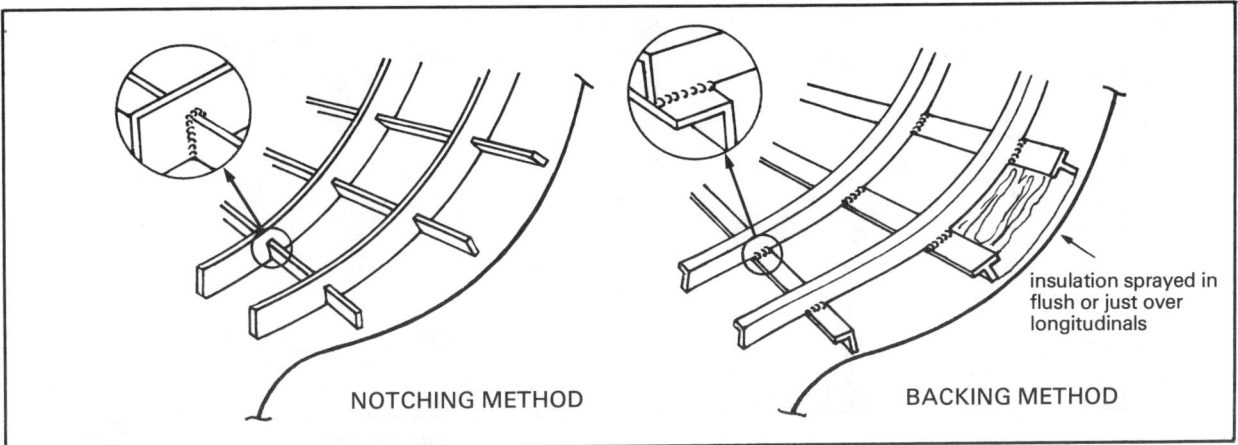

NOTCHING METHOD

BACKING METHOD

insulation sprayed in flush or just over longitudinals

Fig. 8-4. *The two most common methods of joining longitudinals to the transverse frames: notching and backing.*

create a change in section in the frame, and, as their name implies, can become stress raisers. The additional framing depth needed for the backing method is not really a problem in terms of limiting interior space, as frames are located at bulkhead positions. Longitudinals that run on the inside of the frames to provide extra stiffness are called "girders" and "stringers," and they are usually backed to the frames.

Flat bar, angle bar, and plate have all been used successfully for transverse frames. Flat bar allows the most access to the area around it, and is the simplest, cleanest, most available choice. It can be difficult to handle, since it tends to wobble sideways. Angle bar has greater stiffness than the same size flat bar, but is more difficult to bend, since it tends to flop more in one direction. The backing method must be used with angle bar transverses, because the foot of the angle bar isn't deep enough for good notching.

Cut plate is used for the deep or oddly dimensioned frames that are difficult to bend. The outer edge of

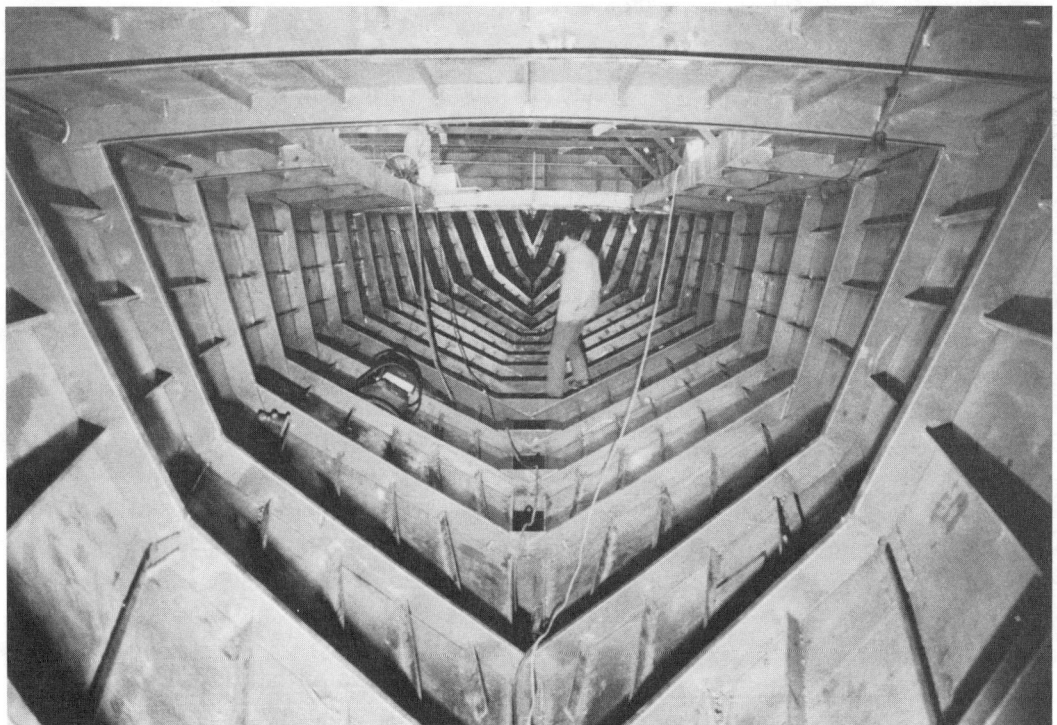

Fig. 8-5. *The 64' cutter,* Ruby, *was built with deep flange plate frames with notched-in flat bar longitudinals.*
Courtesy of Coast Marine Construction (Millerick Bros.)

127

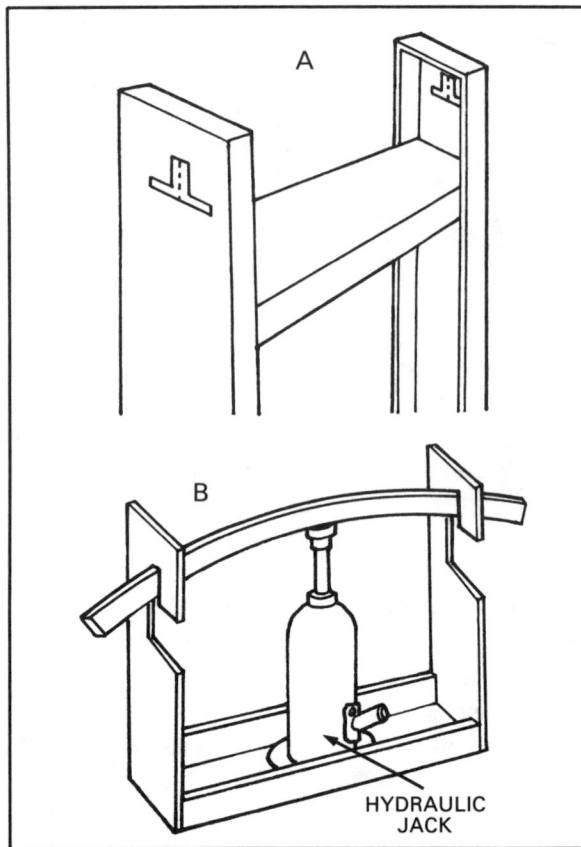

Fig. 8-6. A. *The reciprocal angle-bar frames for each side of the hull can be tacked together and bent simultaneously in this jig. B. This simple hydraulic frame bender is practical for flat bar.*

the plate can be cut to fit the curved shape of a round hull, and small sections can be welded together to produce the frame. Since the edges of the plate are sharper than prefabricated bar stock, extra grinding will be needed to bevel the edges for good coating adhesion. Flange plate is also cut from flat plate, but a flange is then put in by a braking machine. This flange creates a very strong shape, and the frame can be cut to any depth to increase hull stiffness and allow the notching method to be used. Because the plate edge next to the hull can

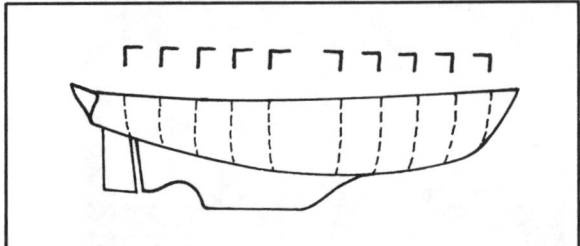

Fig. 8-7. *The arms of angle-bar frames should point toward amidships for the greatest stiffness and easiest access.*

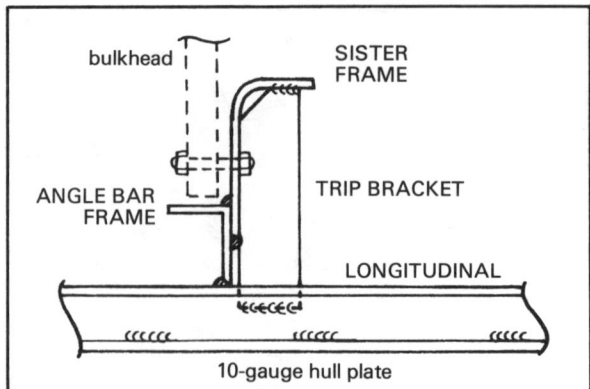

Fig. 8-8. *Sister frames made of flange plate are added after the hull is plated. Trip brackets can be welded in at every other longitudinal. These frames are so deep that bulkheads can be attached easily.*

be cut to a curved shape, flange plate works well for round hull frames.

There are more choices for longitudinals. In addition to the flat bar and angle bar used for transverses, T-bar, channel bar, half or solid pipe, and rod can be employed for longitudinals. (Cut or flange plate is not used.) Flat and angle bar are the most commonly used, and the choice depends on the method of attachment to the transverse. Flat bar is more practical than angle if the notching system is used, since a large notch would have to be cut to accept the angle bar; angle bar is preferable for the backing method. T-bar is a good second choice for the backing method, since the section modulus will be about the same as with angle bar. T-bar bends equally well in both direction and won't flop or wobble. However, it is sometimes hard to find in the proper sizes and adds a bit more weight than the equivalent angle bar. It can also be difficult to coat T-bar properly; it is often used pre-primed for this reason. Channel bar is difficult to find and is rarely used today. Like T-bar, it is very easy to handle and can be installed on its side, back, or front. But since there is always a wide, flat surface or enclosure against the plate, with channel bar the risk of corrosion is higher. Split pipe is also rarely used because of the corrosion potential. It should be limited to guard rails, sheer guards, soft chines, and cabin corners. Solid pipe and rod are almost always used only at chines and sheers.

Transverse Frames

The skeleton of the boat consists of a number of frame "hoop" assemblies composed of frames, floors, and deck beams or spawls. Cabin frames and beams can also be incorporated into the frame hoop, although if the hull

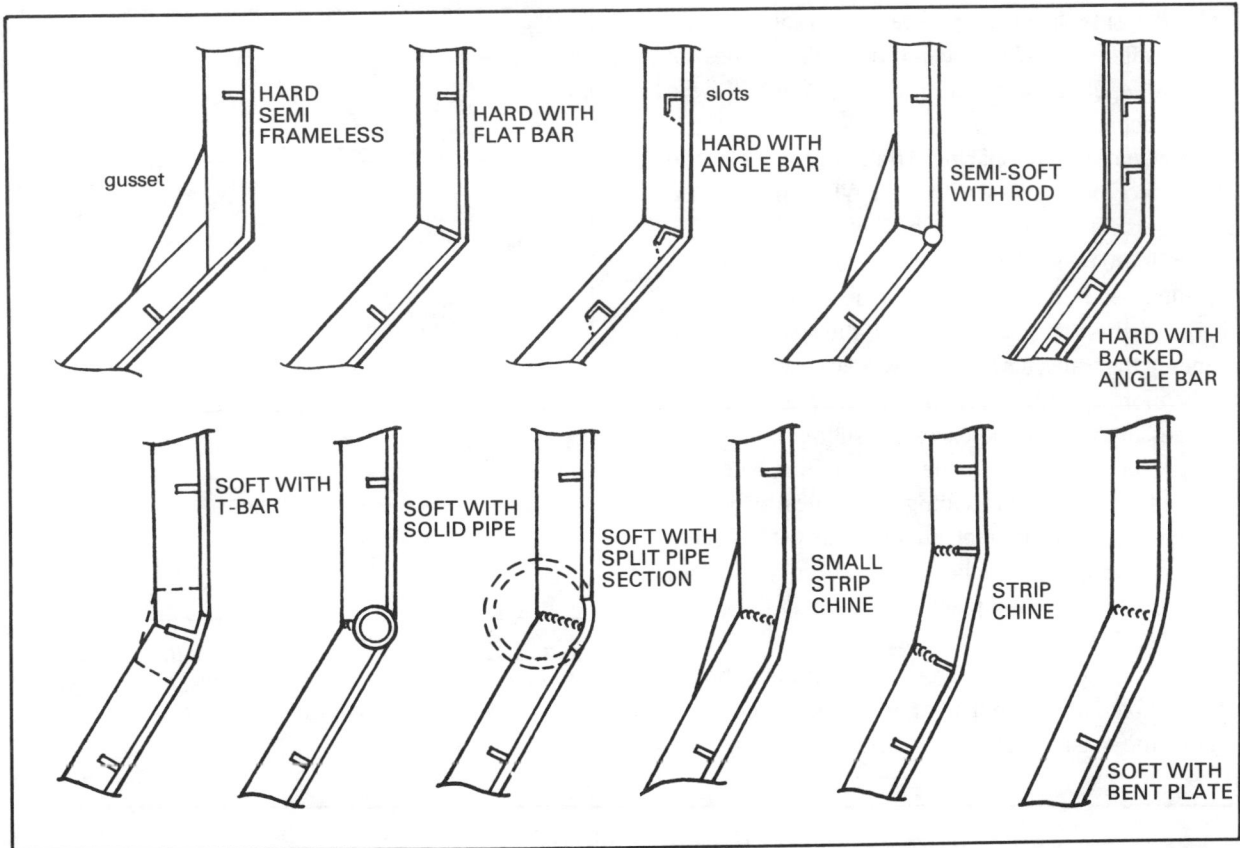

Fig. 8-9. *The different ways to construct framing for chine hulls.*

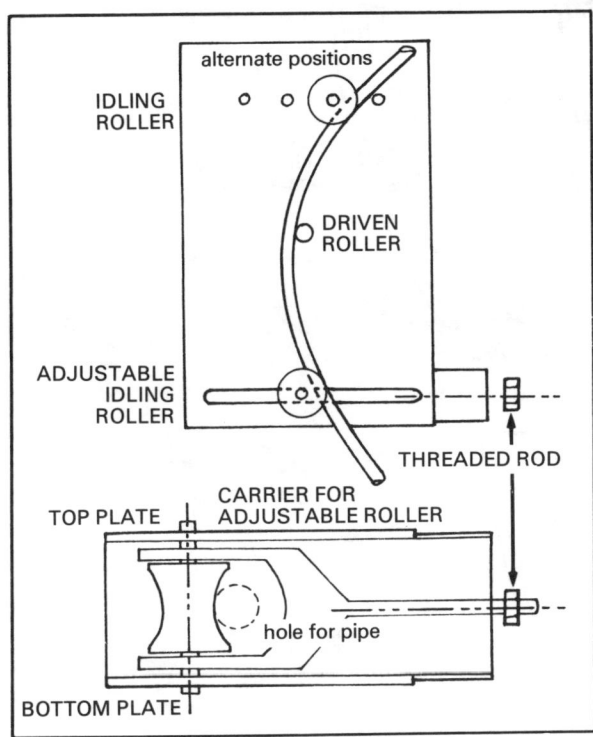

Fig. 8-10. *The pipe shaped on this bender is useful for rails, sheer pipe, cabin corners, and cockpit edges.*

Courtesy of Cecil Boden

Fig. 8-11. *Deep framing is used for this large schooner being built at Haglund Boat Works. The tractor in the background moves large pieces of plate.*

is plated upside-down, it is preferable to install the cabin framing after the hull has been turned. The fairness of the hull depends on the accurate alignment of these frame hoops.

The actual size and spacing of frames depends on the thickness of the hull plate to be used. When thicker plate is used, frames can be somewhat lighter, while heavier frames are needed with lighter plate. Proper section modulus and hull stiffness are the desired ends. Ease of construction is closely related to the spacing of the frames: if the transverses are too widely spaced, plating will be more difficult, but too many transverses will add unnecessary weight and excessive stiffness.

The steel master plate made during lofting is used as a guide for cutting and welding the frames, as well as for marking the position of longitudinals with a recess template so that the notches can be cut in the frames before they are fixed in place. It is much easier to cut or weld and, if necessary, to straighten a warped frame when it is lying flat on the ground. The frames should be assembled on the shop floor and each one checked against the master plate.

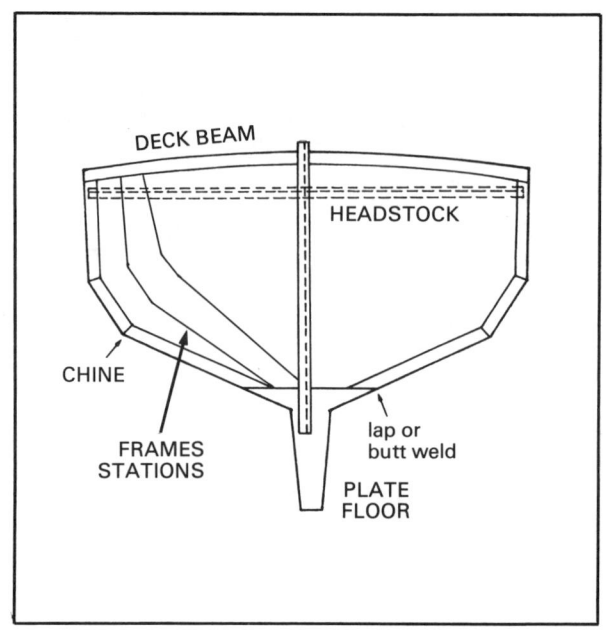

Fig. 8-12. *The master plate guides the shaping of frames. If the hull is built upside-down, headstock are tack-welded in place of deck beams.*

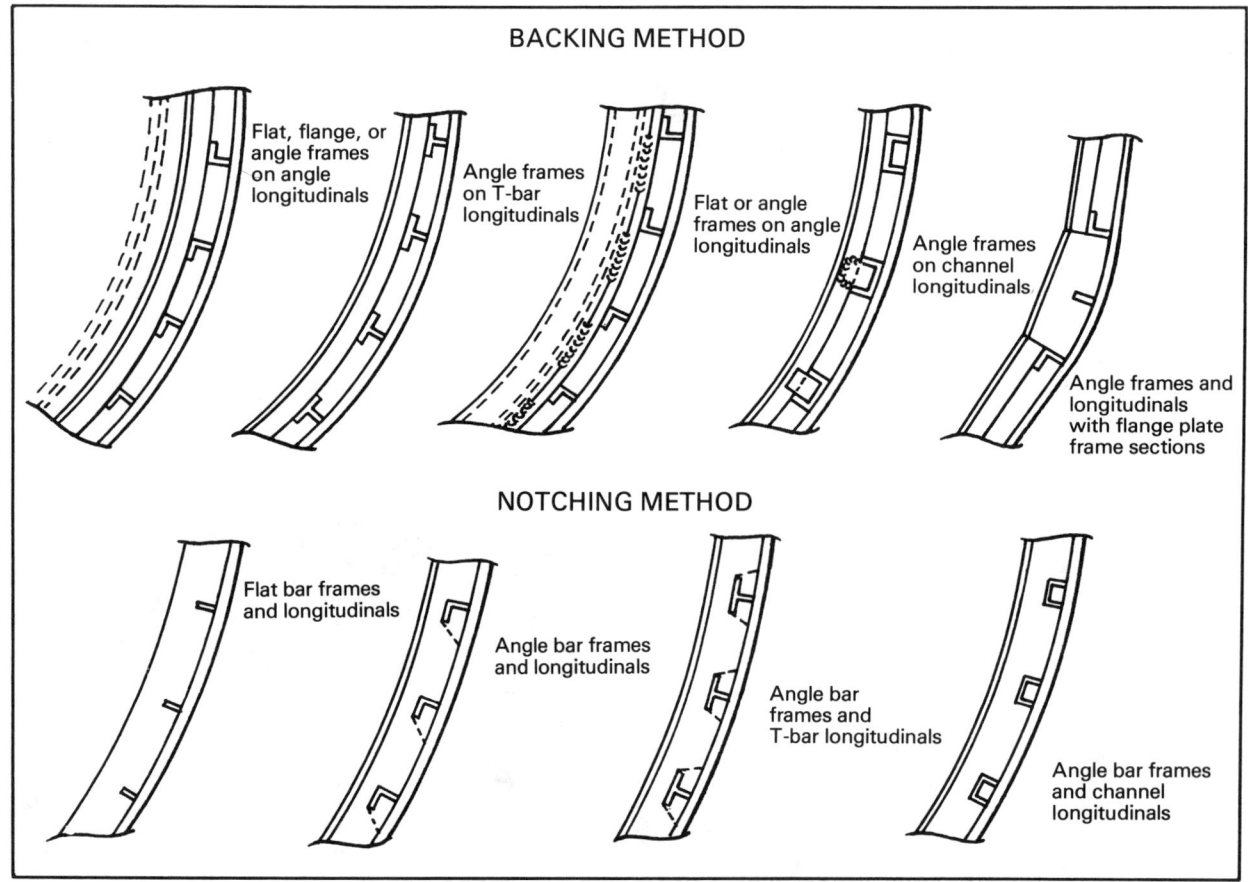

Fig. 8-13. *Different methods for fabricating round hull frames.*

130

Steel floors are often welded into the frame hoop assembly. Ideally, they should be of the same thickness as the frames so that there is no sectional change at the joint, creating a notch-sensitive spot. The floors also can serve as stiffeners for the keel plating, keel tank baffles, and tank walls, and can support the cabin sole. (Angle bar, flange plate, or flat bar can be welded to the top of the floors to support the cabin sole if the floors are lower than the sole.) Floors aligned with frames can be lapped for a quick, strong joint, but a welded butt joint is cleaner.

Intermediate floors also can be used to help spread out the load and the stresses caused by the change in section where the keel and the hull meet. They also can serve as tank baffles and provide additional support for the sole, although extended frames and longitudinal girders can perform these functions as well. Longitudinal girders are especially important below the engine and mast step and above the skeg and keel.

Gussets or brackets can be welded on edge where deck beams meet frames, at the chine, or at the frame station where the mast is located. They help to stiffen and strengthen the frames, and thus the hull shape. The use of girders is a carry-over from old wooden designs, and in many cases they are unnecessary unless the area is under extreme stress. Trip brackets are rarely seen on small designs, but they can be welded between a transverse cut from flange plate and a longitudinal to keep the transverse from buckling sideways.

If deck beams form the top of the hoop, they first are cambered by bending them over a jig, just as frames are bent. The correct camber is obtained from the loft floor. The most common method is shown in Fig. 8-14. When the beam is bent correctly to match the lofting, it is welded to the frames.

If the hoop is assembled with headstock instead of deck beams, the headstock is usually tack-welded to the frames. It can also be attached with bolts to elliptical slots cut in an extension at the top of the frame. The frame positions can then be adjusted before deck beams are welded on. Although this method is not usually necessary, it can be helpful when building a flush-deck design.

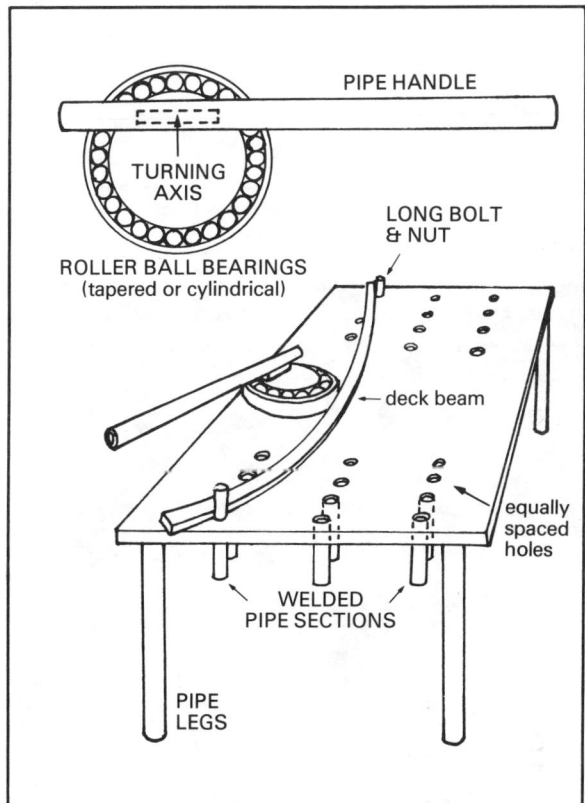

Fig. 8-15. *This manual frame bender can be used for flat bar, angle bar, pipe, or T-bar. It is especially good for shaping deck beams.*

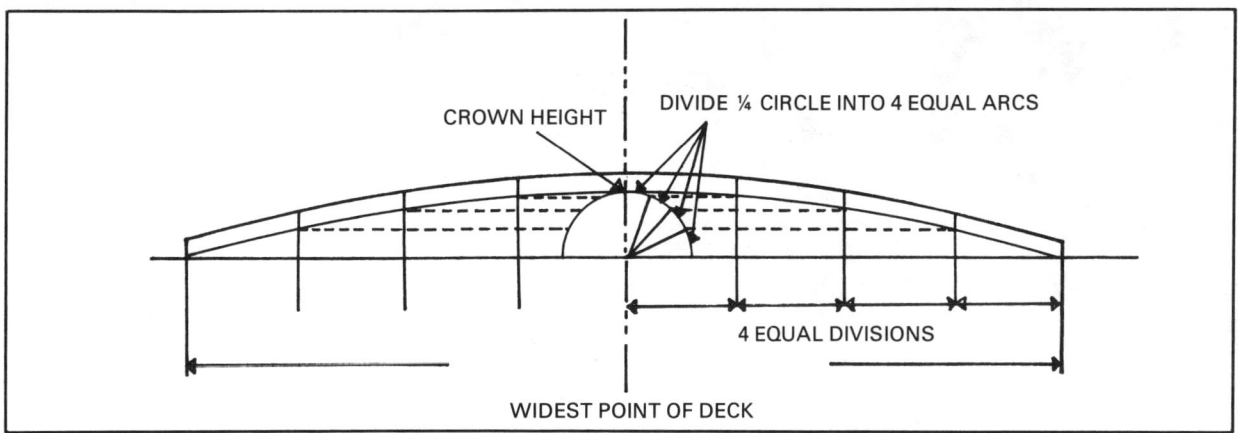

Fig. 8-14. *Once the width of the deck and the height of its crown are known from the plans, a pattern can be made for bending and checking the beams.*

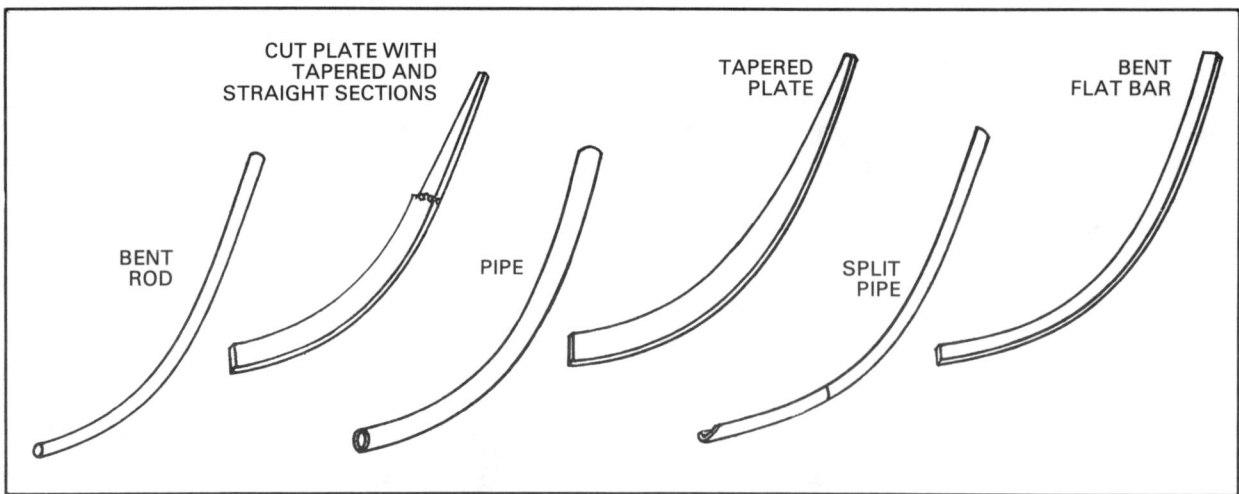

Fig. 8-16. *Different methods of fabricating the stem.*

Fig. 8-17. *A cone made of braked plate will be installed in this bow. The cone is supported by the bent flat bar stem and angle bar shown in the photograph.*

Once each frame is matched against the master plate, it can be stored without fear of distortion until the fabrication of the stem and transom is completed and the skeleton erected. The master frame plate will no longer be needed except for small miscellaneous parts. You could keep wood patterns for fabricating the frames and use the master plate as part of the hull plating.

As each frame is erected and aligned vertically with a plumb bob, it should be braced with angle bar welded to the cradle or to the building so that the frame stays rigid fore and aft. Angle bar tacked on the centerline between the floors and the top of the hoop will also keep the frames (especially flat bar) from shifting out of alignment. Whatever the method, the bracing should be planned so that room is left for installation of the longitudinals and for plating.

Bulkheads

Although bulkheads of steel can help to stop fire and, if watertight, will reduce flooding if the hull is damaged (unlikely, of course, with steel), they do add both unnecessary weight and the chance of distortion from the continuous welding required to make them watertight. The change in section also is an unnecessary stress-raiser and potential hard spot. There are other ways to strengthen stressed areas besides full-steel bulkheads. Partial or frameless bulkheads can be used, and pillars or rod also work in specific areas subjected to high stress (for example, under the inner forestay or below the cockpit). A compression rod (or "pumping strut") installed between the deck and keel is essential when the mast is stepped on the deck or cabin top. Plywood bulkheads installed at frame stations or attached to tabs just

132

make more sense since, with a steel design, bulkheads aren't required for structural integrity.

However, if watertight bulkheads are desirable, they can easily be placed at the bow and stern. The spaces thus sectioned off can be used as a chain locker and lazarette, if drain holes are provided. A watertight inspection hatch of steel should be installed, and a closable vent can be put high on the bulkhead with a screw cap attached by a small chain. The engine area is one spot where a watertight bulkhead could be considered. It would cut out noise and fumes and keep any spilled oil or fuel in the engine area, as well as add an enormous flotation area. A watertight access door with stiffeners would be needed here.

Stem and Transom

There are many choices of materials for the stem: round bar, tube, flat bar, angle iron, or plate, and each is used by different builders. Round bar is easily bent and gives a fine entry. But it isn't very strong, doesn't retain its shape, and can kink, so flat bar is generally used for small boats. Bending this flat piece into the shape of the stem is one of the most difficult forming jobs in steel boatbuilding, especially on a larger boat. Cut plate, which has good stiffness, also can be used for the stem. The stem should be properly tapered to fit the keel so that the joint is not a notch.

The upper stem on larger boats can take a cone shape that tapers out as it runs down to the waterline. These cones are commonly formed from flat plate with brakes or rollers. If the stem profile has a nice concave curve instead of a flat run, the edges of the cone may need to be slit so that it can be drawn into position.

Transom shapes vary immensely, and the plate must be properly supported to hold its shape. Flat bar or angle bar are most commonly used for centerline support; T-, angle, or flat bar longitudinals bent to the proper curve are good lateral stiffeners.

Longitudinals

Once all of the frames have been erected, correctly aligned in all directions, and firmly braced, the longitudinals can be installed. Since lighter weight stock is generally used for longitudinals, they are rarely bent on a machine, but instead are pulled down to each transverse and tacked there. Flat bar should be used if the longitudinals are to fit into slots in the transverses because with it the notches can be welded up better. It is generally easy to curve flat bar around the frames, although it does have a tendency to wobble. Angle or T-

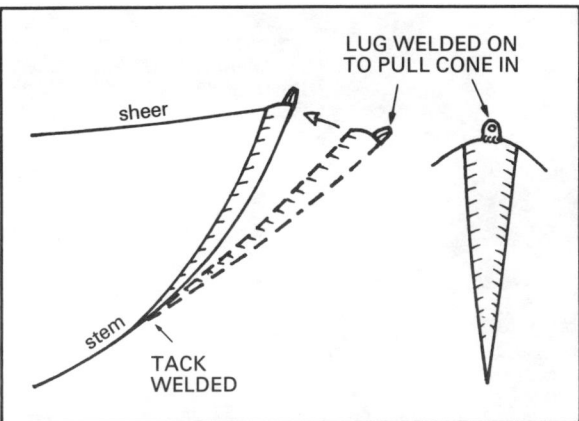

Fig. 8-18. *The bow cone is first shaped on a braking machine and then slit so that it will bend into place. The cone is pulled into the stem with a come-along or chain hoist. Then the slits are welded up.*

Fig. 8-19. *The stem on this flat-bottomed chine hull is another example of the use of a braked-plate bow cone.*
Courtesy of Danny Greene

133

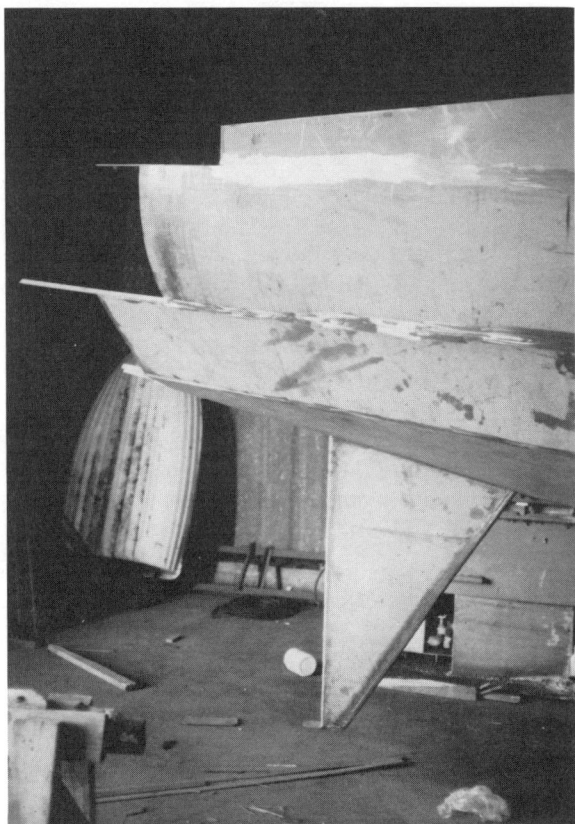

Fig. 8-20. *The transom of this Shannon* Amazon 36 *will be installed next, after the hull plate run-off is trimmed away.*

Since longitudinals by their nature prevent water from flowing down the inside of the hull, they can become water traps. Smooth elliptical limber holes should be cut to allow any condensation or spilled water to run freely down to the bilge. V-shaped drains should never be used, since they are notches. Slanting the frames down inboard so water can drain is a suggested solution, but it is very difficult to place the longitudinals correctly without affecting hull fairness. Limber drains are not really necessary if foam insulation is sprayed flush to the tops of the longitudinals.

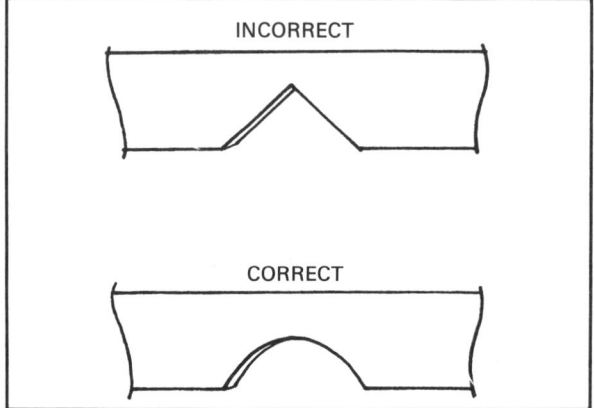

Fig. 8-21. *Limber holes cut in the longitudinals must be correctly shaped so that they are not stress-raisers.*

bar is preferable for the backing method, because the slots in the transverses would have to be larger than with flat bar longitudinals. If angle or T-bar is used, it may have to be forced into place and clamped there, because it is stiffer and more difficult to bend than flat bar.

The use of angle and T-bar for longitudinals is often frowned on, the argument being that, once installed, the edge butting against the plate, the underside of the longitudinals, and the plate underneath the frame are hard to blast and coat properly. This is somewhat true, but it need not be such a problem if pre-primed plate and a sprayed-on coating of a good-flowing paint are used. A special angled brush can also help to do the job properly. Similar problems arise when flat bar is used with notched transverses since the longitudinals and transverses are then so close to the hull that it is difficult to treat their edges. Using pre-primed frames would be wise here too. But if sprayed-foam insulation is installed flush to the top of the longitudinals, these areas are sealed up anyway, so no oxygen or water should get in there to start corrosion.

Like the transverses, the number, size, and spacing of the longitudinals depends on the particular design and the desired stiffness and panel strength of the hull. Sometimes their position is dictated by the position of the plate seams. Longitudinals are commonly spaced closer together (10–16″ centers with 12–14″ most common) than frames (3–5′). Longitudinals don't necessarily run parallel with the sheer, and they need not run the full length of the boat. In some designs, the rub strake or guard rail acts as a longitudinal.

The chine bar in chine hull designs and the sheer in any boat are special-purpose longitudinals. Flat bar or rod is generally used if the chine is sharp. Angle bar works best at the sheer since it gives extra stiffness where it's needed and can be used to help align the deck plate. Split pipe and T-bar can be inserted to help soften the turn.

As the longitudinals are installed, each must be faired properly. This will be the last chance to make any adjustments before the plate goes on, and to determine where the difficult plating sections will be. A wooden batten clamped down at various locations can be sighted along to check fairness. A thin sheet of plywood can be laid against the frames to give you a sense of how the plate will lie down against them.

PLATING THE HULL

Plating is one of the most important jobs in the building process, but if the design is well developed and proper techniques are used, it need not be too difficult. Good plating takes time. Done well, it will make the vessel as fair as the frame alignment permits; done poorly, it will make it as foul as a "hungry horse." Washboard distortion is a common result of a poorly plated hull.

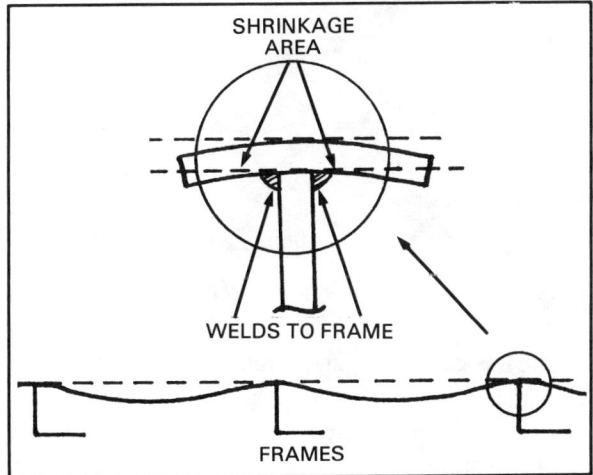

Fig. 8-22. *The "hungry horse" look is caused by shrinkage due to improper welding or overwelding.*

Cutting the plate to the right size is a critical matter, especially if there are rolled sections at the turn of the bilge. The "right size" for flat plate sections depends on the lifting tools available and the shape of the hull where the sections will lie. The rule of thumb is "cut to the line and leave enough to grind" (unless, of course, you're using a plasma arc cutter).

Plate Fitting

The easiest way to get a good weld joint is with plates that fit together perfectly. First the position of the horizontal seams is determined. For chine hulls, this is usually the chine line, and in molded-radius hulls the rolled and flat sections meet at the tangent lines. Then, at least for flat plate, the location of the vertical seams is determined based on the size of plate that can be safely lifted and accurately placed. Although it's good practice to minimize welding and working time by using the largest

plate possible, getting a good fit that will weld up properly is more important than building the boat fast.

After the planning is complete, the steel plate must be marked and cut into the necessary sizes and shapes. There are three basic ways to mark out the plate for fitting: 1) using templates of thin plywood to mark plates; 2) offering plates to frames and marking them in place; 3) taking the plates straight off the lines plan. Each builder uses the technique that works best for his or her skill level.

Many builders use templates, especially in tricky areas or where large sections of plate are going to be cut. Doorskin, hardboard, or plywood similar in thickness to the plating duplicates the bending characteristics of the steel. The template material is cut a little smaller than the plate will be and is laid in the proper position. Dividers or spiling sticks are used to mark the shape on the template. The template is laid on the plate, and the scribing is reversed so that the correct seam lines are marked on the plate. The steel plate is then cut and lifted into place. Although the templates are easier to handle than steel plate, sometimes the plate will handle just differently enough to be $\frac{1}{8}''$ too short. Since large gaps should not be filled with weld metal, the builder may end up with a cut plate that can't be used (however, it can be saved for another section). Experienced builders can use a smaller spiling batten to mark the plate; beginners should use a larger template to reduce the chance of error.

The "trim-and-fit" method is also used by professionals for both round and flat plate sections. A plate section is cut roughly to shape but is left a bit oversized. It is hoisted and dogged into place, touching all the

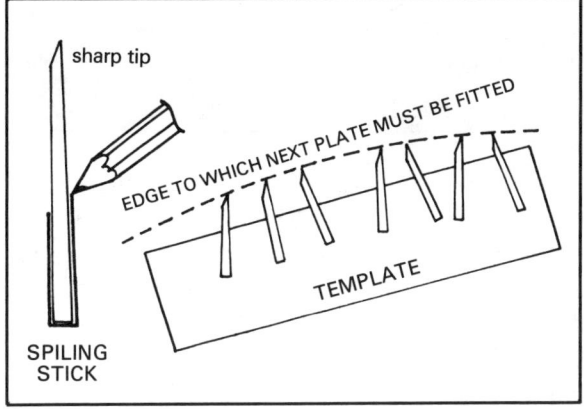

Fig. 8-23. *A spiling stick is moved to different positions on a template to mark the shape of the plate edge. The position of the stick is drawn on the template each time the stick is moved.*

Fig. 8-24. *A thin piece of plywood ("doorskin") is used to determine the height of the next radius section.*

frames, and the correct shape is scribed out with chalk or scribers. The plate is then removed, cut, and returned to the frames. Sometimes the builder can trim to the scribe mark while the plate is in place (or nearly so), especially if he or she has a plasma arc cutter. This saves the effort of hauling the plate up and down, a welcome relief when large pieces of plate are being handled. Although extra time is spent cutting with this method, the fit is more often correct.

Getting a good three-sided fit is tricky, especially with rolled plate sections that want to move in several different direction. Rolled sections must be laid directly on the frames so that the plate itself can be marked and cut

where it begins to run off the frames because of the fore-and-aft curvature of the hull. Builders avoid four-sided fits by installing the last plate at one of the ends of the boat and cutting off the overhang.

Fig. 8-26. *A heavy-duty truck crane is used to hoist large pieces of plate at the Sutton yard.*

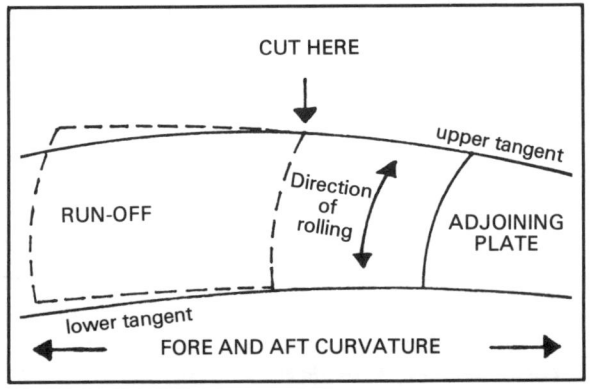

Fig. 8-25. *The run-off of rolled plate sections.*

136

The most difficult of the fitting methods is to take the plate shape straight off the lines plan, cut it to size, and erect it for a correct fit. This method depends on the perfect accuracy of the lines, and it is rarely used.

Once the plate is cut, it is lifted into place and tack-welded there. Steel is heavy, so good dragging and lifting gear are needed to move large pieces of plate from the cutting-out floor to the frames. An easily-fabricated rolling wagon or dragging clamps help to move the plate close, and various tackle, hoists, and jacks can be used to lift it. The last few inches are the most difficult, but dogging or clamping the plate into place often works. Many builders have special tricks for moving the steel that little bit (for example, a piece of angle bar welded on perpendicular to the plate can be used to gain leverage and hold small sections of plate flush for tacking).

Table 8-3. TOOLS FOR MOVING AND LIFTING
BASIC
Dollies
Staging made of pipe or angle
Chain fall hoist (manual, electric, or pneumatic)
Snatch blocks and tackle
Turnbuckles
Lifting lugs and eyes
Plate gripper
OPTIONAL
Pinch bar
Adjustable trolley
Winches (manual and electric)
Fork lift
Tractor
Truck crane

No matter what fitting method is used, even on a chine hull some areas of plating will need coaxing to lie against the frames, especially if the hull shape isn't conically developed. Clipper bows, extreme flares, or wineglass shapes require that the plate do some twisting. (Many of the methods of shaping steel discussed in Chapter 5 can be used to provide encouragement to the steel.)

Plating Sequence

The plating sequence is as important to the fairness of the finished hull as the welding sequence is. You can't just plate one side completely and then do the other without distortion occurring. Each builder follows a slightly different sequence, and that sequence should be determined by the particular design and how rigidly the frames are held in place.

Table 8-4. TOOLS FOR ASSEMBLY
BASIC
Toolbox on wheels
Metal work table
Clamps
Dogs
Saddles
Wedges
Leverage tools
Bench vise
Jacks (screw or hydraulic)
Pipe jack
Low-height hydraulic jack
OPTIONAL
Gear pullers
Hold-down bolts

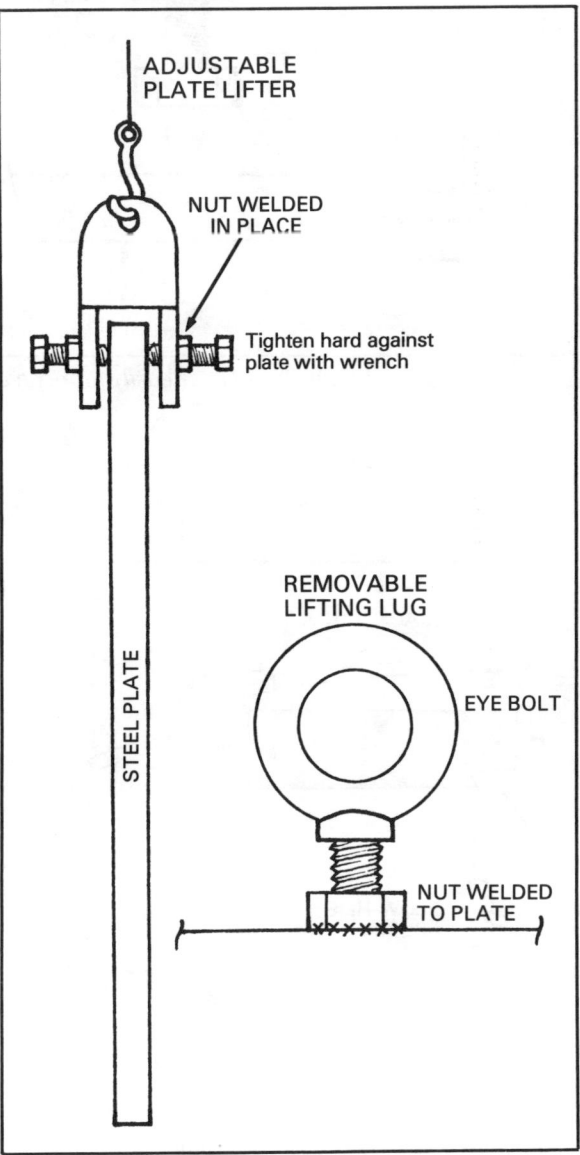

Fig. 8-27. *A sample of homemade lifting tools.*

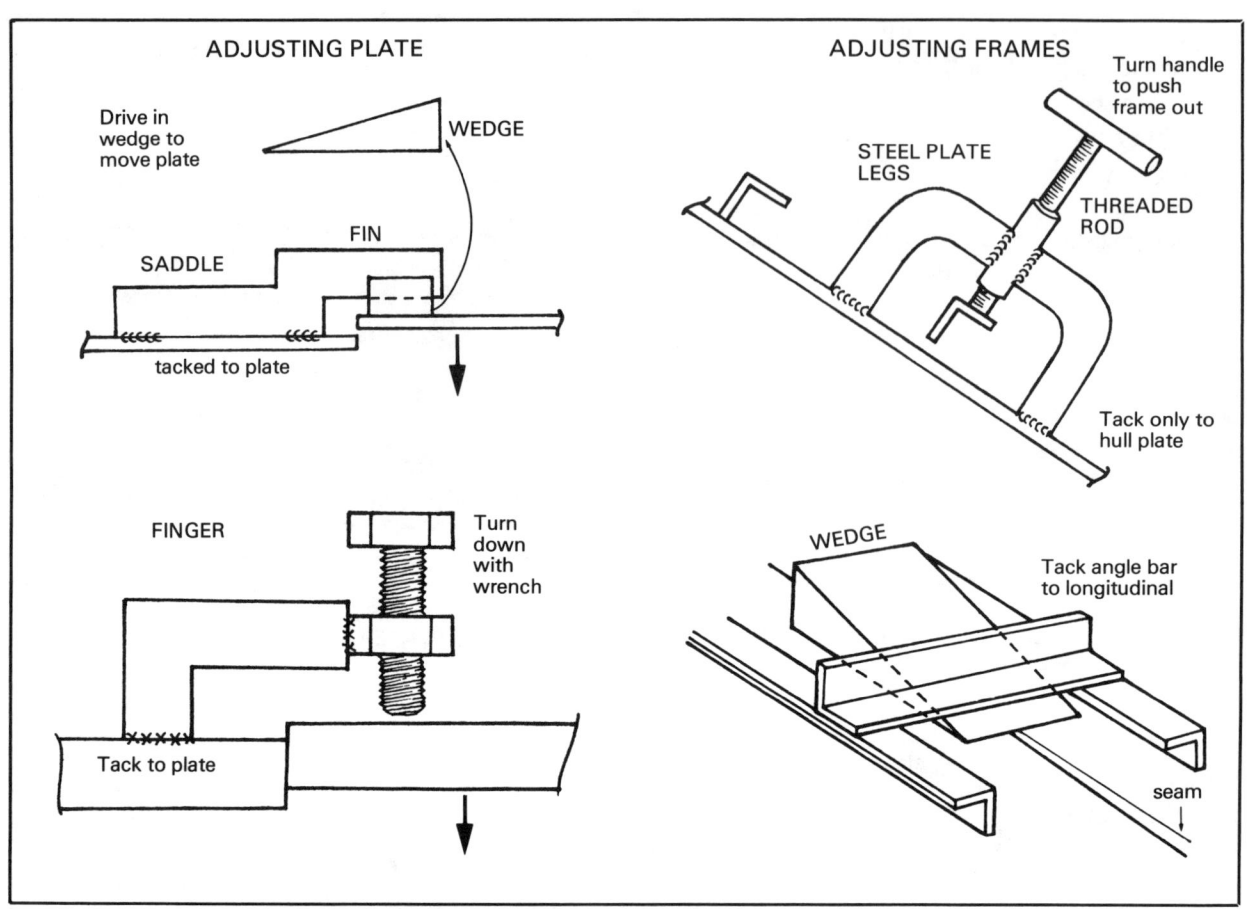

Fig. 8-28. *These easily fabricated tools can be used to align plate and frames.*

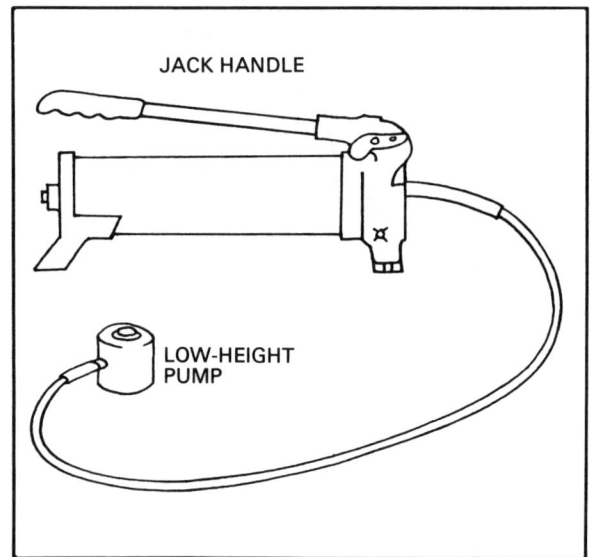

Fig. 8-29. *A low-height jack assembly is handy for fine adjustments.*

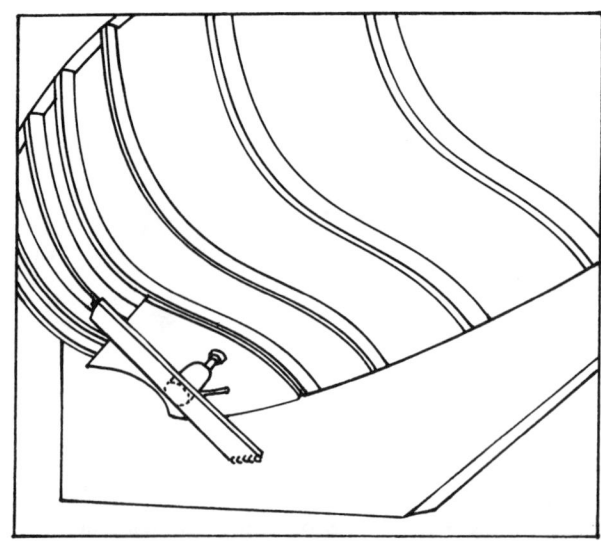

Fig. 8-30. *The curved "garboard" plate on a wine-glass hull can be deformed into shape with a temporarily braced jack.*

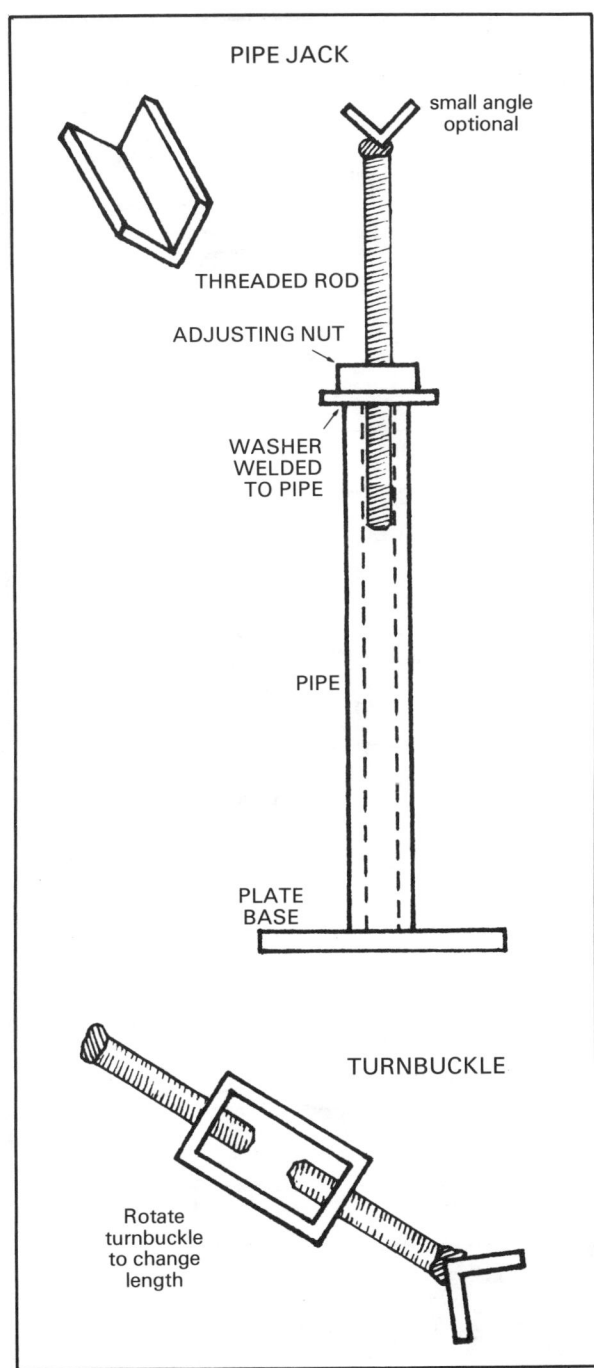

PIPE JACK

small angle optional

THREADED ROD

ADJUSTING NUT

WASHER WELDED TO PIPE

PIPE

PLATE BASE

TURNBUCKLE

Rotate turnbuckle to change length

Fig. 8-31. *Simple homemade tools like this pipe jack and turnbuckle can help to push or pull steel into position.*

In general, if the hull is built upside-down, either the sheer or the "garboard" plates are installed first. Most builders start in the middle and work out towards the ends, doing both sides simultaneously. When building rightside-up, the deck is sometimes tacked on first to stiffen the skeleton. The edges can also be trimmed more easily this way. For strip-chine assembly, the strip goes

Fig. 8-32. *The keel and the hull are plated simultaneously on* South Sea. Courtesy of Cecil Boden

on first. Then the sheer and bilge plates are welded on alternately. (Plating sequences for round hulls are discussed in Chapter 5.)

The position of the plate seams in relationship to the location of the transverse and longitudinal frames also has to be considered. It is best if plates do not meet over frames, because better penetration can be achieved if the seams are welded independently. Some builders plan the location of the fore-and-aft seams so that they are near longitudinals, since the support of the frames facilitates fitting the plates in correctly. Other builders choose to weld the seams to the longitudinals, although this involves more welding.

When the plate has been fitted in place tight against the longitudinals, it is then tack-welded to the adjoining plates and to the longitudinals. Especially when large pieces of plate are used, keeping the plate correctly aligned during tack welding may be difficult. Some builders use bolts tightened down with large nuts between the plates to keep the correct gap and minimize shrinkage, overlap, and buckling. However, this is a time-consuming method. Sticking thin spacers, rods, or bolts in the gaps is an easier method, but the easiest of all is using a straight edge and a lot of patience.

The Welding Sequence

Final welding is done only after all the hull plate is tacked up and checked to make sure that the correct gaps have been left and that the plate is fair. The welding sequence is as important as welding technique if the aim is to produce a fair hull without having to use fillers. The only way to ensure fairness is to prevent or at least limit distortion in the plating.

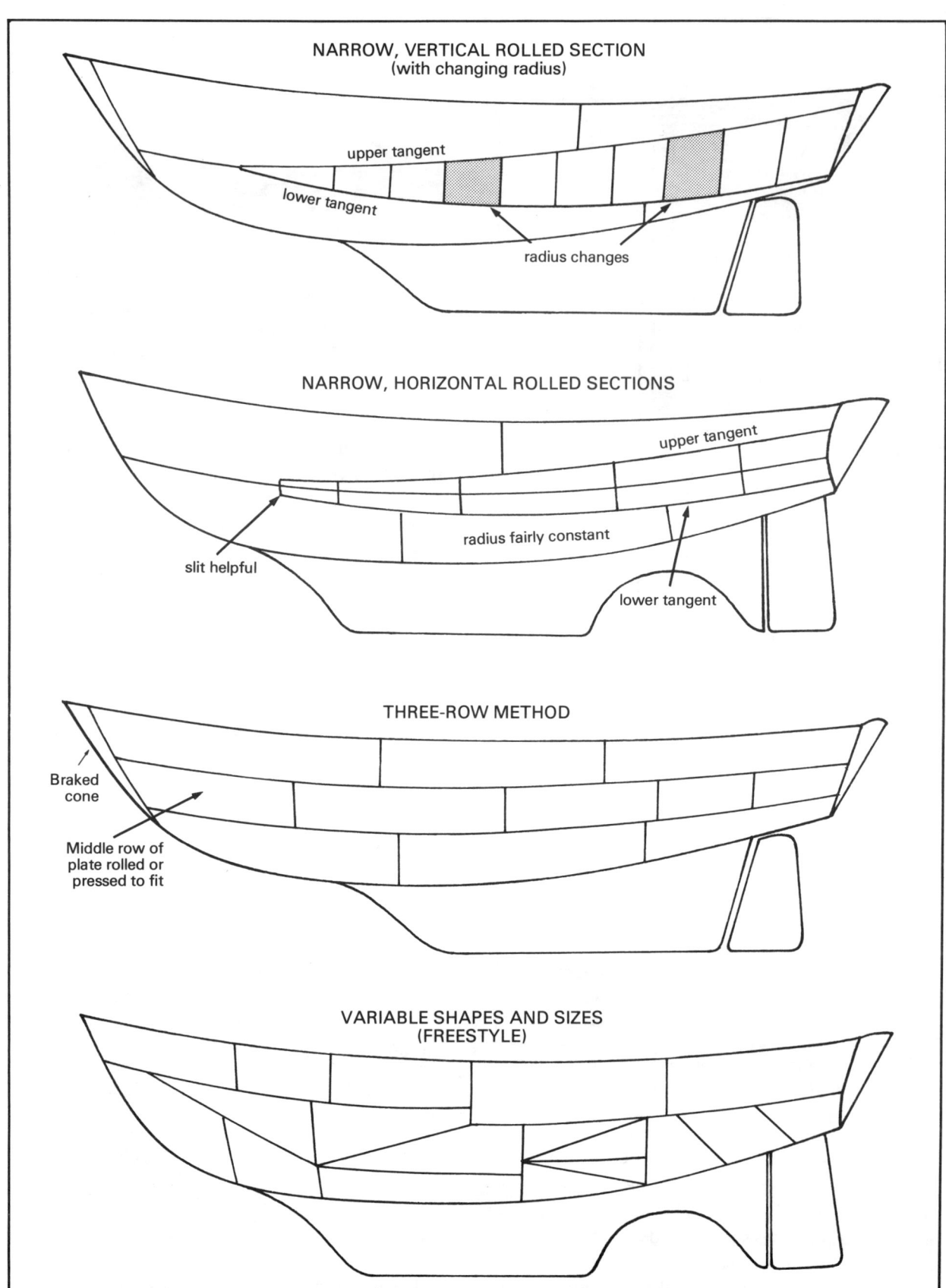

NARROW, VERTICAL ROLLED SECTION
(with changing radius)

upper tangent

lower tangent

radius changes

NARROW, HORIZONTAL ROLLED SECTIONS

upper tangent

slit helpful

radius fairly constant

lower tangent

THREE-ROW METHOD

Braked cone

Middle row of plate rolled or pressed to fit

VARIABLE SHAPES AND SIZES
(FREESTYLE)

Fig. 8-33. *Different styles of plating a round hull. Plate sizes and shapes are only approximate.*

140

Fig. 8-34. *Interior and exterior shots of Brewer's* Corten *under construction at Mooney Marine. Note the headstock and centerline bracing.*

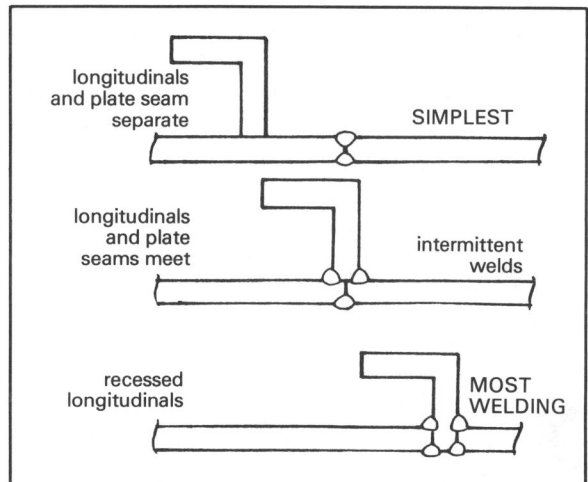

Fig. 8-35. *Different joinery options for longitudinal/hull plate seams.*

Distortion can be defined as improper stretching or shrinkage of the metal after heating. The amount and type of distortion is primarily influenced by the heat generated during welding or torch-cutting. When plate is welded into position, it is restrained and cannot fully contract as it cools. This restriction sets up stresses in the metal that lead to distortion. Shrinkage also occurs in the weld zone itself, and can produce tensile stresses near yield-point magnitude, which can cause the adjacent plate to bend. When bending occurs in two planes, twisting results.

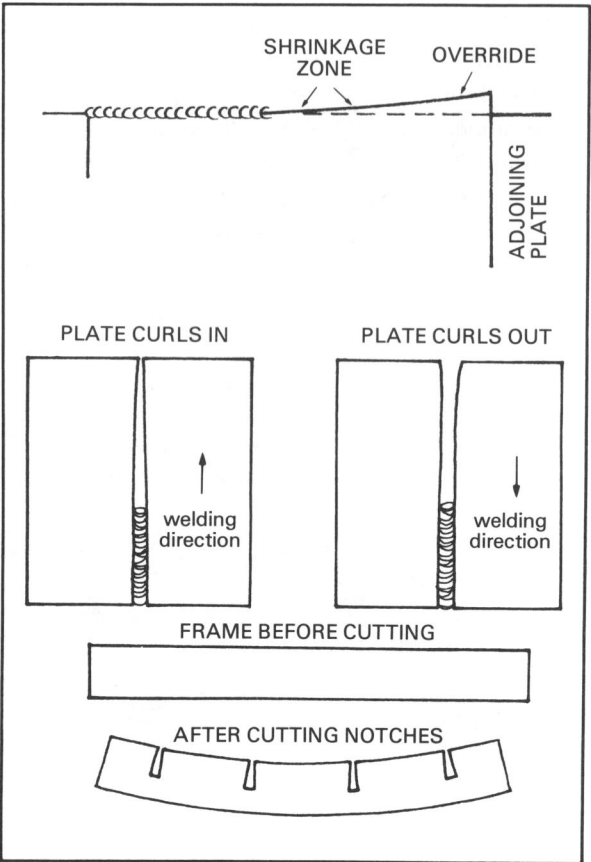

Fig. 8-37. *Some examples of distortion in plates and frames. The degree of distortion is exaggerated for clarity.*

Fig. 8-36. *The clamping device is tacked right to the plate for handling a tricky area in the bow.*

The best way to prevent distortion caused by heat is not to overheat or overweld the metal. Proper adjustment of the welding voltage and current, choice of welding position, and welding sequence are all important in this effort. The joint itself must be of the proper size to prevent overheating. MIG welding helps to lessen distortion because it is faster and operates on a lower current, so the metal does not heat up as much as with arc welding, and the area affected is smaller. Using nibblers or a plasma cutter rather than a torch for cutting also reduces distortion since no heat is involved.

The fit of adjoining plates is the other important part in building a distortion-free hull. If the proper allowance is left on the plate at the fitting stage, the plate will shrink into the correct position. An allowance of about 2% for contraction is needed to reduce deflection and distortion. Clamps and jigs can be used to counteract the tendency of the metal to shrink as it cools, but they may not always fit where they are needed.

The welding joint must be properly designed to avoid stressed members, notches, and local rigidity. Extra members should not be attached where the geometry may increase stress. Weld congestion should be reduced wherever possible.

The correct welding sequence allows each piece of metal as much freedom as possible to move during heating and cooling. Hull plate is never welded continuously, but instead a series of welds are made, using methods such as continous back-step, symmetrical back-step, stitch, block, and cascade. Proper sequence controls shrinkage and prevents defects like cracks, at the same time making sure there is no increase in residual stress. The method chosen depends on the type of structure, the assembly, what is being attached (for example, bulkheads, frames, stiffeners), and the welding position. If a necessarily tight fit does not allow freedom of movement for the plate, then proper welding technique and choice of rod are even more important.

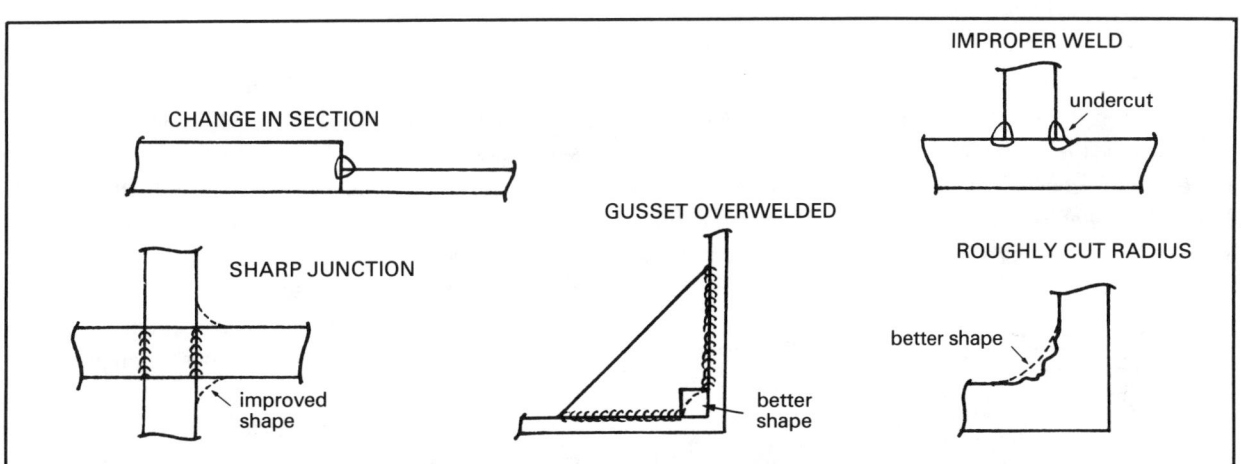

Fig. 8-38. *Stress raisers and notches.*

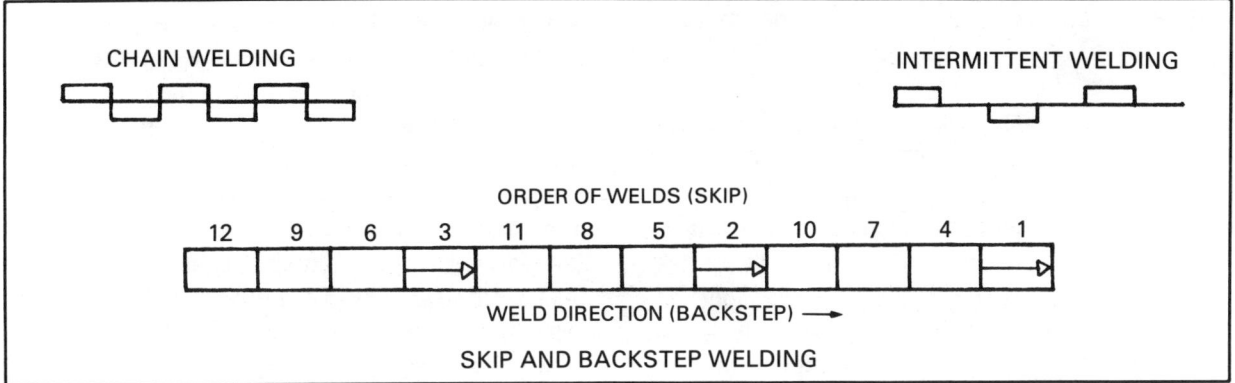

Fig. 8-39. *The correct welding sequence varies with the application. Chain welds are commonly used in stressed areas; intermittent welds join longitudinals to plate. Continuous welding on hull plate must use skip and backstep welding techniques.*

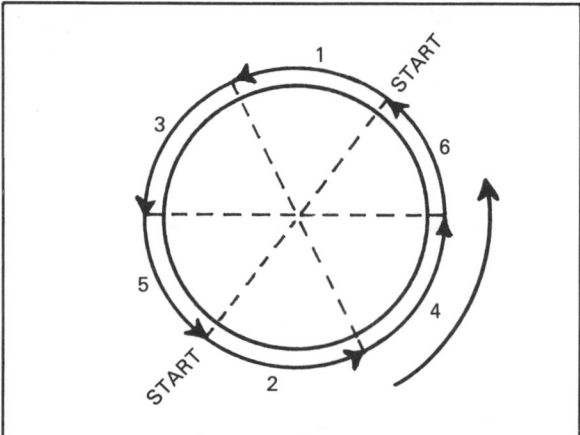

Fig. 8-40. *Pipe welding sequence. The number of welds varies with the diameter of the pipe.*

Back-step welding is commonly used for final welding of the hull plate. Weld bead runs of no more than 2″ on 10-gauge plate are best, although 3″ runs can be used on 7- or 8-gauge plate. When MIG welding is used, the length of the weld bead can be increased slightly, to 3″ or 4″. Longer runs can also be used in reinforced areas. Gaps of the same length as the runs are left between to be filled in on the next series of runs. The old welds must be completely cool before starting adjacent welds. When new welds meet old ones, a ½″ overlap of the two welds is desirable so that porosity is minimized and continuity maximized.

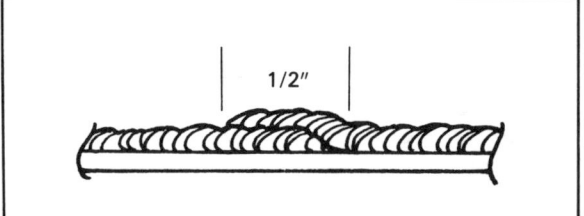

Fig. 8-41. *Each new weld must overlap the previous weld bead.*

If the plates could be tacked together only on the inside of the plate, all final welding on the outside could be done without interrupting the tack blobs. This would be a difficult technique to apply throughout the boat, so it's fortunate that there are other ways to handle the tack welds. The outside run must have full penetration, and a lightly penetrating tack weld should never be left as part of the final weld. The easiest method is to weld through the tack, although MIG welding cannot blow through stick-welded blobs unless low-hydrogen stick electrodes have been used. The tack can also be ground

off. The final outside weld must be close to perfect so that final grinding to fairness is not too difficult.

When all the plate seams are welded up, the hull plate is next welded intermittently to the longitudinals. Some builders then weld short sections of the plate to the transverse frames, but this can ruin fairness; any distortion that occurs vertically to the hull is much more apparent than when it is horiztonal, especially with vertically rolled plate. One of the attractions of the backing method is that only the longitudinals are welded to the transverse frames, not the hull plate.

Heat can also be used in a constructive way to *prevent* distortion. The process of tacking the plate into place builds up stresses, but the heat of welding helps to relieve stress if a proper welding sequence is followed. Preheating the weld zone reduces the cooling rate during welding, which lowers the stress concentration and the hardness of the heat-affected zones. Slower cooling may also decrease brittleness, preventing cracking and increasing the notch toughness of the welded joint. Preheating during cold weather is often specified for welds in thick plates, for example, in a keel.

Another way of reducing distortion is to lower the residual stresses in the weld zone. Hammering a hot, newly deposited weld will relax the adjacent area, stretching it to counteract the tendency to shrink as it cools. Post-weld heat treatments are also occasionally given to heavy weldments to decelerate cooling. However, high-strength, low-alloy steels like Corten may suffer loss of strength and impact resistance when post-weld heat treated.

A very experienced builder can weld flat bar stiffeners to the backside of plate that may distort. But this is a chancy business at best and may cause distortion in nearby plate.

When the plate is all welded up, the builder may discover some areas that have distorted despite efforts to prevent this effect. Some corrective measures can be taken, although none guarantee fairness.

Selective heating is one of the most common ways to correct plate distortion. The distorted plate is heated to cherry red on the opposite side of a dish or across from the weld that caused the distortion. Heating is done either in a regular pattern of spots or along a line. As the metal cools, it shrinks, pulling the plate back into shape. The metal can be cooled with a spray of water, but this may cause embrittlement. There are limits to how much distortion can be corrected with this method, and it should only be attempted on hull plate by someone with experience in the techniques.

The weld itself can be stretched with a large hammer and dolly, but this is a last-resort method and isn't recommended since it can significantly weaken the weld zone if improperly performed.

If all else fails, filler can be used. On a first boat, some lack of fairness may be regarded as inevitable, no matter how much care is taken. But using fillers on hull plates can cause major problems later in a boat's life when they blister, crack, and fall away, leaving depressions under which water can eat, eventually causing rusting. The problems caused by filler may not be worth a little unfairness. Using some epoxy filler (polyester filler doesn't bond well to steel) to fair out the fillet welds where the deck meets the cabin or at the cockpit sole corners is quite common, and it actually provides a smooth surface that enhances paint adhesion. On a well-designed, fair hull, this may be the only area requiring filler. The best builders use only a few pints on the whole boat, and only as coving filler.

DECK, CABIN, AND COCKPIT

A good cabin design should be raked inboard, especially on the ends. This gives a softer corner that is easier to join and that reduces the chance of injury. A fairly pleasing and easy-to-build corner with enough radius for good paint adhesion can be made with simple plate joints, especially with raked cabin sides. The corners can be softened even more with split pipe or rod, but this is extra work. Very soft cabin corners made with rolled or braked plate are very expensive and time-consuming, but the results can be pleasing.

A properly designed deck should be cambered for added headroom, good appearance, strength, and proper drainage of spray and splash. The camber should be uniform throughout, so that same bending jig can be used for all the frames.

Although Lloyd's and ABS rules require deck beams to be quite heavy, most builders and designers realize that heavy scantlings are unnecessary for small yachts, in which the frames are spaced relatively closely. The transverse frames and longitudinals for the cabin are usually lighter than the hull framing. The cabin top can be plated with 12-gauge plate, although MIG welding will probably be needed to avoid distorting this lightweight plate. As long as proper stiffness and panel strength are maintained by the combination of plate and frames, the result should be strong enough. Keeping topsides weight down is important for a sailboat, and the

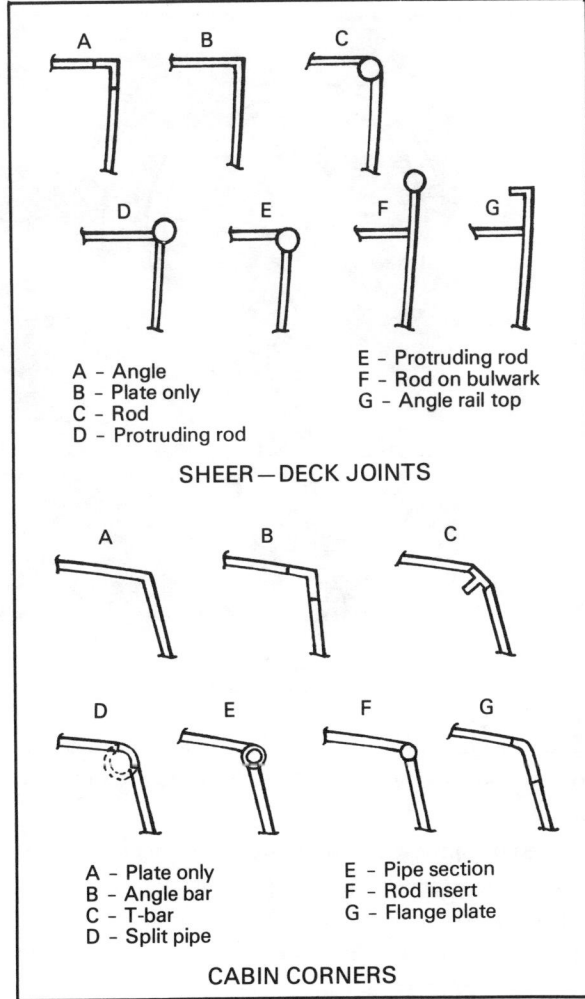

A - Angle
B - Plate only
C - Rod
D - Protruding rod
E - Protruding rod
F - Rod on bulwark
G - Angle rail top

SHEER—DECK JOINTS

A - Plate only
B - Angle bar
C - T-bar
D - Split pipe
E - Pipe section
F - Rod insert
G - Flange plate

CABIN CORNERS

Fig. 8-42. *Different options for the sheer-deck joint and cabin corners.*

smaller scantlng dimensions also allow for a bit more headroom.

If plates butt at the cabin centerline, the joint is usually braced with a gap-welded longitudinal that is backed to or slotted into the transverse deck beams. Flat-bar notched framing is the simplest, but angle and T-bar are commonly used for deck and cabin beams. Angle bar is best used in composite boats with wood decks or cabins, since fastening is easier. (The special joinery techniques used for attaching wood decks to steel are discussed in Chapter 15.)

Beams for the deck and cabin that were not included in the frame hoop are welded to the hull sides, sometimes with additional brackets. Longitudinal stiffeners need not be as frequent or as closely spaced as for the hull. The plate is installed like the hull plate, using the largest sections possible to minimize welding. To re-

Fig. 8-43. *Many small flat bar frames are needed to achieve proper deck stiffness on this lapstrake hull.*

duce the number of seams and increase the possibility of fairness, the plates for the cabin top are best laid athwartship.

The cockpit sole should be a minimum of 9″ above sea level and have cross drain pipes at the forward end, unless the sole will be above the waterline during excessive heeling, in which case the drains can be led out the same side. Proper drain lips should also be incorporated into lockers and seat rakes. Gentle curves in the cockpit coaming and sides can be put in the plate with a small plate-bending jig, brake, or roller.

Fig. 8-44. *The superstructure of a cabin with a curved coachroof.*

BALLAST

At this point, it seems appropriate to discuss ballast. Ballast can be added at many different stages of construction, depending on the type used and the method of securing it. However, it is usually installed after the welding of the hull, deck, and cabin is complete. The ballast can actually be put in the keel early on if the keel is built separately, but it's easier lifting if you wait until the hull is turned upright and the keel is attached.

Box keels can be filled with melted and/or placed ballast. Bolted-on or cast-ballast keels should not be used, since they are subject to electrolysis. It is wise to put in only 75–85% of the ballast initially and keep the remainder for trimming the boat fore and aft after it's in the water. The remaining ballast can either be poured or placed into the keel through an access lid.

The top of the ballast can be sealed completely with a tar or bitumastic paint, nylon dip, epoxy coating, or a welded steel plate. The latter method is by far the best since it makes the area air- and watertight. The U.S. Coast Guard frowns on bitumastic paint because, even though it is flexible and has good adhesion, it is flammable and is dissolved by diesel fuel. It is also affected by salt water.

There are many choices for ballast material. However, the following are the most practical:

Iron ballast is very cheap and fairly heavy. It is not recommended for smaller boats because it must be held

Fig. 8-45. *Now that this hull has been turned over, the headstock will be removed as the deck beams are installed.*

Fig. 8-46. *The rolled sections on* Perelandra *go on after the large underbody and topsides plates. The hoist will then turn her over.*

in place with fillers and takes up a lot of space. But larger boats with big keels might save money using iron instead of lead. Since the most common fillers are bitumastic paint, tar, or cement, the inside of the keel really does not need to be blasted and painted, but it should be dry when the ballast is installed. If tar is used for the filler, the keel box could be heated first to promote good adhesion. Cast-iron ballast can be dipped in boiling pitch to seal corrosion out.

Scrap steel is also cheap and can be used for ballast, but, like iron, it is not very heavy, and a large volume is needed. Steel castings, punchings, or pigs, well packed and sealed in tar, have been used successfully. Heavier tractor track pins set in resin can also be installed, but the epoxy resin is very expensive. Pigs dipped in epoxy or nylon and sealed in heavy plastic bags of oil have also been tried with success. The loose ballast will need to be held down either with brackets or angle iron or with a steel cover plate welded over the keel.

Steel mixed with concrete is a successful combination for ballast since these two materials bond well. Concrete is not dense enough to be used alone; if steel punchings are used, they must be degreased before being mixed with the concrete. One part fire clay can be added to every four parts of cement to make a more waterproof, resilient adhesive mix. One drawback to this method is the chance of cracking and loss of adhesion when there is a sudden impact on the keel. However, cement does make a good top sealant. This method, like the first two, takes up room in the keel that might be better used.

The old favorite, *lead,* is still the best choice, especially if scrap lead in the form of ingots, sinkers, pigs, shot, tire weights, or plumbing pipes can be found and purchased almost as cheaply as steel. Since lead weighs 705 lbs./cu. ft., the space savings in the keel can be used for sumps and integral tankage. Using lead also helps to lower the center of gravity and even the cabin sole, so performance, stability, and comfort are improved. Lead can either be poured or placed in the keel. If it is placed in, the pigs should be small enough (15–25 lbs.) to be easily handled, and filler (such as tar) should be poured around them.

When molten lead is poured into the keel, timing is important. If it is poured too fast, the keel plate can be distorted by the heat. (This heat does help to relieve stress, but fairness is more important.) Pouring too slowly takes too much time, and the cooling layers don't bond well to adjoining pours. Solid pigs can be used with melted lead to reduce the heat and the resulting distortion. Impurities should be skimmed off the top of the lead with a ladle, and airholes caused by too-rapid pouring should be prevented.

Both poured and placed lead ballast should be installed with a slope aft to a sump in which bilge water can collect. This slope can be difficult to achieve with placed lead. With poured lead, a slanting steel cap plate welded on before pouring helps shape the slope.

If the lead is placed in, the inside of the keel plate should be painted beforehand with either strontium chromate, epoxy primer, coal tar epoxy, zinc primer, or bitumastic paint with an epoxy overcoat. Even though lead is more noble than steel and quite inert in sea water, any interaction of consequence occurs in the presence of bare steel, water, air, and their combinations. So it's best to seal the keel with paint in case air or moisture become present. Obviously, a coating won't be needed if molten lead is poured in, especially if it is sealed with a steel cap.

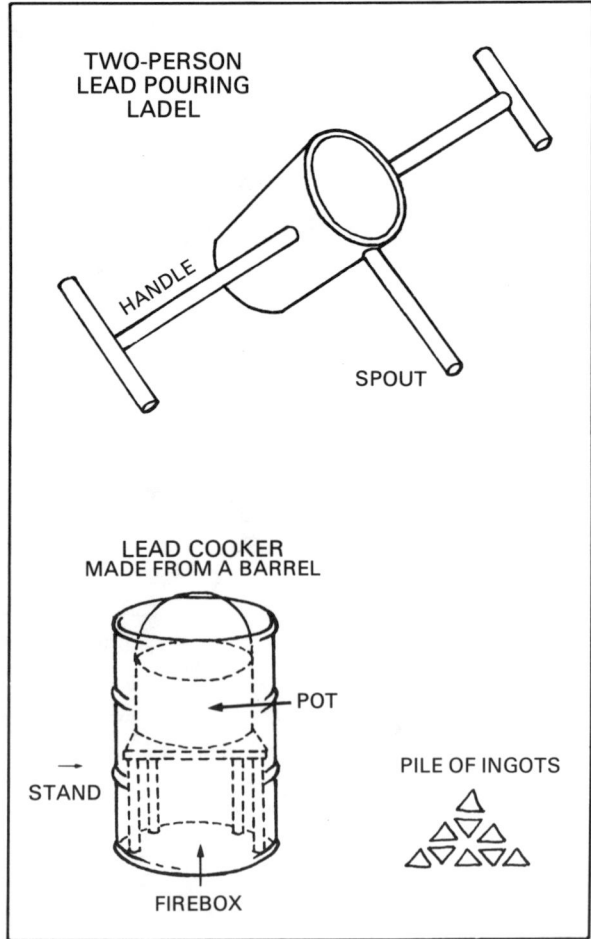

Fig. 8-47. *Lead can be melted and poured with simple tools like these.*

—Chapter 9

Integrals

The advantages of building a boat in steel are most apparent when the discussion turns to integrals: those pieces fabricated of steel or stainless steel that are welded to the hull before blasting and painting. These integrals are as large as a bowsprit and as small as a bobstay eye, and many (like tabs, eyes, flanges, brackets or pipes) are used for attaching other pieces of equipment to the hull. On a wood or fiberglass boat, expensive alloy fittings must usually be purchased and attached after the hull has been reinforced to support them. The integral attachments on a steel hull are as strong as the hull itself and won't work loose or cause leaks.

Although welding is stronger, cheaper, and cleaner, some fittings are better fastened mechanically even on a steel hull, so that they can be moved or removed for repair, maintenance, or inspection. The method of fastening (and the amount of work that must be done at the integral stage) depends on the piece of equipment being attached.

All integrals should be welded to the hull before it is blasted and primed so that they can be treated properly. Although attachments can be added later, the area around the weld will have to be ground clean and recoated, which can impair the continuity of the coating and lead to failure. Any large holes to which equip-

ment is welded or fastened should also be cut out before blasting.

When a bare hull assembly with "all basic welding complete" is being purchased, the building contract should clearly specify which attachments are included. Major appendages (such as rudder, bowsprit, chainplates, and engine bearers) and basic cutouts are often part of the hull package; integral tanks, flanges, eyes and tabs may or may not be. Some builders also include mast step(s), winch mounts, and samson posts. Bare hull assemblies rarely contain detail fittings, unless the designer has included their exact designs and locations in the construction drawings, and the contract specifies their completion. If you have specific ideas about additional attachments, the builder may be willing to weld them on, and their cost can be covered in an addendum to the original contract.

CHOOSING THE MATERIALS

Only certain materials can be welded to a steel hull: steel, stainless steel, or cast iron. Other metals must be mechanically fastened and insulated from the hull to prevent galvanic corrosion. (In areas that are prone to corrosion, it also may be preferable to bolt down stainless steel fittings, since they are more noble than the steel hull.) Cast iron is difficult to weld because of its brittleness, so that leaves steel and stainless as the most appropriate choices for integrals. (Chrome-plated fittings are good for nothing but show.)

These days, most mass-produced fittings are made of stainless, answering the desire of dockside sailors for a shiny, yachty look. Certainly stainless is appropriate in heavy-chafe areas because of its corrosion resistance and durability, but mild steel will serve well in many other places. Many of the production stainless fittings are not well-designed and cannot meet the heavy use requirements of the cruising life.

Large stainless items, like windlasses or winches, are usually bolted down through a wood insulating pad, which prevents any galvanic corrosion, while eyes, lips, and fittings like cleats are integrally welded. Sections of the rudder post and the propeller shaft are also usually stainless, since other practical alternatives are either more expensive or have corrosion problems when used underwater. All stainless integrals should be covered with tape before the hull is blasted so that they are not damaged, although the design of some production stainless fittings makes them difficult to cover adequately.

Different builders have fabricated many strong and practical appendages (like anchor roller assemblies, railings, or cleats) from stainless plate, pipe, or rod. However, the difference in the cost of the production fitting and the labor costs in fabricating a similar piece are often negligible. Perhaps a better consideration is the design of the production fitting and whether there is a chance of failure or corrosion because of poor design or workmanship.

Steel fittings are much more difficult to find on the mass market because there is not as much call for them, even though they are strong and less expensive than stainless ones. Drop-forged, galvanized cleats, hawsers, and bollards are the only steel fittings that are widely available. Drop-forged steel is preferable to cast steel for welding to the hull (see Chapter 6), and cast items like portholes are usually fastened mechanically. However, there is really no limit to the kinds of steel fittings that can be fabricated through forging and casting, and perhaps foundries will respond to the growth of interest in steel boats by producing more steel fittings.

Many steel shapes, such as L's or T's, tubing, pipe, or rod, can be bent and shaped into fittings. Steel plumbing pipe of various schedules can be used for ventilators, throughhulls, fuel fillers, standpipes, pedestals, and bollards. Chainplates can be made of heavy steel plate

and welded into the hull so that they are stronger than any bolted-on chainplate could be. As with stainless, there is a certain amount of labor (and labor cost) involved in making steel fittings, but since they are not readily available, custom fabrication may be the only way to get what you want. At least the steel is less expensive than stainless.

Although attachments and areas of the hull that are subject to chafe are often sheathed with or fabricated of stainless, mild steel can hold up well in these areas if it is protected by a durable coating. A good epoxy paint will withstand mild chafe, and steel fittings can also be metallized with stainless, aluminum, or zinc, although this can be costly unless your hull is being metallized. In certain chafe areas the steel can also be impregnated with epoxy powder, which, though very durable, is only available in black or brown.

Steel attachments (for example, chainplates) can be fitted with stainless eyes, although the labor involved in fitting and welding in the eyes may raise the price near that of a stainless chainplate, which would be stronger. With, for example, a bobstay eye, where only a small piece of metal is used, it would be easier and cheaper to weld on a piece of stainless with a hole drilled in it than to weld a stainless insert eye into a piece of steel.

JOINING STEEL APPENDAGES

The correct method for joining a particular attachment depends on the material of which it is made and whether it must be removable. Lips, flanges, brackets, tabs, eyelets, cleats, bollards, and other small parts are usually welded on, whether they are plain steel or stainless. Stanchions, travelers, pulpits, fairlead eyes, or railings, on the other hand, are commonly fastened mechanically. Any dissimilar metals (including large pieces of stainless), of course, must be insulated from the steel, and so are secured to the steel with studs or bolts. (Non-integral methods of securing various items for the boat systems will be covered in the chapter devoted to that system.)

Welding steel attachments to the hull is a relatively easy process, although the joints must be carefully designed to prevent stress concentrations and notches. When welding cast-steel fittings to a steel hull, the proper electrodes and welding temperature (usually lower than for welding plain steel) are critical. Any galvanizing must be ground off to prevent inclusions in the weld, so if it is possible, purchasing fittings from the

Fig. 9-1.   *The builder of this single chine hull made good use of steel pipe and tubing.*

Fig. 9-2.   *Steel pipe sections are welded in to enhance the sweep of the steel bulwarks on this George Buehler design. The builder, an amateur with excellent welding skills, fabricated most of his own fittings and used pipe to soften many corners.*

manufacturer before they are galvanized makes sense. For welding stainless to mild steel, special electrodes are required.

Doublers are traditionally welded behind attachments like the windlass that operate under heavy loads. Depending on the doubler's location, though, the continuous welding required to prevent its becoming a water trap may distort the hull. In this case, it would be better to cut out a hole and insert a doubler of heavier plate. An even better idea is to use a flange box (see Fig. 9-3) instead of a doubler.

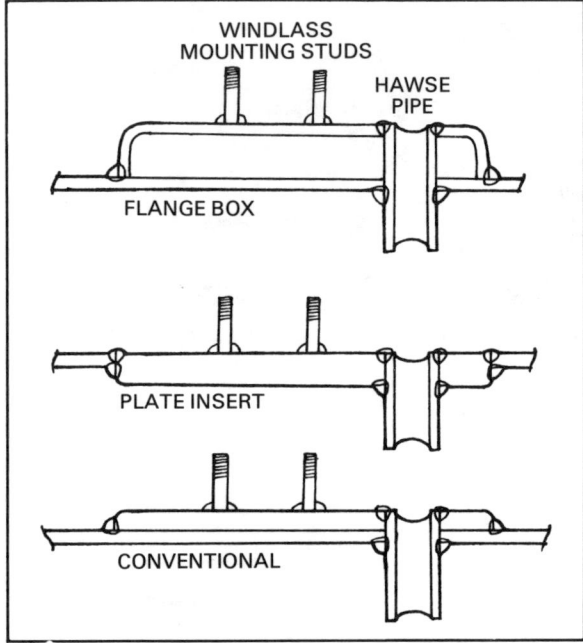

Fig. 9-3. *Doublers under the windlass can take many forms. The plate under the flange box type can be cut out for access to the bottom of the doubler, and the lower end of the hawse pipe could be flared out so that the chain doesn't catch.*

If a fitting is to be fastened mechanically on the deck or cabin, either studs can be welded on the deck or cabin to receive it or holes can be drilled so that it can be bolted on. Stock fittings (like travelers or windlasses) can be purchased ahead of time and held in place so that the location of studs can be marked. (Patterns can also be used, but the pattern may vary slightly from the piece of equipment eventually purchased.) On the other hand, when the exact position is not known (for example, for fairlead eyes, whose positions may need to be changed when the rigging and sails are tested), it will be wiser to bolt the fitting down through holes drilled in the hull.

The small holes needed for mounting fittings and woodwork can be drilled with a good tap-and-die set either before or after blasting and coating, since the area of steel exposed inside a ¼ " hole is so small and since the fastener can be bedded before it is inserted. Thread compound can later be applied to the hole to protect the steel. Some "countersink" beveling of the edges of the hole with a metal file or peanut grinder is a nice touch, but blasting will remove some of the sharp edges. Much drilling time and effort will be saved if holes in the many tabs that may be needed for wood joinery are drilled on a drill press before assembly. However, there is no hard-and-fast rule for when to drill small holes.

The holes should be threaded when a tight grip is needed to prevent leaks or when a nut cannot be used because of poor access. Threading the hole should be postponed until after painting because blasting can damage the threads, and the paint can gum them up. Sometimes threaded holes are taped off before painting, but this makes for extra work. Studs and pipes, however, can be threaded before they are coated. Any paint which does adhere to the threads will add to corrosion resistance, although most will be sheared off when the fitting is screwed on.

All of the large holes in the hull plate also should be cut out before blasting, and the large hatch openings are often cut soon after the deck is welded on so that there is access to the interior. A plasma cutter or nibbler or even a jig saw with a metal blade (on 12-gauge plate) does the cleanest job of cutting out large areas, although a torch handled by an experienced operator can do wonders. When using a torch, a hole cutter tip or circle guide is helpful for cutting smaller holes for throughhulls or dorade vents. If a torch is used, the cut edges should be ground carefully to the proper fit.

If an attachment is to be welded to the cutout, the hole is usually cut before the attachment is welded on, although this order is occasionally reversed. (For example, the hawser hole is cut before the chain pipe is installed.) But large hatch openings can be cut out either before or after the hatch lip pieces have been welded on, although cutting first is preferable, especially if flange plate is used for the lip. Some cutouts like scupper drains have no attachments, although rod can be welded around the hole to soften the edges. Holes must also be cut for portholes, stove pipes, ventilation cowls, and pipe weldments like the stern tube.

Any piece of equipment that is attached to a hole must be a very precise fit to allow for good welding or, if the attachment is mechanically fastened, so that there is no leakage around the hole. In most cases, the specific fitting must be purchased or patterned so that the cutout is the right size. If you are building your own hatches, you should be very sure of their designs so that the correct size holes are cut.

THE LIST OF INTEGRALS

Table No. 9-1 is a list of the integral attachments most likely to be used, arranged by areas of the boat: hull (below sheer), deck and cabin top, and cockpit and interior. These groups of attachments are then separated into use categories: plumbing and engine, ventilation and light, moorage and steering, rigging and sail handling, and other (safety, electrics, woodwork, storage, comfort, and navigation). Preparing a similar list for your boat can save costly changes after blasting and painting.

The discussion to follow on each attachment will focus on design, material, preparation for joinery, and whether or not it should be made integral. We also offer some construction suggestions for home builders.

HULL ATTACHMENTS

Plumbing and Engine

Integral or non-integral—that's the main question with *tanks*. In integral tankage, the hull itself forms the fourth side of the tank, increasing the amount of living space in the vessel. Integral tanks are especially attractive in the keel, since they use otherwise dead space and also help to keep the boat's center of gravity low. But

a hull rupture at the tank location can ruin the contents. Removable, non-integral tanks can also be built in the odd shapes required, and they protect the tank contents regardless of the integrity of the hull.

Part of the answer may come from considering what the tank is to hold. Out at sea, water is definitely more precious than fuel. And, although properly painted steel tanks should keep water potable, you may want to invest in better material for water tanks. If any material other than mild steel is used, the tank will have to be non-integral.

The location and weight of tanks are used in a boat's design to help keep the hull stable. All tanks should be located low in the boat because of the weight of their contents, and they should measure no more than one-third of the beam. An integral tank can provide some extra margin of safety by acting as a kind of watertight bulkhead if the hull is ruptured. However, the chance of rupture occurring at the usual tank location amidships rather than at the forefoot is unlikely.

With integral tanks, there is a much greater chance of hull distortion caused by the complete welding of the tank to the hull. This is hard to counteract and easily spotted from the outside. The amount of distortion is influenced by the thickness of the hull plate and the type of welding equipment. However, if the tanks are built into the keel, which is of heavier plate, distortion is less likely and won't be seen in any case.

Although some interior space may be lost with non-integral tanks, this loss will be minimized when the tanks are placed down low (for example, under the cabin sole) and in odd corners. It may be difficult to find

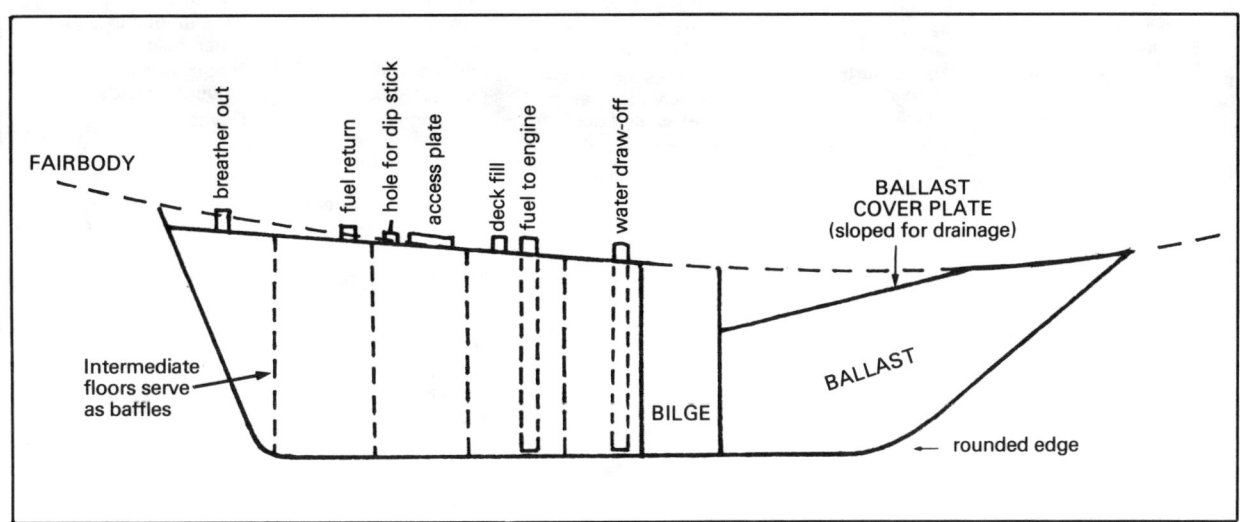

Fig. 9-4. *An integral fuel tank built into the keel. The access plate should be as large as possible.*

Table 9-1.   PLANNING THE HULL ATTACHMENTS AND CUTOUTS

PLUMBING & ENGINE	VENTILATION & LIGHT	STEERING & MOORING	RIGGING & SAIL HANDLING	OTHER
HULL				

Tanks
  fresh water
  fuel
  other
  mounting tabs
  /brackets
Throughhulls
  engine salt water
  head intake
  head outflow
  galley intake
  galley outflow
  cockpit drain
  2 engine outflow
  engine exhaust
  flange
Sea chest (opt.)
Limber drain holes
Enginer bearers &
  girders
Engine mounts
Stern tube
Stuffing box &
  bearing
Tube boss
Shaft log
	Portholes
	Underwater view-
	  ing port
		Rudder w/steering
		  eyes & pintles
		Rudder post & re-
		  ceptors or
		  gudgeons
		Shoe bearing
		Rudder stopper
		Emergency rudder
		  hook-up
		Emergency steer-
		  ing eyes
		Chain locker/tabs
		  with 2 eyes
		Rub rail
		Wind vane
		  mounts
			Chain plates &
			  doublers
			Eyes for bobstays,
			  boomkin & bow-
			  sprit stays
			Mast step or
			  tabernacle
			Compression rod
				Gussets & webs
				Bulwarks/rail-
				  tabs for wood
				  joinery, scupper
				  drains
				Watertight bulk-
				  head, stern
				Ballast straps or
				  welded cover
				  plate
				Stern ladder
				Studs for zincs
				Throughhull for
				  electrolysis
				  meter
				Transducer hole
				  or mount
				Hole for speed log
				Holes for fasten-
				  ing wood on
				  transverse frames
				Generator prop
				  (opt.)
				Additional sole
				  beams

DECK				
If composite, add tabs, lips, cross bars or holes, covering board and carlin				

Filler/cap outlets for
  fuel & water tanks
Tank pump-out
  deck outlet
Propane locker,
  holes, bracket
Engine cowl vents
	Hatch openings with
	  flange lip
	  lazarette
	  fo'c's'le (can be on
	    cabin)
	  skylight
	  main companion-
	    way
	  tabs for turtle
	  latches
	  hinges
	Prisms (deadlights)
	Cowl vents, dorade
	  box tabs, pipe lip
		Cleats/eyes
		Samson post or
		  bollard
		Stern bollard
		Stern roller chock
		Bow roller assembly
		  and doubler
		Windlass mount as-
		  sembly (dogs and
		  brakes) and doubler
		Hawse pipe with lip
		Emergency tiller
		  outlet
			Bowsprit/boomkin
			  bracket
			Forestay plate and
			  doubler
			Connecting rod
			Running backstay
			  lever
			Jib pedestal
			Fairlead eyes for
			  sheeting mizzen
			  staysail, jib; deck
			  eyes for safety har-
			  nesses, dinghy, life
			  raft, vangs, others
			Cleats (also for
			  towing
			Travelers for jibs,
			  main and mizzen
			Genoa slide track
			Winch pads (base
			  mounts), doublers
			  and bolt holes
			Boom chock
			Mast pulpit and be-
			  laying pin rail
				Stanchions and
				  eyes/bases
				Pulpits, bow and
				  stern (opt.)
				Electric hook-ups
				AC plug-in and insu-
				  lated hole
				Dinghy or life raft
				  mounting pads
				Davits

154

Table 9-1. (CONTINUED)				
PLUMBING & ENGINE	VENTILATION & LIGHT	STEERING & MOORING	RIGGING & SAIL HANDLING	OTHER
CABIN AND COCKPIT				
Tank breather outlet holes Cockpit scupper drain lips Engine panel Engine controls and throttle Engine access plate and bolt holes Shaft lock control	Porthole lips and flanges Stove stack lip and air box Heater vent opening and flange	Pedestal/binnacle stand, holes for bolting down Steering lead cutouts or hole in access plate to lead inside For vane: wheel drum pulley outlet & block in coaming	Mast collar and cutout for mast Handrails or tabs for attaching rails Whisker and spinnaker pole mounts	Dodger tabs or flanges Spray shield tabs or flanges Coaming or tabs Companionway ladder hook Cockpit spotlight cutout Drink box Locker opening Tabs for attaching wood cockpit locker Sail locker & flanges Eyes/lips for grating Cockpit table socket Cushion tie eyes Holes for eyebrows

portable tanks in the shapes best for your boat, but they can easily be custom-made. Non-integral tanks can be removed and repaired if necessary, although the weight of a tank can make removal easy or difficult. They do cost more, even when made of steel, since more metal is needed for both the tank plate and the mounting brackets.

Stainless steel, aluminum, and monel are the best choices for nonintegral *water tanks*, and none need to be painted. However, there are some questions about the long-term health hazards associated with aluminum tanks, and monel is quite expensive. That leaves stainless steel as the most likely choice. But plain or galvanized steel, copper, fiberglass, rubber, polyethylene, and polypropylene have also been used for water tanks. The copper tanks that work well on wooden boats may cause corrosion in a steel vessel, and anyway they are expensive and getting harder to find. Fiberglass may tint the water, and rubber or PVC are hard to clean. Polyethylene and polypropylene are non-corroding, but can change the taste of the water and will melt in a fire. (They work well for sumps or holding tanks, though.)

Plain or galvanized steel can be used successfully for water tanks, as long as the steel is properly painted.

Plain steel water tanks should be coated with vinyls, inorganic zinc, phenolics, or the brushable types of coal tar or polyamide epoxies. There are also special paints manufactured for water tanks; for example, International Paints has a black water tank paint that dries well and is approved by the Food and Drug Administation. Cement washes should not be used since they can leave lime in the water. Galvanized tanks should be carefully cleaned before use so that no zinc comes off in the water.

Steel produces the cheapest diesel *fuel tanks*, and it can be used untreated if the tanks are kept full, since diesel will stop rust. Of course, steel tanks can be coated for longer lifetime. Epoxy paints are best, and bituminous mineral paints should never be used since they dissolve in fuel. The breather vents can be plugged to prevent condensation when the tank is empty or not in service.

Other materials can be used for fuel tanks, depending on whether they are designed to hold gasoline or diesel. Diesel reacts with both galvanized coatings and copper, fouling the fuel. Stainless, aluminum (preferably an alloy with minimal amounts of magnesium), or monel are fine choices, if expensive ones. Fiberglass fuel tanks have been used, but if there is a fire onboard, the fiberglass will burn and add fuel to the fire. Brass will de-zincify rapidly when in contact with either gas or diesel. Finally, old black iron fuel tanks are still in service, although it makes more sense to use steel for new tanks.

Stainless tanks should be carefully inspected at the corners to make sure that conditions causing crevice corrosion are not present. A nice type of stainless tank can be made using a braking machine to fabricate the corners rather than welding pieces of plate together.

The tank should be designed with a slightly cambered top so that it can shed any exterior condensation. An access plate of a minimum of 2 sq. ft. at the top or side is recommended for clean-out and inspection, although in stainless tanks an access plate is not absolutely necessary. For integral tanks, it may be practical to make the whole top removable for easy servicing. The gasketed access plate should be secured with stainless steel bolts spaced every 2–3″. If galvanized bolts are used on a steel tank, they should be well-sealed and painted to prevent their being locked in place by corrosion.

For diesel tanks, only neoprene or other fuel-resistant materials should be used for the access plate gasket, since diesel causes rubber to deteriorate. Rubber gaskets can, however, be used for water tanks. Whichever material is used, the gasket must seat the access plate securely so that no leaks develop. The gasket should be secured with a flexible bedding compound.

Fuel tanks generally have six different openings besides the access plate: 1) deck fuel fill opening; 2) fuel outlet line to the engine; 3) fuel return from the engine; 4) breather line outlet located near the top of the tank with a spring-loaded check valve in the line to keep water out; 5) draw-off opening for removing any contaminants; 6) fuel dipstick level. Water tanks have only four openings, since no return line is needed and a sink outlet can be used to drain out contaminated water. To prevent sloshing, all tanks should have baffles every 24″ that extend only part of the depth of the tank.

A well-designed fuel tank should provide a means of drawing off water, grit, or the residue from bad fuel. The draw-off openings should be located at the top of the tank to prevent leaks, but the pipe itself should extend to near the bottom of the tank. Tanks can also be built with sumps where the unwanted substances can collect and be drawn off. But a sump is sometimes difficult to put into integral tanks, especially those in the keel, so a pump-out arrangement is more practical.

All non-integral tanks should be bolted down to steel tabs or brackets extending from frames, floors, or the tank itself.

Fig. 9-5. *The tank breather vent and filler openings for fuel and kerosene are built into a watertight opening in a design by Waterline Yachts. The angle bars on each side drain water onto the deck, and a gasket will also be installed to keep water out.*

Throughhulls and the seacocks that close them deserve considerable thought and attention to detail. Six throughhulls are common: engine water intake, engine exhaust (some vessels have two), saltwater intake for galley sink, head saltwater intake, head discharge, and galley gray water outlet. Discharge throughhulls must be located so that the black or gray water can't flow into the raw-water intakes. Throughhulls may also be needed for cockpit drains, although some designs have cockpits that drain aft above the waterline, using a rubber flapper secured to a small tab to prevent water from backing up into the cockpit.

The design of a throughhull is fairly simple. A hole is cut in the hull, and a pipe of the proper schedule, fitted with a lip or flange on the end that will be inside the hull, is welded into the hole. If the pipe protrudes slightly outside the hull, its edge should be rounded. The pipe should be long enough inside so that the seacock can be properly secured to it. Since the pipe itself is welded to the hull, failure would only be caused by improper seating of the seacock to the pipe or by a faulty seacock.

A recessed sea chest, which consolidates some of the throughhull openings (usually raw intakes) can be used to reduce the number of throughhulls. (This arrangement is discussed in Chapter 13.)

Throughhulls can also have a strainer or flapper secured on the outside to keep debris from clogging the works. However, a separate in-line strainer is simpler, easier to maintain, and less liable to corrode than is a grill on the outside of the hull.

Limber drain holes cut out in the lowest parts of the boat are essential for proper drainage of any water collecting inside, especially along the longitudinals, which could corrode under wet conditions. However, limbers aren't necessary if urethane insulation is sprayed in over the level of the longitudinals. Chain lockers or watertight bulkheads should also have limber holes, which can be fitted with a plug or cap to make them watertight and allow controlled drainage.

Several attachments are directly related to engine operation. A hull kit should include well-designed *engine bearers* (beds) spanning a number of frames fore and aft. These are generally made of steel T-bar, angle iron, or flange plate, welded integrally to the hull. On larger boats, flange plate or angle bar *girders* also run longitudinally outboard of the bearers. The location of the holes for the *engine mounts* that are welded onto or cut into the engine bed must be found either by measuring the specific engine to be used or by consulting the spec sheet for that engine. The *stern tube*, through which runs the drive shaft that connects the engine and propeller, is easily fabricated by welding steel pipe of the proper schedule in place. The stern tube should be long enough to allow for insertion of a flexible shaft gland or to receive a *stuffing box*. The tube must also be able to accept the bearing that supports the propeller shaft. In some larger boats, a steel *tube boss*, made of larger-schedule pipe than the tube, can be installed to strengthen the stern tube. The welding and fitting of all these components must be carefully done so that the shaft alignment is not jeopardized.

Some water-driven generating systems use a separate shaft and propeller attached to a generator. In this case, another throughhull with tube and bearing will be needed for this assembly.

Ventilation and Lighting

Portholes are occasionally seen in the hull forward of amidships on high-freeboard designs, but are more often located in the cabin side. Most access hatches are also built into the deck or cabin. Fixed portholes can easily be fastened mechanically flush with the hull or bolted to angle bar welded into the hull. Ample bedding is important here to prevent leaks or to isolate dissimilar metal portholes.

An *underwater viewing port*, installed like a sea chest, can be a nice optional addition to a steel hull, and is often a feature on charter boats. A high-tensile clear plastic window (for example, Lexan), rather than a bell cap, is fastened on top of the standpipe.

Steering and Mooring

The *rudder* is one of the basic appendages included in a hull-deck assembly. An outboard rudder is simple to construct, but not all designs have outboard rudders. Building the rudder will be more complex if it extends inboard with the rudder post entering under the stern.

Fig. 9-6. *A single plate rudder with stiffeners is easy to make, but it doesn't have a particularly good foil shape. The skeg would be improved if its leading edge were slanted at more of an angle.*

In a steel boat, the rudder is usually a hollow box design with a good foil shape to reduce turbulence. However, a single plate with stiffeners also can be used for the rudder, and a wood rudder (for example, plywood sealed with epoxy) could also be built. The box design should be constructed with proper internal stiffeners, and it can be filled with oil or tar to prevent corrosion, although no filler is needed if the rudder is welded up completely. A hollow rudder can also be filled with foam for added flotation, although sealing the rudder then becomes very tricky. A drain plug in the rudder can be used to pressure-check for leaks. If the vessel has a full keel, a slot should be cut in the rudder stock so that the prop and shaft can be removed without having to pull out the rudder.

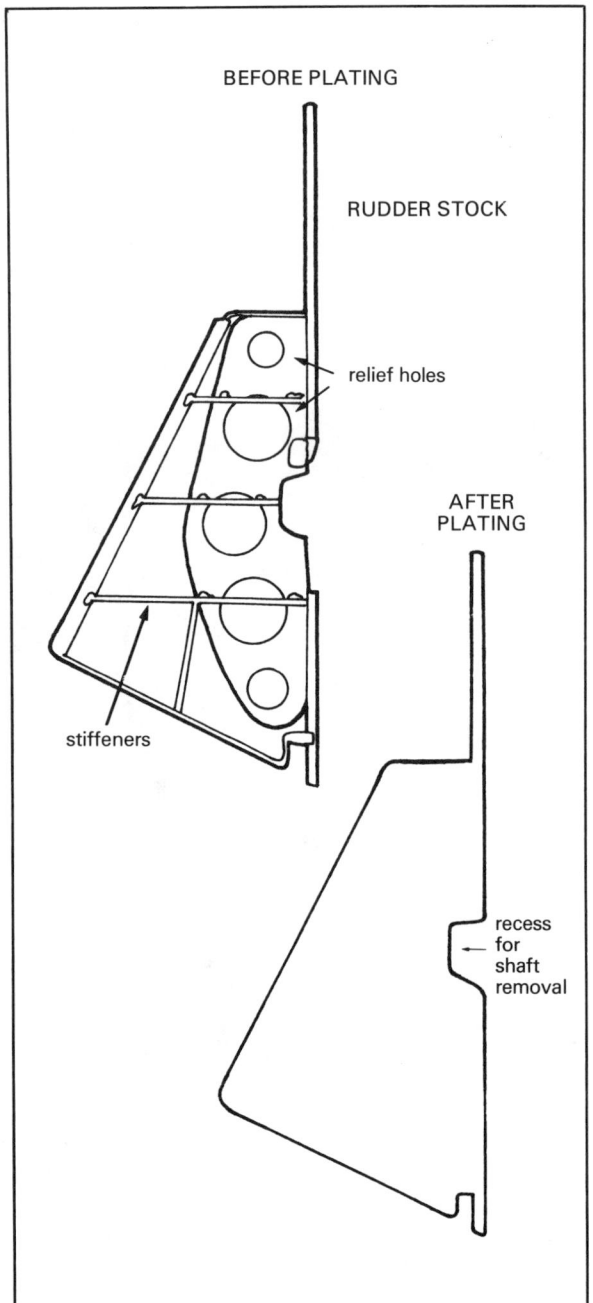

BEFORE PLATING

RUDDER STOCK

relief holes

AFTER PLATING

stiffeners

recess for shaft removal

Fig. 9-7. *This reinforced box rudder should not create much turbulence since it has a good foil shape.*
Courtesy of Waterline Yachts

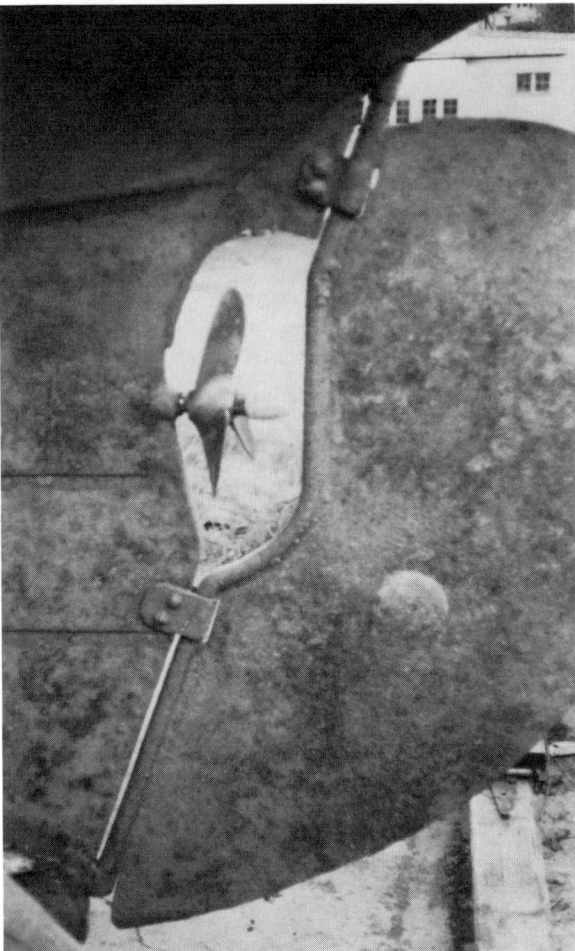

Fig. 9-8. *The simple single-plate rudder is easily attached with bolt-on gudgeons. This black-iron hull is built with riveted lapped plate.*

The *rudder post* for a hollow rudder can be tube or pipe stock (schedule 80 or higher). The upper and lower sections of the rudder post, where the bearings are located, should be made of stainless steel. The rudder stock is usually attached to the hull with either a bolted flange coupling or a welded rudder port tube, made of the proper schedule pipe, fitted with a bearing. The lower end of the post is seated on a *shoe bearing* extending from the skeg or keel. This bearing can easily be made removable so that the rudder can be slid down off the post. A bronze cutlass bearing or one made of durable plastic (for example, Nylatron) or phenolic-encased neoprene should be installed on the rudder post; ferro-asbestos ball bearings should be avoided since they are susceptible to corrosion. The rudder post could also rest on a stainless steel nub welded into the bottom of the lower bearing. A *rudder stopper* arrangement should be included to keep the rudder from turning too far. The stopper can be designed to be part of the steering quadrant or the interior bulkheads.

Emergency steering eyes should be fitted in the aft top half of the rudder. A small pipe or a half chain link can be welded through the top aft edge of the rudder for this purpose. If the rudder stock breaks, lines or a yoke and chain can be attached to the eyes to allow steering.

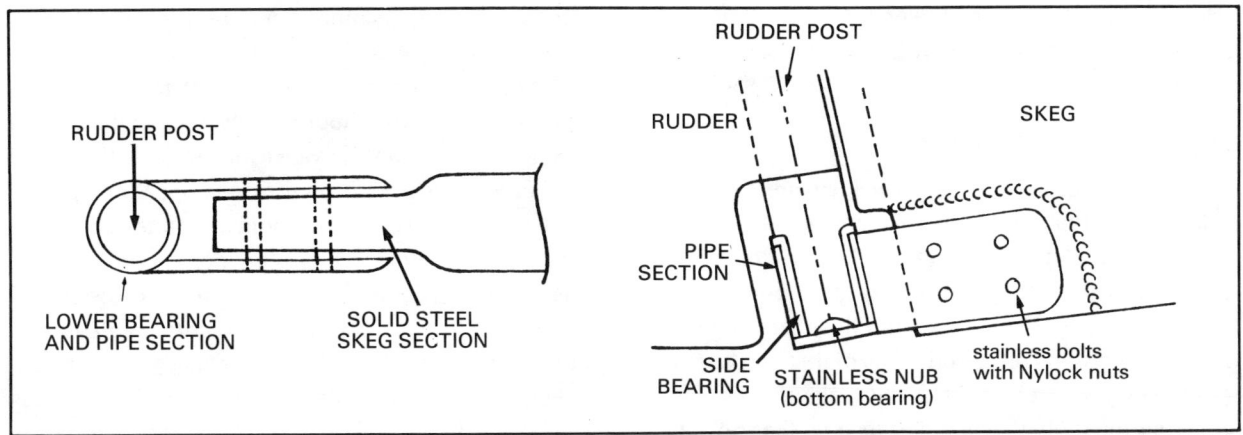

Fig. 9-9. *Bottom and side views of a removable lower rudder bearing.*

These eyes can also be used for lifting the rudder out, if need be.

Gudgeons to receive the rudder pintles are usually found only on outboard rudder designs. A section of steel pipe is welded to the transom for this purpose, and is generally part of the hull kit. A good reinforced nylon or neoprene/phenolic bearing is later pressed into the pipe section to prevent corrosion caused by chafe on the gudgeon. This simple mounting method is what makes outboard rudder mounting easier and cheaper than inboard.

A *rub rail* protects the hull from chafe when docking or rafting up, and it provides some longitudinal strengthening. Steel longitudinals can sometimes be omitted in this area. Rub rails for steel boats are commonly made of steel, wood, or the more expensive cupronickel.

Although wood rails look good when new, in time they can get quite beat-up and will need to be replaced. The wood can be either attached to studs or bolted to the hull. It can be a bit difficult to fit long sections of hardwood or fir rail to studs, and the studs can also interfere with topside paint fairing. If the rail is bolted down, steel cap nuts can be welded inside the bolt holes to seal them and prevent leakage. No matter how the rail is attached, the bolt heads or nuts must be well-recessed to protect them from damage.

A welded steel rail gives a superior longitudinal strength to the hull. There are basically two types, depending on who is building the hull with what tools—cut half pipe or molded plate sections. Both are welded directly to the hull, but the former requires less equipment and generally appeals more to the amateur. However, getting a proper fit with the changing fore-and-aft twists of the side of the boat can be tricky. Professionals with access to a stamping machine press can have a plate shape molded and later tapered. A braking machine can also be made to produce a shape that looks more yachty and is easier to install.

If *tabs, sockets, or flanges for mounting the wind vane* must be welded into position, it may be necessary to purchase the vane to be used so that measurements for location of the mounts can be made. Stainless steel rod can be used if the wind vane mounts are made of stainless tube. A deck mounting can be extended by welding

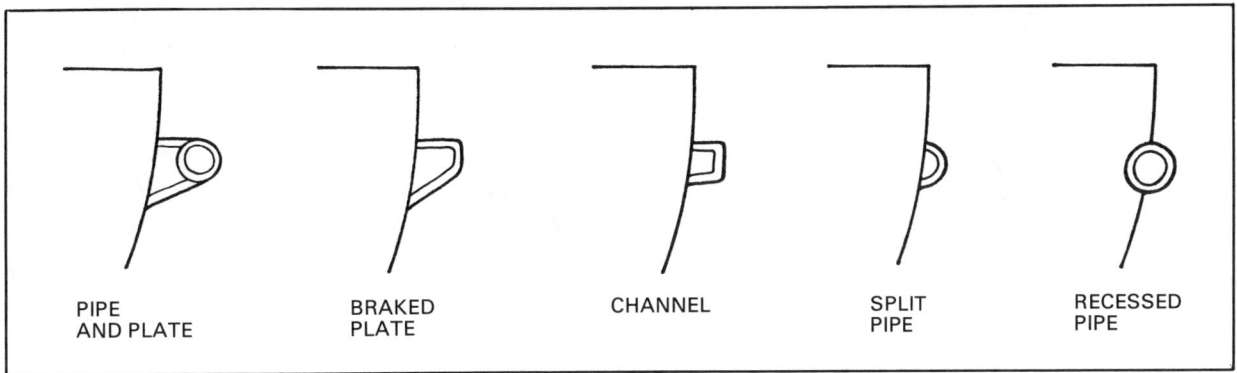

Fig. 9-10. *Different steel shapes can be used for different styles of integral rub rails.*

a steel pipe in place. If you prefer, you could wait and bolt on the mounts supplied with the vane, thus assuring a perfect fit.

Rigging and Sail Handling

Chainplates are almost always welded directly to the hull—in fact, that is one of the advantages of building in steel. Chainplates welded to a hull are so strong that a steel boat can easily be hoisted by them. Some extra stiffening may be required around the chainplates to distribute the stress placed on them, or they can be tied into the hull with a steel strap and longitudinals. The stiffening must be carefully designed so that no hull distortion is introduced. As mentioned above, the job of fitting stainless inserts into the eyes of mild steel chainplates is so time-consuming that most professionals find it easier to use an all-stainless chainplate. Chainplates are generally part of a hull kit.

Various *stay eyes* will also be needed if a fairly long bowsprit or boomkin is part of the design. Three tangs with eyelets should be welded on: one at the stem near the waterline for the bobstay and one on each side near the sheer for the shrouds. As with chainplates, they should either be all stainless or mild steel with stainless insert eyes.

A steel *mast step* made of the proper-radius pipe section or bent flat bar should be installed at the correct position, with proper allowance for wedges, either in the keel or as a *tabernacle* on the deck or cabin top. The mast step on a larger boat should be connected to steel floors; proper reinforcement can include girders welded to extended floors. A drain hole in the lowest part of the step is a wise addition. A *compression rod* or pumping strut made of steel pipe can also be used between the cabin sole and the mast step if the mast is stepped on deck. Even though a steel deck is strong, the rod helps to spread out the compression loads on the mast. If the mast is aluminum, a good insulator (like reinforced plastic) will need to be installed on the top of the step before the mast is lowered into place.

Other Attachments and Cutouts

Extra *gussets and webs* may also be called for in some designs. These "knees" are commonly found where the hull meets the deck or where the cabin sides and roof meet, especially at the mast station; they are also occa-

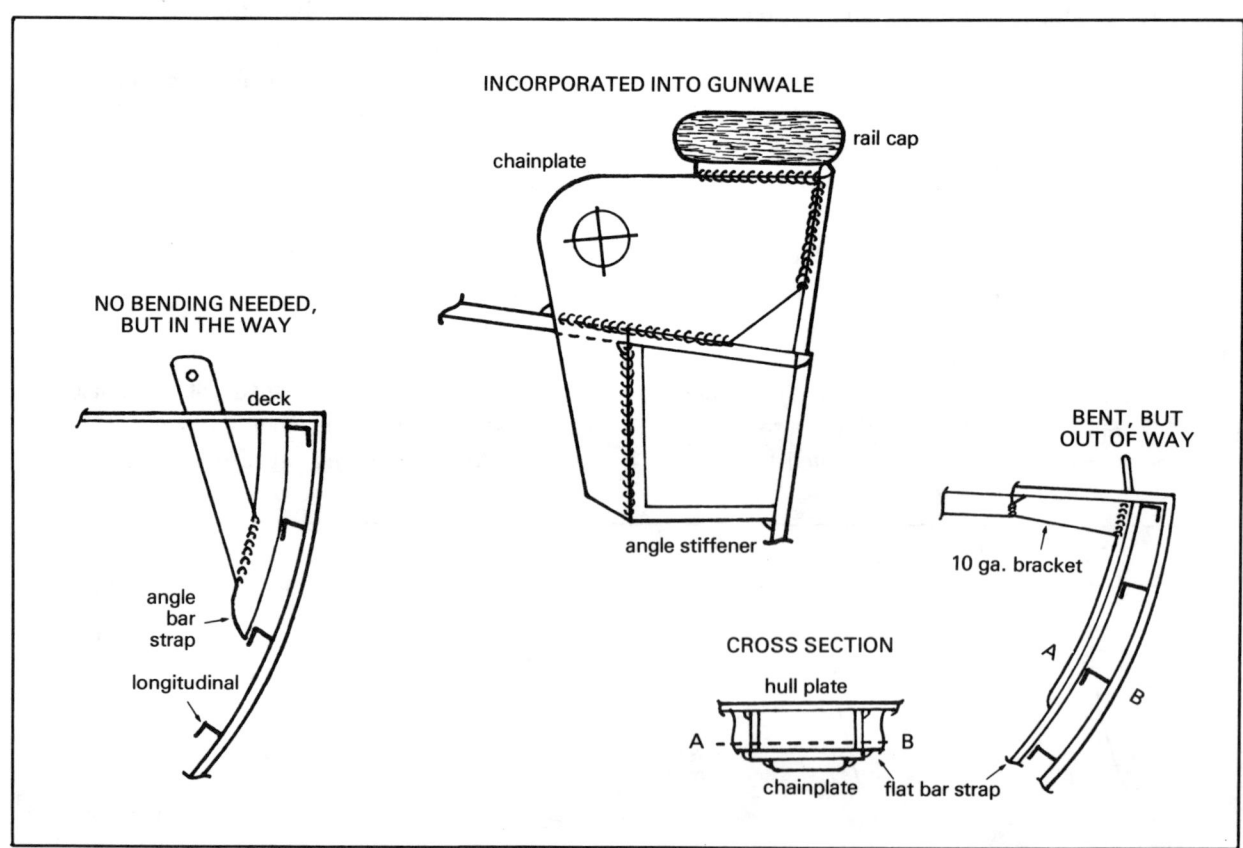

Fig. 9-11. *Different options for welding chainplates to the deck. Notice that none of the chainplates are welded to the hull plate. The load can be easily dispersed to the hull by using the methods shown above*

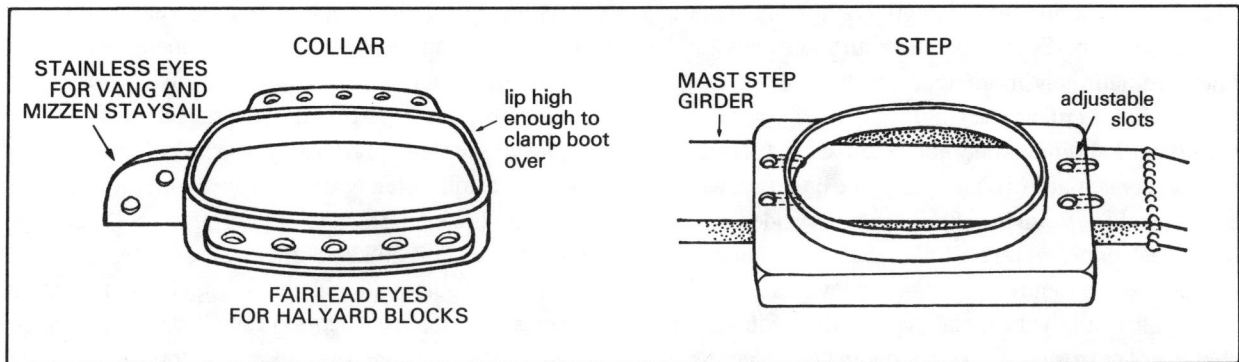

Fig. 9-12. *The collar and step for a keel-stepped mast. The adjustable slots in the step are nice but optional. The mast step girder spreads out the load, and water can drain out underneath the step itself.*

sionally installed near chainplates. Their purpose is to help support high-stress areas. Although there may be some question of their importance on a steel boat, they should be installed if the designer calls for it. Sometimes web frames are used instead of gussets for this purpose.

Steel *bulwarks* or deck rails will be completed before blasting as part of the hull kit and should be designed both for safety and beauty. There are many joinery choices, including those shown in Fig. 9-14. Proper *scupper drains* located at the lowest point of the bulwark must be cut out, and are best rimmed with steel rod. Rod gratings can be installed to prevent losing small items overboard. If scarfed wooden bulwarks are bolted a few inches above the deck to steel tabs welded to the deck, long natural scuppers will be formed. These wood bulwarks look nice, are lighter than steel ones, and allow full-length drainage of deck wash.

A *watertight steel bulkhead* can be located in either the bow or the stern, or both. Watertight bulkheads can also can be used to secure the engine room, but don't

Fig. 9-13. *This home builder installed a nice, heavy-duty tabernacle mast step on the deck of his boat.*

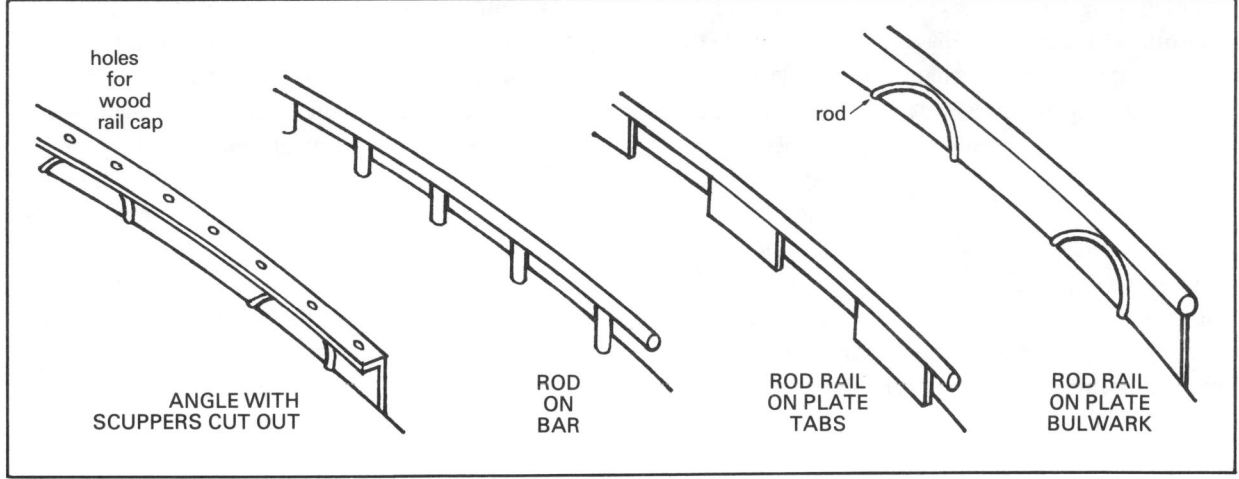

Fig. 9-14. *When the deck rails and bulwarks are welded integrally, many different looks can be achieved by combining steel shapes.*

add much to the structural integrity of the hull and are difficult to drain. (See Chapter 8 for further discussion.) They are definitely more appropriate for large cargo ships than for cruising yachts.

Another important safety item is some kind of *ballast strap or cover* made of plate to hold the ballast down in case of a rollover. Angle or flat bar can be welded across the ballast, or holes can be drilled in the floor flange for bolting down a removable strap. However, sealing the ballast off totally with a plate cover also reduces the chances of corrosion. If some of the ballast is left movable for trim adjustment, an access plate can be installed in the cap for any additions to the ballast.

A *stern ladder* is a safety feature that can be welded onto the stern for climbing aboard or servicing the wind vane. An integral bent pipe or rod ladder can be made either of stainless or plain steel. A detachable extension can also be bolted or simply hooked onto integral tabs. Steps of steel pipe welded onto the transom are also seen on sterns that slant inboard.

Studs for securing zinc anodes are needed on the outside of the hull. Backing washers can be used on the stud to keep the zinc away from the hull. Three to six zincs will be required on a steel hull, depending on its size. If an *electrolysis meter* is installed, a small through-hull, only big enough for a wire enclosed in a phenolic casing to pass through, will have to be cut and possibly fitted with a small steel pipe.

Hull cutouts for electrical equipment may also be necessary. If a depth sounder is to be mounted, a hole will be required for the *transducer*. The closed-box depth sounders without a throughhull fitting that are used on fiberglass hulls won't work on a steel boat, because the signals can't pass through metal. The transducer is best mounted on a steel pipe section recessed in from the hull surface. Transducers that hang over the side can be used, but these types are more appropriate for power craft. If you are using an electric rotary *speed log* encased in nylon or phenolic, another hole will be needed. The alternative is a taffrail log, although they tend to foul on weeds.

Holes for fastening wood need to be drilled in the transverse frames, deck beams, the bottom of the cabin side plates, and, occasionally, in longitudinals. The easiest way to put these holes in is to drill or punch them before the frames are assembled. However, they can be drilled in place. A good mechanical, jawless nibbler punch with a right-angle fitting can be used, as well as a power drill or cutting torch with a hole-shooter tip. Firring strips for wood joinery could be attached with a spe-cial power drill that shoots fasteners, welding them in place by friction. However, this is an expensive tool that is difficult to handle, and in the marine environment, the corrosion resistance of the fasteners is questionable.

Designs for larger boats may also include *floor extensions* and additional *girders* to spread out the load and stress on the keel, skeg, or engine bearers. These supports are usually made of angle bar or flange plate.

On larger boats whose floors are much lower than the cabin sole, *cabin sole beams* of steel angle bar must be welded at the proper level above the tops of the floors so that the sole can be attached. (This procedure is described more fully in Chapter 15.)

ON-DECK ATTACHMENTS

There are many items that can be integrally welded to a steel deck. If your design uses composite construction with a wood, steel, or fiberglass deck or cabin, the attachments and cutouts mentioned in the rest of this chapter can only be used as a checklist, since the method of securing them will depend on the material used. To attach the composite deck or cabin to the hull, a *covering board* of flange plate or angle bar must be welded to the hull and have numerous holes drilled in it for bolting on the deck. Some composite designs are steel all the way to the *carlin*, and a flange with holes punched in it will be required where the deck meets the cabin, unless a transition block is used (see Chapter 4).

Engine and Plumbing

Filler holes and caps for fuel and water must be installed either on the deck or, possibly, on the cabin or cockpit coaming, depending on the design. Steel or plastic can be used for most of this assembly. It's important to have a tight opening that doesn't allow saltwater infiltration. Some builders incorporate the fillers into the spring-line cleat by fabricating the cleat of pipe with a removable cap on top. This is a nice way to simplify deck fittings.

A *holding tank pump-out outlet* can also be placed on deck. As with other tanks, the filler caps should be flush with the deck. This item is more appropriate for boats that stay in port for a long while.

Propane locker drain holes will be needed if propane is used for the galley stove or water or cabin heater. *Brackets* can be welded to steel to hold a fiberglass or wood box for the propane tanks. A locker could also be enclosed in steel coaming with a drain running overboard through the hull.

Engine ventilation cowls require cutouts and then a means of attaching a plastic ventilator or dorade box. Even a good steel or plastic "clam" vent works well when bolted in place in a fairly dry area, such as in the cockpit or cabin top. All ventilation openings should be located as high up as possible, but water must be prevented from flooding in through the vent with either a screw-on cap or a dorade box.

Ventilation and Lighting

Special provisions have to be made for proper lighting and ventilation onboard so that it is pleasant to be below when the weather is bad outside. The hatches, skylights, prisms, and vents that bring air and light inside can be located either on the cabin or the deck, but, for the sake of simplicity, all will be discussed below. Portholes will be covered under *Cabin and Cockpit Attachments*.

The number of *hatches* and *companionways* depends on the boat design, but commonly it will include a lazarette, a cockpit companionway, a skylight, and a foredeck hatch. A lip or flange is welded into the hatch opening, and this piece of steel extends down below the hatch so that wood face pieces or cleats can be attached if desired. The riser can be made either of flat bar or flange plate. Flange plate, made on a brake, has a soft corner which is quite attractive, and either a production or a custom hatch can be bolted down to the flange. (A custom steel hatch can be designed to cover the flange.) The riser for a sliding hatch must be able to resist continual chafing, so a stainless steel flange is usually welded onto flat bar for this purpose. Risers welded to the deck are also required for *skylights*. If a *turtle cover* (or sea hood) is used, it can be made of welded steel or lighter-weight wood, fiberglass, or aluminum, and the turtle is then fastened to pre-drilled steel tabs or bolted down through holes in the cabin top.

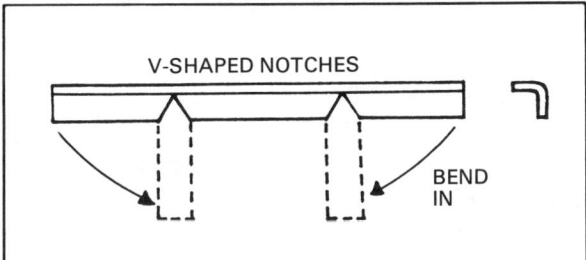

V-SHAPED NOTCHES

BEND IN

Fig. 9-15. *Flanged plate can be notched and bent to form the base of a hatch. Two of the assemblies pictured here will be welded together to make the base of the opening.*

Latches and *hinges* will be needed for hatches unless they are included with a production hatch. Latches or tabs/eyes for latches should be welded to the deck or cabin. If wood hatches are used, the latch should be on the hatch and a simple eye in the deck. Regular galvanized hinges from a hardware store can work well if the galvanizing is removed before welding, and local foundries will sometimes fabricate steel hinges to weld to the steel deck. Stainless steel hinges can be either welded on or bolted through an insulator. The push rods that hold up certain hatches may also need an eyelet on the flange to which they can be secured. Two-way opening hatches are another nice option. Hinges are installed on opposite sides of the hatch, and a stainless rod that can be moved from one set of hinges to the other is used to secure the hinges. Other clamp eyes for extra security are helpful, and can be welded or cut out of steel flange on the opening.

Deadlights and prism cutouts must have a lip on which the glass can rest. A steel flange welded on an angle works well, although a wood pad is simpler. Small items like this are commonly bolted in place. Proper bedding for deck prisms is extremely important to prevent leaks.

Ventilators with cowls allow fresh air into the cabin, but shouldn't let water in at the same time. The best way to install them is with a dorade box arrangement. Proper *dorade vent tabs or fastening holes* will be needed at the various ventilator locations, probably four to eight. All-steel dorades can be used, but wood is more appealing and easier to assemble using flexible rubber cowls, and it is not subject to corrosion, like steel.

Steering and Mooring

Various *cleats* or *chocks* are needed on deck for securing docking, mooring, spring, or anchoring lines. Chocks can be incorporated into the rail rather than installed as separate fittings. Although galvanized steel can be used, stainless is preferred because these fittings are often chafed. A *samson post (bollard)* is the primary place to secure bow lines, tow lines, and emergency deck lines. There are various designs for the samson post, and, as usual, stainless is preferable for this highly chafed fitting. Undoubtedly, a bollard in the stern will also come in handy. A *stern roller chock* to guide tow lines, stern anchor rodes, and line for towing warps can be bolted onto the stern bulwarks or welded to the deck.

A *bow roller assembly* is important for stowing and handling the anchors. This assembly can be made of steel, but stainless will handle the chafe better, since this

Fig. 9-16. *This unique bollard, fabricated of steel pipe, incorporates the fuel fill opening, which is hidden under a removable bell cap.*

area gets a lot of it. A good design will incorporate two rollers so that two anchors can be carried on the bow. A *windlass mount with dogs and brakes* should be included near the bow roller. Since the windlass might need to be removed, it is best bolted down on a insulator pad to studs welded in the deck. An inset steel doubler or flange box is often welded under the windlass to increase the stiffness of the steel deck. The *hawser hole cutout* should be completed before installing the *hawser pipe and lip,* which may be included when a windlass is purchased. Mountings for spare anchor pads can also be welded to the deck.

An *emergency tiller outlet* is an important part of the steering system, since it's the primary back-up for wheel steering. The exact arrangement can vary, but a hole is usually cut in the deck so that a pipe extension can be slipped onto the head of the rudder stock. A tiller is then fastened to the pipe extension. The hole is fitted with a threaded pipe, so that a screw cap can cover the hole when it is not in use. A small doubler plate and a simple sleeve bearing could be added to the outlet.

Rigging and Sail Handling

The use of a *bowsprit* is mostly a matter of personal preference and design. Its practicality in design is more apparent with a split rig than with sloops or cutters, because the main mast is farther forward and more room

is needed for headsails. The exact length and shape of the sprit should be decided during early planning with the designer.

There are many different ways to build a sprit that is both strong and simple. Whether it is long or short, properly sized steel pipe or tubing can do the job. Although some people may prefer stainless for its looks, the extra expense is not really necessary. Some wood secured to the top of the sprit is a nice touch, especially if it is part of a usable platform. There are several different ways of attaching the sprit, for which different mounts must be welded on.

Traditional sprits can be made of a long section of heavy-schedule pipe that is either welded to the stem or mechanically fastened in a socket on the samson post with a special support bracket at the stem. Sections of angle bar can be welded across the bow, and a wood platform attached. A wooden bowsprit can also be used and will require similar weldments.

In a less traditional but strong method, a sprit can be fabricated of two steel pipes that extend forward from the sheer just aft of the stem and meet in a V. The end can be softened by installing a "tube turn" made of bent pipe, and cross pieces can be welded in for attaching a safety platform. A short, U-shaped bowsprit can also be made of big angle iron, in which case a wood platform can be bolted down to the steel. The bow anchor roller

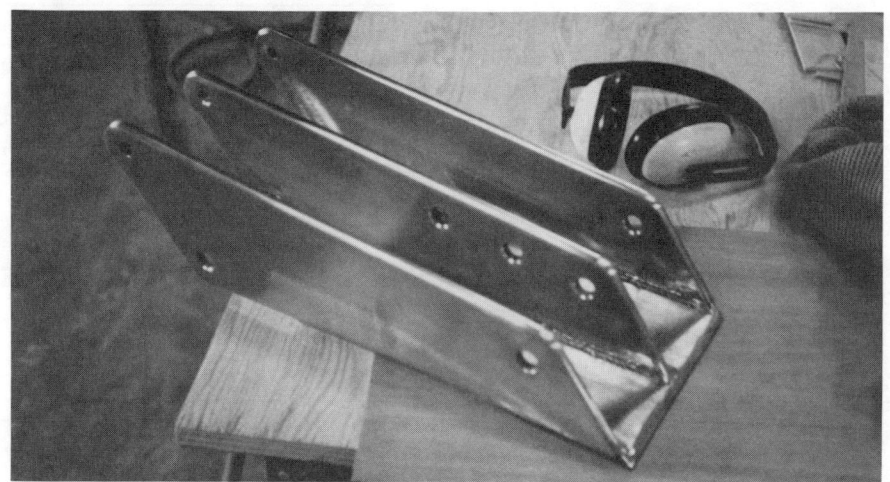

Fig. 9-17. *A stainless bow roller, fabricated at SP Metalcraft.*

Fig. 9-18. *A short bowsprit made of steel pipe is held down by a rod bobstay.*

Fig. 9-19. *A long pipe bowsprit fits right in with the clipper bow on this schooner.*

can be incorporated into the bowsprit attachment design, and can even rest on the sprit. Any stay eyes that are needed should be made of stainless.

A *boomkin* is uncommon, but if the design calls for one, it can be constructed like a bowsprit, although it will be simpler since there will be no anchors to house.

Various weldments of steel or stainless steel will be needed for rigging and sail handling. *Forestay deck or stem plates* ("deck irons" on a wooden boat) for attaching headstays are best made of stainless or mild steel with stainless sleeves, in the same way that chainplates are fabricated. When the forestay is secured aft of the stem, a doubler or a steel *connecting rod* (similar to a compression rod) running to the stem may be required to add reinforcement and disperse the load. Two *running backstay levers and lock-downs* are often used in heavy weather conditions on larger cruising boats. They can be made of mild steel pipe with eyes of either galvanized or stainless steel. The sheave for the backstay wire can be mounted between two large curved tabs welded on deck. The assembly must be properly spaced, so that the stay will drop forward enough when not in use.

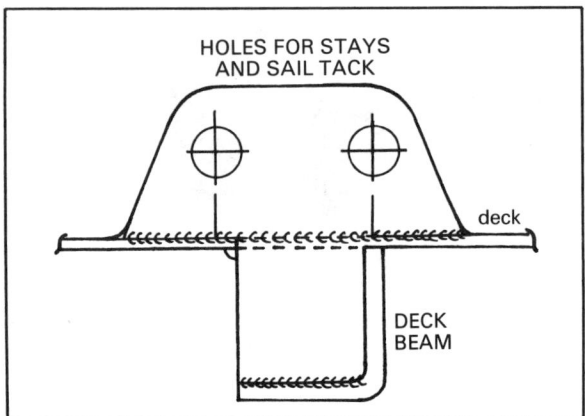

Fig. 9-20. *In this design, the forestay deck-eye plate is tied into a deck beam.*

A *jib pedestal* for the working jib is another integral found in some designs. It makes handling self-tending, loose-footed club staysails easier, and it can be made of steel pipe either welded to the deck or secured with bolts or studs. A good, simple homemade pedestal is shown in Fig. 9-22.

Deck eyes have a variety of uses onboard a steel hull. Fairleads for headsail sheeting can be secured to eyes, as can boom vang block assemblies. The mizzen staysail is tied down to an eye, and dinghies, rafts, and other items are lashed to eyes. Safety line can run through eyes, and the safety harness can be clipped directly to

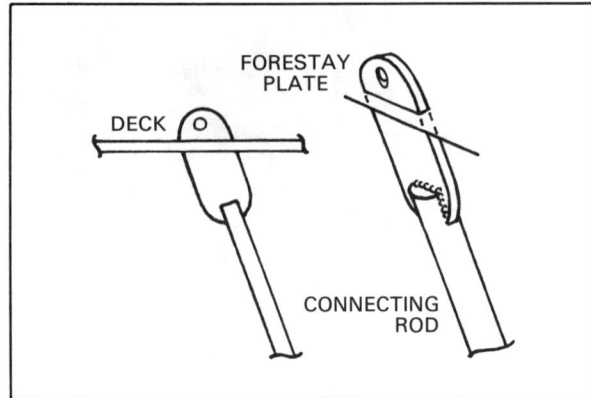

Fig. 9-21. *A steel connecting rod transmits the load on this stainless inner forestay eye to the stem.*

a deck eye if necessary. Emergency gale lines and aft lines can be secured to eyes, although a stern bollard can also be used. Eyes with stainless bushings should not be used on deck, since they are subject to corrosion fatigue and failure due to varying loads; it's best to use either an all-stainless or an all-steel eye. Chain links cut in half and welded on work well. Fig. 9-23 shows various methods of making eyes. If the exact location for a fairlead is uncertain, it can be bolted on later.

Various *cleats* may also be required in certain areas for securing the sheets, halyards, and other running rigging. A steel or stainless cleat is easily made by bending pieces of tubing and welding them together, but cast cleats are designed to belay sheets correctly. As we mentioned previously, steel cleats can be coated with epoxy powder to increase their chafe resistance. Cleats made of cast iron should only be bolted on, since they are too brittle to weld. Steel and stainless cleats can be welded onto the deck, or, if their location is not quite set, can be bolted in place after the winches and running rigging are installed.

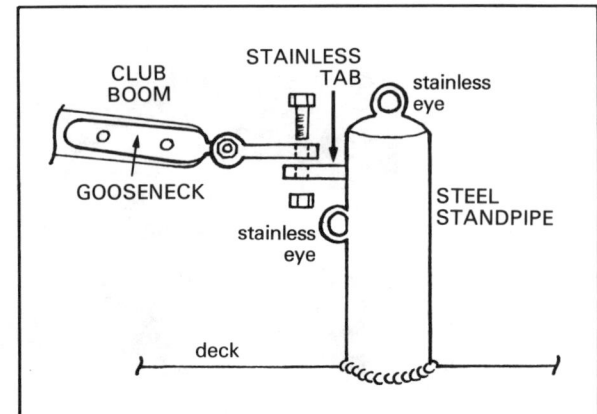

Fig. 9-22. *A simple design for the jib pedestal.*

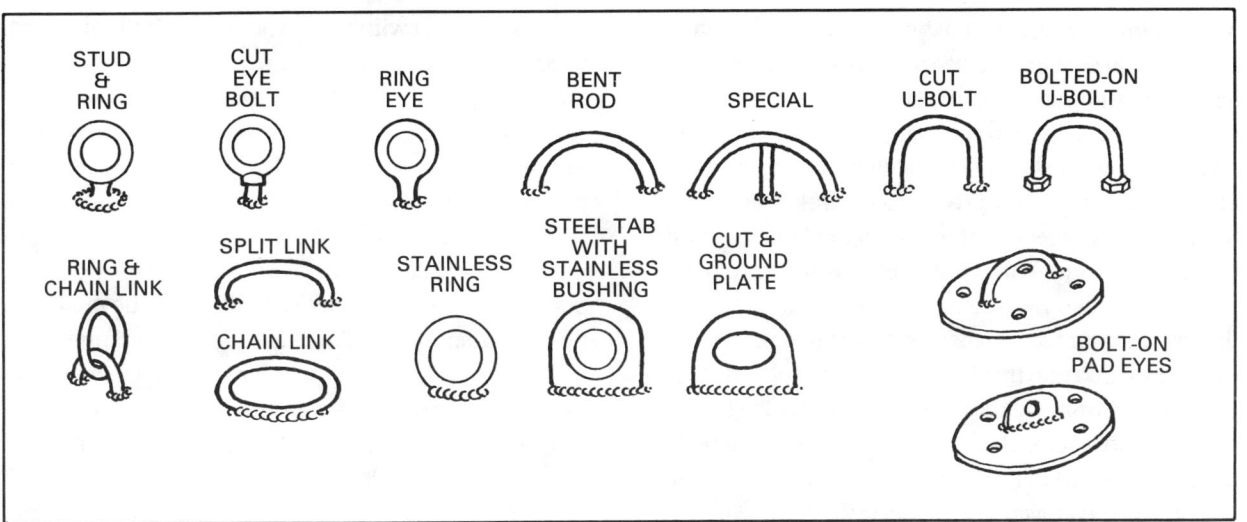

Fig. 9-23. *The many methods of fabricating eyes.*

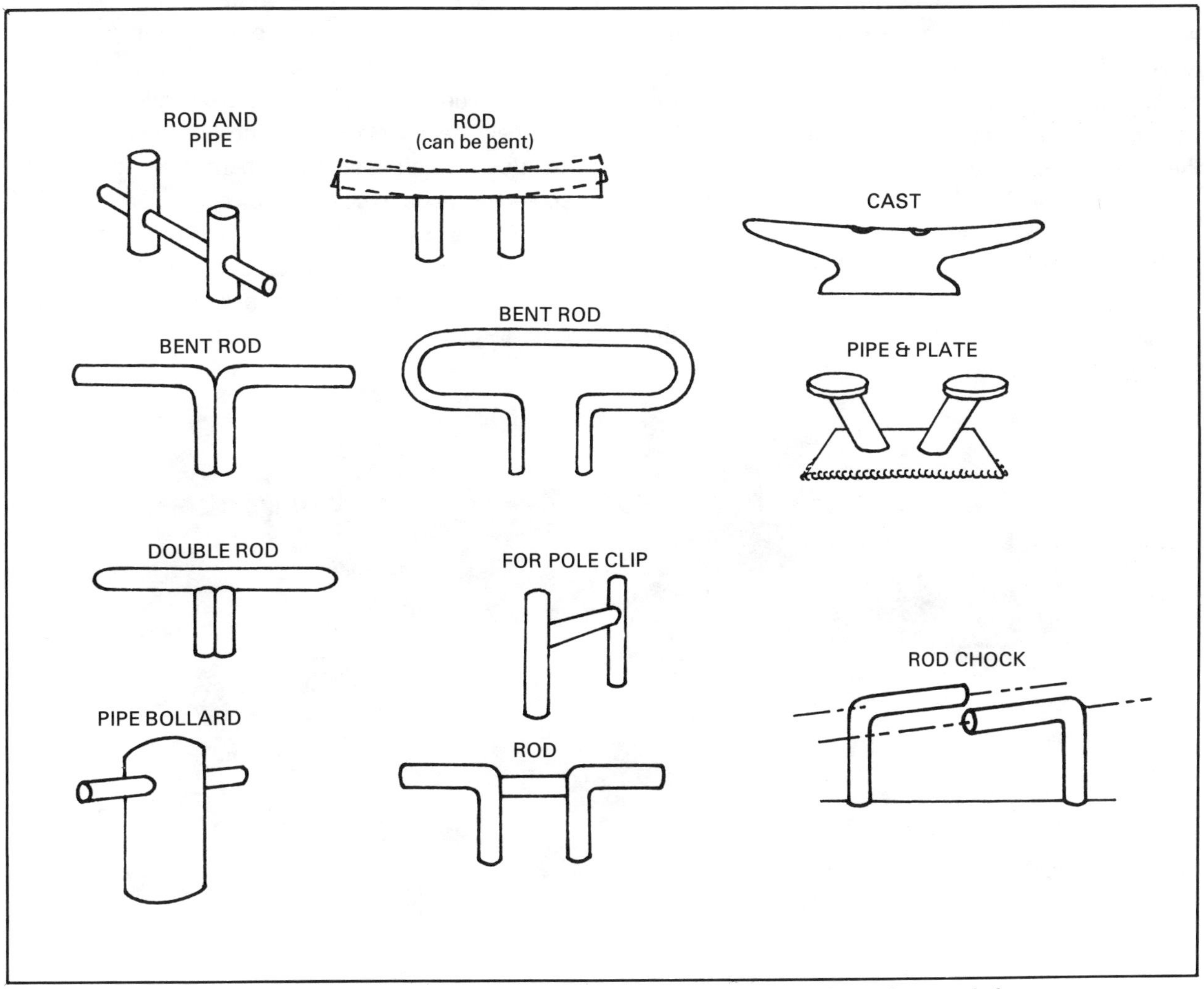

ROD AND PIPE

ROD (can be bent)

CAST

BENT ROD

BENT ROD

PIPE & PLATE

DOUBLE ROD

FOR POLE CLIP

ROD CHOCK

PIPE BOLLARD

ROD

Fig. 9-24. *Cleats can be fabricated out of a variety of steel and stainless steel shapes.*

167

Sheet *travelers* are also basic items that are usually non-integral so that they can be removed for repair. A self-tending jib should have a small traveler, similar in design to the one used with the main. For split rigs, another traveler should be installed for the mizzen. Stainless or aluminum production traveler tracks are preferable, but steel rod or pipe bent to a fair curve can be used. The center area of a steel traveler could have a stainless section welded in to handle the chafe. Although this saves some cost, using an all-stainless rod traveler welded into the deck would be simpler. A stopper could be welded at each end of the top of the traveler; these can be covered with a decorative turk's head or other ropework. The *genoa slide track* or fairlead eye may need to be moved, so it is usually bolted down with ample bedding to the deck or gunwale. These production tracks are usually made of stainless or aluminum and have fairlead blocks that lock into the track as they slide along.

Winch pads are easily fabricated of steel, but wood pads mounted on the coaming with studs or bolts are nicer. Solid rod can be welded to the deck, threaded on top, and inserted through the plate mount to receive the winch, although proper alignment of the winch makes the bolt-on method more practical.

Boom chock gallows for the main and possibly for the mizzen vary immensely in design, and, like travelers, can be made of steel pipe or rod. The best designs use a mount welded to the hull and removable pipe sections attached to the mounts. 4–6″ high pipe sockets of the correct diameter with a drain hole at the bottom can be welded on for the mounts. If wood is used for the gallows, a bracket or tab must be welded to the proper place so it can be secured. The traditional cast bronze can also be used, as long as it is properly insulated from any steel mounts, since it does not have as many corrosion problems when used above the waterline.

A *mast pulpit* to hold belaying pins and provide support when a crew member is working can be mounted near the main mast. This fitting is most common on flush-deck designs, but it is handy on any sailboat. The most common design is stainless tubing bent fairly into a loop and welded or bolted onto the deck, although steel can be used if it is well-coated. A diagonal cross-support in the middle of the loop will help to stiffen the assembly. A wooden bracket to hold the belaying pins can be fastened to tabs welded to the pulpit.

Other Attachments and Cutouts

Stanchions are one of the primary safety features on a cruising boat, but loose, wobbly, or bent stanchions are all too common. It is much easier to eliminate these problems on a steel boat. A steel rod welded to mounts that have been welded to the deck is the best design. Stainless stanchions tend to get bent more often, so they should be made removable, since dents are very hard to remove when the stanchions are in place. Steel sockets can be welded to the deck and possibly connected to the bulwarks for added support. If hollow tubing is used, all the openings must be welded shut, whether the

Fig. 9-25. *A homemade car runs along this sheet traveler. Notice also the fine workmanship on the hand rail.*

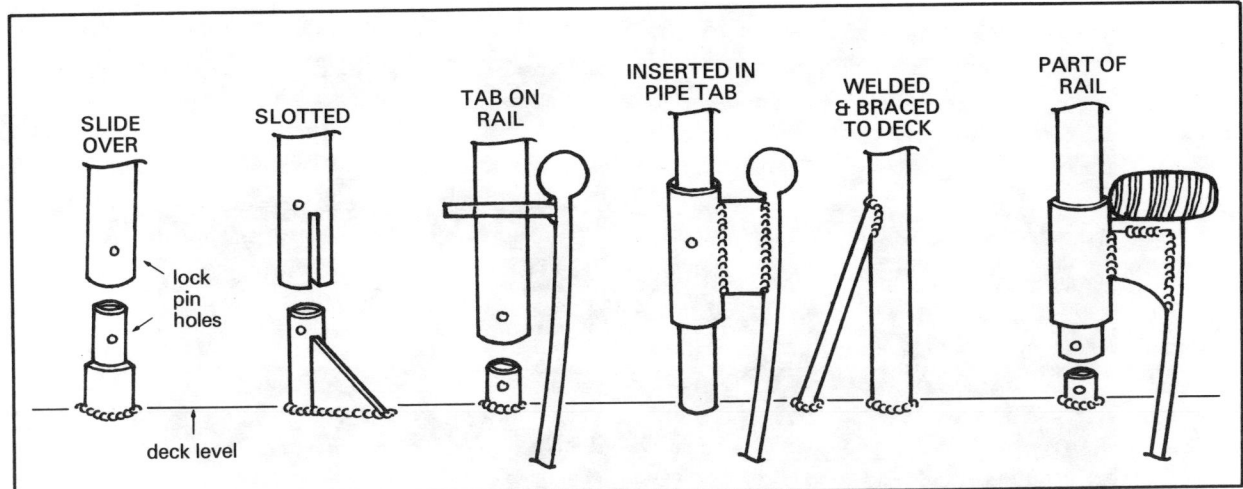

Fig. 9-26. *A variety of designs for the stanchion mounts.*

tubing is stainless or mild steel. Stanchion bases can be constructed in many ways, as shown in Fig. 9-26.

Pulpits can be found at both the bow and stern (where they are called pushpits), depending on the length of the bowsprit and boomkin. Stainless steel is generally used for pulpits, although mild steel can be used if the yachty look isn't important. The tube can be bent by a builder, so that those expensive production pulpits don't need to be purchased. However, thin-walled tubing tends to buckle when it is bent (see Chapter 22).

Electrical hookups for running lights, masthead light, bow, anchor, and stern lights, and spotlights will require cutouts and small pipe inserts in the proper places, usually in the cabin sides. If possible, the wires for different lights should be grouped so that they can exit through the same opening.

The *AC power hookup* will be important to some boat owners. A good-sized hole will need to be cut out to allow for an extra insulation sleeve around the AC plug-in box, unless the outlet box already has a phenolic casing. These plugs can be either screwed or bolted in place with lots of bedding all around them.

Dinghy or life raft mounting pads are usually made of wood. They can be secured to welded studs or bolted on. *Davits* for securing the dinghy are rarely used on cruising boats. However, if you choose to have one, a

Fig. 9-27. *This* Departure 35 *has a pushpit welded to deck tabs. The stanchions are also mounted on tabs to which a wood gunwale will be attached. All the hatches have been covered for painting.*

Fig. 9-28. *Sturdy davits are welded to the stern of this pilothouse schooner.*

steel pipe assembly like a very tall traveler works well. Take a look at how ferry boats secure their lifeboats.

CABIN AND COCKPIT ATTACHMENTS

For a vessel with a steel cabin and cockpit, most of the cabin and cockpit attachments and weldments are easily completed. If the boat design combines a fiberglass or wood cabin, bolt holes will be needed along the carlin to secure the cabin to the deck, and most of the items mentioned below would be bolted or screwed in place.

Plumbing and Engine

Most of the work for the plumbing and engine involves cutting out sections of plate. Cutouts needed for plumbing are *tank breather outlets* in the cabin wall and *cockpit scupper drain outlets* on the cockpit sole. Tank breathers can be sandwiched in place with a threaded backing ring, much as a car ignition switch is held in place. The cockpit scupper drains are commonly short pieces of pipe to which flexible tubing is clamped and led to a seacock. However, in a cockpit with a high sole that required no bends in the tubing, a schedule-80 pipe can run from the scupper drain straight down to the bottom of the hull. With this design, there is, in effect, a hole straight through the boat, but the water never rises far enough to flood the cockpit. These scupper drains are inexpensive and eliminate one seacock.

For the engine, cutouts will be needed in the cockpit for the *engine ignition panel* (if designed to be visible from the helm), *engine controls and throttle*, and *engine access plate*. A nice engine panel can be mounted in a recess in the side of the cockpit and fitted with a glass (Lexan) cover to protect the instruments from spray. The controls are often mounted on the binnacle, which usually is fastened mechanically over the pedestal. If an engine access plate is cut in the cockpit floor, it should be secured with bolts drilled through holes spaced 2-3″ apart, gasketed with neoprene, and stiffened with flat bar or angle bar underneath. This access plate can also be made of aluminum so that it is easier to remove.

The only other hole that might be required in the cockpit would be for a *shaft lock control*. Shaft locks

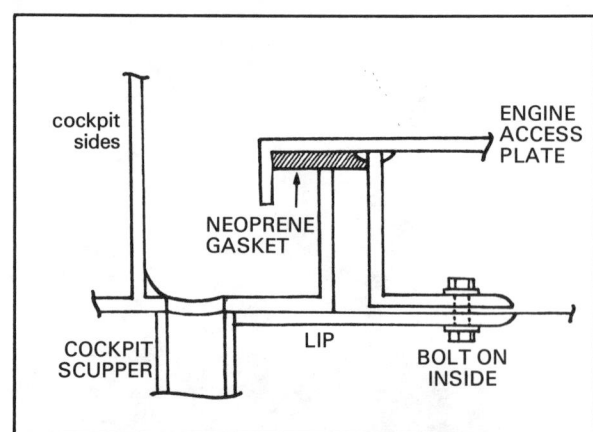

Fig. 9-29. *The engine access plate must be carefully joined to the cockpit sole if it is to be watertight. The scale is greatly exaggerated in the illustration.*

Fig. 9-30. *The soft corners in this cockpit will be appreciated by the crew. Shown on this boat built by Waterline Yachts are the stern propane locker, cockpit locker opening, and engine panel. Each are designed with proper drainage in mind.*

keep the shaft and propeller from revolving when the boat is sailing. This helps to extend the lifetime of the transmission and decreases propeller drag.

Ventilation and Lighting

Portholes can be purchased, but non-opening ports can be fabricated at a good cost savings. Since it is almost impossible to find galvanized opening ports, bronze or aluminum is usually chosen. Portholes can either be bolted on flush or to *porthole flanges* welded in place. The lip design of the flange depends on the type of porthole used, but steel angle bar bent around the inside of the opening is a very simple and effective method. The spigot cast into production portholes serves no purpose on a steel boat, so it must be cut off. Then the ports are bolted to the steel angle bars. Exterior cover rings can be machine-screwed in place or excluded altogether. The only tricky part of installing opening ports in slanted cabin sides is making sure that water is not trapped around the porthole. Some portholes are designed with slanting spigots, and in this case the angle bar frame can be bent to conform to the angle of slant. For a non-opening port, Lexan can be bedded firmly and secured to the steel. Once again, a cover ring is nice but not necessary.

A *stove stack cutout* will be needed for the cookstove or heater, and, if you are using a propane flash water heater, it also must be vented to the outside. A steel lip made from a cut pipe section will serve nicely here for attaching a stack. Small holes for securing a charlie noble or similar ventilator can be drilled in the lip. Another variation incorporates an air box to keep water out. A flush-mounted fitting into which the stack pipe can be screwed can also be installed.

Fumes from your cookstove or head also must be led outside through a vent. The hole must be cut to the correct size for a proper leakproof fit.

Steering and Mooring

A pad or doubler can be used in the cockpit around the cutout for the *pedestal/binnacle stand*, but bedding the pedestal and bolting it directly to the cockpit sole is simple and adequate. If a pedestal is not used, holes for the steering leads will have to be cut where the leads enter the hull. For tiller steering, a schedule-40 or -80 pipe insert with the proper bearing will be necessary. If a self-steering wind vane is used, eyes or stainless steel *fairleads* will be needed for connecting the tiller lines to the wheel drum or tiller. These fairleads are usually integral, but a lot depends on the cockpit layout.

Rigging and Sail Handling

Exterior hand rails on the cabin top can be made of wood, which is pleasant to handle and softens the lines of the steel cabin. These rails are either bolted down or fastened to studs. Mild steel tubing can also be used for rails, since on them chafe is not a problem and welding is quite simple. A *mast collar* on the cabin top is easily constructed of a steel pipe section or bent flat bar or angle bar. Fairlead blocks mounted either directly on the cabin or attached to welded eyes or tabs can be used to run halyards to the cockpit. Wooden or stainless rod *whisker pole and spinnaker pole mounts* bolted on or attached to studs help prevent chafe on the sails.

Other Attachments and Cutouts

If a removable dodger is installed ahead of the cockpit, *dodger tabs or flanges* with holes drilled in them will be needed to bolt the dodger down. Studs work well for securing a wood base as long as the design is correct. *Spray shields* can be handled similarly. It doesn't make much sense to have the actual dodger or shield integral.

Holes or tabs may be needed for securing the *cockpit spotlight socket, drink box,* and *non-integral coaming or cockpit lockers.* Except for the spotlight, these items are usually made of wood. All *cockpit locker openings,* including the *sail locker,* need proper flanges or drain lips to keep water out. Eyes or lips will also be required for securing wood *gratings* on the cockpit sole and for keeping *cushions* on the cockpit seats. Lighter items like cushions, awnings, and plastic covers can also be fastened with stainless steel snaps, one end of which is fastened in a small threaded hole with machine screws. A *cockpit table* could be mounted with a flange on a pipe section secured to the cockpit sole. However, a simpler arrangement uses a slip-in or flip-down table secured to the pedestal.

For a nice, purely decorative touch on a steel boat, wooden *eyebrows* can be fastened on the upper cabin sides above the portholes to enhance the lines and lower the apparent height of the cabin. These are usually through-bolted to the cabin side. The holes in the plating should be threaded for extra holding power.

PRE-BLASTING CHECK LIST

Although the list of 96 integrals discussed in this chapter may be incomplete, it covers most of the items attached to the hull, deck, and cabin. The forethought and planning required to make a list like this for your boat will help to prevent unnecessary problems with installation. However, there is always more than one way to do something, and trial and error, although not the best method, is very common.

You can ask yourself the following questions to make sure that nothing is missed as you're developing a list of attachments or preparing for the coating process.

1. Is stress relief built into all the areas of stress concentration? Doublers, inserts, or stiffeners may be needed underneath davits, winches, mooring bitts, chainplates, windlass mounts, or mast steps. The answer to this question can be found in the construction plans.
2. Have you decided on the type and size of the wind vane, windlass, portholes, vents, and stanchions that will be used so that tabs are correctly placed and the proper-sized holes are drilled?
3. Is the ballast completely installed? Is there a way to secure it?
4. Have all integral fuel and water tanks, the skeg, and the rudder been installed and pressure-tested?
5. Are the mounts for all non-integral tanks correctly cut, assembled, and positioned?
6. Are the stern tube and engine mounts correctly positioned for engine/shaft installation?
7. Are all necessary stainless items welded on, ground smooth and covered with duct tape?
8. Are all tabs and holes ready for non-integral joinery?
9. Are all integral steel appendages complete?
10. Are all necessary studs and tabs welded in?
11. Are all holes drilled for mechanical fastening? (Remember, there is some flexibility in when the holes can be drilled.)
12. Has the welding been done well enough so that nondestructive testing isn't necessary (for example, there are no pinholes in the welds)?
13. Are all sharp corners rounded off enough to hold the paint?
14. Is there a way to install the engine and interior bulkheads?
15. How fair does the hull look? Will filler be needed to help fair the hull or only at fillet joints around the cabin and cockpit coaming?

Once all these questions (except the last one) are answered "yes," the hull can be prepared for blasting and painting.

—Chapter 10

Coating Systems

In the last few decades, incredible improvements have been made in marine coating systems, leading to a confusing array of products. No boat is given only a single coat of paint; many different layers form a paint system that is a barrier between the steel hull and the corrosive marine environment. Each part of the system must not only perform certain functions but must be compatible with the coatings which precede and follow it. This system may include layers of metallizing or galvanizing, and special coatings are also available for insulation, tanks, fire resistance, and anti-fouling.

Different systems, specially formulated to work together, are available from many of the major paint companies under their special brand names, but the generic products are about the same. However, some companies have more expertise with one type than another: some deal more in "yachty" paints (polyurethanes and enamels), while others specialize in paints for work boats (zincs and epoxies). Of course everyone is looking for the perfect bottom paint.

Paint manufacturers usually prepare a product data sheet for each of their different formulations. These spec sheets are available either from a chandlery handling the brand or from the maufacturer or distributor. A data sheet is a gold mine of information, listing the paint ingredients, required surface preparation, application procedures, coverage and the range of service for the paint.

The special properties of the paint that make it appropriate for certain uses are also included.

FUNCTIONS AND PROPERTIES OF PAINT

The primary function of a coating system is to protect steel from the harsh elements of a corrosive environment. But it doesn't have to be ugly to protect—coatings can be decorative too. The essential properties of the paint and the specific performance desired from it determine the proper coating system for a steel vessel.

The marine environment poses some of the most severe challenges to a paint system. Constant washing with spray, immersion in salt water, sunlight, fouling, high humidity and condensation, chemical pollution in ports, extremes changes in temperature, severe mechanical abuse, corrosive attack—all are constantly present. A marine coating system has to be tough to protect a metal hull.

Every paint has certain essential properties that allow it to function in a specific way: density, dispersion of solids, percentage of solids, viscosity, film thickness, tack (liquid behavior), sandability, and drying rate. These properties are combined to create marine paints with the characteristics shown in Table 10-1.

Other paint properties affect application of the coating. The shelf life of a paint determines how long it can be stored safely in its container at normal temperatures (it can be many months). Pot life regulates how long after opening and mixing the paint will be usable. Drying time is subdivided into three stages: tack time, when the paint is not affected by dust; overcoating time, which varies with each paint; and final cure time, after which it's ready to meet the elements. A paint's flash point (the temperature above which the vapors will ignite) can influence application procedures and safety precautions.

Paint does have weight, and there is enough paint on a boat for the weight to add up. Spec sheets generally list the weight per gallon, and this figure can be used to determine the total weight of the paint used. Designers often add this figure into the designed displacement of a vessel.

The specific performance desired from the coating system depends on the area on which it is used. The vessel can be divided into different areas with different coating requirements: bottom, boot top or splash zone, topsides and freeboard, weather deck, exterior superstructure, and interior. Boot tops and splash zones are exposed to polluted surface water, wave slap, oxygenation, ultraviolet light, and mechanical damage from docks, floating debris, and the like. Temperature changes are also more extreme in this area. Therefore, a very durable paint with good chemical resistance and adhesion is needed here. For topsides, gloss and color retention are more important, while the deck area must be tough

and able to resist UV rays. Although the interior is somewhat protected, the coatings used on the interior steel must provide excellent corrosion resistance, especially in the bilge. The paint used under an anti-foulant must prevent any electrochemical reaction between the heavy metals in the anti-foulant and the steel hull. It must also have excellent adhesion and hardness to resist scratches and peeling underwater. Each area can be analyzed in a similar fashion to determine the specific functions that the coating must perform.

But no matter how carefully you plan the coating system, unless the steel is properly prepared to accept the paint, the lifetime of the coating system will be reduced and the time required for maintenance increased.

SURFACE PREPARATION

In almost all cases, premature coating failure is due to faulty preparation and improper application of the primer. The steel surface must allow a continuous coating to develop, since discontinuities, even in the primer coat, will eventually lead to failure. The surface must be smooth; the slightest protrusion will disrupt the coating continuity. But it must also have the right surface profile for physical adhesion of the first layer of paint.

Pits, pinholes, and gouges must be welded shut, and they and the weld zones ground smooth before beginning final surface preparation. All sharp and irregular

---

Table 10-1.   THE FUNCTIONS OF PAINT

► Compatible with both the material being covered and the coatings that will follow, acting as a barrier coat if necessary.

► Good adhesion to the underlying surface.

► Easy to apply by commonly used methods.

► Continuous and nonporous film with no weak spots or holidays when dry.

► Consistent spread.

► Neutral and nonconductive so that no electric current can pass through the coating (especially important for primers).

► Flexible enough to withstand thermal expansion and contraction without rupturing.

► Resistant to abrasion so that the coating will not scratch, mar, or wear down.

► Capable of providing a proper anchor pattern for coatings that will follow.

► Reasonable resistance to weathering, sunlight, UV rays, chemicals, oils, detergents, contamination, grease, acids, alkalis, water vapor, high-speed loss of adhesion, and temperature changes.

► Decorative texture and gloss (primarily required of top coats).

► Readily available at a reasonable cost from sources in different ports. (If it's not, a supply will need to be carried on board.)

Fig. 10-1. *This* Chatam 34 *is ready for blasting and painting. All weld zones have been ground smooth, and all corners beveled.* Courtesy of Metanav

edges and corners should be beveled to promote paint adhesion, since coatings tend to sag away from sharp corners, both concave and convex. Crevices and corners often show the first signs of coating failure, so careful attention here will be repaid.

There are many ways to prepare the steel surface mechanically and chemically. Some mechanical methods smooth rough areas and imprint a surface profile on the metal, as well as clean the surface. Others must be followed with chemical treatments to ensure cleanliness. All mill scale and rust must be removed, and the metal must be spotlessly clean, since any oil or grease will interfere with film forming. Chemicals can be used to etch the correct anchor pattern into the surface or to change the surface pH, since all paints except catalyzed epoxies demand a neutral surface for good adhesion. The acidity or alkalinity of the surface can be found by testing with litmus paper, and can usually be changed by flushing with fresh water or steam. However, sometimes chemical treatment is necessary.

Mechanical Methods

Hand Cleaning

The wire brushes, scrapers, knives, chisels, chipping hammers, and sandpaper that go to sea in a maintenance kit should all be available during construction for quick clean-up. Using these hand tools can be frustrating on large jobs, but they are very practical for smaller ones. Tightly adhering paint and rust are difficult to re-

move by hand, but paint remover followed by an old wood chisel can work on restoration projects. Old paint can also be loosened by carefully torching the surface or using a heat gun.

Power Cleaning

A wire brush attached to a rotary drill will not remove intact mill scale, but it will clean out loose materials and rust. It is especially useful over irregular surfaces such as bolt heads. Wire brushes and disks are available in a variety of sizes and shapes to fit in odd spaces. Buffing pads can also be attached to shine up any stainless fittings.

Grinding is the most common way of preparing small surface areas. This procedure smooths out all rough edges, protruding weld beads, bits of slag, and rough corners, allowing the paint to adhere well. Grinding will also remove intact mill scale. But care must be taken not to overgrind an area to a polished, glossy surface to which paint cannot hold. Eye protection with goggles is essential when grinding.

Impact tools like chippers, scalers, and needle guns work well on hard or brittle contaminants like rust, mill scale, or weld slag, but they are very slow, and the impact can drive particles into the metal. High-quality rotary impact scalers are expensive but do a better job. However, even they may leave gouges with sharp burrs.

Water-Blast Cleaning

In water-blasting, a high-pressure stream of water is directed on the area to be cleaned. Its best use is for removing old paint, not for washing away tightly adhering rust. Water-blasting is particularly efficient on irregular surfaces. The results are comparable with those obtained using power tools, but no dust is produced and no abrasives are needed. But this method leaves the surface of the steel wet, and the hull must be dried prior to painting. One of its advantages is that water-blasting can be used in commercial areas that do not allow sandblasting. Low-pressure water-blasting is often used to clean hulls during haul-outs.

Sandblasting

Sandblasting (abrasive blast cleaning) is simply the best surface preparation method, since all contaminants and corrosion products are removed from the surface and a good anchor pattern of microscopic ridges is left for the primer coat. If pre-primed plate is used, only the weld zones need a full blasting. The rest of the steel receives a light sweep-blasting to clear away any oil, grit, or other contaminants.

Although the process is usually referred to as "sandblasting," different types of abrasives are used. The surface profile or anchor pattern (that is, the roughness of the steel) depends on the type of abrasive used, measured by mesh size, and the force with which it hits the surface.

Sand (siliceous abrasive) is the most inexpensive and commonly used abrasive. It has a semi-sharp shape, but it breaks down too rapidly to be reused. (Besides, it's faster and cheaper to use a new bag.) Mesh size 16-30 silica sand gives an anchor pattern approximately 1½ mils deep. Strained, washed beach sand can be used, but it will leave a residue of salts on the surface. No. 16 sand, available at lumber stores, is more practical. The clean-up after blasting with sand is a lengthy process, although the blasting itself goes quickly.

Table 10-2. TOOLS FOR SANDBLASTING

BASIC
Sandblasting unit with hoses, nozzles, and
   water separator
Generator (diesel or gasoline)
Sandblasting suit with respirator and hood
Abrasives
Screens

OPTIONAL
Tumbler for small items like fittings

Refractory slag or grit, although a bit more expensive than sand, contains none of the free silica that can cause lung disease, and copper grit gives a deeper surface profile than sand. This abrasive is available under the trade names Copper Blast, Copper Slag, Green Diamond, and Garnet. It does take longer to cover the same surface area with grit than with sand.

Crushed steel shot is irregular, sharp, crushed iron or steel, with capabilities comparable to those of sand. Although these metallic abrasives are more expensive initially, they can be reused many times.

Choosing the abrasive that will give the proper surface profile for the selected paint system is important. A surface that is too rough has peaks that break the coating continuity, but if the profile is too shallow, adhesion will be poor. The paint manufacturer may recommend a certain anchor pattern—pay attention to it. An anchor pattern 1½ to 3½ mils deep is suitable for most coating systems. Thick coal tar epoxies tolerate a deeper, rougher surface profile, while the thinner vinyls and urethanes demand low profiles. A depth micrometer, Elcometer, surface profile comparator, or replica tape can be used to check the profile.

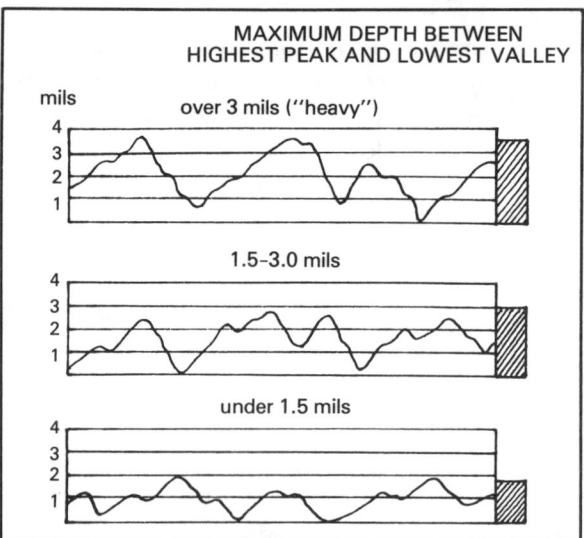

Fig. 10-2. *These somewhat exaggerated examples of surface profiles (also called "anchor tooth patterns") show the surface of the steel after blasting with abrasives.*

A special type of wheel-abraded blasting is done at plate warehouses, especially for plate that is going to be pre-primed. When plate thinner than 10-gauge is wheel-abraded, distortion is common because of the heat generated during the process, so some shops won't guarantee the fairness of even 10-gauge plate. 12-gauge steel will definitely distort when wheel-abraded.

Steel hulls are commonly dry-blasted in the open air with portable direct-pressure or gravity systems. In the direct-pressure method, a mixture of air and abrasive is forced together through a hose and out the nozzle. Gravity-blast systems use separate lines for air and abrasives. Gravity-blast has the wider spray pattern but hits the steel with less force than direct-pressure blasting, so it is more efficient before coatings that require a relatively smooth anchor pattern. Various nozzles, abrasives, and air pressures can be combined to get the correct surface profile, but a minimum of 80 psi should be delivered at the nozzle, and the nozzle should be properly rated for the air output of the compressor.

Vacuum-blast cleaning is a method by which the abrasive is reclaimed by a vacuum, leaving the work area clean and free from contamination. This method is very expensive and slow, and is mainly used in applications where a high degree of cleanliness is required or where delicate instruments could be contaminated by airborne dust. Small parts and fittings can be cleaned up in small vacuum-blast units called "tumblers."

Wet-blast cleaning, in which water is used to reduce dust, is also an option, but this method leaves a pile of wet, heavy sand to clean up. A rust inhibitor (usually solutions of chromic acid or sodium and potassium dichromates with a trace of phosphate and nitrate) can be added to the water. But rust inhibitors only protect the metal for a limited time, and the surface must be blown dry, wiped clean, and painted as soon as possible.

Any sandblasted surface must be coated as soon as possible, since rust can begin to form in as little as four hours, especially if the humidity is high. Unless the entire hull, inside and out, can be blasted, the abrasive cleaned up, and the primer applied within these time limits, the blasting will have to be broken up into stages so that the steel can be properly coated.

The hatches, portholes, and other openings allow the abrasives to flow from the outside to the inside and, to a more limited extent, from the inside out. Therefore it may be more practical to blast the exterior first. Any sand or grit that gets inside can be cleaned out after the interior is blasted, and there is no risk of damaging the interior primer. The exterior primer should be allowed to cure before anyone climbs over into the interior. The small amount of abrasive that may leak out when the interior is blasted can easily be swept away. If the interior must be blasted first, special clamps (illustrated in Fig. 10-3) can be fitted over large openings to keep out the sand and grit from the exterior blasting. Small holes can be covered with navy-grade duct tape; parti-

ally cured silicon sealant is also reputed to work well for this purpose.

Once the blasting is complete, the sand or grit must be completely removed before priming begins. Dust can be wiped from the steel surface with a clean rag, but blowing it away with dry compressed air is a better method. Using buffing pads on drills or grinders to clear away dust may change the surface profile of the metal. Acid etching with a 5–10% solution of phosphoric or muriatic acid helps to remove dust that cannot be blown away, but it should not be necessary if the blast job was done properly. For small areas that might be treated during repairs, a good wipe-down with alcohol or mineral spirits is a simple method to use; oily cleaners will recontaminate the surface.

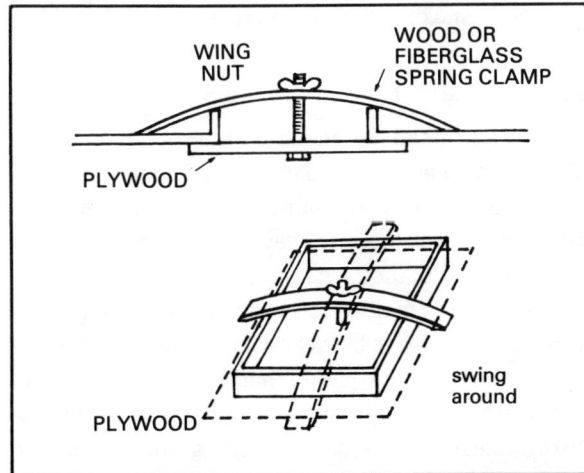

Fig. 10-3. *Side and top views of a type of home-made clamping device that can be used to cover large openings during blasting. A wood spring clamp can be cut with a bandsaw, and the clamping arm rotates to different positions so that the area under the clamp can also be painted.*

Special safety precautions are a must during the sandblasting and clean-up. A good abrasion-proof canvas suit with a built-in respirator is required, since inhaled abrasives cause lung disease. There are a variety of helmets to choose from, some of which are better than others. Professional sandblasters work hard for their wages, and there will rarely be a case in which it's not worth the money to contract the job out.

Chemical Methods

Oil and grease can be removed from small areas by chemical means. With the exception of solvent cleaning, the chemicals react with the base metal and leave a deposit on the surface. In some cases the surface compound must be removed, while in others it enhances coating adhesion.

Solvent Cleaning

Solvents, which can be applied by wiping, dipping, or spraying, dissolve oils and greases, and the residue is then wiped off the metal surface with a rag. Mineral oil and turpentine are often used, but they do leave their own oily deposits. Naphthas and ketones remove oil better, but are very toxic; they will not remove rust, mill scale, or non-oil contaminants. None of these chemicals can be reused, and all are highly flammable and explosive. Most paint removers must contain strong chemicals, although denatured alcohol is sometimes successfully used to remove vinyls, chlorinated rubbers, thermoplastic coatings, and varnish.

Alkali Cleaning

Synthetic alkali detergents with a sodium or potassium base convert oil and grease into a water-soluble soap. Most commercial paint strippers are caustic sodium hydroxide solutions. They are efficient and free of toxic fumes, but they are not very effective for removing heavy oils. Small objects that have been coated with oil-based paints can be cleaned by immersing them in a tank of detergent solution that is heated to speed up the action. Other application methods include spraying, using a steam gun, or hand-brushing small areas. The clean surface must be neutralized with acid after using any alkali solvent.

Acid Cleaning

Acid cleaners remove surface contaminants including rust on steel surfaces by reacting with the oxide corrosion products. Acid cleaning also etches the surface and leaves a corrosion-resistant deposit. Etching enhances the anchor pattern, and the surface film that is deposited is a good base for subsequent paint applications.

These cleaners usually have phosphoric, hydrochloric, or muriatic bases. The hydrochloric and muriatic types generally must be diluted before application. Allowed to dry overnight, Ospho (a trade name for phosphoric dichromate) converts rust into inert iron phosphate. Acid-cleaning is a good substitute for blasting when a small rusted area is to be treated, and it can be used successfully for restoring old steel hulls whose surfaces are in varying conditions. Acid cleaners are extremely caustic, so dilution directions should be carefully followed and hands protected with gloves.

Pickling is a more sophisticated type of acid-cleaning in which the item to be cleaned is immersed in a dilute acid solution, such as sulfuric acid. Since entire hulls can't be pickled, this process will not be very useful in boatbuilding, although pickled plate is available. Most coating systems perform well over pickled plate without blasting, although zinc primers require the anchor pattern left by abrasives.

Chemically cleaned and pickled surfaces are often pretreated before painting with conversion coatings such as zinc phosphate (for ferrous surfaces) or zinc chromate (for aluminum or zinc surfaces). These conversion coatings vastly improve the adhesion of organic coatings.

Other Cleaning Methods

In flame-cleaning, an oxyacetylene torch flame is passed over the surface to be cleaned. The intense heat lifts loose rust and mill scale and some tight mill scale by thermal expansion and explosive action. The results fall way short of blast-cleaning, but the method can be used to remove old paint from a surface or to drive moisture from the pores in the steel before priming. Gentle heating also can open up these pores and allow a primer to penetrate below the surface. Care must be taken so that the metal does not deform as it cools.

Steam-cleaning, which washes the surface with a jet of steam, is generally used to remove heavy contamination with oil, dirt, and grease, and in areas that are hard to wipe with solvents. Tightly adhering mill scale and rust are not removed, and a strong alkali must be added to the steam to lift off old paint. Steam-cleaning is inexpensive but more suitable for cleaning the engine than the hull.

Choosing the Cleaning Method

The right cleaning method depends on the material to be cleaned, how clean you want it, and what paint system will be used. For example, although zinc and other primers will adhere to freshly galvanized steel without pretreatment, the steel must be etched with acid or lightly sandblasted before coating with certain other paints. On the other hand, older galvanizing should not be etched, but rather should be chemically cleaned to remove contaminants and then primed.

For low-carbon steel, certain paint systems, like the vinyls, epoxies, and phenolics, require more stringent preparation (in other words, blasting) than do the alkyds

Table 10-3. CLEANLINESS STANDARDS	
WHITE METAL	All visible rust, mill scale, paint and foreign matter is removed from the surface.
NEAR WHITE	The surface is 95% free of any visible matter.
COMMERCIAL	Two-thirds of the surface is clean.
BRUSH OFF (OR SWEEP)	The base metal shows through tightly adhering mill scale, rust, or coatings as tiny, evenly distributed patches.

and epoxy esters. Sandblasting is usually required on new construction, although water-blasting may be sufficient for some coating systems.

Stainless steel should not be cleaned by any abrasive methods, since the protective oxide film would be removed. It should be masked off from blasting with navy-grade duct tape, and cleaned with solvents if necessary.

So how clean is clean? The Society of Naval and Marine Architects and Engineers, the Steel Structure Painting Council, the National Association of Corrosion Engineers and other groups have set internationally recognized standards of cleanliness. Hand tool-, power tool-, solvent-, and flame-cleaning all are expected to remove loose paint, rust, and mill scale. Blasting, which is recommended for corrosive atmospheres, is regulated by four standards, all of which are based on how clean and white the metal is (see Table 10-3).

Information about these standards is available in the reference materials published by the standard-setting groups. The organizations distribute photographic samples that can be compared with a blasted surface to determine the degree of cleanliness. Although a freshly blasted surface should not be touched, if you were to rub a clean, dry hand over it, your hand should come away clean.

Preparation of a new hull will probably include: inspecting the hull to make sure all pits and crevices have been welded up; hand- or power-smoothing all rough spots and sharp edges; sandblasting to the cleanliness standard recommended by the paint manufacturer for the primer coat; blowing dust away with compressed air where necessary; and applying the first primer coat immediately after blasting.

A GOOD PAINT JOB

Good paint application techniques on a properly prepared surface allow the paint to perform as expected. Once again, the product data sheets give information about the recommended techniques, including proper drying and curing times, overcoating times, and correct solvent and/or thinner. Each type of paint handles differently and may require special application methods. Many experienced painters have hands-on experience with these techniques and may depart slightly from the manufacturer's recommendations, but they make this decision based on knowledge of the past performance of the specific paint.

Proper film thickness, both wet and dry, is critical, since paint performance and corrosion resistance are directly related to this film thickness. In addition, some of the paint's desired functions can be weakened because of porosity caused by too thin a layer or because poorly cured spots have been created by uneven application. Excessively thick film can result in a different set of problems (especially with primers), that can include solvent entrapment, runs, orange peels, blistering, and shrinkage. Depending on the paint type, the recommended thickness ranges from a minimum of 1 mil (for pre-primers) to up to 30 mils (for anti-foulants). (A mil equals one-thousandth of an inch, i.e., 1 mil = .001".)

Each manufacturer formulates coatings to be applied in a certain film thickness and lists this information in product data sheets. If a thicker layer is desired, two or more coats of the proper film thickness should be applied or a high-build coating used instead.

The surface to be painted must be at the proper temperature before the coating is applied, usually 50–70°F or as recommended by the manufacturer. The moisture content of the air is also important, and painting should not be done at temperatures less than 5° above the dewpoint. Moisture condensation on the surface contaminates the paint, as does wind-blown dust and dirt.

Before painting begins, the paint must be mixed to make sure that all of the solids are suspended in the liquid vehicle. Some paints, especially high-solids paints like some zinc primers, require the use of an agitator so that mixing is continuous and the heavy particles cannot settle out of solution.

Table 10-4. DEFECTS IN PAINT

Like design, paint technology has its own vocabulary to describe the different appearances of paint. Some of these conditions are inherent in the paint, some are caused by deterioration due to outside influences, and some are caused by poor application techniques.

Bitty Paint contains bits of skin or foreign particles which project above the surface. "Peppery" describes small, evenly distributed bits. "Seedy" denotes bits which have developed in the paint or varnish during storage. Good filters and strainers are recommended to remove the bits from top coats.

Bleaching Loss of color in paint or varnish due to internal chemical action. Also, intentional lightening of the color with oxalic acid for decorative purposes.

Bleeding Undesirable staining or discoloration caused by the undercoat. Bituminous paints, wood preservatives, pigment dyes, and stains may cause this defect.

Blistering Formation of blisters in the paint caused by local loss of adhesion. The blisters can contain liquid, vapor, gas, or crystals.

Bloom Deposit that sometimes forms on glossy enamels or varnishes. It causes loss of gloss and dulling of color. Bloom can sometimes be removed by wiping the surface with a damp cloth.

Blushing A milky film caused by moisture condensation or precipitation of one of the solid components of the paint. It commonly occurs in lacquers.

Bridging Covering over an unfilled gap, crack, or corner with a film of paint. This leads to weakness in the coating that may eventually cause cracking.

Bubbling A temporary or permanent film defect in which bubbles of air or solvent vapor are present on the surface.

Chalking Formation of a powdery coating on the surface of the paint, caused by disintegration of the binder due to weathering. This is most common with epoxy top coats.

Cheesy Characteristic of a paint film that is mechanically weak and soft on top.

Cessing Defect in which the paint recedes from certain areas of the surface, leaving too thin a layer.

Clouding Development of cloudiness in a clear film; caused by precipitation of insoluble matter.

Checking Also called "cold checking." Development of hair cracks in a lacquer film when it is subjected to alternating temperatures.

Cracking Splitting of paint as a result of aging. There are five distinct types: 1) hair cracking, in which fine cracks usually do not penetrate the top coat; 2) checking, in which fine cracks are distributed in a pattern all over the surface; 3) cracking, in which the cracks penetrate at least one coat; may result in complete coating failure; 4) crazing, which resembles cracking with cracks that are deeper and broader; and 5) alligatoring or crocodiling, a more drastic type of crazing in which the many cracks produce the appearance of an alligator hide.

Erosion Paint is removed from the surface by the harsh environment. Results from the choice of a paint that is too soft.

Fading Process in which paint loses shine or gloss, usually because of the effect of UV rays.

Flaking Lifting of paint from underlying surface in the form of flakes or scales.

Holiday A gap in the film continuity.

Peeling Paint falls off in long peels.

Sagging Downward movement of paint after application and before drying; caused by uneven and excessive paint application.

Yellowing A change in the paint color due to age. This occurs with many varnishes and with some epoxies.

180

The choice of the proper tool, whether brush, roller, or spray gun, depends mostly on the type of paint, but also on the surface that is being coated.

Brushes are used for paints that are thick enough to stay in the brush but fluid long enough to flow out of the brush marks and then harden before the paint sags or drips. Brushes should be used for some primers so that the paint can be worked into the rough sandblasted surface. Many different sizes and shapes of brushes are available. The best quality brushes are easiest to work with, and they don't shed bristles into the paint.

For roller application, the paint must stay wet long enough to flow out of the roller pattern, but should be less fluid than when a brush is used so that it doesn't drip when picked up on the roller and applied. For flat, smooth surfaces, rollers can save time. They are available in different materials and thicknesses, from thin to thick. The disposable foam types can be used with success, especially with epoxy paints.

Table 10-5.   PAINTING EQUIPMENT

BASIC
    Sandpaper, wet and dry
    Sanding blocks
    Sanding disk pads for use with drill
    Paint filters and strainers
    Paint containers
    Brushes
    Rollers
    Roller tray
    Proper solvents

OPTIONAL
    Paint spray gun with hoses, canisters, regulators, pressure pot, and accessories
    Compressor with minimum of 8 cfm and 80 psi
    Generator (gas or propane)

Spraying is best for covering irregular surfaces, and the speed of application makes this method the best choice when a large area must be covered quickly. Two types of equipment, both powered by an air compressor are used for spray painting: air sprayers and airless sprayers. Airless sprayers aren't really airless; they work by atomizing the paint under high pressure rather than breaking it into droplets by mixing it with air at the nozzle, as air sprayers do. The compressor pump is usually powered by electricity or gas, although hydraulic and diesel compressors are also available. The compressor must be large enough to create sufficient pressure at the nozzle (a minimum of 8 cfm at 50 lbs.) to do the job ef-

ficiently. No matter which method is used, drop cloths and shields will prevent environmental contamination from overspray.

Airless spraying equipment is generally found only in large paint yards, since it is not as portable as air sprayers and is more expensive. Because of the high pressure involved, this method is very dangerous to the painter, especially if any part of the system should fail unexpectedly. The film thickness is more difficult to control since the paint is mixed in the tank rather than at the nozzle.

The primary advantage of airless spraying is supposedly less overspray, but the correct type of air spraying system, properly regulated, can also cut down on overspray. Doug Knight of Sierra Yachtwerks offers the following explanation of the pressure pot system:

Typically, a conventional sprayer will have too much overspray to be worthwhile for production painting of a boat. This is mainly because the sprayers that are used are left over from the automotive trades, where overspray is contained in a booth. The automotive sprayer with a siphon cup is only useful for really small jobs and touch-up work. The ideal conventional spray set—the pressure pot system—has no more overspray than airless systems.

The pressure pot setup consists of either a 2-, 3-, or 5-gallon paint tank (although for a portable system to take on the boat for maintenance a 2-quart pot is sufficient) that is fed with clean, dry air from a compressor. Moisture traps and filters must be used at all times.

Many pressure pot systems fail to work properly because the operator has failed to put together a proper system. The older-type air caps used in the gun are not capable of atomizing the fluid properly. Air caps are internal or external mixers, and the external types are more popular. The fluid needle and nozzle should be properly matched to the paint being used (manufacturers will often recommend a certain size nozzle). If the air cap, fluid needle, and nozzle are not properly matched, low production output or overspray can result. The air and fluid pressure must be regulated separately, and the regulators should be connected so that the spray air can be set from 40–70 psi and the fluid between 4 and 25 psi. The correct pressure to use again depends on the type of paint. Many pressure pot systems are sold with only one regulator for controlling both the air and fluid pressures at the same time. The end result is overspray, either on your car, your body, or someone else's boat.

The pressure pot system only functions properly with strained and filtered paints and clean equipment. The gun adjustments are easy once the complete setup is attained. Remember, overspray is a function of an improper or incomplete setup or dirty equipment.

Commercially built pressure pots are available for between $75 and $100, and guns can be purchased new for under $200. It's a good idea to have two guns, one for primers and epoxies and one for top coats.

All paints dry at different rates, and, naturally, the high-build coatings take longest. Low air temperature will slow down the drying process even more. Full curing of many paints may take days, although the paint will reach the dry-to-touch stage much sooner; some epoxies keep curing for a much longer time. The proper interval for overcoating depends on the exact formulation of the paint. It can be as little as one hour (zincs and chlorinated rubbers) or several years (some epoxies). The minimum overcoating time is more important than the maximum, since solvent entrament can occur if the paint is covered before all the solvent has evaporated.

Some paints, like epoxies, require that the previous layer be mechanically roughened with sandpaper before application. If overcoating has been delayed past the minimum overcoat time for any paint, some sanding may also be necessary.

Paint definitely involves you in the chemical world, and there are many nasties waiting to get you. Gases, liquid, powders, and dusts produced during paint application are health hazards, especially to the lungs and skin. Safety equipment like gloves, goggles, and masks are your defense. Flammable solvents used in some paints produce fire and explosion risks during storage, transportation, and use. Read the manufacturer's safety precautions and follow them very carefully.

When your good paint job is finished, be good to yourself. Many ingredients used in coatings are highly toxic, and safety precautions should be followed as closely during clean-up as in application. Resist the temptation to clean spatters off your skin using methyl ethyl ketone (MEK), trichlor ethylene (TEKE), or similar solvents. They do take the paint off quickly, but they are also absorbed through the skin and can carry toxic materials into your bloodstream. Acetone is also a strong solvent, and contact with it should be avoided. Mechanic's protective creams, like Invisible Glove, are very useful, since they wash off easily, carrying the stains and toxic chemicals with them. If you clean the paint off before the film is cured, turpentine, Goop, or granular cleansers can also be effective. Vinegar or lacquer thinner can be used to clean up epoxy.

SELECTING A PAINT SYSTEM

As we said at the beginning of this chapter, a boat receives not a single coat of paint, but rather is protected by a paint system. This system is composed of a number of layers, each of which has a specific function to fulfill. The exact number of layers and the thickness of each varies with the area of the boat that is being protected, so selecting the proper paint system can be a demanding task. Many people use whatever brand happens to be available at their local chandlery, and for most hull materials that works out well. But, since the coating system is one of the main ways to control corrosion in a steel hull, it is more important to choose a paint for its specific properties than because it's readily available.

The paint system for a steel hull can be divided into four categories: 1) primers, including wash primers and pre-primers; 2) intermediate coats; 3) top or finish coats; and 4) specialized coatings (as for anti-fouling or fireproofing). The coatings that will be carried onboard for touch-up and maintenance should also be considered part of the system, since they must be compatible with the original paints.

The first layer of any paint system is the primer coat. Primers basically fulfill two functions: protecting the metal and ensuring good adhesion of the paint system. But specific requirements for primers depend on whether the interior or exterior is being primed and whether the steel is above or below the waterline of the boat. An exterior primer must have good adhesion to the metal, appropriate flexibility, and the ability to retard corrosive action on the metal surface. In addition to these traits, an interior primer must also flow well so that it can get under frames and into corners and crevices. Some top coats require that specially formulated primers be used, and some primers demand specific top coats.

Traditional metal primers contain zinc pigments because the zinc provides galvanic protection to the steel if the coating is scratched through to bare metal. These primers have been proven successful above the waterline. However (as we will discuss later in this chapter), there are some questions about the advisability of us-

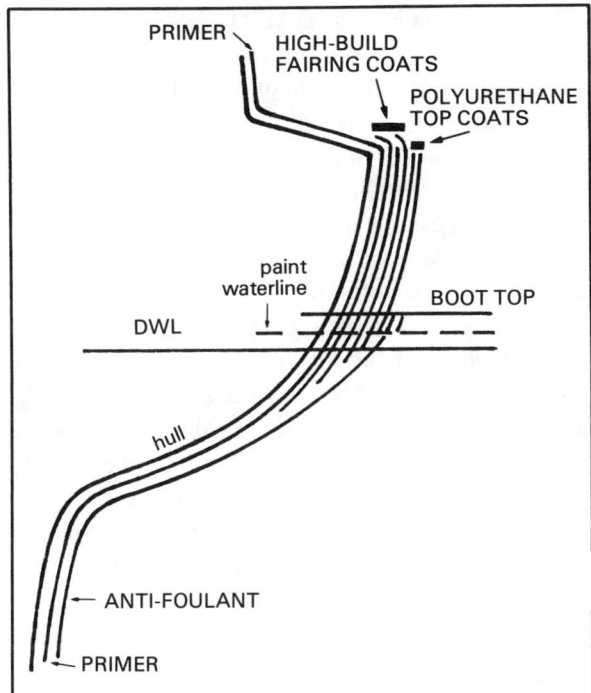

Fig. 10-4. *The different layers of a coating system for a steel hull. The topside layers are tapered out below the waterline, and the anti-foulant continues up over the design waterline. The boot top is generally given an extra coat of paint.*

ing zinc below the waterline, since contact between the zinc and salt water may cause top coats to blister. Some of the new epoxy formulations, especially the high-build and coal tar types, offer a similar level of protection without the problems of blistering, and they are being used increasingly on submerged steel surfaces. Theoretically, a zinc primer could be used above the waterline and an epoxy below, but the coating continuity might be compromised at the waterline, where these two primers meet.

If the plate has been pre-primed before construction, the primer must be compatible with the pre-primer used. The best pre-primers are those that can be welded through so that the paint does not have to be ground away from the weld zones. The zincs and epoxies used for primers are not good pre-primers, since they emit toxic fumes under the heat of welding and, in the case of zinc, cannot be successfully welded through. Most pre-primers are based on phenolic resins and are applied as very thin layers. Some of the pre-priming coat is removed when the steel is sweep-blasted to prepare it for receiving the primer coat.

Wash or etch primers were developed during World War II to provide quick, temporary protection during the

rapid construction of battleships. The thin film only protects the steel for a short time. Wash primers can also be used over metallized surfaces to promote adhesion of top coats.

On other substances, such as wood or concrete, primers act as sealants to bind, fill, or seal the base material so that the other layers of coatings are not drawn into its pores. The traditional alkyds or oil-based paints used for this purpose have fairly good bonding characteristics but somewhat limited resistance to corrosion and exposure. They cannot be followed satisfactorily with vinyls, epoxies, or other synthetic coating systems.

Fig. 10-5. *This hull, built with lap seams, has been given her first primer coat. The simple angle bar bracing tacked to the rub rail holds the hull up without interfering with the painting process.*

If "coving" filler is going to be used (for example, at the deck-cabin joint or to fair out the cockpit joints), it should be applied after the primer and before any other coats. If the filler should crack or peel, the steel underneath will remain protected by the primer.

The intermediate coats in a paint system can have several different functions. Often a coating is needed between two layers of paints, either because they are incompatible or because they do not bond well. This coating is called a "barrier" or "tie" coat, depending on its purpose. Tie coats are usually based on premium resins, such as those used in high-build vinyls and epoxies. They are very handy when incompatible paints must be used for repairs. Barrier coats are most often used between the hull and anti-foulants, which contain heavy metals that could react galvanically with the hull; the barrier coat prevents such interaction. Zinc primers must be overcoated with a barrier coat, both to protect the zinc and to allow a variety of top coats to adhere. On the other hand, epoxy primers also act as barrier coats, and anti-foulants can be applied directly over these paints. Epoxies can also be used as barrier coats over aluminum metallizing.

Intermediate coats can also be used to fair the topsides, although, realistically, only minor imperfections can be smoothed out. Up to three coats of epoxy are generally used for this purpose. After each coat has dried, the paint is sanded with a sanding batten or board to remove a small amount of paint from the high spots. Each subsequent coating and sanding tends to smooth out the hull by equalizing the high and low spots. Enough layers are applied to ensure that the minimum film thickness is present over any high spots even after sanding. If necessary, low spots can be further filled by local paint application. This process is a much better way to fair a hull than by using filler putty, especially when the plating is as fair as possible. It is really only critical when high-gloss, thin top coats (like polyurethanes) are used.

Top coats may contain the same resins as the primer and any intermediate coats, but they are formulated for gloss and hardness. However, top coats containing different resins than undercoats can be applied as long as they are compatible. For example, polyurethanes can be successfully applied over epoxy primers or intermediate coats as long as the epoxy color is close to that of the polyurethane, which is applied in very thin layers. If the top coat is to be used in the interior, less wear resistance is required, so less-expensive paints like the alkyds can be used. Top coats for decks can be mixed with anti-skid compounds, and epoxy-cork mixtures have been used for this purpose with mixed results. A non-skid sheathing (discussed in Chapter 12) can be glued down instead.

With so many different choices, the selection of a coating system can take some time and a great deal of research. The key to choosing the correct system is to find the simplest one. Then there are few problems with incompatibility, which will also help with maintenance.

COMPONENTS OF PAINT

Paint is a mechanical mixture of solid particles suspended in a liquid that dries to form an adhesive film, bonding the solid pigments and other additives to a surface. The liquid portion, called the vehicle, is a solution containing the binders or film formers that remain after drying and a volatile solvent that dissolves the binder and allows the paint to flow on smoothly. It is the binder that gives a paint its essential properties.

Although many different film formers can be included in a vehicle, oils or resins are used most frequently. Some vehicles contain both, some only oil, and some only resins. The generic name of the paint often tells what the film former is: for example, epoxy ester (epoxy resin and oil), vinyl (vinyl resin), oleoresinous (oil and resin), or coal tar epoxy (epoxy resin and pitch). These substances are also incorporated into other marine products such as glues, bedding compounds, insulating gaskets, and sheathings.

If only oil is used in a vehicle, the paint will be soft and slow-drying, with good flexibility, gloss, and resistance to water, soaps, chemicals, and other corrosive products. The most useful types are the drying oils, such as tung, linseed, or oiticia oil. Oils also improve the wetting properties of the paint and the leveling of the film so that application is easier. Most oils are derived from fatty acids, and their properties depend on the type of fatty acid used.

Resins are organic compounds (compounds containing carbon) that can have either a natural or a synthetic origin. Rosin is the most important of the natural resins, and it was traditionally used in bottom paints because it can be dissolved by water, allowing the anti-foulant to leach out. The many synthetic resins (alkyds, epoxies, polyurethanes, phenolics, vinyls, chlorinated rubbers, and others) are formed by chemical reactions. As with oils, different resins impart different properties to the paint. Synthetic resin-based paints are more suited to the marine environment than oil-based paints because they have better drying times, hardness, gloss, adhesion, and resistance to chemicals. However, applica-

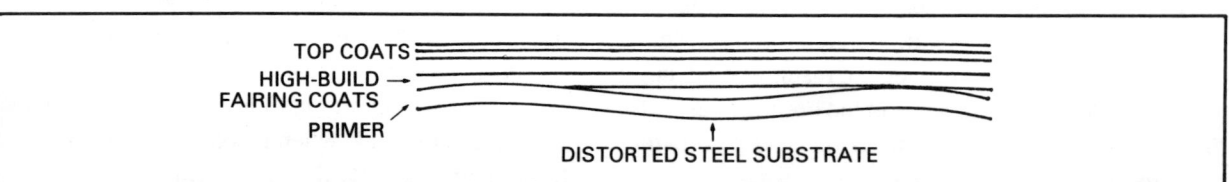

Fig. 10-6. *A section through an area of the hull that has been smoothed out by applying high-build fairing coats after the primer and before the top coats.*

tion temperature and time between coats is often more critical for resin-based paints.

Most resins are solid, and to become part of the liquid vehicle they must be combined with a solvent. Some solvents cause the resin to go into solution, while others produce emulsions or colloidal suspensions in which globs of liquid or particles of solid resins are suspended in the solvent. These volatile solvents also can act as thinners, if necessary reducing the paint viscosity for easier application. The solvent and thinner specified for a particular paint may be of different make-ups.

Either water or organic compounds are used as solvents. The major organic solvents include hydrocarbons (e.g., mineral oil), aromatics (e.g., distilled coal tar hydrocarbons), alcohols, esters, ketones (e.g., acetone or methyl ethyl ketone [MEK]), ethyl alcohol (used for dissolving shellac), or the terpenes (e.g., turpentine). The type of solvent and the percentage of the vehicle it makes up both influence the drying time, and solvents also contribute properties such as leveling and gloss.

Paints also differ in the method by which they dry—whether it's physical or chemical. Physical drying occurs as the volatile components of the vehicle evaporate, as happens with lacquers, emulsions like latex paints, and paints containing natural resins, vinyls, acrylic esters, chlorinated rubbers, or bitumen resins. In emulsion-type paints, the solvent (usually water) evaporates and the drops of film left behind float into each other. The film that is formed can be easily redissolved by solvents.

The most durable paints dry by chemical reactions like oxidation or curing. Paints based on drying oils harden as the oil changes from a liquid to a gel by absorbing oxygen from the air at room temperature. Oleoresinous varnishes and oil-modified alkyds are the most common examples of coatings that dry by oxidation. The various types of chemical curing can cause existing molecules to join together, can create new molecules, or can use catalysts to produce polymers (synthetic super molecules). For some resins (polyesters, amine-cured epoxies, and polyurethanes), the reaction takes place over a wide range of temperatures, but the catalyst in paints with thermosetting resins (epoxies, alkyds, acrylics, silicons) is only activated at specific temperatures. Some curing methods also require moisture to activate the catalyst. Many of these chemical curing methods produce what are called "convertible coatings"— coatings in which the binder in its final form differs chemically from the binder as it was originally applied.

Some resins are also thermoplastic. These solid resins (polyvinyls, polystyrenes, polyethylenes) are melted for application and then solidify as they cool. Paints based on thermoplastic resins stay plastic when cured and are easy to recoat, while thermosetting paints dry to a very hard finish.

In non-pigmented, clear coatings, nothing else will be added to the paint. But pigments are often used to give hiding power, decorative color, and specialized qualities, such as fire resistance (from antimony oxide), fluorescence, electrical insulation, or poison (tributyl tin

Fig. 10-7. *Choice of top coat color is a personal one; this photo shows that light and dark work well on fine steel hulls.*

on a ship's bottom). Pigments also fill space to help film continuity. The proportion of pigment to vehicle determines the type of gloss; as the percentage of pigment increases, the gloss diminishes. Varnishes and lacquers contain little pigment and dry to a high-gloss finish.

Many additives in various combinations are used in paint. Plasticizers are commonly added to increase the flexibility of the paint film. Some additives keep the paint stable in the can before use by preventing pigments from settling or separating and by keeping the paint liquid. The largest group of additives enhance paint application. For example, leveling agents help the paint to flow properly, while anti-settling agents prevent sagging of the paint as it dries. Wetting agents improve adhesion, and foaming agents inhibit the formation of bubbles. Driers speed up the oxidative drying process, which otherwise might take days. (Metallic soaps of cobalt, lead, manganese, calcium, zirconium, iron, zinc, and cesium are commonly used as driers. They act by increasing the paint's absorption of oxygen from the air.) The last group of additives acts after the paint is dry (for example, mildewcides prevent the growth of fungi on a painted surface).

Each type of paint is composed of a particular combination of vehicle, solvent, pigments, and additives. Lacquers are usually pure, cellulose film formers with solvents and additives, while stains contain a small amount of pigments and film formers. Gloss enamels have a high concentration of film formers with significant amounts of opaque pigments, while semi-gloss enamels contain fewer film formers and more pigments than high-gloss. Flat paints contain a great deal of pigment and a reduced number of film formers, so the pigments come off easily when the painted surface is washed. Primers are designed to make the surface more paintable, so they have a higher percentage of pigments. Primers are usually flat paint because the color and gloss seen in top coats would be wasted in a primer. Sealers seal off porous surfaces so that the suction caused by the porosity cannot affect subsequent coatings, and they therefore contain more film formers and less pigment than do primers.

TYPES OF PAINT

Oil-Based Paints

Oil-based paints have been the stand-bys in the marine trades for many years. The vehicle is a combination of natural or synthetic resins and oil; water resis-

tance decreases and durability increases in proportion to the oil content. These paints have poor resistance to acids and alkalis.

Oil-based paints cure by oxidation, and addition of drying oils to the paint increases the drying rate. Linseed oil, derived from flax seeds, is the oil most commonly used by itself as a wood preservative and as a component of a durable, non-sagging paint with fair weather resistance and medium gloss. Soybean oil, commonly used as the modifying oil in alkyds, has good drying properties. Tung oil, found in the fruit of a Chinese tree, has the most-resistant film of any of the common paint oils and has good gloss and durability. It is used where resistance to weathering is important, as in deck paint and spar varnish. Tung oil produces a better paint than oiticia oil, also derived from a fruit. Tall oil, a byproduct of the production of cellulose from pine chips, is another commonly used drying oil. Fish, safflower, and dehydrated castor oils have also been employed in the manufacturing of oil-based paints.

Oil-based paints are not recommended for use on steel hulls, but they could serve well as low-cost coatings for interior woodwork.

Latex Paints

Latex paints are water-based emulsions of rubber particles, which can be washed and thinned with water. Latex paints are available in all finishes, and many house paints are latexes. Some are sealants and can be used on canvas and asphalt surfaces. Latex paints offer an inexpensive option for interior top coats, but they aren't recommended for anything else. They definitely do not do well underwater or on exposed exterior surfaces.

Latex paints are often thought of as the only water-based emulsions. However, acrylic, styrene butadiene, and polyvinyl acetate resins are also contained in water-emulsion paints. Some primers that contain rust inhibitors are water emulsions.

Acrylic Paints

Acrylic resins are found in all types of coatings, and are both thermoplastic and thermosetting. The term "acrylic paint" commonly refers to a water-based emulsion of acrylic resins, although these resins are also soluble in some organic solvents. They have good gloss and color retention, and stand up very well to ultraviolet rays. However, acrylics cannot withstand severe weathering, and, although they are often used on exterior surfaces on land, they cannot be expected to hold up under severe marine conditions. However, the addition of silicon to acrylics does improve their weather resistance. Acrylics are often used as a clear finish on bright metals to prevent tarnishing. They can be applied over most other paints and are good on wood, but alkyd paints are better for this application.

Alkyd Paints

Alkyd paints are second to none in overall performance in areas with low abrasion and chemical contact, and represent the conventional primers, undercoats, and enamel top coats used on wooden boats. Most marine enamels are based on alkyd resins. These resins are very brittle, so alkyds are often modified with oil, producing a paint with excellent drying properties combined with good flexibility and durability. They are easy to use, repair, and maintain. Curing is by solvent evaporation; mineral spirits are generally the solvent.

Alkyds are excellent primers, since they can be covered by many types of paints and can be used on many different materials, including steel. Since the colors are generally stable, alkyd enamels perform well on decks and topsides. Oil alkyds containing either red lead, iron oxide, or zinc chromate are quite frequently applied to interior surfaces. The use of alkyd paints as a top coat on steel hulls, underwater or at the waterline, is not recommended because of their particularly low resistance to alkalis.

Alkyd paints are at the bottom of the list of choices for a paint system on steel hulls, but they are on the list. Although not the most durable, they are economical, and certain formulations have proven satisfactory. Since they are compatible with many paints, alkyds are handy to carry onboard for repairs.

Zinc Paints

Zinc paints with either inorganic or organic vehicles are generally used directly over bare steel as primers and wash primers. Depending on the paint formulation, the dried film can contain up to 96% zinc. It provides corrosion resistance similar to galvanizing, since the contact between the zinc and the steel surface causes the zinc to become the anode if the coating system is scratched through to bare steel. The zinc corrosion by-products form a protective blanket over the underlying steel, preventing further corrosion, although there are questions about the long-term protection provided by this blanket. The zinc sulfate produced is hard to overcoat, and it must be removed by etching and the surface re-primed.

High-temperature-resistant zinc paints called "zinc dust primers" are used in areas exposed to high temperatures (up to 850°F), like ship chimneys, fireplaces, or exhaust stacks. However, aluminum-flake coatings retard fire better than zincs.

Inorganic zinc-rich coatings are fast-drying paints containing up to 96% zinc dust. These paints are classified according to their type of curing. Post-cured zincs have a lead silicate vehicle and are cured with acid. Self-curing zincs are based either on water with a water-soluble silicate vehicle or on alcohol with an ethyl silicate vehicle. (Although the alcohol-type zincs could be considered organic, the dry film reacts like the inorganic types.) The self-cured zincs are superior to the post-cured ones because the acid used in post-curing can affect adhesion and cause blistering.

Inorganic zinc paints are very hard and tough, and they resist abrasion. They are not, however, very flexible. Although they will eventually react with strong

Table 10-6.	**COMMON ALKYD PAINTS**
SILICON-MODIFIED ALKYD	Modified for good gloss retention for top coats. Easy to apply; can be applied over conventional paints. Good weather resistance because of silicon. Abrasion resistance not as good as polyurethanes or epoxies.
ALKYD PRIMER	Best used before alkyd paints. Sometimes pigmented with red lead or red iron oxide; if lead, not recommended for interior or over inorganic zinc primers. Zinc oxide or zinc phosphate pigments preferred for steel primers.
OIL-MODIFIED ALKYD	May also have styrene, urea, amine or phenolic resins. Copolymer based on petroleum products and pigments of aluminum. Good impact and abrasion resistance. Aluminum gives high heat resistance (up to 350°F).
EPOXY ESTER ALKYD	Gloss finish. Mildy durable. Applies easily.

acids and alkalis if not covered, these paints display the best resistance to petroleum and chemical solvents of any known coatings. Inorganic zincs perform well in high-temperature areas because of their silicate vehicle. They equal hot-dip galvanizing in terms of hardness and abrasion resistance and can last three times longer (although, to be fair, it should be pointed out that in hot-dipping only one coat of zinc is applied, while two coats of primer are generally used). Although the zincs are less flexible than some other paints, they will adhere to any expanding and contracting steel surface.

Organic zinc paints combine zinc dust and a wide range of organic resins, including vinyl epoxy, epoxy polyamides, catalyzed epoxies, chlorinated rubbers, styrenes, polyesters, acrylics, polyurethanes, and silicons, as well as phenoxy resins. The solvent is usually either methyl butyl ketone or methyl ethyl ketone. For the best protection, the zinc content should be at least 90% by weight.

Both inorganic and organic zincs are proven effective above the waterline, but there are questions about the advisability of using either underwater. If the top coat is scratched through to the primer, the zinc corrodes galvanically, and the zinc sulfate byproducts can cause the surrounding top coat to blister and lose adhesion. If an organic zinc is used, the organic vehicle in which the zinc dust is embedded may prevent contact between the zinc and the steel so that the zinc is not called on to sacrifice itself. Of the two, inorganic zincs are best below the waterline, especially if protected by a barrier coat with good resistance to the alkali nature of the silicate vehicles.

Inorganic zincs require a jagged anchor pattern with a surface profile ranging between 1.5 and 3.5 mils. Most of these paints are two-part mixtures which are sometimes difficult to mix. They are best applied with brush or roller, and are difficult to spray. An agitator pot is essential for spraying, although special one-pot products that don't require mixing are available. Most zinc paints can be applied and cured at low temperatures, and some inorganic types can be used at temperatures as low as 14°F. Organic zincs tolerate a poorer surface preparation than inorganic ones and need fewer coats, both of which can save labor.

When either inorganic or organic zincs are used underwater, a top coat is required to protect the zinc from galvanic corrosion. Choice of the right top coat can help to prevent any loss of adhesion in the zincs, although the high zinc loading in the primer can affect intercoat adhesion.

The irregular surface of the cured inorganic zinc film offers a good anchor pattern for heavy top coats like the high-build epoxies. Some of the best top coats are amine-catalyzed epoxies, since their catalysts are organic alkalis that favor the alkaline surface of the zinc paint. Other epoxies, acrylics, chlorinated rubbers, and vinyls can also be used as top coats. Oil-based paints should not be used, since the oils they contain can be affected by the alkaline components of inorganic zinc coatings.

When organic zincs are used in the marine environment, like the inorganic zincs they should never be top-coated with paints containing oils (oil-modified alkyds or epoxy esters). Organic zinc-rich primers are easily softened by the solvents in vinyl or epoxy top coats, so the two layers fuse together to produce an almost-ideal bond. For top coats based on other resins, a wash primer or tie coat may be needed to provide the proper surface.

Although professionals have generally used inorganic zinc primers, there is a trend toward greater use of the organics, especially epoxies and coal tar epoxies, although the effectiveness of both is questionable in salt water. For freshwater immersion, organic vinyl zinc primers coated with vinyl anti-foulants are quite satisfactory. When inorganic zinc coatings are top-coated with polyamide epoxies, chlorinated rubbers, and vinyls, they represent a coating system that will last long and be easy to maintain, especially in chemically polluted waters.

Vinyl Paints

Vinyls are quick-drying, opaque paints containing various additives, including red lead, zinc, aluminum, and zinc chromate. The resins making up the vehicle are mixtures of polyvinyl chlorides, polyvinyl acetates, or polyvinyl butyrals. The paints are available as solutions, dispersions, and emulsions with a wide range of properties. Methyl ethyl ketone is generally the solvent, and it is very toxic stuff.

Vinyl coatings have the best versatility of all commonly used resin-based paints. They have good chemical resistance across the pH scale, excellent water resistance, and the lowest chalking rate. They are very flexible, and, in fact, have greater strength in tension than in adhesion, although they will not peel if applied on a properly prepared surface. Vinyls also put up good resistance to salts, splash, and fumes, and therefore are appropriate for boot tops and exterior use at the waterline. They are, however, temperature-sensitive above 150°F, and are very sensitive to intercoat contamination, making repair difficult, since atmospheric conditions are rarely perfect outside a paint shop.

Vinyl paints must be applied in good weather, but their application temperature range (15–100°F) is wide. They have limited solvency, which can be a problem, since they also need a lot of thinning for application. Curing time is short, which makes them good for quick work. The thermoplastic films are easy to recoat. High-build vinyls are also available, and can be applied by spraying.

These paints are primarily used for barrier and top coats, although primers are available. Rosin vinyl antifoulants can also be found. Vinyls are generally compatible with zinc primers, although the zinc surface must be etched before coating with a wash coat containing the vinyl base, phosphoric acid, and pigments. Vinyls should not be used over oil-based paints because the vinyl will lift off, but they work well over chorinated rubbers. When used as top coats, many layers are required to achieve the desired thickness. The primer must be followed by five coats plus a finish coat of either a decorative or anti-fouling nature. A barrier coat of vinyl must be 8–10 mils deep. Many interior latex paints are based on vinyl resins; fewer coats are required for interior applications.

Epoxy Paints

The thermosetting epoxy resins are among the most useful to the steel boatbuilder. Epoxies are generally two-component paints, and are divided into two groups: 1) oil-modified, also known as "epoxy esters" or "epoxy polyesters," which contain both drying oils and resin and which dry by oxidation; and 2) catalyzed epoxies in which one of the two components acts as a catalyst during curing so that a tough polymeric coating is created. The catalyzed epoxies cure under the influence of either plain or adduct polyamides, amines, or isocyanates. (An "adduct" is a crystalline mixture of components rather than a true compound, and its purpose is to help make the coating plastic.) Although all epoxy resins impart excellent durability, hardness, and chemical resistance to a paint, other resins can also be included to add special properties to epoxy paints. Very strong solvents (like MEK) must be used, although some epoxies are 100% resin and have no solvent.

The percentage of epoxy resin in the vehicle determines its resistance to water, salts, solvents, oxidation, alkalis, and acids. The oil-modified epoxies are truly chemical resistant, while all have good resistance to alkalis and solvents. They are, however, weak in acid re-

Table 10-7.   COMMON VINYL PAINTS

VINYL COPOLYMER	Water-based emulsion. Very water-resistant. Durable finish coat but used primarily as interior wood primer. Can be high-build. Fast-drying. Can be applied at low temperatures. Good over inorganic zinc silicates.
BITUMINOUS VINYL	A tough paint applied at low temperatures. Excellent water resistance. Used for ship bottoms. Can be recoated after long periods.
VINYL ACRYLIC	Contains thermoplastics and tends to soften at high temperatures. Easy to apply as undercoat. Durable finish coat. Adheres to epoxies. Appropriate below waterline.
PHENOLIC MODIFIED VINYL	Used in pre-primers and primers. Can be left uncoated up to 9 months. Good as tie coat between inorganic zinc and top coat. Spray application preferred. One- and two-component systems available.
VINYL ACETATE	Good color retention. Not recommended below waterline.
POLYVINYL BUTYRAL	Two-component paint used as wash primer for aluminum.
VINYL EPOXY	Very durable, high-build coating used as barrier coat between incompatible primers and top coats. Special solvent required.
POLYVINYL CHLORIDE	Primer or finish coat. Available in high-build form. Very resistant to acids, minerals, alkalis, and salt. Can be sprayed. Many layers required, but dries quickly. Stays flexible. Recoats easily.
PHOSPHATIZED POLYVINYL BUTYRAL	One- or two-component wash primer that enhances adhesion of next coat. Two-component contains zinc chromate pigments and can be used as tie coat over zinc paints.
VINYL ESTER	Strong resistance to acids. Applied like polyester coatings.

sistance. Catalyzed epoxies are splendid vapor barriers and are among the most water resistant of all paints. All epoxies have high impact resistance.

Epoxies are less expensive than vinyls and polyurethanes because they are high in solids and can be applied in fewer, thicker coats. There is a special class of high-build epoxies that use inert fillers to give a thicker coating and thus a denser barrier. They are available in all three types of curing. High-build epoxies have excellent impact and abrasion resistance, very low moisture vapor transmission, and the best chemical and sol-

vent resistance of any epoxies. Their marred finish may not be desirable for topsides, but they are excellent for intermediate coats, interiors, and tanks holding caustic solutions.

The main disadvantage of epoxies is chalking, although some of the new resins reduce this effect. Chalking is really only an appearance problem, since the chalk itself forms a barrier against further deterioration. Another tendency may be some intercoat peeling if the recoating time isn't properly observed. Epoxies may shrink a little until fully cured, and the repeated expan-

---

Table 10-8.   COMMON EPOXY PAINTS

POLYAMIDE-CURED EPOXY	Commonly used as primer. Contains hydrocarbons but no coal tar. Best saltwater and weather resistance. Adheres well to difficult surfaces. Excellent resistance to most chemicals. Will chalk in sunlight, but good for underwater hull priming and interior of chemical tanks. Resists peeling and undercutting. Primer usually contains rust inhibitors and can be applied directly on galvanized surfaces. Top finish coat is usually glossy and quite durable. Must be applied in good weather at temperatures above 50°F. Polyamide adduct types are high-build; some coats up to 12 mils thick. Used for float coats inside rudders and skegs. Longest overcoat interval of all epoxies.
AMINE ADDUCT-CURED EPOXY	Generally used as top coat. Underwater primer available. Catalyzed epoxy with inert extender pigments. Some pigmented with silica glass; others have zinc chromate and rust inhibitors. Available as two-component tar epoxy for underwater anti-corrosion priming. Extremely durable, tough, and smooth. Resists peeling and undercutting. Strong adhesion to properly prepared steel, but blasting to white metal not necessary. Resists chemicals, but fuel has some effect. High tolerance to contaminants.
AMINE-CURED EPOXY	Used as top coat. Also good primer. Generally has best solvent and acid resistance, which can be increased by modification. Like other epoxies, can have high solids content and high-build film thicknesses.
MODIFIED EPOXY RESIN	High-build. Contains selected non-reactive resins. Used for one-coat, long-lasting protection of steel structures. Solvent-free coating.
ZINC-RICH EPOXY PRIMER	Polyamide-cured. Generally used with organic zincs. Other zinc-rich epoxies follow it well. Used as primer and for tank coatings.
EPOXY ESTER (EPOXY POLYESTER)	Modified with drying oils. Dries by oxidation. Only used above water as anti-corrosion primer. Excellent sealing properties. Better gloss retention than most epoxies. Pigmented with zinc chromate; adheres well to zinc primers. Good on cement. Available as one-part mix.
ACRYLIC EPOXY	Water reducible. Corrosion-inhibiting protective coating generally used for finish coating. Gloss finish as top coat.
COAL TAR EPOXY	Polyamide- or amine-cured. High-build coating with solids content up to 78%. Used in single coating primer. Primer should be overcoated quickly. Good on concrete ballast. Excellent anti-fouling coating when combined with organo tin toxicant. High chemical resistance. Not appropriate for exterior underwater.
ISOCYANATE-CURED EPOXY	Modified, solvent-free type with high volume of solids and high-build thickness. Used as primer. Good chemical resistance and no smell. Works well in fuel and drinking water tanks.

Recent developments include modified hydrophobic hydrocarbon polyamide epoxies used on submarines. They are very thick, tough, and abrasion resistant, and are appropriate for heavy workboat surfaces. Many other epoxies are available, especially for tank coatings, including ketimine epoxies, which are very resistant to chemicals and weathering, and epoxy urethanes. An epoxy casting resin with excellent adhesion is also available.

sion and contraction of the hull can lead to cracking. They do not have good color or gloss retention over a long period of time, but this can be improved with a coat of polyurethane or vinyl acrylic enamel on top. If used as top coats, a UV stabilizer should be included in the epoxy formulation.

The curing process for the catalyzed epoxies is highly temperature sensitive, and the paint must usually be applied at temperatures of 60–80°F; some have a minimum application temperature as low as 42–50°F. The curing time depends on this temperature: the lower the temperature, the slower the cure. At a temperature of 50°F, the curing time is about 4 hours.

Otherwise, epoxies are ideal to use since they can be applied with roller, brush, or spray gun, dry quickly, and are simple to touch up. Spray application definitely requires protective gear, and epoxy will burn and be absorbed by the skin if protective gloves are not worn. A maximum desirable film thickness of 6 mils per coat is about average, although the specifications supplied by the manufacturer should give this information. Epoxy primers are best applied in a series of thin coats, and they adhere best to a fairly rough metal surface.

Most epoxy coatings should only fingernail hard before overcoating, especially with anti-foulants, since epoxy bonds chemically as well as mechanically with the preceding layer. If more time has passed, the surface should be lightly sanded to roughen it before subsequent coating.

Epoxies are available for both primer and finish applications, and are also occasionally used for barrier coats. Epoxy mastic can be used to fill holes and pits (such as under the anchor locker).

Coal Tar Paints

Coal tar is a thick black liquid derived from coal which is combined with resins to produce coal tar paints. Coal tar is thermoplastic with only fair drying properties; isocyanate additives are used to make the coating pliable at low temperatures. These paints are very useful over both concrete and steel, and are handy for quick repairs at sea. The main drawback is that the coal tar paint may bleed through any overcoats.

Coal tar and epoxy resins are combined to create a marine paint with excellent adhesion and chemical resistance, with the coal tar increasing the flexibility of the epoxy. Up to 35% epoxy resin is used. These paints are either amine- or polyamide-cured with a 24-hour curing time. Coal tar epoxies are very hard and durable,

making them valuable for splash zones. These paints can tolerate a wide range of temperatures and can be submerged because they are very water resistant.

Coal tar epoxies are available in black and brown only, have a tendency to chalk in sunlight, and are difficult to cover with a top coat. They are also messy to apply and clean up. Therefore, their best use in a steel boat is probably in the bilges, where they will show good resistance to any caustic spills and not offend the eyes. They can also be used as anti-fouling top coats and in water tanks.

Vinyl coal tars containing aluminum, are also available. These paints can be used over epoxies, are compatible with anti-foulants, and are generally used below the waterline.

Polyurethane Paints

Linear polyurethanes like AwlGrip set the standard for "yachty" finishes these days. Both modified and unmodified urethane resins are used to produce paints that dry quickly, retain colors and gloss well, and are very hard. The hard, smooth surface resists dirt (unless it has been combined with an anti-skid compound), stains, chemicals, solvents, abrasion, and UV rays. Polyurethanes maintain good flexibility and hardness within a wide temperature range, and dry quickly, although several days are required for complete curing. Since they retain colors so well and have a glossy finish, polyurethanes are commonly used as top coats on the topsides and cabin. However, the finish also shows up any minor imperfections, so several epoxy fairing coats will be

Fig. 10-8. *Round stems like the one shown above are difficult to plate, and the paint tends to emphasize any distortion, especially if polyurethanes are used.*

needed to smooth away defects. (By the way, green and red hide unfairness better than white and blue.)

On the other hand, their hardness means that the polyurethanes are difficult to repair and maintain because they are difficult to sand or scrape. Except for the coal tar urethanes, they are not suitable underwater, and can stain near the waterline. Defects include a tendency to peel and blotchy, uneven colors.

Two types of linear polyurethanes are widely available: polyester and acrylic. Both are moisture-cured with an isocyanate catalyst. Polyester resins produce a harder surface than acrylic ones, because more molecules are linked together in the curing reaction, but, of the two, acrylic poyurethanes are easiest to apply. Polyol curing agents are sometimes used, and they produce the most chemically resistant coatings. These paints must be applied in very thin layers, since the isocyanate curing agent must be able to react with water vapor in the air. The relatively thin films do not hide undercoat colors, which must therefore be similar.

Urethane oils and urethane alkyds are not as durable as the other types. There are also amine-catalyzed two-part urethanes.

The polyurethanes almost demand professional application, since they are very sensitive to both temperature and humidity and require a controlled environment. One-component paints are available, but the two-component types are better. They must be mixed very accurately and require special, highly volatile thinners. Such thin layers are required that the paint is usually sprayed on, although brushable types are available. Fortunately, polyurethanes have excellent leveling properties. They are very sensitive to surface smoothness during application, although there is no need to sand between coats. Used as a primer, they must be overcoated within 24 hours or nothing will adhere.

The primary drawback to using polyurethanes is cost. It's not the paint itself that is so expensive, although it does cost a little more than other types. But the labor costs involved in the fairing coats that must be applied beneath the top coat can boost the price of the paint system to between $75 and $100 per foot, for a total of about $6,000 for a 40′ boat. The isocyanate vapors given off by the paints can cause a lung condition resembling bronchial asthma, sensitizing the painter to further exposure. The only real reason to use these expensive paints is the durable, glossy surface they produce. But epoxies will protect the hull as well at a much lower cost, and won't dazzle the eyes of the islanders when you anchor in their harbors.

Fig. 10-9. *The bracing for this Waterline Yachts design is reflected in the shiny polyurethane top coat. The recessed portholes and gunwale tabs are ready for the next construction stage: wood joinery.*

Phenolic Paints

In phenolic paints, phenol resins are combined with tung oil or toluene. The most common use of phenolics is in rosin-modified phenolic spar varnishes, which are hard, chemical- and wear-resistant varnishes that dry rapidly. Modified phenolic vinyls are also commonly used as primers and weldable pre-primers. As pre-primers they are applied as a thin protective coating that acts as a good base for subsequent coatings with epoxy or coal tar primers, and they can be left without an overcoat for many months. Phenolic vinyls are also used as a tie coat between inorganic zincs and top coats.

Phenolics have good hardness and abrasion and water resistance, but are only moderately resistant to chemicals. Even baked phenolic coatings (like Bakelite) are weak in an alkaline environment. Phenol resins are used in aluminum paints and in metal topcoats in extremely humid areas. Since they will darken or yellow with exposure to light, the darker colors are preferable.

Although the cost of the phenolic paint is low, many coatings are necessary, a fact which increases the total cost. The phenolics are also not easy to repair. They are not recommended for use on a steel hull, except as pre-primers.

Bituminous Paints

Bituminous coatings (bitumastic, tar, asphalt, etc.) are inexpensive thermoplastic coatings that are appropriate below the waterline because they have good water and chemical resistance and excellent abrasion resistance. These paints have poor resistance to solvents, heat, diesel oil, and strong acids and alkalis. Because they are thermoplastic, sunlight tends to cause alligatoring of exterior coatings, so they are better for interiors. Bituminous paints cure by solvent evaporation and can be applied with a brush, roller, or spray gun.

Bituminous paints bleed through top coats, so on the exterior they are used mainly as underwater primers beneath the anti-fouling paint. Most anti-foulants adhere well to them, and modified bitumens with aluminum pigments are particularly good exterior primers. These paints are also excellent interior primers, since they flow very well and have good adhesion. The coating is a flexible base for sprayed urethane foam insulation. However, bituminous paints should not be used in the bilge, where the probability of fuel or oil spills is high; epoxy will give better protection. The U.S. Coast Guard questions the use of bituminous coatings on interior metal since, in a fire, flames will spread rapidly along the surface of the paint. These paints are often used inside keels, rudders, and tanks, though never in water tanks.

Chlorinated Rubber Paints

These elastomeric paints contain chlorinated rubber resins derived from natural rubber, and are usually modified with alkyd resins. They are most often available as high-solids solutions containing plasticizing pigments. There are also unmodified chlorinated rubber coatings that contain no alkyd resins and have outstanding protective properties. Some of these are also high-build formulas. Xylene is the most commonly used solvent, and the paint cures by solvent evaporation.

Chlorinated rubbers provide a tough, thick, leathery coating that shrinks to grip the metal as it cures. They are flexible and abrasion resistant. These paints are very resistant to chemicals, but are affected by strong acids. Their primary drawback is that they are expensive and difficult to find, as well as being somewhat hard to remove and repair.

Chlorinated rubbers are used as primers, tie coats, and top coats both above and below the waterline. They are good over zinc primers, and, with iron pigments, are used as primers themselves. As top coats, they have good ultraviolet resistance, and their high chlorine content contributes fire-retardant qualities and excellent chemical resistance. They are inferior to well-formulated vinyls as primers for anti-foulants, but their good resistance to water and corrosion makes the chlorinated rubbers useful in anti-foulant formulations.

Application temperature is not particularly critical, since these paints can be appplied at a temperature as low as 14°F. They do need proper mixing to flow on well; but they are not sensitive to intercoat contamination, are easy to apply and fast drying, and can be recoated easily. A dry film thickness of 4–8 mils is usually obtained with two coats. The best adhesion is achieved over old coats of vinyls and epoxies; they do not adhere as well to alkyds and phenolics.

Synthetic rubber coatings are also available for special applications. Parlon is a chlorinated rubber resin that is sensitive only to strong acids. It has poor adhesion and requires a special primer. Hypalon is an unusual high-build coal tar formulation with better corrosion resistance than coal tar epoxies. It is used as a fire-retardant coating over foam insulation. Spantex can be used as a non-skid deck coating.

Less Common Paints

Limpetite paints are similar to chlorinated rubbers. They have tremendous abrasion resistance, are impervious to water, and grip steel well. They were designed especially for use in wash pipes, and have also been used on wood. Limpetites are very poisonous and not practical for general use.

Silicon paints are noted for their high heat resistance as well as their excellent durability and resistance to water, electric current, and corrosion. Straight silicons are the most heat- and water-resistant types but have poor solvent resistance, so most are modified with alkyds, polyesters, acrylics, or phenolics, available as a colorless coating. Alkyd-modified silicons perform better than straight alkyds and are more economical, although they are a bit less heat resistant than the pure silicons. The alkyd types can be used over properly primed steel. Silicon paints with aluminum resist temperatures up to 1200°F, but have limited chemical resistance in severe exposure areas. Silicon paints provide good color and gloss retention, and weather better when pigmented than when used as a clear finish. They have good adhesion to wood, but steel must be sandblasted to accept them. They are useful as coatings for cement, since they allow the cement to breath; and they are appropriate for coating dry exhaust stacks.

Furan is a new, very versatile and resistant organic coating that uses epoxy resin cured by a strong acid catalyst. Once cured, the paint becomes extremely hard and almost impossible to maintain. It is difficult to apply and does not adhere well, a characteristic which makes it impractical for marine uses.

Polyester resins, primarily employed in the fiberglass industry, are also used in a relatively new type of coating: thick films of catalyzed polyester resin loaded with glass fiber or flakes. The cured coating is tough, smooth, and water resistant. Although expensive, it seems to last a long time, and has found good service on the hulls of icebreakers. The steel must be blasted to a near-white condition, after which a wash or epoxy resin primer is applied. The cured coatings seem quite compatible with premium top coats, such as vinyls and epoxies. Safety precautions must be taken during application because the highly toxic styrene solvent has a flash point of only 90°F. The peroxide catalyst and the styrene additives are both also highly combustible.

SPECIAL-PURPOSE COATINGS

Anti-Fouling

Anti-fouling paints are used to prevent attack by the over 4,000 known species of fouling organisms present in the sea. The worst of these include the borers (toredo worms) and crustaceans that attack wood; sea urchins, which can destroy steel by abrading it to bare metal vulnerable to corrosion; mollusks, like mussels or pholads, which attack creosote and can penetrate lead sheathing; and barnacles, which pit, corrode, and foul metal near the surface. Although slime, caused by bacteria, can also pit bare metal, it primarily provides a surface on which other organisms thrive, and reduces the toxic effect of anti-fouling coatings. Each group of organisms that forms provides a surface to which the next set can attach, creating a fouling community. Factors like water temperature, light, oxygen content, current, salinity, and the presence of nutrients all affect the growth of this community. Of course a steel hull is not vulnerable to all these organisms; the dread toredo worm is not a problem. But fouling organisms also produce drag, lowering the potential speed of your vessel.

The ideal anti-foulant should: be active against a wide range of foulants; have a low leach rate so it remains effective without maintenance; be easy to apply and compatible with the paint system; be nonpolluting, biodegradable, and low in toxicity to humans; have good air-exposure time; and be economical and accessible for cruisers. However, there is no known anti-foulant that can meet all these requirements.

Anti-fouling paints are generally divided into two categories: soft and hard. The soft anti-foulants based on mineral spirits include most of the traditional types of bottom paint. While underway, they are smoothed by the flow of water across the hull. The hard anti-foulants have a vinyl base, and were developed for racing. These paints resist wear, thereby giving a longer service life; many can be wet-sanded very smooth. They are, however, more expensive than the soft types. Anti-foulants are also available in a controlled-release formula: the paint is covered by a smooth co-polymer membrane that absorbs water and controls the release of the toxin. Their service life falls between that of the soft and the hard.

Anti-foulants work by releasing soluble toxins that interfere with the biochemical processes of the fouling organisms. Lead and zinc sheathings were used before the 1800's, when copper sheathing was found to be more powerful. Cuprous oxide is still the traditional toxin included in these paints, although the new organo tins are proving effective. If possible, neither lead nor mercury paints (many of which are outlawed anyway) should be used on a steel hull.

All copper anti-foulants are effective, but when used on a steel hull, two barrier coats or one high-build coat are needed to insulate the metal substrate or zinc-rich primer from the copper toxicant to prevent galvanic corrosion. This barrier coat must be highly resistant to water, since the anti-foulant may wear away in some spots, exposing the barrier coat to sea water. Copper-based anti-foulants have a normal service life between 9 and 24 months, the higher figure if they're kept clean. They should not be exposed to the atmosphere for long periods before launching.

Although they are more expensive, the organo tins are safer for steel boats, since tin is closer to steel on the galvanic scale than copper is, reducing chances of corrosion. They also have a slower leach rate than copper, with a service life of up to 5 years. However, their service is less predictable than the cuprous oxide types. Since many organo tins include other additives and compounds, a barrier coat is also a good idea. Those paints containing lead, arsenic, or mercury are banned for use in the U.S. because they are too toxic. Epoxy primers seem to work the best under organo tins, but the anti-foulant must be applied within certain time limits for good adhesion.

There are certain problem areas which are subject to erosive attack by the sea water rushing past. These include sea chests, transducers, heat exchangers, speed logs, and the area around the rudder shaft. Extra coats of anti-foulant should be used in these places, and special waxes and tapes are also available.

Table 10-9.   ANTI-FOULANTS

CUPROUS OXIDES:

OIL-BASED	The traditional anti-foulant. Safe use depends on barrier coat. Not generally recommended for steel boats.
VINYL RESIN	Similar to oil-based but harder because of vinyl resins. Contains a great deal of cuprous oxide, so hull must be well primed.
ROSIN-BASED	A soft type that can be applied over a variety of primers. Sometimes contains other inorganic metals. Will crack in air and can't be scrubbed. Must be applied soon after proper primer with roller, brush, or spray. Limited exposure time out of sea water.
MODIFIED VINYL RESIN COPOLYMER	Pigmented with organic metallic compounds. Scrubbable. Can be used for boot tops. Applied with brush, roller, or spray over most epoxy primers or barrier coats. If paint contains copper, don't use on aluminum; some have no cuprous oxide so pose no problem with steel or aluminum.

ORGANO TINS:

TRIBUTYL TIN OXIDE (TBTO)	Safety precautions must be used. Can be applied months before launching. Best choice for steel.
VINYL TRIBUTYL TIN FLUORIDE (TBTF)	Formulated for fiberglass and aluminum hulls. Hard racing finish. Not highly abrasion resistant. Anti-foulant effects more predictable than for TBTO.
CHLORINATED RUBBER TRI-BUTYL TIN FLUORIDE (TBTF)	Acceptable over barrier coat of either vinyl, chlorinated rubber, or epoxy. Expensive.
COAT TAR EPOXY WITH TRI-BUTYL TIN ACETATE (TBTA)	Good abrasion resistance. Economical, since minimal coating is acceptable. Don't allow contact with gasoline, naphtha, or white petroleum, since paint will deteriorate. Very good except at waterline when pollution is present.

OTHER:

POLYURETHANE COPOLYMER RESIN (MICRON 22)	Reportedly lasts up to 3 years. Very toxic resin pigmented with metallic compounds. Some brands use copper as anti-foulant; others are pigmented with organo tins.

New anti-foulants are constantly being developed. PTFE, a fluorinated polymeric coating, is very effective against barnacles, but is not yet mechanically strong enough to be useful, and is difficult to apply. Electrolytic hypochlorination, using an impressed current and a platinum anode, has been tried, but is best for small, specific areas. Hydrolysable co-polymers containing chemically bound toxicants permit progressive dissolving of the toxicant binder, and there is no time limit to atmospheric exposure before launching. These paints may prove practical in the future.

Surface preparation is important for the heavier anti-foulant layers, which are as thick as 30 mils per coat. A surface profile of 1–1.5 mils provides the best adhesion. Crevices, edges, seams, welds, and boot tops should be given a thicker coating of epoxy primer than the rest of the hull.

Proper application procedures and safety precautions must be followed with anti-foulants; the toxins they contain are very dangerous. Brushing or rolling the paint on is much safer than spraying, during which some of the toxins can get into the lungs. Good respirators are also necessary if you are sanding anti-foulants.

Maintenance can double the life of the anti-foulant. As we've mentioned, slime provides a foothold for other organisms and interferes with the release of the toxins. When at sea, water rushing past the hull will wash off some of the slime, but scrubbing the hull once or twice a year, depending on the boat's activity, is recommended. Copper-based anti-fouling coats also develop an insoluble green layer of cuprous salts on the paint surface, blocking the release of toxins. During any scrubbing operation, no more than 2 mils of paint should be removed, and care must be taken not to damage the paint

Table 10-10. COST COMPARISON OF ANTI-FOULANTS		
INEXPENSIVE	**MODERATE**	**EXPENSIVE**
Oil-based cuprous oxide Vinyl-resin cuprous oxide Rosin-based cuprous oxide Coal tar epoxy with TBTA	Modified vinyl with TBTF Polyurethane copolymers	Vinyl TBTO or TBTF Chlorinated rubber with TBTF

below. If the barrier coat shows signs of deterioration, it should be renewed. Blasting is only necessary if a significant amount of primer is also gone. At the very least, the hull should be periodically inspected for damage to the anti-foulant.

Fluorocarbon varnishes are exceptional clear finishes that can be used over anti-foulants. Fluorocarbons (organic compounds in which the hydrogen is replaced by fluorine) are very inert polymers with high resistance to weathering, acids, and alkalis. Their erosion rate is low because of their high water resistance, and their gloss retention is high, so they provide long life without maintenance. Although they are not toxic, they resist barnacle growth and can be used as a speed coat on the ship's bottom. They are expensive, but the spread rate is high, so a gallon covers a large area. At present, their use is not common and research findings about them are inconsistent.

Tank Coatings

Tanks onboard a vesel can generally be divided into those carrying water, those carrying fuel, and those carrying other chemicals and waste water. The primary difference among the coatings required is their chemical resistance.

For steel water tanks, the US Food and Drug Administration standards recommend vinyl epoxy and inorganic zinc or aluminum-pigmented phenolics with a tungsten-linseed binder. Vinyls are easy to use since they can be easily patched. However, many coats with proper curing between are needed, and flammable solvents are required. Epoxies are generally cheaper and easier to apply; chlorinated solvents are sometimes added to the epoxies. Inorganic zincs are inexpensive, need only one coat, and no flammable solvents are required. Fiberglass, aluminum, or stainless steel tanks are also suitable, and need no coating.

The metal in fuel tanks, particularly diesel tanks, can be left bare. But moisture often enters fuel tanks, so an epoxy coating could be used to protect against any corrosion. Zinc should never be used in fuel tanks because the zinc will react with the fuel.

Bare steel tanks can be used for the following chemicals, which are not considered corrosive to carbon steel at any temperature except in high concentrations: chlorinated solvents, hydrocarbon solvents, ketones, concentrated sodium hydroxide, and phenols.

Bitumastics, neoprene coatings, or nickel cladding are effective protection for chemical tanks. Neoprene is highly resistant to diesel fuel, acids, and alkalis, although somewhat susceptible to water. Using stainless steel or polyethylene tanks ensures protection from corrosion; plastics can also be used for holding tanks and sumps. Onboard the vessel, acetone, diesel oil, gasoline, kerosene, or turpentine should be kept in their own separate metal or plastic containers.

Float coats are often used to prevent corrosion in dead spaces, like skegs and rudders, and in tanks. This coat is a blend of biodegradable vegetable and mineral oils that seal out water and oxygen, and passify the steel. They need to reapplied occasionally. Bitumastics and thin epoxy coatings are also used as float coats.

Fire-Resistant Coatings

Fire-resistant coatings fall into two classes: those that act as a barrier to prevent heat from spreading to underlying materials and those that have a very slow rate of burning so that the fire can be controlled.

When this first group is heated, a chemical reaction is set off, forming either a powder residue or a nonflammable gas such as carbon dioxide, ammonia, or water vapor. The heat produced by the fire is used in these chemical reactions, so the material beneath never becomes hot enough to burn. Poured-in concrete also acts as a barrier by directly absorbing the heat while producing water vapor.

In the second class of fire-resistant paints, pigments and resins act to slow the rate of burning. Most inorganic pigments will retard the spread of fire; organic pigments, on the other hand, are generally flammable. But resins such as polyvinyl chloride, nylon, polyester, chlorinated rubber, neoprene, and epoxy cause the paint either to burn slowly or to become practically self-extinguishing. A high fluorocarbon resin level supposedly makes the paint non-burning. Both silicon and aluminum are added to paints on dry exhaust stacks because they are non-flammable at high temperatures.

Fireproof sheathing materials, such as lead, copper, aluminum, asbestos, and concrete, are often used in the engine room and around smoke stacks and exhaust pipes.

Special fire-retardant coatings can be used over sprayed polyurethane foam insulation (see Chapter 11).

CLEAR COATINGS FOR WOOD

Many different resins are used in clear coatings. Rosin is a low-cost, natural resin distilled from the sap of trees. It is popular among inexpensive finishes, but has relatively poor resistance to water and chemicals. Penta resin is used with rosin to give it a higher melting point and better color retention and gloss. Ester gum is also used mostly in low-cost gloss lacquers, and has better color retention and resistance characteristics than rosin. Modified phenolic resins are commonly used in spar varnish, and offer good drying and a high gloss finish. Sanding lacquers often contain maleic resins. Polystyrene resins, which are used in varnishes and for waterproofing paper, are thermopalstic and have high electrical resistance, good strength, and resistance to moisture.

Clear finishes dry by solvent evaporation, oxidation, or moisture curing; some are available as catalyzed two-part mixes. Varnishes are classified by oil length, the ratio of oil to resin. Long-oil varnishes are very flexible and are used for exteriors. Medium oils are harder and are used on cement or woodwork. The short-oil type is very hard and brittle, and is used on furniture since it can be sanded easily.

In exterior applications, clear coatings do not have the durability of paints, even though they contain ultraviolet absorbers. Cracking and peeling are common failures. They are generally used only on wood, and can be applied by many methods, including spraying.

Table 10-11. COMMON CLEAR COATINGS	
ALKYD RESIN VARNISHES	Can be used on all surfaces except alkaline ones. Lack the durability of pure phenolic varnishes in marine conditions, but do well in less aggressive environments.
URETHANES	Good resistance to abrasion, solvents, marring, chemicals, and oxidation. Cure quickly.
EPOXY VARNISHES	Outstanding resistance to caustic substances like chemicals and detergents. Excellent adhesion. Can also be used on metals. Usually two-part mixes that cure by chemical reaction. Can be made highly flexible, and so have good impact resistance and adhesion. Oil-modified epoxy ester varnishes that dry by oxidation are cheaper than the catalyzed types.
PHENOLIC FORMALDE-HYDE VARNISHES	Highly resistant to caustics and acids. Have tendency to yellow, but rarely crack or peel. Can be washed with soap and water.
MODIFIED PHENOLIC VARNISHES	Less resistant to weathering, but can be used for interiors.
POLYVINYL FINISHES	Based on a combination of vinyl acetate and vinyl chloride. Excellent chemical resistance. A wash primer containing polyvinyl butyral must be used first to ensure adhesion.
ACRYLIC AND NITROCELLU-LOSE LACQUERS	Limited to interior use.
SPIRIT VARNISHES	Dissolved in alcohol. Include shellac, manila gum, zein, fumaric resins, and nitrocellulose. Poorer resistance to abrasion, water, and detergents than other types.

Other types of clear finishes such as styrene-modified alkyds, vinyl toluenes, and polyesters have found certain uses, but they are not very common.

OTHER COATINGS FOR STEEL

Metallizing

One question that the boat owner or builder will ask when considering a coating system is "Should I metallize my steel or just coat it with a good paint system?" The primary consideration in making this decision is that sooner or later any paint system will develop cracks, scratches, or gouges that may go right through to the steel, which will then begin to corrode. But when a metallized hull is scratched to bare metal, the "giving" zinc or aluminum will galvanically protect the steel from corrosion; metallizing can double the life of a steel hull. Although some professional builders argue against its usefulness, others recommend it highly. Poor results may be due to inadequate or uneven preparation of the steel surface.

The American Welding Society's study, *19-Year Tests with Flame Sprayed Coatings,* shows the superiority of metallizing. Various test panels were submerged in sea water or placed near the water. All of the steel panels were blast-cleaned and covered with coatings of flame-sprayed zinc or aluminum. Some were also sealed with a coat of zinc chromate wash primer, clear aluminum vinyl, or chlorinated rubber.

The results of these tests showed that sprayed aluminum coatings, .003–.006″ thick, both sealed and unsealed, gave complete base metal protection from corrosion in sea water and severe marine atmospheres. Unsealed sprayed zinc coatings required a maximum thickness of .012″ for complete base metal protection in sea water for 19 years. A thinner zinc coating was sufficient in atmospheric conditions. In severe marine atmospheres, the application of one coat of wash primer plus one or two coats of aluminum vinyl enhanced the appearance and extended the life of the zinc coatings by at least 100%. However, the aluminum vinyl sealer itself deteriorated, suggesting its inadequacy in marine environments. Chlorinated rubber was also found to be an unsatisfactory sealant.

The most important finding was that, although the metallizing showed some damage in the form of chips or scrapes, the base metal did not corrode, suggesting that the metallizing had provided galvanic protection. The AWS now recommends zinc or aluminum flame-sprayed coatings for steel in marine environments. Aluminum is three times more effective than zinc and less expensive, since a thinner coat can be applied.

Metallizing is a hot-spray process in which metal wire is fed through a special gun, melted, and atomized on-to the surface through special nozzles. The equipment and wire are available from Metco, Inc. or Metallizing Company of America (Mogul equipment). Heat is provided with either oxygen and acetylene or an electric arc, and a compressed air system feeds the coiled wire and sprays the molten metal. The heat is controlled by the amount of oxygen or the amperage of the current. A blasted surface is essential for proper adhesion of the zinc or aluminum, because the coating will not adhere to a surface that has oxidation products on it. Atmospheric conditions must also be right; salty, humid, or foggy conditions are not suitable.

Both zinc and aluminum are commonly used for corrosion-control applications, although stainless and other metals can also be flame-sprayed. The splash zone could be metallized with monel, but this metal is very expensive and also cathodic to steel, so it is not recommended. If economically possible, the interior of the boat should also be blasted and metallized to prevent corrosion. If only part of the interior can be metallized, the bilge is most important.

Table 10-12. TOOLS FOR METALLIZING

BASIC
Metallizing gun (Mogul or Metco)
Compressor and generator
Flow meters for gas and air
Air drier
Extra caps
Stands for hoses and wire coil
Wire (comes in reels)
Shop cart

OPTIONAL
Elco meter to measure coating thickness (certain micrometers can also be used)
Pyro meter for check on preheat temperature of substrate

Flame-sprayed zinc coatings can corrode underwater, especially when the water polluted with hydrogen sulfide. Therefore, the zinc must be overcoated. Since zinc tends to react with alkyds and other paints, a wash primer must be used to neutralize the surface and enable paints to bond well. Flame-sprayed aluminum can be followed by a wash primer, a thin coat of vinyl to prevent leaching of chromates from the wash primer, and finally an anti-fouling or finish coat. The air-drying zinc chromate wash primer is an acid-resin combination in which the acid component contains phosphoric acid and ethyl, butyral, or isopropyl alcohol. The binder generally is zinc chromate, and insoluble inert pigments are often included.

Good safety precautions are necessary when flame-spraying any metals, since the dust (especially zinc dust) is a hazard to the eyes, lungs, and bones. An air-fed helmet is the best safety precaution.

An aluminum metallized coating followed by epoxy paints is probably the best way to go with a steel hull. Even insurance companies sometimes give better rates on metallized hulls. However, the decision about metallizing will depend partly on how much you want to pay for a coating system. Even though metallizing costs less than a complete polyurethane paint job, you still have to buy the paint system to put over the metallizing. On the other hand, the cost of maintaining a coating system and repairing the steel where the coatings fail may prove more expensive than the cost of metallizing. But today's epoxy paint systems can do a very good job, as long as you pay close attention to repairing any scratches or gouges soon after they occur.

On the west coast, metallizing is available through Knight Mobile Metal Spray, listed in the Directory under Sierra Yachtwerks. Doug Knight, founder of the company, offers the following look at a typical metallizing job:

> Most jobs (boats 35–45') usually take around a week to complete, from initial set-up to break-down and reloading of the equipment. I have spent as much as 5½ months on a single boat, but that entailed interior blasting, painting, and an immense amount of detail work, all done by a single worker.
>
> Metallizing requires a top-quality blast job, and I use only top-quality materials from start to finish. Since I specialize only in steel boats, the customer doesn't have to worry that a house blaster will ruin the job. Blasting a steel boat requires a great deal more effort and expertise than blasting a house. The steel must be brought down to bright white metal finish with the proper anchor pattern so that the metallizing will adhere properly.
>
> I've sprayed both aluminum and zinc, but I prefer to spray aluminum. It is cheaper and adds less weight to the hull and is three times more effective than zinc on an equal coating basis. For aluminum, the current specifications are two passes with the gun to achieve about 4–6 mils coverage, while zinc will require three passes for a coverage of 7–9 mils.
>
> The usual job would be to completely metallize the entire exterior of the hull with aluminum and follow that with a primer-sealer. Additional paint-

> ing can be done by the owner or as part of the metallizing contract.
>
> Typical pricing of jobs is as follows: for a 35' boat with approximately 1650 sq. ft., the total cost would be $3,382.50 at the current rate (Jan. '85) of $2.05 per sq. ft. for sandblasting, aluminum flame spraying, and one primer/sealer coat. Zinc is currently priced at $3.25 per sq. ft. Travel time and expenses are charged at actual costs. Additional sandblasting and painting can also be contracted out by the job or by the hour.

Galvanizing

Hot-dip galvanizing is the process of immersing small steel items like fittings, chain, anchors, and wire into a zinc bath heated to approximately 780°F. This molten zinc bonds very well to the steel, though thin items like wire lose some tensile strength in the process. Sometimes fittings are double-dipped, but this process only seems to melt the first coat, therefore there is no gain. A single dip at a lower temperature will result in a thicker layer. Any galvanized steel used below the waterline must be coated to prevent the zinc from leaching out. Galvanizing costs about 25 cents per pound, so regalvanizing old fittings is fairly practical if they're in good shape otherwise. Any sharp edges should be ground down before galvanizing, and some items need to be cleaned with a muriatic acid solution to remove surface impurities. Unfortunately, it is just about impossible to hot-dip a complete hull, although some Navy lifeboats have been totally galvanized.

The zinc chromate paint available in cold-spray aerosol cans should not be used to cover fittings in place of galvanizing, since the covering is too thin and will corrode rapidly. It is all right, however, for those emergency repairs.

In Chinese or Swedish galvanizing, the steel is heated red hot and plunged into a bath of boiling pitch (roofing tar can be used). The end product is like a cold bituminous paint, and lasts a long time. However, this process is not as effective as hot-dip galvanizing.

Powder-Dip Coatings

A new process using epoxy powder for coating fittings has recently been developed. This powder is impregnated with compressed air, making it liquid. Fittings are then dipped into the container of powder. The coating is very durable, so it is useful on fittings that are subjected to chafe. The process costs a little more than galvanizing, but holds up better. Although the coating mars, it doesn't chip.

Steel and aluminum must be blasted and then etched with phosphate and chromate, respectively, before being dipped. A metal blast tumbler works well to prepare fittings, and this piece of equipment is relatively inexpensive.

Powder-dipping is more pratical for a foundry or professional yard than for the home builder. The required 50-gallon jug and meters cost between $3,000 and $4,000. (The equipment, called a VibroFluidizer, is available from Armstrong Products Company.) The cost of the powder is between $2 and $3 per pound; for a 50-gallon jug, this will run between $200 and $250. (A good fabricator may be able to build some of the equipment more cheaply.) An air compressor with at least a 90-psi output is needed, as well as a good air filter to prevent powder from being sucked into the compressor. Black coatings are generally used, but other colors are available.

Miscellaneous Coatings

There are many other processes used to give metal a protective coating. In weld-cladding, the metal surface is built up with a series of welds using a more noncorrosive metal such as cupronickel or monel. This method is used on propellers and shafts as a repair technique.

Nylon-dipping has been employed with some success on things like propeller shafts, but once a leak in the coating occurs, corrosion could proceed rapidly underneath the nylon.

Hulls can be sheathed with fiberglass or epoxy, but the metal also corrodes rapidly underneath if the coating is breeched.

In electroplating, an electric current is used to deposit a more-noble metal onto the surface of another metal. Nickel-chromium plating is a fine preservation method, but only as long as the surface remains unscratched. If oxygen gets under the surface, the coating will peel and the steel underneath will rust.

Sherardizing is the process of impregnating steel with a thin coat of zinc powder by centrifugal action in the absence of oxygen. It is not recommended for underwater use, but it does offer steel protection in the atmosphere.

Tin or lead coatings are very corrosion resistant and have been used successfully for tin cans and the like.

Terne plate holds up well on the inside of fuel tanks; however, if it is scratched, the exposed steel becomes anodic and corrodes rapidly. Since scratching is inevitable, these coatings are rarely used for steel hulls.

COATINGS FOR OTHER METALS

The other metals used on a steel boat may or may not need to be coated. Stainless, bronze, and copper (used on the interior) do not need any treatment other than an occasional polishing.

Although galvanized steel is commonly left bare, it should be painted for added corrosion protection, general appearance, heat reflection, and protection from alkali contamination. Zinc-rich coatings are excellent primers for galvanized surfaces; alkyd or oil-based paints should not be used on galvanized surfaces, since they react with the zinc. Latex paints develop good adhesion, especially in interior applications. Paints with polyvinyl acetate or acrylic vehicles also give satisfactory results, but not in areas of high humidity or extreme temperature change. Asphalt coatings over galvanized steel are not recommended, even though the heavy coatings protect against highly acidic environments.

Aluminum items like masts, winches, or blocks, can be left uncoated. They are often anodized through an electrochemical process that thickens the oxide film on the aluminum, giving extra corrosion protection. If the aluminum is to be painted, a zinc chromate primer or a conversion coating will improve the performance of any finish coat applied. A 10% phosphoric acid solution is used for cleaning aluminum. Copper-, arsenic-, or mercury-bearing paints should not be used on aluminum.

As lead ballast ages, an oxide forms on its surface, preventing further corrosion. Since lead has very good chemical resistance, it generally does not need any protection from chemical spills in the bilge. If it is to be coated, bitumastic paints are best, but an epoxy zinc primer with an alkyd top coat or a vinyl primer with a chlorinated rubber top coat can be used. Red lead epoxy or acrylic primers are also suitable, but alkyd or oil-based paints will peel or flake.

Polyurethanes have been used successfully to coat copper, which should be cleaned with muriatic or hydrochloric acid before painting.

TEMPORARY CORROSION INHIBITORS

There are a number of products that can be used to prevent corrosion for a short time. Many are only for emergency uses, and none can be depended on to truly protect metal.

Petroleum-based protectors come in numerous types, some soft, some hard. They can be sprayed, brushed, or dipped onto the surface. The soft kinds usually contain lanolin or petroleum as a base, while the hard varieties contain resins, bitumens, and zinc naphthates. One type contains additives that neutralize acid residues, and it is used in engine lubricating oil. Other types are tacky, have a soft film, and contain volatile solvents; they can be brushed on or the object can be dipped in them. A good thread goop, like that used on pressurized hot water tanks, will inhibit corrosion on threads. Silicon grease or oil can be purchased in aerosol sprays; they are applied mostly to engine parts and moving fittings. Engine oil can be used inside rudders and tubing. Anhydrous lanolin will temporarily seal rigging and small exposed rusting areas.

Dessicants such as silica gel are ideal for the protection of precision instruments, since these substances absorb the water vapor in the air.

Vapor phase inhibitors (VPI) are organic chemicals in powder or solution form that cover the metal in a thin layer. They are good for toolboxes and protection of the engine, since they work well in confined, airtight spaces.

Strippable coatings are usually derivatives of cellulose which are applied hot; they are easy to remove. Vinyl plastisol is one type. These coatings are better used in environments other than marine.

CONCLUSION

There is no question about it: a good coating system determines the lifetime of a steel vessel. Although cost is often a consideration, high initial cost may actually produce a system that lasts longer with less maintenance, so that the cumulative cost is lower in the long run. Metallizing is an added expense, but it will pay off over time. If the hull is not metallized, then a premium coating system is even more advisable.

There are very different requirements for coatings above and below the waterline. The appearance of the bottom isn't that important, but the topsides must look good and perform well. For good performance, you will probably choose either a polyurethane or an epoxy top coat. For appearance, the hard, glossy finish of a polyurethane can add a touch of class to a fair steel hull. However, when a polyurethane top coat is used, the hull (no matter what material it's made of) must be faired with several coats of a high-build paint (epoxy works best on steel). The labor costs for the fairing operation are high, although you can decide to accept a few surface imperfections to keep the price down a litte. Epoxy is not as pretty as polyurethane, but it is less expensive and performs equally well.

There are a number of different ways to combine paint into a coating system, and the paints are available from a number of companies, including Petit, International, U.S. Paint (AwlGrip), Devoe, Sigma, Dietzler, and Porter. The following system is a combination that will provide excellent protection to a non-metallized hull, and will require minimal repair and maintenance.

INTERIOR:	Pre-primed with phenolic modified vinyl (except 12 ga. cabin top).
	Weld zones blasted and rest of plate sweep-blasted.
	One coat of high-build bituminous primer except in bilge, where three coats of high-build epoxy primer are used.
	Urethane foam insulation sprayed to level of longitudinals, except in bilge and engine areas. Foam coated with fire-retardant paint.
EXTERIOR:	Pre-primed with phenolic modified vinyl.
	Blasted to near-white metal.
	Three thin coats of high-build catalyzed epoxy primer.
Topsides:	Two to four intermediate sandable fairing coats of high-build epoxy.
	One or two hard-surfaced epoxy barrier coats.
	Three thin coats of polyurethane applied in quick succession, with an extra layer on the boot top.
Below water:	Two coats of organo tin antifoulant.

Fig. 10-10.   *Careless painting can leave drips and drools of paint that may peel off.*

SOURCES

Metallizing Equipment

Metallizing Company of America
321 S. Hamilton St.
Sullivan, IL 61951

Metco, Inc.
1101 Prospect Ave.
Westbury, NY 11590

Powder Dip Coatings

Armstrong Products Company
P.O. Box 647
Warsaw, IN 46580

—Chapter 11—

Insulation

Some sailors, especially those cruising the tropics in wooden boats, may choose to do without insulation. But other hull materials are too thin to have an insulating effect—temperature changes and noise are easily transmitted through the skin to the interior. Even some wooden hulls are not thick enough. Insulation in a sailing vessel can definitely enhance comfort by blocking these intrusions from the outside, and, as a bonus, certain types can increase the corrosion resistance of a steel boat. Local insulation is also a safety requirement: the areas around exhaust pipes, stoves, heaters, and stacks must be insulated from the high heating temperatures that could start a fire or cause injury.

Noise on a sailboat comes from both inside and outside. Although the romantic slapping of waves in a gale may be an annoyance if you're trying to sleep, the unmuffled roar of a diesel engine is worse. Noise produced inside the boat can travel through the hull plate, but insulation keeps sound where it belongs. Special types of sheathing may be needed to dampen the sounds of engine and generator.

Steel has high thermal conductivity (though not so high as aluminum), so the metal responds quickly to any temperature change. Insulating the hull allows you to maintain the air inside the hull at a different temperature from that outside: warmer or cooler. A well-insulated hull will not need a powerful heater (al-

though a small one will be welcome), which can save you money. Steel boats are generally insulated to just below the cabin sole or to the level of the lowest longitudinal, and insulation is needed most above the waterline, in the cabin roof and topsides. The bilge is generally not insulated, since if any water should happen to get in there, the insulation would be sitting in water and would deteriorate. Panel insulation can be attached to the bottom of the cabin sole if desired. The area below and around the engine should not be insulated with anything that will burn.

Condensation is a problem that can be greatly helped by good insulation. In the tropics condensation rarely occurs even on an uninsulated boat, because, with good ventilation, the interior and exterior temperatures stay about the same. However, in the colder air and sea of more northern latitudes, the difference in temperature between the metal hull and the interior air (warmed by galley stoves, kerosene lamps, and cabin heaters) can cause heavy condensation. A layer of insulation prevents the cold metal and the warm, moist air from coming into contact with each other.

On small boats, insulation can be used to add buoyancy, so that the hull will float if capsized. The amount of insulation needed for flotation is determined by calculating the weight of the hull and the weight that each cubic foot of insulation will support. Most of the insulation is placed at the end and up high, with enough down low to increase initial flotation characteristics. Unfortunately, steel cruising boats weigh so much that the whole hull would have to be filled with foam insulation for it to float.

If sprayed foam is used, the insulation may also help to protect the steel from corrosion. When correctly applied, the foam bonds tightly to the steel and acts as another layer in the coating system. It can also be used to fill dead spots and voids (for example, under tanks or in the forepeak), so that they do not become water traps. (Sometimes cement, tar, or bitumastic compounds are used to fill dead spots, but foam is much lighter.) Rudders and skegs can also be filled with foam, but not if welding needs to be done later (for example, to attach a cover plate), since the foam will burn.

Actually, any type of insulation provides some corrosion protection, since loose metal objects, such as jewelry or coins that may get behind the paneling, are isolated from the steel. The steel is also protected from scratching.

No space is really lost to insulation, since it is no thicker than the frames to which the interior woodwork is attached. An average of 2″ of insulation is the maximum that would be applied, and 1½″ are quite adequate, especially if your cruising itinerary is in the tropics.

INSULATING MATERIALS

Over the years, many materials have been used for insulation, some more successfully than others. The fire hazards posed by the different types of insulation are important to consider. Almost all of these linings will burn, but usually only if exposed directly to flame for a period of time.

Sawdust is good only for absorbing moisture and reducing condensation for a short while. It has been used, but really is not worth considering for a steel hull.

Cork is usually mixed with an adhesive and sprayed on, although cork board, which is very light and easily cut and installed, can also be used. The use of cork does help to minimize condensation, but it absorbs water, is subject to rot, and deteriorates. Many older steel boats used this method.

Rock wool and the mica insulation used for houses have been tried successfully on boats, but these types are fairly impractical, since they absorb water.

Fiberglass wool is a fair insulator which doesn't rot in water, but it doesn't bond well and does loosen up,

creating an itchy mess. Fireproof fiberglass, used for loft insulation, soaks up water.

Polystyrene can be glued to metal or wood and has a fair R-factor. This is the so-called fire-resistant insulation that contains bubbles of fire-dampening carbon dioxide. It comes in sheets and does absorb some water, though not much.

Placed styrofoam is commonly used for ice chests, since it has a good R-factor. This method of insulation is inexpensive, and the sheets can be easily installed, although they break if bent too much. It is certainly not as flexible as polyethylene foam.

Polyethylene foam is impervious to water because of its close-cell nature. If placed-foam insulation is used, this is the type to buy. It is available in thin sheets, which are quite flexible and easy to apply. Polyethylene foam is also used in life vests. It will burn, but only if a torch is continuously applied to it. This type of insulation costs between $1 and $3 per board foot. (Ethafoam by Dow Chemical is a popular brand.)

Polyurethane foam is the close-cell, water-resistant type of insulation most commonly used today. The foam can be either sprayed or poured onto the steel and can also be injected into closed spaces. One of the major criticisms of polyurethane is that toxic fumes are given off when it burns. Although polyurethane foam does not burn easily, fire-retardant paints should be applied over it.

Neoprene foam provides insulation similar to sprayed polyurethane. It has excellent adhesion, but is twice as expensive as polyurethane foam, which can add up when a whole boat is insulated.

There are many other types of insulation, some of which may become useful on steel boats in the future. These include phenolic foams, electrostatic coatings, cellular cellulose acetate (presently used for ice boxes), and hot plural epoxy sprays. The Plegicel (expanded PVC) used to insulate fiberglass boats should not be used on steel hulls.

SPRAYED-FOAM INSULATION

There are many arguments about the best way to install insulation, whether to glue it in place or spray it onto the steel surface. The primary area of disagreement is how easy it is to inspect the interior steel. Because sprayed foam bonds so tightly, it must be scraped away with a slick or chisel to expose the steel. Placed insulation itself can be removed easily, but all the woodwork must be dismantled first, so the inspection process really isn't much easier, although it is reversible. If, as some suggest, sprayed foam acts as part of the coating system, the condition of the foam surface should reflect the condition of the paint and steel below it.

Separation of the insulation from the steel is another worry associated with sprayed foam. Proper surface preparation is important before urethane foams are sprayed. Foam seems to hold best when applied over epoxy paint, although some newly built boats are insulated without being blasted. (It seems that this is asking for trouble.) There is still some question about the possibility of the foam developing hairline cracks due to the expansion and contraction of the steel to which it is bonded. If these cracks should occur and water get behind the foam, the steel should be protected from corrosion by a good high-build primer and perhaps an intermediate coat. Most insulation failures seem to occur in fish-holding tanks and freezer compartments, where extensive expansion and contraction has taken place.

How you decide to deal with condensation is also a factor in choosing placed or sprayed insulation. Even an insulated boat will occasionally run into conditions under which water vapor will condense. Space must be left for any condensation to flow to the bilge, so that water does not lie against the steel, the insulation, or the wood paneling. Sheet insulation is usually glued directly to the hull, but if, instead, it is stuck onto the backside of the paneling, water can run down the hull plate

through limber hulls cut in the longitudinals. With sprayed insulation, the insulation must cover the longitudinals so water is not trapped on top of them. Space must also be left between the surface of the foam and any paneling. Special anti-condensation paints (for example, International's Corkon or Blake's anti-condensation emulsion) are available for use on foam.

Because of the additional corrosion protection given by sprayed foams, their use is probably more appropriate for a steel hull, but placed polyethylene foam is much easier, cheaper, and less toxic to apply. A serrated knife (electric carving knives are ideal) or saw is the best tool for cutting through the stiff foam, which is usually 1½″–2″ thick. If the foam is glued to the hull, the glue layer must be thick and continous, so that water is not trapped behind the insulation. Some hulls have been sprayed with epoxy glue, but this job is almost as messy and toxic as spraying foam insulation. When the foam is glued to the back of the lining, installation can be awkward unless the panel are designed to be removable.

The thickness of a sprayed foam layer depends primarily on the depth of the longitudinal framing, since the foam should be level with the tops of the longitudinals. Of course the foam thickness will be thicker when the insulation is being used to fill pocket areas.

If the longitudinals are notched into the transverse frames, wood cleats (used for attaching interior woodwork) and bulkheads may need to be fitted before spraying, since the foam will cover up much of the transverse

Fig. 11-1. *Polyurethane insulation has been correctly sprayed in over the longitudinals. Note also the access lid on the integral fuel tank.*

frames. Even if the longitudinals are backed to the transverses and the full width of a transverse is available for cleating, when the wood strips are put in first they can be neatly sealed in place with the foam. When bolt holes for deck fittings must be drilled after the foam is in place, a small area will have to be cleared, but the job isn't difficult.

The foam should never be compressed by walking or leaning on it. However, this kind of insulation can't be sheathed with fiberglass, the polyester resins of which can melt the polyurethane foam. In the living quarters, the insulation will be covered by paneling or cupboards, and you will just have to be careful until these linings are fitted.

As the sprayed foam cures, it develops a tough outer skin that becomes a moisture barrier and a protective coating. However, because foam sometimes expands when applied to uneven or too thick a depth, this skin must occasionally be shaved away to a certain preferred level. The foam can also be sanded smooth, but this is a much more time-consuming task. Where the skin has been removed, the foam will be more liable to absorb water and any contaminants. Protective coatings can be used to provide a tough second skin.

Polyurethane foam gives off potentially lethal cyanide fumes when it burns because the resins of which it is composed are created by reactions with isocyanates. The foam must be scraped away before steel is either cut or welded, which can pose a problem to alterations. The foam contains some fire retardants, which slow down the rate at which it will burn, but to guard against onboard fires, a fire-resistant coating should be applied over the foam.

Yes, it is possible to combine protection and fire resistance in a single coating. Theoretically, the foam could be metallized with aluminum, but this method is a pretty expensive solution to the problem. Many of the coatings developed for use on roofs and decks subject to high degrees of weathering will also do the job.

Chlorinated rubbers (Hypalon) and urethane rubbers can be applied directly to foam insulation as fire retardants. The urethanes are fast-curing elastomers with good acid and solvent resistance and fair alkali resistance. Hypalon has better resistance to water vapor transmission, fair resistance to solvents, and good resistance to acids and alkalis. Foam insulation can also be coated with a liquid neoprene that, should it begin to burn, is self-extinguishing. However, neoprene has poor resistance to some solvents and does not weather

well. A combination system could use several undercoats of neoprene and a top coat of Hypalon.

All of these coatings should be applied over the foam as soon as the skin is cured, so that the surface is dry and clean. In as little as two days the foam can begin to become dirty enough that it will have to be cleaned before coating. When foam must be trimmed away, the trimmed area should be given an additional coat of paint to act as a sealer. The urethanes can be sprayed on, and all of the fire-retardant coatings can be applied with brush or roller. Three coats may be needed to achieve a total film thickness of between 20 and 30 mils. The rougher the foam (that is, the more surface exposed), the more paint will be needed for complete coverage.

Spraying insulation is another one of those tasks for which it really might be best to hire a profesional who has the proper application and safety equipment. The emphasis here is on safety equipment. Toxic fumes are given off during the installation of sprayed polyurethanes, and a heavy-duty respirator is more than a luxury. Like professional sandblasting, professional insulation is not cheap, but both are nasty jobs that require special equipment to perform safely.

However, if you are determined to spray the insulation yourself, you can make small batches of foam in a clean 5-gallon drum. The foam should be whipped with a paddle blade on an electric drill at at least 1400 rpm (the faster the better). Try to keep a brownish skin on the foam, since this makes it more waterproof and less sticky. A portable nozzle is best for spraying foam, and a heavy-duty compressor generator can be rented. For small repairs, a spray gun can be used, and spray foam is also available in aerosol cans.

INSULATING THE ENGINE ROOM

There is only one way to describe the noise from a diesel engine—terrible. The most effective way to muffle this sound obviously will depend partly on where the engine is placed. If it is located in a separate, closed engine room, the whole room can be insulated with sound-deadening material to prevent the noise of the engine from traveling through the hull. If, on the other hand, the engine is located in the cabin or underneath the companionway, it can be covered with an acoustically insulated box. The correct engine mounting pads and shaft alignment, coupling and muffler also help to keep the noise down.

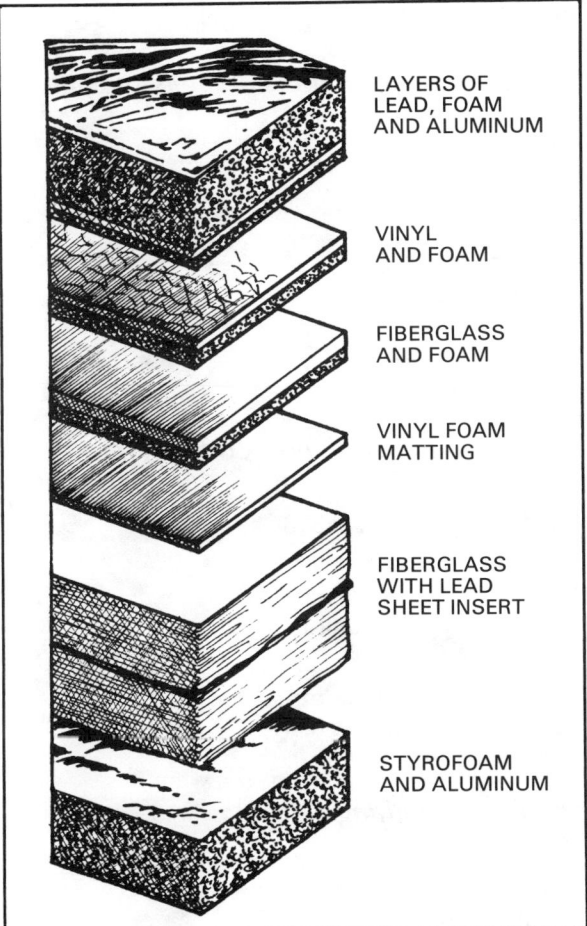

LAYERS OF
LEAD, FOAM
AND ALUMINUM

VINYL
AND FOAM

FIBERGLASS
AND FOAM

VINYL FOAM
MATTING

FIBERGLASS
WITH LEAD
SHEET INSERT

STYROFOAM
AND ALUMINUM

Fig. 11-2. The various types of insulation for the engine room.

Insulating the area around an engine also traps the heat generated by engine operation. Therefore, it is even more important to assure adequate ventilation to insulated engine areas. Engine rooms are easiest to ventilate properly while keeping the noise from intruding on the cabin. Special vent pipes and/or louvers may need to be added to boxes that cover engines.

The insulation used in the engine room can also be chosen to help restrict the spread of any fire to the rest of the hull. Lead, which is the best sound deadener, is also effective as a fire retardant. (This function is especially important if gasoline engines are being used.) However, you can't rely on any insulation to serve this purpose. The engine room should be fitted with a CO_2 or halon fire extinguishing system, or, at the least, a good CO_2 extinguisher should be located just outside the engine room.

Acoustical insulation that also retards fires is expensive, so the smaller the area to be sheathed, the better.

There are less expensive ways to do it, but they don't work as well. If the area to be sheathed is fairly small, you may be able to scrounge the insulation material at surplus warehouses. Most sound-insulation materials can be applied to bulkheads or panels with contact cement; some are stiff enough to be screwed in place with sheet metal screws.

The materials that can be used for engine room insulation are listed in Table 11-1, with some indication of cost (summer 1985). Most of them incorporate some kind of barrier sheathing to increase fire resistance.

Table 11-1. ENGINE ROOM INSULATION	Price/ sq. ft.
THIN, FLEXIBLE ROLL MATERIAL	
Polyethylene (some sound and heat insulation capabilities, but not fire-resistant)	$2.00
Filled vinyl-foam matting	$3.50
Loaded vinyl mat with glass cloth backing (very thin rolls)	$3.50
Heavy filled vinyl (thicker but still flexible; used commercially underneath carpet)	$4.00
Lead-loaded vinyl mat	$5-6.00
Galvanized steel (very thin sheet, 20 gauge)	
Lead foil	
Sheet neoprene (good sound dampener, but expensive; attached with sprayed glue)	
THICKER SHEET MATERIAL	
Close-celled styrofoam with aluminum foil cover	$1.50
Polyurethane foam with thin lead liner	$3.60
Fiberglass and foam with thin lead liner	$3.60
Foam and lead (thin layers of each; available in different thicknesses)	$4.00
Vinyl mass barrier (foam with polyester finish)	$4.50
Two layers of fiberglass with lead insert	$5.00
Neoprene foam filled with lead powder	
Layers of aluminum, foam, and lead	
Layers of lead, foam, and lead (best soundproofing, but costs the most)	$7-8.00

When a hot pipe, stove or vent must be insulated from the surrounding area, sheathings made of asbestos, stainless steel, fire-resistant ceramic tiles, galvanized steel, or a lead-foam-fiberglass combination may be required. Asbestos has been used for years but has been proven a health hazard, both to apply and to live with, so it should be avoided unless it is sheathed with another material, such as rubber. Asbestos can be painted wtih an arabol-rubber compound to seal the loose fibers.

A new sheet product, called Pyrodur, has recently been introduced from Germany. Pyrodur has all the good qualities of asbestos, without the health hazards. It is reasonably priced and has a pleasing appearance. This may be the new wonder insulation.

If an air-cooling system is used on the engine, the exhaust pipes carrying the combustion gases can be quite hot. If these pipes go through bulkheads, the bulkheads should be insulated where the pipes pass. The pipes themselves should be wrapped wtih insulating material to prevent burns if someone happens to touch one. A fiberglass-covered, ceramic-fiber blanket can be used for insulation, as can asbestos and rubber wraps.

The appearance of the insulating material can be a factor for consideration when it is used around stoves or heaters in the cabin area. Sheet stainless steel has been used successfully in these areas, as have decorative fire brick, slate or other special materials.

SOURCES OF INSULATION

All types of insulation for hulls, engines & exhaust

Cork Insulation
1943 1st Ave. S.
Seattle, WA
(206) 627-1094

West Coast Insulation
34008 18th Place
Seattle, WA 98003
(206) 838-1198

Spray Foam Installation Contractors

American Ocean Services
Port Townsend, WA 98368
(206) 385-3576

Harbour Foam & Coatings
9330 15th Ave. S.—Unit F
Seattle, WA

Metal Clad Insulation Corp.
4233 W. Marginal Way S.W.
Seattle, WA

Pyrodor Sheathing

Tech Transfer, Inc.
P.O. Box 412
Renton, WA 98057
(206) 271-0060

—Chapter 12———————————

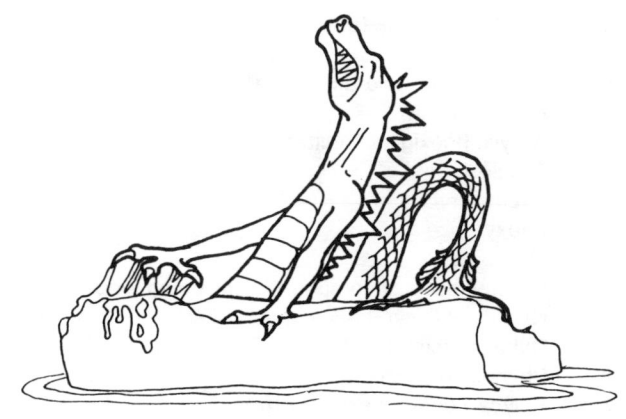

Other Construction Materials

Many different materials besides wood and metals are used in boatbuilding today, no matter what the hull material. Adhesives, bedding compounds, gaskets, insulators, fillers, lubricants, preservatives, sealants, and other chemically based components have a multitude of uses onboard a vessel. On a steel boat, adhesives are used to secure wood or rubber to metal and to laminate wood for spars, tillers, or cabinetry. Plastic insulating gaskets are important to isolate dissimilar metal fittings, and bedding compounds prevent water from becoming trapped between surfaces. Sheathings and coverings are used in various places, from the galley to the deck; sealers and preservatives are often required to treat woodwork. There are so many available materials that it can be difficult to decide which is best, whether for new construction or for repair work.

Most of these construction materials are based on resins, polymers, and elastomers (polymers with the elastic properties of natural rubber). The resins used in paints (especially epoxies and polyurethanes) are also found in these compounds, as are the different solvents. Many are hard plastics (complex organic compounds produced by polymerization). Materials made from the same basic components can take many forms: liquid adhesives, hard gaskets, flexible tubing or bedding compound, and woven cloth. Table 12-1 shows the most common materials and their uses.

Synthetic resins are used much more frequently in these compounds than are natural resins, although asphalt, petroleum resins, and natural rubber are applied as sealants. Synthetic rubbers (neoprenes and polysulfides are the best known) are frequently used for marine applications, especially for flexible gaskets, tubing, exhaust hose, and bedding compounds. Butyl rubber has excellent gas impermeability and is utilized as caulking material. Chlorinated rubbers are good marine sheathing materials, and, as Kevlar, are also fabricated into sail cloth. Butadiene acrylonitrile (Buta-N) is used for plugs, and butadiene styrene (GR-S) is a hydrocarbon used in plastic utensils. Fluorocarbons are primarily found in rigid pipes designed to carry chemicals, although there are some adhesives based on fluorocarbons.

Many of the thermoplastic resins are used to form other plastic products. Acrylics are found in plastic awning material. Polyvinyl acetate (PVA) is used to fabricate clear waterhoses, as is vinyl. Polyethylene is a component in inexpensive plastic fittings and hoses. Polyvinyl chloride (PVC) is often utilized for reasonably priced plumbing tubing and for rigid hoses and connectors. It is also used for flexible vent cowls and, when reinforced with polyester-welded seams, for flexible tanks.

Nylon and vinyl are very important components of high-strength plastics. Nylon is used for fairly high-priced plastic hoses and plumbing fixtures. It can also

GENERIC NAME (trade name)	Adhesives	Bearings	Bedding	Cloth/Awnings	Deck Fittings	Fillers	Gaskets	"Glass"	Insulation	Lubricants	Plumbing	Sheathing	Sleeves	Tanks	Tubing & Hose
Table 12-1 OTHER CONSTRUCTION MATERIALS															
ABS (acrylonitrile-butadiene-styrene)							X								X
Acetal (Delrin)							X				X				
Acrylic (Plexiglas, Lucite)	X			X	X	X		X				X			
Cellulose											X				
Cyanoacrylate	X														
Epoxy	X					X									
Fluorocarbons	X														X
Natural resins & compounds, including wood	X						X			X		X			
Neoprene & synthetic nitrile rubber	X						X								X
Nylon polyamide (Nylatron, Monocast, Zytel)	X	X		X			X				X	X	X	X	X
Phenolic (Micarta)	X	X					X					X			
Polycarbonate (Lexan, Tuffak)				X				X							
Polyester (Mylar)	X			X	X				X			X			X
Polyethylene	X			X							X			X	X
Polypropylene				X							X	X			
Polystyrene									X		X				
Polysulfide			X												
Polysulfone											X				
Polytetrafluoroethylene (Teflon)		X								X		X			X
Polyurethane		X	X				X		X						
Polyvinyl acetate (PVA)	X														X
Polyvinyl chloride (PVC)	X						X				X			X	X
Rubber & synthetic rubber	X		X				X						X	X	
Silicon			X							X					
Urea formaldehyde	X														
Vinyl				X	X							X			X

be modified or reinforced for gears and bearings. Bearings are also made of phenolics, polytetrafluoroethylene and polyurethane. Glass substitutes, like Lexan and Plexiglas, are high-impact-resistant plastics based on polycarbonate and acrylic resins, respectively.

In this chapter, we discuss those construction materials that are used for securing (adhesives), insulating (gaskets and bedding compounds), sheathing, and filling or preserving. (Hoses and tubing are discussed in Chapter 13. Chapter 17 includes a description of the different bearing materials that are appropriate for shaft protection.)

ADHESIVES

Adhesives theoretically can provide four types of bonds: wood to wood, plastic to wood, wood to steel, and other metal to steel. On a steel-hulled vessel, however, there are only certain areas where glues are used, and these places are more often in the interior than the exterior. In the interior, adhesives can be found in fancy woodwork inlays and veneers, galley fixtures (chopping blocks, formica counters, or table coverings), cabin sole coverings, shower stalls, plumbing, bulkhead laminations, and ladders. The most important exterior application is laminating spars of Sitka spruce. Adhesives are also used to apply plastic or rubber deck coatings to steel decks, to make wooden rail caps and tiller laminates, to apply leather chafe protection to wood, and to repair sails.

Adhesives have many advantages over metal fasteners. Dissimilar metals can be joined without risk of corrosion, since the adhesive has no electrical conductivity. Using adhesives is faster and cheaper than welding, brazing, soldering, or screwing, and it is a good choice in areas where other types of joinery are impractical. Tools can be repaired and safety glass and veneers fabricated with strong, thin laminates, which distribute stresses over larger areas.

A good marine adhesive should be resistant to water, oil, heat, cold, light, fungus, and loss of adhesion. The correct adhesive must satisfy the demands of both surfaces being joined. Like any other material, each type offers certain advantages and has certain limitations.

Types of Curing

Adhesives, like paints, are composed of a vehicle, a solvent, and various modifiers and additives. Either an organic solvent or water is used to thin the compound. Many epoxy-based adhesives, as well as others, require a curing agent mixed in just before application. Water-soluble types need only to have water added in the correct proportion.

Solvent-based adhesives can be a liquid, paste, tape, or film composed of elastomers and thermosetting resins. They require pressure and/or heat or solvents to bond properly. These adhesives flow well, are easy to apply, and work best on porous materials. However, the solvent may react unfavorably with certain types of plastics. Generally these types have good flexibility and impact strength.

Water-based adhesives are a mixture of reclaimed rubber, asphalt, casein, or thermosetting resins (like urea formaldehyde) suspended in water. They require either heat or pressure to bond. This type is the least expensive, and includes the contact cement used by carpenters for bonding plastics like formica on counter tops. The consistency can be changed by adding water.

Thermosetting adhesives contain epoxies, polysulfides, polyurethanes, and other resins in the form of pastes, films, or liquids. Constant pressure at a temperature within the required range is all that is required for bonding. These glues are commonly supplied as two components requiring mixing. The thermosetting types have high heat resistance and good void-filling ability. They are very suitable for metal-to-metal bonds, since their shear strength is relatively high.

Resin Composition

Adhesives containing *natural resins* are mostly water-based, although some cure by solvent evaporation. With the exception of those based on asphalt, petroleum resins, or natural rubber, these glues have limited use in the harsh marine environment, since they have limited moisture resistance. The animal-origin glues (hide and casein) can be used for bonding wood to wood in the interior. With a few exceptions, glues of plant origin (coumarin, dextrine, gum arabic, rosin esters, wheat flour, soya, shellac rosin, and other oleoresins) are generally used only for paper-to-paper bonds or as sealants, although zein, derived from corn, is a common component in hot-melt glues.

The list of adhesives based on synthetic resins is much longer, and their make-up can be quite complex. They are generally stronger and more resistant to deterioration than glues based on natural resins.

Adhesives containing *elastomers* have low strength but high flexibility and are hard but not brittle. Therefore, they are best for flexing, unstressed joints. Most cure by solvent evaporation, but some are self-curing and require moisture and a particular temperature for curing. *Neoprene* is a flammable one-part liquid available in cartridges; it is also used in contact cement. With its high weather resistance and stability in changing temperatures, neoprene is good for laminating plywood, veneers, panels, studs, woods, and formica. *Latex adhesives*, like Patch Stick, are one-part liquids that can be brushed on fabrics like canvas; they also waterproof the material.

Many of the adhesives based on *synthetic resins* are "multi-purpose" glues. *Polyvinyl chloride* (PVC) and its co-polymers are used in clear, fast-drying liquid cement that is impervious to gas, oil, and alcohol. It is flammable, but used properly, it is good for home repairs. *Anaerobic glues* are one-part compounds which cure very quickly by oxidation. They are reported to be good for metals. *Nylon glues*, usually available as epoxy-nylon mixes, bond well to metal. *Cyanoacrylate glues* are special-purpose, water-based contact glues used on rubber, fiberglass, plastic, and metal. These quick-setting polymers require no clamping, have good chemical and oil resistance, and hold up well under heavy shocks. *Aliphatic resin glues* are creamy one-part liquids which are not waterproof and are used to bond woods.

Adhesives based on synthetic *thermoplastic resins* are best for bonds other than metal to metal. These adhesives become soft when heated and then harden on cooling. They are available as either solvent-based or water-emulsion types. *Acrylic resins* and *acrylonitrile* are used in liquid or powder glues. This creamy, elastomeric adhesive can be used on porous and non-porous material, and is very strong, fast setting, and waterproof. It can be used for bonding some metals. *Cellulose nitrate* (gum) is a flammable, one-part liquid used in cements. It has a honey-like consistency and is water resistant. *Polyvinyl acetate* (PVA) are used to produce a milky-white, water-based glue that is used on woods and in fabrics and foams. It is not strong, nor is it waterproof. *Polyethylene* is used in hot-melt glues, available in cartridges and jugs. These multi-resin glues bond to plastic, vinyl, wood, metal, and tile.

Synthetic *thermosetting resins* either harden permanently or solidify when they are heated. They bond by heat or pressure and sometimes require a catalyst for this bonding. These glues come in all forms, and have good strength characteristics. Epoxies, phenolics (resorcinol), and polyesters are the best for metal-to-metal bonds. The thermosetting adhesives include some of those most commonly used in boatbuilding.

Epoxy adhesives are two-part systems with a vehicle and a catalyst. Once epoxy has set, nothing will dissolve it, and the joint cannot be seen. Moisture-cured epoxies are some of the most waterproof adhesives available. These glues are useful on a variety of materials, including wood, foam, fiberglass, plastic, rubber, and metal, and they can also be used to fill gaps. A rougher surface helps application and they can cure at low temperatures. Epoxies are easy to use, since no clamping is needed. Fillers such as cabosil, micro-balloons, chopped glass, sawdust, or aluminum powder are sometimes added to help the adhesive go farther, thus saving cost. Epoxies are available under the following brand names: T-88, Cold Cure, Systems Three, Marine-Tex, and West System 105. Although the chemical in the catalyst may cause allergic reactions such as rashes, with proper safety precautions they should pose no health hazards.

The *phenolic resin blends*, which include phenolic vinyl, phenolic polyvinyl butyral, phenolic polyvinyl formaldehyde, phenolic nylon, phenolic neoprene, and phenolic butadiene acrylonitrile rubber, are thermosetting under high pressure and have very high heat resistance. *Resorcinol* is probably the best known of these glues. Resorcinol and phenolic resorcinol adhesives are easy to mix, using three parts of resin to one part of powder hardener to make a thick cream. The glue can be washed from surfaces with water before it dries, is not affected by many solvents, and is not weakened by boiling. Application requires tight joints held together with clamps or fasteners. A minimum temperature of 65°F is needed for curing, so these glues are particularly useful in the tropics. The resorcinols do stain wood, and the glue line is visible through varnishes. They are not recommended for use on oak and other acid woods, although teak can be successfully glued.

When adhesives are used for cold-molded laminates, the builder must make a choice between the less-expensive resorcinol glue or the more-expensive but more-durable and moisture-resistant epoxies. The structural importance of the lamination is usually the deciding factor, as well as whether it will be exposed to the elements. Epoxy is better for structural integrity and water resistance, even though resorcinol is waterproof and resistant to chemicals. Resorcinol can be used for smaller items and interior joinery work, and is less hazardous to work with.

Urea formaldehyde resin glues (the best-known of which is Weldwood) are sometimes confused with the resorcinols. This adhesive is a less-expensive powder that is mixed with water in the ratio of five parts powder to one part water. The joint has good water resistance but is not 100% waterproof. Urea formaldehydes are often used on boats, especially for bunging, but require good clamping for laminations and a fairly warm temperature for curing.

Polyester resin glues are two-part mixes of liquid resin and hardener that are used primarily on fiberglass boats, but they can also be applied successfully on steel boats. These glues are considered waterproof, and are most useful for plywood-to-fiberglass bonds. They are also utilized to secure drain holes and tubing.

Table 12-2. TOOLS FOR APPLYING ADHESIVES
Paper or cloth jumpsuit
Gloves (butyl rubber or neoprene)
Boots
Apron
Respirator
Barrier cream for hands
Knives
Trowels
Brushes
Spray gun
Hot melt gun
Mixer for epoxy (see West System)

Methods of Application

Adhesives can be applied to a surface in many different ways: with air knife, spatula, roller, or gun; by dipping or spraying; or in tape form. Hot-melt guns, although expensive initially, are often used in marine production. Small tubes of epoxy are inserted into these tools, which act like soldering guns to make fast bonds to plastic, vinyl, wood, metal, or tile. The epoxy substances are generally very toxic, and the manufacturer's instructions on self-protection and application methods should be followed. A well-ventilated working space is probably the most important safety precaution, followed by proper protective clothing.

INSULATORS AND ISOLATORS

On a steel ocean cruiser, insulators (isolators) are needed so that dissimilar metals and steel do not come in contact, forming an electrical connection that can lead to galvanic corrosion. Isolating materials also prevents selective corrosion of the metal in the dissimilar fitting. When steel and wood are joined, water must be prevented from sitting in the joint, where it can cause the steel to corrode and the wood to rot.

Both rubber products and plastics can be fabricated into the hardnesses and shapes required for different applications. These materials have good isolating properties, since they are non-corroding and have very low electrical conductivity. An insulator is a hard pad placed between a fitting or fastening and the steel, while gaskets or sleeves are softer and are used, for example, around fasteners. These soft gaskets can also be employed to seal hatches or porthole openings. A flexible bedding compound has some isolating ability but is used more often to keep water out of crevices and for items that may need to be removed. Cost and availability may dictate which is used; the flexible compounds are more available and can serve a function similar to a hard pad or gasket.

Bedding compounds used between seams and under mechanically fastened fittings can either be soft or hard, but a good bedding compound should always stay a bit flexible, even after curing. The traditional bedding compounds applied between wood joints require primers such as anti-fouling paint or red or white lead paint. Seam compounds can be used with fillers like cotton or oakum, but a better choice would be tar. However, they are not really suitable for wood-to-steel joinery. It would be better to use a rubber or plastic bedding compound formulated for that purpose, since for these the rate of deterioration is lower.

Polyurethanes are probably the best bedding compounds for sealing wood and dissimilar metal fitting and fasteners on a steel hull. Products like 5200 and Sika-

Flex are the best-known polyurethanes. They are slow-curing compounds (though SikaFlex cures faster than 5200) that are good for all-purpose applications, and they harden to a tough, flexible finish. These products flow well into crevices, and any excess can be easily cleaned off the surface before the compound is cured. Polyurethane bedding compounds can also be used in conjunction with neoprene gaskets to seal access plates in tanks.

Of the rubber-based compounds, the *polysulfides* are the most common. Thiokol is a two-part rubber deck-seam compound frequently used on wood boats. It does not bond as well to metal as the polyurethanes, but it is best between flexing seams. Dectogrove, Lifecaulk, and Boatlife are two-part compounds, similar to Thiokol, which are fine for use under fittings. SikaFlex also is available in a polysulfide formulation, and 3M produces single-component tubes of a polysulfide called 101. Rubber butyl caulking compound, another rubber-based compound, adheres well to most materials, except polyurethanes, and is noted for its fast curing time. Silicon rubbers are very elastic and are used for bedding and as sealants, although they are not appropriate seam compounds. They can take high temperatures and have good flex at low temperatures.

Silicon sealants, which take 24 hours to cure completely, are best used for glass and plastic, although they have limited use for metals when press-fit. They are not recommended for extremely wet areas, for underwater use, or for sealing fuel tank lids.

A new type of adhesive bedding compound with a *polycarbonate* base has recently appeared on the market under the brand name, Seal-Once. It is available in a variety of colors, is easy to handle and apply, and is advertised as sealing through water and oil films. It is too early to know for sure whether this compound will prove effective in the marine environment.

Other elastic putties, like Dolphinite, are made with special antifungal properties and contain pentachlorophenol to prevent rot. These are mostly used for wood-to-wood joinery.

Coal tar compounds are also used as patch cement for flooring and chimneys. Combined with asphalt or asbestos or in emulsion form, they are ideal for both wet and dry areas. These pitch compounds are good fillers for dead spaces such as under locker floors.

The harder, less-flexible insulating gaskets are more commonly used as sleeves around dissimilar metal fasteners, under permanent fittings (like seacocks, windlasses, or engine mount pads), and for plumbing and electrics. Rubber, neoprene, special mastics, plastics, and wood products are the material ingredients. These hard compounds are also used in areas where resistance to high-load friction is required (as in shaft bearings, couplings, and steering columns). Plastic insulators (especially nylon) can also be used as bearings on fittings where a stainless steel pin goes through a steel mounting tab (as in gooseneck fittings, fairleads, blocks and bow anchor rollers).

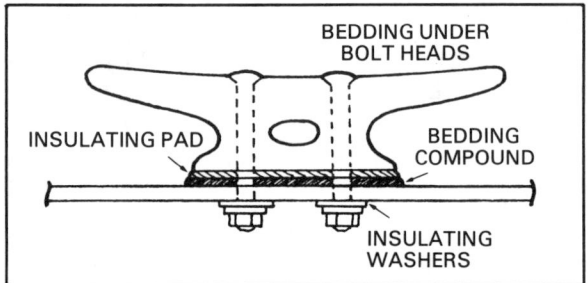

Fig. 12-1. *The correct method of bolting a dissimilar metal fitting (in this case, a cleat) to a steel deck.*

Neoprene and Tufnol are rubber products seen as weather stripes on hatches, washers, bearings, and bolt sleeves. Neoprene is the most commonly used gasket material on a steel yacht. It is often used under access lids, fuel tank lids, and hatches to keep water out. It works well for this purpose as long as the mechanical fasteners are tightened down hard.

Plastics like Nylatron (reinforced nylon), acetal, Teflon, Thorden (a polyurethane), Hypalon, ABS polypropylene, Micarta (phenolic), and PVC are all used for hard and semi-hard isolators. For example, Micarta is commonly used when bronze seacocks are mounted on a steel hull. Both acetal plastic and Micarta encase transducers and neoprene shaft bearings. Vinyl and nylon are also used for bolt sleeves. Almost all of these plastics can be further reinforced and molded into particular fittings like seacocks, hoses, and connectors. These fittings can be used without further insulation, unlike the more traditional dissimilar metal fittings.

Wood can also be used as a permanent isolating pad below mechanically fastened fittings. These pads can be made of plywood and pressboard, although neither is very durable. Hardwoods are definitely better as pads under deck fittings.

The only metal appropriate for use as an insulator is zinc, because it is lower than steel on the cathodic scale. Zinc pads can be placed under metal deck fittings to protect the steel beneath.

Fig. 12-2. *The deck iron for this rotating exhaust ventilator is isolated from the cabin top with a simple wood pad.*

Proper isolating gaskets or pads are most important underwater or in areas subjected to heavy weathering. Bedding compound provides sufficient insulation in less-exposed areas, and can be used in conjunction with gaskets in most exterior applications.

SHEATHINGS

Sheathings not only improve appearance and safety but offer protection from heat, cold, corrosion, moisture and heavy traffic, and they provide some insulation. They are especially important in high-chafe areas. Although fiberglass cloth or roving predominates today, many other materials are also used, even for a steel yacht.

There are certain areas onboard that need sheathing, and the requirements of each area must be matched with the properties of the sheathing material and the type of adhesive or fasteners with which it is secured. In the old days, copper sheets were nailed on the underbodies of tall ships to protect them from fouling organisms. Today, however, sheathing is more apt to be used in shower stalls or around heaters.

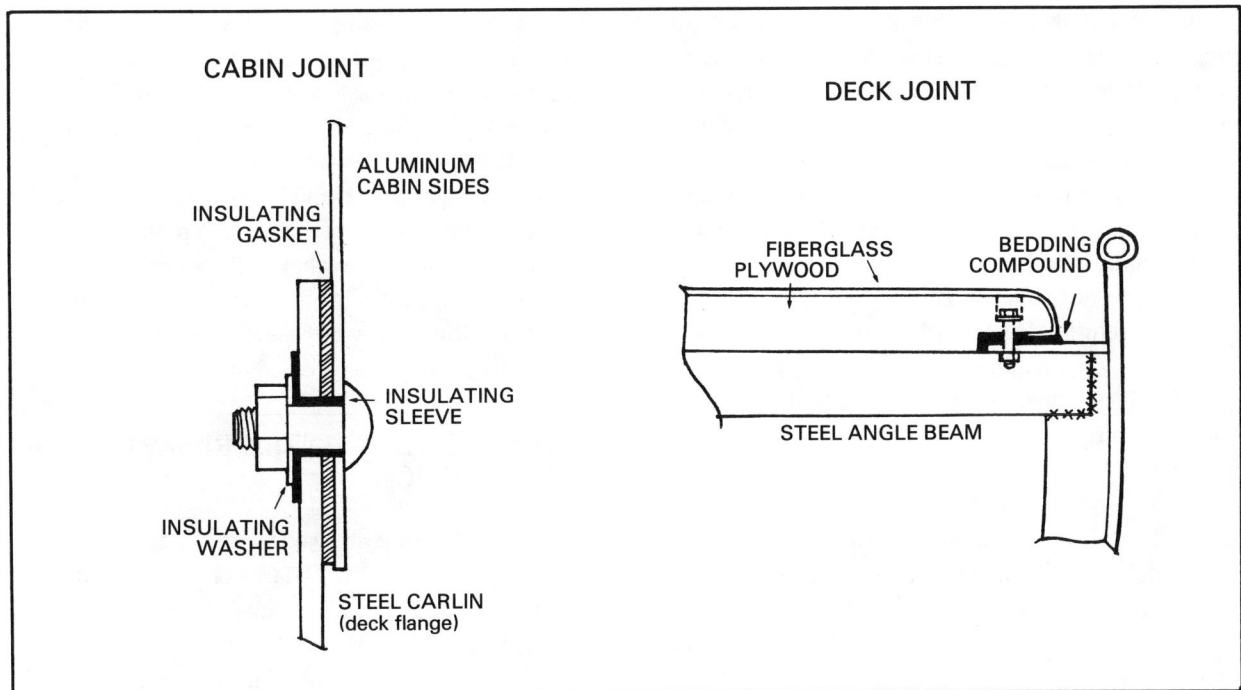

CABIN JOINT

ALUMINUM
CABIN SIDES

INSULATING
GASKET

INSULATING
SLEEVE

INSULATING
WASHER

STEEL CARLIN
(deck flange)

DECK JOINT

FIBERGLASS
PLYWOOD

BEDDING
COMPOUND

STEEL ANGLE BEAM

Fig. 12-3.   *In composite joinery, the type of insulation needed depends on the material being joined to the steel. An aluminum cabin requires gaskets and sleeves, while a plywood deck (or cabin) should be solidly bedded to keep water out of the joint.*

In the boat interior, sheathings are used primarily to insulate, to protect from moisture, to make clean-up easier, and to please the eye. Insulation (see Chapter 11) is a special-purpose sheathing which keeps heat, cold, and noise in their proper places. Special insulating materials also protect woodwork from heat generated by stoves and heaters. A refrigerator will need an insulating lining of fiberglass, foam and foil. Galley and head counters and shower stall floors can be covered with fiberglass, formica, ceramic tile, linoleum, or linotile so that these areas can be properly cleaned and are protected from moisture. Special rubber compounds can also be poured into the floor of the shower stall to prevent leaks. Where the primary concern is esthetic, decorative tiles, formica, and bricks can help to protect as well as to beautify the area. These sheathings are generally stuck down with contact cement.

Non-slip sheathings made of cork, rubber, and plastic mixtures (like Vetus, Treadmaster or Polygrip), antiskid TBS (polyurethane resin and granules), and mastic overlays are used to cover and protect decks, shower floors, ladders, and other slippery areas. When glued to the deck, these non-skid coatings also help to insulate the interior from heat. Such materials make a lot of sense for steel boats, since, although they are not cheap, they are long lasting and provide a nice-looking, comfortable surface. The surface is easy to clean, unlike non-skid paint or cork-epoxy coverings. This sheathing comes in rolls that can be cut to fit and glued down wherever desired. Vinyl/rubber non-skid pads can be used for small areas.

Moisture-sensitive materials, like electrics and navigation charts, can also be sheathed in plastic or resins. A thin layer of plastic can be rolled over paper to form a calendar coating. The cascade method involves dropping powder over a preheated object and can be used to coat electrics with epoxy. Some materials can be dipped into resin. A plasma welding unit with a special spray gun can be used to spray a very thin (.0001") coating of plastic onto metal. Electrostatic spraying can protect electrics that must be installed in damp areas, but its use is rare.

Natural sheathings are also useful. Wool or felt liners are placed under wood to repel moisture. Leather antichafe patches can be sewed to sails. Chlorinated rubber (Kevlar) and latex rubber linings can be applied directly to hulls. Natural fibers like cotton canvas have their uses for sail covers. Cement and tar mixes are generally bedding compounds, but can also sheathe tanks and dead spots. Wood is a natural for interior sheathing of a steel hull. It can also be laminated into complex shapes and curves.

Many materials based on synthetic resins are appropriate for sheathings. Flexible sheets of vinyl can be installed to cover cabin ceilings. They are secured with glue or metal fasteners. A loosely woven acrylic mat, like Dynel, is used with an epoxy resin to cover wood. Acrylics and vinyls also serve for awnings; combined with PVC, the material becomes rigid. Polyester cloth (for example, Nexus cloth) is thin and easy to handle, and can be used to cover plywood. Fiberglass matt and roving is strong but has limited ability to stretch; it must be applied over a stable surface. Fiberglass lamination can effectively sheathe exterior surfaces that require long-term protection from the elements. Arabol resin is especially handy for holding down cloth, both natural and synthetic. Polypropylene cloth has better strength than polyester, and it will stretch. Protective sail covers can be made of nylon, dacron, or rayon cloth. In this plastic world of ours, many new products are constantly coming out, and once tested, they may find various unforeseen applications in the marine world.

Sheathing must be applied properly to hold correctly. The proper adhesives and methods of application must be used. For example, when applying formica with contact cement, a certain amount of pressure is necessary. Only certain mastics or paste glue can be used on tiles. Non-slip Vetus deck coverings adhere best to painted metal when certain epoxy adhesives are applied after the deck is sanded and the edges of the sheathing are bull-nosed. Elastomers like neoprene can be difficult to laminate, so a mechanically fastened press fit is required, even if a flexible bedding is used with the neoprene sheathing. In each case, the manufacturer's instructions must be followed carefully.

FILLERS, LUBRICANTS, PRESERVATIVES AND CHEMICALS

Fillers are commonly used for fairing and to fill gaps, holes, and cracks in the surfaces of wood, plastic, and cloth. The traditional fillers for wood include glazing compounds, phenol wood filler, Duritite bedding (for bungs), Plastic Wood, Boat Fil, putty and varnish in wood seams, and paste filler (for example, Silex for filling wood pores).

Fig. 12-4. *How many different materials can you find on this boat?*   (At least 10)

The newest formulations generally adhere well and are most durable. If it's absolutely necessary to use fillers on a steel hull, good epoxy fillers are best; for wood, there are many possibilities. Special fiber fillers for repairing high-impact plastics like ABS and Lexan are also available. Some of these compounds "weld" the plastic together.

The modified polyamide epoxy fillers preferred for metal include Red Hand (International), Gluvitt by Travaco (clear or colored), Marine Tex, and Poxy Putty (Permalite Plastic Corp.), which hardens quickly and is good underwater. Cabosil, chopped glass, graphite, fine sawdust, micro-balloons, alum powder, epoxy paste, cabofill, or phenolics can be added to epoxy fillers to make them go farther. Fast-cure epoxy fillers can also be used for bunging. Vinyl plastics work fairly well for mending wood, but are not useful on metal. Polyester fillers, like fast-curing, two-part Bondo, are all right on fiberglass cloth or mat or on wood, but should not be used to fair a steel hull. Some of these polyester fillers include fiberglass strands saturated with resin. Cementitious acrylic emulsions are two-component cement fillers that are hard and very durable. Heat can help to speed up the curing process, and many of these synthetic fillers dry to a sandable surface within an hour.

Table 12-3. TOOLS FOR APPLYING PRESERVATIVES AND SEALERS

Gloves
Mask
Respirator
Masking tape and duct tape
Emery cloth
Sandpaper
Buffing pads
Grinding discs
Paint buckets and jars
Brushes
Rollers
Spray tools

Some patching compounds are specially formulated for use in wet areas and underwater. They work by displacing water, and will not dissolve or float away. These fillers have high strength and adhesion characteristics, and many are quick drying. They also work well on hull fittings, pipes, fuel tanks, and areas subject to corrosive attack.

Preservatives are used primarily on wood to seal surfaces and prevent rot. Kerosene, although it can be a preservative, is better used as a fuel because of its strong odor. Cuprinol or a mixture of linseed oil, kerosene, varnish, and Japan drier is often used to preserve wood. Pine tar is a preservative that keeps fabric, manila line, and steel cable in good shape. Coal-tar solvents and paints can be used for the same purpose. Penta (pentachlorophenol; trade name Woodlife) is very nasty stuff and can be deadly at high exposure rates. The clear type is best, but it will leach through paint.

Some preservatives can also be used on metal and plastic surfaces. Save-Cote is a liquid plastic that can be applied on all materials. Varnish can be used on metal for emergency temporary repairs. But good metal primers are the best preservatives for steel. Metal polish and waxes can be helpful in keeping stainless steel and other alloys shining.

Other protective coatings seal the pores in the surface of wood to prevent contamination by moisture or other materials. These include creosote (an antiseptic), tung oil, salt and salt water (the old "pickling" practice on wooden hulls), Marine Mate (teak sealer), tributyl tin oxide (Flexabar, Flextin), teak oil (Deks Olje is one type), paste wax, lacquer (used instead of paint for natural finishes), shellac (especially on knots and pitch pockets before painting), varnish, paints, fish oil, and copper naphthanate (very toxic, but a good penetrant). Epoxy resin sealers are excellent in critical areas.

Lubricants are used on bare metal surfaces in machinery, electrics and plumbing. They do have temporary anti-corrrosive properties, but only as long as the lubricant remains on the metal. Common lubricants include Teflon Lub (W.G.L.), Lubriplate, Aqua-guard, Fluid Film, Amasol-Lub (fuel additive), Lubrimatic, Moovit (belt dressing), silicon spray, ether, LPS, WD-40, petroleum jelly, and grease. Gear oil will also come in handy. Hydrocarbons (like Never Seize) and thread compounds have good anticorrosive properties, and fasteners can be dipped into them prior to installation. Teflon tape is handy for sealing plumbing fixtures and stainless steel seacocks, but it does not provide the galvanic insulation of a thicker gasket.

Most of the other chemical products carried onboard are used for maintenance or for solvent cleaning. Acetone is a strong solvent especially useful for cleaning fiberglass. To clean stainless, dilute nitric acid or an emery cloth work well. Since rubbing alcohol contains no oil, it is good for stove fuel and for cleaning parts. It should be used in the shade, since it evaporates quickly. Paint thinner, besides cleaning paint, can be used in kerosene lamps; it is smokeless if thinned with Tovlul.

Mineral spirits is another low-oil cleanser that is good on bare metal. A grease cleaner (like kerosene) is good for engine parts, and a bilge cleaner will also emulsify both grease and oil. Paint removers, rust removers, and dilute muriatic acid will clean impurities from metals; all must be handled carefully. Other toxic solvents that might be carried include heptane, methyl ethyl ketone (MEK), glycerol, ethylene glycol, or toluene. It would be wise to stick to one or two that will serve most needs rather than carry many of these toxic chemicals.

Other less-harmful chemicals likely to be found aboard are detergent cleansers for sails, wood, upholstery, and bilges. Good hand cleansers with lanolin or pumice help to restore the body to normal after a long working day.

CONCLUSION

As this overview indicates, many items will serve but only a few are really necessary, especially in a maintenance kit to be carried on-board. You would be wise to stick to those materials used during the boat's original construction. A repair kit might include two kinds of adhesives (epoxy and resorcinol), polyurethane and polysulfide bedding compounds, epoxy fillers, some hard insulators (nylon and Micarta), some flexible neoprene gaskets, a wood preservative (like Cuprinol), various sheathings, and the necessary solvents for adhesives and lubricants for parts. With these materials, you'll be able to repair anything anywhere and even to carry out a number of alterations to the various systems.

Chapter 13

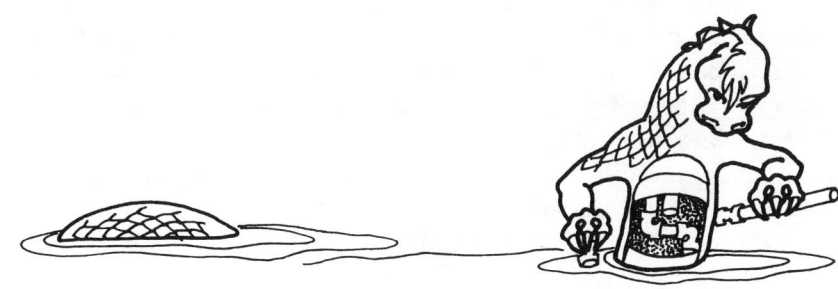

Plumbing

This chapter focuses on the materials used for the hoses, fittings, tanks, pumps, and miscellaneous containers that are part of the plumbing system. The engine exhaust system, integral throughhulls, and the marine toilet are each discussed separately in other chapters.

The plumbing system onboard a steel sailboat is basically the same as that used in any other hull type, with the proviso that dissimilar metals should be avoided whenever possible. When they must be used, special gaskets, both rigid and flexible, will be needed between the steel hull and dissimilar metal fittings. Certain items like tanks, throughhulls, and topside breather vents can be welded integral with the hull, thus simplifying the system.

Installing the plumbing is relatively simple, and it can be done with a few basic tools. Even if you hire a professional to do the job, it's good to know the basics, since plumbing failures at sea can create major problems. Failures in seacocks are the most critical, but a leaky fuel line, a reverse-siphoning head, or polluted drinking water can also be "disasters" at sea. Careful attention must be given to the location, the layout, and the material for all throughhull fittings, and the whole system should be as simple and centralized as possible. If you are purchasing a secondhand vessel, potential problems may be close to happening, so a thorough inspection and replacement of questionable parts is definitely in order.

Plastics, rubber products, and metals play an important part in plumbing. Plastics are especially suitable, since they neither corrode themselves nor promote galvanic corrosion in the steel. ABS, Teflon, PVC, polypropylene, polyethylene, Viton, polyester, reinforced nylon, vinyl, neoprene, and glass-reinforced nylon are all available as molded fittings or hoses. When fitted with isolating gaskets, bronze and stainless steel can be used successfully for fittings like seacocks, especially since the small area of the fitting in relation to the large hull area helps to control corrosion. However, steel and galvanized steel are sometimes suitable. Neither copper nor monel should be used, since both are much more noble than steel.

SEACOCKS

Like any opening below the waterline, seacocks need special attention to ensure that they are sound and completely leakproof. Both the material and the method of installation are very important. The integral throughhulls to which they are attached usually have been fabricated with an insert of schedule-80 steel pipe that protrudes into the interior. The end of the pipe is either fitted with a steel flange, to which a bronze or stainless seacock and its gasket can be bolted, or threaded so that

219

a plastic seacock can be screwed in. Spare softwood plugs should be carried onboard to plug up the through-hull if a seacock should fail.

Seacocks have either ball or gate valves; the ball valve is preferable, since there is less chance of its clogging. Lever handles are better than the threaded, screw-down types that may freeze up at critical moments. No matter which type is used, seacocks should be strong, easy to install, maintenance free, and easily accessible at any time during a voyage.

Cast silicon or aluminum bronze is the traditional sea-cock material because of its strength and durability underwater. On a steel hull, a hard plastic, nylon, or phenolic (Micarta) insulator must be installed between the bronze seacock and the hull. Bronze bolts should be painted, covered with a plastic sleeve, and inserted into oversized holes with nylon or neoprene washers at both ends. The entire assembly is bedded with a flexible polyurethane compound, although grease will work for fast emergency replacements. The zerk fitting used to lubricate the seacock should be made of bronze or 316 stainless, not steel.

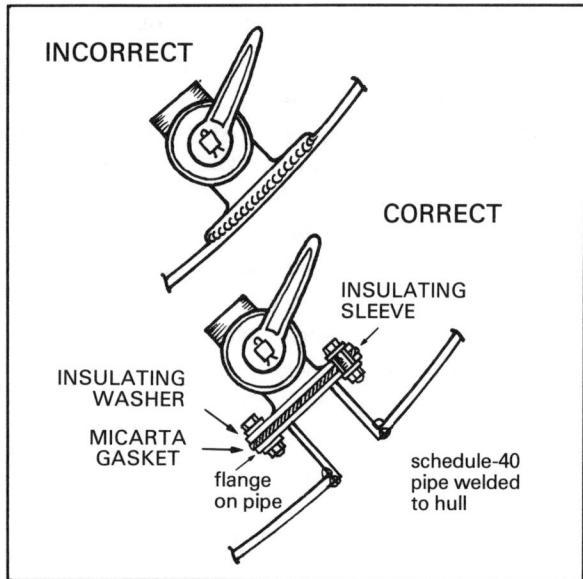

Fig. 13-1. *Successful installation of seacocks depends on proper insulation. Although a stainless seacock could be welded to the hull (above), this procedure is not recommended.*

Stainless steel is also used for seacocks, and since it's closer to steel on the galvanic scale than bronze, it requires less insulation. (Some professional builders use only Teflon tape on the threads of the throughhull pipe for insulation, but an isolating gasket would be safer.) There is little chance of the seacock being subjected to

the stresses that cause fatigue in stainless, although there is a risk of crevice corrosion, since its protective oxide layer is partially deprived of oxygen. The low-grade types of stainless should not be used, but if a seacock is made of type 316 or 17-PH stainless and is bolted on an insulated flange, there will be few problems.

Plastic seacocks have an unnecessarily bad reputation for breaking off under stress and for melting during fires. However, most such catastrophes befell the relatively stiff, brittle plastics of the past. Today there are new formulations of plastic which, while relatively inexpensive, have very high strength characteristics and can be used more safely in critical areas. They are very practical on steel hulls because they are non-conductive. Even these "miracle plastics" will melt during a fire, but they do so slowly, and only if the fire spreads to the area directly around them. The best insurance is to make sure that your electric and heating systems will not cause a fire; fire retardants added to insulation will also lessen the danger of melting seacocks.

The new plastic seacocks are made of Zytel or Marelon. Marelon—reinforced nylon with fluoroplastic polymers—has passed extensive testing by Underwriters' Laboratory. It weighs and costs less than bronze seacocks and has high chemical resistance. Zytel is a glass-reinforced nylon, and is also used in strong hoses. The only maintenance required is periodic lubrication with light oil or vaseline. (This kind of maintenance should be carried out on seacocks of any material so that they don't freeze up.) A plastic seacock can be screwed directly into a threaded throughhull pipe or onto a galvanized elbow fitted to the pipe, but these seacocks are subject to cross-threading, so care should be taken when installing them.

Modern plastic seacocks are definitely worth considering for a steel hull, but well-insulated bronze fittings may stand up better over time. You trade the risk of corrosion and freeze-ups for the risk of melting during a fire.

As Chapter 9 indicated, there are an average of nine places where throughhulls and seacocks will be needed onboard a cruising yacht. A head needs three: toilet intake, toilet outflow, and sink outflow. Saltwater intake and gray water outflow are needed in the galley. The engine requires a saltwater intake and an exhaust pipe opening. Two cockpit scupper drains may also need seacocks if throughhulls are used to drain the cockpit.

A sea chest can be used to consolidate a large number of seacocks into one area, especially those for raw water intake. Properly designed, it has a standpipe rising well above the waterline with a removable cap on top and a number of nipples welded to it for attaching seacocks. If the standpipe does not rise above the waterline, it should be protected with zinc anodes or a ½" threaded union with a nut that has a zinc collar.

Schedule-80 pipe welded into the hull forms the sea chest. A doubler plate can be inserted around the base, but this extra-heavy plate can be omitted if the pipe is supported by steel gussets. The standpipe should be located as close to all intakes as possible so that the hoses that must be run to plumbing fixtures need not be too long.

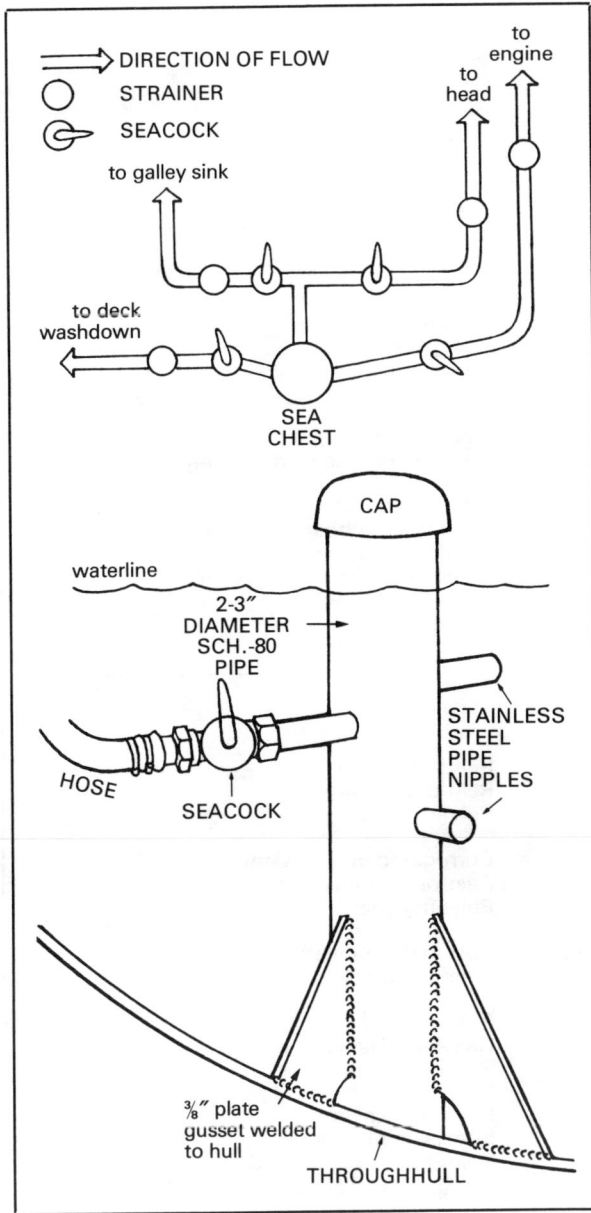

Fig. 13-2. *Hoses are connected to the sea chest to route water throughout the boat.*

A sea chest can be hard to maintain because of frequent fouling. The diameter of the pipe should be large enough that the sea chest can be easily inspected and cleaned with a mop or plunger. The opening can be fitted with a screen, but screens often corrode or clog, and can be difficult to clean. A simple rod grate, to keep weeds and floating debris out of the standpipe, and in-line strainers (fitted after the seacock junction) may work best.

Seacocks should be removed and inspected at least every three years. During regular haul-outs, the area around the throughhull can be checked for corrosion; if any is found, the seacock should be removed and inspected. The seawater circulating through the plumbing system most likely won't affect the seacock, but crumb or crud, temperature changes, stray currents, and corrosive action will.

VALVES AND FITTINGS

Tank and hose shut-off valves are needed in many places onboard, and their number and location depends on the design of the plumbing system. Y-valves and elbow vent loops of PVC are used in the head and elsewhere. T-valves of PVC or polypropylene may also be required. Bend fittings, both 45-degree and 90-degree, are needed for plumbing installation, as well as joints and hose cuffs. Adapters are also commonly made of PVC. Teflon makes good valve seats, and ABS plastic is used mostly for valve handles. Buta-N rubber is fabricated into valve plugs and impellers. Bronze shutoff valves should be installed in all fuel lines.

HOSES

The number of hoses required in a plumbing system seems almost endless, since hoses are used to connect everything to everything else. Intake hoses from seacocks are needed for saltwater connections to the engine, galley, and head. Hoses for fresh water and fuel run from deck fillers to the tanks. Leading lines then take fuel to the engine and water from tanks to fixtures, sometimes with a detour through a hot water heater. The engine exhaust is also carried through a hose or pipe. Drain hoses run to holding tanks from all sinks, heads, and showers, and then from the holding tanks out. The bilge pump uses hoses at each end.

Hoses can be divided into two groups: those which carry water and those which carry fuel or other chem-

Table 13-1. HOSE MATERIALS

RAW WATER INTAKE

Engine	Neoprene Reinforced neoprene Nitrile
Galley	Corrugated polyethylene Reinforced polyester
Head	Corrugated polyethylene Reinforced polyester

CLEAN INTAKE

Freshwater deck fill	Vinyl Copper Galvanized steel Glass-reinforced nylon (Zytel)
Diesel deck fill	Nitrile-reinforced neoprene

LEADING LINES

Fuel tank to engine	Neoprene ¼″ copper tubing Carlisle (reinforced neoprene)
Water tank to sink	Vinyl PVC Glass-reinforced nylon (Zytel)
Hot water to sink	Reinforced PVC Reinforced rubber Reinforced polyester Glass-reinforced nylon (Zytel) Reinforced vinyl Copper

DRAINS

Bilge pump	Reinforced vinyl Reinforced nylon Polyethylene
Head to holding tank and out (black water)	Corrugated polyethylene Reinforced polyester Polybutylene
Sinks and showers to holding tank and out (gray water)	Corrugated polyethylene Reinforced polyester
Cockpit scuppers	PVC Galvanized steel pipe Reinforced polyester
Engine exhaust	Reinforced nylon Special reinforced nitrile Reinforced neoprene (Carlisle) Galvanized steel pipe

icals. Different degrees of chemical and temperature resistance and wall thickness are needed for each type. Depending on the geometry of the area in which the hose is installed, it may also need to flex. To make thick, strong hose capable of bending, it is often corrugated or reinforced with metal or fibers.

In hoses, plastic really comes into its own. PVC makes the stiffest drinking-water hoses (although water quality tests have raised some questions about its suitability for carrying potable water); a polyethylene hose is more flexible. Polyester (even dacron polyester) yields a hose that is strong and flexible, while fiberglass-filled materials produce harder hose; nylon-reinforced hoses are commonly used in bilge pumps. Clear vinyl hoses that can be visually inspected are good choices for water hoses, while high-strength vinyl hoses have good chemical resistance, making them valuable for gray and black water or for chemical drainage. Vinyl-coated flexible tubing can be used for pumps and hot water.

Rubber products, both natural and synthetic, are best for heavy-duty hoses. Fuel lines, head hoses, and bilge pumps all require strong, reinforced hoses that won't collapse under the suction caused by pumping action. Rubber hoses are often reinforced with metal. Synthetic nitrile rubber (Carlisle) is one of the best bets for engine exhaust. Neoprene can be used for diesel fuel lines, engine raw water intake, and some exhausts. Plain rubber hoses are stiff but don't have good resistance to diesel. Polybutylene is another type of synthetic rubber used for flexible hose and connectors.

Different types of metal pipe can also serve for some hoses. The most common materials are galvanized steel and copper. Galvanized steel is an inexpensive option for freshwater lines and engine exhaust; it should never be used for diesel fuel lines, since the zinc galvanizing will react with the diesel. Chrome- or zinc-plated steel will also deteriorate quickly. Copper can be used for both hot and cold water lines, although there is a risk of hull corrosion if the copper pipes are in contact with the steel hull. If galvanized water tanks are used, copper piping should not be installed, since the tanks will corrode rapidly.

Obviously, some hoses cost more than others. The more-expensive types can be used only for short distances in order to save money. Here is a list of hose materials in order of cost (starting with the least expensive):

1) polyethylene
2) vinyl
3) clear vinyl
4) PVC

5) reinforced nylon
6) reinforced polyester
7) polybutylene
8) neoprene and neoprene combinations
9) synthetic nitrile-reinforced nylon
10) rubber

Stainless steel is really the only practical material for hose clamps and clips. All hoses should be double-clamped at each end for safety.

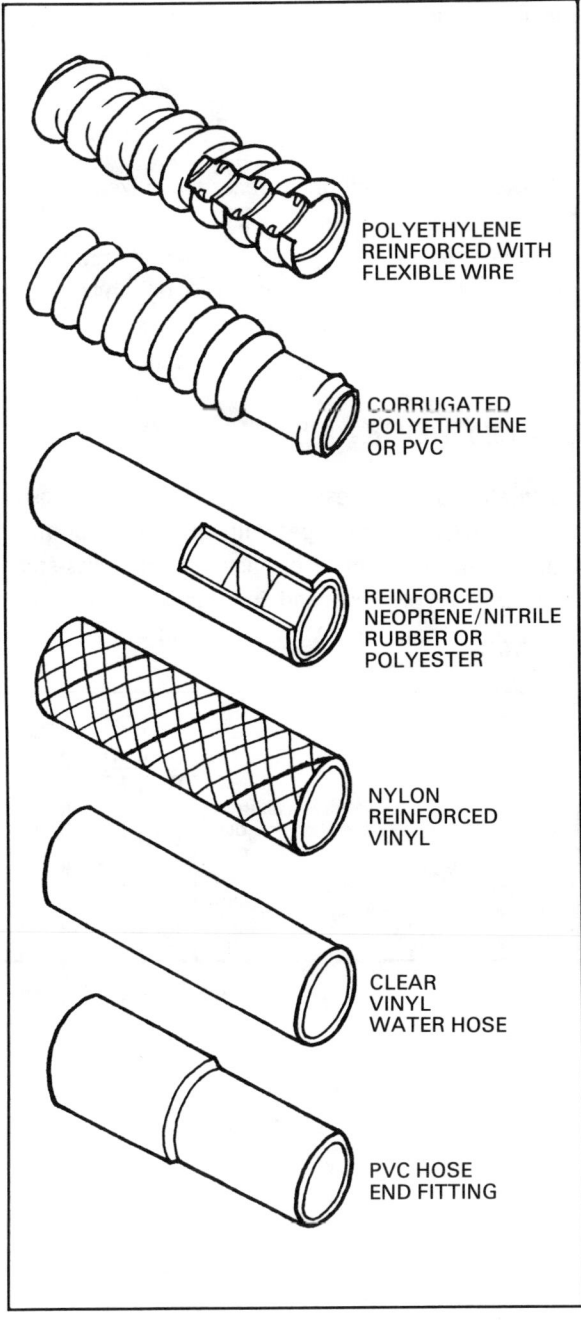

Fig. 13-3. *The hoses used in onboard plumbing come in many shapes and sizes.*

STRAINERS AND FILTERS

In-line strainers or filters located just after the seacocks should be installed on intake lines for both engine water and potable water. When in-line filters are used, there is no need for a screen welded to the throughhull opening. Such screens make cleaning and painting the throughhull much more difficult. In-line strainers and filters can easily be cleaned out from the inside when the seacock is closed. The strainers are usually made of metal or plastic.

VENTS

Glass-reinforced nylon, bronze, galvanized steel, or PVC can be used for vent loops in the head. Breather vent lines may be of clear materials so that they can be visually inspected for clogging. Inverted fittings should be installed where the breather lines pass through the plate, so that water cannot get into the lines.

GALLEY HOOK-UPS

After the raw and fresh waters are brought by hoses to the galley, a sink equipped with foot or hand pumps, faucets, and filters must be installed. Stainless-steel sinks are most practical, and, in the galley, twin basins facilitate dishwashing. A propane flash water heater,

like that manufactured by the Paloma Company, can also be put into the line to provide hot water. This is a fairly economical system that uses fuel only when heating the water. If an electric hot water heater is used, lines must be led between it and the hot water faucet. Drainage lines from the sink can lead directly to a seacock and throughhull; if the sink is located low or far off-center to either side, the drain line should lead to a throughhull on the opposite side.

HEAD HOOK-UPS

In the head, as in the galley, there must be sinks, shower heads, pumps, faucets, and filters. A hot water heater also can be connected to the lines bringing water into the sink or shower. The black water from the toilet and the gray water from the shower are both carried to their own holding tanks. A bypass valve is necessary for discharging directly overboard when outside inland waters; a deck pump-out will be needed if you only operate on inland waters. The head drainage system must be properly vented with a sufficiently large breather tube fitted into the line.

PUMPS

Pumps drive water, waste, or fuel through the hoses that make up the plumbing system. Both manual and

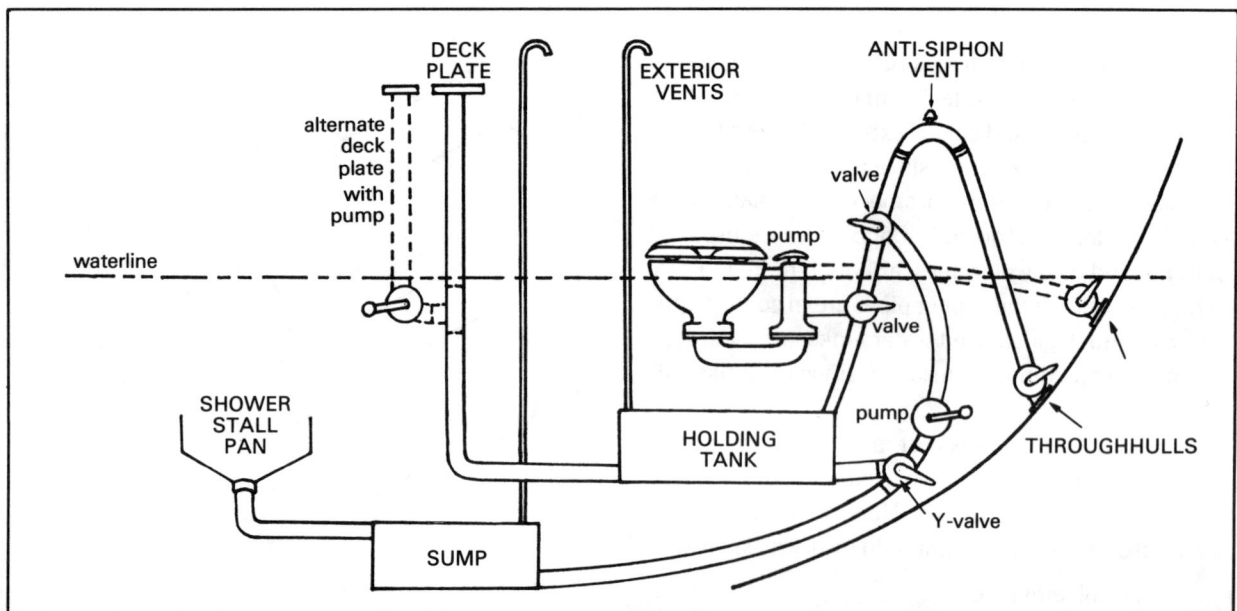

Fig. 13-4. *Plumbing for the head is complicated by requirements for holding tanks and deck pump-outs. The toilet itself should be above the waterline; the intake seacock could come off a sea chest.*

electric pumps are available, but if electric pumps are used, manual backups should also be installed, especially for the critical bilge pump. Foot pumps, equipped with strainers, are most practical for sinks, although pressurized water systems with electric pumps are also available. A pressurized system with its own electric motor is an unnecessary, costly, and elaborate assembly, although it could run off the engine. But some may feel they want this luxury.

Bilge pumps, though rarely needed on a steel vessel, are an important safety item. Most are made of metal or high-strength plastic (like glass-reinforced polypropylene). The diaphragm-type pumps are most practical, since they are self-priming and let small bits of bilge crumb pass through without plugging up. A "strum box" filter should be installed in the line ahead of the bilge pump to keep large pieces of debris out of the pump. A bilge pump can also be rigged to run off the engine's clutch if large-volume pumping is required. Good bilge pumps are manufactured by a number of companies, including Rule, Park, Edson, and Jabsco.

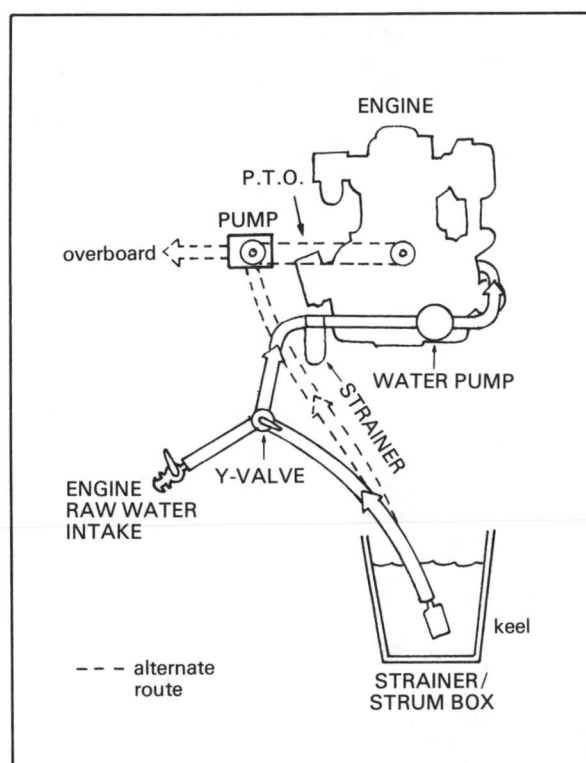

Fig. 13-5. *Engine power can be harnessed in several different ways to pump the bilge: the engine's own water pump can provide suction, or a separate pump can be run by a power take-off. The bilge pump hose can also be routed to the galley or head sink, from which the water will flow out a throughhull*

Reinforced plastic or neoprene tubing can be used for the bilge pump hose. Although it is not fireproof, it will hold up well when hot water is pumped through it. Galvanized pipe is cheaper than some plastics, and may be used if space allows.

Manual or electric pumps will be needed to clean out all holding tanks, and small pumps can also be used to clean out integral tanks. The same pump can be used on different tanks, although the pumps used for fuel and water should be kept separate. A separate pump for the engine oil removal is also a good idea.

If watertight bulkheads are installed onboard, there should be a small bilge pump for each compartment. They are particularly handy for removing water from a trapped area in the bottom of an anchor locker.

The wise sailor carries along a pump repair kit containing spare valves, diaphragms, hoses, clamps, O-rings, and PVC conduit. Conduit can be used for protecting vent hoses where they pass through bulkheads, although the protection may not be necessary.

Table 13-2. PLUMBING MAINTENANCE AND REPAIR KIT

One or two buckets
Spare hose sections
Hose clamps
Hacksaw
Nippers
Pliers
Tape
Wire
Hose glue
Teflon tape
Conduit
Cleansers
Disinfectants

TANKS

On a steel hull, many tanks can be made integral, especially in the keel (see Chapter 9). However, non-integral tanks also have their place. These tanks can be metal (stainless, mild steel, black iron, aluminum, or plastic). For flexible water tanks, reinforced nylon, PVC, neoprene-coated nylon, or polyethylene can be used. Spare flexible tanks can easily be stored in odd-shaped spaces, and a few small plastic 5-gallon water jugs will also probably prove useful. Kerosene can be stored in 2-5-gallon plastic, copper, or galvanized jugs or tanks with spigots. Reserving a few spare plastic 5-gallon jugs for transporting diesel is also sensible.

Holding tanks must have fairly high chemical resistance. For these, rigid PVC, polyethylene and neoprene-nylon combinations are useful because they do not react with their contents.

All integral tanks must be fitted with properly located breather valves, filters, valves, and hoses. A clear tubing (vinyl or glass) level gauge, often seen on the outside of water tanks, is also a good idea. A proper pump-out leading on deck or into the head's holding tank may be required. In U.S. coastal waters, you need to comply with the various changing water pollution regulations.

—Chapter 14—

Openings

The various openings found in the hull, deck, cabin, or cockpit of any sailboat are not only necessary for ventilation, but also for plumbing, drainage, access, light, and engine operation. These openings are cut out of the hull skin before blasting and painting, and each must be covered securely (especially in heavy weather) so that the interior of the boat stays dry and comfortable. The overall cost of these covers can be reasonable, especially if the more expensive alloys and production fittings are avoided. Steel and wood can be used to fabricate attractive covers that are both strong and simple. But the joinery is a bit different on steel boats than on those built of other hull materials.

Gaskets, bedding compound, and fasteners play important roles in securing and insulating the various covers. Wood, neoprene, Micarta, nylon, or rubber (refrigerator gaskets work well) are effective gasket materials. Good polyurethane bedding compounds will also be necessary, along with a supply of the proper-sized bolts, washers, and nuts, either stainless or galvanized steel. Machine screws or drift bolts can be used for securing hatches, ventilators, and portholes; studs are not really necessary for this joinery.

HATCHES

The largest, and therefore the most vulnerable, openings are those which allow the crew (or large amounts of water) to move from the exterior to the interior. In order to guarantee the integrity and security of any cruising sailboat afloat on the wild blue sea, these openings must be fitted with strong, watertight access hatches that will keep water out during a broach, a one-eighty, and even the rare 360-degree roll. Although many hatches have small leaks that are very annoying, the best ones only let in small squirts of water, if any at all, during a knock-down. On the other hand, even well-built hatches have occasionally been carried away by the crashing waves, much to the dismay of an anxious crew below.

The design of the hatch must also take into account the safety of the crew as they move around the deck. Manufacturers like Bomar, Atkin and Hoyle, and Lewmar produce ready-made hatches that lie very flush to their mounts, but they still protrude far enough to trip someone. Unfortunately, there are also some second-rate plastic hatches that won't stand up to rough weather; don't bother to buy and install them.

A very strong and inexpensive hatch can easily be made of steel. However, because of its weight, a steel hatch could have a dangerous accidental impact on a crew member's head. Wood doesn't deliver quite the blow that steel does, and it looks better. Aluminum also can be used, and, because of their light weight, aluminum hatches are especially easy to open and close.

A well-built, traditional wooden hatch with proper gaskets and latches will perform very well on a steel

Fig. 14-1. *This builder has readied his vessel for even the ultimate gale with a completely watertight steel companionway hatch.*

hull. Building your own wooden hatches is the least expensive way to go, and besides adding a touch of class on deck, it can be an enjoyable joinery project. Securing wood hatches to a steel deck is fairly easy, as long as allowances are made for any swelling of the wood.

The *main companionway* leading below from the cockpit or deck is usually the largest access opening. If the hatch opens up at the wrong time, a great volume of water could get in. You could be pumping for a long

time—even for the last time, since a steel hull full of water will go down a lot faster than a wooden one. Therefore, the design of the hatch should emphasize both strength and watertight closure.

Companionways are generally shaped like a sideways L; that is, the opening is in two planes. The longer top opening is covered by a hatch which usually runs on a slide. The front opening should have a riser or lip at deck level to keep splashes out of the interior. A fairly hefty set of removable drop boards can be inserted above this riser for heavy-weather sailing; a small viewing port made of clear plastic is handy in the top drop board. Many sea-going designs use well-secured swinging doors instead of dropboards. A turtle made of laminated wood, wood planks, fiberglass, aluminum, or steel is installed over the hatch to help keep rain and spray out, and to provide a safe place to step. Turtles can easily be made removable by bolting them on over gaskets.

If a wood hatch is used over the companionway, the hatch opening should be built with a flange sufficiently wide to allow the wooden lip that fits under the slide to be wide and strong. Failures of wooden hatches commonly occur because this section does not have enough meat. Metal hatches do not need as wide a slide section, because their material is stronger.

Builders often neglect to provide a way to get large pieces of wood (for example, bulkheads) below after the hull is plated up. One good solution to this problem is to have a removable access panel located forward of the companionway opening under the removable turtle.

Fig. 14-2. *This aluminum hatch was fabricated with very simple hinges. The homemade traveler to the right is machine-screwed to a long doubler plate.*

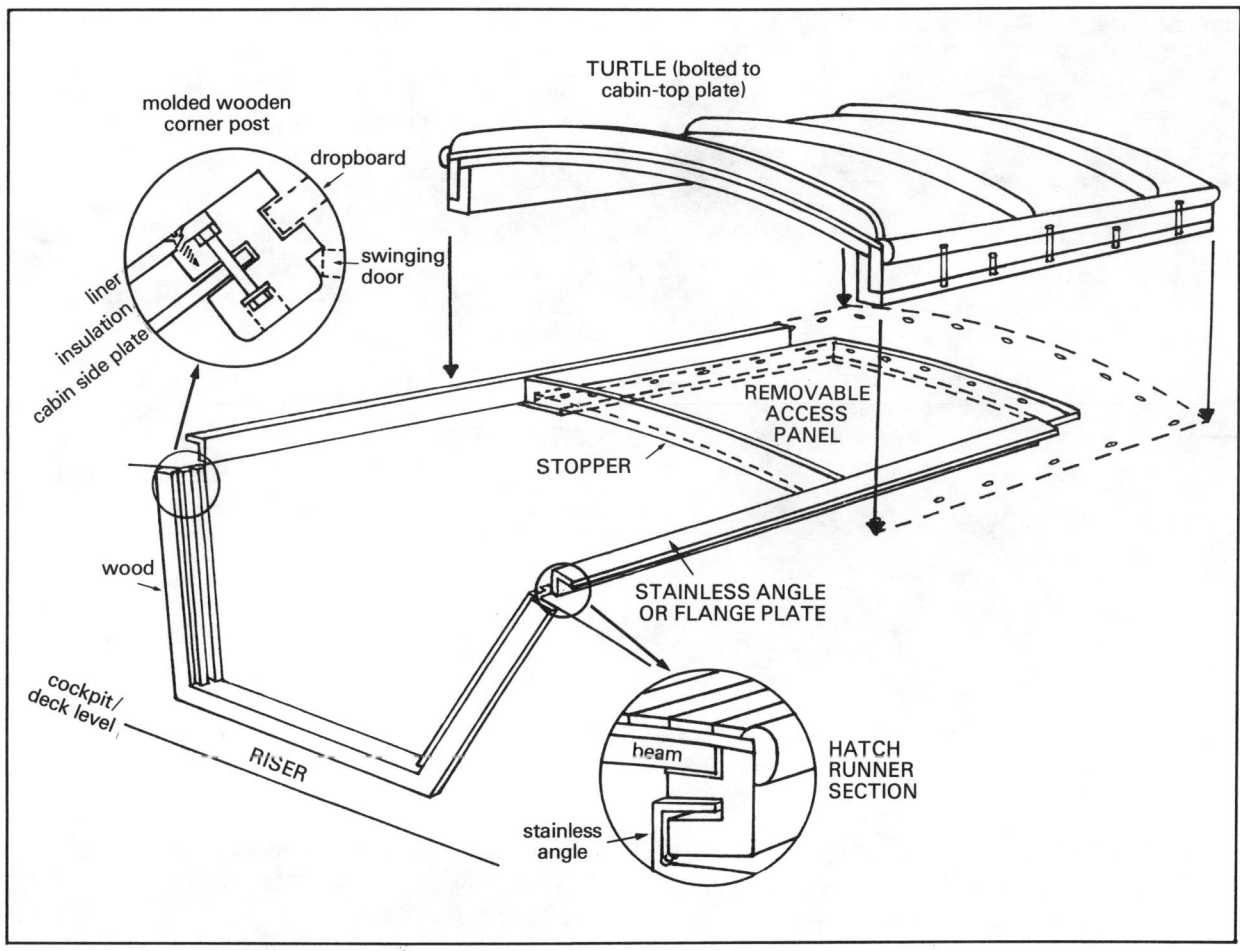

Fig. 14-3. *An exploded view of a companionway design that allows large objects to be placed below.*

When the turtle, the hatch cover, and this panel are removed, a fairly large opening is available.

A piece of clear or tinted plastic (Lexan or Plexiglas) can be inlayed into the top of the hatch to allow light below. The plastic can be lightly sandblasted to get a frosted look, if desired. Prisms and fixed deadlight ports can also be used to admit light; they are quite inexpensive and easy to install. These prisms and deadlights can also be mounted separately at appropriate locations on the cabin or deck.

The weight of the hatch assembly is a factor both for ease of handling and increased stability of the vessel. (Too heavy a hatch will increase the weight up high, and every little bit of weight reduction helps.) An aluminum turtle secured to studs, a removable aluminum access panel bolted down underneath the turtle, and a wood hatch is a combination worth considering.

Access to the engine from above for installation or removal is a desirable often overlooked. A steel engine-access plate can be installed in the cockpit sole for this purpose. It should be well secured to a flange in the cockpit with strong interior Henderson clamps or dog latches, or it can be fastened with stainless steel studs or bolts placed a maximum of 3″ apart. A laminated neoprene gasket together with a good polyurethane bedding compound will prevent any leaking. Of course, the steering pedestal must first be removed before the access plate is lifted off.

Cockpit scupper drains are always required in the corners of the cockpit. If an engine access plate is installed in the cockpit sole, the scuppers should be located on the original cockpit floor, since the flange that remains is slightly lower than the access plate. A minimum of two drains placed diagonally across from each other are necessary, but if four drains are used, the holes can be smaller. Hole size depends largely on the depth and area of the cockpit. Generally four 2″ diameter holes allow rapid drainage from a 75 cu. ft. cockpit. If the cockpit is high enough above the waterline, the scupper drain hose can lead directly to a throughhull on the same side

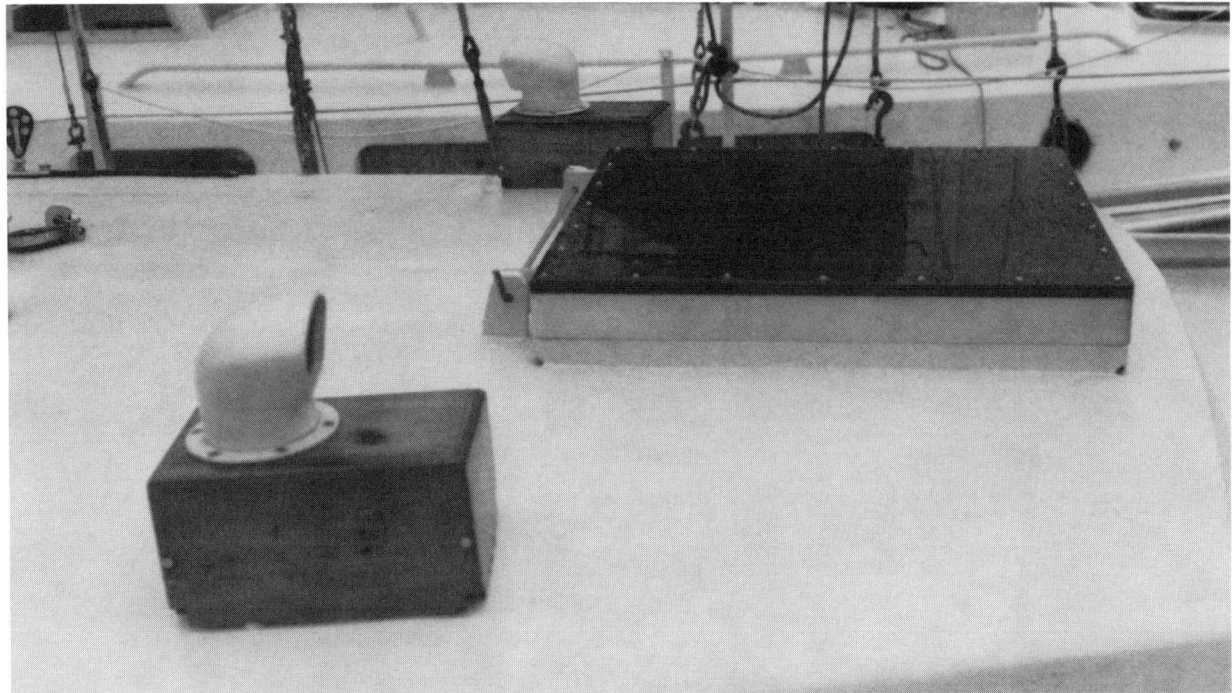

Fig. 14-4.   *Bedded and bolted Lexan forms the top of this deck hatch, which can be lifted off completely when the latch pin is removed. Notice also the handsome wood dorade box.*

without worrying about water backing up into the sole. Cockpits whose sole is at or below the waterline should have drains that cross underneath the cockpit sole so that water doesn't back up at extreme heeling angles.

Other hatches commonly found on the deck or cabin are the forepeak or fo'c's'le hatch, lazarette hatch, and small cabin ventilator hatches. Their design varies from that of the companionway hatches in that they lift open instead of sliding. Flush-mounted custom or production hatches make sense on the working deck.

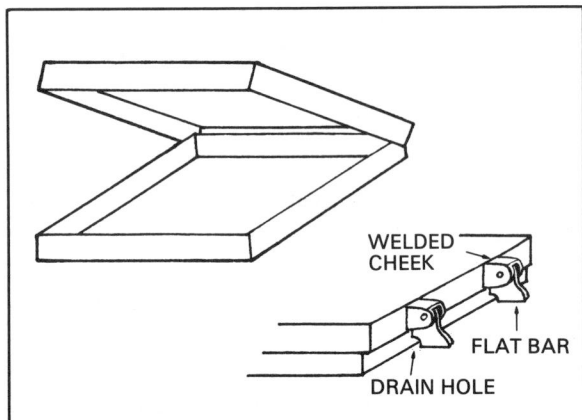

Fig. 14-5.   *The detail of this simple steel hatch shows how hinges can be fabricated.*

Fig. 14-6.   *These round steel access hatches are definitely watertight. A steel toe rail has also been welded in place.*

If the boat is a center-cockpit design, an aft-cabin companionway is an option that allows quick access to and from that area. This opening does face forward, and splash water could easily enter. A tight-fitting deck hatch would provide almost the same access as a companionway without the danger of leakage. If a fire occurred in the engine room, this aft access route could save someone from being trapped inside the boat.

Skylight hatches can be either the fixed or opening types. Opening skylights require good design and fitting, since they are susceptible to leaks. Deadlights like plastic ports or prisms are simple, cheaper, and let almost as much light into the interior.

Hatch tops can also be used for other purposes. For example, solar panels can be installed in hatches to generate power, and, if dorade vents are fitted in the hatch top, the hatches can serve as ventilators even when they are closed. In this case, the dorade must be designed so that the hatch can be opened fully, and the deck may need to be padded where the dorade will rest. Electrical panels with depth sounders and other navigational aids have also been designed into the molded tops of companionway hatches.

PORTHOLES

Portholes are used to light boat interiors and, in some cases, to provide fresh air and ventilation. They also allow a view of the outside from the inside. Portholes can be of the fixed or opening types, but opening ports are much more expensive. Like hatches, they too need to be well secured with bedding and gaskets if they are not to leak.

Portholes are commonly cast of iron, bronze, stainless steel, aluminum, or plastic. Although any of these materials can work well, simple galvanized steel ports are the most practical and economical, if you are able

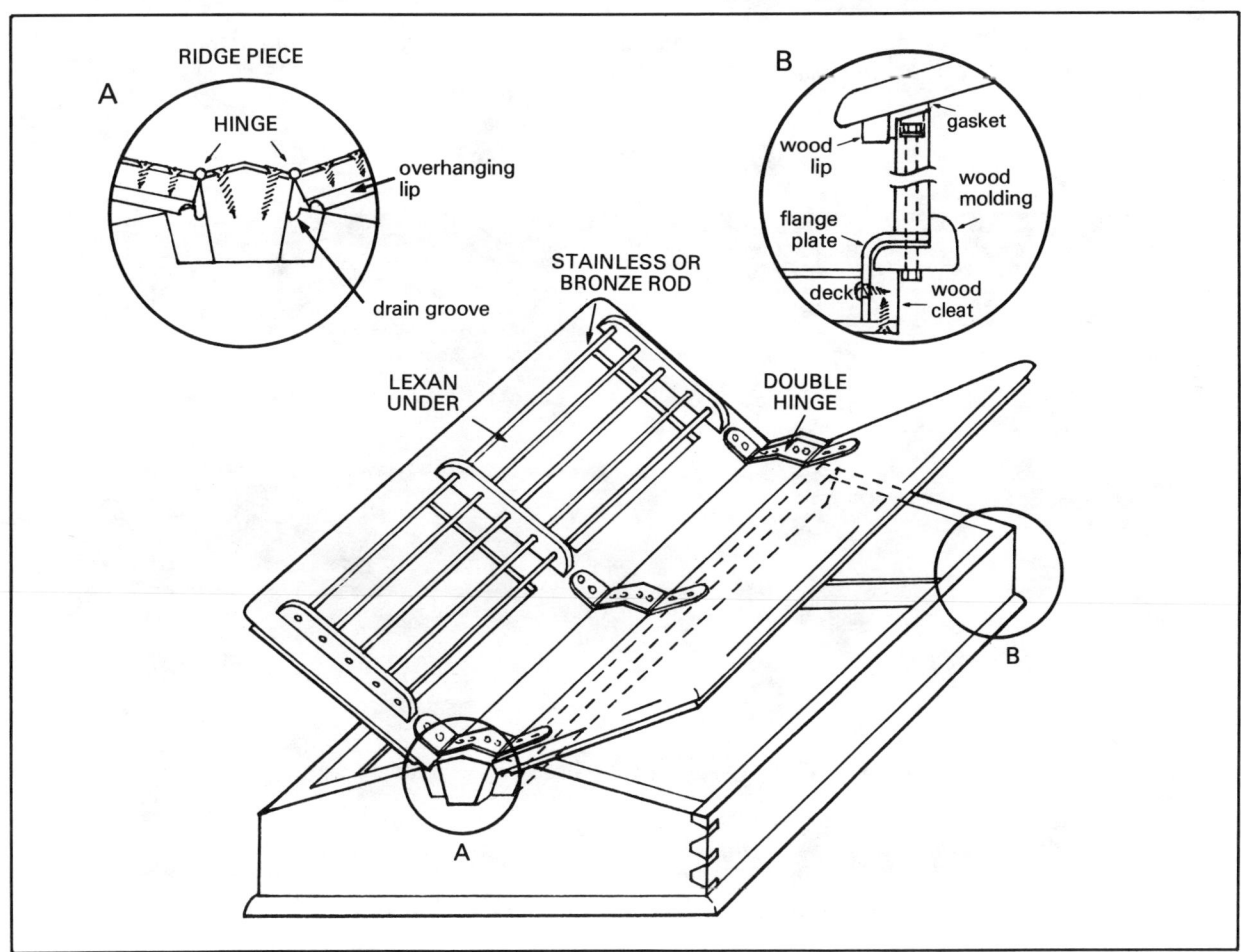

Fig. 14-7. *This sea-going skylight uses overhanging lips and gaskets under the lid to prevent leaks. Notice the grooves for drainage cut underneath the hinged edges of the opening panels.*

231

Fig. 14-8.   *This simple but good looking skylight can be built of either steel or aluminum. The soft corners should prevent any injuries.*

Fig. 14-9.   *Flush-mounted production portholes, a pair of nice wooden hatches, and a stainless steel handrail set off this cabin.*

to find them. Some of the plastic models are not safe for stormy sailing.

Large windows usually are not found on an ocean-going yacht, although some pilot house designs incorporate fairly large ports. The type of glass used is important, whether for a small porthole or a large window. The clear or tinted high-impact plastics now on the market are the best choice. Although Plexiglas can and has been used, it tends to fade and is easily scratched. Polycarbonates, like Lexan and Tuffak, are more expensive, but have better strength and durability. If glass is used, it must be heavy-duty, shatterproof safety glass, similar to that used for car windows. Large windows and even small portholes should be fitted with metal or wood shutters for protection in heavy-weather conditions.

Steel angle bar can be used to make an inexpensive fixed porthole. The bar stock is bent to shape and welded to the hole that has been cut in the cabin side. Numerous bolt holes are drilled on the inboard side of the flange. A piece of Lexan is then bedded and secured to the flange with machine screws. A wood cleat is placed behind the angle bar before it is bolted down, and the interior ceiling is then secured to this cleat.

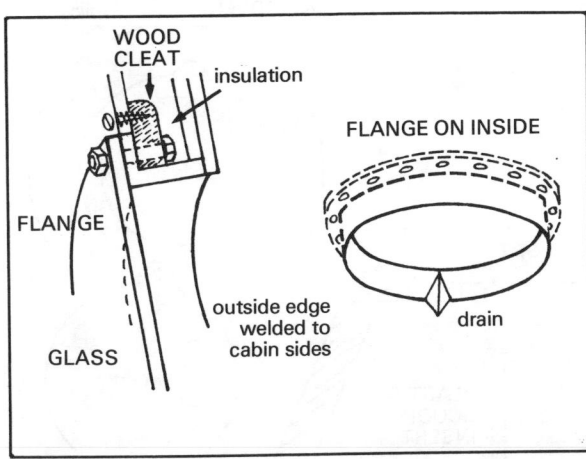

Fig. 14-10. *Integral porthole mounts can be fabricated of angle bar, flat bar and cut plate, or flange plate. If the lower edge of the porthole is not tilted, a drain should be built into the mounting flange.*

Opening portholes made of galvanized steel or bronze can be installed in a similar fashion. A flange of the correct size and shape must be chosen to fit the porthole, and any dissimilar metals require extra bedding or isolating gaskets. Some opening ports have deep spigots appropriate only to thick-walled wooden boats. These spigots should be cut off so they don't protrude outside the opening. If the cabin sides slant inboard, the porthole mounting must be designed to drain water, unless the port is mounted flush to the cabin side (see Chapter 9).

Accessories like port screens or inserts are also very handy for the tropics. Spare pins, bolts, Lexan, and bedding compound should be kept on hand for repairs.

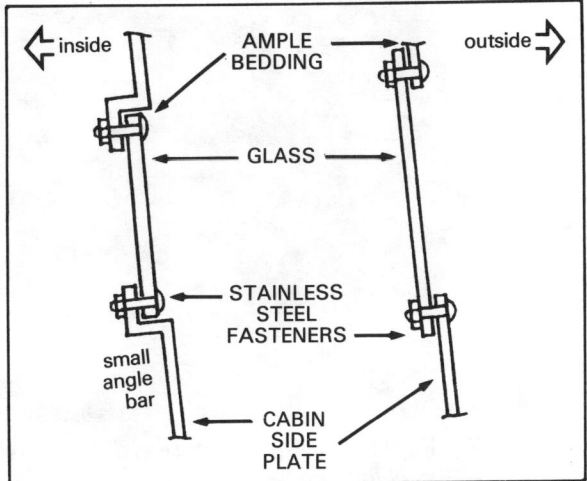

Fig. 14-11. *Two different methods of fabricating non-opening portholes. Ample bedding is required between the glass and the steel to prevent leaks.*

VENTILATORS

Good ventilation is important for preventing condensation and providing fresh air below decks. Holes must be cut for ventilation cowls, which are used both to draw in fresh air and to expel exhaust fumes. A dorade or mushroom ventilator assembly is the best way to allow fresh air in while keeping water out. The dorade assembly can be made of plastic, fiberglass, or metal, but a wood box looks and works very well. It can easily be mounted to integral steel tabs or cleats welded to the steel deck. A raised lip should be inserted into the hole to keep any water that enters the dorade box out of the interior. A steel pipe can be welded in place, but a plastic (PVC or ABS) tubing insert would be better, since it will run no risk of corrosion. The cowls fitted on the dorade box are usually available in strong plastic or bronze.

A ventilator will often be required for removing galley fumes and smoke from stoves and heaters. A spinning metal mushroom vent (charlie noble) connected to a stainless- or galvanized-steel pipe should be used for the hot air being vented from stoves or heaters. Charlie nobles usually come with a recessed deck iron to insulate the deck from the hot pipe. For exhausting fumes from

Fig. 14-12.   *These large steel dorade boxes also serve as storage lockers. Note the sturdy steel tabernacle.*

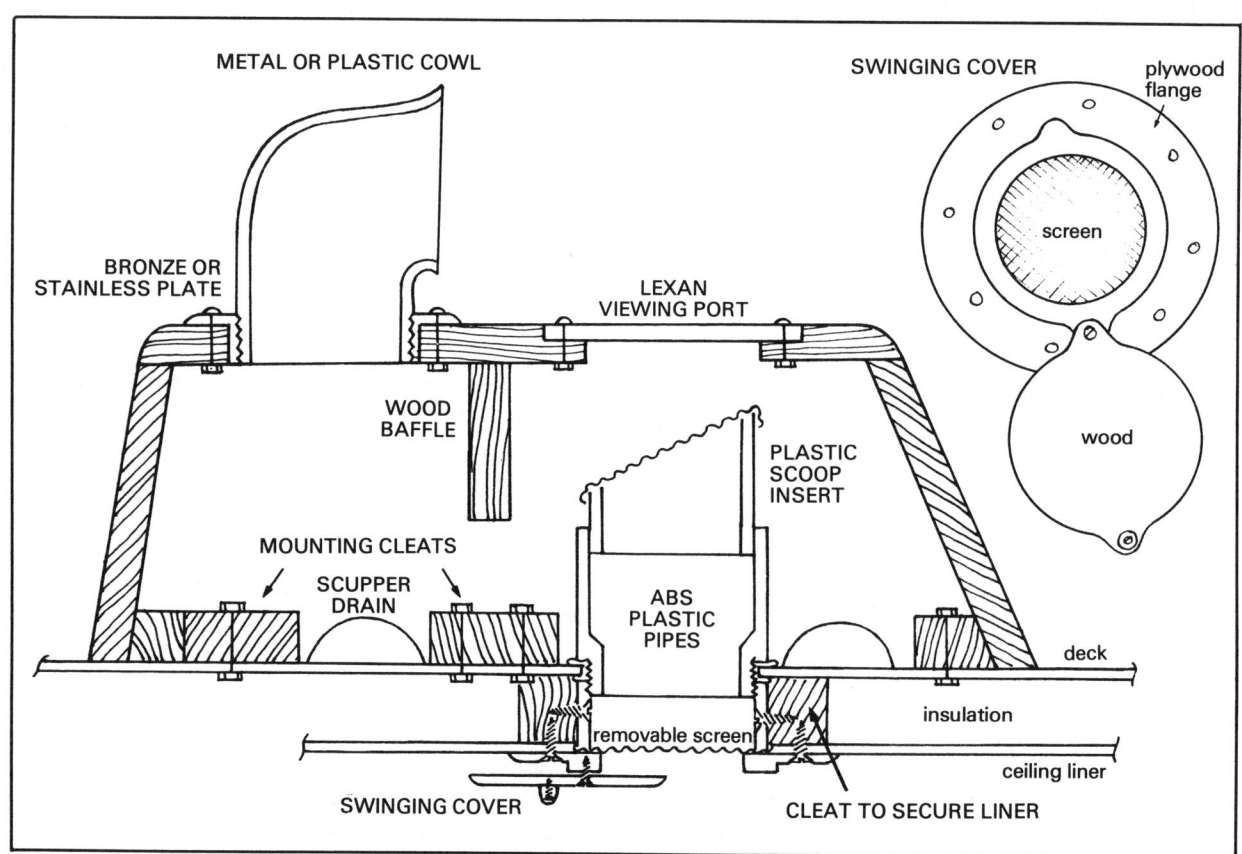

Fig. 14-13.   *This wooden dorade box is bolted securely with ample bedding wherever the steel touches another material. Although a production insert could be purchased, ABS plastic plumbing fittings can also be screwed together for a more economical assembly.*

cook stoves, there are several types of vents available, most of them plastic. The most efficient ones have fans that help to draw the fumes out of the cabin; the fan can be operated either by solar power or by electricity.

Ventilation of the engine area is extremely important to avoid explosions if gasoline is used for fuel, and diesel engines also require good airflow. Two plastic clam vents, one facing forward and one facing aft, set up a good air circulation pattern. Some types are mounted so that they can be turned in different directions to increase air flow. Clam vents also can be installed in the cabin sides with their mouths facing downward to keep water out of the ventilation system. Vents of steel pipe welded into the deck or cabin sides are an inexpensive way of providing ventilation. All vents should be fitted with some kind of screw-on or snap-in cover or with a flap, so that they can be closed tight when the engine is not being used or in heavy seas. Flexible duct tubing leading down low to the front of the engine channels the air provided by a ventilator to where it's needed. A blower will also be required if a boat with a gasoline engine is to be used for commercial ventures.

OTHER OPENINGS

The locations and coverings for smaller holes (for example, deck filler caps, fuel and water tank vents, hawser holes for chain, electric light sockets, and AC power outlets) must also be well thought out. All openings, no matter what size, must be watertight and properly joined to prevent possible galvanic or electrolytic action.

All fuel tanks must be vented to the outside, and the vents are commonly made of stainless steel or bronze. However, a simple, steel 90-degree-elbow pipe welded in place and fitted with a threaded cap can do the job. The pipe opening should face downward and be located as high as possible to keep water out of the fuel tank. Plastic tubing leading to the tank can be clamped to the pipe lip inside the cabin side or cockpit coaming. Water tank vents do not need to lead outside, but they must end high in the interior.

Fuel and water tank filler plate assemblies are commonly located on the deck, but they can also be mounted on the cockpit coaming or cabin sides. A double-cap arrangement with a drainage hole, installed inside the coaming, could also be used. High-tensile plastic filler outlets also work well and will not corrode.

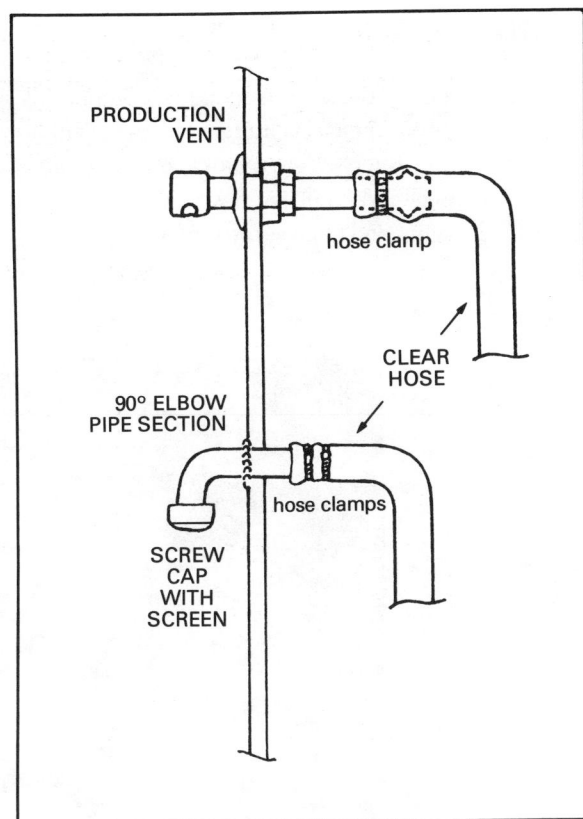

Fig. 14-14. *Breather vent outlets can either be bought commercially or fabricated from plumbing fittings. They must, however, be designed to keep water out of the tanks.*

It is hard to totally seal hawser holes if the anchor chain is left connected for emergency use. Old socks, sponges, and rags always seem to wind up as plugs in this location. It's best to plan for a small amount of water entering here by installing some kind of catch basin under the anchor line. Watertight chain lockers can be fitted with small pumps, and portable pumps can also be used to draw off the accumulated water.

Electrical sockets and wire leads that pass through the cabin or deck must be isolated from the hull and designed so that water does not get inside them. If the sockets are plastic, there will be no problem with corrosion, but stainless steel hook-ups are common, and neoprene, nylon, or Micarta gaskets are required with them. If possible, all electric outlets should be located high on the cabin instead of on the deck. Running lights could be mounted directly over the outlet, and spotlight sockets can be installed high in the cockpit where they would be easy to reach in an emergency.

MAINTENANCE

A supply of all of the gaskets, bedding compounds, and fasteners used when installing covers over openings should be carried onboard in a repair and maintenance kit, along with general metal and woodworking tools. Even if the hatches and dorades are the best quality, any good skipper routinely keeps a sharp eye out for any signs of problems. If the openings have been properly maintained, when the skipper yells "Batten down the hatches," all the crew will need to do is pull the latches and secure the portholes. Since they can rest assured, they can then relax and put a tot of rum down their own "hatches."

Fig. 14-15. *Many different openings and covers can be seen in this Nils Lucander design. The flush ports are sealed with rubber gaskets, and a nice wooden spray shield protects the center cockpit.* Courtesy of the designer

—Chapter 15———————————

Wood Joinery

No matter what their hull material may be, most cruising yachts have nice interior and exterior woodwork. Some steel yachts even have enough wood on the outside to fool an onlooker into thinking that the hull itself is wood. However, wood should only be used in suitable places, or problems can result. Many people favor wood decks, but when installed over a steel deck, they may cause corrosion. The interior is always an appropriate place for wood, but the joinery should be careful and the wood beautiful if the boat is a full-time home. The resale value and appearance of any boat increases with well-done woodwork.

Many people decide to do the woodwork themselves, partly because they enjoy doing it, but also because they can save money, since professional labor costs for the lengthy joinery work can add up quickly. On a steel hull, there are also other ways to cut costs with woodwork.

Since the steel hull and superstructure guarantee the structural integrity of the vessel, the wood does not have to bear much weight. (Although wood bulkheads add stiffness, this is only structurally important in frameless designs.) Therefore, at least for interior joinery, less-expensive kiln-dried, common-stock wood can be used. However, exterior woodwork and hatch covers demand high-quality, tight-grained, air-dried wood for its durability and rot resistance.

Theoretically, the required scantlings for interior woodwork can be reduced, thus reducing weight and overall cost. The change will be slight, however, since a certain degree of stiffness is required. Bulkheads and settees shouldn't flex or collapse; decent-quality marine ply must be used. But hidden cleats and liners can be made of construction-grade wood.

On a steel yacht, the wood-to-wood joinery is similar to that on any boat. The differences come in joining wood to steel. Stainless or galvanized bolts and screws are used to attach interior woodwork to cleats, liners, or battens that are bolted, screwed, or occasionally glued to the steel frames. Bulkheads are usually bolted to transverse frames or tabs. Exterior woodwork can be bolted through the steel or fastened to tabs or studs that have been welded to the plate.

Since tabs, studs, and flanges should be welded on before the hull is blasted and painted, advance planning of specific joinery is required. Exterior woodwork can be added on anytime after painting is completed, and small holes can be drilled and threaded as the wood is fitted to the steel. The construction sequence for interior woodwork depends on how the boat to be is insulated. If sprayed-foam insulation is used, the spraying operation usually follows painting, and then woodwork is begun. However, cleats or bulkheads may need to be attached to the frames before the insulation is sprayed in (see Chapter 11). If sheet insulation is used, it can be attached to the ceiling, lining, or hull as the wood interior is being built. Some parts of the plumbing system and wiring for electrics may need to be installed early in the interior construction process.

PROPERTIES OF WOOD

The woods used on a boat come from many species of trees, and each species has different working characteristics due to grain structure and growth habits. Wood is primarily rated in terms of density, static bending, stiffness, crushing strength, and shear strength. Explanations of other traits can be found in one of the many books written specifically about wood.

The different strength characteristics of wood have been discussed in Chapter 1, but a brief summary here may be helpful. A piece of wood is strongest when stress is applied parallel to the grain, so the joinery should be planned to use this characteristic to best advantage. The modulus of rupture measures the ability of a piece of wood to bend without breaking; it is similar to tensile strength in metals. Crushing strength determines how the wood reacts to compression stresses applied both parallel and perpendicular to the grain; the compression strength of a wood is lower than its modulus of rupture. Shearing strength is determined parallel to the grain,

since it is very weak in the perpendicular direction. It is usually about 10% less than the modulus of rupture. Stiffness reflects the modulus of elasticity; the higher the modulus, the stiffer the wood.

No matter how "dry" wood appears, it always retains some moisture within its cells. Since strength is related to moisture content, the weight and strength characteristics of wood are always calculated with reference to a particular moisture content. The moisture content also determines how well paint will adhere to the wood; with greater than 20% moisture, paint failure will probably result. How the wood is dried (whether in a kiln or in the open air) also affects its properties. In kiln drying, moisture is removed from the wood so quickly that its cellular structure can be damaged, increasing the chance of rot and making the wood more brittle. Kiln-dried wood with a moisture content of 12% is perfectly adequate for dry interiors, but for exterior woodwork, air-dried wood is preferable.

The moisture content of a piece of wood also affects its specific gravity (the ratio of the density of wood to the density of water in it). As wood dries, its specific gravity increases, and strength and workability change. Woods with high specific gravities are strong, though somewhat brittle. The lower the specific gravity, the easier the wood is to cut and work.

The weight of a piece of wood also depends on its moisture content. Most boat lumber weighs 25–50 lbs./cu. ft.

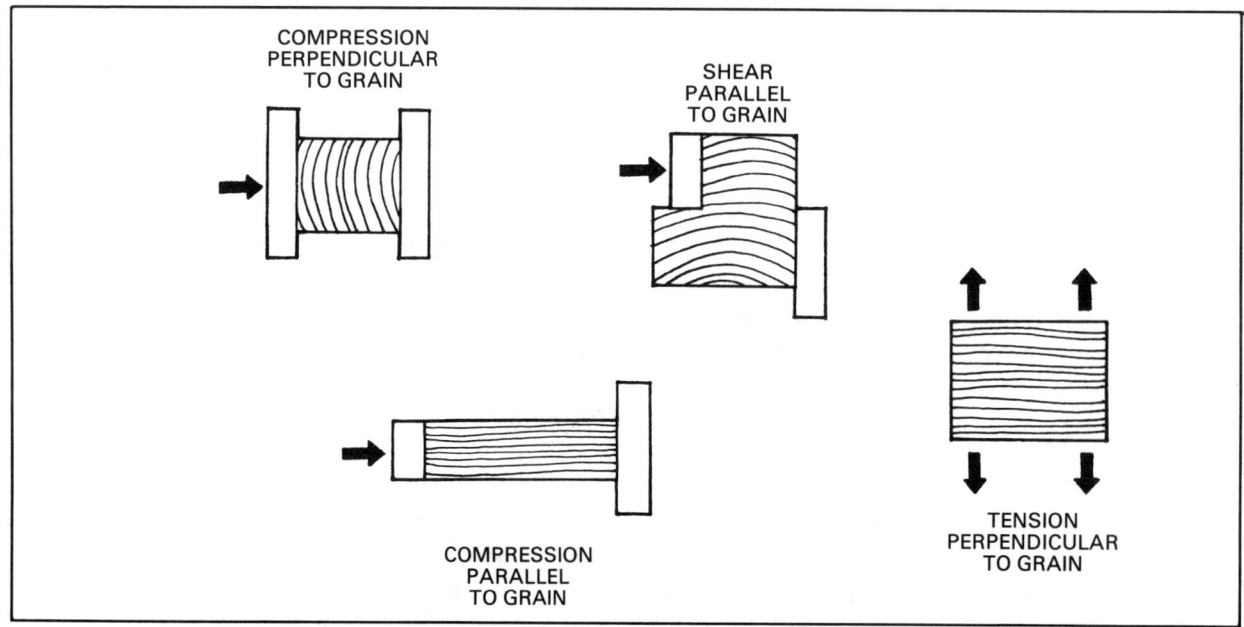

Fig. 15-1. *Some examples of the relationship between the forces acting on wood and the grain.*

Vertical-grain wood is preferable for structural members like bulwarks and hatches, since it has greater dimensional stability and better finishing qualities. However, flat-grain boards are stronger. Sapwood should be avoided, since it is liable to rot, and wood sawn from the very center of a tree is often defective. Heartwood is the best there is.

Wood joinery includes drilling, sawing, planing, shaping, sanding, and painting. How well a species of wood performs during these operations (its machinability) helps to determine its usefulness. Of course, tool blades that are sharp and well-maintained make working any wood easier. The wood must also have good screw-holding capabilities to be suitable as boat lumber.

The service life of wood depends on its resistance to rot and other forms of deterioration (like staining and attack by fungus, molds, metals, insects, chemicals, and fouling organisms). High moisture levels will cause both wet and dry rot; using dry, coated wood is the standard way to prevent rot. Although conditions leading to rot are rare on a steel boat since there are no seams to work and admit moisture, all wood should be properly coated. A durable wood will stand up to the wear and tear of a working life on the sea. Its hardness gives it this durability. Those woods that crack and check as they dry can be ruled out from the start.

BOAT WOODS

Of the thousands of species of wood in the world, only a handful are suitable for boatbuilding. Some have the strength and durability needed for structural joints. Some have especially high resistance to weathering. Others, though not as strong, weigh less, and so add less weight above the waterline; these woods can be used for non-structural woodwork. Boatbuilders are constantly trying out new woods (the search for inexpensive substitutes for teak is one such venture), and some are proving valuable.

Marine plywood is a reasonable choice for large panels and bulkheads. The chief advantages of marine plywood over the type used for house construction are better glue, fewer voids, and better mechanical strength. The term "marine ply" includes many different grades of plywood; fir is the standard wood used for laminations. If the defects are sealed with epoxy filler, shop-grade marine ply can be used for non-structural joinery (for example, benches, cabinets, and bunks) and in the places where appearance is not important. Plywood cov-

Table 15-1. OTHER BOAT LUMBER		Specific Gravity at 12%	Modulus of Rupture
Softwoods	White cedar (Atlantic)	.32	6,800
	Cottonwood (Eastern)	.40	8,500
	White pine	.35	8,600
	Basswood	.37	8,700
	White spruce (Eastern)	.40	9,800
	Tamarack	.53	11,600
	Port Orford cedar	.43	12,700
	Larch	.52	13,100
Hardwoods	Maple (big leaf)	.48	10,700
	Cherry	.50	12,300
	Black walnut	.55	14,600
	Rock elm	.63	14,800
	Beech	.64	14,900
	Yellow birch	.62	16,600
	Red scarlet oak	.67	17,400
	Hickory	.75	20,100

ered with an attractive wood veneer can be used where it is visible (for example, bulkheads or panels). The strength and durability of the super marine plys like Bruynzeel are rarely needed on a steel hull.

Oak is a very popular and durable structural wood that is pointed to with pride as a framing material on wooden boats. It does crack on occasion and, contrary to popular belief, will rot if it is allowed to remain wet for a long period of time. But it bends well when green and is easily worked.

Other domestic hardwoods like ash, beech, maple, bird's-eye maple, cherry, and hickory have strength and durability comparable to oak, although generally their resistance to decay is lower. These woods don't warp like oak and are very enjoyable to work. But most have a low strength-to-weight ratio, and they are relatively inaccessible and therefore more expensive. They aren't really necessary except where good anti-chafe qualities are needed (e.g., exterior rails or mounting pads).

Softwoods are generally lighter and easier than hardwoods to drill, fasten, shape, and plane, but they are not as strong. However, in most dry areas of a steel boat, softwoods perform well. Douglas fir is a good, general-purpose softwood that can be used for many parts of a boat (cleats, corner posts, framing for cabinets.) It is easily worked and moderately durable. On the west coast of North America, it is still quite accessible for a reasonable cost; larch can be substituted if fir is not available.

Table 15-2. CHARACTERISTICS OF COMMON BOATBUILDING LUMBER

Species	Type	Spec. Grav.	Appearance	Wt. lbs./ ft.³	Modulus of Rupture	Screw Holding	Hand Planing	Life, wet	Life, dry	Bending	Toughness	Warping	Cracking	Some uses
Ash	Hard	.60	Straw to white	43	15,400	Fair	Fair	Short	Long	Excellent	Good	Rare	Rare	Hatches, oars exterior
Western red cedar	Soft	.32	Brownish red	24	7,500	Fair	Easy	Long	Long	Fair	Poor	Rare	Occasional	Ceilings, lockers
Yellow cedar	Soft	.44	Light yellow	30	11,100	Fair	Easy	Long	Long	Fair	Fair	Rare	Rare	Ceilings, molding
Douglas fir	Soft	.48	Tan-yellow	35	12,400	Fair	Easy	Medium	Medium	Good	Fair	Occasional	Occasional	Cleats, strips, liners
White oak	Hard	.68	Tan-brown	47	15,200	Excellent	Fair	Medium	Long	Good	Very good	Occasional	Occasional	Stringers, coamings, structural
Longleaf pine	Soft	.59	Yellow-brown	41	14,500	Excellent	Fair	Long	Long	Fair	Very good	Occasional	Occasional	Cabin sole, cleats
Sitka spruce	Soft	.40	White-yellow	28	10,300	Fair	Easy	Short	Medium	Excellent	Poor	Rare	Occasional	Spars, oars ceilings
Afrormosia	Hard	--	Brownish	50	--	Good	Hard	Very long	Very long	Fair	Good	Rare	Rare	Rub rails, coamings
Balou	Hard	--	Yellow-dk. brn.	52	--	Excellent	Hard	Very long	Very long	Fair	Excellent	Rare	Occasional	
Greenheart	Hard	.93	Dk. brn.-green	70	25,500	Excellent	Hard	Very long	Very long	Fair	Very good	Rare	Very rare	Rub rails
Iroko	Hard	--	Brown/yellow	44	--	Good	Fair	Very long	Very long	Fair	Very good	Rare	rare	Teak substitute
Honduran mahogany	Hard	.45	Brown to red	40	11,600	Fair	Hard	Long	Long	Fair	Fair	Rare	Rare	Handrails, exterior, interior
Philippine mahogany	Hard	.41	Light red	35	11,300	Fair	Good	Medium	Long	Good	Fair	Rare	Rare	Interior, trim molding
Teak	Hard	.64	Brownish	44	12,800	Good	Fair	Very long	Very long	Fair	Very good	Rare	Very rare	Decks, exterior, hatches

IMPORTED (Ash through Sitka spruce)

DOMESTIC (Afrormosia through Teak)

On the East Coast, pine is the standard boat wood. Both longleaf and white pitch pine are very workable, durable woods with good screw-holding capabilities.

Cedar and cypress are softwoods with very high resistance to rot. Western yellow and red cedar are nice to work, and, because they are lightweight woods, they are very appropriate for non-structural joinery, such as closets, lockers, and interior trim. Port Orford cedar is the strongest of the softwoods, but also the most expensive, and it is often used for planking on wood boats.

True mahoganies are excellent boat woods, combining the strength of hardwoods and the easy working characteristics of softwoods with a medium strength-to-weight ratio. They hold fasteners well, don't warp much, and their cost is sometimes less than native fir. The only problem with mahogany is that the occasionally squirrely grain can make it hard to plane the wood to a smooth finish. Many Philippine "mahoganies" (lauan, meranti, and seraya) are not true mahoganies, although their appearances are similar; the dark-red Philippine type is the best choice if you can't get the real thing. The real thing (Honduran, Brazilian, or African mahogany) is very attractive and can be used in many places throughout the boat. Honduran has the edge over African in most respects, especially hardness. Kapur or balou can be used instead of mahogany, and both have better abrasion resistance.

Sitka spruce is the boatbuilder's favorite for spars because of its high strength-to-weight ratio and high modulus of elasticity. Its interlocking grain structure reduces splitting under stress. Sitka spruce is light, easily worked, holds fasteners well, and can be successfully laminated. Other exterior uses for spruce are limited, since it is soft and prone to rot; it does make attractive interior ceiling and lining material.

Teak is the current favorite hardwood for exteriors because of its good resistance to weathering. However, it is heavy, not particularly strong, and quite expensive. Alternatives like iroko, afrormosia, and utile have similar qualities but cost less. These substitutes generally are a bit harder to work than teak.

More and more varieties of wood are being imported today, leaving many forests almost totally logged over and their ecologies irreversibly devastated. In response, some countries have placed high export tariffs on their wood or have banned export completely. It seems that more use of domestic woods and less dependence on imports would be wise. However, some of the imported teaks, teak substitutes, and true mahoganies are hard to beat. Other imports worth considering include Span-

Table 15-3.   WOODWORKING TOOLS

1. SAFETY EQUIPMENT

Protective goggles
Gloves
Face masks (one for dust, one for vapors)
Portable work lights
Knee pads
Ear protectors

2. MEASURING AND MARKING TOOLS FOR LAYOUT

Tape rules (10′, 25′, 50′)
Yardsticks (metal is best)
Spirit level (one short, one long)
Combination square
Large framing square
Adjustable tri square
Bevel gauges (large and small)
Trammel points for scribing circles
Calipers
Pencils
Plumb bob
Chalk and line
Protractor
Wing dividers
Spiling battens
Template material (hardboard, doorskin, thin ply formica)
Punches
Awls
Spikes
Nail set

3. ASSEMBLY TOOLS

Clamps (C, bar, pipe, finger)
Bench vise
Wedges
Pliers
Vise grips
Needle-nose pliers
Sawhorses
Work bench

4. SHAPING TOOLS

BASIC
Chisels (from ¼″ to 2″)
Wood files and rasps (round, oval, flat, Surform)
Electric hand router with various bits

OPTIONAL
Table mount for router
Gouges and carving tools for fancy woodwork
Table shaper
Lathe

Table. 15-3. (cont.)
WOODWORKING TOOLS

5. PLANING TOOLS

BASIC
    Planes (block, low-angle block, smoothing, jack, rabbet)
    Spokeshave
    Draw knife
    Electric hand planer

OPTIONAL
    Bull-nose plane
    Thickness planer
    Electric jointer/planer

6. CUTTING TOOLS

    Handsaws (crosscut, rip, backsaw, keyhole, fine-toothed backsaw, hacksaw, coping saw)
    Knives
    Ax
    Splitting wedge
    Nippers
    Electric saber saw
    Electric circular saw
    Electric mitre chop saw
    Band saw
    Table saw with mitre clamp and dado blade
    Ripping bar
    Electric hole saw

7. DRILLING AND FASTENING TOOLS

BASIC
    Brace and bits
    Doweling jig
    Dowel and plug cutters
    Hammers (ball peen, claw, soft head, sledge)
    Wood mallet
    Screw starter
    Electric hand drill
    Electric drill bits
    Hole cutters
    Countersink set
    Screwdriver bits (square drive, phillips, slot)
    Staple gun

OPTIONAL
    Drill press
    Drill press vise
    Hilty gun

8. FINISHING TOOLS

    Cabinet scrapers
    Putty knives
    Sanding blocks
    Sandpaper and belt sandpaper
    Scissors
    Waxed paper
    Utility knife
    Sponges
    Vacuum cleaner
    Electric belt sander
    Electric rotary sander
    Disk sander with foam pads
    Table-mounted sander
    Electric grinder with various disks
    Cleaning agents like turpentine, mineral spirits paint thinner, acetone
    Paint tools listed in Chapter 10

9. TOOLS FOR MAINTAINING TOOLS

    Sharpening stones or wheel
    Wrenches and sockets
    Allen wrenches
    Lube oils
    Cleaning abrasives
    File card and brush

ish cedar, apitong, kapur, angelique, and balou, as well as jelutong.

JOINING WOOD TO STEEL

Wood can be joined to steel using simple techniques and studs, bolts, and stainless or galvanized fasteners; the steel should be blasted and painted before any of the woodwork is begun. On the exterior, a good bedding compound must be used between the wood and the steel to keep water out of the joints. Since wood is a very porous material, it expands and contracts with chang-ing moisture levels in the air. As it moves, it can loosen the bedding compound in the wood-to-steel joint, and allow water to seep behind the bedding compound.

The best way to reduce the dimensional instability of wood is to seal it completely, creating an artificial environment of constant humidity. (This is the basis of cold-molded construction.) The wood's degree of stability is determined by how well it is sealed. Exterior wood should be totally sealed to protect it from waves, rain, and salt spray. Epoxy sealers are the most effective vapor barriers, and their higher price is offset by their durability.

On the interior, bedding compound is not absolutely required, but any wood surface that touches metal should be coated with at least a marine primer (alkyds, acrylics, or epoxies). Latex house paint is unacceptable for this purpose. End grains should be sealed with cuprinol, linseed oil, paint, or epoxy. Epoxy sealers are particularly effective for sealing the end grain of plywood, especially in areas that will become inaccessible once the woodwork is in place (for example, bulkheads and floors). Woodwork around the galley sink, head, and shower has high rot potential; a good epoxy sealer in these area will help the wood to last longer.

Exposed interior woodwork can be coated with two to four layers of paint. Alkyd enamel is the standard type used, but the inexpensive latexes can be used on interior wood if cost is really an issue. Vinyls and epoxies (sealers or paints) are not really necessary except in areas that might be exposed to moisture. Spar varnish and Varathane can be used to enhance the natural look of the wood used in trims, for moldings, or as veneers on plywood bulkheads.

Proper measuring, cutting, and fitting are just as important here as on any boat. Where wood touches the steel, it should fit snugly. However, the less surface contact between the wood and the steel, the better, since the possibility of moisture entrapment is lowered. For example, floors do not need to be butted up against the surface of the hull, nor do other joints that will not be visible.

Because wood can and does absorb moisture at sea, proper allowances for expansion must be included in the joinery of locker doors, drawers, and other moving parts. In wood-to-steel joinery (for example, fitting wood hatch covers over steel lips), a smaller allowance is needed than for all-wood joinery, because steel is more stable than wood. Heavy, oily woods like teak, or woods with high pitch content like apitong and balou, do best where the moisture level fluctuates.

Fasteners

The type of fastener you use depends on whether the wood is being attached to the interior or exterior of the hull. Exterior woodwork is often secured to the hull plate itself, while frames or tabs usually provide the base whereby wood is fastened to the interior. Studs welded to the hull are preferable in areas that may get wet (like rub rails and spray shields), while bolts running through holes drilled in the steel are adequate for the interior and certain exterior applications (like handrails or fairing pads). Anytime a hole is drilled through the hull plate, the fasteners must be securely bedded and tightened down. A machine nut or metal strap punching can also

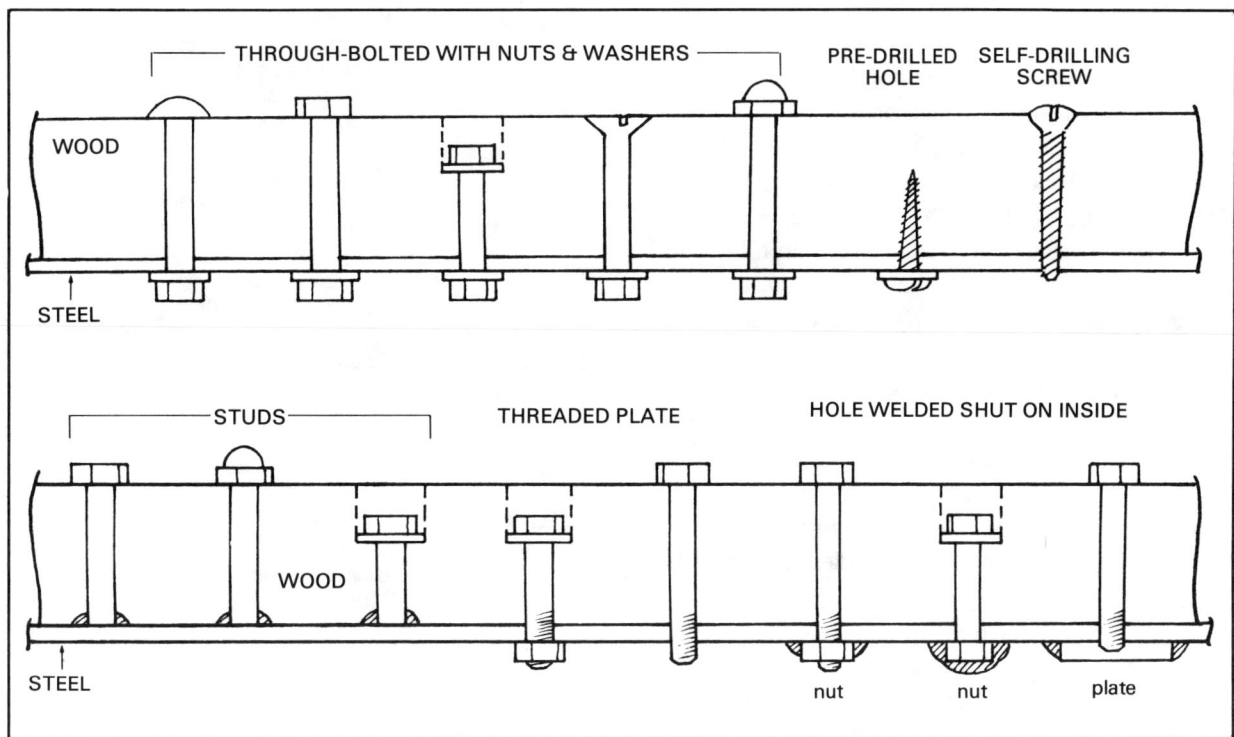

Fig. 15-2. *Wood-to-steel joinery can be accomplished with a number of different fasteners.*

be welded to the backside of the hole to create a watertight joint.

Studs are easily made of steel or stainless steel rod that is first threaded and then welded integrally with the hull. Studs are very strong, since they are essentially part of the hull, so they are appropriate for fastening down pieces of equipment like windlasses that operate under a heavy load. They can also be used for wood pieces that will need to be removed and replaced—especially the rub rails, whose function is to wear away as they protect the plate.

Good-quality stainless steel or hot-dipped galvanized machine screws (which are actually bolts) are the best types for wood-to-steel joinery. Galvanized fasteners are likely to corrode if the galvanizing on the surface of the threads is worn away. They are better for joining wood to wood, although they can be used with steel. Stainless steel is best for fastening exterior joints that will be exposed to extreme weathering. Both are close enough to steel on the galvanic scale that corrosion problems will be minimal. Sheet metal screws, cheap bolts, and copper- or cadmium-plated fasteners should all be avoided. If ungalvanized steel bolts must be used, they should be the high-quality machine types.

When a bolt is to be inserted through steel, a hole of the proper size must first be drilled out. If the hole is threaded, the machine screws will grip tighter, which is important in areas where, because of access problems, the bolt cannot be secured with a nut. A machine nut or a piece of metal that has been welded to the back of the hole will also improve holding power. In addition, threaded holes keep the bolt from wobbling, reducing the chance of leakage. Another option is to use self-drilling screws, which drill their own holes as they are driven into place with a strong electric drill. In years past, on large ships most of the wood-to-steel joinery was done with a hilty gun, which drove in large, self-drilling screws. However, because these self-drilling or self-tapping screws are chrome-plated rather than galvanized and are not available in stainless steel, corrosion is more likely to affect them than studs or bolts. Their availability is limited to certain sizes, and self-tapping screws have been known to break.

Before being inserted in their holes, bolts can be dipped into a corrosion inhibitor or polyurethane bedding compound to help insure against corrosion problems. Heavy-duty plumber's compounds like Never-Seez or Slic-Tite, which contains Teflon, also work well on threads. These compounds don't harden, so fasteners can be removed easily.

INTERIOR JOINERY

Most of the interior joinery must be done in a somewhat confined space, so in some cases, the rough assembly is fitted in place and then disassembled and carried to a work bench outside the boat, where the finish work (sanding, painting, etc.) can be done more efficiently. Although this method saves a lot of trips in and out of the boat, the assembly time is increased. An alternative is to build a work area level with the sheer, where power tools like bandsaws and shapers can be placed. Small components and those designed to be removable (like hatches) can easily be fabricated at another location.

Although the specific sequence of interior wood joinery varies, the first step almost always is attaching cleats (also called "firring strips"), battens, or liners to the met-

Table 15-4.	EXTERIOR APPLICATIONS FOR WOOD
HULL	Rub rail
	Rudder (especially outboard)
	Bowsprit
	Boomkin
	Sprit platforms or gratings
	Seacock plugs
DECK OR CABIN	Bulwarks
	Rail cap
	Boom gallows (crutch)
	Spars (masts, booms, poles, spreaders)
	Samsom posts
	Dorade vent boxes
	Hatches and turtles
	Skylights (on deck or cabin)
	Eyebrows for cabin trim
	Hand rails
	Emergency tiller
	Decking (optional)
COCKPIT	Coamings
	Steering wheel
	Pedestal and binnacle
	Cockpit lunch table
	Seats and lockers
OTHER	Gratings
	Boat hook
	Belaying pins
	Mount pads for winches, windlasses, and dinghy
	Flag pole
	Dinghy chocks
	Anchor chocks
	Whiskerpole deck mounts

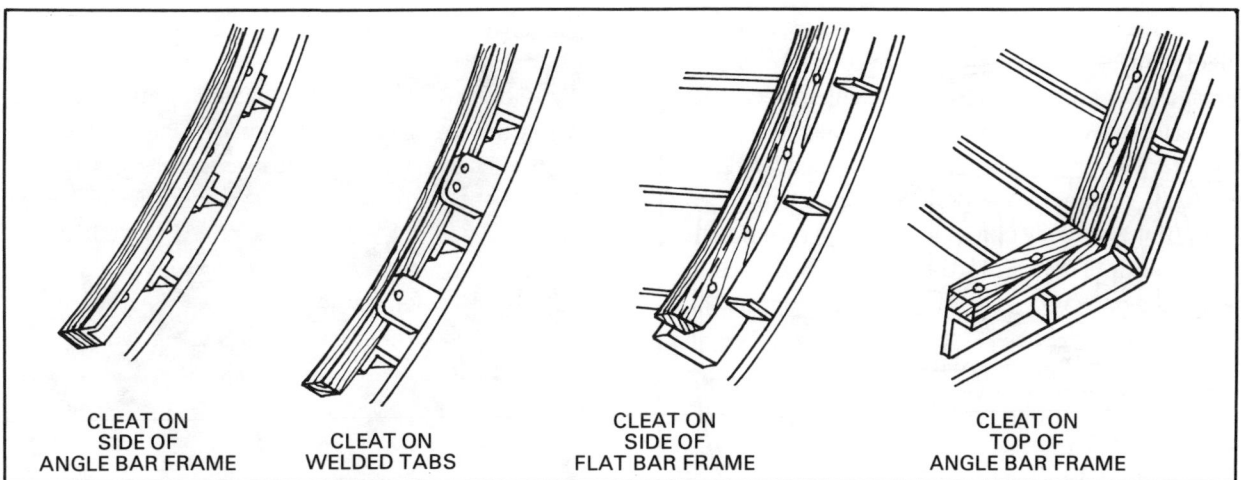

CLEAT ON
SIDE OF
ANGLE BAR FRAME

CLEAT ON
WELDED TABS

CLEAT ON
SIDE OF
FLAT BAR FRAME

CLEAT ON
TOP OF
ANGLE BAR FRAME

Fig. 15-3. *The method of attaching cleats depends on the type of framing used and on the cleat's location.*

al frames, beams, and floors. The rest of the woodwork will be fastened to these strips. The major plywood bulkheads can also go in simultaneously, secured to frames, tabs, or, less frequently, to cleats.

Next, the cabin sole is fastened to the floor cleats or directly to the metal sole beams. The floor then provides a safe, level place from which to work on the remainder of the joinery. It is better to attach the floor to strips, since with this method there is less wood in direct contact with the metal, so there will be less chance of moisture entrapment. It makes sense to use plywood for the floor, since access panels for the inspection of the bilge are easy to cut. If plank flooring is used, it should be at-

tached to a plywood subfloor where the access panels are to be located.

Most of the production plywood flooring made of teak or holly is very expensive. But you can easily make your own traditional-looking sole. ⅝″ plywood should first be laid down to make the floor properly stiff. Then strips of ½″ teak, fir, holly, spruce, or other durable wood are fastened over the ply in whatever combination you find attractive. If the finish strips are too thin to be screwed and bunged, bronze ring-barb nails can be used. Traditional seam compound between the ply and the wood

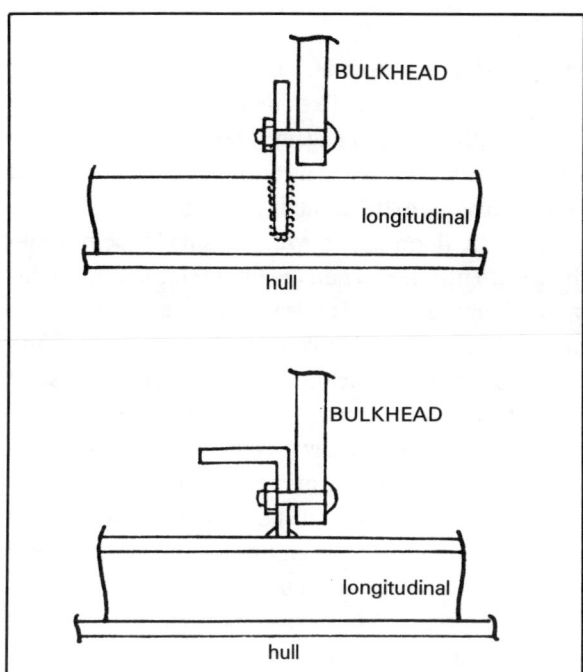

Fig. 15-5. *Major bulkheads can be bolted to the sides of either angle or flat bar frames when either the backing or notching method is used.*

Fig. 15-4. *Close-up views of three methods of attaching wood cleats for interior joinery.*

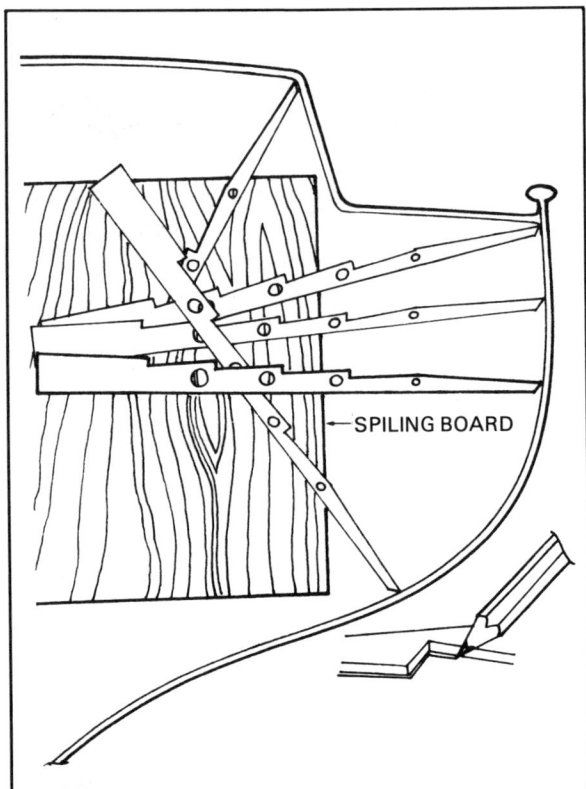

Fig. 15-6. *A tick stick can be used to spile the shape of the inside edge of a bulkhead. The exact position of the tick stick is marked each time it is laid down, and the process is then reversed to transfer the shape to the bulkhead stock.*

Fig. 15-7. *Cleats and bulkheads were installed on this hull before the insulation was sprayed on.*

strips helps to keep water out and looks good, too. Although a polysulfide like Thiokol can be used, epoxy mixed with a coloring agent (graphite fibers make it black) also works well. The entire floor can be sealed with epoxy for extra durability.

After the flooring is down, the smaller semi-bulkheads are installed. Then the linings for the hull sides and ceiling are secured to cleats. It is easier to fit the ceiling and lining to the bulkheads than vice versa, and cleats fastened to structural bulkheads provide a solid place to fasten the thin panel material. Since the purpose of the lining is simply to cover the insulation, metal, and firring strips, the material can be thin; the only stresses on the material will be a leaning crew member or stored equipment. When the span between frames is great, extra steel tabs should be installed for extra firring strips. This will keep unsupported ceiling sections from overflexing or drooping. If there is no other place to fasten them, cleats can be attached to longitudinals (if they are not covered with insulation); holes in the hull plating should be avoided.

For a traditional look, the hull can be lined with strips of fir, pine, spruce, or yellow cedar whose edges have been bull-nosed. Various types of thin sheet paneling such as plywood, nylon, formica, or hardboard can also be used; ceilings are commonly made of these materials to allow for greater headroom. Thin sheets of plywood can also serve as lining material; if grooves are cut in the plywood with a router, the lining will bend easily into place and take on a more traditional look.

After the floor, major bulkheads, and lining are installed, pine or fir cleats are attached to them for fastening plywood partitions, semi-bulkheads, and the rest of the wood-to-wood joinery which is like that in any boat. The wooden items most commonly found in interiors include corner posts, bunks, counters, shelves, salon tables, settees, cabinets, lockers, drawers, desks, galley

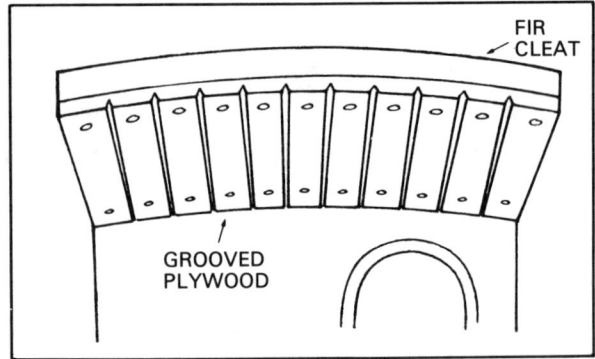

Fig. 15-8. *Grooved plywood makes a traditional-looking ceiling when attached to overhead cleats. A router can be used to put in the V-shaped grooves.*

counters, storage racks, fiddles, companionway ladders, doorways, doors, medicine chests, cutting boards, hand holds, battery boxes, and finish molding.

Finish trim and molding are commonly made of mahogany, teak, oak, cedar, or one of the other beautiful woods. Many builders use the combination of varnished moldings with white paneling for a nice effect.

It's beyond the scope of this book to detail all the interior joinery options that are so well outlined in other boatbuilding books. Take a look at them for more ideas.

Stainless steel square-drive screws are the best choice for interior wood-to-wood joinery. The square drives are less likely to deform than slotted or phillips screws, so it is easier to drive them in rapidly with a power screwdriver. Hot-dipped galvanized screws and bolts can be used, but they won't cost much less than the stainless ones that may last longer. Although bronze fasteners can be used in woodwork, especially when bunged or sealed, they are the most expensive and are best avoided. However, bronze or brass locker hinges, doorknobs,

or decorative pieces can be used without fear of corrosion, since they are attached to wood, not to steel. It's good practice to use the same type of metal fasteners throughout. Purchasing them in bulk will also save money.

In areas where space is at a premium (for example, around portholes or in cabin ceilings), thin wood strips are sometimes glued directly to the plating with epoxy adhesives. The results seem satisfactory; however, the strength of the adhesive bond over time has not yet been verified. Of course this method won't work if the steel plate has already been insulated with sprayed foam.

EXTERIOR JOINERY

Some steel hulls have very little wood on the exterior but instead use pipe sections for guard rails, grab rails, and cabin eyebrows. However, there are many places where wood can be used to great advantage for appear-

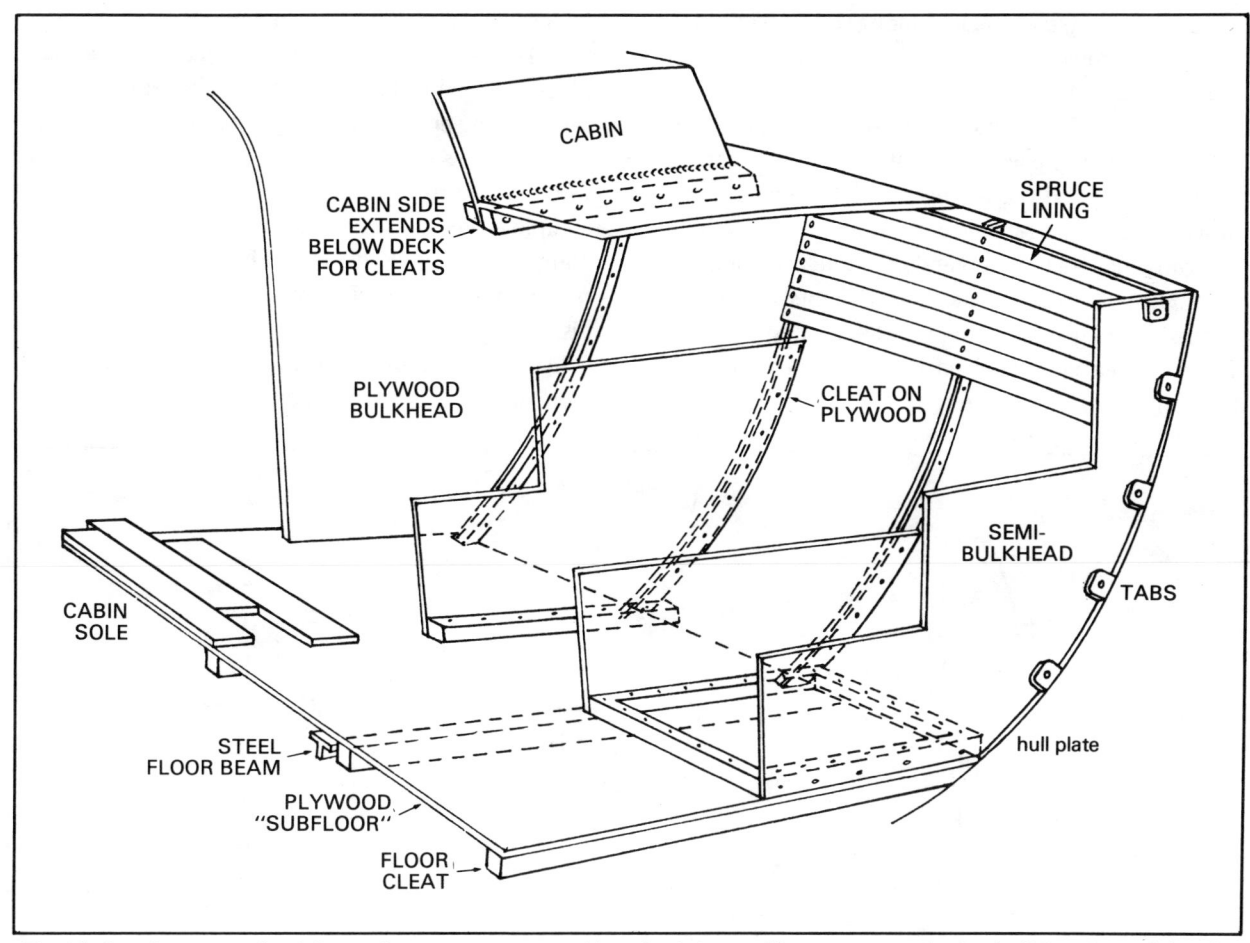

Fig. 15-9. *An example of the various components of interior joinery. Cleats are attached to bulkheads and the plywood "subfloor" as a base for joining the lining, ceiling, lockers, settees, and cabinetry.*

247

ance, weight savings, and good service. (Weight is only saved when wood is used in place of steel; using teak decking over steel plate is not such a case.)

Some of the items we will discuss can also be fabricated of integral or non-integral steel or stainless steel or, in some cases, of non-integral aluminum (see Chapter 9). Here we'll look at what can be done with wood. You may have to move back and forth between the chapters to make your final decisions.

Guard or rub rails are the wooden items most commonly attached to the hull. Using wood is very appropriate here, because the sound of wood crunching or rubbing against a dock or another boat is more pleasant than the sound of steel doing the same. Heavier steel rub rails are prone to dents and rust if continually banged, and removal, repair, and replacement are all easier with wood than steel. Besides, a wood rub rail looks much nicer and doesn't bleed rust like a steel rail. A good, durable hardwood should be used.

The rub rail can be fastened to the hull on studs or with a nut-and-bolt arrangement (see Fig. 15-10). Studs work, but if they are damaged along with the rail they cannot be removed without cutting or drilling. If high-build fairing coats are used as part of the paint system, the studs will also be in the way. Although it is tricky to align the curving wood rail with the studs, it can be done. The nut-and-bolt arrangement allows for easy removal of the guard rail and bolt without leaving a hole that can cause leaks, as in standard through-bolting. No matter how it is secured, the wood rail must be heavily bedded with a good polyurethane bedding compound, since this area will be washed with sea water more often than any other part of the boat.

Wood is also the most appropriate material for a long *bowsprit*, since a long steel sprit weighs too much. Shorter sprits are often made of steel pipe, which, in short lengths, weighs about the same as wood but is stronger. Wood bowsprits can be removed much more easily, but might cost more to replace. The choice here between steel and wood is a close one. The same factors also apply to the boomkin on the stern.

There are many ways to install a wooden bowsprit, and the method illustrated in Fig. 15-12 works particularly well. In this case, a section of steel pipe of the proper diameter can serve as the gammon iron, and another section can form a socket into which the sprit is inserted.

A *platform* supported on metal brackets or tabs will need to be added for easy maneuvering out on the sprit. If steel pipe or tubing is used to support the sprit, most of the support structure already exists. A nice wood grating can be installed as the platform itself. An arrangement that allows water to pass through the platform if it dips into a wave uses tabs to secure the wood (see Chapter 20).

Occasionally you will see a wood *rudder* on a steel hull. They work well, but cost more than rudders made of steel. Wood rudders are best laminated and totally sealed using epoxy and nexus cloth.

Many items on the deck and cabin can be made of wood. The most common are *rail caps, gunwales*, or complete *bulwarks*. As Fig. 15-13 indicates, there are many variations. Rails are definitely one of the best places to use wood, since the sheer always catches a visitor's eye.

In one of the most practical gunwale designs, a wide wooden plank is raised above the deck level and se-

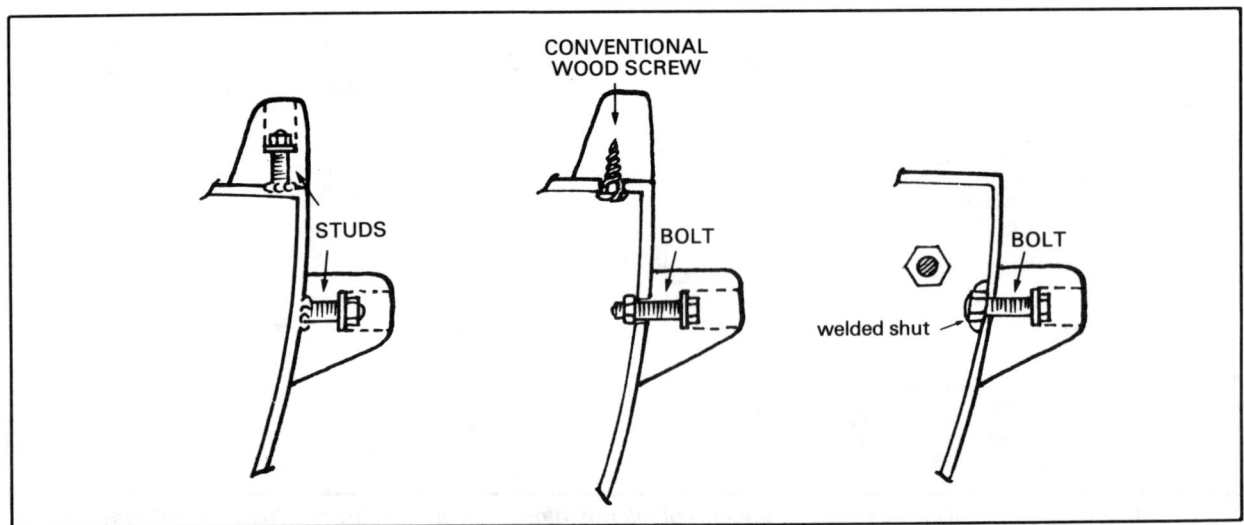

Fig. 15-10. *Some options for joining the toe rail and rub rail to the steel deck and hull.*

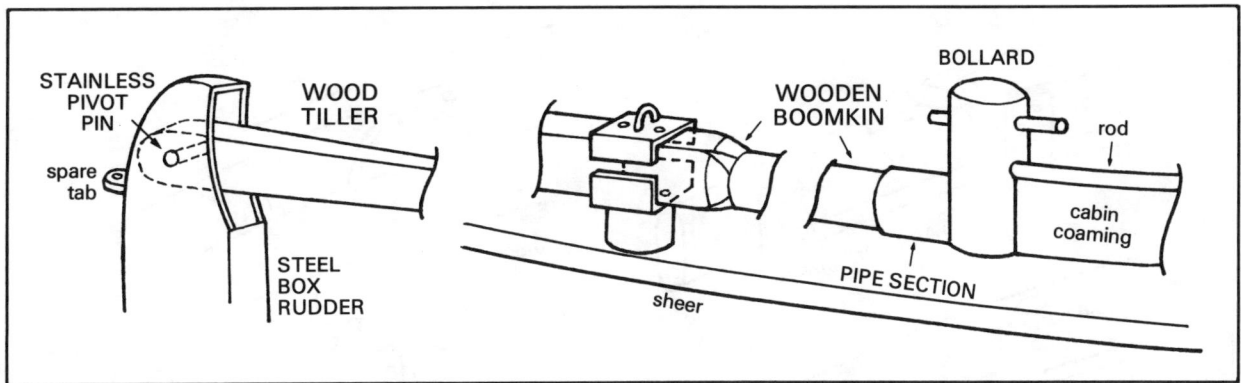

Fig. 15-11. (Left) *A method of attaching a wooden tiller to a steel rudder.* (Right) *A wood boomkin can be secured by inserting it into a pipe section welded in place.*

cured to appropriately spaced tabs. With this arrangement scuppers are not needed to drain deck wash, which flows quickly out under the gunwale between the tabs. Construction is very quick and inexpensive, and topside weight is reduced. The tab spacing must be matched to the strength properties of the wood, so that the gunwale doesn't flex and break. Fir, mahogany, oak, and teak are good choices of wood for this type of gunwale. The tabs can also double as stiffeners for the stanchion mounts, or the stanchion mounts can double as tabs for the gunwale.

If a steel gunwale is chosen, a wooden cap rail over the top will add both to looks and comfort. In this case, proper scuppers must be cut in the steel.

Boom gallows (crutches) can be fabricated in wood in a number of ways. Crutches commonly use steel or stainless tubing or pipe for the legs and a good, durable hardwood for the top. The cross beam between the two legs will likely have three half-round notches in it to receive the boom in different positions. The bottom of the legs can be secured to a base that is either welded

or bolted to the deck or cabin top (the welded base can't be removed). This base can be a solid steel or stainless socket, a pin, a curved angle- or flat-bar tab, a rod, or a pipe. If the base is bolted down, it should be well bedded, especially if it's stainless. The entire assembly can also be made of wood, bolted down to an integral curved flange or flat-bar tab that fits the legs. But a piece of inlaid angle iron would be strongest. (See Chapter 21 for illustrations.)

Other small wooden deck fittings include the emergency tiller, samson post, decorative caps, hardwood pads for winches and windlasses, dinghy chocks, anchor chocks, whiskerpole mounts, and flag poles. Don't forget the miscellaneous boathooks and belaying pins, even though they are only secured with line or clips.

Dorade ventilator boxes, hatches, turtles, and skylights are all commonly made of wood and are discussed in greater detail in Chapter 14. However, Fig. 15-16 illustrates some hatch details.

Various *hand rails* and *grab rails* are important safety features on the cabin top. They can be made of steel,

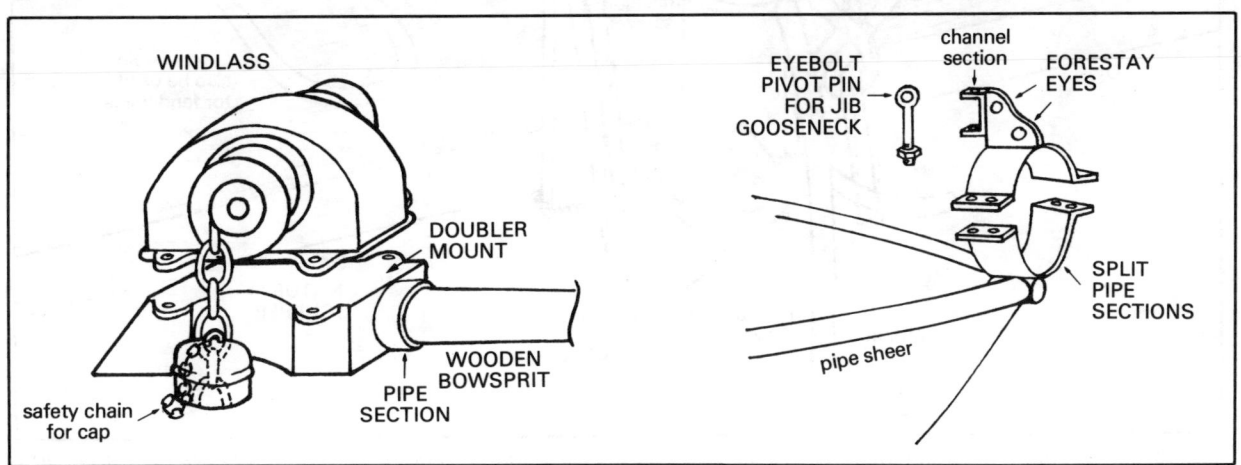

Fig. 15-12. *Pipe sections find employment as a secure mount for a wooden bowsprit*

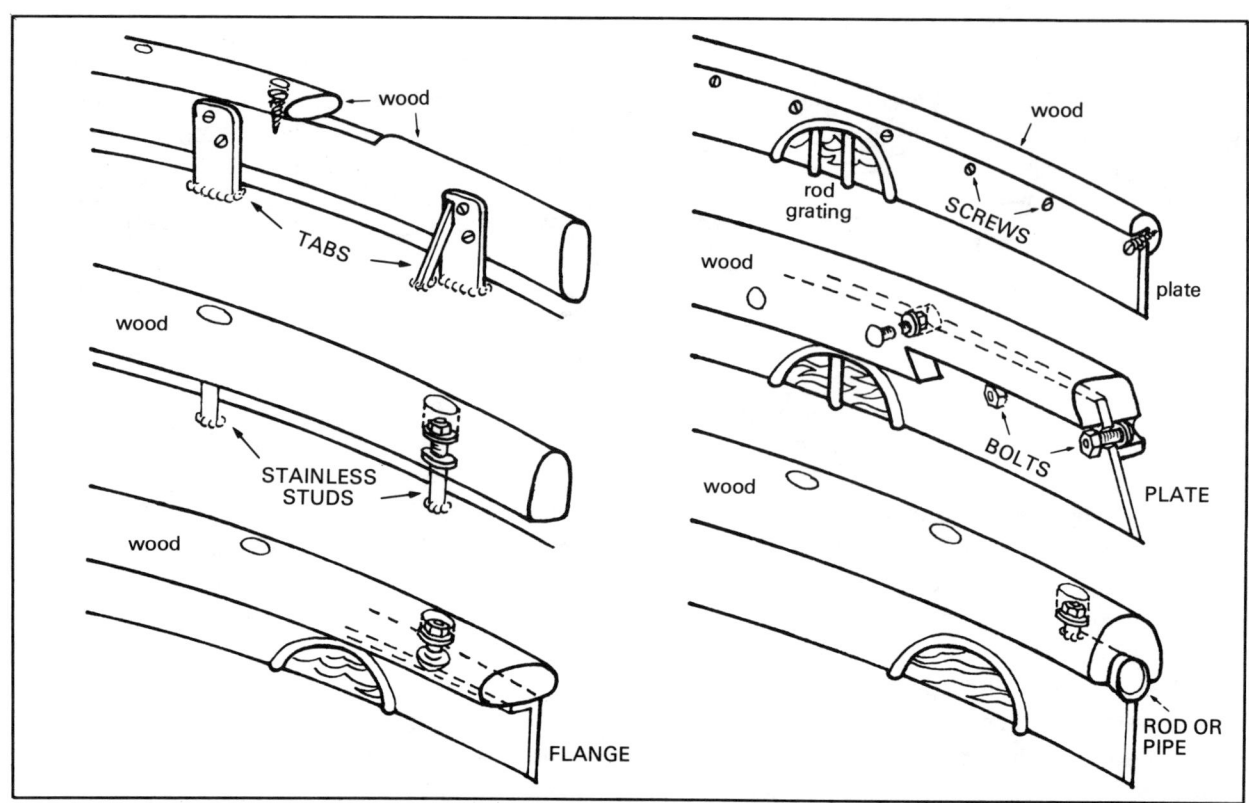

Fig. 15-13. *Attaching wood rails on bulwarks or to the hull can be accomplished in a variety of ways. In the top two examples, natural scupper drains are formed by the joinery; in the others, scuppers must be cut in the steel bulwarks.*

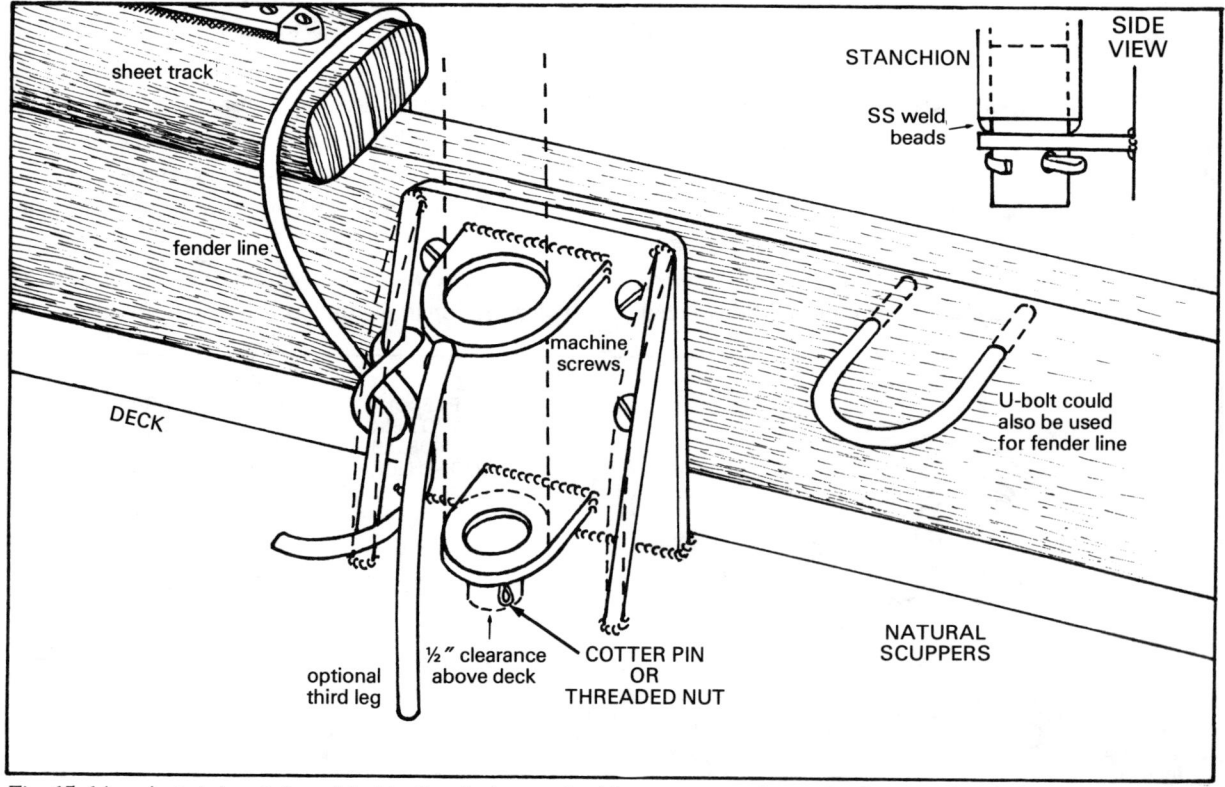

Fig. 15-14. *A stainless tab welded to the deck can double as a mounting point for wooden bulwarks and a stanchion mount. The stanchions must be fabricated with a tapered end to fit securely into the mount.*

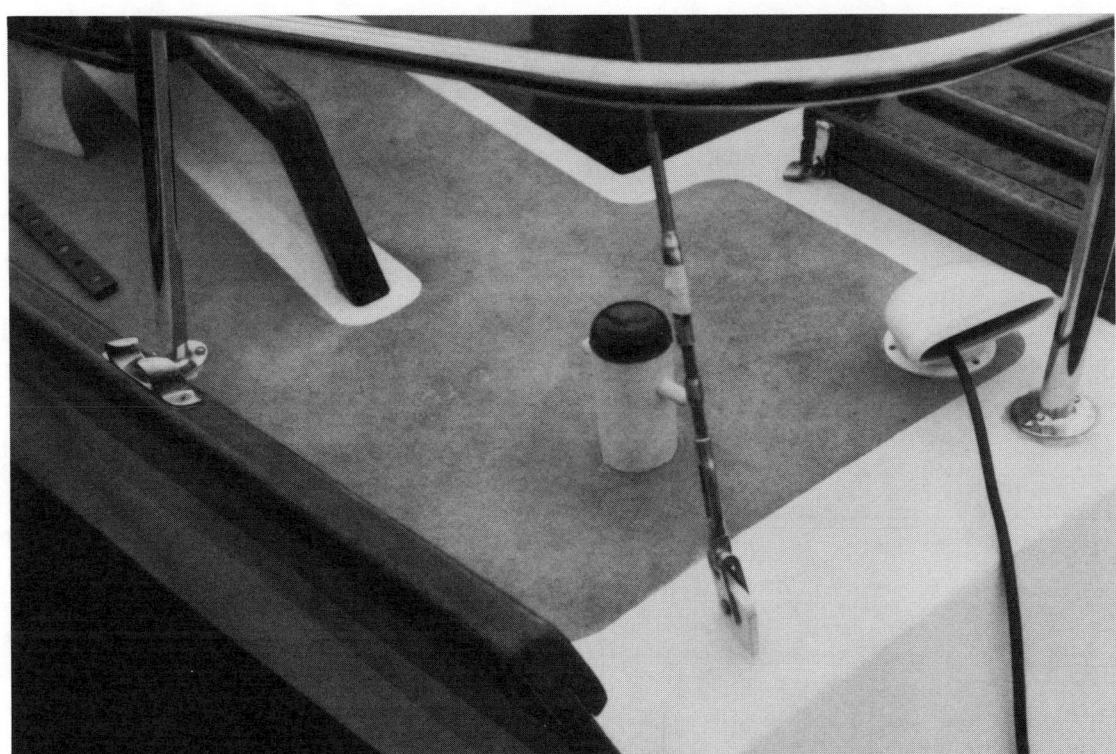

Fig. 15-15. *Wooden cap rails add a nice touch to the coaming and rail. Notice also the wooden cap on the bollard.*

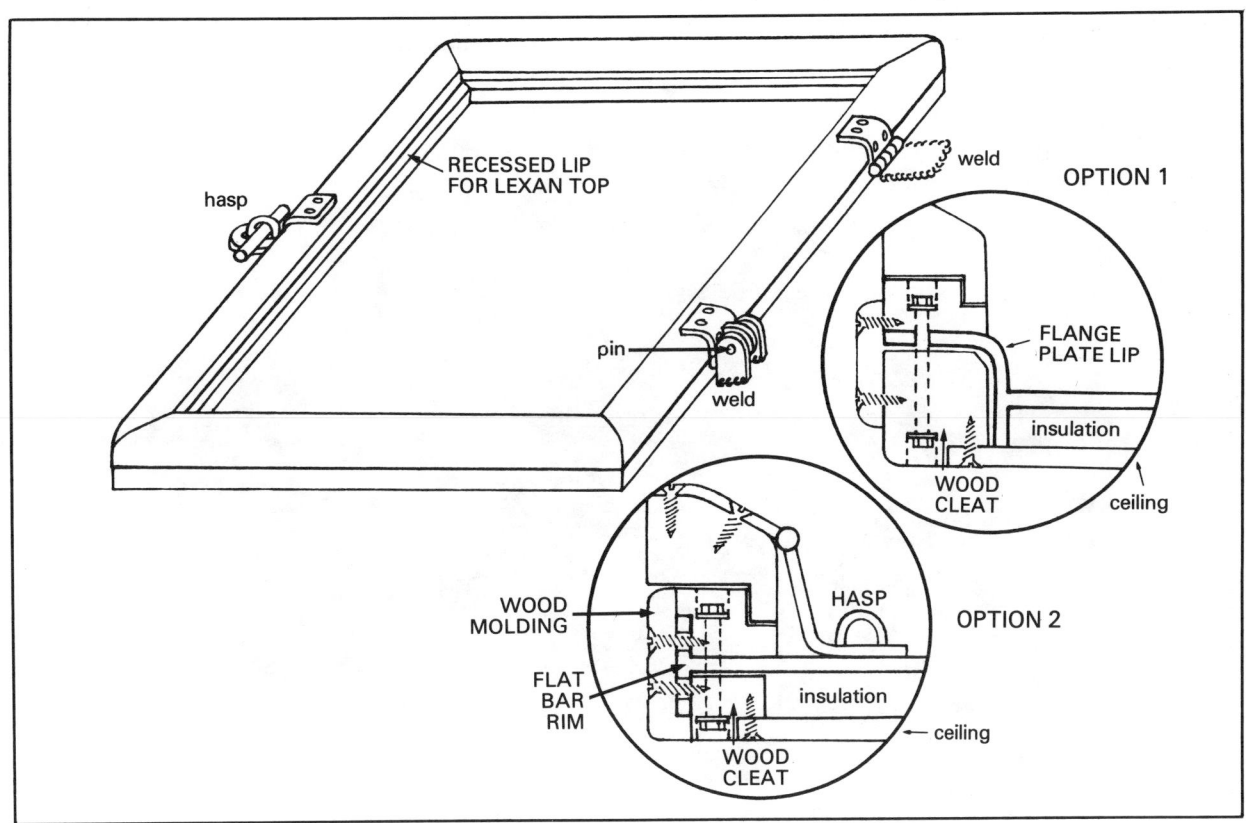

Fig. 15-16. *Joinery option for a hatch. The top can be either wood or Lexan.*

stainless steel, aluminum, or wood without much argument for or against any particular material. Wood is attractive but not expensive. Aluminum is lightest, though wood comes in second, and stainless wears well. Steel, of course, is quickest and cheapest to build.

Like handrails, *eyebrow trim* on the upper cabin edge helps to soften the boat's appearance. Eyebrows can be through-bolted or fastened with small countersunk bolts secured to a threaded nut welded on the back (as shown in Fig. 15-17). Obviously, their position depends on the shape of the cabin.

On any boat, a wooden mast requires a major expenditure of time and money. But making all spars of wood makes a lot of sense (see Chapter 20).

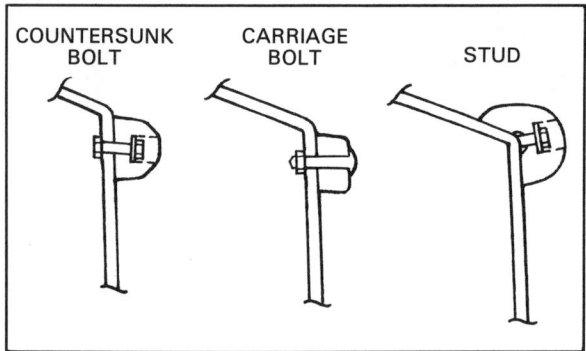

Fig. 15-17. *Eyebrows can be attached to the cabin sides with bolts or studs.*

Almost everyone loves *wood decks,* and many people want to know how they can be incorporated into steel hulls. Unfortunately, wood decks fastened over steel can easily become a problem.

The most common method of laying wood over a steel deck parallels the traditional planking method. In order for the fasteners to hold properly, thick planks must be used, adding extra weight to the boat. These planks, tightly fitted at the bottom edge but grooved to resemble seams on the upper surface, are secured to the deck with either studs or bolts. The "seams" are then filled with a flexible compound. But decks take a lot of abuse from people and the elements. No matter what kind of "seam" compound is used, eventually water will leak into the seams and around the fasteners. If the paint coating of the steel is scratched through even in one place, this trapped water will promote corrosion. The rust that is produced will lift up the decking, allowing more water to seep in, which, in turn, will increase the corrosion. Once rusting and pitting starts in the steel, the wood joinery will go to pieces rapidly. Wood decks will hide the rusting steel until corrosion has become so bad that a new steel deck is needed. Rusty drainage bleeding over the "covering board" (outboard deck area) and uneven lifting of deck planks are signs of corrosion. This is something to look for if you are buying a second-hand hull.

Fig. 15-18. *This steel schooner built by Haglund Boat Works sports traditional wooden masts and booms.*

The best solution to these problems is not to put wood decks over steel. It's a lot of extra work and weight. Other types of deck covering, like Vetus or Treadmaster (both are rubber/plastic mat-like materials), can create a comfortable, attractive deck. However, if you're still determined to lay on teak, there are several methods that may be more successful than the traditional one. There are two different approaches: either recognize that water will get below the wood and provide a way for it to flow out, or place some kind of barrier between the wood and the steel.

In a simple variation on the traditional method, the strips of wood are not fastened to the steel deck but instead are clamped down with straps of thin, painted steel bar stock, spaced every 3–4 feet, running athwartship. Both ends of each strap are welded or fastened to a stud. The straps can also be inlaid into the wood so that they are flush with the deck. There still will be a chance of water collecting underneath the wood, but the straps can be removed occasionally to inspect the steel deck.

The deck can also be elevated so that the wood and steel do not touch; any water that leaks through can thus drain away completely. Transverse cross pieces of bar stock or wood can be fastened to tabs or studs welded to the steel deck, and the wood fastened to these transverses. Wood is best for them, since metal cross pieces may rust themselves. A wood deck is also more easily secured to wooden transverses. Although there will be some chance of corrosion under the cross pieces, it will be more limited than if the wood were in contact with the steel across the whole deck.

Another way of elevating the deck is to insert quarter-inch steel rods through the deck planks, much as doweling is used in furniture. The rods, which will run the full width of the deck, are fastened down at either edge.

The next group of methods, though still experimental, take advantage of the strength of the new epoxy adhesives. The problem is that there is no data on the long-term adhesion of epoxy and steel.

One technique, developed by the Gougeon Brothers for use on cold-molded hulls, can be adapted to fastening wood decks over steel. In this method, the bottom and edges of $\frac{1}{4}$" or $\frac{3}{8}$" plywood are sealed with epoxy and then the plywood is laid down over the steel deck. The top surface should not be sealed, since UV rays can cause the epoxy to chalk or crack. A few bolts, countersunk to the top of the plywood, will be needed to help hold the ply in place. Then $\frac{3}{32}$" teak boards spaced $\frac{1}{4}$" apart are bonded to the plywood with epoxy. The spaces are filled with a black epoxy-graphite mixture to give the traditional appearance of tarred seams. The use of thin deck "planks" not only saves weight but prevents delamination problems.

In another method using epoxy, the deck planks are bonded directly to the steel hull. Either thick or thin planking can be used. When thin strips are used, they

Fig. 15-19. *The wood deck on this boat stops short of the bulwarks so that water can run freely along the covering board.*

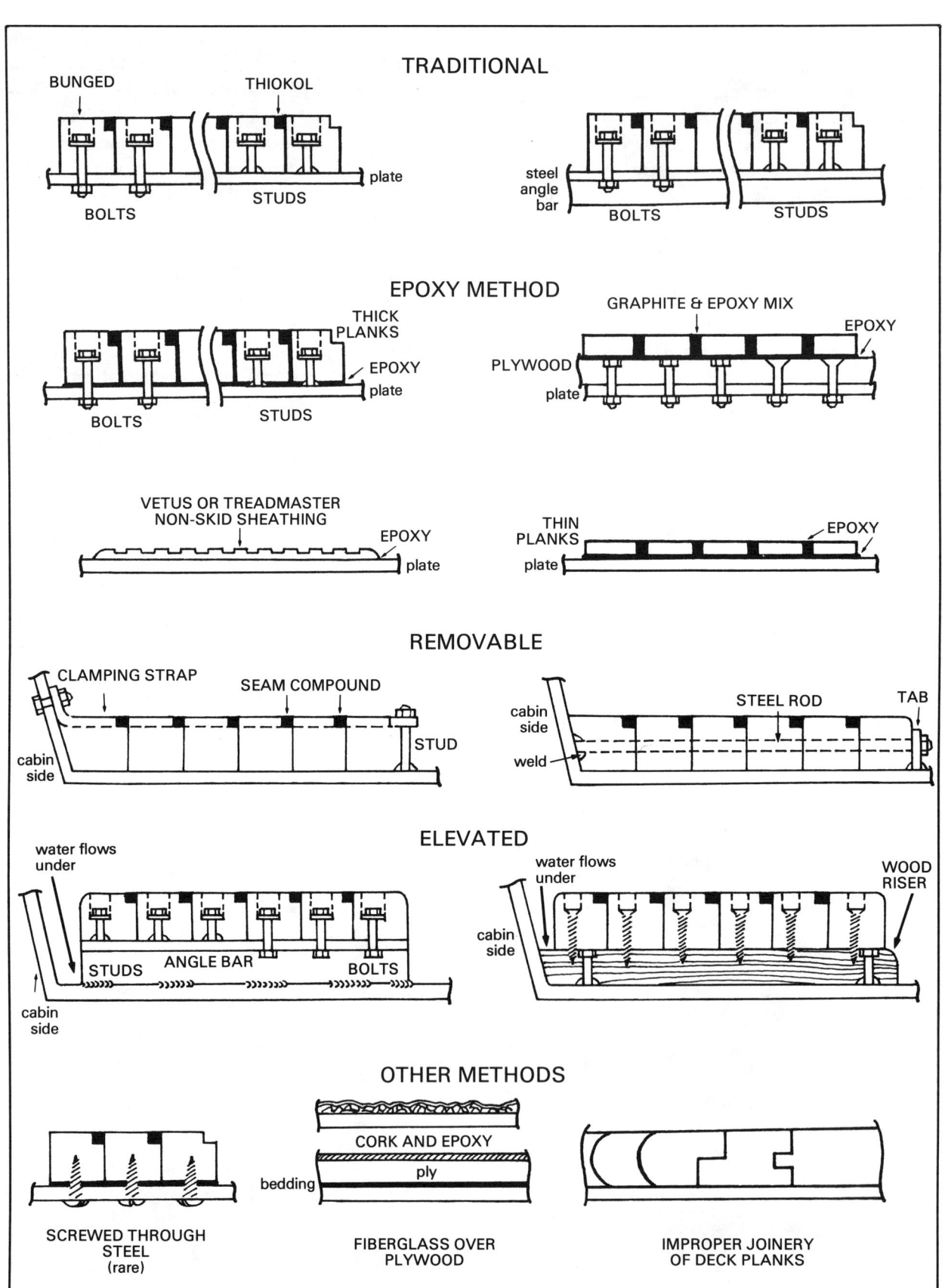

Fig. 15-20. *Methods of installing wood decks on a steel boat.*

254

are glued to the hull and the spaces between are filled with a polysulfide seam compound. For thick planks, the epoxy adhesive is continued halfway up the sides of the planks, and then a bead of seam compound is laid down on top of the epoxy. The thick planks are also bolted down, although the bolts are spaced more widely in this method than in the traditional one. For this method, fir is preferable to teak, since it is more successfully glued with epoxy.

The final approach is to avoid the problem of wood over steel by using a composite construction method. As is done on wooden boats, the wooden deck planks are joined directly to the deck beams with bolts or studs. The difference is that these beams are steel angle iron instead of wood. If teak decking is used, a plywood layer should be sandwiched between the teak and the beams. Plywood covered with a fiberglass sheathing can also be used for a composite deck. The joinery of the deck to the hull can be done at the sheer or over a steel covering board (see Chapter 9).

Wood can be used in many locations in the cockpit. The *coaming* and *spray shield* are very good possibilities, depending on the design; in some designs, steel is more appropriate. With a center cockpit, a wide steel coaming can cover a walkthrough below, between the forward and aft cabins. On smaller boats and those with aft cockpits, wood coamings make sense and keep the weight down. They can be secured to studs or tabs. Teak, fir, and mahogany are excellent woods for cockpit coamings.

Many amateur builders make their *binnacles* and *pedestals* of wood. Otherwise, the stainless or aluminum pedestals manufactured by companies like Edson or Merriman are quite acceptable. Pedestals should be bolted or secured to studs so that they can be removed.

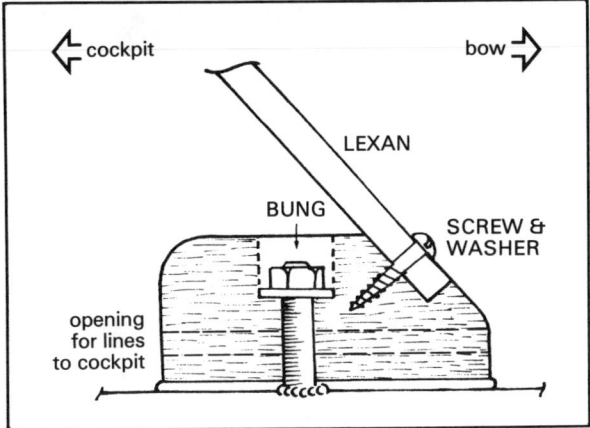

Fig. 15-21. *A wooden mount is an attractive way to join a removable spray shield to the cabin top.*

Fig. 15-22. *This custom-made wooden pedestal is both attractive and practical, since many accessories can be attached to it.*

Stainless steel *steering wheels* are commonly purchased from production manufacturers, but using nice woods like mahogany or teak for a wheel is very appropriate, since this item is handled a lot. A wooden wheel can be easily built with only a router and epoxy adhesives, and the result can be a work of art. If a stainless wheel is used, leather or fancy ropework is commonly added to improve appearance and prevent the hands from slipping on the wheel.

Cockpit lockers always take in some water, no matter how watertight they are supposed to be. So it's important to have proper drainage into the cockpit sole. Wood used here makes a soft, pleasant sitting area, and it saves on weight. The tops of wooden *lazarette and storage lockers* should be constructed of a durable, stable wood, like teak or one of its substitutes, that has good weathering properties. The rest of the lockers can be made of epoxy-sealed or painted plywood. In large cockpits, long settees and lockers can be attached to a longer flat-bar flanges; however, most often steel tabs or studs are strategically placed for joining cleats to which the lockers can be attached. In the cockpit, as in many other areas, drilling holes through a horizontal steel surface for attachments should be avoided because of the potential for leakage.

Other miscellaneous uses for wood in cockpits include teak wood sole gratings, lunch tables, and portable boxes for equipment, some of which may clip onto the pedestal guard.

CONCLUSION

Although wood can often be used to replace steel, you shouldn't get too carried away. Steel work is quicker and in most cases less costly. The various factors must be carefully weighed in deciding which to use.

In choosing the correct wood, keep in mind how chafe and the elements will affect the fitting. Is it going to rub against another boat or just the ship's cat? As a general rule, hardwood should be used for the "heavy" areas and softwood for interiors. If there is a chance it will be damaged, the item should be made removable; most of the joinery methods mentioned here allow for easy removal when repairs are necessary.

The installation of woodwork can be very enjoyable, and won't take that long, since joining wood to a steel hull is easier than joining wood to any other hull material. As on any boat, finishing out can take quite a while: fairing, sanding, and coating will likely take as much time or more than the initial installation.

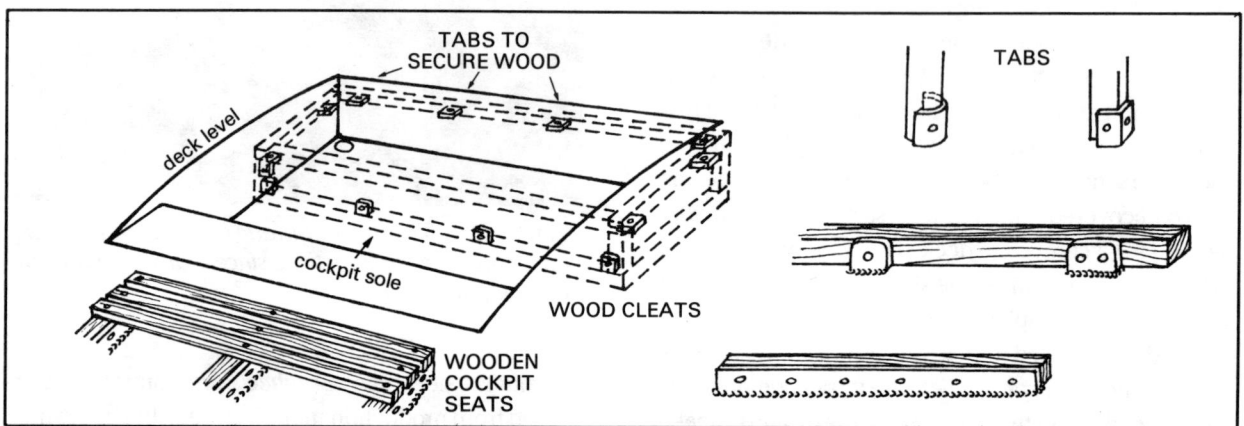

Fig. 15-23.   *Various type of tabs can be welded to a steel cockpit for securing wooden seats and lockers.*

—Chapter 16

Electrics and Navigation

Sailors today seem to carry more electrically powered equipment than ever before. This trend reflects the increasingly high standard of living, often based more on prestige than on practicality, that is promoted by sales personnel. More equipment usually means more problems; if you want all the conveniences of home, you must be prepared to pay for extra generators and deal with breakdowns in both the equipment and the tangled maze of wires. However, there is no limit to what you can run if the power is there.

Electrical equipment used for safety rather than comfort should be considered most important, and a margin of safety should always be built in for emergencies. After power is secured for running lights, starting the engine, and navigation equipment, you can think about adding outlets for electric pumps, hot water heaters, stoves, and appliances. But once you pass a certain power requirement, AC power will be needed to supplement the DC output.

The electrical equipment that will be used dictates the number and size of batteries, as well as the charging requirements. Although the main engine is usually called on for charging, other power sources like solar panels, shaft-driven alternators, wind generators, and auxiliary generators are good supplements or alternatives.

Minimizing electrical needs will help to simplify the system, which will lower its overall cost. Simple mechanical methods can often be substituted for electrical equipment. To check their contents, tanks can be fitted with visual gauges rather than electric ones; a good ice box can take the place of a freezer; foot and hand pumps aren't really so difficult to live with. Some equipment, like windlasses, can be powered with hydraulics instead of electricity. The clever sailor can probably devise lots of other power-saving gadgets such as a refrigerator compressor that runs on an engine power take-off instead of a separate electric motor.

On a steel hull, proper isolation of the electrical system from the hull is the key to preventing electrolysis. So you will need to become "enlightened" about the science of electricity and how to keep current where you want it. The placement and installation of each item must be carefully planned to prevent corrosion.

Once the basics of electrical installation are understood, it isn't very difficult, as long as the system is kept simple. It might be wise to hire a professional to help plan the wiring system to insure against stray current and accidental grounding to the metal hull.

Power invariably fails when it's needed most; portable spotlights and flashlights will help to brighten the dark. Many wise sailors also carry kerosene lights on board. They can be used as a good back-up and as a primary source of lighting and heat for cooking at sea.

This chapter will offer just an overview of marine electrics and guidelines for planning your electrical needs. Since almost all navigational equipment these days requires electricity, it is discussed here. Power-generating sources like solar, wind, and power take-offs are all grouped with the engine in the next chapter.

POWER REQUIREMENTS

The four terms used most often by electricians are "watts," "amps," "volts," and "ohms." Watts indicate the amount of power drawn by a piece of equipment. Amps (short for amperes) measure the amount of electric current running through the wire. A volt shows the potential energy of an electrical charge (for example, in a battery). An ohm is the measure of the electrical resistance in the wire (or other conductor) through which a current is running. These four principles are interrelated through a series of equations, called Ohm's Law, that allow you to convert from one to another:

$$\text{Watts} = \text{Volts} \times \text{Amps}$$
$$\text{Amps} = \text{Watts/Volts (or} = \text{Volts/Ohms)}$$
$$\text{Volts} = \text{Amps} \times \text{Ohms (or Watts/Amps)}$$

Some examples: a 25-watt bulb (the brightest that need be used) operating on a 12-volt circuit will require a current flow of about 2 amps:

$$\text{amps} = 25/12 = 2.08$$

A 500-watt cabin heater running on a 120-volt AC circuit will need 4.5 amps of current; on a 12-volt system, the heater will use almost 42 amps. A 1-hp motor draws 12 amps from 120-volt AC systems and about 90 amps from 12-volt DC. That's the reason 120-volt AC systems are required if you want to run high-wattage equipment.

Amp-hours (the amount of current drawn in an hour) relate the power drawn by a piece of equipment to the battery capacity. Most 12-volt batteries have a capacity of between 50 and 300 amp-hours of service. If the 25-watt bulb mentioned earlier is run for 4 hours a day, it will require 8 amp-hours from the battery. Connected to a battery with a capacity of 84 amp-hours, the light could be run continuously for about 42 hours before the battery has no charge left in it (the infamous "dead battery"). That 500-watt cabin heater, on the other hand, would drain the battery in 2 hours. It's wise to analyze the amp-hour drain of an electrical item before you purchase it.

The first step for determining power requirements is to graph out all the electrical items that will be used on board, the wattage they demand, the amps they draw, and the approximate number of hours they will be used per day. You can add 20% to compensate for the fact that you estimated the usage and to allow you to add equipment later. The total amp-hours will help you to determine whether a DC system is sufficient or if AC power should be added. The number, capacity, and type of batteries and a charging schedule can also be determined from these totals. The sizes of cables and switches that will be needed also depend on the load requirements.

Table 16-2. WIRE AND BREAKER SIZES VS. LOAD		
Total load in amps	A.W.G. wire size	Breaker rating in amps
7.5	16	10
10.0	14	15
12.5	12	20
20.0	10	25
28.0	8	35
40.0	6	50
53.0	4	60
70.0	2	80
83.0	1	100
96.0	1/0	120
110.0	2/0	150
130.0	3/0	180
150.0	4/0	200

Next, the maximum electrical load can be determined by adding up the power requirements of all equipment that will likely be in use at any given time. If this figure is higher than can be delivered by a single 12-volt battery, you have five options: 1) You can cut this "will likely be on" to a more practical "must be on." 2) You can use batteries with a greater amp-hour capacity. 3) You can increase the charging time by running the engine or charger longer (this can become very obnoxious). 4) You can hook two or more DC batteries in parallel; connecting batteries in parallel provides more amp-hours of service at the system voltage. (Two batteries connected in series deliver twice the voltage of a single battery, so more power is delivered at the same rate of battery discharge. However, connected in series, any number of batteries last only as long as one.) 5) If none of these four ideas produces enough power to handle your electric needs, you will have to consider additional charging sources or install an auxiliary generator to provide 110-volt AC power.

You will have to juggle many factors before it will be possible to determine what your final electrical system will look like. For the cruising sailboat, 12-volt systems are the safest, simplest, and most economical; 24- and 32-volt systems are only used on larger craft. Most

Table 16-1. ELECTRIC CONSUMPTION ONBOARD A CRUISING VESSEL

Watts	Amps	Equipment	Typical Quantity	Total Amps	Hours/Day	Total Daily Amp Hours	Comments
			LIGHTS & COMFORT				
6	.5	Compass light	1	.5	5	2.5	All lights are mostly used at night.
6	.5	Companionway light	1	.5	3	1.5	
9	.75	Masthead lights	2	1.6	1	1.6	
9	.75	Stern light	1	.8	1	.8	
12	1	Running lights	4	4	1	4	
12	1	Plug-in spotlight	1	1	½	.5	
12	1	Anchor light	1	1	2	2	
15	1.25	Cabin lights	4	6	1	6	
15	1.25	Fluorescent lights	2	3	½	1.5	
24	2	Other interior lights	3	6	½	3	
24	2	Spreader lights	1	2	½	1	
24	2	Emergency trouble light	1	2	½	1	
24	2	Stereo cassette deck	1	2	4	8	
48	4	DC television	1	1-4			
48	4	Fan (optional)	2	8			
72	6	Ice box conversion kit	1	6	4	24	Better to use engine-driven compressor (3 hp)
96	8	Search light	1	8			
			WATER & PLUMBING				
6	.5	Tank level gauge (opt.)	1				Use dipstick
	3	Automatic bilge pump	1				Could use manual
48	4	Freshwater pump (opt.)	1	4	¼	1	
60	5	Sump pump	1				Could use manual
60	5	Holding tank pump	1	5	½	2.5	
			FUEL & ENGINE				
6	.5	Fuel tank gauge	1				Use dipstick
*	50-300	Starting engine	few seconds				
*	*	Blower for gas engine	1				

Note: All engine power take-offs can run without draining batteries.

Watts	Amps	Equipment	Typical Quantity	Total Amps	Hours/Day	Total Daily Amp Hours	Comments
			NAVIGATION & PILOTING				
6	.5	Digital depth sounder	1	.5	4	2	
6	.5	Anemometer	1	.5	2	1	
6	.5	Speed log indicator	1	.5	2	1	
24	2	RDF	1	2			Can have own battery
24	2	Loran	1	2	½	2.5	
36	3	Ham radio	1	3	1	3	
36	3	Hailer (optional)	1	3			Try a portable hailer
54	2	VHF (transmit: 5.5 amps; receive: 2 amps)	1	2			
60	3	Single side band radio (transmit: 15 amps)	1	3			
72	6	Radar	1	6			
96	8	Auto pilot (optional)	1	8			Use wind vane
360	30	Anchor windlass	1	30	½	15	May need AC backup

Note: newer digital equipment may have less power drain.

| | | | | | | TOTALS | 84½ | |

* Varies with model; amps should be monitored

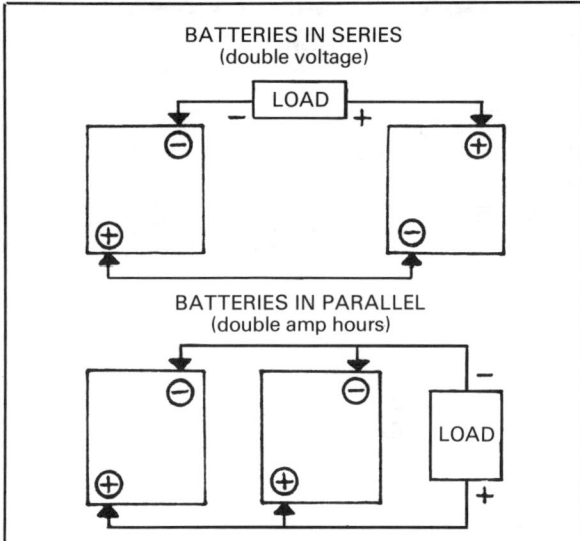

Fig. 16-1. *Batteries can be connected in parallel or series for different effects.*

Table 16-4.	USAGE SCHEDULE
Under 2 amps	Use daily or nightly (e.g., running lights)
5–10 amps	Use occasionally
10–20 amps	Use rarely
Over 20 amps	Use only for a short time (e.g., anchor windlass)

marine equipment is available for use with 12-volt DC, and many shoreside extras like TV's, can openers, and blenders, are now available for use with DC current. But if a 12-volt DC system must run that 1-hp Sears motor drawing 90 amps of current, an auxiliary generator or alternator will be required for battery-charging at sea.

You can also put some limits on your high-watt equipment use. If the usage suggested in Table 16-4 are followed, a reasonable charging schedule can be set up.

If you frequently run equipment demanding over 50 amps and a 12-volt system can't be kept charged economically, it may be better to use an alternator to provide 120-volt AC current. These units can be costly,

but they may pay for themselves over time. Because of the higher voltage involved, 120 is much more dangerous than 12, especially if it is improperly grounded. Stray current from a 110- or 120-volt system will also eat up steel faster than 12 volts will. Call in a professional if you don't know how to install and ground AC power.

You can't store AC current, since there are no AC batteries. So the AC generator or alternator must be run while the AC equipment is being used, unless you use an inverter to change DC current into AC.

BATTERIES AND CHARGING

The actual use of power equipment and the storage capacity of your batteries in amp-hours determine how often you will need to charge them. The balance to strike here is between the cost of the batteries (which do wear out) and the cost (and noise) of keeping them charged. In any case, the main engine starting system (especially for diesel engines) should be powered by its own battery, since starting the engine draws a tremendous momentary current (75 to 300 amps). The other batteries should deliver enough to run emergency equipment, as well as accessories. A properly designed two-battery system could do both jobs on a small cruiser; on larger boats with higher power demands, a two- or three-bank system of batteries connected in parallel would be appropriate.

Standard marine batteries are lead-sulfuric acid types; nickel-cadmium (Nicad) batteries can be recharged rapidly but are very expensive. Better than regular auto or marine batteries are the deep-cycling, lead-acid types. A regular battery is designed to deliver a large number of amps for a short time, while deep-cycling batteries deliver fewer amps for a longer time. Because these batteries have thick plates and a better plate make-up than regular ones, they can be fast-charged and discharged repeatedly without damaging the plates. Deep-cycling batteries last longer, but they may be rated a few amp-hours lower than a regular battery. Spending extra mon-

Table 16-3.	HEAVY CURRENT USERS	
	Typical Wattage
Depth recorder	150
Horn	224
Burglar alarm	240
Small refrigerator	250
Freezer compressor	500
SatNav equipment	600
Battery charger	700
Air conditioner	800
Electric space heater	1,200
Hot water heater	1,200
Water maker	1,400
Clothes washer and dryer	3,000
Cook stove (4 burner)	4,000

ey for good batteries will reduce the headaches of power failure.

A good battery system could use a regular marine battery for starting the engine and include a bank of 12-volt deep-cycling batteries to run other equipment. All batteries should be of equal size and capacity so that one is not favored over another, which would cause that battery to wear out faster. Six-volt batteries are easier to handle than larger ones, and can be wired in series to get a 12-volt output, but they are hard to find. The increased number of connections need to use 6-volt batteries also increases the chance of problems.

If batteries are kept in a fully charged condition at all times, they will last longer. This is almost impossible to achieve, but a reasonable charging schedule will lengthen the life of any battery. Different batteries demand different charging rates: a trickle charge is best for regular marine batteries, while a deep-cycling battery can accept a faster charging rate.

The battery bank must be well-ventilated and secured to the hull. The batteries should be kept as cool as possible, dry, clean, and clear of corrosion. A removable battery box is handy, but the base must be sealed to contain any acid leaks. Since hydrogen gas is given off during charging, ventilation is important; a fan can be installed for better air flow. The batteries should be fitted with special vented, leakproof caps so that there won't be any acid spills during excessive rolls.

The key to happy experiences with onboard electricity is being able to keep the batteries charged. The easiest

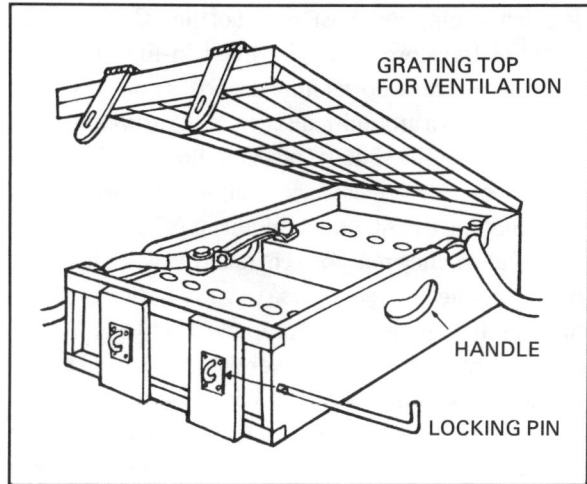

Fig. 16-2. *A wooden battery box can be used to secure and protect the batteries*

way is to run the engine for a few hours each day. At sea, running the engine will help to keep it in condition in case it is needed. But both the noise of the engine and the cost of fuel have to be considered. When at anchor, you don't want to have to crank the engine up full, so the engine alternator should be capable of good charging at low rpm's.

If you are at dockside, AC shore current can be used both the power AC equipment (like power tools) and to charge batteries. A step-down transformer, located between the AC source and the ship, may also be necessary, especially in foreign ports where the system voltage may be different. Shocks from an AC circuit can kill,

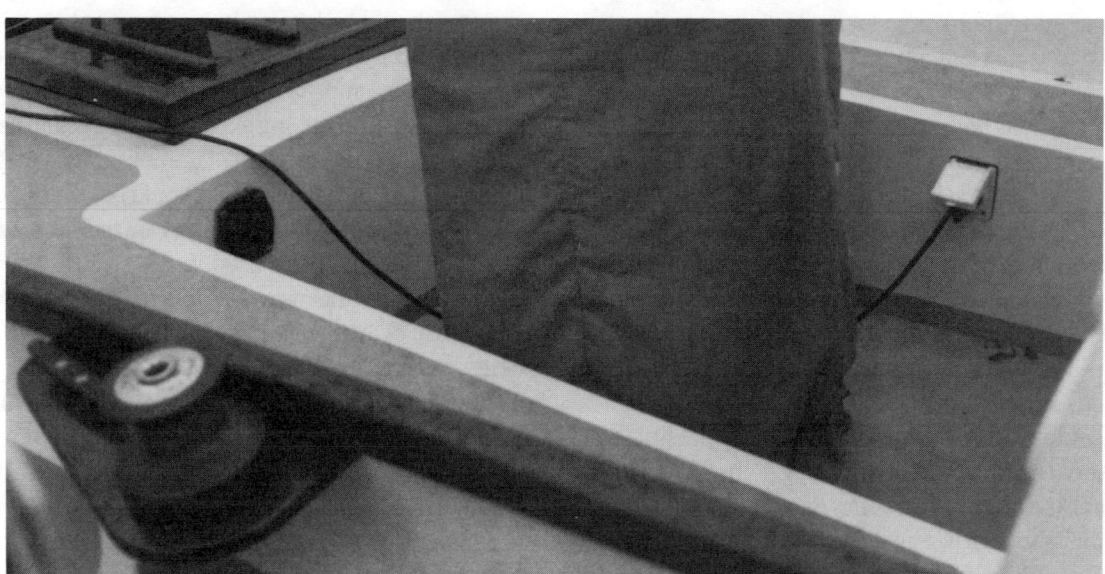

Fig. 16-3. *This plastic-encased electric outlet with its own lid is located in the cockpit, out of the splash zone. But if the cockpit were flooded, the outlet might get wet.*

so safety equipment must be part of the AC system. An isolation transformer can be fitted in-line to totally separate the shore power from the boat's power system. Even better is a ground-fault current interrupter (GFCI) that automatically shuts off power if short circuits or current imbalances are detected. It should be installed directly behind the AC outlet. When an AC plug and line are installed, they must be kept totally isolated from the hull and tested with a reverse polarity indicator to see that the shore plug is wired properly. If a GCFI is not installed, a master circuit breaker should be used to disconnect all shore power.

The correct charger must be used if the battery is to live out its expected service life. The charge delivered by standard battery chargers commonly tapers off as time passes. A super-charger that delivers a continuous current with an equalizing phase is better, especially for deep-cycling batteries. The unit chosen must deliver enough current so that the batteries can be charged in a reasonable amount of time.

A small, portable, gas-driven auxiliary AC generator (like those made by Honda and Sears) is commonly added to a 12-volt system. These generators produce power (some up to 1000 watts) at a reasonable cost, and can be used to run power tools and accessories and to charge batteries. The required fuel is flammable gasoline, so proper safety precautions must be taken. Gasoline for the generator (and for small engines for the dinghy or inflatable) can be safely stored in jugs on deck or in a vented lazarette locker. If the generator is allowed to run out of fuel before it is stored, it can be safely secured below, and can be covered for protection from dampness. These small generators are a lot quieter than the main engine, and they can be moved to various locations on deck as well as carried ashore.

Permanent auxiliary DC diesel generators are more expensive, but are safer to have around. If the boat is big enough to stow one and the electrical demands are high, the purchase makes sense. The most appropriate diesel generator on a steel boat may well be a portable AC/DC welder/generator. The Miller "Starfire," which delivers 170 amps of current and has four AC outlets, is a good example. It's not cheap, but this unit is a safe, dependable workhorse that could make it possible to trade services for goods on remote islands.

AC or DC equipment powerful enough to run an electric compressor can be very handy. The compressor can be used for filling diving tanks (1500 psi of air), for using air tools (120 psi), for spray painting (80 psi), or, if the output is high enough, for metallizing or blasting. Gasoline- or diesel-driven compressors can be used instead of electric ones to decrease electrical demands.

When the ship's engine is running, it generates more power than can be used to charge the batteries. A power take-off can take advantage of this extra energy by supplying power to an auxiliary generator, by running hydraulic motors for anchoring, fishing, or steering, or by powering a refrigerator compressor. Some diesels have a stud at the front end for hooking up the pulleys and clutch assemblies needed to set up a power take-off system.

Power can also be supplied by externally mounted generating systems. Solar panels can easily be installed on hatches or the deck. Though a bit expensive, they will provide the battery with a constant trickle charge, even on cloudy days. Wind- and water-driven power sources generate about the same number of amps as solar power. Any of these methods, as well as power take-offs, can supplement fuel-consuming charging systems like the engine or generator.

INSTALLATION

Installing the electrical system is easiest if it is done before the inside paneling and ceiling are finished. Good planning with preliminary lay-out drawings of all electrical equipment and wiring will save you a series of headaches during installation. This planning should also consider where and how the wiring will be secured, because it must be kept totally isolated from the hull.

The electrical panel, the main switchboard for your system, should be located in a convenient place away from salt spray. Space should be left in the panel for spare circuits and for additons or alterations to the system. Instead of buying expensive production panels, you can make your own out of the appropriate parts. All of the bolts, nuts, and washers should be made of brass, bronze, or copper; stainless, galvanized, or steel fasteners should never be used in the electrical system. Panel covers can be made out of formica or Micarta. The back cover of the panel should be hinged so that the circuits are accessible for repair and installation.

The number of circuits and outlets that the boat requires depends on the kind of equipment that will be plugged in. For safety, each circuit should be fitted with a fuse or circuit braker in the electric panel. Some pieces of equipment may require so much current that the circuit and its fuse can only handle one item. On the other hand, low-amp users like interior lights can all be put on one circuit.

Once the location of all electrical outlets is decided, you can plan exactly where to run the wires. If the wires are color coded according to their system and labeled as they are installed, you can avoid problems deciphering them later.

Proper wiring is what installation is all about. Choosing the correct-sized wire is the most important part, both to make sure that the wire can carry the current that will be drawn through it by the different pieces of equipment connected to its outlets, and to prevent stray currents that can lead to electrolysis. Wire size is a function of both the amp load the wire is to carry and the length of the wire. Stranded, tinned copper wire is the best kind, although #14 AWG is more appropriate.

Copper wire is a good conductor of electricity, but it isn't perfect. Current meets some resistance (ohms) as it travels through the wire. The voltage available at the battery is reduced by the time it reaches the outlet—a voltage drop. Voltage drop is a serious matter because it can cause stray currents in the electrical system, which

can lead to corrosion. It can also damage electrical motors that are designed to run at certain rpm levels. (Voltage drop is calculated using Ohm's law: voltage drop = currents in amps × resistance of the wire.) The larger the wire is, the lower the resistance and thus the lower the voltage drop. Wire must be chosen to minimize this drop, using charts like the one reproduced in Table 16-6. Basically, thicker wire will prevent voltage drop to large current users.

Wire splicing is critical on a boat, because shorts in the wire can produce the dreaded stray current that will cause corrosion. Also, at some time or another, moisture will probably collect around the splice. Wire splices should be soldered with tin solder and then wrapped with electrical tape or heat-shrink tape. Petroleum jelly or other compounds (like 3M's Scotch Coat), can be used to coat the junction to keep water out, and lacquer can be used to coat the cable. If the splice is in an area that will almost certainly get wet, it should be enclosed in a box. In fact, if you can afford it, all splices and con-

Table 16-5.	A.W.G. WIRE SIZES FOR A 12 VOLT SYSTEM										
Total current on circuit (in amps)	Length in feet, source to fixture										
	10	15	20	25	30	35	40	45	50	55	60
5	16	14	14	14	14	14	14	14	12	12	12
10	14	14	14	12	12	12	10	10	10	10	8
15	14	14	12	10	10	10	8	8	8	8	8
20	12	12	10	10	8	8	8	8	6	6	6
25	10	10	10	8	8	8	6	6	6	6	4
30	10	8	8	8	8	6	6	6	6	4	4
50	2		0		00		000				

Based on maximum voltage drop of 10%

Table 16-6.	WIRE RESISTANCE
A.W.G. wire size	Resistance in feet/ohm (at 25°C)
00	12,330
0	9,804
1	7,752
2	6,173
4	3,861
6	2,439
8	1,529
10	982
12	617
14	389

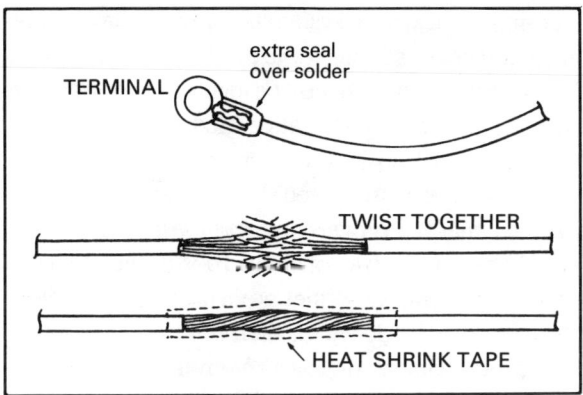

Fig. 16-4. *A good electrical splice includes twisting the wires together, soldering the connection, and protecting the soldered joint with heat-shrink tape or a watertight seal.*

nections should be made inside boxes. The box can then be potted with silicon foam to seal the connections.

Aircraft wire is easier to solder than regular copper wire. Aircraft wire is also less likely to corrode, and, if you can find it at a surplus warehouse, it can be used instead.

Wiring on a boat has to stand up to substantial vibration levels. All wire should be properly insulated with rubber or plastic sheathing; neoprene, PVC, and polyethylene are commonly used. Stranded wire absorbs these vibrations better than solid-core wire, and it will not break as easily. Wires that are passing through wood or metal bulkheads or steel decks can be protected from chafe by running them through plastic conduit, nylon sleeves, or cable casings.

On-deck outlets need to be carefully planned to exclude moisture. Flat deck sockets should not be used, and splices and junctions should be located well below. A good nylon stuffing gland and bedding compound should be used where the wires are led through the decks. And, if possible, the outlet should be located on the cabin top or sides rather than on the deck itself.

If your vessel is going to be used for commercial or chartering purposes, the Coast Guard has special wiring requirements for you. In this case it would be better to have the installation done by a marine electrician. *U.S.C.G. Regulations, Subchapter T* lists the requirements for boats under 100 tons.

PREVENTING CORROSION

Electric current, if not properly controlled, eventually can be fatal to a steel hull. Proper grounding and a well-insulated wiring system free from voltage drops and short circuits is the key to preventing electrolysis.

The electrical system must be totally isolated from the hull except at a single negative-ground point, usually at the engine. A positive-ground system should never be used, and, if possible, you shouldn't even tie up next to a boat that is positively grounded. All ground wires should be connected to a ground bus in the electrical panel, which is also connected to the negative side of the battery. A single wire is then run from the ground bus to the engine mounts or a nearby frame. A bonding strap running the length of the boat, as is used on wood boats, is not recommended. Fittings, like zincs, don't need to be grounded back to the engine, since they are already part of the hull.

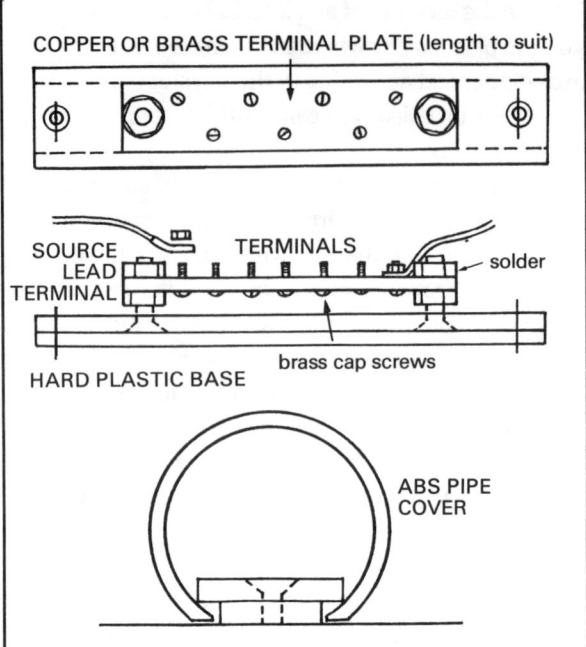

Fig. 16-5. *A bus bar can be fabricated from copper or brass plate, brass screws, and an insulating pad. A cover made of a section of ABS pipe will protect the bus bar.* Courtesy of John Simpson

A two-wire return system with the positive hot and the negative grounded must be used; the hull should never carry any current. The master battery switch should be fitted on the battery's positive terminal. Every time a wire or piece of equipment is connected, you must make sure that positive is connected to positive and negative to negative to preserve the proper polarity, since reverse polarity contributes to electrolysis. Worse, with an AC system, reverse polarity can cause very nasty shocks.

You should take all the steps discussed under installation—proper wire size, good splicing, good insulation, protection from moisture, protection from chafe—to prevent any stray current. It only takes a potential of .25 volts to start electrolysis. A current will follow the path of least resistance, and if this path leads through the hull, corrosion will begin.

As extra insurance, current monitors (discussed in Chapter 3) can be hooked into the system to show if there is any stray current, and to measure the stray current present in the water of an anchorage.

A voltmeter can also be used to check for current leaks. When all equipment is turned off, there should be no current running through the system. If a voltmeter connected to the positive terminal of the battery registers a current flow, you know that there is a short cir-

Table 16-7. ELECTRICAL SUPPLIES, PARTS, AND TOOLS

INSTALLATION SUPPLIES

Battery bank, including:
- Batteries
- Battery box
- Battery cables
- Cable terminals
- Voltage regular
- Master battery switch
- Ground cable

Main panel with:
- Switch-type circuit breakers or fuses
- Switches
- Various terminals
- Brass bus bar

Wire: A.W.G. Nos. 10, 12, 14 (and possibly 16)

Lights:

Interior	Exterior
Galley	Bow
Salon	Mast
Fo'c's'le	Running (2)
Closets	Stern
Lazarette	Compass
Engine room	Cockpit
Navigation	Spreaders (2)
station	Spotlight
Staterooms	Strobe
	Anchor

- Light clips for exterior mounts
- Switches
- Junction boxes
- Waterproof deck sockets for exterior lights
- Sockets for interior outlets

AC equipment:
- Battery charger
- Portable charger
- Shore power adapter connections
- Circuit separator and inverter
- Rectifiers
- Step-down transformer

PARTS

Plastic cable ties	Screws
Screw clips	Washers
Straps	Tubing (conduit, plastic, PVC)
Lacing	Insulators (mastic, nylon, rubber, neoprene,
Various terminals	plastic)
Clips	Spare 30′ AC power cord
Fuses	
Crimp connectors	
Spare wire	
Sockets and plugs	
Switches	
Labels	
Tags	

TOOLS

- Flashlights
- Combination wire cutters
- Hydrometer
- Crimping tool/wire stripper
- Mirror
- Needle-nosed pliers
- Soldering iron
- Heat-shrink tubing
- Silicon or Scotch Coat sealant
- Ampere meter
- Volt meter
- Baking soda for cleaning batteries
- Steel battery post brushes
- Distilled water
- Water funnel
- Petroleum jelly, grease, or wax
- Anti-corrosive wire spray
- Black electrical tape
- DC plug-in work light
- 12-volt circuit tester light
- Battery jumper cables
- Plug-in polarity tester for AC receptacles
- Feeler gauges

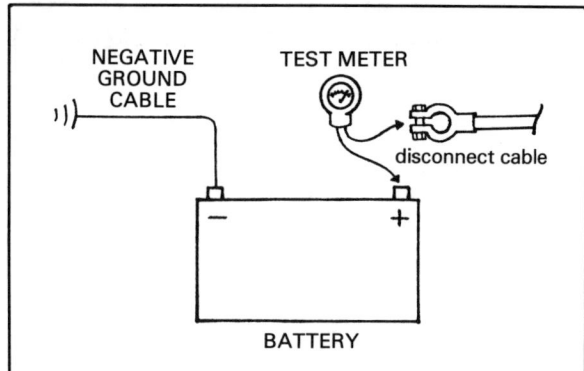

Fig. 16-6. *A method of testing for current leaks in a DC system. The test meter is connected between the battery and the positive lead, and all equipment is turned off.*

cuit somewhere onboard. You can then check each system to find the culprit. An ampere meter can be used to check electrical supply and generator output.

KEROSENE BACK-UP SYSTEMS

Many sailors use kerosene lights at sea to conserve energy, even when electricity is available. A kerosene back-up system requires fuel and a good 5–10 gallon tank, preferably one with a spigot. Kerosene can be found in most parts of the globe, and paint thinner can be substituted as a fuel if kerosene isn't found. Paint thinner is less expensive and works well, but it smokes more than kerosene does.

The number of kerosene lanterns on a boat can vary, but a big gimballed salon lantern and half a dozen portable lights for reading, navigation, or cooking are sufficient for the interior. (They can add a little romance to the voyage, too.) Topsides, a good anchor lantern is the most important, along with emergency running lights. A special kerosene compass light and a cockpit lantern may also prove helpful.

Besides kerosene, plan to carry spare parts for the lanterns and equipment for filling them. These include funnels, filaments, chimneys, bases, scissors for trimming wicks, pliers, and rags. A spare jug of kerosene is also wise for long trips.

NAVIGATION EQUIPMENT

Sailors today seem to rely more than necessary on electronic navigation gear. But you can get by with only a compass, sextant, and RDF, along with the sixth

sense that experience with dead reckoning brings. The navigator who pushes a button to find his or her position may still have to fall back on celestial navigation when the power fails. But electronic navigation aids provide a margin of safety, and in that sense can be looked upon as a sort of insurance policy for your boat. Navigational technology is advancing by leaps and bounds, and prices for sophisticated equipment keep falling.

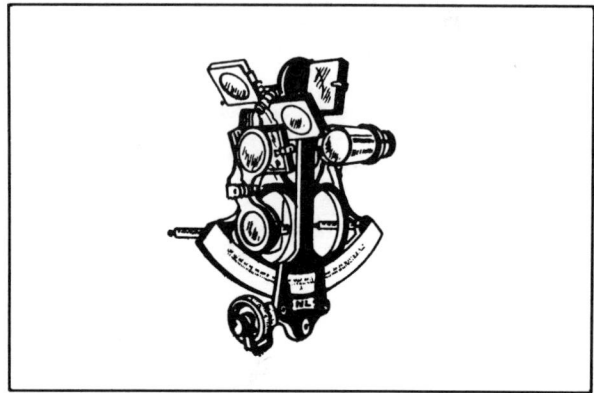

Fig. 16-7. *The traditional sextant.*
Courtesy of Nils Lucander

A good compass is usually first on the list of necessary items. Even on a steel hull, the usual methods for treating on-board deviation can be successful. However, special compasses with external magnetic adjustors that reduce extreme deviations can be purchased for added assurance of correct compass readings.

The usefulness of a navigation aid depends on the type of cruising being done. For a coastal cruiser, a good VHF radio is high on the list, and a radio direction finder, depth sounder, and Loran set would also come in handy. Depth sounders are especially useful for coastal cruising, and the new units come with all kinds of fancy features like digital read-outs and alarms. Transducers can be installed easily on a steel boat by welding in a schedule-80 pipe vertical to the waterline. A threaded bell cap with a hole for the transducer wire is screwed onto the pipe with ample bedding. The transducer itself should have a rounded shape and should be sheathed in phenolic, Lexan, or a similar durable plastic.

For offshore navigation, a single-sideband (SSB) radio or a ham set would be more appropriate than a VHF, although a VHF can also be handy for ship-to-ship communication out at sea. A ham radio can link you to a worldwide network of operators with a proven record of successful rescue operations. The ham licensing and operating regulations are described in a large body of literature, and SEA, Inc. has a great guidebook available

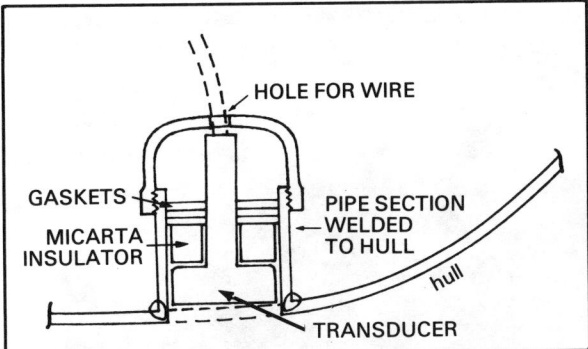

Fig. 16-8.   *The transducer for a depth sounder can be installed in an opening fabricated of steel pipe. The transducer itself is recessed into the pipe section, and a bell cap with a hole for the wire is secured to the top of the pipe.*

for people interested in SSB operations and equipment. SatNav has replaced radar as the "ultimate" position-finder, but apparently it will be outdated in another decade by a new system presently in development. Loran-C is becoming less popular because many cruising areas aren't covered, but coverage is slowly increasing. Both offshore and coastal equipment will probably be needed on a cruising yacht.

All electronic gear should be grounded to the common engine ground, and the ground wires should have low-resistance conductors. Each piece of equipment should have its own circuit breaker in the main electrical panel. Radio and speaker supply wires should be a shielded, twisted pair that is as short as possible and located away from machinery. Radios and speakers should not be placed anywhere near the compass, since they can cause magnetic interference. Although good radios have screening filters, the radio should be placed a fair distance from the engine. To prevent electromagnetic interference when the radio and engine are operating simultaneously, the aerial or antenna should be far from the engine, and can be hoisted up on the mast or attached to an insulated stay.

CONCLUSION

With proper installation, the electrical system on your boat should give little trouble, as long as routine checks are carried out and maintenance and repair performed promptly. A realistic charging schedule and the equipment to carry it out will allow you to run the equipment you need. A master switch to be turned off as you leave the boat will save you worries when ashore.

Table 16-8.   NAVIGATION GEAR

BASIC
    Compass (white card, 30°, binnacle mount)
    Hand-bearing compass
    Ship's clock
    Chronometer (digital wrist watch will do fair job)
    Ship's bell
    Horns, manual and butane
    Binoculars, 7 × 50
    Radio direction finder
    VHF radio, 24-55 channels
    Antenna for VHF, 3 dB, and extra cable
    Depth sounder with transducer
    Sounding lead with 12-fathom line
    Sextant, metal
    Sextant, plastic back-up
    Taffrail log or electric knotmeter
    Anemometer
    Shortwave radio (may be included in RDF)
    Loran-C with antenna
    Ham radio
      or
    Single sideband radio
    Radar reflector
    For calculating position:
        Charts
        Pilots
        Reduction tables
        Nautical Almanac
        Parallel rulers, dividers, protractor
        Calculator
        Log book
        Cruising guides
        Light lists

OPTIONAL
    Gyro compass
    Telltale compass
    Handheld RDF (could be kept with survival kit)
    Handheld VHF with weather alert (for dinghy and
      ship-to-shore talk)
    Short VHF antenna for emergencies
    Bottom graph recorder
    Radar
    Auto pilot
    SatNav
    Omega
    Weather facsimile
    Inclinometer
    Hailer

Fig. 16-9. *These older-style electrical outlets must be well sealed and insulated to prevent water from invading the box.*

—Chapter 17——

Engine and Power Sources

Although some die-hard sailors don't want anything to do with engines, there are so many benefits to the power they provide that it's hard to exclude them from a cruising vessel. Engines add both to safety and comfort by enhancing maneuverability, providing power to get out of currents and calms. They can also run power take-offs for operating hydraulics, for running refrigerators, compressors, and electric windlasses, and for charging batteries. Other power sources such as auxiliary generators or solar and wind generators can augment power supplied by the engine.

MARINE ENGINES

An engine's strength is measured in horsepower, and the required horsepower is usually determined by the designer. If this information is not available, you can calculate it by several methods. The classic method—described in *Skene's Elements of Yacht Design*—uses the speed-length ratio, the resistance caused by hull displacement, and the efficiency of the propeller to arrive at a shaft horsepower figure.

The speed-length ratio ($V/\sqrt{LWL}$) can also be used to determine maximum hull speed. At the maximum optimal hull speed, the speed-length ratio for a displacement hull is 1.34 (planing hulls can have ratios ranging from 2.5 to 8). If the LWL is multiplied by 1.34, the product is the maximum hull speed in knots. Most vessels operate a bit below this speed at a speed-length ratio of 1, called an "economical hull speed." Although a generous margin for safety (at least one-third more power) is needed to compensate for the fact that engines are rated as they perform in calm seas, it's still a waste of fuel to install an engine that delivers far more power than it takes to achieve hull speed. However, there are some advantages to having a few more horses in reserve. If power take-offs are to be attached to the engine by a drive belt, they may require more torque at lower rpm's or an increased horsepower rating, although there is a limit to how much power can be taken off a particular engine.

Once you know the horsepower that an engine must deliver to achieve the desired speed, you can examine specific engines and their power curves. Look at the "maximum continuous speed" curve to find at what rpm's the required horsepower is produced. If you can achieve maximum hull speed without running the engine at high rpm's, there will be less engine wear and lower fuel consumption. Fuel consumption tables covering a range of rpm's are often available in the engine specifications. Having a sturdy, well-built engine with high torque at low rpm's makes sense in terms of fuel efficiency.

Diesel engines are preferable to gasoline engines for reasons of both safety and economy: diesel fuel is less expensive than gasoline and is much less explosive. Diesels do cost more initially, but their hourly fuel consumption is considerably lower than that of gas engines: diesels are more heavily constructed and burn fuel more slowly. There are fewer electrical connections to malfunction, and, if the oil and filters are changed regularly, the diesel engine is less likely to need replacement of its relatively expensive parts. Diesels are noisier, but this minor drawback can easily be overcome by insulating the engine room.

Diesel engines last longer if they are run continuously, so you don't need to worry about using one freely. Most failures occur in filters, pumps, alternators, and, occasionally, starters, so you should always carry spares along.

Two- and four-cycle diesels are commonly used for boat engines. They are air or water cooled, and are rated as slow, medium (less than 2500 rpm), or high speed, depending on how many revolutions it takes to yield optimum horsepower. Slow-speed engines are very heavy for the amount of horsepower delivered, while high-speed diesels can be very light.

Diesels come in many different sizes, measured in cubic inches. Large diesels can't be crank-started (a shortcoming if the battery is dead) because their compression is too high. These large engines usually depend on batteries and electric ignition systems.

"Standard" equipment on a new engine can vary from nothing to everything. So when you're pricing different engines, you should also look at the standard equipment list. Sometimes the cost of all desirable accessories (especially the reduction gear) is equal to that of the engine alone.

Parts for some engines are easier to find and less expensive in different parts of the world. If you are cruising long distances, the accessibility of parts is important, even though you carry spares.

With so many variables to consider, the choice of which engine to buy may be difficult, but your knowledge can be supplemented by chats with manufacturers and mechanics and by keeping an ear to the waterfront grapevine.

The following companies manufacture diesel engines suitable for cruising sailboats: BMW, Bukh, China Diesel, Detroit (series 53 and 71), Deutz, Farymann, Ford Lehman, Graymarine, Lister, Murphy, Perkins, Pisces, Saab, Universal, Volvo, Westebeake, and Yanmar. For larger sailboat engines, Perkins, Ford Lehman, Yanmar,

Universal, and Westerbeake are the most respected manufacturers, and their parts are usually accessible worldwide.

ENGINE LOCATION AND INSTALLATION

Although you should follow the designer's stipulations for locating the engine, since engine weight figures and position have been used in calculating the trim of the boat, you may want to check your design against the following points.

If possible, an engine room should be created by placing bulkheads fore and aft of the engine. This engine room should be as large as possible so that you're not forced into contorted positions while working on the engine. The area should be well ventilated, with the air intake vent leading well forward of the engine and located above any possible bilge water. Soundproofing insulation that is fire- and moisture-resistant will help to keep engine noises in the engine room. If a bulkhead partition is not possible, as on smaller boats, a cover or panel can be used to separate the engine from the rest of the interior.

An engine has to go in and come out of the boat, so some kind of access should be designed into the engine room. In a center cockpit design, the cockpit floor can often be used as an installation opening. This access way can be bolted down securely to remain watertight.

A strong engine bed with well-secured transverse stiffeners should run at least twice the length of the engine to spread out its weight. On a steel yacht, the engine bed can be integrated into the hull using plate, flange plate, or angle bar; in some steel designs, vertical keel plates are extended up to make engine-bed bearers. If the bearers are welded instead to steel bulkheads, some stiffeners should be added. The engine bed must hold the engine above any bilge water and at the proper angle for shaft installation and operation. There must be room underneath for bolting the engine to the bed; clearance for mounts and shims; and space to install the coupling and possibly a shaft lock, and to service the stuffing box. Many engines have adjustable bases, and if elliptical slots are cut in the bed, aligning the engine with the mount will be easier. Adequate space should be left around the engine so that the transmission can be removed for repairs, if necessary. An oil drip pan under the engine and gearbox will help to keep oil out of the bilge. If there is space, a separate bilge sump in the engine area is an even better way to collect oil and grease. Steel collision stops (chocks) on the front face of the

Table 17-1. A COMPARISON OF DIESELS FOR CRUISING SAILBOATS

HORSEPOWER AT CONTINUOUS RPM

MAKE	10	15	20	25	30	35	40	45	50	55	60	65	70	75
BMW	at 3000 (1 cyl.)				at 3000 (2 cyl.)			at 3000 (3 cyl.)						
Bukh	at 3000 (1 cyl.)		at 3000 (2 cyl.)		at 3000 (3 cyl.)	at 3600 (3 cyl.)			at 3600 (3 cyl.)					
Deutz				at 2300 (2 cyl.)				at 2300 (3 cyl.)			at 2300 (4 cyl.)			at 2300 (5 cyl.)
Farymann		at 2500 (1 cyl.)	at 2100 (2 cyl.)	at 2500 (2 cyl.)		at 2500								
Ford Lehman								at 3000 (4 cyl.)	at 3000 (4 cyl.)		at 4000 (4 cyl.)			
Graymarine				at 2200 (2 cyl.)	at 3000 (2 cyl.)			at 3000 (3 cyl.)			at 3000 (4 cyl.)			
Isuzu					at 2800 (2 cyl.)			at 2800 (3 cyl.)	at 3600 (4 cyl.)		at 3000 (4 cyl.)	at 3000 (4 cyl.)		at 2600 (4 cyl.)
Lister		at 2200 (2 cyl.)			at 2200 • at 2200 (3 cyl.)			at 2200 (3 cyl.)				at 2200 (4 cyl.)		
Lugger		at 2500		at 2500			at 2500							
Murphy		at 2300 (2 cyl.)		at 3000 (2 cyl.)				at 3000 (3 cyl.)	at 3000 (3 cyl.)		at 3000 (4 cyl.)			
Perkins						at 3000 (4 cyl.)				at 3000 (4 cyl.)		at 2250 (4 cyl.)		
Pisces							at 3400 (4 cyl.)				at 3400 (4 cyl.)		at 4500 (4 cyl.)	
Sabb	at 1800 (1 cyl.)		at 2250 (2 cyl.)	at 1800 (2 cyl.)	at 1900 (2 cyl.)								at 2200 (4 cyl.)	
Universal	at 3000 (2 cyl.)	at 3000 (2 cyl.)	at 2800 (2 cyl.)	at 3200 (3 cyl.) • at 2800 (3 cyl.)		at 2800 (4 cyl.)		at 3000 (4 cyl.)						
Volvo	at 2500 (1 cyl.)	at 2000 (2 cyl.) • at 2500 (2 cyl.)		at 2200 (3 cyl.)	at 2300 (3 cyl.)	at 2400 (3 cyl.) • at 2500 (3 cyl.)				at 3000 (4 cyl.)		at 4500 (4 cyl.)		
Westerbeake		at 3000 (2 cyl.)		at 3000 (2 cyl.)	at 2400 (4 cyl.)	at 3000 (4 cyl.)		at 3000 (4 cyl.)		at 3000 (4 cyl.)	at 4000 (4 cyl.)			
Yanmar		at 3600 (2 cyl.)		at 3600 (3 cyl.)		at 3400 (3 cyl.)	at 2000 (3 cyl.)	at 2200 (4 cyl.) • at 2200 (3 cyl.)			at 1800 (3 cyl.)	at 2000 (4 cyl.)		at 2500 (4 cyl.)

Fig. 17-1. *The large aft-cabin windows on this Merrit Walter design offer a good view of the newly installed engine.*

engine bearers will help to keep the engine in place in the event of a collision.

Installing the engine is not too difficult if the proper procedures are followed and the right wrenches, a feeler gauge, and shims are at hand. Using flexible mounts and couplings makes the exact alignment of the engine less critical, but less-than-perfect alignment is bound to cause unnecessary wear on either the bearings or the transmission seal.

Shaft and Propeller

The power produced by the engine is transferred to the propeller by the shaft, which is attached to the reduction gear by a coupling. The reduction gear slows down the speed at which the shaft revolves so that the propeller has better thrust and drives the boat efficiently. The reduction gear is usually included as part of the engine package, although an engine also can be bought without the gear.

The shaft material must be strong and chafe resistant. But some of the best materials are also susceptible to corrosion, because, at least for part of their length, they are constantly submerged in salt water; the smaller the shaft, the more noble the material should be. Stainless steel, the most popular shaft material, can pit and crack if its surface oxide film is deprived of oxygen. But it is strong and wears very well, especially types 316 or 17-PH; type 304's wear resistance is lower. (If you're buying a used stainless shaft, spectrographic analysis of a

few shavings can determine the exact type of stainless the shaft is made of.) Steel can be used for the drive shaft if it is metallized with stainless at least at the stuffing box and stern tube, but corrosion can be a problem. Coating the steel with fiberglass is not recommended. The best shafts are made of monel or titanium, but both are very expensive.

When more noble shafts and propellers are used on a steel boat, the hull should be fitted with zinc anodes near the stern tube for protection from corrosion. The shafts, too, should be protected from electrolysis with zinc collars bolted around them and electrically connected to the shaft.

The shaft is held in alignment by bearings and glands as it goes through the stuffing box and out the stern tube. If the shaft is very long, additional "spring" bearings will be needed to prevent its wobbling. Bronze is the traditional bearing material, but some question its use on a

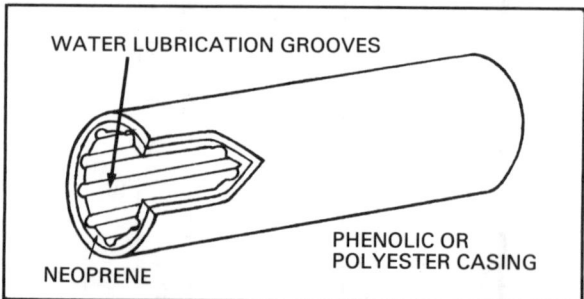

Fig. 17-2. *This type of cutlass bearing contains no dissimilar metals and so is very appropriate for a steel boat.*

steel boat because of galvanic corrosion at the stern tube, where the bronze is in contact with the steel. As we said in Chapter 3, since the bearing has a very small surface area in relation to the steel hull, corrosion should be fairly minimal. However, this is a point to consider. Water-lubricated neoprene cutlass bearings with polyester or phenolic casings could be used instead of bronze; their cost is only marginally higher. The new heavy-duty, high-impact plastic bearings (like Nylatron or Monocast), which are inert, are also worth considering. No matter what the material, proper allowance must be made for the correct tolerance between the shaft and the bearing. A certain shaft size requires an exactly sized bearing; there are charts of compatible shafts and bearings.

Since plastics have lower melting points than metals, plastic bearings must be protected from heat build-up. (The heat, of course, is generated by friction as the shaft spins inside the tight-fitting bearing.) Heavy-duty plastics can normally operate without lubrication (although it helps), but under severely abrasive conditions the proper clearance between the shaft and the bearing is critical.

At any time, proper clearance between a shaft and a bearing prevents seizing or unnecessary wear. It can be determined by using the formula $P \times V$. P is the pressure

exerted on the bearing, and is foun[d] total load in pounds per square inch V, velocity, is 262 × the engine rpm eter. The length (and therefore the a is the easiest variable to change.

Over time, any bearing material replacement will eventually be necessary. This is not always an easy job, so proper care should be taken in selection, assembly, and maintenance to prolong bearing life. Grit and sand can sometimes pass through a bearing and collect inside the stern tube. If plug holes are installed on the stern tube forward of the aft bearing, during haul-out the holes can be unplugged and a pressurized water hose connected to clean out the grit.

The stuffing box can be made of bronze, possibly with a plastic or neoprene isolator between the stuffing box and the stern tube. A good, water-lubricated, waxed wicking will do fine for the packing gland. A flexible stuffing box arrangement can also be fabricated with a section of sturdy hose clamped between it and the stern tube. A new watertight variation on this system is the Lasdrop stuffing box, which uses two shaft rings, one of stainless steel and the other of polyacetal. No water drips out of the stuffing box with this arrangement.

Schedule 40–80 pipe welded integrally to the hull can be used for the stern tube. On larger boats, a tube boss

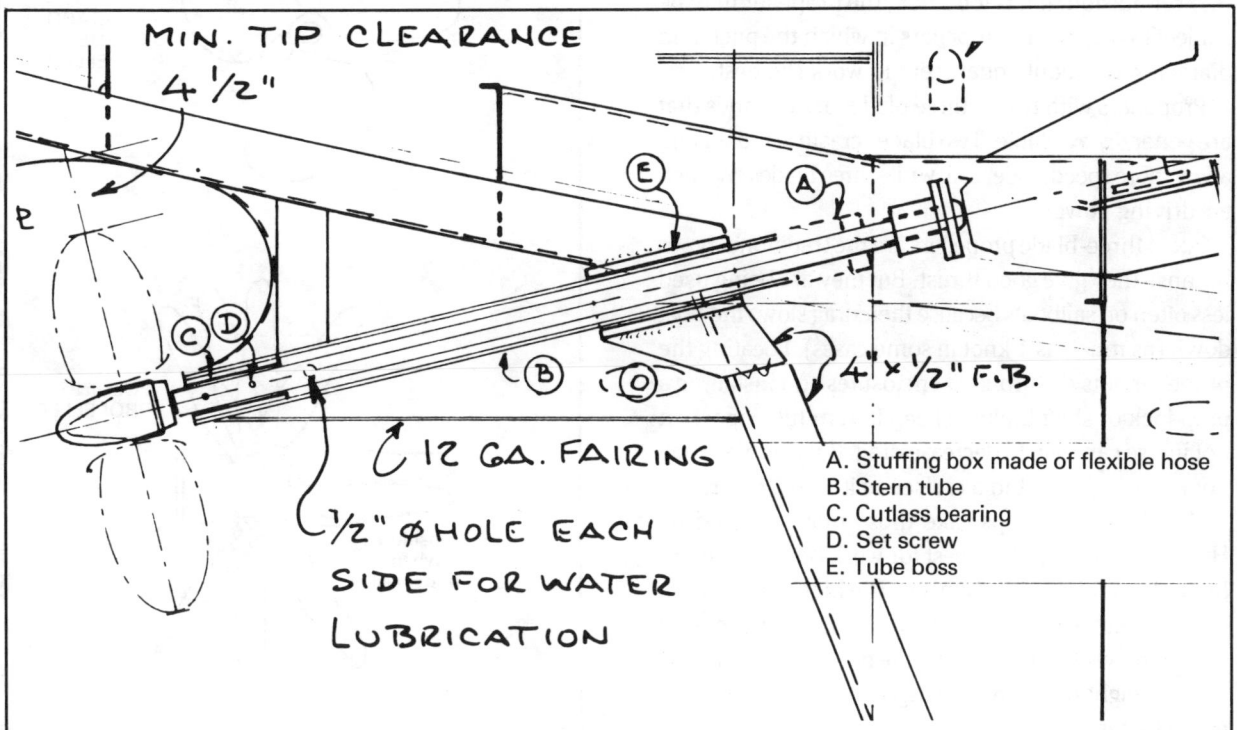

Fig. 17-3. *A centerline profile showing the components of the shaft asssembly when it is installed between the keel and a skeg rudder.*
Courtesy of John Simpson

(heavier schedule pipe) is commonly added around the stern tube for extra stiffness.

The proper propeller is the key to getting the most efficient use of the engine's power. Some power has already been stripped away by the reduction gears, so you can't afford to lose any horsepower to a bent or oversized propeller. All propellers are attached directly to the shaft using a locking nut, pin, or key.

In order to get the most efficient use of the blades, propellers should be placed in an area with low turbulence. The traditional location is in an aperture just forward of the rudder; unfortunately, this is not the best place to put a propeller. In a design with either a fin keel or a reduced deadwood area and a skeg, the propeller can be placed between the hull and the rudder, clear of turbulent waterflow. A skeg deflects the flow of water from the propeller so that irregular pressure is not put on the rudder; this is the most efficient location. However, for easy removal, the shaft must be aligned (either skewed at an angle or off-center) so that it can be pulled out alongside the skeg without moving the engine. If the propeller is located just forward of the rudder, a cutaway in the rudder is required for the same reason.

Efficient operation also depends on both the diameter and the pitch of the propeller blades. If the diameter is too large, not as much engine power will be translated into propulsion. If it is too small, the propeller may be subject to cavitation. Propellers in which the pitch and diameter are about equal seem to work the best.

Propellers with two or three blades are the ones that are generally available. Two blades create less drag and allow more speed under sail, while three blades give better driving power.

Fixed three-blade propellers are the traditional types because they give good thrust. But they are being used less often on sailboats because their drag slows the boat down (as much as 1 knot in some cases). Locating the propeller outside turbulent enclosures and installing a prop lock or shaft brake to keep it from turning when not in use can help to decrease drag. But this drag may not be as important to a cruiser as it is to a racer.

Variable pitch props (like those manufactured by Hundestadt or Sabb) are best for work boats that carry heavy loads of varying tonnage. The high-pitch adjustment works well with the heavy, low-rpm engines that usually power these boats, and the pitch can be changed as the weight of the load changes, helping the boat to move better.

Full-feathering fixed props, like the Max Prop, are very expensive, but are good for a sailboat because of

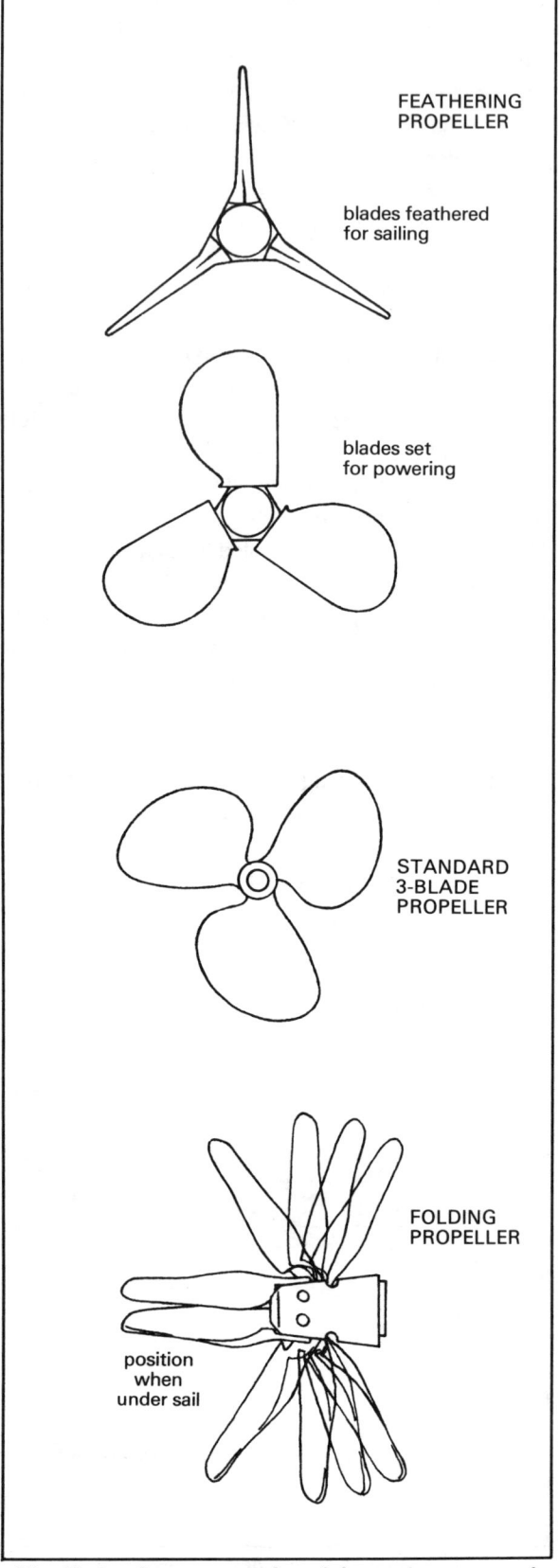

Fig. 17-4. *Some examples of the various types of propellers available for cruising sailboats.*

their reduced drag. In some cases, their pitch can be changed during haulouts.

Folding props, (Gori or Martec) are most suited to small boats because their blades are generally too small to drive a large one. Sailors who are willing to get along with less thrust and want maximum speed under sail will appreciate the fact that these propellers produce the least drag. The Gori prop is actually the best type of folding prop, because the blades are geared and can be set to different angles for optimum efficiency in reversing, sailing, or motoring.

Although the choice of a propeller design involves considering many variables, the choice of materials is pretty straightforward: manganese bronze is the type most commonly found. Steel is a poor choice, since it is subject to cavitation, although it performs somewhat better if metallized or coated with epoxy. Gunmetal has good corrosion resistance but is weak. Nickel aluminum bronze has better corrosion resistance than manganese bronze, but costs twice as much. Stainless steel props are also very expensive, but are sometimes found on expensive yachts. Other special types of props, like rubber, resin-bonded bronze or nylon, are used for special purposes.

Fuel System

The best fuel lines for a diesel engine are made from reinforced neoprene or equally high-quality reinforced tubing. When diesel fuel is in contact with copper, brass or galvanized iron, the hydrocarbons in the fuel oxidize, and gum then forms in the diesel. This action occurs over a long period of time, especially in stored fuel. Additives retard this process but do not stop it. Therefore it is best to avoid these materials in tanks and tubing for the fuel system. If copper is used, it should be brazed, not soldered, at the joints. If it is available, black (wrought) iron is an inexpensive alternative for fuel lines; its exterior can be painted in the same way as steel.

In-line filters should be used in the fuel system to strain out both particulate matter (like rust from old fuel storage tanks) and water. It is best to have both a primary and a secondary filter on the line from the tank to the engine, and one of these filters should have a glass bowl so that the fuel can be inspected visually. Two fuel-filter cartridges (a pre-filter and a paper one) should be used for each tank. A strainer placed between the deck filler cap and the tank will help to keep the tank clean; fuel can also be strained through chamois or an old nylon stocking as it goes into the deck filler.

The fuel tanks themselves are discussed at length in Chapter 9. If two or more tanks are used, a T-valve can be installed below the deck filler cap to route fuel to the tanks. Tank breather vents of clear vinyl tubing should lead from the top of each tank to an outlet placed high on the cabin sides.

Fuel pumps are usually supplied with the engine. They should not have bottom taps, since these sometimes leak.

The parts box for the fuel system should include spare fuel injectors, fuel pump parts, and diesel fuel additives. Injector nozzles can foul up, so carry some spares. Fuel and oil filters will also have to be replaced periodically.

Cooling Systems

Four different engine-cooling systems can be used onboard a cruising sailboat. Although different equipment is required for each, every cooling system is connected to the engine by intake (suction) and exhaust (discharge) hoses. (The many different materials that can be used for these hoses are discussed in Chapter 12.)

An air-cooling system uses a fan to cool the engine. The system must have adequate ducting for air intake and outflow. These systems are mostly seen in well-ventilated craft, like open lifeboats. Air-cooled engines must be used with dry exhaust hook-ups.

In freshwater cooling systems, hot water from the engine is pumped through a heat exchanger, which is cooled by salt water that enters a throughhull and circulates around the heat exchanger. Copper is the traditional material, but in contact with the hot, fast-flowing salt water that cools the heat exchanger, corrosion can result. Cupronickel, though expensive, will have fewer problems; stainless steel can be used, but even 316 stainless is not as corrosion resistant as cupronickel. Some systems use a cooling reservoir instead of a heat exchanger; these self-contained systems are most commonly used with large diesels. To maintain freshwater cooling systems, filters should be attached to all lines. Anti-freeze should be added to the system in colder climates and to prevent boil-overs.

Raw saltwater cooling is common for the relatively small engines used on sailboats. Seawater enters the manifold, circulates through the engine, and exits out the exhaust. Although there are some questions about the possibility of corrosion with this method, a copper heat exchanger (which has a higher corrosion potential) is not needed. An in-line strainer should be fitted after the seacocks to keep debris out of the engine. A water pump is necessary, as are spare pump impellers, extra thermostat parts, and pump spares.

The fourth cooling system is most common on metal boats. In this method, the hull itself acts as the heat exchanger in a freshwater system. This cooling method works well, although integral reservoir tanks must be of the proper size. On non-metal boats, metal "keel coolers" can be bolted on. However, since with this method there is more chance of obstructed waterflow during heeling, it is more common on powerboats.

Exhaust System

An exhaust system should silence the engine as well as vent combustion products. In order to be safe, it must also be leakproof. Four types of exhaust systems are used for marine engines: 1) a wet system with the engine above the waterline; 2) a wet system with the engine below the waterline; 3) a dry system with the engine above the waterline; and 4) a dry system with the engine below the waterline. In most cases, the engine of a sailing vessel will be near or below the waterline, and a wet system is preferable, but a partially dry variation on the system may work as well.

When either a wet or a dry exhaust system is used, there must be some way of keeping sea water from backing up into the engine. The exhaust line should run in an inverted U, the top of which is located at least 10 to 12 inches above the waterline, and then through a water trap muffler, also placed above the waterline. The exhaust line then joins an exhaust pipe, which has a check valve or rubber flapper where it exits the hull. The system should be fitted with a drain cock at the lowest point or be self-draining, and the muffler (especially the water-injection type) also should have a drain or vent.

The material used for the exhaust pipe must withstand the high levels of heat produced by exhaust gases. Galvanized steel, iron, and stainless steel can be used, but the stainless must be isolated from the engine with rubber or neoprene hose sections. Nickel alloy 625 or 825 pipe is the most non-corrosive material, but it is expensive. Brass and copper should not be used, since they can de-zincify or deteriorate. Pipe joints should be brazed rather than soldered to withstand heat. Because dry-exhaust systems have very hot air running

through them, metal pipes should be insulated with at least ¾" of asbestos, ceramic-glass fiber, or other heat-resistant cloth wrappings to prevent nasty burns.

Wet-exhaust systems can use rubber, nitrile (Carlisle) or neoprene hose instead of metal pipe, cutting down on the chance of corrosion. Flexible tubing also withstands engine and hull vibration better than metal pipe. Any rubber tubing should be the heat-proof, reinforced type similar to that used in automobile radiators, and it should be secured with stainless steel clamps. High-tensile nylon or polypropylene bearings can be used to support the exhaust hose, although hanging pipe brackets with pads also works well.

Starting and Electric Systems

Diesel engines can be started in a number of ways: hand crank, electricity (e.g., Dynastart), spring start, hydraulics, inertia, compressed air, gas, and recoil. But electric and hand-crank starting methods are the most practical. A hand-crank system is the best back-up there is, as long as the engine has been installed so that the crank can be fitted and used. Small diesels can be hand-cranked because they have a compression-release valve; in larger diesels, the compression is too high for hand-cranking, so other starting devices, usually an electric ignition run off the batteries, are used. Of course the smaller diesels usually have electric ignition, too.

The electrical system used to start the engine begins with the battery bank or with the engine's own starting battery, which should be the type that can provide a burst of high-amperage current. As with the main electric system, proper size and length of wire and good splices or terminals are required. The wires to and from the engine are connected through the engine panel, which includes a voltmeter, amp meter, tachometer, oil-pressure gauge or alarm light, water-temperature gauge or alarm light, and ignition. If glow-plug ignition is used, it also runs to the engine panel. An engine shut-down switch should also be installed in the engine panel; it can be either an electrical switch or an air choke.

Lubrication and Accessories

If fuel is food for an engine, oil is its blood. Good-quality engine oil will pay for itself many times over. Two oil filters should be installed for safety, and rust-inhibiting agents can be added to the oil. A portable pump fitted under the engine block will make easier the messy but necessary job of changing oil. Funnels with strainers also make sure that nothing but oil goes into the engine. Spare parts for the oil pump should be carried onboard, along with spare hose clamps, nuts, bolts, screws, locknuts, and cotter pins. It's better if they are all made of the same material (for example, machine steel or stainless steel).

Various types of engine controls are available in chandleries and junk yards. The location of both the throttle and steering controls depends on where the helm console or pedestal is located, as well as the type of controls used. Flexible wire, chain, or self-lubricating cable can be used to attach the controls to the engine. All cable should be nonmagnetic if it runs near the compass; stainless steel is often used. The cable must also be accessible for inspection and repair, and is easily hung on aluminum or plastic hangers. Any flexible wire (non-conduit type) should be fitted with turnbuckles for adjusting the tension.

Table 17-2. ENGINE SPARES AND TOOLS
Metal-working tools
Wrenches
Feeler gauge
Glow plugs
Fuel filters
Oil filters
Fan belts
Air filters
Hoses
Exhaust tubing
Switches
Fuel pump
Zinc anodes
Hydraulic adapters (optional)

OTHER WAYS TO GENERATE POWER

Today almost any household luxury can be installed onboard as long as your pocketbook can stretch far enough to include the equipment to generate power for it. Some auxiliary power sources are simple, innovative, and economical, while others are quite elaborate and unnecessary unless you're pretty spoiled. As Chapter 16 explained, if you want to run AC equipment, like power tools or toasters, you will need a source of power other than the engine. This AC current may be used directly by AC equipment or converted to DC and stored in batteries.

Today there are many ways to generate usable power, but some are more logical than others and have been tested at sea. If the various power sources were rated in terms of power output, the list would look like this:

Low: solar, wind, water

Medium: engine, power take-offs, auxiliary generator

High: large, fixed auxiliary generator

A low-power source that's clean, quiet, and constant is not to be ignored. However, if your energy needs are high, a high-output auxiliary source may be the answer.

Attaching a power take-off to the main diesel makes sense, since all of the engine's power is not needed to charge the batteries. The many, often innovative systems are a good alternative to installing heavy, expensive generating plants. Any slack can be taken up with a *small* AC generator. The types of PTO's include: 1) a V-belt directly off the clutch; 2) a hydraulic clutch unit (which is very expensive); 3) a long shaft with a clutch and a 3–5 hp diesel motor (separate shaft and prop or use same); 4) a front-end drive with a universal joint (common on some good diesels like Perkins); 5) a shaft charger (which can be noisy and cause some loss of speed).

Power take-offs can drive DC alternators with diodes, AC alternators, AC/DC generators, rectifiers converting AC to DC, bilge pumps, AC inverters, and hydraulics for steering, anchors, windlass, and fishing. PTO's can also run mechanical compressors which in turn can operate a refrigerator, run other motors, supply air to diving tanks, run air tools, and even operate spray painting equipment. The compressor's capacity is related to rpm's; the more rpm's, the more power.

The capacity of a PTO varies according to the shaft rpm's and the clutch adjustment, and the most efficient rpm's vary with each unit. A 110-AC generator rated at 1000 watts and run by a PTO can drive several items at a time (for example, hand power tools and a small refrigerator). These can be quite handy, although they are inefficient compared to an inverter.

One of the simplest ways to get AC power is with a DC-AC inverter. These run off the ship's battery, and can be purchased for $200 to $400. They are quiet and fairly efficient, and allow you to run a few power tools or a TV for a limited period of time. Although their amperage is low, they'll still drain the battery fairly soon. So the charging schedule needs to be matched with the amount of time the inverter is used. The Dynamote inverter is a type that creates differing amounts of AC voltage; they are limited only by output power. Some types of inverters work off an AC generator that runs off the main engine.

A PTO or generator for operating a hot water heater isn't really necessary, since in-line propane flash heaters do a very efficient job. However, for those who desire it, hot water can easily be pumped from the engine cooling system, although the coolant flow and temperatures will have to be adjusted with a secondary ball valve. If water is diverted from the coolant line directly after the engine, the engine's water pump will force the water along so that another pump is not needed. There are many variations on this system.

Separate auxiliary generators come in a wide range of sizes, cost, and weights, and can be powered by gas, diesel, or even propane, although diesel is preferable. Auxiliary generators can also be used to start the main engine in case of power failure. They have many merits, but they definitely tend to destroy the peace of a quiet harbor.

Large fixed generators (like those manufactured by Onan) are popular on power boats. These units are generally quieter, more efficient in charging and fuel usage, and cooler than the main engine. On the other hand, they are expensive, require a large space, and need proper beds and exhausts. Mid-sized diesel generators are more practical, and they usually provide enough power for moderate electrical requirements.

On small cruising yachts, 1- to 4-cycle portable generators are most common. At a price of $300–400, these quiet-running units are a good charging back-up for the main engine. Larger 5-hp models that can run a power tool or a TV at the same time can be purchased for under $1000. The lower-rpm generators are easier to handle, while the higher-rpm models are quieter and lighter. As Chapter 16 indicates, a portable diesel arc welder can also be used as a good mid-sized generator. These are very practical carried onboard a steel yacht.

Water power can be harnessed by taffrail generators with DC motors. A water-driven propeller that produces low rpm's is towed behind the hull, and can generate 6–7 amps at a 6-knot boat speed. These can cost as little as $400, and, like solar and wind systems, make a fine charging back-up that can reduce the necessity of running the main engine. Some types have a separate fixed prop on the hull connected either to a motor or to an alternator that trickle-charges the battery. In both cases, there will be some reduction in speed because of the prop drag and a chance of fouling by weeds.

Solar power is one of the cleanest, quietest, most efficient ways of providing a trickle charge to the batteries. It cannot, however, be used to generate AC power. Depending on the size of the solar panel, between 4 and 12 amps can be supplied each day. A solar panel can be inlaid into the typical hatch cover; portable panels that can be moved about to various locations increase the efficiency of the system.

Wind generators are fine alternatives to solar cells, although they are more practical when moored than when out at sea. They can be mounted on deck (although they will probably be in the way), installed on a line and raised out of the way when sailing, or permanently fixed to a mast. Their output in amperes is similar to that of solar. Many sailors with moderate electrical needs use both solar and wind as back-ups, depending on whether they are sailing or at anchor.

SOURCES

Solar Generators

AEG-Telefunken Corp.
P.O. Box 3800
Somerville, NJ 08876
201/722-9800
—solar generator sets

Atlantic Solar Power, Inc.
6455 Washington Blvd.
Baltimore, MD 21227
301/796-8094
—solar panels

AQUA-SOL
Box 18646
Ft. Worth, TX 76118
—*Solar Boat Book*

ARCO Solar, North America
20554 Plummer St.
Chatsworth, CA 91311
213/700-7393
—solar photovoltaic modules, batteries, battery protectors

Boat Electric Co.
6303 Seaview Ave. N.W.
Seattle, WA 98107
206/784-5908
—solar panels

Edmund Scientific
7877 Edscorp Bldg.
Barrington, NJ 08007
— solar cells, generators,
and solar-powered equipment

Free Energy Systems, Inc.
P.O. Box 3030
Lenni, PA 19052
215/459-2158

Ron Wilson
Glass Energy Electronics
Seattle, WA
206/632-1645
— deck panel

Kyocera International, Inc.
7 Powder Horn Drive
Warren, NJ 07060
201/560-0060

Solar Energy Company
P.O. Box 649
Gloucester Point, VA 23062
— solar cells, solar generators,
solar-powered equipment,
wind generators

Solarex Corporation
1335 Piccard Dr.
Rockville, MD 20850
— solar cells, solar generators,
solar-powered equipment

Spectrolab
12484 Gladstone Ave.
Sylmar, CA 91342
— solar cells, solar generators
solar-powered equipment

PDC Labs
P.O. Box 603
El Segundo, CA 90245
— thin deck- and hatch-mounted
solar chargers

Water Power Generators

AMPAIR Products
76c Meadrow, Godalming
Surrey, GU73HT
England
— water-driven generator

"Hydrocharger"
Regent Marine and Instruments, Inc.
1051-B Clinton
Buffalo, NY 14206
— water generator

Wind Turbine Technologies, Inc.
4035 Oceanside Blvd., Bldg. 51
Oceanside, CA 92056
— large line of wind
and trolling generators

Free-Wheeling Propeller-Shaft Generators

Warner Gear
P.O. Box 2688
Muncie, IN 47302

Sail Charger, Inc.
2895 46th Ave., Bldg. B
St. Petersburg, FL 33714
813/522-9417
— propeller shaft-driven alternator

Wind Power Generators

C.I. Bock
2321 Washington
Marina del Rey, CA 90291
— wind generator

"The Cruising Sailboat Generator"
Hamilton Y. Ferris
Box 219
Dover, MA 02030
— wind generators

J.S. Haft
8925 N. Tennyson Dr.
Milwaukee, WI 53217
— wind generator

IMTRA Corporation
151 Mystic Ave.
Medford, MA 02155
— wind generator

Mother's Bookshelf
P.O. Box 70
Hendersonville, NC 29739
— *Wind and Windspinners* by
Michael Hackelman and David Hause.
Build your own.

Windlight Workshop
Rt. 2, Box 271
Santa Fe, NM 87501
— catalogue of parts, props,
controls, and motors

279

—Chapter 18

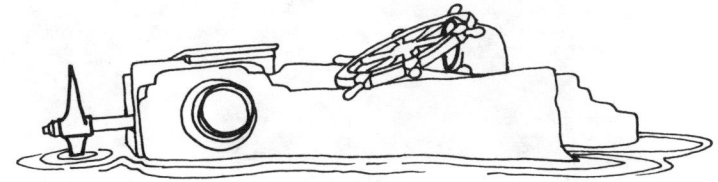

Steering and Anchoring

Unlike most other boat systems, both steering and anchoring use only a few important pieces of equipment, but they are apt to be costly; safe anchoring of larger boats requires several expensive anchors and a high-priced windlass. Cost decreases as the weight of the vessel goes down, since smaller anchors can be used and a windlass becomes a luxury rather than a necessity. Although the steering system must also be matched to the size and design of the boat, you usually have a choice between the more economical tiller and the more easily handled wheel. Installing these systems on a steel boat is about the same as on any boat, except that some parts can be welded integrally with the hull and mounting the anchor-roller assembly is easier.

STEERING SYSTEMS

A boat is steered with a tiller or a wheel linked with the rudder (see Chapter 9). Either can be hooked up to a self-steering vane or an auto pilot. Although the hookup is simpler with a tiller, a drum and lines can be fitted on the wheel to transmit the commands of the self-steering device.

Tillers are simple to install and easy to repair, and they permit the person at the helm to feel the rudder movement directly. However, in a heavy-displacement boat, handling the tiller in stormy weather can be quite a struggle, because the person at the helm must fight the pressure put on the rudder by wind and waves. Tillers can only be used with an aft-cockpit design.

If a tiller is used, a well-made wooden one is best. Several layers of wood are commonly laminated to provide the necessary strength, but a long natural crook of the correct dimensions could also be used, if you can find one. The method of joining the tiller to the rudder depends on whether the rudder is an inboard or outboard design. Outboard rudders are the simplest and most economical, since the rudder is easily attached to the hull and the tiller can then be fitted directly into the top of the rudder. However, this is not necessarily the most effective arrangement. Inboard rudders are built with a rudder post that runs up through the hull to the tiller location.

Wheels are easier to handle, since the system that connects the wheel to the rudder absorbs shocks and reduces the pressure felt by the person at the helm. Although contact with the rudder is not direct, an experienced sailor soon learns to relate the sensations produced by the wheel with the movement of the rudder. Wheel steering requires more equipment, so it costs more. This and the maintenance it demands may be considered its only real drawbacks.

Fig. 18-1. *A simple tiller design can be used with outboard rudders. Note the nice, clean pushpit mounts, permanently welded in place.*

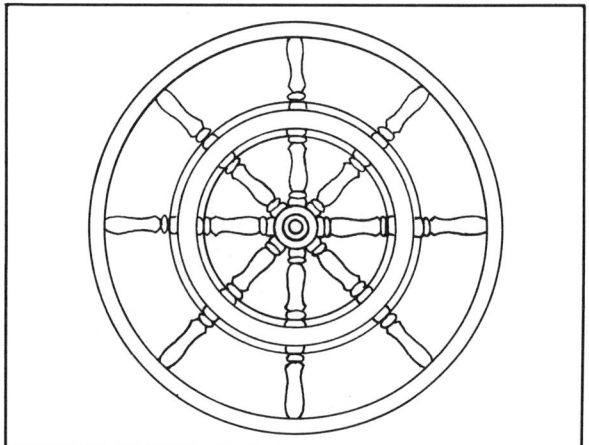

Fig. 18-2. *A good-looking, traditional wheel with wood spokes and stainless steel trim.*

A wheel can be installed in either an aft or a center cockpit and can be mounted on a bulkhead or pedestal. The compass and engine controls can also be placed here, centralizing operations. The location of the wheel determines the type of steering system that can be used, and vice versa. There are three basic systems—direct-geared, cable-and-quadrant (or wheel-and-cable, on small boats), and hydraulic—although there are many variations of each.

Direct-geared steering systems are usually limited to aft cockpit designs, since the gear box must be placed over the rudder post and the wheel connected directly to the gear box. These systems are commonly used when there is not enough space under the cockpit floor for a quadrant to be installed. Traditional worm gear

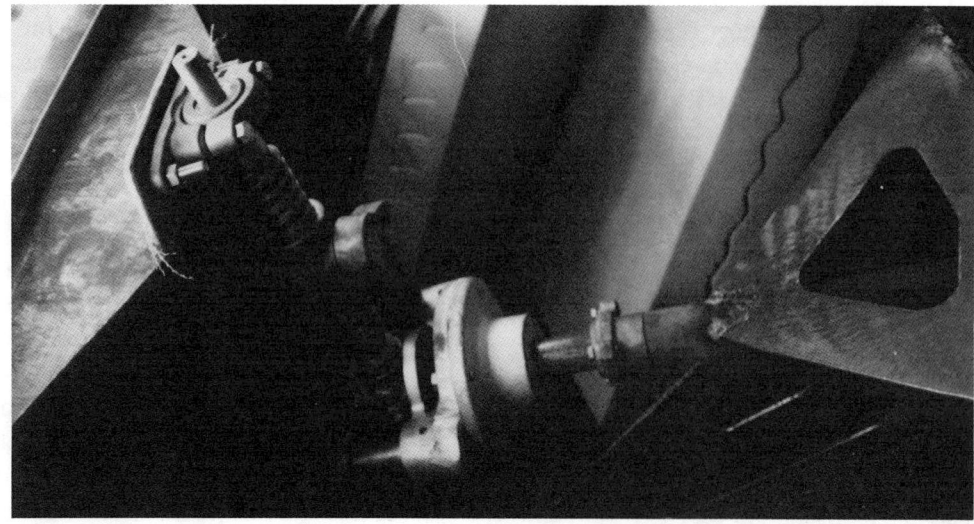

Fig. 18-3. *An unusual home-built worm-gear steering device.*

assemblies are very simple and trouble-free systems with only a few moving parts, but they require many turns of the wheel to put the rudder hard over. Rack-and-pinion assemblies are similar to worm gears, but are designed so that fewer turns of the wheel produce the same result. Both of these systems are relatively inexpensive and easy to install.

The cable-and-quadrant system is the one most commonly installed in both aft- and center-cockpit designs. Although there is some play in the cables that causes a slight delay in responsiveness, the cable-and-quadrant system requires few turns of the wheel to affect rudder position. The wheel can be mounted either on a pedestal or a bulkhead, and the quadrant is fitted over the top of the rudder post.

There are a number of ways of connecting the wheel and the quadrant. The simplest uses cable run through sheave blocks. Other systems, like Edson's Radial Drive and the pull-pull system, have specialized applications (for example, pull-pull systems, in which the cables are run through flexible conduits, are best for center-cockpit designs, since the cable must run a long distance to reach the quadrant). Bulkhead-mounted wheels require slightly different connections than pedestal mounts, and commonly use a sprocket mechanism or needle bearing linked to the quadrant by cables.

Choosing the correct cable-and-quadrant system requires juggling information about the angle at which the rudder post rises, the wheel location, the vessel's displacement, power requirements, and installation space.

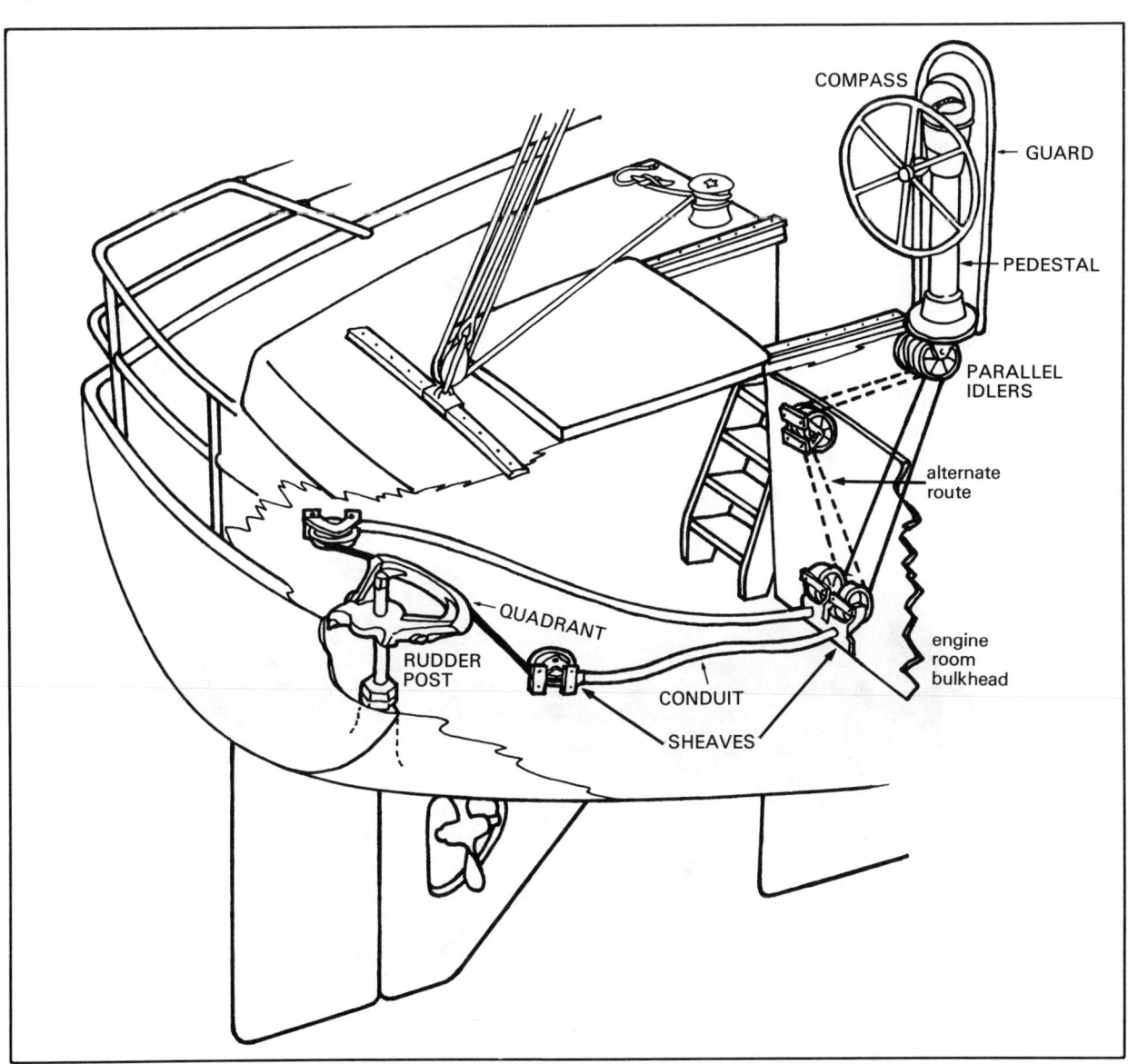

Fig. 18-4. *The basic parts of a cable-and-quadrant steering system with the pedestal mounted in a center cockpit.*

Most companies that manufacture these systems provide information to help you select the proper components, and on request will recommend a specific system. Installation drawings for stock designs may also be available.

Many steering wheels are mounted on pedestals installed on the cockpit floor. The wheel shaft is fitted with sprockets, and the cables are attached to the ends of a chain running over the sprockets, which translates the rotary motion of the wheel into cable movement. Many pedestals come equipped with a pedestal brake so that the wheel can be locked into position. The steering cables run down through the pedestal and are directed back to the quadrant by various sheaves. The pedestal is a convenient place to mount the compass and binnacle, and the engine throttle controls can also be placed here. There are many accessories that can be attached to a pedestal, including a pod containing a depth sounder, a speed log, and a windspeed indicator; auto pilots; cup holders; binocular holders; and lunch tables. A stainless steel pedestal guard should be fitted around the pedestal to protect it and also to provide a handhold for crew members.

Most of the parts used in the steering system are built to last and are made of nonmagnetic materials that will not cause compass interference. Quadrants are commonly made of manganese bronze or aluminum, and stainless cable is standard. Pedestals are usually fabricated of stainless, aluminum, or plastic; the metal ones must be isolated from the steel deck at the base with a wood pad, bedding compound and/or a rubber gasket.

The opening for the pedestal should be cut in the cockpit floor before blasting and priming, and small holes will need to be drilled in the steel for mounting the base.

Although complete steering systems can be bought from various manufacturers (Edson and Merriman are the best known and supply excellent catalogs), you can save money by building some parts yourself. Making your own wheel from laminated wood isn't difficult, and it will be a unique addition to your boat. Pedestal guards can be fabricated of steel or stainless pipe, while the pedestal itself could be made of wood. Although the sheaves could be turned on a lathe, the time that it takes to do so is probably not worth the cost savings. Gear parts and cable will have to be purchased from suppliers, but may be available through discount warehouses.

Although it is the most expensive of the steering arrangements, hydraulic steering is very attractive because of its smooth, trouble-free action and great mechanical advantage. This system is simple, clean, easy to assemble, and the lines do not require a straight run to the rudder. However, hydraulic steering does not give the person at the helm much direct contact with the rudder, and the system can be difficult to fix or replace in case of failure. (For example, if dirt gets in the seals, the entire system will become inoperable.) It seems that those who praise hydraulic steering have never had a failure to deal with, because those who have had problems don't have much good to say about hydraulics.

An emergency tiller hook-up should be included with any wheel-steering system, and extra tillers should be carried onboard for tiller systems. The emergency hook-

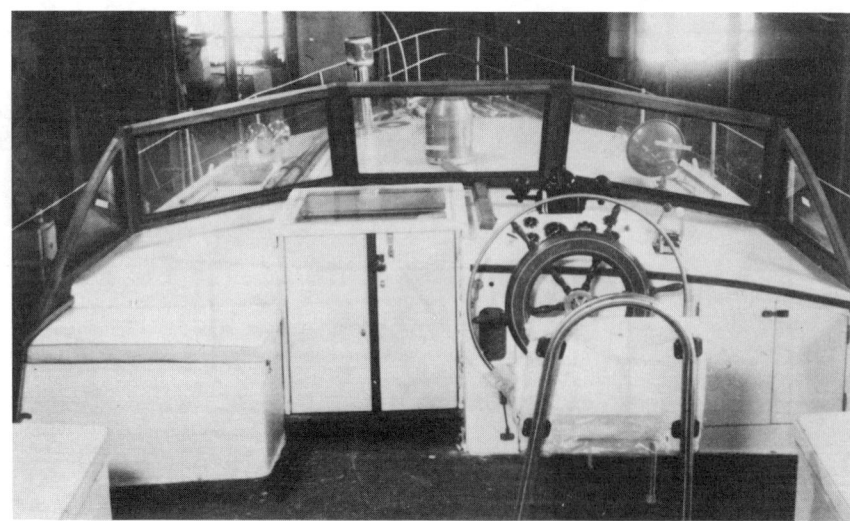

Fig. 18-5. *An attractive, wood-framed spray shield and a padded seat make this a comfortable steering station.* Courtesy of Nils Lucander

Table 18-1. THE PARTS OF A TYPICAL CABLE-AND-QUADRANT ASSEMBLY	
WHEEL	Various diameters available. Stainless or wood. Turk's heads and leather or twin binding make wheel less likely to slip through hands.
PEDESTAL	Various heights available. Often includes binnacle for compass. Commonly made of aluminum or stainless steel.
PEDESTAL GUARD	Protects compass and allows accessories to be mounted. Usually made of stainless steel.
CABLE	Generally ⅛" or ³⁄₁₆" wire rope; also 7/19 stainless
SHEAVES	Various sizes for directing wire rope. Types include parallel idlers, doubles sheaves, and conduit idlers.
QUADRANT	Bored out to specific size of rudder post and keyed for locking in place. Made of manganese bronze or aluminum.
SMALL PARTS	Terminals, toggles, wire clamps, in-line conduit greaser with zerk fitting, grease, wire eyes, Teflon lubricant, bolts.
OPTIONS	Throttle and shift controls, depth-sounder mount, self-steering drum.

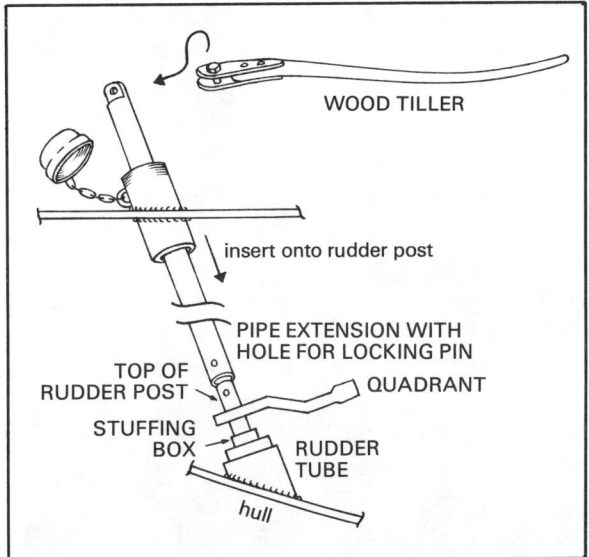

Fig. 18-6. *A pipe welded through the deck and fitted with a bearing serves as the outlet for an emergency tiller. A screw-on cap seals the opening when not in use.*

amazed! Although the sails of a well-balanced cruising design often can be adjusted to hold a course, when control is needed at the helm, a modern self-steering system does better than a person can, especially over long periods of time. As long as the sails are trimmed properly, the best vanes work well in almost all sea conditions. Although sail adjustments may be necessary, standing

up can be provided by a pipe extension on top of the rudder post. For on-deck steering, an opening will have to be cut in the deck, and a screw-on cap fabricated to close this hole when the emergency tiller is not in use; a bearing can be fitted to seal the hole when the tiller is being used. Some singlehanded sailors also make simple arrangements for steering from below (for example, by fitting a dome just forward of the emergency tiller hook-up). If you are planning to do much rough-weather sailing, this set-up might be appealing. Usually, however, two steering stations aren't necessary.

SELF-STEERING DEVICES

Since the advent of self-steering devices like wind vanes and auto pilots, deck watches are not the ordeals they used to be. Those sea dogs of yesteryear would be

Fig. 18-7. *The enclosed pilothouse on this Merritt Walter design keeps the steering station nice and dry. The large, snap-on plastic window panels can be removed when ventilation is more important than staying dry.*

Fig. 18-8. *This deck-mounted wind vane directs the course of the boat through a linkage to trim tabs on the rudder.*

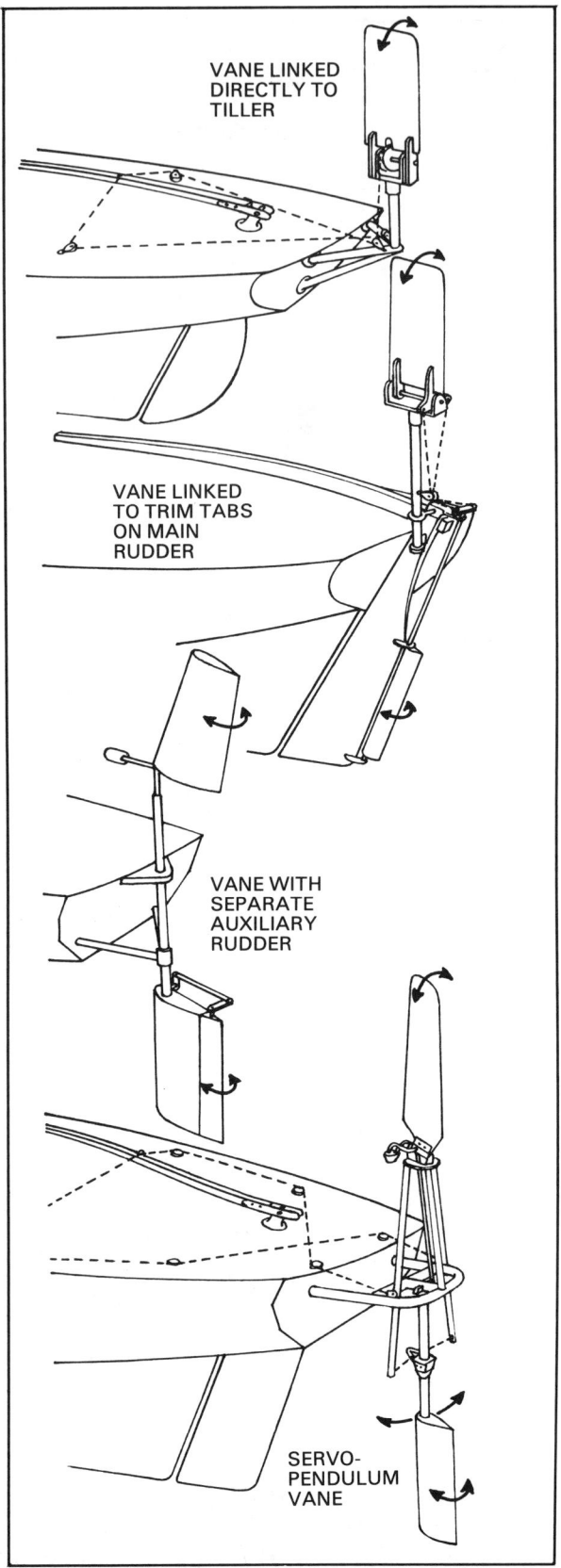

VANE LINKED DIRECTLY TO TILLER

VANE LINKED TO TRIM TABS ON MAIN RUDDER

VANE WITH SEPARATE AUXILIARY RUDDER

SERVO-PENDULUM VANE

Fig. 18-9. *The basic types of wind vanes. The arrows show the direction of movement.*

watch doesn't mean standing at the helm, so watch-keeping is more efficient and less tiring. Wind vanes and auto pilots may also allow you to set sail with a smaller crew. However, self-steering should be not be used as an excuse for not standing watch or as a substitute for experience.

A wind vane is composed of the airfoil vane and the linkage or gears that transmit the movement of the vane to trim tabs, the tiller, the wheel, or the rudder. Wind vanes came of age during the trans-Atlantic races of the early 1960's, when men like H.G. Hasler proved their effectiveness (he only spent 1 hour at *Jester's* helm during the entire crossing). Although there have been many different vanes invented and used, they have sorted themselves into four basic types, on which the vane is mounted either vertically or horizontally:

1) The simplest vanes have gears and linkages that directly move the rudder or tiller. The earlier version of this assembly was developed in the early 1900's by George Braine for use on model boats.

2) Some vanes move a trim tab attached to the aft end of the main rudder. These have more power than type #1, and the mechanism has more underwater parts.

3) Other vanes move an auxiliary rudder, which is separate from the main rudder and hung over the stern. The auxiliary rudder counteracts the force of the main rudder to help keep the boat on course. Trim tabs are often used to transmit directions.

4) The servo-pendulum vane, which has worked well for many cruisers, makes powerful, advanced use of an auxiliary rudder. Its vertically hung rudder is balanced and moves fore and aft and sideways, making it very efficient and, of course, expensive.

The basic requirements for a good wind vane design are strength, simplicity, and enough versatility to meet changing conditions. It must be powerful enough to resist the force of the wind, but sensitive enough to transmit small direction changes to the rudder. Simplicity calls for few moving parts; the less friction there is to affect it, the greater the mechanism's accuracy and the lower its chances of breakdown will be. Servicing a simple design is easier, and fewer parts have to be carried for repairs.

Extruded stainless steel is the preferred material for a wind-vane steering system, since the assembly is more durable and often stronger than one with cast parts. A rupture in a cast aluminum or stainless vane system will be difficult to repair; stainless steel tubing can be bent, drilled, and jury-rigged easily. For the small bearings and cotter pins that are part of the assembly,

high-strength alloys or high-tensile-strength plastics are best because of the stress exerted on these small pieces.

Choosing the correct vane involves analyzing a specific boat—its displacement, freeboard, and the design of the rudder and transom. Yachts with conventional transoms and inboard rudders have a number of brands to choose from. However, two wind vanes with many success stories are the Monitor (with a stainless tube body) and the Aries (with a cast aluminum body). Vane manufacturers and experienced sailors will often let you know if a particular vane can be successfully installed on your boat.

Proper installation of the vane is quite simple: it is mounted to the stern and lines are run to the tiller or wheel. Wind vanes work best with a tiller, but a wheel can be fitted with a drum to which the control lines are run. If the boat has a center cockpit, the length of the lead lines from the vane may introduce some slop and drag into the system. If the vessel has high freeboard at the transom, a shaft extension will be needed for servo-pendulum vanes.

On a steel boat, the mounting position of the specific vane to be used may have to be decided before the hull is complete, so that mounting tabs, eyes, or sockets can be welded into the hull before it is blasted. However, the vane assembly can also be through-bolted to the transom at any time after construction. But integral eyes

Fig. 18-10. *This Aries vane is set up on its own sturdy boomkin mount, which is secured to the deck*

may be needed for the linkages that run between the rudder and the steering device and between the vane and the wheel or tiller.

Most wind vanes have a few faults. They are not particularly efficient in light wind conditions, especially off the wind or in lumpy sea conditions. A wind vane also cannot look out to sea and ascertain the coming wind changes, as a person at the helm can do.

Good wind vanes are equal in cost to major items like anchor windlasses. *Wind-Vane Self-Steering* by Bill Belcher includes plans for some good do-it-yourself vanes. For a skilled fabricator, this job is relatively simple if there is a model to work from.

Modern electric auto pilots are very efficient and hold a course quite well, even in light winds and when under power. Although they cost about the same as a vane system, they draw power from the batteries, and if they should fail, repairs could be both difficult and expensive. Auto pilots can be connected to almost all steering systems.

Auto pilots steer by the compass or with a small vane, and various adaptations allow them to be mounted either in the cockpit or out of the way down below. The auto pilot acts like an electric eye or an electronic sensor that changes the helm position by activating a small motor which moves the steering control with either a hydraulic arm (typical of tillers) or a belt connected to a drum on the wheel. They are much more compact than a vane system. Auto pilots for an average 40′ cruiser cost $1,000–3,000, almost the same as production wind vanes.

The power drain of an auto pilot on the batteries can be considerable. This kind of equipment can draw between 1 and 10 amps, depending on the make; this adds up quickly if the auto pilot is on 24 hours a day. An increase in the charging schedule or some sort of auxiliary power source will undoubtedly be required to keep the batteries charged.

Of course the ideal self-steering system would have both a wind vane and an auto pilot, so that each could back up the other.

ANCHORING AND MOORING GEAR

The peace of mind that makes cruising a pleasure depends on having good-quality mooring and anchoring equipment of the proper size and type. This system should have no weak links, since a failure in any part can have devastating effects. Most accidents happen near land, in anchoring depths, and carrying a wide range of the best equipment you can afford can be considered a substitute for the expensive and hard-to-come-by world cruising insurance.

Successful mooring and anchoring depends as much on good seamanship as on the correct gear. When anchoring, the skipper should determine the bottom conditions as accurately as possible so that the appropriate anchor can be chosen. But it will do no good to use the proper kind of anchor if it is too small. Of course, you can argue that since yours is a steel-hulled boat, a grounding would not disastrous. That's true, but in the event of grounding you'd be stuck with kedging off or waiting for the tide to change, not to mention repair work on the dents and scrapes in the steel. Having a steel hull can't prevent all the consequences of carrying the wrong equipment.

With a steel hull there are some initial cost savings in the anchoring assembly, because the bow-roller assembly, hawsers, chain pipes, and chocks can be easily fabricated and integrally welded to the hull. However, with a steel hull there is little difference in equipment requirements, since boat size and displacement, not the hull material, determine them.

In order to generalize about equipment, we'll describe the requirements of a 40′ steel cruiser with a moderate displacement of 25–35,000 lbs. There will always be times when unusual situations will cause uncommon problems and equipment failures, but the equipment described here should be adequate in most conditions.

Storage

Having the right storage space for anchoring gear means that you can carry plenty of equipment without cluttering up the decks or tripping up the crew. The foredeck, the forepeak locker, the lazarette, and the bilge are the primary places to stow anchors and chain. There are many different designs for these areas, and a walk on any dock will reveal numerous examples, but remember that of the designs you may see, many have never had their lay-outs tested by a long voyage.

A good forepeak locker needs ample room for chain and line storage, as well as space for spare anchors and fenders. A lazarette or stern locker can also be used to store spare anchors and lines, which can be used for stern moorage; the extra weight aft will help to counteract the weight of the gear stored in the forepeak locker. Two solid eyes can be welded to the stem, and the bitter end of the anchor chain can be shackled to these eyes so that it can't all run out the hawser pipe opening. Eyes can also be welded high on the side of the locker for storing extra line and buoys. The forepeak doesn't really need to be insulated, since no one but a mouse could live there. However, to increase corrosion protection, insulation can be sprayed on here when the rest of the interior is insulated. Both the forepeak and stern lockers, insulated or not, should be lined with plywood or rubber sheathing to protect the steel against damage from anchors or chain.

The floors of the forepeak and lazarette should be made watertight with asphalt, epoxy filler, cement, or other sealants. Drip water can collect in these areas, and a small bilge pump, a drain valve in the bulkhead, or a sponge can be used to remove the puddle. Because it is not always possible to wash off the chain before storage, these lockers will need to be cleaned occasionally to get rid of weeds and mud. A moderate-sized access hatch from the fo'c's'le is the easiest way to service the forepeak; access to the lazarette can be through a hatch on deck.

A chain pipe (hawser) leading to the locker should be welded through the deck. Below, heavy rubber or PVC tubing can be attached to the lip of the pipe to lead the chain into the locker. (Galvanized pipe can be used instead of plastic, but the repeated chafing by the chain will eventually lead to corrosion.) If two hawsers are used, a separator of sheet rubber or plywood mounted

Fig. 18-11. *Bow roller assemblies can be mounted through steel bulwarks instead of on the centerline. This roller design also incorporates a stainless steel anti-chafe doubler plate.*

on the centerline of the locker will help to prevent tangled chain and line.

On deck, the whole area from which anchor work is done should be as free from obstructions as possible, and the anchors should be stowed so they don't turn into hazards themselves. The two main anchors can be mounted on twin bow rollers made of hard, high tensile-strength plastic that are supported by a stainless steel bracket welded to the stem head or the bowsprit. The anchors will thus be ready to use but out of the way. The pin holding the rollers in the bracket should also be made of stainless because it must withstand a great deal of chafe. The bow roller assembly should include a way to secure the anchors; CQR's and some other anchors have eyes near the fluke that can be used for this purpose. Since there should be more than one way to dog or secure the anchor, a pawl, stopper, pelican hook, chain dog, or tie-down eye should be attached directly aft of the anchor or on or near the windlass. A nice hardwood or rubber chafe strip can be mounted on deck to protect both the steel deck and the ears of the crew, since the continual scraping of sliding anchors or chains on deck in heavy-weather conditions is unpleasant.

Anchors

The CQR plow is the first anchor most sailors choose. It is useful on many bottoms, especially hard coral sand, and buries itself deeper as the pull on it grows stronger. It will also trip over and bury itself again if the direction of pull changes. However, a CQR does not always hold well in soft mud or a loose, sandy bottom. The true CQR is drop-forged from hot steel billets and is balanced with most of its weight in the flukes. Beware of poorly made imitations.

The most common second choice is the Danforth-type anchor. This works especially well in thin, sandy bottoms and mud because its large fluke doesn't have to be buried deeply to hold well. Danforths will trip when the direction of pull is changed, but they have limited use in hard, rocky bottoms, since they aren't as strongly built as CQR's.

A CQR and a Danforth complement each other nicely, so it's definitely worth it to have both onboard. In fact, these two are the minimum necessary for any cruiser, since one or the other (or both) can be used in varying conditions.

The Bruce anchor is a relatively new type, originally used for oil rigs. Its stockless, efficient design gives good

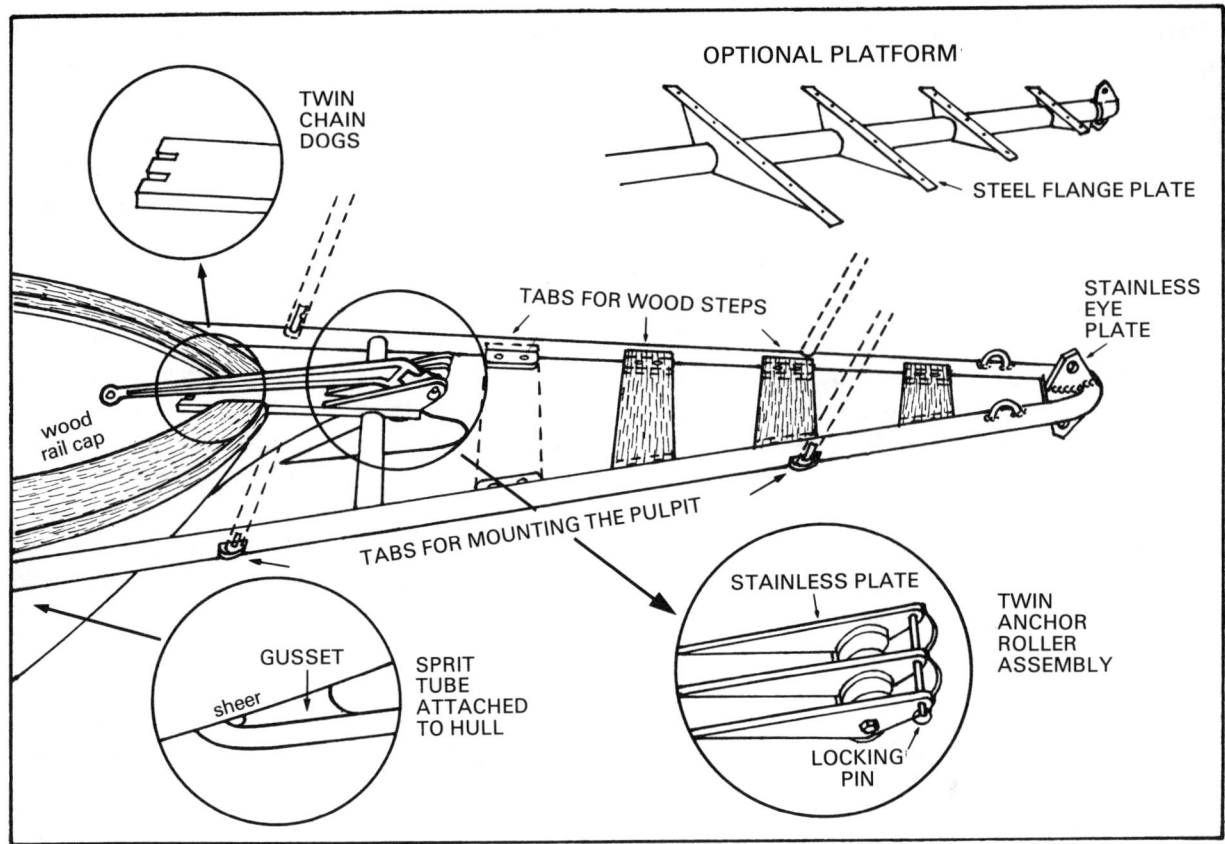

Fig. 18-12. *This bowsprit, made of steel pipe with a tube turn at its forward end, has a built-in anchor-roller assembly and tabs for attaching the pulpit and platform.*

holding power, so small Bruces are becoming more popular as both primary and secondary anchors. These anchors hold well at various angles of pull, but do not trip over like CQRs and Danforths and occasionally will drag when they pick up a rock. However, they are easier to break free and, because of their size, are easily handled.

In particularly bad anchoring conditions, backing up the primary anchor with a heavy yachtsman anchor (also called a "fisherman" or "Herreschoff") is wise, especially for foul, rocky, or weedy bottoms. Although these anchors are cumbersome to stow, some do fold up. You may use one only a few times, but it will be a blessing to have in those emergencies.

Other anchor designs, both large and small, will also have many uses: as a lunch hook or for kedging, grapnelling, or dinghies. Names like Northhill, Davis, Attwood, or Forfjord and shapes like mushrooms, seahooks, and coral hooks are tried and true. Each has particular holding, handling, and storage attributes. Most of these anchors are made of either cast or welded carbon steel and are commonly galvanized.

For the primary anchor, you should pick a size somewhat larger and heavier than that required by normal conditions, so that if conditions worsen, it will continue to hold. It's good to avoid using two anchors whenever possible, because of the possibility of their fouling each other's lines, but the number-two anchor should be ready to go if necessary. Hauling a relatively large anchor isn't that much more difficult than hauling a small one, especially if you have a good windlass, and knowing you have extra holding power lets you sleep more soundly.

Table 18-2. ANCHOR INVENTORY FOR A 40′ WORLD CRUISING SAILBOAT

#1	60-lb. CQR plow on chain and line for general use (larger CQR could be used)
#2	45-lb. CQR plow on chain only for light or back-up use
#3	35-lb. Danforth on line for sandy bottoms
#4	33-lb. Bruce for mixed bottoms
#5	75-lb. Yachtsman for rock bottoms or extreme conditions
#6	Small grapnel or mushroom for dinghy and miscellaneous use

The number of anchors you carry will depend on your cruising ground. Good-quality, galvanized, cast-steel anchors are a sizeable investment, but one that will repay you many times over.

Chain and Line

Both galvanized chain and nylon line are appropriate for anchor rodes, and both have an important place aboard ship. Chain withstands chafe and abrasion, and its weight helps to keep the rode at the correct angle to the anchor. Nylon line has elastic qualities that reduce shock-loading. The number-one anchor is best fitted with an all-chain rode; other anchors can use both chain and line. About 25–50′ of chain is usually attached between the anchor and the long nylon line. In many typical tropical cruising areas, the coral bottom can destroy nylon line, so an all-chain rode must be used. If you're not anchoring long in clear, soft mud, a rode of 90% nylon line and 10% chain should be sufficient.

The size, type, and length of chain and line required by a boat depends on its size. Table 18–3 pairs the recommended anchors with their rodes.

Three-stranded nylon line, ½″ or ⅝″ thick, is the best for both anchoring and dock lines on an average 40′ cruiser, although the heavy yachtsman anchor needs ¾″ line. Buying line by the 600-ft. reel is most economical, and any leftover line will surely find other uses.

There are no set guidelines for chain size, because loads vary depending on the particular situation, the amount of scope, the vessel's displacement, and the windage topsides. Working load for most chain is rated at a quarter of its ultimate breaking strength, so there is quite a margin for safety. As a general rule, depending on displacement, for the average 40′ cruiser ⅜″ chain is standard. ⁵⁄₁₆″ is adequate for 25–35′ boats, and ¼″ chain can be used if the boat is under 25′.

Basically, there are two different types of chain used for boats and available in the U.S.: BBB and proof-coil. BBB is strongest and has passed the most stringent testing, but proof coil is usually strong enough for cruising yachts and costs less. A third type, high-test chain, is also available, but it is manufactured for special purposes and in the required lengths is far to expensive to be practical. There are also different grades (schedules) of chain in any given size. When purchasing chain, try to get well-galvanized and certified (tested) chain; it can be purchased by the drum for extra savings. Chain strength varies with the manufacturer and with the alloy make-up, so don't assume that the working-load rating of chain manufactured by different companies is the same.

When line and chain are to be joined, the line should be spliced around a thimble, a shackle inserted, and wire stoppers tied to the pins of the shackle. Each line should also be fitted with a swivel where it joins the chain.

Various short lengths of extra ⅝″ nylon line can be attached to chain rodes to absorb shocks and protect the chain when, in a given anchorage, sea conditions are stretching it. Stretching occurs especially in conditions that demand the use of a short rode. A similar arrangement can reduce the load on the windlass.

Windlass

A windlass is simply a sophisticated winch, but it can make cruising easier and safer. Because the windlass hoists the anchor for you, you are encouraged to use the heavy anchors that mean extra security. Windlasses can also be used to kedge off an obstruction or hoist someone aloft to perform repairs.

There are many different windlass designs, which can be powered by hand, electricity, or hydraulics. Manual

Anchor	Weight	Type of Rode	Rode Length
CQR	60 lbs.	300′ of 5/8″ or 3/4″ nylon line and 50′ of 3/8″ chain	350′
CQR	45 lbs.	350′ of 3/8″ chain	350′
Danforth	35 lbs.	300′ of 5/8″ or 1/2″ nylon line and 25′ of 3/8″ chain	325′
Yachtsman	75 lbs.	275′ of 3/4″ nylon line and 25′ of 3/8″ chain	300′
Bruce	33 lbs.	250′ of 1/2″ nylon line and 25′ of 3/8″ chain	300′
Grapnel	20 lbs.	200′ of 3/8″nylon line	200′

Table 18-3. ANCHORS AND RODES

Table 18-4. WORKING LOADS OF ANCHOR LINE AND CHAIN

SIZE	NYLON LINE		GALVANIZED PROOF COIL CHAIN	GALVANIZED BBB CHAIN	GALVANIZED HIGH-TEST CHAIN
	Ultimate strength	Safe working load	Working load 4:1 safety factor	Working load 4:1 safety factor	Working load 3:1 safety factor
1/8″	—	—	375 lbs.	—	—
3/16″	1,000 lbs.	500 lbs.	750 lbs.	800 lbs.	—
1/4″	1,700 lbs.	850 lbs.	1,250 lbs.	1,400 lbs.	2,500 lbs.
5/16″	2,600 lbs.	1,300 lbs.	1,900 lbs.	2,000 lbs.	4,000 lbs.
3/8″	3,600 lbs.	1,800 lbs.	2,650 lbs.	2,850 lbs.	5,000 lbs.
7/16″	5,000 lbs.	2,500 lbs.	3,500 lbs.	3,700 lbs.	6,500 lbs.
1/2″	6,600 lbs.	3,300 lbs.	4,500 lbs.	4,850 lbs.	8,000 lbs.
5/8″	10,300 lbs.	5,150 lbs.	6,900 lbs.	7,200 lbs.	11,500 lbs.
3/4″	14,000 lbs.	7,000 lbs.	9,750 lbs.	10,200 lbs.	16,000 lbs.

Note: Strengths and working loads vary with the specific alloy make-up of the chain, with the grade, and with different manufacturers.

operation is the most economical and reliable, and it gives you a little welcome exercise. Electric windlasses are much more costly, because they need a heavy-duty motor with thick electric cable leading back to the battery. They are also a very heavy power drain on the batteries (as much as 100 amps), so their use should be limited as much as possible. Hydraulic windlasses have less chance of failure than electric types and have fewer operating problems. However, their initial cost is even higher than that of electric ones. A combination hydraulic-manual unit would be great, but this type isn't commonly made. Both electric and hydraulic windlasses should have manual back-ups for emergencies. Some units have double-speed action, which makes the job go faster, a particularly useful attribute on electric windlasses since the time during which the windlass is drawing power is reduced. Windlass assemblies often come with hawser, pawls, and chain stoppers included.

Windlasses are made to be mounted either horizontally or vertically. Traditional horizontal mounts are most common and are easiest to operate manually, because the best leverage is obtained when the crank is worked vertically. However, they limit the number of other jobs for which the windlass can be used. Vertical mounts, on the other hand, allow line to be led off in any direction so that hoisting can be done anywhere onboard or overboard without the line binding. However, either type will allow easier anchoring.

The best windlasses are made with a cast-iron or bronze body and stainless steel gears; stainless bolts are used for mounting the unit. Cast-aluminum windlasses are more apt to break, and there may be problems with corrosion where the stainless bolts pass through the aluminum base.

The windlass should be fitted with a chain gypsy on one side and a rope capstan on the other, although some are available with gypsies on both sides. With certain windlasses, you can lock the gypsy and use the capstan separately. When purchasing a windlass, you should make sure that the model you're buying is compatible with the chain you're using. Some foreign-made windlasses have gypsies designed for metric chain rather than for chain sized by the U.S. customary system.

Since a windlass is a very costly item, an amateur builder might consider making one, but fabrication requires proper tooling and skill. Choosing to make one is rather like choosing to make your own chain or rigging wire. It's probably better to buy a proven product from a manufacturer. But where a builder draws the line between what to make and what to buy will depend on the temperament and skills of the individual.

The windlass is easily mounted on studs with a gasket placed between its base and the steel deck; a hardwood pad with bedding makes a very pleasing gasket. The deck should be reinforced with either a plate or flange-box doubler underneath the windlass so that the deck

Fig. 18-13. *This handsome assembly combines a sturdy windlass mount with twin anchor rollers. Notice also the chain gate, hose outlet for washing down chain and the deck, mooring cleats and chocks, and a clamshell vent for the forepeak.*

Courtesy of Treworgy Yachts

will be reinforced and the loads spread out over a wider surface. In some designs, the hawser hole through which the chain runs is incorporated into the base of the windlass.

Tools and Supplies for the Mooring System

Tools like a hacksaw, marlinspike, bolt cutters, grease gun, and needle-nose pliers will probably be used during a long voyage. Spare parts like shackles, wire, chain links, small wire swivels, thimbles, cotter pins, dogs, and tie assemblies should also be carried onboard.

Mooring buoys and small anchor floats are both handy items, and can be attached to anchor lines on occasions when you plan to return to the same anchorage. They are also used to float an anchor tripline if it is needed to break out an anchor that is fouled or tightly dug in.

A good selection of fenders is also basic. They are a cheap means of protecting the sides of the steel hull when at a dock or when rafting up with other boats. Whitewall tires can do the job but tend to mar the hull.

Two boathooks of different sizes are standard equipment, and will be useful in many situations. A boarding ladder or step on the deck is handy, but not necessary.

Nylon dock lines (either ½″ or ⅝″) can be made of the unused anchor line. Chocks for docking and spring lines are easily welded integrally with a steel rail.

SOURCES

Gear and Quadrant Steering Systems

Edson Corporation
460 Industrial Park Rd.
New Bedford, MA 01745-1292

Merriman
301 Oliver St.
Grand River, OH 44054

Hydraulic Steering Systems

Wagner Engineering, Ltd.
40 Gostick Place
North Vancouver, BC
Canada V7M 3G2

Wind Vanes

Atoms Ocean Gear
2442 Mississippi Ave.
Tampa, FL 33609
— servo-pendulums

Auto-Helm
4051 Redwood St.
Marina del Rey, CA 90291
— separately mounted wind vanes

Thomas Foulkes
4A Samson Rd., Leytonstone
London E11 3HB
England
Tel. 01-435 5627
— Aries wind vanes and other marine equipment

Larwyk Development
17330 Raymer St.
Northridge, CA 91325
— servo-pendulums

Madeira Marine and Mfg.
P.O. Box 1218
Pinellas Park, FL 33565
    — RVG, separately mounted wind vanes

Marine Vane Gears
Cowes, Isle of Wight
England
    — Aries servo-pendulums

Scanmar Marine Products
298 Harbor Dr.
Sausalito, CA 94965
    — Monitor and Navik servo-pendulums

Chain Manufacturers

Campbell Chain Division
McGraw-Edison Company
3990 Market St.
P.O. Box 3056
York, PA 17402

Washington Chain and Supply
2901 Utah St.
Seattle, WA

—Chapter 19—

Down Below

The basic comforts, that's what you want on a boat, especially a live-aboard cruiser. You need to eat, sleep, and stay healthy and clean; at sea you will have to be your own doctor, plumber, engine mechanic, and entertainment committee. The list of items that are "basic" varies greatly depending on the lifestyle you choose to adopt. These days it seems that you can buy almost any shoreside amenity for use on board—TV, hairdrier, blender, heater, microwave, computer. At the other end of the scale, you could probably sail around the world with a can opener and a sleeping bag. The accommodations described in this chapter fall somewhere in between these two extremes.

STORAGE

The available storage space on your boat really determines what you can carry. Storing things onboard a boat is different from storing things elsewhere, because you must assume that the boat will be in constant motion in a seaway, so everything must be secured to prevent breakage or injury. Storage must also be designed to keep weight low in the hull so that its center of gravity is not affected. Therefore, storing gear underneath fixed objects has always been popular. Under bunks, under settees, under tables, under cockpits, under sinks—all

these places can be designed to secure gear. An ingenious design will have storage lockers and bins built into every conceivable space.

No matter what is being stored, the contents of a storage locker must be kept dry. In a home with the high humidity of a boat, the only way to keep things dry is to ventilate the storage space. Locker and bin doors can be covered with louvers, cane, or fabric to allow air to circulate to the goods within. Drawers are a bit more difficult to ventilate, but back, bottom, or sides can have holes drilled into them to let in air and let out moisture.

Equally important is a way of positively securing doors and drawers so that when the boat is underway they cannot open and spew their contents all over the interior. Many different types of latches are available from marine equipment manufacturers. Some are fitted inside the locker or bin and are reached through finger-holes cut in the face. These latches are particularly useful for storage behind seating areas; you can lean back and relax without having to adjust your position around protruding knobs and metal fittings.

There are some special problems involved in storing wet clothes and gear. The wet locker is the classic answer to this problem; it keeps wet clothes from getting everything else on board wet too. The ideal wet locker would have a watertight floor, sealed with a mastic compound, that slants to a small sump. If, as is common, the

Fig. 19-1. *Motorsailors, like this one designed by S.L. Petchul, generally have large engine rooms and pilothouse steering stations. There is plenty of room below in this 44' cruiser.* Courtesy of the designer

An engine room can also be an excellent spot for storing large tools or accessory power equipment. However, these things should be stowed so that there is still plenty of working space around the engine. Built-in storage lockers will help to keep tools and equipment in place. As Chapter 11 indicates, the engine room must be well insulated for sound to be a good traveling companion.

Anchors, chain, fenders, lifejackets, and anything that must be grabbed quickly from on-deck, are best stowed in a forepeak or lazarette locker, accessible through a hatch. (Layouts and suggestions for these lockers are discussed in Chapter 18.) Emergency equipment should also be stored where it is easy to reach.

The bilge is another area to consider for storage, especially the dry bilge of a steel boat. The amount of room in the bilge will depend, of course, on the height of the cabin sole and the location of any non-integral tanks. Access holes can easily be incorporated into a wooden cabin sole to get to bilge storage areas.

wet locker shares a bulkhead with the engine compartment or engine room, the warm, dry air from the engine area can be let into the wet locker through louvers or holes, and the wet gear will dry more quickly. Wet lockers are generally located as close as possible to the main companionway so that dripping oilies and boots don't have to be dragged through the cabin to be stowed. Therefore the wet locker is also a practical and accessible place to keep an abandon-ship kit.

SLEEPING QUARTERS

Whether it's an aft cabin, fo'c's'le, or pilot berth, nothing beats a dry bed on a stormy night. The trick, of course, is to keep it dry. Adding to the moisture-laden nature of the air inside the boat is the propensity of the human body to warm up the air around it during sleep. The warm, moist air travels down through the mattress

Fig. 19-2. *The high freeboard in this boat means more room in the interior for storage. This design also features portholes in the topsides of the hull.*

and condenses when it hits the cold wood underneath. Fortunately, with a steel hull you rarely have water dripping onto the bunk from leaky seams, though a poorly designed and constructed hatch could be the culprit. Mattresses are usually made of close-celled foam, some types of which have better resistance to water absorption than others. A practical solution to the damp-mattress problem is to put some kind of mat or grating under the mattress—expanded plastic or plywood with holes—to raise it above the bunk surface and allow water to collect underneath.

All berths should be fitted with either wide webbing straps or wooden bunk boards so that the sleeper is not tossed out onto the floor during a gale or when the boat is heeling.

Blankets, sheets, pillows, and sleeping bags are all standard issue for sleeping quarters, although sleeping bags do tend to get a bit odoriferous when used without airing. It is not difficult to fit sheets and blankets to oddly-shaped bunks, and these homey touches can be a very affordable luxury. (See Bob & Karen Lipe's *Boat Canvas from Cover to Cover* for one method.) The mattress itself can be protected by a sturdy cover that wraps around the foam and is fastened underneath by a full-length plastic zipper or velcro.

Depending on the position of the lockers and seats around the berth, drawers or bins accessible from the front can be fitted underneath. This area can also be reached by cutting access holes in the wood platform on which the mattress rests. The lids can be secured with latches that are either recessed or reached through a fingerhole. If both drawers and top-access bins are built underneath a berth, partitions should be used so that objects stored in the bin don't interfere with the action of the drawers. Heavier items should be stowed down as low as possible.

Sleeping quarters are often the only place where you can get away from everyone else. A reading light over the bed and stereo speakers can make this area a true place of refuge. Doors or curtains can be used to close off a fo'c's'le or aft cabin from the rest of the boat when privacy and quiet are desired.

THE HEAD

The word "head" came into the nautical vocabulary when sailors were sent to "the heads" (the area forward of the forecastle on old sailing ships), which served as the counterpart of the modern lavatory; sometimes the

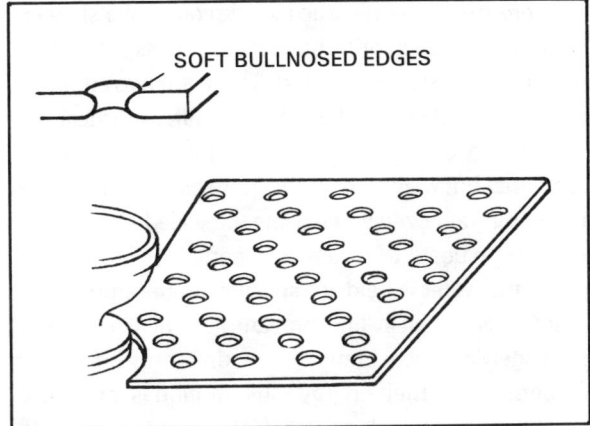

Fig. 19-3. *Plywood gratings are a simple and inexpensive way to provide drainage in the head or wet locker. Equally spaced holes are cut in the ply and then rounded off to a soft, bullnosed edge. The grating can be cut to any shape required.*

heads were fitted with seats and tubes, sometimes only gratings. Although today many sailors at sea rely on this time-proven method and the equally simple bucket, a modern marine toilet connected to a holding tank is required in most ports and also makes sense for liveaboards. When purchasing a toilet, you often get what you pay for: some of the less-expensive brands seem to clog up or leak more often than those that cost a bit more; the quality also varies greatly with the different makes. Although toilets that flush electrically are available, a model with good valves and a foot-operated pump is simple to operate and maintain and won't leave you depending on a bucket if power is not available. A head repair kit with spare parts is a must and can be stowed near the toilet.

A wash basin with a freshwater hook-up is also a basic fixture in the head. Showers, though less basic, are becoming more and more common on live-aboard boats; some people won't even buy a boat if it doesn't have a shower. The area around the wash basin and the walls of the shower stall must be protected from splash by formica, linoleum, decorative tiles, fiberglass, or other waterproof materials; if wood is used, it should be sealed with epoxy or painted. The shower stall must either be built with its floor lower than the floor of the head or be fitted with a low sill to keep drain water inside the stall. The floor should be watertight and slope to a drain connected to a sump; self-leveling mastics can be poured onto the floor to seal it. A plastic or rot-resistant wood grating on the shower stall floor will make showering safer; a piece of plywood with bull-nosed holes for drainage is a cheap and easy way to go.

There are few people who include cold-water showers in their lists of favorite pasttimes (unless, of course, they're in the steamy tropics). There are two common ways to provide hot water, and they differ drastically in their energy demands. A pressurized system with a conventional hot water tank is the more expensive and demanding way. Even when using the scaled-down tanks installed in boats, the drain on batteries can be high, because the water is held at a specific temperature. More practical is a small in-line, propane flash heater (Paloma is a widely available brand). These units only heat water on demand, so their energy consumption is much lower, although they put out alot of BTU's when they're going. These heaters must be fitted with an exhaust stack that is well insulated where it passes through the deck or cabin top. Other systems that use a thermo-syphon from the main engine or the stove to provide hot water may also be worth considering. No matter what system is installed, short showers make sense to reduce consumption of both water and energy.

Good ventilation is a must for the head since the moisture content of the air will inevitably be high, and the air will sometimes carry unpleasant odors. Opening portholes and deck-mounted ventilators should be installed; solar-powered vent fans improve the rate at which air is exhausted from this area.

The head should also contain storage lockers for consumables such as soap, toothpaste, shampoo, deodorant, paper towels, toilet tissue, and cleanser. Racks for drying wet towels and bins for holding dry ones are also convenient.

The head seems to be the natural place to store the medicine chest. A good medical kit is a top priority for healthy life at sea, since the doctor's office is often a lot farther away than a car ride. There are many excellent books and first-aid manuals covering medical care at sea, and seminars on the subject can give you good basic information. Subscription services are also available that will give you medical advice at sea over the radio. Some of the drugs that are recommended for a medical kit are only available by prescription, and a visit to the doctor will also provide you with an opportunity for a complete physical so that you start the voyage knowing you're in good health.

There is another school of thought on treating minor ailments: many of the tried-and-true herbal remedies can be a good addition to your medical chest. One of the best books on the subject, which also includes a list of supplies for an herbal medicine kit, is *Healing Yourself* by Joy Gardner, which is listed in the Recommended Reading section. Herbs are lightweight and can be obtained all over the world, making carrying and restocking the kit easy.

It's also important that you know whether any crew members have special medical needs and that any prescription drugs they may need are on board in sufficient

---

Table 19-1. SUPPLIES FOR THE FIRST AID KIT

EQUIPMENT	TREATMENTS AND MEDICATIONS
Thermometer	Antibiotics and antibiotic ointments (e.g., penicillin and Neosporin ointment)
Tourniquet	Burn and sunburn ointment
Bandages	Insect repellant
Adhesive tape	Calamine lotion or Campho-Phenique for insect bites
Absorbent cotton	Seasickness remedy
Cotton swabs	Pain killers (e.g., Demerol)
Gauze	Laxatives (e.g., Milk of Magnesia)
Forceps	Diarrhea remedies (e.g., Paregoric, Lomotil)
Scissor	Decongestants
Tweezers	Eye drops
Safety pins	Hydrogen peroxide
Scalpel and blades	Ammonia
Eyewash cup	Vasoline
Hot water bottle	Baby powder for wet, chafed skin
Ice Bag	
Mirror	
Tooth-pulling tools	

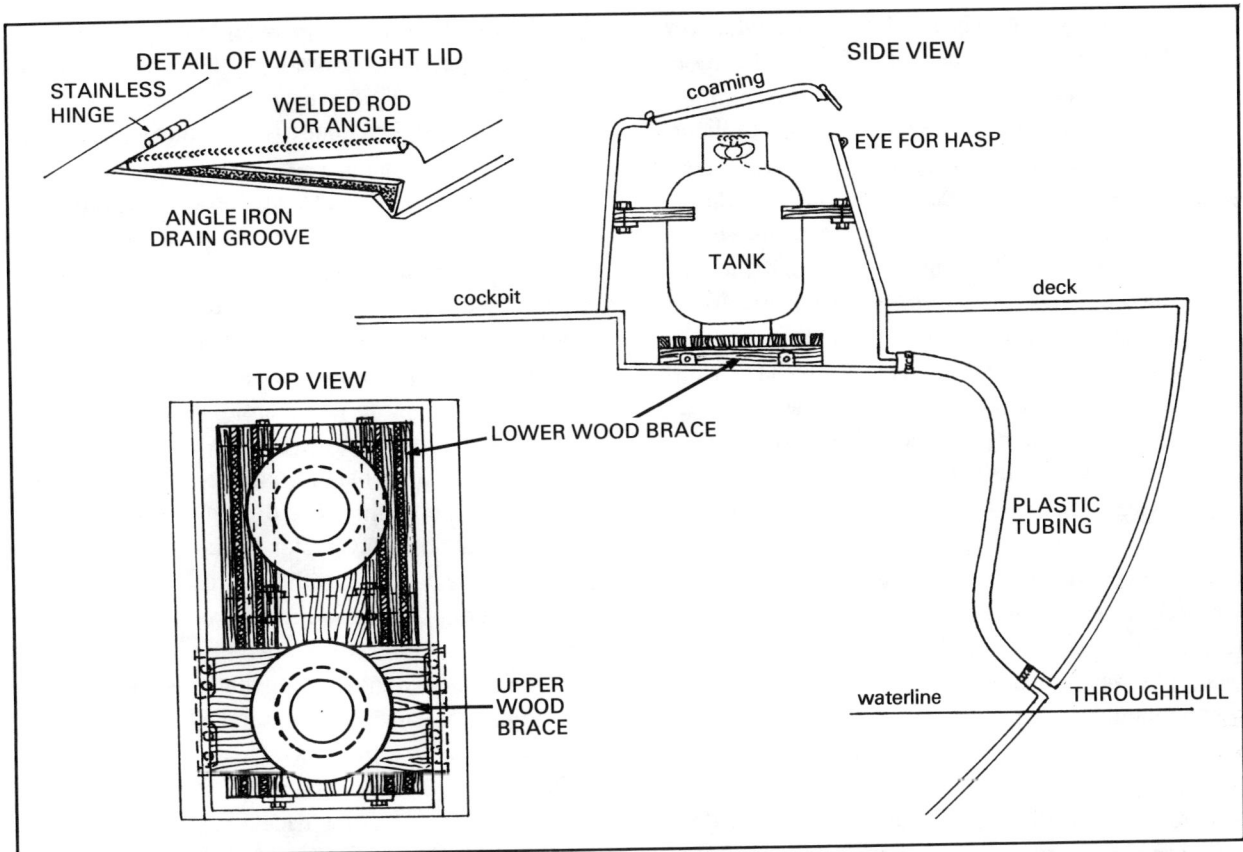

DETAIL OF WATERTIGHT LID
STAINLESS HINGE
WELDED ROD OR ANGLE
ANGLE IRON DRAIN GROOVE

SIDE VIEW
coaming
EYE FOR HASP
TANK
cockpit
deck
PLASTIC TUBING
waterline
THROUGHHULL

TOP VIEW
LOWER WOOD BRACE
UPPER WOOD BRACE

Fig. 19-4. *The coaming of a center-cockpit design is the perfect place for a self-contained propane locker. The tank braces are mounted on tabs, and the floor of the locker slopes outboard to a drainage tube and throughhull.*

amounts. All drugs should remain in their original bottles with prescription labels to avoid any problems from Customs. Any narcotics must be stored in a locked cupboard, which can double as a place to secure bonded stores like liquor for Customs inspections.

THE GALLEY

The galley is an important area onboard the ship—some would say it's the most important. It should be centrally located but out of the way of the main companionway and walk-throughs. If the galley is built at either end of the boat, the cook will be quite uncomfortable in heavy seas.

The most expensive and important piece of equipment in the galley is the cookstove. Depending on the size of the crew, its size can range from a single burner to a three-burner, gimballed stove with an oven. The more important decision is what type of fuel to use. Although CNG, diesel, alcohol, white gas, electric, coal, and wood stoves are all available, kerosene and propane

are the two most practical choices in terms of availability, expense, and ease of handling.

Propane is potentially a very dangerous fuel, but handled correctly it is very efficient and clean, and it is widely available. The National Fire Protection Association's pamphlet No. 362 gives good guidelines for proper installation and use of propane, and the American Boat and Yacht Council (ABYC) also has written guidelines for the use of propane included in its booklet, *LPG Systems for Boats.* A revision of the ABYC guidelines is due out in early 1986.

Since propane is heavier than air, if any leaks out of the system it will sink to the lowest point, usually the bilge, where it can explode if ignited. The tanks should be enclosed in a locker located topsides, and the locker should be vented overboard. On a steel boat this locker is easily incorporated in the cockpit coaming, or a self-contained cockpit seat box that vents out the transom can also be used. The locker or box should have a tight-fitting access lid so that the regulator and valves can be inspected often. If the lid is sealed with a gasket, no water should get into the locker. The tanks themselves should be solidly braced inside the locker so that they won't be damaged if the boat is bouncing around in a seaway.

LPG systems include the tank, fitted with a regulator, pressure gauge, and fuel-level indicator; the electric solenoid; and the lines that carry the gas from the tanks to the appliances. All should be located in the sealed propane locker, so that the only points where inboard leaks can occur are where the propane line is joined to the appliance or in the appliance itself. If two or more tanks are used, the T-valve that channels the gas into the leading line should also be located inside the propane locker. A solenoid switch should be mounted near the appliance so that the gas can be switched on and off easily. A leak detector or "sniffer" can be placed in the bilge and connected to the electric solenoid to automatically shut off the system if a leak is detected; however, leak detectors are easily damaged if any water gets into the bilge. The solenoid could have a bypass in case electric power is lost, but the system can also be shut down manually at the solenoid. When these kinds of precautions are taken, propane can be employed very safely onboard a boat.

Kerosene, the other practical fuel, has been used for many years. Although it is inexpensive and available around the world, kerosene stoves are more difficult to keep clean, and dirty burners (usually caused by the fire's burning too low) can render the system inoperable.

Regular cleaning of the burner nipples is important to successful operation. Kerosene burners must be properly preheated, usually with alcohol, or a dirty, smoky fire will be produced. Kerosene has a definite odor that can sometimes pervade the vessel.

Sea-going stoves should be installed on the fore-and-aft axis and should be gimballed so that meals can be prepared when the vessel is heeling. Cooks will need some way to brace themselves, either with a rail just across from the stove or with a padded strap looping across the front of the stove. If a strap is used, the cook should be able to unfasten it easily if he or she needs to move quickly away from the stove. The stove itself should have a safety bar in front to keep the cook from being thrown onto the stove during heavy rolls.

As we described in Chapter 11, the area around the stove must be insulated with heat-resistant sheathing, and a vent or opening porthole located above it to exhaust fumes and moisture-laden air.

Cold storage is another issue that must be dealt with in planning the galley. Freezers and refrigerators can be run on propane, electricity, kerosene, or diesel, but generally they require a large amount of fuel to maintain their temperature. A simple icebox, properly built and insulated, can keep fresh food from spoiling for many days. A combination of wood, foam, and plastic can be used to insulate the icebox, and drip water can be removed with a pump or drained into a removable sump. On long crossings, you can rely on staples that don't require freezing and still get a balanced diet, especially if you're able to do some fishing. An icebox conversion kit, which consumes less energy than a traditional refrigerator, is one of the best compromises. It's inexpensive, easy to install, and doesn't take up much room in the icebox. A refrigerator compressor that runs off a power take-off from the main engine is another alternative used by some cruisers. A portable ice chest for cold drinks, especially one that can be stored in a cockpit locker, will be handy to have onboard when extra people are along on a short day trip.

A stainless steel double sink, located near the center of the boat so that it will drain on either tack, is another basic piece of kitchen equipment. A foot pump can supply seawater for washing dishes while leaving your hands free, and if hot water is desired, a line can be led from the flash heater installed for the shower.

Galley countertops can be made of wood, left bare or covered with water-resistant formica or tile. Low, removable fiddles should be fitted to keep things on the counters, and storage cabinets for dishes, pots, and pans

---

Table 19-2. BASIC GALLEY EQUIPMENT
Pressure cooker
Coffee pot
Baking dish
Loaf pans
Muffin pan
Steamer
Potholders
Mixing bowls
Measuring cups and spoons
Thermos
Knives (fish, carving, bread)
Whetstone
Funnels
Soup ladle
Can opener
Bottle opener
Corkscrew
Sprouter
Meat grinder
Ice tongs and pick

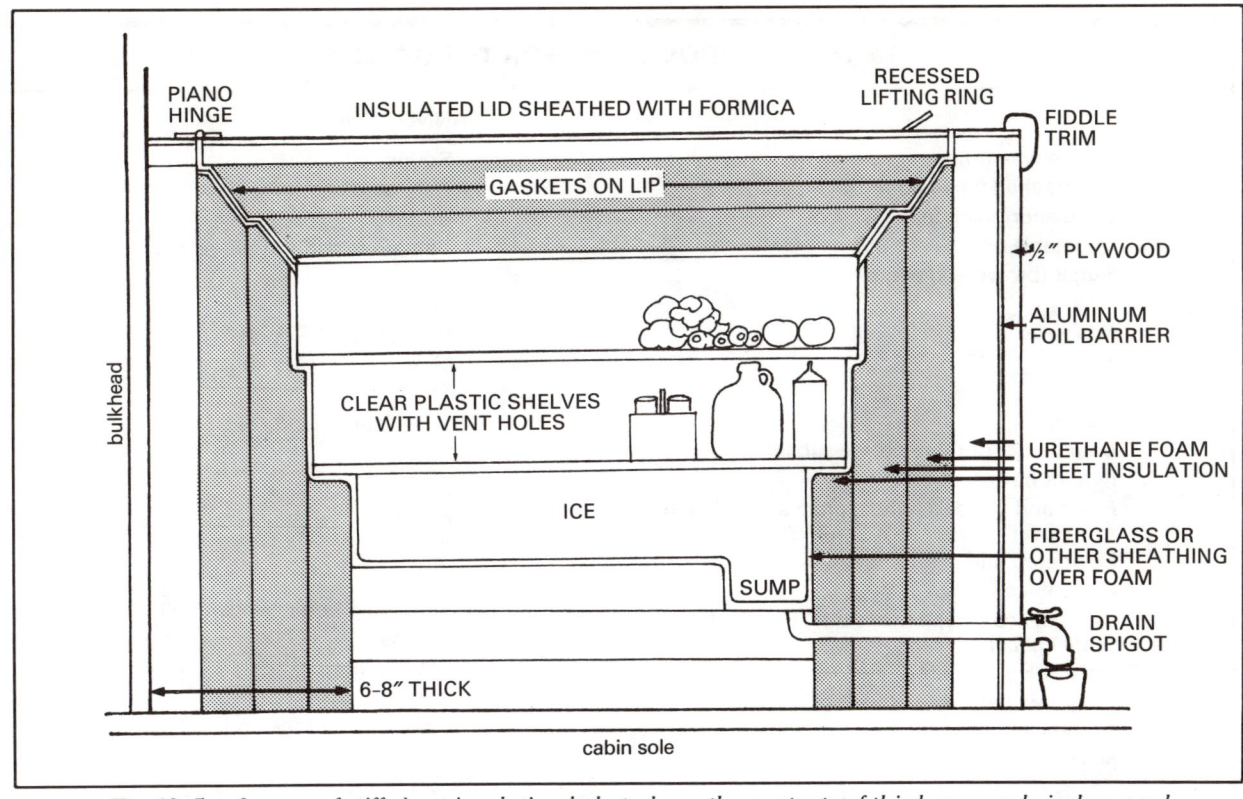

Fig. 19-5. *Layers of stiff sheet insulation help to keep the contents of this homemade icebox cool.*

should be built with compartments to keep everything in its proper place. A garbage locker can be installed under the sink.

Tableware can be plastic, ceramic, wood, metal, or disposable. Nesting sets of pans and bowls can be used to save space while including a variety of sizes. Accessories that require running the engine to charge the batteries may be more trouble than they're worth; these include toasters, electric frying pans, microwaves, and icemakers.

"What's for lunch?" is a classic question on land or sea. Answering that question becomes a lot more complicated when you and your corner grocery are separated by hundreds, even thousands, of miles of salt water. But a hot, nourishing meal on a blustery day can put heart into the weariest sailor.

Knowledge of basic human nutritional needs is important onboard a cruising vessel, since limited stores must meet those needs. There are many excellent books on nutrition; one of the best, which is oriented to vegetarian cooking, is *Laurel's Kitchen* (Nilgiri Press). Many of the principles of this type of cooking make sense on a boat, and grains and beans can be supplemented with fresh-caught fish. Menu planning should be based on food that the crew likes to eat, since if they won't eat it,

all of the nutritional planning in the world won't do a thing.

When planning how much food to take with you, you must take the speed of the boat into account, since a faster vessel will need fewer provisions to get from Point A to Point B. However, a reserve of 2 to 3 months' food should be stowed on board in case the vessel is disabled and must try to make port under a jury rig that drastically reduces its speed.

Fresh produce must be stored in a dry locker especially designed for good air flow. Although hanging nets can fulfill this function, the swinging of an unsecured net can bruise the food and lead to spoilage. Wire bicycle baskets or plastic-coated wire storage bins are very handy in this situation. Dry goods should be double-sealed in plastic bags or placed in plastic buckets with tight-fitting lids and stored in a dry location.

THE MAIN SALON

The main salon is the "living room" on any cruising boat. Many off-duty activities center here, and there should be enough space to accommodate all crew members. Most salons include comfortable settee seating

Table 19-3. PROVISIONS FOR THE GALLEY

STAPLES

Whole wheat flour
Unbleached white flour
Solid shortening (e.g., Crisco)
Vegetable oil
Sugar (brown and white)
Honey
Molasses
Tea
Coffee
Cocoa
Cafix, Inca, or other coffee substitute
Peanut butter
Pasta and noodles (whole grain and spinach
 are best)
Powdered milk
Brown rice
Dried beans (soy, pinto, azuki, kidney, lentils,
 split peas)
Oats
Bulgar wheat
Cornmeal
Nuts
Seeds (sesame, sunflower)
Bouillon cubes
Sprouting seeds (alfalfa, cabbage, mung bean)
Granola
Yeast

CONDIMENTS AND SPICES

Salt
Pepper
Vinegar
Mustard
Ketchup
Tamari
Miso
Mayonnaise
Sesame oil
Chili salsa
Favorite spices
Garlic (fresh and powdered)
Bakon yeast (smoked torula yeast)

CANNED GOODS

Soups
Fish (sardines, tuna)
Butter
Tomatoes and tomato sauce
Broth
Fruit
Vegetables
Milk

DRIED FOOD

Apricots
Apples
Peaches
Pears
Raisins
Red and green pepper
Onions
Potato flakes
Milk
Soy milk (for making tofu)

FRESH FOOD

Potatoes
Onions
Sweet potatoes
Winter squash
Carrots
Cabbage
Fruit
Fresh greens
Cheese
Eggs
Milk

SPECIAL TREATS

Candy
Chocolate
Canned cakes and puddings
Crew's choice

around a large table. The table often has sides that can be raised or lowered and storage compartments built into its center section. Various lockers are built into the walls and under the settees to hold books, games, TV, tape recorder, VCR, craft supplies, hobby equipment, spirits, and whatever else you wish to indulge in. Pilot berths are often built behind settees, and can be used as extra berths or for crew members on call for the next shift on deck.

Lighting is important in the salon, and several small lamps in convenient locations will work best. Kerosene lanterns can be used to avoid unnecessary drain on the batteries. A skylight or deadlight prism in the cabin top above the salon will provide welcome daylight.

Nice woodwork, art work, comfortable cushions, and simple prints and fabrics will increase the enjoyment of the crew as they sit around the table eating, reading, or talking.

WORK AREAS

A separate navigation station with a seat and slanted chart table gives plotting the ship's position and course the importance it deserves and the space it requires. The table top can lift up to allow access to a storage compartment underneath. The amount of required chart storage space will be determined by your cruising plans, but you should estimate high so that all charts can be stored in the same place and charts added as new cruising spots are explored. The electrical navigation equipment (discussed in Chapter 16) should be located as high as possible so that it is out of the way and protected from people falling against it. A gooseneck desk light is very practical here; a red light for night work will also come in handy.

If there is room onboard, a small shop with a work bench and tool storage lockers will facilitate onboard repairs. In a center-cockpit design, this work area can be located under the cockpit coaming. All of the repair kits (sail, electric, plumbing, etc.) can be stored in this central location so that there are never any questions about their whereabouts. Good lighting is essential here. This area can also double as a photo darkroom, small cargo space, or whatever specialty you might want to include. In a pinch, the work bench can be converted into a spare bunk.

Fig. 19-6. *The* Pavane II, *designed by Sparkman and Stephens, graces the waters outside her southern base. Accommodations onboard are as nice as on shore.*

Photo by Rey Scott, courtesy of the designer

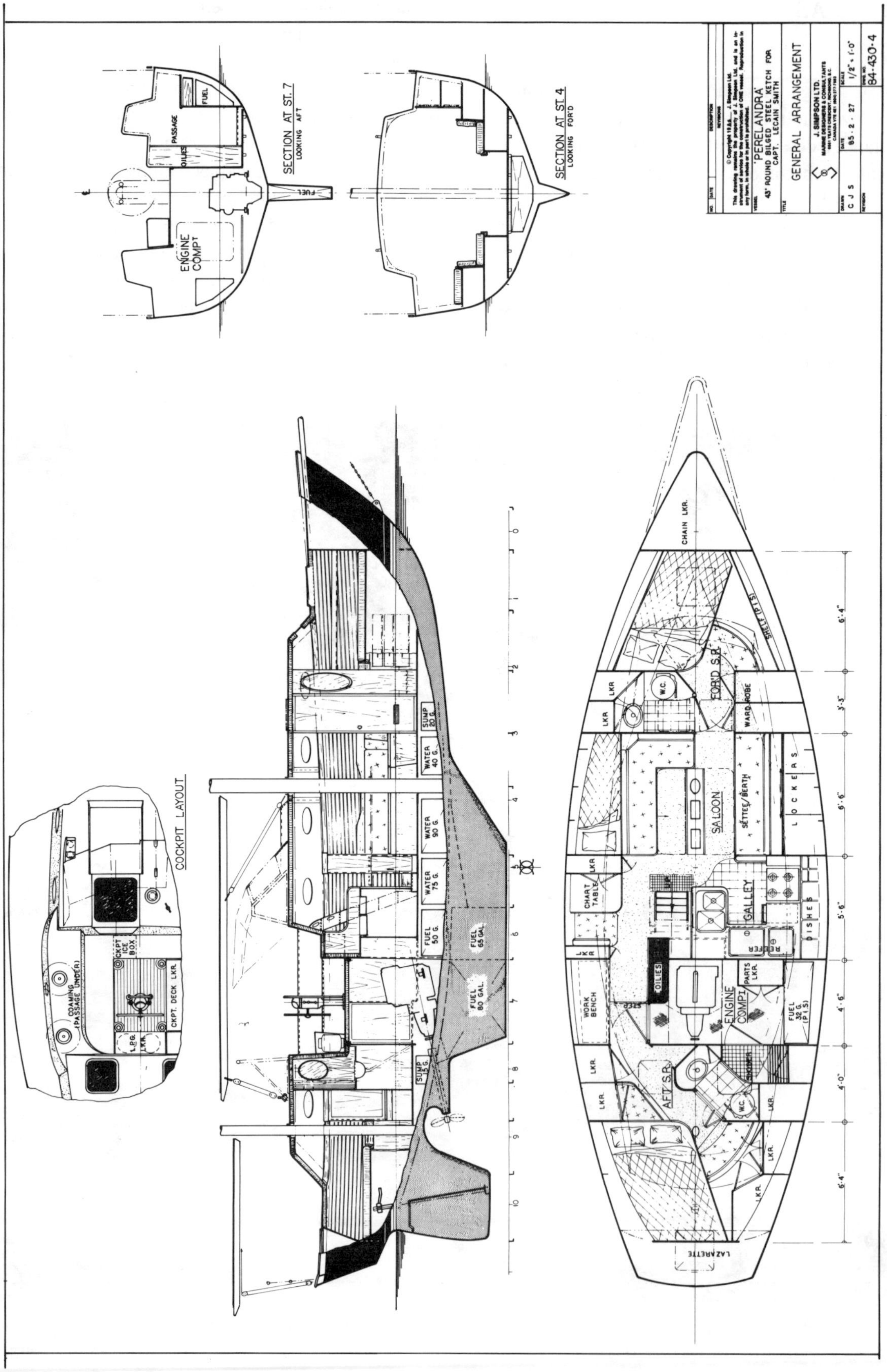

Fig. 19-7. *The accommodations plans for Perelandra, designed for the authors by John Simpson.*

Courtesy of the designer

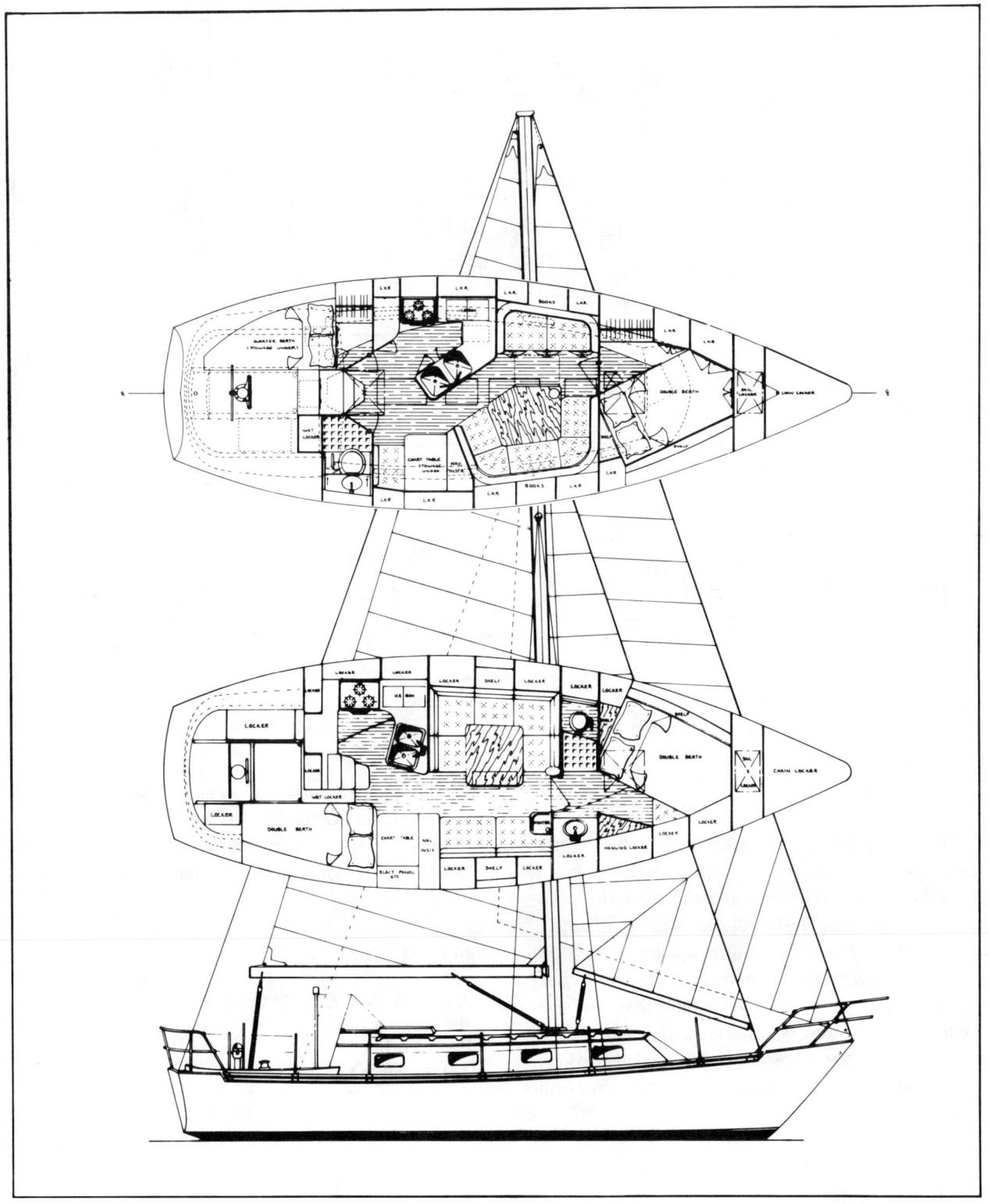

Fig. 19-8. *Different interior arrangements reflect the different perspectives of the designers of the* Waterline 333.

Courtesy of Waterline Yachts

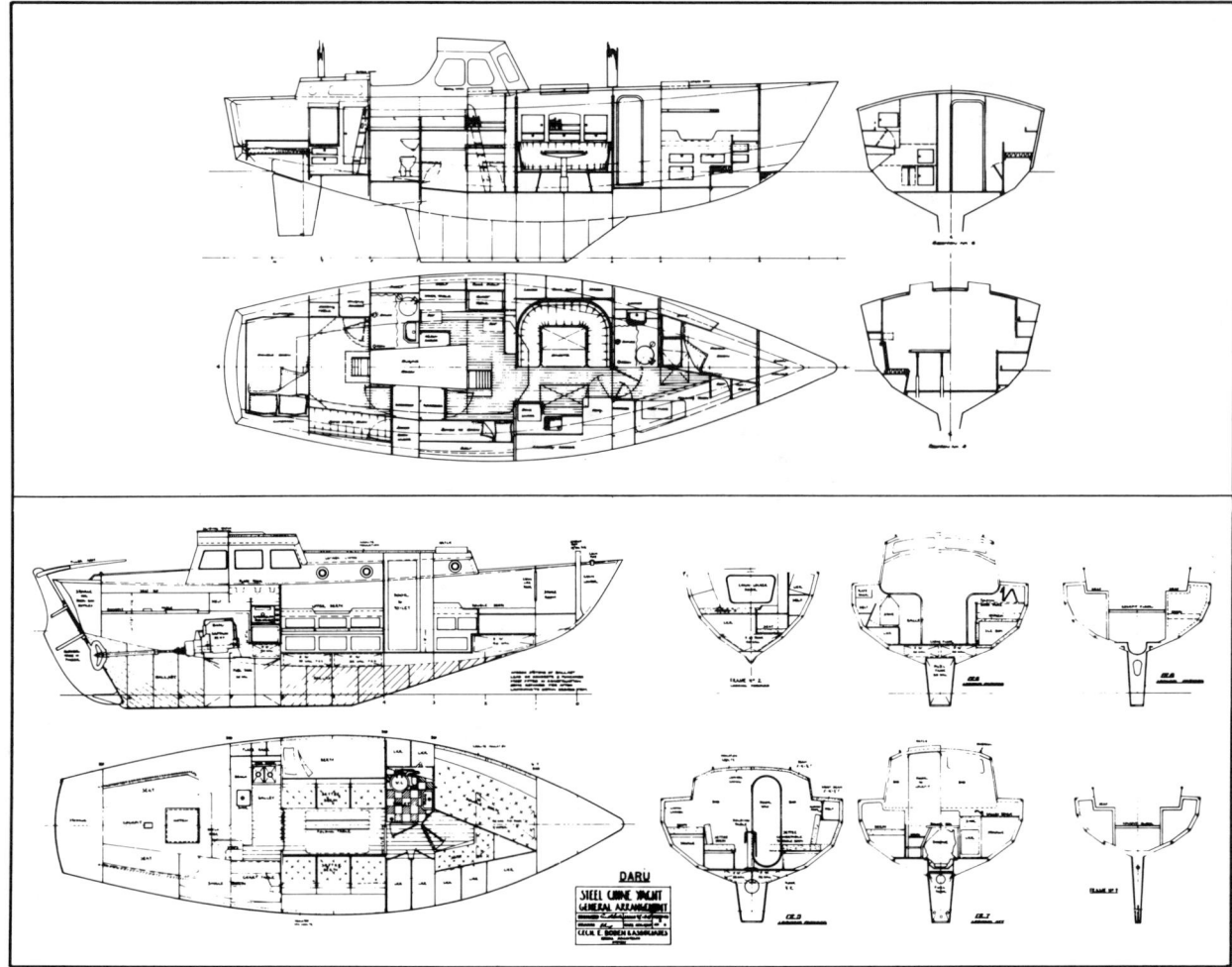

Fig. 19-9.   *Accommodation arrangements designed by Cecil Boden.* (Above) *South Sea;* (Below) *Daru.*

THE COCKPIT

The cockpit definitely forms part of the living quarters, especially in the tropics, where meals are often eaten on deck and the cockpit and deck are used for sleeping under the stars. The layout should be clean, simple, and practical. Non-skid coatings applied to the deck allow safe movement anywhere. Amenities like a cockpit drink locker and a removable table that can be attached to the steering pedestal are convenient, help to keep the area clear of obstacles. It's a good idea to keep access to the deck from the cockpit clean and free from obstructions.

CONCLUSION

The layout of accommodations will vary with each cruising design, as the figures in this chapter illustrate.

The important thing is to allow enough storage for your needs without overloading the boat. Generally, the larger the crew or family, the larger the boat that will be needed to provide comfortable living space for them.

SOURCES

American Boat & Yacht Council
190 Ketcham Ave.
P.O. Box 806
Amityville, NY 1170-0806

Chapter 20

Spars and Standing Rigging

Most of today's cruising yachts are rigged with aluminum spars and stainless steel wire. But most is not all. There are other options for materials—some more expensive than others. Wooden masts and galvanized steel rigging wire can be cost-effective alternatives that work very well when properly installed and maintained. But the desired performance of a given material may influence your decision more than cost.

The spars and standing rigging are the third most expensive system on a boat. If you choose a freestanding rig, like the Freedom or a junk, you may not have to invest in winches, rigging cable, or costly spar fittings; but, the spar itself will be expensive. The more masts you have, the more rigging and spar material you'll need, and special rigs like gaffs or fish boats require additional fittings. As with the other systems, the cheapest isn't always the best, and the most expensive isn't always necessary.

The steel hull to which the rigging is attached doesn't flex like other hull materials. Therefore, there is little additional stress on the rigging, so it can be set tighter and will last longer. There is also no danger of the hull seams opening up due to tension and compression stresses transmitted from the rigging through the chainplates to the hull.

SPARS

A spar is defined as a support that is used in rigging a ship, and a list of those most commonly used will include: main mast, main boom, mizzen mast, mizzen boom, staysail club boom, spreaders (two sets for taller, thinner masts), jumper struts (mostly used on three-quarter rigs), single or twin whisker pole (for running downwind), extra genoa pole, bowsprit, and boomkin. Of these, the masts—the spars most critical to a sailing vessel's performance—will be our focus here.

Masts must be properly placed to balance the boat. This balance is designed into the vessel, and you can't arbitrarily move a mast or change the position of the spreaders on the mast without affecting performance or strength. It may be tempting to convert a sloop into a ketch, but the conversion should only be done on the designer's drawing board. Many stock plans are available with different rig options for which the masts are correctly placed.

Masts can be stepped on deck or down in the keel, and both methods have been used successfully. But, for a world cruiser, stepping the mast in the keel is safer, because here the mast is supported as it goes through the deck or cabin top: this makes the mast stiffer and less

Fig. 20-1. *When a boat is used for fishing, extra stays are needed to support the fishing spars.*

likely to break. If a stay or shroud should part and the mast break, it will probably stay with the boat, and the break usually occurs far enough above the deck so that another spar can easily be jury-rigged to the stub. A mast stepped on the deck can be lowered for passing under bridges in waterways or canals, and with this design more space is available below, a point worth considering for small boats. Deck-stepped masts are a bit less expensive and lighter than those stepped in the keel, but they have a higher failure rate in heavy sea conditions, as the results of some around-the-world races attest. The mast step or tabernacle is under enormous compression stress, and even a strong steel deck must be supported by a compression rod when the mast is stepped on deck. The load on a keel-stepped mast is spread throughout the entire framing system by the floors and, sometimes, by floor extensions and girders.

The material used for masts must be somewhat flexible and have a good strength-to-weight ratio. The maintenance the material will require is another point to consider, as is the ease with which the fittings can be attached. The most logical choices are wood and aluminum. Each can do the job well, and access to one or the other at a reasonable cost may be the deciding factor. Designs usually specify aluminum masts, because they are most commonly manufactured, and the weight and strength of production aluminum spars is easily calculated. Wooden mast drawings take more work, but a designer may work out the specifications for a slight additional fee.

It is possible to use a combination of materials for the different spars on a vessel. For example, a mast could be made of aluminum and its boom of laminated wood.

However, it makes more sense to keep the same material for major spars so that the strength characteristics and the required fittings are the same for each.

Wood

Wood is the traditional spar material, and with good reason. It is stiff, yet able to flex without buckling, so is more forgiving than aluminum. Wooden masts also look good. They are easier to repair than aluminum, and attaching fittings to them is less complicated. Some maintenance is required for wood spars, but a properly painted mast will hold up well. It's not necessarily true that sailors with wooden masts have one hand for the boat and one for the varnish pot.

The traditional mast is solid fir or pine. These solid spars are quite heavy and have large diameters, which increases windage aloft; both of these characteristics can affect performance. However, in certain places in the world, solid spars are the least expensive option, and they're worth considering especially for a large working sailboat or a lug rig, which uses shorter spars. But checks and cracks may develop as the wood ages or dries, and the swelling and shrinking due to the changing atmospheric moisture content can increase cracking. These blemishes will not cause the spar to fail, although some people like to saturate cracks with a fungicide to prevent any rot. Painting the spar can help to seal the wood from the atmosphere around it.

Today, laminated spruce masts are more common than solid spars. They are not as heavy as fir or pine masts, and can be shaped to a better foil plan. Sitka spruce is usually chosen because it is light and has a very high modulus of elasticity, so it returns to its original shape after heavy flexing stresses. The interlocking grain structure of spruce also gives it good resistance to compression stress. Spruce does tend to rot under damp conditions, but the masts are high enough above the water that no real problems should occur. As a precautionary measure and to prevent water stains, a good coating or sealer should be used to stabilize the wood and protect it. These spars are generally hollow, but are reinforced with filler blocks where the base, gooseneck, spreaders, and masthead band will be located.

Failures in laminated spars can usually be traced to the use of poorly seasoned woods, cheap glues, or mistakes in the lamination process. Straight, air-dried, clear, tight vertical-grain spruce must be used, and it's getting harder and harder to find. Although resorcinol and urea formaldehyde glues have been used for lamination, the epoxy glues now on the market do a superior job (although they are more expensive).

Of course, wooden spars do require maintenance, and the time required depends on the type of coating used. Varnishing and oiling are the methods used to retain the natural look of the wood. Maintenance for both methods is about equal (although it's easier to oil than to varnish), and in the tropics the spars may need to be recoated every few months unless you are prepared to sand down to bare wood and start over again. On the other hand, spars painted with epoxy or polyurethane will only need to be recoated after a few years, especially if the wood has first been covered with an epoxy primer or sealant so that it doesn't swell and cause the paint to

Fig. 20-2. *Large solid fir spars are appropriate for this traditional schooner built by Haglund Boats.*

lose adhesion. The method costs more initially but pays for itself in maintenance labor saved. Certain buff colors can look quite natural, too.

The cost of a professionally built wooden mast may be equal to that of the average aluminum spar kit. However, if you build a wood spar yourself, you can save two-thirds of the cost of an aluminum mast that is purchased complete. A home-built spar bench and lots of clamps are the only required investments besides wood

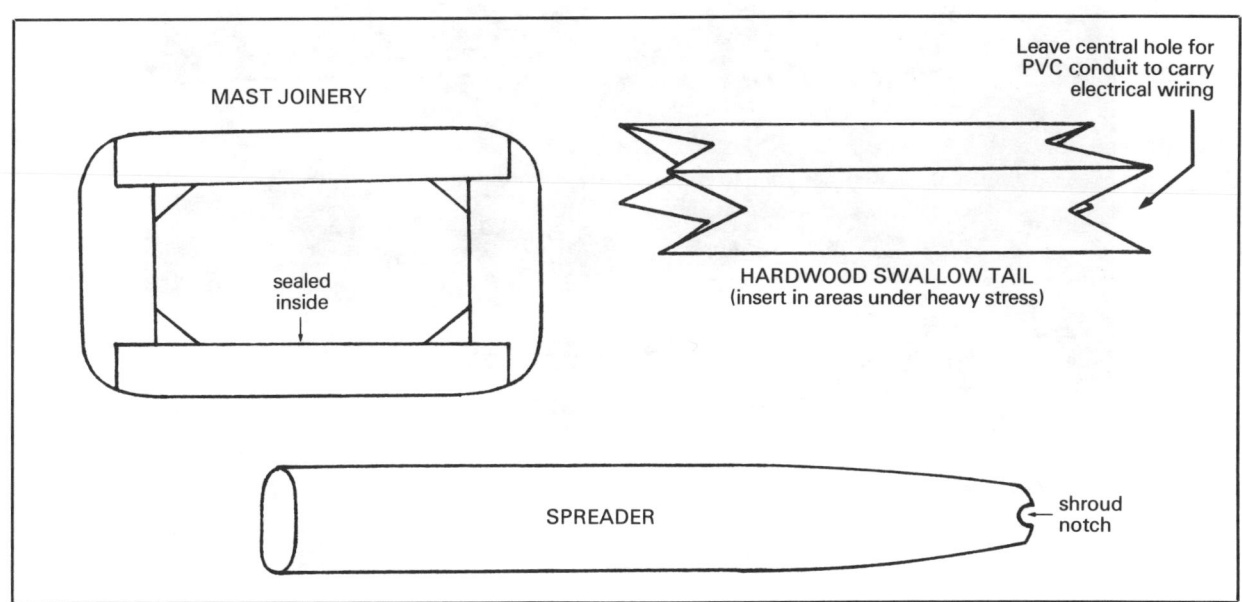

Fig. 20-3. *Close-up views of some details of box spar construction.*

and glue. The important considerations for home-built wood spars are whether the builder is qualified and whether the right kind of wood is available at a good price in your area. In different parts of the U.S., the cost of spruce can range from $2 to $10 a foot.

Aluminum

Aluminum masts have ruled the seas in recent years. The material has a very high strength-to-weight ratio (especially when heat-treated), is very strong, and requires little maintenance. However, aluminum masts buckle more often under high compression loads than will laminated spruce, and are more apt to break if a stay parts. In other words, although aluminum is stronger than spruce, it will take less bending to break it. Over a period of time, the oxidation of the surface of the aluminum may freeze the fittings into place so that they can't be removed.

Aluminum masts are generally made of 6061, 6063, or 6066 aluminum that has been anodized to increase its protective oxide layer. The extruded tubes are only available in certain lengths, and for taller masts, sections of tube may have to be joined together with internal sleeves or welds. (Remember, the weld zone of aluminum is only about 60–70% as strong as the surrounding metal.) Spar kits are available at a lower cost than a complete mast.

Although aluminum does not need to be coated because of its oxide layer, the color can be varied with an epoxy or polyurethane paint designed for use on alum-

Table 20-1. COST COMPARISON OF WOOD AND ALUMINUM SPARS			
	Low	Medium	High
Aluminum	$4–6,000 (kit)	$6–7,000	$7–9,000
Wood	$2–3,000 (self-built)	$3–4,000	$4–7,000 (professionally built)

inum. A clear polyurethane finish can also be used. The aluminum should be treated with an etch primer before painting.

Aluminum is lower than steel on the galvanic scale, so an aluminum mast must be protected from galvanic corrosion. Under certain conditions, aluminum can pit rapidly. In general, however, this doesn't effect the usefulness of aluminum for spars. It should be insulated from the steel deck and step with neoprene or nylon pads. High-strength aluminum or stainless fittings must be used, and the stainless must be well bedded.

Other Spar Materials

Although steel masts are the least expensive variety, their heavy weight, thick diameter, and the inefficient sail foil behind them are detrimental to sailing performance. But large boats with low-aspect-ratio rigs have successfully used steel pipe for spars, and these hollow masts can even double as exhaust pipes. It is hard to find

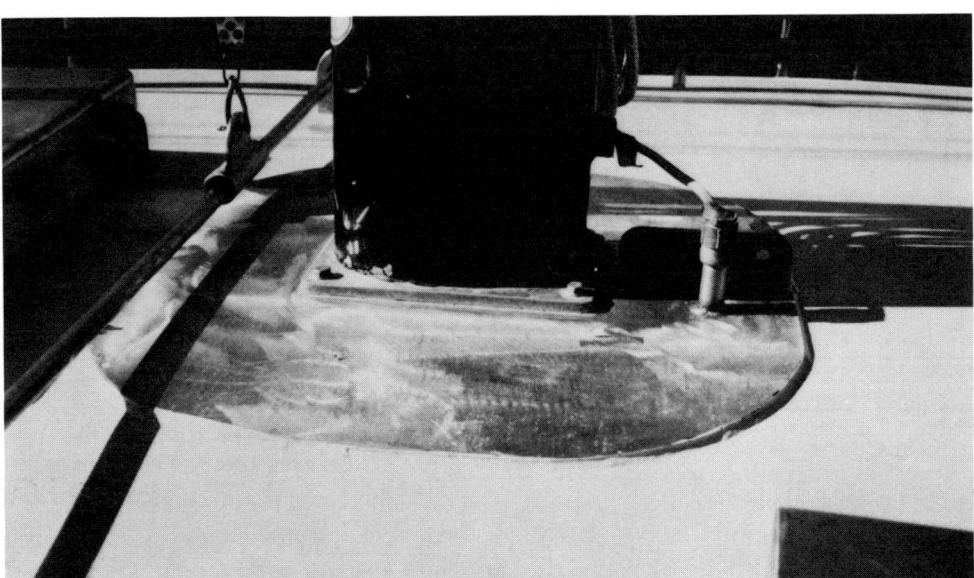

Fig. 20-4. *This aluminum mast is stepped over an internal stainless steel collar, and a stainless doubler below the mast helps to spread out the load.*

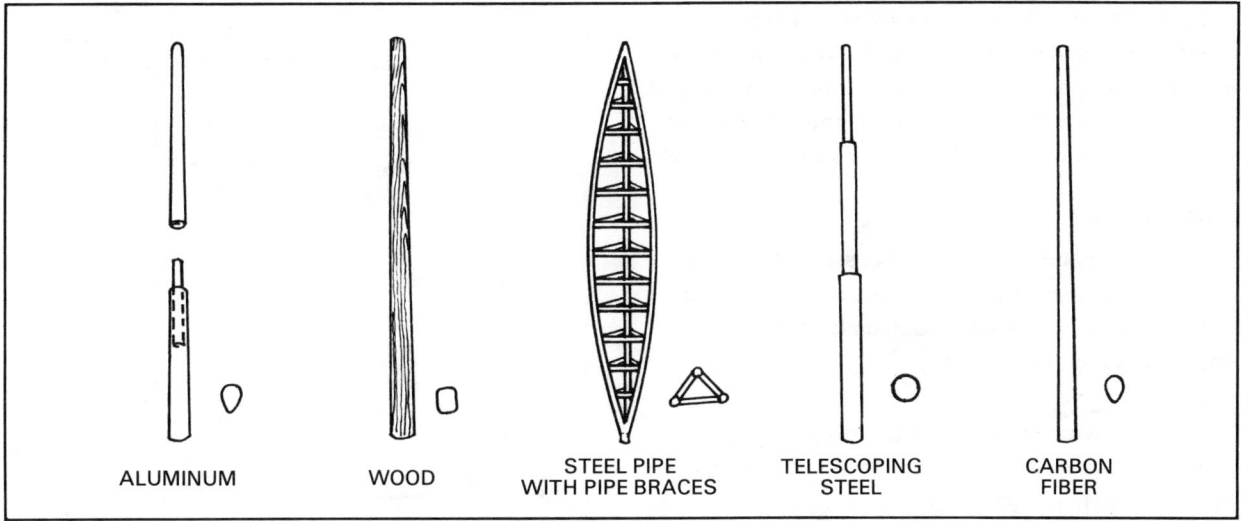

Fig. 20-5. *Some examples of the different types of masts that can be purchased or fabricated. (No attempt has been made here to draw them to any particular scale.)*

good, tapered, cylindrical shapes; different-sized tubes connected in telescope fashion, with the heaviest schedule on the bottom, have been employed on some tall ships. Corrosion is not too problematic if the mast is properly coated, although if corrosion were to develop, the frequent recoating required could become a chore. Stainless steel should be welded in at chafe points (for example, tang eyes), but inexpensive steel fittings can be fabricated and welded to the mast.

Titanium is a very strong, light metal and would make excellent spars, but at present it is too expensive to be considered. Magnesium is also strong and light, but it does not have compression strength sufficient to resist the heavy stresses acting on a mast.

The new "miracle masts" are made of carbon fiber, and are incredibly expensive; they are fabricated by setting heated fibers in epoxy. The great strength of these spars allows them to be used unstayed in freestanding rigs. However, they have not been around long enough to prove their long-term worth. Fiberglass-epoxy laminations have also been used for masts, but so far have not been successful for larger cruising spars.

SPAR FITTINGS

Many different fittings are required on the spars and the deck so that the wires that hold the masts in place can be rigged. When the boat is made of steel, deck fittings can be welded directly to the deck, making them an integral part of the hull. (These deck fittings are discussed in Chapter 9.) Less expensive galvanized steel fittings can be used for both spar and deck fittings, although bronze and stainless steel are sometimes more appropriate. Table 20–2 lists the fittings required for most masts.

Because most of today's custom fittings are produced for aluminum masts of standard diameters, you may have some difficulty in finding the correct-sized fittings for a wood spar. And most of the mass-produced fittings are made of the stainless required for aluminum masts. However, many small foundries are very capable of casting fittings of other materials at a reasonable price.

The best fittings for wooden spars are made of manganese bronze (a high-strength brass). It is stronger than stainless and also less brittle, so it doesn't fracture under stress as stainless can; it doesn't corrode like steel when it is chafed. Since the bronze is well above the water line, de-zincification, the major form of corrosion to which it is subject, is not a problem. Silicon bronze is not generally used for spar fittings, since it is not as strong as manganese bronze, though it is slightly more corrosion resistant. Both silicon and manganese bronze can both be easily cast because of their low melting points, and foundries can make complex shapes by welding simple castings together with a heli-arc welding machine.

Manganese bronze castings are available in three different strength grades, with tensile strengths ranging from 32,000 to 120,000 psi depending on the particular alloy. The medium strength range of manganesse bronze is higher than that of steel or stainless, and is ideal for most spar fittings. These fittings are usually secured to a wood mast with silicon bronze fasteners, which have a tensile strength of 55,000 psi.

If you are using an aluminum mast, you'll be limited to stainless fittings, although some strong aluminum gear is suitable. Most stainless fittings are made of strap material, since stainless is difficult and expensive to cast. Cold working can harden the stainless, making these fittings more susceptible to fatigue, cracking, and sudden rupture. Stainless fittings must be carefully designed to prevent notches. Although, since stainless is strong, the scantlings required for fittings can be reduced a bit, this practice has gone too far, and many production fittings are too light to be safe.

Table 20-2. SPAR FITTINGS

Masthead bands with brackets for lights, anemometer, antenna, etc.

Halyard sheaves at mast head

Tangs (check block optional)

Sail slide track with slide stopper

Spreader strap connectors (flexible mount type allows for some pivoting fore and aft)

Pulley for lanyards or spreaders

Spreader tips with anti-chafe rubber boot, tape, plastic roller, etc.

Assorted cleats

Storm sail track and switch

Whiskerpole/genoa/spinnaker pole track

Mast ladder steps or ratlins on shrouds (crow's nest is optional, but nice)

Winch mount pads and cleats

Gooseneck mastband with belaying pin mounts

Gooseneck boom assembly

Boom vang band and eye

Jiffy reef blocks and cleats

Boom bail to attach sheets

Outhaul car assembly with cleats

Boom sail track

Mast-mounted winches for halyards

Club jib gooseneck or pedestal assembly

Hardwood mast shims for wood spar or flexible neoprene or rubber gaskets for aluminum spar

Mast boot of flexible rubber or treated canvas

Step insulator pad (if mast is aluminum)

Stainless fittings are installed on an aluminum mast either with machine set screws inserted into previously drilled and tapped holes or with pop rivets set in with a gun. The machine screws seem to hold larger fittings best. All fasteners should be well bedded, and all of the threads should be lubricated so that the fittings can be removed.

Galvanized steel can be used for spar fittings if the most economical route must be taken. For example, the masthead band or various tangs can be fabricated of

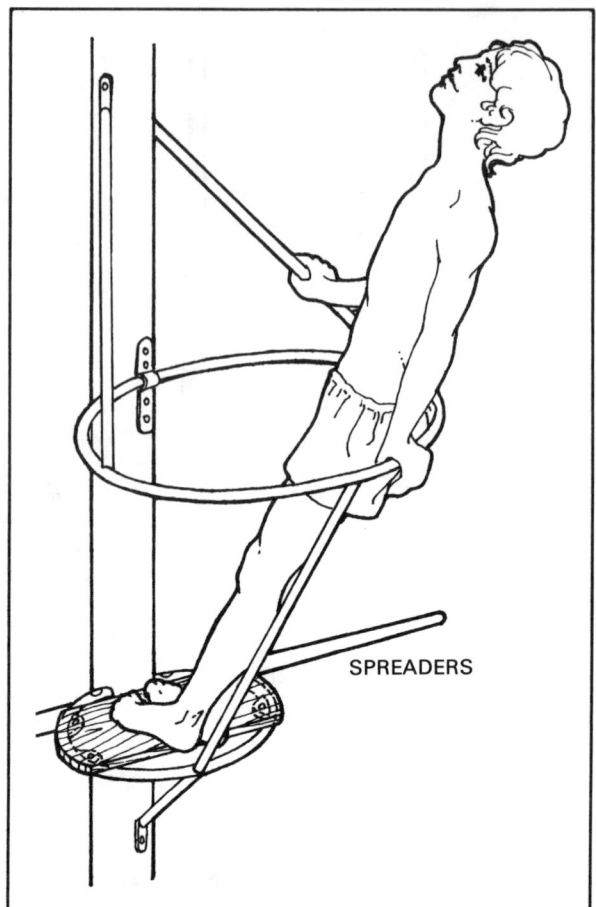

Fig. 20-6. *A simple but safe crow's nest can be put together with stainless tubing and strap.*

steel strap. However, steel fittings are not as strong as high-tensile manganese bronze or stainless, and they do require more maintenance. Cast-steel fittings are rarely found in the marketplace, but a good foundry can make them up quite inexpensively. Steel fittings should be galvanized or coated with epoxy powder. Fittings that can chafe under a load, like goosenecks, toggles, and eyes on deck gear, can be fitted with nylon (Nylatron) bearings or stainless steel bushings to protect the steel.

All fittings must be properly designed with a particular mast in mind. They must have the correct scantlings and holes that match the standing rigging, running rigging, or sails that will be attached. A fitting should always be rated stronger than the rigging wire to be used.

STANDING RIGGING

All of the shrouds and stays that support the mast and keep it in the correct position are part of the standing rigging. Of course, the number of stays increases with

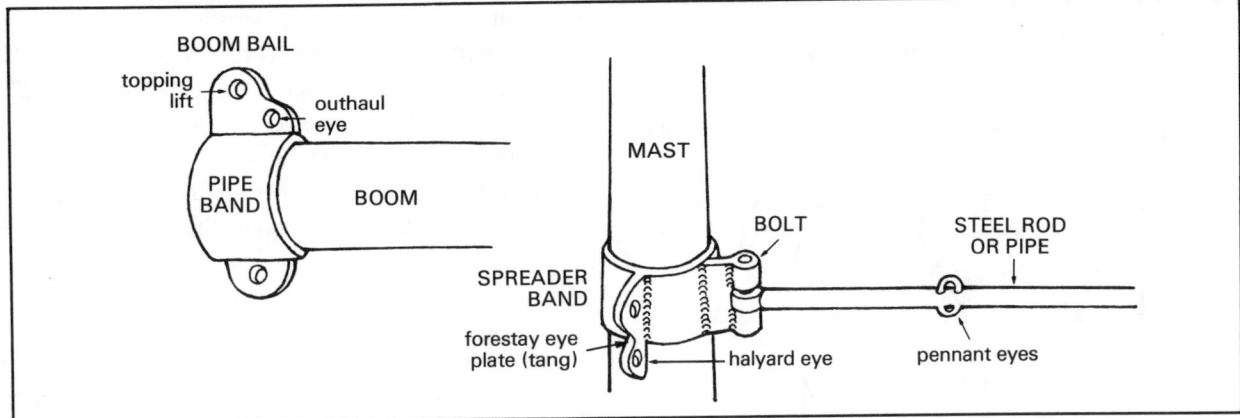

Fig. 20-7. *Steel spar fittings are easy to create with plate and tubing.*

the number of spars. The points at which the rigging wires are attached to the masts and to the deck or bowsprit are calculated in the design: the wider the angle the shroud forms between the masthead and the chainplate, the easier it is for the rigging to keep the mast from bending to leeward and the less strain there is on the shrouds. And outboard chainplates are not in the way of someone moving along the deck. Table 20–3 describes standard running rigging for a ketch.

The integrity of all standing rigging is tested by its weakest link, usually a cotter pin, shackle or sheave bearing, so the size and material of each part must be chosen carefully. The wire itself must be strong enough to withstand the ultimate gale or possibly a knockdown, despite the fact that the boat won't encounter these conditions often. Overrigging a boat with wire that is stronger than normally necessary can slightly increase the windage aloft, but it adds extra security.

A bobstay or whisker stays on the bowsprit can also be considered as part of the standing rigging. Bobstays can be made of stainless wire or rod or galvanized chain. Although rod is more expensive, it will cause less chafe on the anchor chain or line. For this reason, a rod does not need to be covered with a rubber boot as a chain bobstay must. A rod bobstay can be designed as a long turnbuckle by inserting rod with opposing right- and left-hand threads at the clevis ends. Since chain or cable bobstays require turnbuckles, terminals or shackles, thimbles, and toggles at each end, there is a definite cost savings when rod is used instead. Whisker stays will also be needed unless a steel tube bowsprit is used.

Table 20-3. TYPICAL STANDING RIGGING FOR A KETCH
Outer jib forestay
Inner single or double forestay
Two lower shrouds
One main upper shroud
One intermediate shroud or main and mizzen masts, depending on size of boat,
One permanent backstay (two if mizzen is in the way)
OPTIONAL
Jumper strut on three-quarter rig
Two running backstays with clamp-down lever or tackle
Triadic stay from top of main to mizzen instead of permanent backstay
Backstays for for mizzen on boomkin (only needed on certain designs)

Fig. 20-8. *Of the many ways to stay a boat, this design uses one with crossing shrouds between the upper and lower spreaders on a wooden mast. Note also the small platforms that have been built on the lower spreaders, which are made of steel pipe.*

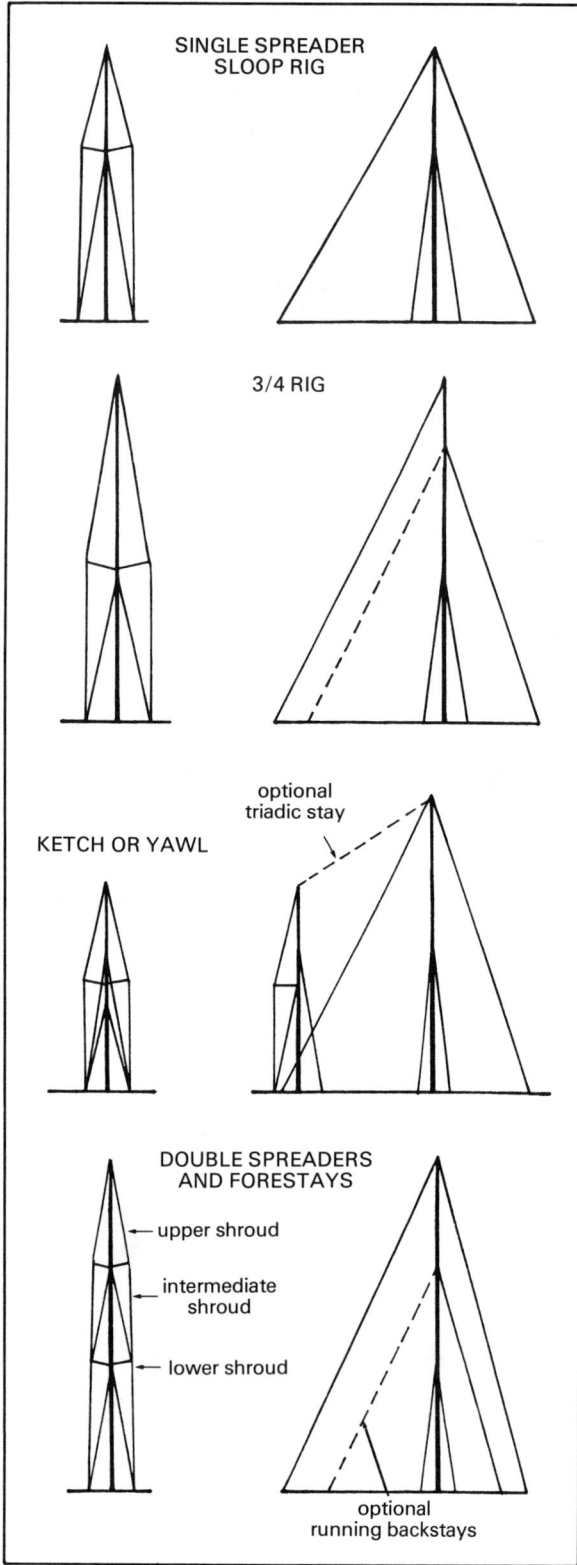

SINGLE SPREADER
SLOOP RIG

3/4 RIG

KETCH OR YAWL

optional
triadic stay

DOUBLE SPREADERS
AND FORESTAYS

← upper shroud

intermediate
shroud

← lower shroud

optional
running backstays

Fig. 20-9. *The most common ways of staying a boat. When a high-aspect-ratio mast is used, double spreaders and forestays may be necessary to allow lighter mast scantlings and better support.*

An interesting but more expensive way of adjusting the bowsprit has been developed by New Found Metals in Port Townsend, Washington. It is shown in Fig. 20-12. The method reduces the necessity for turnbuckles on the bobstays by adjusting the sprit tension at the samson post. It also allows the bowsprit to be pulled inboard so the boat can fit into a smaller slip, saving moorage charges.

Wire Materials

There are really only two choices of wire material: galvanized or stainless steel. Any two sailors will probably disagree on which to use, but stainless seems to have an edge on the market at present. The main considerations are strength, stretch factor, lifetime, types of failure, and difficulty of installation and maintenance.

Rigging wire is categorized by the different arrangements in which the strands are bundled and wrapped around each other. For stiff standing rigging on yachts, 6/7 or 7/7 galvanized steel wire and 1/19 stainless wire are the best choices. The first number represents the number of wire bundles that are twisted together to form the cable; the second is the number of strands in each bundle. Basically, the fewer wires in a cable, the more rigid it is, and the larger each individual strand is, the stronger the wire. As Fig. 20-11 shows, in equivalent sizes there are many more small strands in 6/7 wire than in 1/19. Therefore, 1/19 wire, whether stainless or galvanized, is stronger and stretches less. (In some sizes, 1/19 galvanized is actually slightly stronger than stainless. The best, and most expensive, types are advertised as aircraft cable.)

However, the flexibility of the wire determines whether or not it can be spliced easily. 1/19 stainless is so stiff that splicing is difficult, although it can be done by an experienced rigger. Since 1/19 cannot be spliced around a thimble, swaged and mechanical terminals must be used. On the other hand, 6/7 galvanized is strong enough and easily spliced, yet is stiff enough to hold the mast in position. The more flexible types like 7/19 or 7/7 are used most appropriately for stanchion safety lines, safety harness lines, and wire luffs on jibs and halyards.

Price also must be considered when purchasing the large quantities of wire needed for rigging. Stainless wire is approximately three times more expensive than galvanized, and the special terminals required can cost more than all the galvanized rigging wire itself. Inexpen-

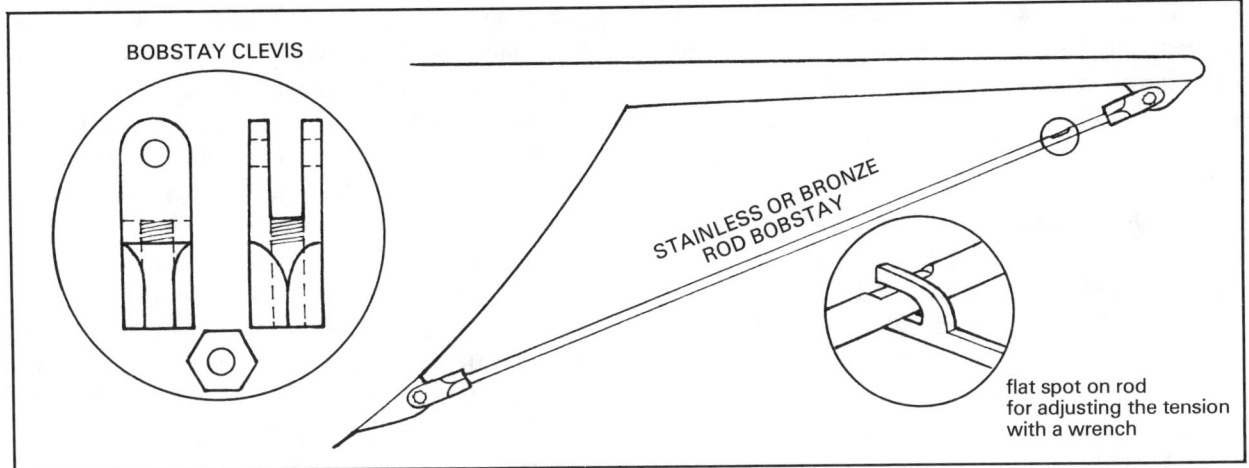

Fig. 20-10. *A rod bobstay with left- and righthand clevises at opposite ends. Another variation uses a turnbuckle at the center of the rod to adjust tension.*   Courtesy of New Found Metals

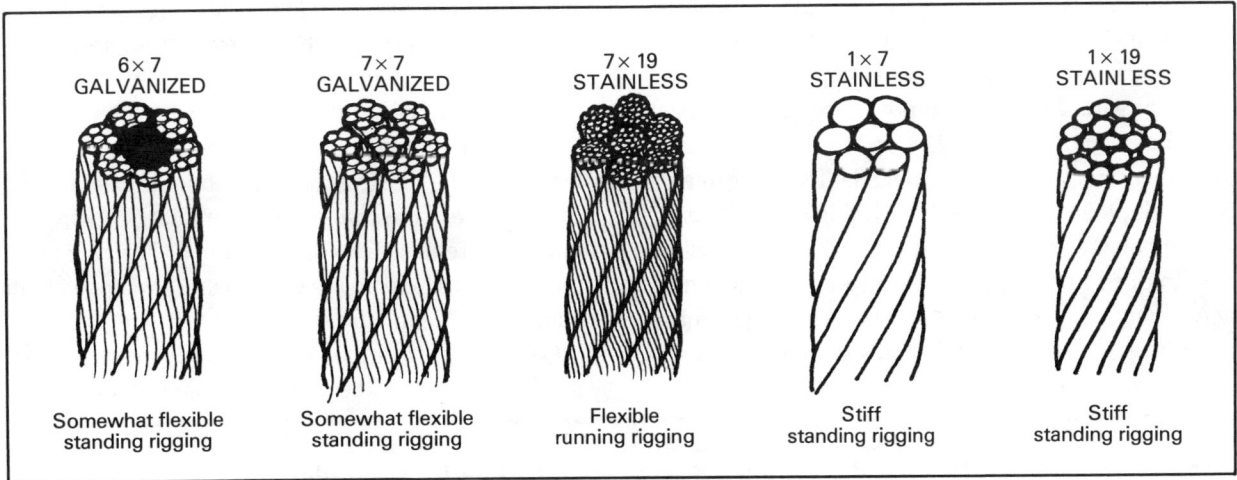

Fig. 20-11. *Rigging wire.*

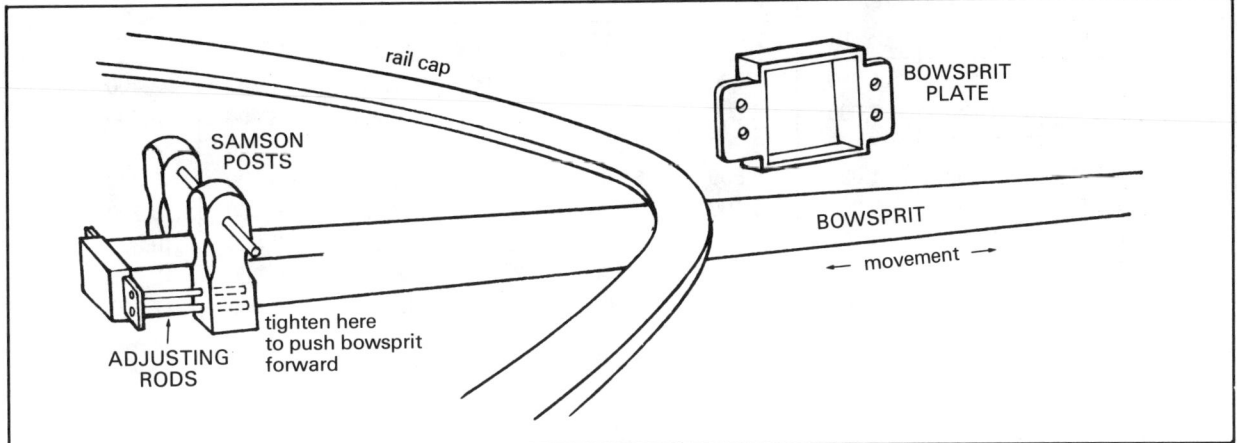

Fig. 20-12. *This fitting, designed and manufactured by New Found Metals, allows the bowsprit to be moved in and out. The plate which grips the sprit is cast of bronze.*   Courtesy of New Found Metals

sive galvanized fittings, however, can be used with galvanized wire. When rigging a boat with galvanized wire, it is common to use stainless for the outer forestays on which the headsail hanks will run, since it stretches least and will resist chafing best.

All rigging wire is available in different diameters, and its strength increases with increasing size. The old rule of thumb is that the breaking strength of the wire should equal half the boat's displacement, but a safety factor of 10% should be added to this. Because 6/7 galvanized is not as strong as 1/19 stainless, a larger size will be required to hold the mast rigid enough for good performance. This larger-diameter wire increases the windage aloft a bit, but not enough to concern a cruiser.

Galvanized rigging wire is available either bright or galvanized. Although the bright wire is 10–20% stronger, it is not suitable for use in the marine environment because the steel is not protected. Galvanized wire is available in three grades: regular, improved (or plow), or extra-improved. The core can be either fiber or a thick strand of wire. Polyethylene fiber cores are stronger than those of polypropylene; strand cores are stronger than fiber ones, and are not as flexible. The 6/7 galvanized wire preferred for standing rigging is usually galvanized plow wire with a fiber core. The old 6/7 wire had an oiled hemp core, stretched a lot, and was not very strong, but it was cheap. Rigid 1/19 or 1/7 galvanized wire can be used if the difficulty of making splices is not a consideration.

Types 302, 304, and even 316 stainless steel are used for rigging wire. They have similar breaking strengths, although that of 304 can be slightly lower; type 316 has a 10–20% lower tensile strength, but is more corrosion resistant. There are also some special super-corrosion-resistant types of stainless wire, such as that manufactured by the Macwhyte Company.

Rigging wire is subjected to considerable operating stress, and the way in which it fails can be a life-or-death matter. Stainless wire is subject to metal fatigue and crevice corrosion, which shows up in the form of hairline cracks that are difficult to detect. In the tropics splinters are a common problem, and kinks in the wire increase fatigue. Stainless wire can rupture without warning because there are no signs of corrosion, like the rust on galvanized wire, although close inspection can reveal signs of fatigue. Since galvanized steel is more ductile, it will bend or stretch long before breaking. Its corrosion is visually apparent long before there is any damage, and it can be remedied.

The number of bundles that make up the wire also influences the service life of the rigging. With 1/19 stainless, which has basically only one bundle of strands, if two or three of the strands break or kink, the wire will have to be replaced. If you are using 6/7 galvanized, a number of strands can break in several bundles without adversely affecting the strength of the wire.

Galvanized rigging must be properly treated so that it will not corrode. Many different coatings have been

Table 20-4. BREAKING STRENGTHS OF RIGGING WIRE
(in pounds)　(based on averages of various brands)

SIZE	Galvanized Improved Plow Steel (fiber core)		Galvanized Steel Aircraft Cable			Type 302 Stainless Steel*		
	6 × 7	6 × 19	7 × 7	7 × 19	1 × 19	7 × 7	7 × 19	1 × 19
1/8″	1,150	1,250	1,700	2,000	2,100	1,700	1,760	2,100
5/32″	1,900	2,000	2,600	2,800	3,300	2,400	2,400	3,300
3/16″	2,700	2,800	3,700	4,200	4,700	3,700	3,700	4,700
7/32″	3,750	4,000	4,800	5,600	6,300	4,800	5,000	6,300
1/4″	4,800	5,000	6,100	7,000	8,200	6,100	6,400	8,200
9/32″	6,100	6,700	7,600	8,000	10,300	7,600	7,800	10,300
5/16″	7,400	7,800	9,200	9,800	12,500	8,900	9,000	12,500
3/8″	10,500	11,200	13,200	14,400	18,000	12,000	12,000	17,600
7/16″	14,200	15,000	16,000	17,500	23,400	15,600	16,300	23,400
1/2″	18,500	19,000	20,500	22,700	31,000	21,200	22,800	29,800
9/16″	23,400	24,000	25,500	28,500	38,500	26,600	28,500	36,200
5/8″	28,000	30,000	—	35,000	35,000	32,500	35,000	46,000

* Type 304 has approximately the same values, though a bit lower. Type 316 is about 10% weaker, although it is more corrosion resistant.

Fig. 20-13. *This low-aspect-ratio Colvin junk design guarantees low-stress sailing and lots of living room.*

ic maintenance. Hard paraffin or turpentine can be used for temporary repairs to the tar coating.

Served wire is not as pretty and shiny as stainless, but it is practical and good looking in its own way. Bernard Moitessier always paints his rigging black anyway, so that it shows up better at night in case he has to grab it to stay onboard. Properly served galvanized wire will outlast stainless, and if you do the serving yourself, it will also cost less. Of course, if the wire is professionally served, the initial cost will be higher.

Although maintenance is not as critical with stainless rigging wire, some is required. One type of treatment uses a vinegar wash and then a wipe-down with a mixture of one-third fish oil and two-thirds black anti-corrosive paint. Since salt spray can decrease the lifetime of the wire and terminals, they should be rinsed with fresh water as often as is possible. The upper part of terminals can also be coated with beeswax for extra protection.

The newest development in material for standing rigging is the use of rod made of Nitronic 50 stainless steel. It stretches very little and is so strong that small diameters can be used, reducing windage. However, it is expensive (about double the cost of stainless wire), and its strength can be lowered where the rod is wrapped around the cross trees. There are still many questions a cruiser would want answered: where do you store a 60'-long spare rod? And how do you repair it at sea?

FITTINGS FOR STANDING RIGGING

Turnbuckles (also called rigging screws or bottle screws) and terminals are the most important rigging fittings, since they are used to attach the rigging wire to the chainplates and to keep the wire in tension. A failure

tried (for example, black paint, fish oil, a boiled linseed oil-white lead mixture, penetrating sprays, liquid latex, and a black tar mix made of linseed oil, Japan drier, and unsulfured grease—all of which can be messy to live with). The method that seems to work best is the traditional one popularized by The Rigging Gang, headed by Nick Benton: parceling and serving the wire.

The rigging is served after all splices have been made and seized with wire. If it is necessary, the wire is first wormed (cord is wrapped with the lay of the cable to smooth out the surface), and then it is parceled by wrapping canvas or friction tape (Bulldog is best) the full length of the wire. Finally, the wire is served by wrapping tar-saturated spring or marlin twine on top of the tape. Stockholm tar is best to use because it is naturally smoked and contains no acids. The only maintenance is a matter of rubbing tar into the twine about every six months; fittings can also be checked during this period-

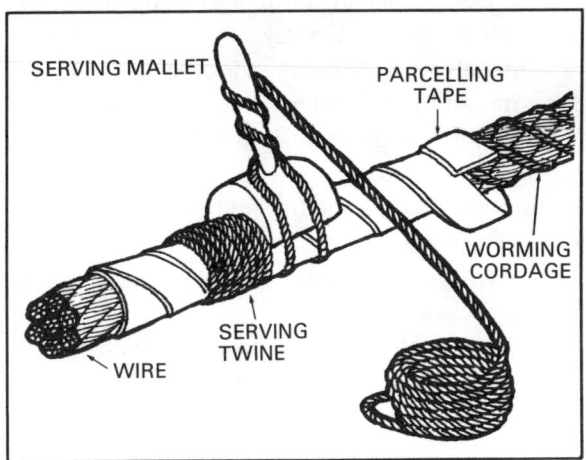

Fig. 20-14. *Serving galvanized wire.*

here can mean a dismasting. The choice of material depends on the kind of rigging wire used, but the fittings should always be rated stronger than the wire. Stainless or bronze fittings can be used on stainless wire, while stainless, galvanized steel, or epoxy-dipped steel are more appropriate for galvanized rigging, but bronze can also be used. Expensive monel turnbuckles and ones made of cast aluminum are also available. Generally, all of these materials are dependable, but prices for each can vary greatly. Other parts and fittings to be used with the standing rigging are listed in Table 20-5.

Table 20-5. PARTS AND FITTINGS FOR STANDING RIGGING
Shackles
Thimbles
Cotter pins
Antenna wire insulators
Anti-chafe rubber sleeves or baggywrinkles
Canvas or rubber boot covers for turnbuckles
Traveler lever to clamp down backstays
Backstay adjuster (hydraulic optional)
Large pelican hook and turnbuckle release mechanism for inner forestay

There are basically two types of turnbuckles: closed- and open-barrel. To keep the turnbuckle from loosening, the closed barrel uses a lock rod and the open barrel a cotter pin. If you choose the less-expensive galvanized turnbuckles, they should be of the closed-barrel type and should be filled with grease. The open-barrel type is preferable for stainless or bronze, which needs to "breath." Every turnbuckle should be fitted with a toggle to reduce fatigue and bending; toggles are especially necessary when the top of the chainplate doesn't line up properly with the stay.

Terminals are fitted to the ends of each wire so that the wire can be attached to the toggle or turnbuckle. The correct type of terminal to use is partly a matter of personal preference, although it does depend on the wire material and the kind of sailing you plan to do. There are six types to choose from: 1) splices, 2) bull-dog clamp, 3) nicropress, 4) socket, 5) swage, and 6) mechanical.

Traditional splices are still used, especially for 6/7 galvanized wire. Splices are very strong, and this terminal method is inexpensive, since the only tools and parts it requires are a metal fid to open the strands, a rigging vise, a thimble to form the eye, and seizing wire

to secure the splice. But splicing does require some skill and time; the technique has been written up in many books available to the sailor. Galvanized splices should be completely served to protect the wire, and the serving can continue around the eye that has been formed. If the effort is made to splice stainless, after seizing the splice need only be waxed and taped.

Galvanized bulldog or U-clamps that hold the wire around a thimble are very good for emergency repairs, but they are not strong enough for cruising. At least two clamps (three is better) should be used, with a space equal to the width of a clamp between each. The bolt side should run over the standing part of the wire so that the free end is held securely in the U. These clamps can be installed with a wrench.

With nicropress terminals, sleeves manufactured of soft copper-lead alloy sleeves are pressed around the wire to hold it in place around a thimble. For cable under 5/16", a hand tool that looks like a cable cutter can be used to install the sleeves; on large cable a nicropress machine is needed. Epoxy can be poured into the ends of the nicropress sleeve to seal the wire. These terminals are more appropriate for small boats, life lines, or dinghy rigs than for standing rigging on large boats.

Sockets, also known as "spelter sockets," "hot-shot terminals," or "cones," are economical terminals that can be used with both galvanized and stainless wires. They are commonly used on construction cranes or elevators, and are very strong. Galvanized cones should

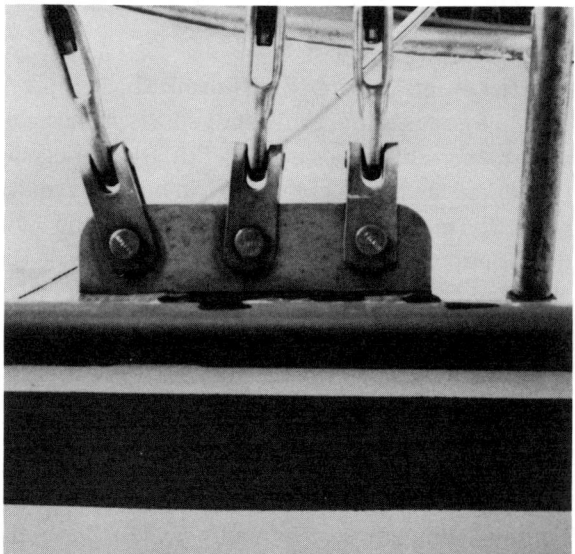

Fig. 20-15. *The stays on this boat come together at a single wide chainplate welded to the hull. The arrangement of the open-barrel turnbuckles and toggles makes this a simple but functional design.*

be used with galvanized wire, and stainless or bronze cones with stainless. The cones are available with either eye or fork ends, but those with eye ends are better, since the fork ends can be bent out of line. The cones can sometimes be difficult to locate, but a local foundry can easily fabricate them. Socket terminals are definitely one of the strongest ways to attach standing rigging, and metal fabricators would be wise to take on their manufacture.

The wire is held in the cone with either zinc or epoxy. The rigging wire is first seized with thin wire a short distance above its end. It is inserted into the cone and the strands are spread out to fit inside the cone with a pair of small needle-nosed pliers, and then are taped in place. When zinc is used, the cone should be cleaned with acetone or diluted muriatic acid and preheated slightly to ensure good adhesion. A torch is used to melt the zinc in a ladle, and the zinc is poured into the cone; soldering flux is sometimes added to help adhesion. Alternatively, two-part liquid epoxy adhesive may be poured into the cone. In this case, the socket cures rapidly and is ready for service minutes later. The epoxy can also be softened and removed by heating, so the socket can be reused. The epoxy method has slightly better corrosion resistance and is easier and safer to install than poured zinc, but zinc-filled sockets are very strong because of the metallurgical bond between the zinc and the wire. Both types of sockets, however, have high strength and resistance to shock and fatigue. Sockets are also easy to use when making rigging repairs at sea.

Stainless steel swage terminals are very common and have been used for a number of years. They are very neat-looking terminals with fork or eye ends. These terminals are very strong, but stainless swages on lower ends of rigging wire are often in contact with salt water and may develop crevice corrosion and cracking. But their main drawback is that they must be put on with an industrial swaging machine. The pressure of swaging can work-harden the stainless, and small hairline cracks can develop. There have also been cases reported in which the eye has pulled out of a swage terminal.

The standard terminals for today's stainless rigging wire are the mechanical ones, like the Norseman and the StaLock. Although expensive, these terminals are easily installed with a wrench, wire cutters, pliers, seizing twine, and possibly a hose clamp to hold the wire in place during installation. The terminal consists of a body and an end piece with either an eye or a fork end. A cone inside the body compresses the wire and holds it in place as the pieces of the terminal are screwed together. The correct amount of torque is needed when screwing the parts together, since the terminals have been known to explode if too tight. Beeswax or lanolin and tape should be used to seal the fitting. These terminals are machined out of stainless bar stock, and are

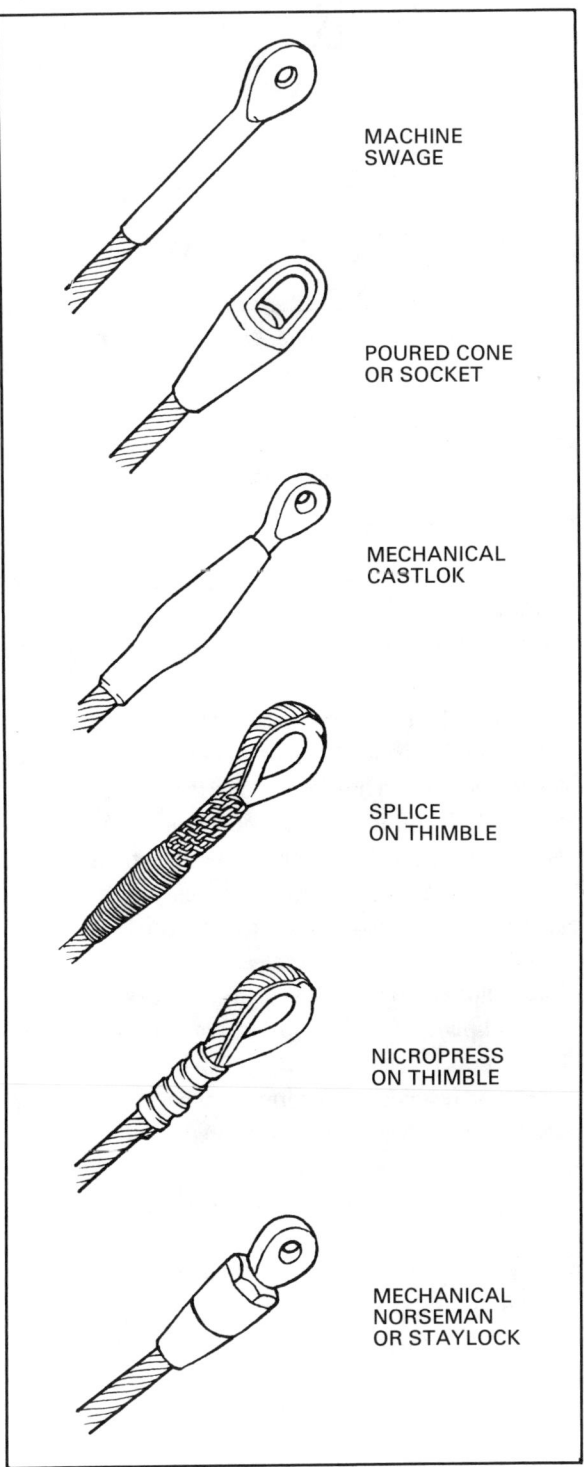

Fig. 20-16. *The various types of terminals that can be used on rigging wire.*

MACHINE SWAGE

POURED CONE OR SOCKET

MECHANICAL CASTLOK

SPLICE ON THIMBLE

NICROPRESS ON THIMBLE

MECHANICAL NORSEMAN OR STAYLOCK

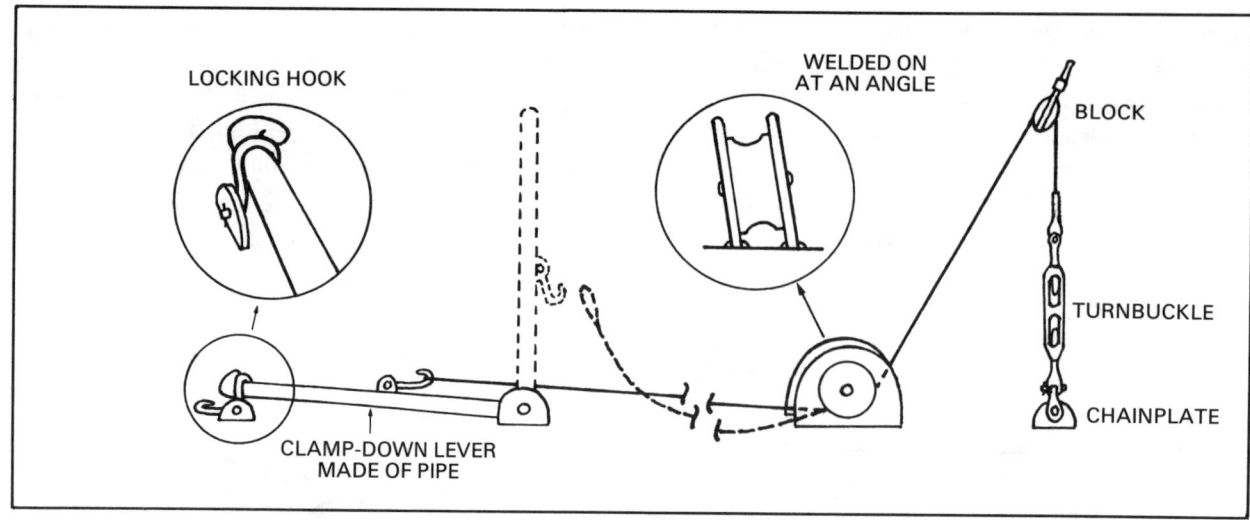

Fig. 20-17. *This running backstay lever can be easily released from the cockpit when the boat must be jibed. A 4-in-1 block purchase on a chainplate could also be led to a winch.*

very strong, but the cost of installing them on both ends of every wire will equal the cost of all the rigging wire you will use. They are handy for quick rigging repairs at sea.

Another type of mechanical terminal, the CastLok, uses an epoxy resin to form a plug that compresses the wire into place in the body of the terminal. It is installed with pliers and seizing twine.

On many boats, running backstays can be set up for extra security during heavy-weather sailing. Some people consider them a headache, since they must be quickly released if you have to jibe downwind, but they do offer extra support to big rigs under the stress of high winds. With the proper design, a quick-release system can be devised. A block and tackle can be led to a conveniently located winch, or release levers fabricated out of steel pipe can be clamped on a steel tab with a stainless steel pivot pin, as shown in Fig. 20-17. Commercially produced assemblies can also be used.

A backstay adjuster on permanent backstays is often used by racers to change tension on the rig, but it's not really needed on a cruising vessel.

On rigs with two headsails and therefore an inner and outer forestay, when a large genoa is being flown on the outer forestay, it is helpful to be able to remove the inner forestay and secure it farther back on deck so it doesnot interfere with the genoa when it is tacked. A special pelican hook is often used for this purpose, but there are many other designs for forestay-release mechanisms. You may need to search for a well-designed unit that doesn't also release a jungle of fittings that will clang around on the deck.

INSTALLATION AND REPAIR

Installing the spars and attaching terminals to the rigging are best done after the boat is launched. If the tidal range in your area is great, you may be able to raise the mast from a high dock at low tide. Otherwise, a crane will have to be used to set the mast in position.

Proper measuring is the key to cutting off the correct length of rigging wire. Although the lengths are commonly given in the boat plans, it's a good idea to double-check the measurements in place. Shrouds and stays are commonly attached to the mast fittings before the spar is stepped, and, if mechanical terminals, splices, or sockets are going to be used at the deck ends of the wire, the wire is left a little long. Then, after the mast is in

Fig. 20-18. *Now that this 30' sailboat has been launched with a crane, her spars will be installed.*
Courtesy of S.L. Petchul

Table 20-6.   REPAIR AND MAINTE-NANCE EQUIPMENT

Rigging tension-reading tool
Turnbuckle adjuster rod and wrench
Wire cutters
Nicropress tool
Cat eyes
File
Fid
Galvanized wire
Serving material
Marlinspike
Rigging knife
Bedding compound like neoperne
Rope and leather for anti-chafe
Steel brush for cleaning fittings
Spray galvanizing or cold zinc paint for
    temporary repairs
Spare rigging wire fitted with eyes
Shackles
Galvanized maintenance material:
    Friction tape
    Spring twine
    Seizing wire
    Three-way vise
    Bearclaw vise
    Nippers
    Waxed thread
    Twine
    Duct tape
    Matches and lighter
    Bolt cutter
    Galvanized terminals
Hole punch to take out old, rusted cotter pins

place, the wire can be cut off the proper length and the deck end terminals attached. If swaged terminals are used, the measurements must be exact beforehand.

Repairs at sea may include both cutting new lengths of wire and attaching terminals to wire. Table 20-6 lists the gear that should be carried for these purposes.

SOURCES

Foundries

New Found Metals
240 Airport Road
Port Townsend, WA 98368

Port Townsend Foundry
739 Lincoln St.
Port Townsend, WA 98368
(206) 385-6425

Rigging Wire

West Coast Wire Rope and Rigging, Inc.
7777 7th Ave. South
Seattle, WA 98108
    —galvanized wire

U.S. Rigging Supply
241 East Stevens St.
Santa Ana, CA 98707

Mcwhyte Company
2906 Fourteenth Ave.
Kenosha, WI
(414) 654-5381

Chapter 21

Sails and Running Rigging

A proper suit of sails sets apart the ocean sailing yacht from any other kind of boat. But a good selection of high-quality sails is the most expensive part of the boat, usually costing more than even the engine. In fact, some sailors chose not to buy an engine so that they don't have to skimp on sails.

Of course, the size and type of rig chosen for a sailboat not only affects its performance but also determines the number, size, and cost of the sails. The proper set and foil design varies with every type of sail, and each must be fitted with line and hardware. There are many variations in rigs and sails, so, for the sake of simplicity, we will focus here on the marconi rig, and only mention other rigs (like junk, lug, Freedom, gaff, wishbone, or staysail) when there is something particular to say about how they perform.

Although racing technology has led to many improvements in sail material and design, the new materials like Kevlar and Mylar are best suited to the demands and pocketbooks of ocean racers. Dacron or nylon are used for most sails today, while awnings are commonly of cotton canvas or acrylic fabrics.

RIG AND SAIL CHOICES

Tall sloop or cutter rigs with large sails are common today, and the racers who favor these rigs carry sails for every conceivable wind condition. However, the sails of a low-aspect-ratio cruising rig can be carried longer in a blow without reefing, if the sail cloth is of the correct weight. Low-aspect split rigs, like ketches and some yawls, require more sails than single-masted boats, but the individual sails are smaller and easier to handle. These additional sails also add versatility for contending with various weather conditions; it's nice to have the option of going jig and jigger (running under only the mizzen and working jib) in storms, or to raise a mizzen staysail in light airs.

A proper reefing system is also very important for safe, easy sail handling. Although some recent reefing developments like zip stops, roller masts, stowaway booms, furling mast stays, and internal reefing are attractive in theory, because a variety of adjustments can be made in sail area, in fact the fittings are complex, expensive, and have a high failure rate. You will often hear of someone with such a system having a sail stuck only halfway reefed; but to be fair, improvements in these systems are always in the works. Roller reefing is more common for headsails, since an elaborate set-up is required to use it on the main. However, the standard worm-gear roller boom works quite well as long as the boom is properly shaped. Mainsail reefing systems that use either a mast stay or the mast itself are becoming more popular, since a specially shaped boom is not necessary. No matter what reefing system is used, the mainsail should always be fitted with a set of conventional reef points for use in emergencies.

A jiffy reef or "slab" reef system makes more sense for the cruising sailboat, since it will not jam and is relatively easy to operate unless you have some physical infirmities. At its simplest, this system consists of two or three rows of reef points running across the sail. Although there are many variations on the actual reefing method, a line generally is tightly secured to cringles at the fore and aft ends of the sails and is pulled down through blocks to the boom; the forward cringle can also be snapped onto a hook on the gooseneck. Then the individual reefing lines, which run all the way across the sail, are secured under the foot of the sail; it is best to tie them around the sail, not around the boom. This method of reefing is definitely the most economical, since it doesn't rely on any complex fittings.

Fully battened sails like some Chinese junk and lug rigs (and variations on them) require many small lines for reefing, but both the reefing and general sail handling can be done without using expensive winches. This is definitely an advantage if you must keep down the cost of the deck hardware.

The designer outlines sail plans for a boat, but a good sailmaker may be able to improve on these by changing cloth weights, sail areas, and other particulars. However, the locations of working sails, the mast, and forestays should not be altered, since this would relocate the center of effort of the sails, in turn changing the lead and therefore the balance of the boat. However, preferences for battenless sails, a certain amount of roach, patch reinforcements, or the number and spacing of reef points can be specified to the sailmaker.

Proper design of individual sails is really the job of a good sailmaker. A sail with the proper foil shape drives the boat most efficiently, and the way that the sailcloth is joined together determines how well the sail will keep its shape and how stress upon it will be distributed. For example, the direction in which the panels run can be different for a mainsail or a headsail. Standard jibs with a low clew can have panels that are sewn horizontally (like the main) or vertically. Headsails with a high clew may have a mitred or "scotch-cut" panel arrangement. There are many technological advances being made in sail design which are beyond the scope of this book, but a sailmaker who specializes in cruising sails may have incorporated some of this new information into his or her sail designs.

The mast height and distance between other parts of the rig are used to determine the sail dimensions and sail area. The sail area and the required cloth weight will be used to bid on the job, with the cost of reef points and other handwork added in. The sailmaker will need to look at the plans and/or make measurements onboard.

Cruising sails have different requirements than racing sails. Longevity, ease of handling, and shape are the most important attributes of cruising sails, while racers

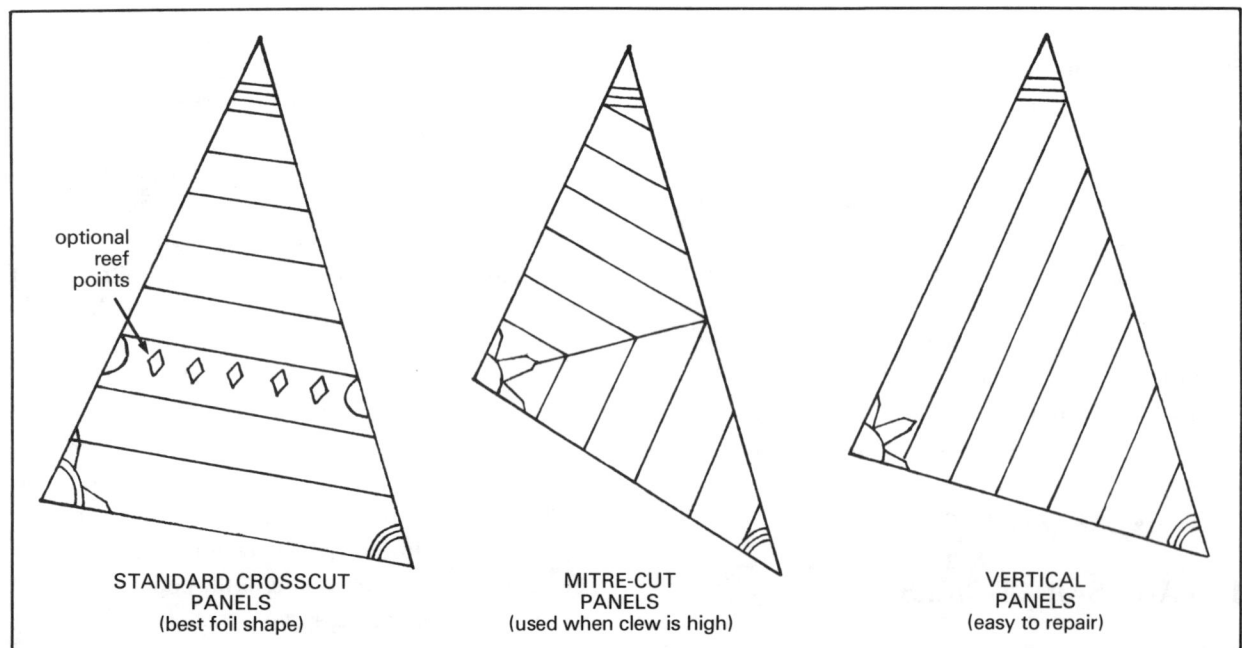

STANDARD CROSSCUT PANELS
(best foil shape)

MITRE-CUT PANELS
(used when clew is high)

VERTICAL PANELS
(easy to repair)

optional reef points

Fig. 21-1. *The headsail cut is chosen by the sailmaker to get the best set for that particular sail.*

may put up with enormous, awkward sails for the sake of speed. Luff curves, roaches, and the rounding of the foot can be much more conservative on cruising sails, which are usually made of heavy-weight Dacron with extra reinforcement at stress points. Three rows of zig-zag stitching is preferable for the seams, and extra hand-work in the right places goes a long way to extending the life of the sails. Rings at the head, clew, and tack of each sail, and at the reef points on mainsails, should be reinforced with hand sewing for extra durability. Leather sewn onto chafe points (for example, at hanks and slides) also prolongs the life of a sail.

Dacron, the standard material used today for working sails, is a cloth woven of synthetic polyester, which

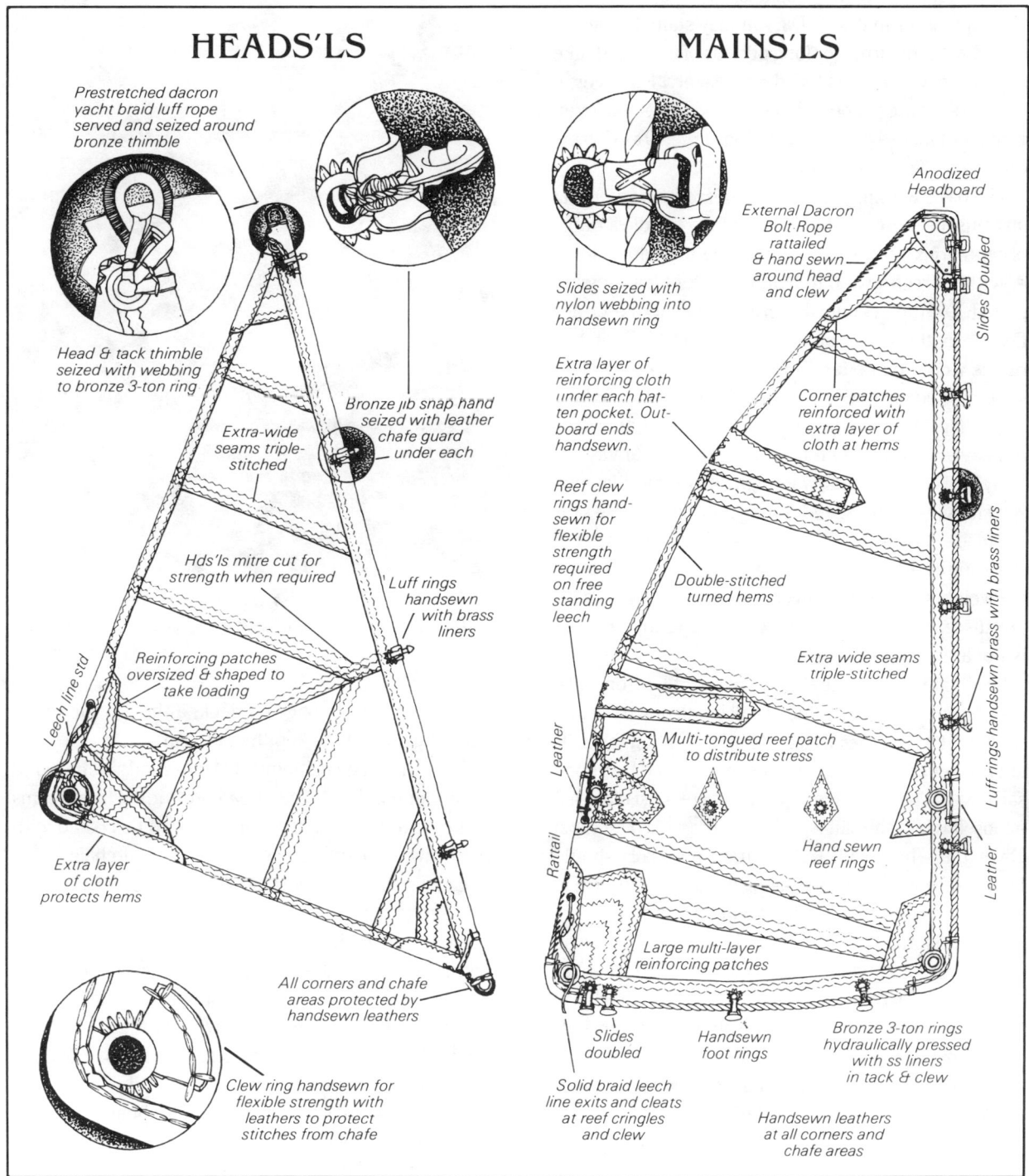

Fig. 21-2. *Good cruising sails require strong and careful hand work.*

Courtesy of Port Townsend Sails

does not have the problems of rot, excessive weight, or chafe that canvas or Egyptian cotton had. It holds its shape well without much stretching, maintaining the efficient foil shape of the sail as it was cut. Over a period of years, however, it can stretch slightly. Dacron is better than canvas or other fabrics because it is far stronger, easier to maintain, lighter, nonporous by nature, and doesn't get heavy when wet. It is also easier to handle than any other material. Dacron may stain if soiled or stored without airing for long periods of time, and, like any fabric, will tear if chafed excessively. However, if Dacron sails are properly handled and protected, even with constant use they will last a long time; 10 to 15 years of service life is not unusual.

The basic working sails (main, mizzen, and working jib) must be strong, yet light enough to handle a range of conditions. Strong cloth allows sails to be flown longer without reefing and to hold up better after they are reefed. For the average 40' cruising yacht, 6.5-ounce Dacron is the minimal weight, although 7.5- or 8.2-ounce would be better. The exact weight of the cloth should be determined by the specific sail area and how and where the sail will be used. Storm sails are made of heavier Dacron cloth or, sometimes, of canvas.

Nylon is used primarily for light-wind sails like mizzen staysails, drifters, and spinnakers. Since these sails are made of lightweight cloth (1.5–2.5 oz.), they are not as strong as the working suit, even though in comparable weights nylon is stronger than Dacron. Nylon sails are susceptible to chafe and tearing, and the material is not as stable as Dacron.

Sunlight is the number-one enemy of Dacron sails; the ultraviolet rays eventually will break down the fabric so that it becomes weak and brittle. When the sails are not being used, they should be protected by a good sail cover. The head, leech, and foot are most often left exposed when the sail is furled, so the sail cover must cover the whole sail. Roller-furled headsails should have protective strips sewn along the edges of the leech, which are exposed to sunlight when the sail is furled.

Proper storage of sails is also important. The most-often-used sails should be easily accessible but kept as dry as possible. Dacron should be rinsed with fresh water before it is stored, so that the abrasive salt crystals are removed, and nylon should never be packed away wet, since its dyes will bleed. Furling and folding sails neatly for storage also helps to lengthen their life. Lockers in the forepeak, cockpit, or lazarette can be designated for sail storage, and during a voyage some head-

Fig. 21-3. *The proper aspect ratio keeps this 35' cruiser from heeling excessively as she flies along.*
Courtesy of W.H. Schwarz

sails can be left in bags on deck, although the decks should generally be kept free of gear.

The number-two enemy of Dacron sails is chafe and improper handling. The thread protruding from seams is most prone to chafing; this area can be coated with protective compounds like Duroseam; anti-chafe patches can also be sewn over the seams. Baggywrinkles on the shrouds and rollers on the spreaders help to reduce chafe on the mainsail and mizzen when going downwind. Proper sail design can also reduce wear (for example, headsails should clear pulpits and lifelines). In light winds it is better to take down sails than to let them luff and slop around. The most important part of good sail maintenance is knowing how to sail properly.

A sail repair kit should be carried onboard and used at the first sign of damage to a sail. Table 21-1 lists the tools and parts that should be gathered into this kit.

Table 21-1.   TOOLS AND PARTS FOR SAIL REPAIR AND ROPE WORK

PARTS	TOOLS
Stainless steel or bronze slides (internal or external) for luff and foot	Portable sewing machine (Pfaff #130-6 recommended)
Webbing for sewing slides to the sail eyes	Sailmaker's needles (#12, 14, and 16, straight)
Plastic inserts and slide shackles (good for temporary use)	Grommet and die kit
Spur grommets for canvas work and sails	Sailmaker's palm
Washer grommets for flags and tarps	Beeswax
Eyelet grommets	Hand-sewing thread (3- and 7-ply Dacron)
Clevis pins and liners	Knee pads
Thimbles (round, oval, open, and closed)	Canvas pliers to help to remove stuck needles
Round rings	Rivet and die set
D-rings for jib clew	Hole cutter
Rivets for headboard plate	Canvas bucket
Sail headboard	Bosun's chair (canvas with flat board sewn in)
Bolt rope ($\frac{3}{8}$" 3-strand Dacron)	Sail repair tape
Reef lines ($\frac{3}{16}$" braided Dacron)	Polyester twine
Leech lines ($\frac{3}{16}$" braided Dacron)	Seine twine
Cunningham line ($\frac{3}{16}$" braided Dacron)	Tarred marlin
Sew-on hanks (hammer-on types are useful for emergencies	Small seizing wire
Spare Dacron for patches (1 yard per sail)	Teflon gel
Luff tape, 10 yards of 3", 4", and 5" (8 oz.)	Sail cleanser (non-detergent)
Webbing, ½" wide for slides, plus 1" and 2" for reinforcing	Guard tape
Leather, chrome-tanned or "pearl-split," 5 oz.	Pine tar and linseed oil
Battens (fiberglass or wood)	Ditty bag
Clips and eyelets	Hot iron or hot knife
Fasteners and snaps for canvas work	Rigger's knife with fid
Wire pennants	Revolving punch
Protective compounds (Duraseam, Seam Kote,)	Rigger's wire and rope fids
Grease for sail track (silicon paste, lub oil, clear grease)	Braider's fid
	Rawhide mallet
	Swivel bench hook
	Stich and pricker awls
	Scissors
	Thread clips
	OPTIONAL: automatic awl, automatic awl

ACQUIRING SAILS

There are basically four ways to get sails: 1) make your own; 2) buy them new from a professional sailmaker; 3) buy them new but do the handwork yourself; and 4) buy them secondhand.

You can make your own sails, but unless you have studied under a sailmaker, you may pay the cost in lowered performance and lifetime. If you do decide to make your sails, take a lot of time to study the design and to consult any sailmaking books that are available. (This is a good idea even if you don't plan to make sails, since you will undoubtedly have to do some repair work on them.)

Proper construction of sails requires not only a heavy-duty sewing machine with zig-zag stitching and a ditty bag full of parts and tools, but also a large floor space on which to lay the sail out. If you don't have much or any experience in sailmaking, practice on a set of sails for the dinghy first. Junk rig sails are the easiest for the amateur, since the foil shape and layout are simple.

You may be able to arrange things with the sailmaker so that she or he does the main layout, cutting, stitching and sewing, while you do all the time-consuming hand work like the grommets, bolt ropes, and reef points. This can save you up to 30% of the cost of a sail, and give you practice at repairing and maintaining it. However, don't expect the sailmaker to teach you how to do the handwork.

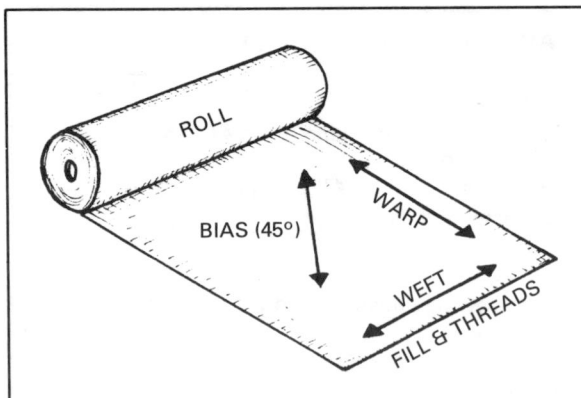

Fig. 21-4. *Sails are cut to take advantage of characteristics imparted to the cloth by the weaving process.*

Depending on the size and rig of the boat, the job of sailmaking may be best handled by an expert. Choose a sailmaker as you would choose any professional. Ask other sailors for recommendations, and see finished work. Then sit down and discuss things like the number and spacing of reef points, the size of the wire luff rope, the spacing between hanks, the various cuts, taping, tabling, leech lines, jack lines, and other specifications like stitching, cunninghams, cringles, and outhaul fittings. If you do not know what is required, let the sailmaker guide you. But always try to keep things as simple as possible.

You may be able to get a discount from a sailmaker if a number of sails are ordered at one time. It's a good idea to have all the main working sails made by one sailmaker so that the sails that must work together will be consistent in material and performance characteristics. The light-wind or storm sails could be made by a specialist or another sailmaker at a later date.

The inexpensive sails available from some foreign sources (for example, Taiwan and Hong Kong) aren't always of high (as advertised) caliber, and poor-grade materials are often used to achieve the low price. You don't often know what you will get until it arrives, and then it's too late. However, many sailors have found good buys on imported sails, especially from Hong Kong. If you are considering buying mail-order sails, check with people who have already dealt with a given company.

Sails are also available from secondhand discount warehouses. Be careful to choose sails that are the correct shape and size. If anything, they should be a little larger than necessary, since it is easier to cut away material than to add it. Some of these outfits are quite reputable and allow you to return sails that weren't quite right, as long as you're willing to pay for the shipping.

Good deals on secondhand sails can also be found by watching marina bulletin boards. Sometimes you'll find a desperate sailor who is willing to part with sails for a very reasonable price.

Fig. 21-5. *The sails on this Colvin Gazelle offer an unusual sight to the onlookers perched on the bowsprit of another steel boat.*

Fig. 21-6. *The* Calliope 339 *moves right along with her sloop rig, which is the simplest to equip and handle.*

Courtesy of Croft Marine

THE SUIT OF SAILS

Day sailors can get by with a main and a jib (plus a mizzen on split rigs), but sails for a variety of conditions must be carried to run a cruising yacht efficiently. The number is really limited only by your pocketbook and the storage space aboard.

The primary sail on any boat is the mainsail. On a 40′ world-cruising sailboat, 8- or even 9-oz. cloth with strong patches and tabling should be used. At least two sets of reef points, which will reduce the sail area to 50%, are best. Battens can be used to keep the leech flat, or a specially cut roachless sail can be designed. (Roachless sails are easier to maintain, but the leech has a tendency to curl, hurting performance to windward.) Battens can be made from wood, plastic, or nylon, and spares can be carried without taking up much space. Most of the battens at the top of the sail should be parallel to the seams, but the bottom batten should be parallel to the boom so that it doesn't interfere with reefing. Bat-

ten pockets tend to be the first area of a sail to wear out, but with care and proper construction they should last fairly well. A chafe patch sewn between the pocket and the sail and proper reinforcement at the ends of the pockets will also increase their lifetimes.

The next basic sail is the inner working jib (fore staysail), and it can be either free-footed or self-tending with a club boom and pedestal. The small club boom is not as hazardous as a conventional large boom, but the crew should still pay attention to its position when they are working the foredeck. Only the clew needs to be fastened to the boom to make the sail self-tending, so the foot can be left free to maintain a good foil shape. Using a club boom-and-pedestal arrangement helps to keep the sail tack and the turnbuckle on the stay from being twisted around and overworked, as can happen when the sail is secured to the forestay. Some new jib designs also have a "boom batten" sewn into the sail, but this arrangement can prevent the sail from acquiring a good, curved foil shape.

329

The outer working jib is generally a 110 to 130% foretriangle, rigged without a boom, and cut to different shapes and sizes. Lighter-weight cloth can be used for the outer jib than for the inner, because it is used mostly in moderate conditions. The smaller flying or yankee-style jib set high on the forestay is not very efficient, since there is not enough sail area relative to the main

to drive the boat along. However, it is easier to handle when tacking than a larger jib, since it will stay clear of the inner forestay.

The last of the working sails, at least for a split rig, is the mizzen. It should be about the same weight as the main and staysail, but cut a little flatter, so that it is less prone to luffing. If the mizzen is made of sufficiently

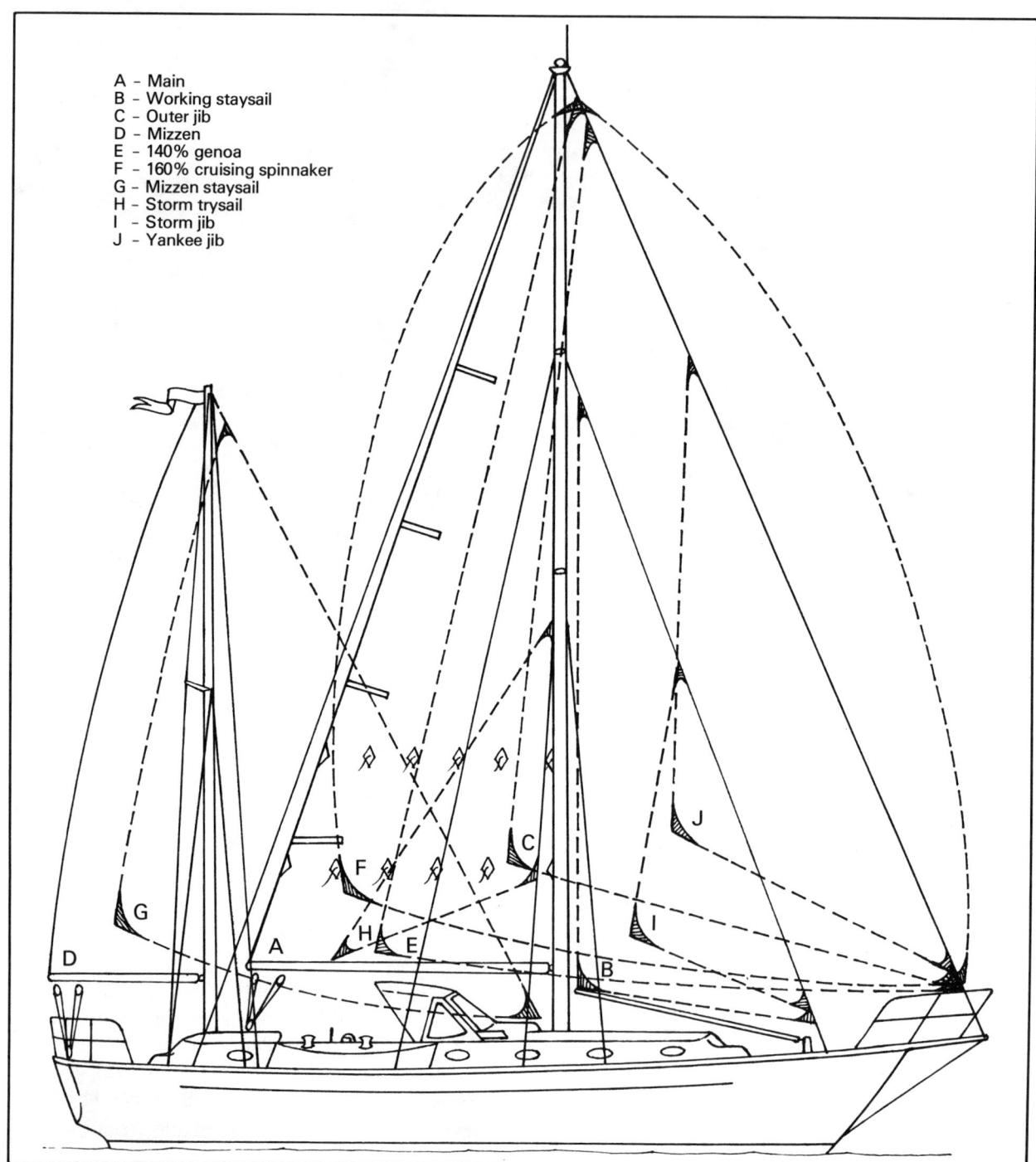

A – Main
B – Working staysail
C – Outer jib
D – Mizzen
E – 140% genoa
F – 160% cruising spinnaker
G – Mizzen staysail
H – Storm trysail
I – Storm jib
J – Yankee jib

Fig. 21-7. *The full inventory of sails carried onboard a performance ketch.*

heavy cloth, it (and the working jib) can be fitted with a single row of reef points so that the two sails can be used in high winds for equal jib and jigger sets.

Sails in addition to the working suit are very useful for improving performance in light or heavy wind conditions, though they will require an extra investment in lines and blocks for handling, as well as additional whiskerpoles and running poles. They're worth it though, because you don't want to be becalmed for days on end or lose maneuverability in stormy seas. These sails can be added to the inventory over a period of time, as your pocketbook allows. Extra sails do require extra storage room, but this should not be much of a problem on a cruising boat.

A genoa is probably the most common light-wind sail, since it can also be used in moderate conditions. It is especially good when reaching, which is common in trade-winds sailing. A 120% genoa gives good driving force and can be used in a wide range of wind conditions, including the 10–20 knots common in the trades. This sail should be made of fairly heavy cloth (6.5–7.5 oz.), so that you can leave it up as long as possible. If the foot of the genoa is too low, it may obstruct visibility from the helm, chafe on the pulpits, and scoop up water.

A drifter or reacher is usually a 165–180% foretriangle sail used in very light winds. These sails, which are good downwind, can also be used on reaches. However, a good cruising spinnaker, which is smaller and easier to handle than racing designs, would be a better choice for dead downwind sailing in light winds. A 160% spinnaker of 1.5-oz. nylon can be secured to the bow and handled without a pole; a "snuffer" is handy for furling these large sails. A cruising spinnaker can also be used in place of twin headsails.

When sailing downwind, many people consider using a twin staysail rig so that two similar sails can be flown from the bow and adjusted for self-steering. But proper placement of double forestays is necessary, as is extra equipment to rig them. Although you could use two sails interhanked on the same forestay, handling and chafing problems will probably arise. If the wind changes directions, some fast and furious work on the foredeck may be necessary to change the sails. A cruising spinnaker is more efficient, has more power in light winds, and is less prone to chafing and handling problems. A twin headsail arrangement can, however, be left up longer in higher winds, because the sails are generally made of heavier-weight cloth than a spinnaker. Some

sailors decide between the two arrangements on the basis of past experience, and there are proponents of both.

On a ketch or yawl, a mizzen staysail made of lightweight nylon is especially useful for beam reaches in light winds. Mizzen spinnakers are also available, but not often used.

On schooner and gaff rigs, many other sails are flown. On some schooners you'll see a big fisherman between the masts, or even a larger gollywobbler. Upper topsails are used on gaff rigs, as are squaresails, mules, and giant drifters. This list of miscellaneous sails is almost endless, considering the different combinations of weights and shapes.

Storm sails are a must for heavy-weather sailing, and chances are good you'll run into a storm. A properly shaped, loose-footed trysail, set on a separate mast track with a switch to the mainsail track, is ideal. The best size is between 25 and 30% of the area of the mainsail, so that after dropping a main that has been reefed to 50%, the heavier storm main will reduce the sail area even further. Storm sails should be made of 9–12-oz. Dacron, depending on the size of the boat, and battens are best omitted. Nowadays cotton canvas of equivalent fabric weight is generally found only in storm sails. The sail will be stronger if it is roped all around, but since the leech will curl when roped, it is usually left free. Reinforcement patches, tabling, and rope should all be quite heavy. A properly designed storm main will enable the boat to keep headway and perform to weather even in

Fig. 21-8. *A split rig like a schooner gives the skipper the option of setting a variety of staysails.*

Fig. 21-9.   *The* Bay Lady II, *built from a design by Wallstrom, Watkins, and Assoc., displays her schooner rig off the coast of Downeast Maine.*

Photo by Arthur B. Layton, courtesy of the designer

high winds. (The boom is often lashed down when a trysail is used, so that there is less chance of damage if heavy seas crash aboard.)

A storm jib is also an important sail, and should be made of the same weight cloth as the storm main. You should be able to set it on either the mizzen or the fore-stay. The clew should not have any shackles, which might injure a crew member working on the foredeck in heavy weather. Sheets or lines can be tied directly to the clew with a bowline knot and led through deck fair-leads to winches or cleats.

FABRICS FOR OTHER ONBOARD USES

Various other fabrics besides Dacron or nylon sail cloth help to make life aboard more enjoyable. Although cotton canvas isn't practical for sails anymore, it has many other uses. Awnings, dodgers, and sail covers of water-resistant, treated canvas (Vivatex is one brand) are fairly common, although in some cases other materials like acrylic, Sunbrella, and nylon will last longer, be lighter, and be easier to store.

Table 21-2. FABRICS FOR SAILS, COVERS, AND AWNINGS

		Price/yard
HEMP	Traditional sail material. Swells and gets heavy when wet. Egyptian hemp resists tears, but still deteriorates. Needs preservatives	$2–3
POLYETHYLENE TARP	Reinforced nylon. Least expensive, but will break down in sunlight. Okay for temporary covers.	$2–4
COTTON CANVAS	Nice to handle. Cheaper than acrylic but won't last as long. Shrinks. Even if treated may eventually rot in sunlight. Vivatex (treated cotton canvas) makes good sail covers and is useful for interior bunk covers.	$5
CANVAS DUCK	Shrinks. Sweats on bunks. Best when treated to resist deterioration	$3–4
DACRON POLYESTER (Terylene)	Doesn't stretch. Stronger than acrylic but eventually weakens in sun. White best for awnings. Best used in interiors.	$4–5
DACRON	Water-repellant. Fades in sun. Used for small ditty bags, duffle bags, bosun's chairs.	$5
SAIL DACRON	Heavier weave. Besides sails, also good for water collectors and covers.	$5–19
RIPSTOP NYLON	Best used in interiors, since it stains, stretches, and reacts to ultraviolet rays.	$8–11
ACRYLIC	Acrilan and Argonaut are common brands. Very resistant to ultraviolet rays. Stable. Easy to work with. Wide range of colors that don't fade. Water-repellant. Breathes. Doesn't stretch. One of the most appropriate awning materials.	$7–10
VINYL-COATED POLYESTER	Commonly called "truck tarp." Strong and durable. Commonly UV-treated. Good awning material. More expensive than acrylic.	$9–10
POLYESTER-REINFORCED VINYL	Stable; holds up in sunlight. Easier to clean than acrylic. Harder to fit because it shrinks and stretches. Does not breathe, so don't create moisture trap with tight-fitting cover.	$9–10
VINYL	Flotilla and Naugahyde are popular brands. Usually backed with cotton or polyester. Commonly used for cushion covers, but bare skin sticks to it. Clear vinyl used in sheet form for awning windows.	$11–12

Canvas can be treated to prevent rotting with a mixture of raw linseed oil thinned with turpentine or Japan drier. Either this solution is brushed on or the canvas is dipped in a hot tank of the solution. Although better results are obtained when the canvas is soaked in a hot bath, the solution must not be too hot or the fabric's natural fibers will be weakened.

Many fabric accessories can be made by hand, but a good zig-zig sewing machine makes the job a lot easier. The sewing kit should include various items to complement the fabrics, including: zippers, clips, turnbuttons, snaps, Velcro, and glues. Close-celled foam for cushions and back rests should also be included. A good waterproofing treatment kit with linseed oil, paraffin, bitumen, or metallic soap (aluminum stearate) is good for canvas and cotton. A rot-proofing solution could contain cod oil, red okra, cuprinol, cupramonium, or wax (Mesowax).

Table 21-3. USES FOR FABRIC ONBOARD A CRUISING BOAT

- ► Awnings for shading deck and cockpit
- ► Dodgers to keep spray out of cockpit
- ► Hoods to keep water off deck equipment
- ► Spray shields for companionway
- ► Spray shields mounted on stanchions
- ► Wind scoops on hatch to improve ventilation
- ► Rainwater catchers
- ► Water buckets
- ► Bosun's chair
- ► Winter storage covers
- ► Interior storage bags
- ► Cushion covers

RUNNING RIGGING

Running rigging includes all the lines (halyards and sheets), blocks, shackles, and deck fittings (like winches, fairleads, and travelers) that are used in sail handling. The deck fittings can often be welded to the deck, but some pieces, like fairleads, are better bolted on so that they can be relocated to improve sail handling.

Strength, weight, elasticity (or lack of it), and ease of handling are the primary concerns when choosing line. How well a line will resist kinking, abrasion, dirt, chemicals, and water determines its durability. With the advent of the hardy, light synthetic materials, yesterday's rot-prone, scratchy manila and hemp lines have become obsolete. Today's working line should also coil easily, resist buckling, hold up to sunlight, and knot and splice well.

Various types of synthetic fibers are available, but Dacron (polyester), nylon, polypropylene, and special combinations of polyethylene fibers are most often used for ship's line. The properties of a line depend on the length of the fibers, how the strands are formed, and the thickness of both the strands and fibers. In general, Dacron line is quite strong and abrasion resistant, and it does not stretch much. Therefore, it is best for sheets and halyards, where stretch must be kept to a minimum. Nylon is a bit stronger than Dacron, but it stretches and loses some strength when wet, so it is most useful for anchor and mooring lines, where some shock resistance and flex are desired. It is also lighter than Dacron. Polypropylene, lighter and weaker than nylon and Dacron, is most subject to UV deterioration and can chafe your hands. But it floats, so it is good for dinghy painters and tow lines, although the floating line may be a hazard, since it can be hard to see.

Keep in mind that the strength of lines of the same size and type varies among manufacturers because different numbers of strands and types of lay are used in the manufacturing process. The strongest line is constructed with a continuous filament; spun-filament line, though not as strong, is easier to hold onto, being less slippery. A soft rope is strongest and easiest to splice, but a firm rope will wear best. Ropes made of blends of different fibers generally are not as strong as those made

Table 21-4. AVERAGE BREAKING STRENGTH OF FIBER CORDAGE (in pounds)

SIZE	LAID 3-STRAND		BRAIDED		
	Nylon	Dacron	Nylon	Dacron	Polypropylene
3/16"	1,000	1,000	1,200	900	750
1/4"	1,700	1,650	2,100	1,700	1,200
5/16"	2,600	2,500	3,500	2,600	1,800
3/8"	3,600	3,600	4,200	3,600	2,500
7/16"	5,000	4,800	6,000	5,200	3,300
1/2"	6,600	6,100	7,500	6,800	4,000
9/16"	8,400	7,600	9,000	8,200	4,800
5/8"	10,300	9,500	11,000	10,000	5,800
3/4"	14,000	12,500	17,000	16,000	7,800
7/8"	18,500	17,000	23,500	21,000	11,000
1"	24,000	21,000	28,500	28,000	13,000

Note: Strengths can vary as much as 30% among different manufacturers. The average strengths listed above are based on a survey of various manufacturers, not particular brands.

of only one material. It's wise to stick to the quality name brands like Samson, Yale, and New England Rope.

Laid three-strand and braided construction are the two principal ways in which modern rope is manufactured. Laid-strand line is usually cheapest and easiest to splice, while braided line resists abrasion best and lies down without buckles. Stranded line is best used for anchoring, mooring, and pennants, while sheets, hal-

yards, and other running rigging are best made of braided line, especially on large boats. Small-diameter braided line also works well for reef lines and ties, while stranded line is preferable when medium- to large-diameter line is required. Both types have about the same strength, can be handled fairly well, and last a long time, but braided line generally costs more.

Racers often use wire rope for halyards because it doesn't stretch and therefore the sail can be set tauter. However, wire halyards can chafe the mast, bind in winches, kink, and clank around in the wind. Dacron line is usually spliced into the lower part of the halyard to make it easier to haul on the halyard. Although Dacron line stretches and increases windage aloft because it is thicker than wire rope, Dacron halyards can be successfully used on cruising yachts. They are easier to handle than wire rope and won't chafe the mast; self-tailing winches can be used with them. The halyard can be tightened up after the sail is raised.

When planning to purchase line, it is wise to use as much of the same size and type as possible so that you can buy 600' reels or spools. This saves money, since price breaks are given only on full reels.

FITTINGS FOR RUNNING RIGGING

In order to use the sheets and halyards, deck and rigging hardware must either be attached to spar fittings or mounted on deck, either welded integrally or bolted down. These fittings can include various fairleads, turning blocks, shackles, thimbles, swivels, snap hooks,

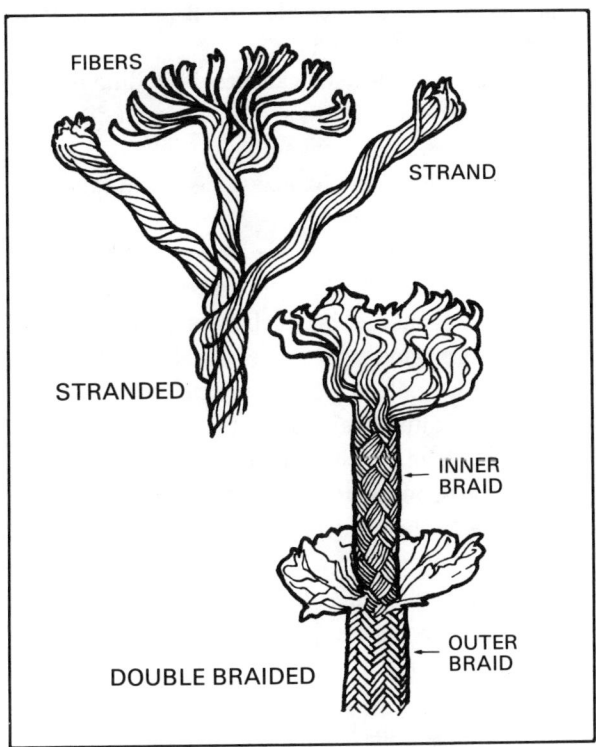

Fig. 21-10. *The two types of line available for running rigging.*

Table 21-5.	USES FOR LINE ONBOARD A CRUISING BOAT
RUNNING RIGGING	Sheets, halyards, downhauls, topping lifts, outhauls, vangs, reef points and slab reefing, ties, cunninghams, sail bolt ropes. Mostly braided Dacron, although some small three-strand Dacron or nylon can be used. Basic requirements are lack of stretch, good strength, and easy handling.
WORKING LINE	Anchoring, docking, towing, rescue work, dinghy, emergencies, safety harnesses, gale lines, water skiing. Basic requirements are strength, flexibility, and stretch. For tow lines, secondary requirement is ability to float so that line doesn't get caught in propeller. In most cases, this large line would be stranded nylon, although polypropylene is used for floating lines.
MISCELLANEOUS	Swimming, extra ties, lazy jacks, pennants, spare line, dinghy lashings, stanchion lines, ratlins. Basic requirements are general strength and workability. Small-size braided nylon or medium-size stranded Dacron are used.
SMALL CORDAGE	Handy for seizing and decorative rope work. If accessible, good-quality marlin is excellent for ratlins, turk's heads, and other knotting projects. Small nylon seizing or seine twine should always be carried.

sheet travelers, boom gallows, vang tackles, jam cleats, winches, and belaying cleats. As with other boat systems, the fitting must be of the right design and size so that it is strong enough to do its job. Small parts (like pins, bearings, and sheaves) must have strength characteristics similar to those of the fittings.

As we mentioned in Chapter 9, deck gear can be fabricated of galvanized steel, bronze, stainless steel, aluminum, or a high-strength plastic. Although corrosion above the decks is not a great problem, good insulation practices should still be carried out: any dissimilar metals must be properly isolated from the steel with insulator pads, mounting sleeves, and bedding. Metal items (like blocks and shackles) that are secured to spar fittings should be made of the same material as the fitting or be close on the galvanic series. On wood spars with bronze spar fittings, bronze or stainless fittings for the running rigging should be used. However, galvanized shackles can be used with galvanized tangs. Aluminum spars with stainless or aluminum tangs and fittings are best combined with stainless shackles or blocks with stainless eyes or beckets. The shackles, thimbles, and swivels used on blocks should also be of material similar to that in the eye or becket of the block.

There are many types of blocks which are mounted as turning blocks on deck or on spar fittings. They include single, double, swivel, becket, snatch, and various combinations thereof. Using the proper type and size of block for each line helps to extend the life of the hal-

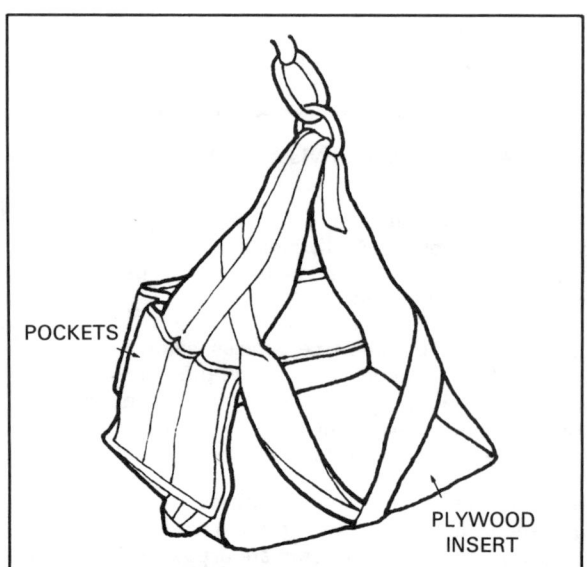

POCKETS

PLYWOOD
INSERT

Fig. 21-11. *A bosun's chair is the safest way to go aloft to check or repair rigging. A deluxe version can be sewn up out of strong webbing and canvas, with a piece of plywood inserted into the seat to stiffen it.*

yards and sheets. Deck fairlead blocks can be shackled directly to integral stainless steel eyes, screwed into hardwood or laminated wooden mounts, or bolted to the deck over bedding compound. Proper location and arrangement is important for correct sail set, to prevent the crew from tripping, and to allow the boat to be singlehanded. Although aluminum and high-tensile plastic blocks are often used, custom-made wood blocks are a nice touch that can be made at a substantial cost savings by a skilled fabricator.

Halyard and fairlead blocks on self-tending rigs can be mounted on a stainless eye or tab protruding from the mast collar. Additional multiple-lead blocks can also be bolted down to organize a clean run to a cockpit winch.

Various cleats will be needed to secure sheets, halyards, vangs, topping lifts, and the rest of the running rigging. This is one area in which marine technology has come up with some nice innovations. Now, along with the traditional belaying cleat, jam cleats, roller cams, and stopper cams are also available. The cleats are usually bolted in place, since their positions may need to be changed as the sail handling is tested.

Other deck fittings can be fastened to steel or stainless steel tabs, flanges, or mounts. Some can be welded directly to the deck, while others, especially those made of cast stainless or aluminum, are best mechanically bolted down with the proper insulating gasket. Some of these fittings (for example, bollards) can be fabricated out of galvanized steel (see Chapter 9), and bronze can be used for freestanding items like blocks and shackles or for winches that are bolted to insulated mounts.

A stainless steel or steel belaying pin rail with wood or stainless pins can be welded or mechanically mounted near the mast. It is quite handy and increases safety when the crew is handling lines. In some cases, a gooseneck similar to a mastband will incorporate the belaying pins.

Sheet travelers may or may not be required, but they are commonly used to allow extra adjustments to the set of the sails. The staysail sheet traveler should be located just forward of the main mast, with two fairlead blocks on either side leading the sheets to the cockpit. This is a simple, clean handling arrangement. Likewise, the main and mizzen travelers should be mounted in the appropriate locations. Traveler designs vary greatly, as Fig. 21-12 indicates. Many of the travelers shown here can easily be made by the home builder, using stainless tubing or galvanized steel pipe bent to shape and welded to the hull.

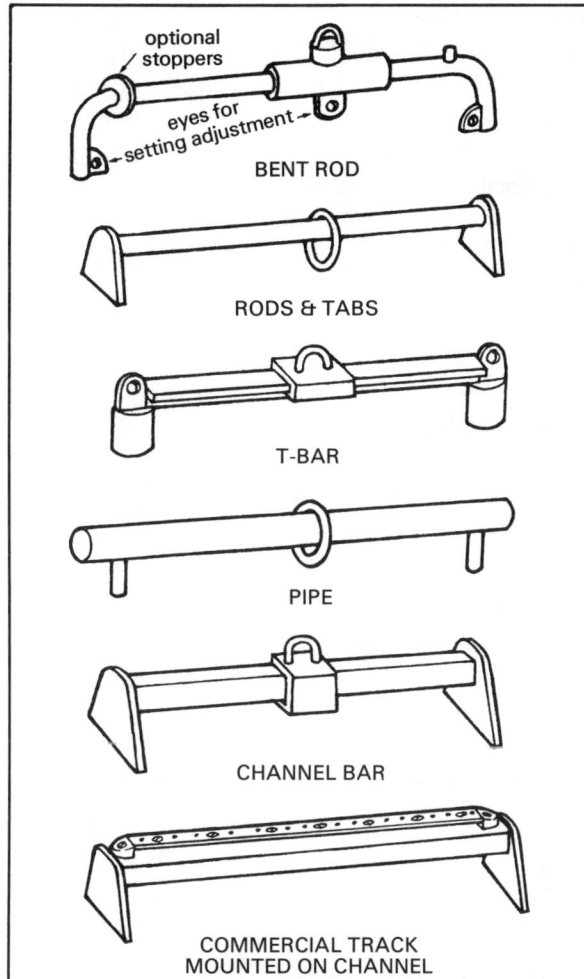

Fig. 21-12. *Travelers for the main and mizzen can be purchased or fabricated from plain steel or stainless. Moving parts should be made of stainless no matter what other materials are used.*

More sophisticated and expensive stainless production tracks may be used instead of travelers. They are usually bolted to a steel flange or the deck with machine screws, with proper bedding or gaskets underneath the track. Genoa sheet tracks are best made of aluminum or stainless steel and bolted to the deck or rail. The track, car, swivels, and block (single- or twin-sheet lead) must be of sufficient size and strength to withstand the pull of the genoa sheets.

A good back-up supply of blocks, shackles, jam cleats, and cotter pins for emergency and auxiliary uses is important to have onboard. Snap hooks and various tackle for vangs and emergencies should also be required equipment.

Winches are the workhorses that are constantly used to adjust sheets and halyards. Since their cost increases dramatically with their size, in choosing which to pur-

chase it's important to study the specifications of the various brand names (such as Lewmar, Barlow, Gib, Barient, and Merriman) and to match them with the size of the line and the area of each sail. Low-aspect-ratio rigs with small sails often can be hauled by hand or with the aid of a handy billy block and tackle. However, winches make the job so much easier that they really are worth the expense. They can be used in many operations besides sail handling, such as installing rudders, kedging off, adjusting backstays, anchoring, and also in emergencies. Of course, some rigs, like lug and junk, don't need winches for sail handling, although some lug variations commonly use winches.

Fig. 21-13. *The pipe and doubler plate assembly that supports this winch is only one of the many ways of fabricating a winch mount.*

The required number and size of winches depends on the number and size of the sails as well as the size of the vessel; winch manufacturers supply reference tables and graphs to help you decide on the appropriate model. Mainsail, halyard, and sheet winches are most common; the self-tailing types are useful. Powerful, two-speed, self-tailing winches are especially handy for larger sails like the genoa. Winches can be fabricated, but it's not an easy job.

Winches must be mounted and cared for properly. Welded tables or metal stands can be used underneath large winches, or they can be attached to studs welded on deck. On a mast, hardwood mounting pads under the halyard winches are common. As always, proper

gasket material must be used between dissimilar metals.
Winches should be cleaned and lubricated as necessary.
A good winch handle is also required.

For securing the main and mizzen, a boom gallows
(boom crutch) is a useful item that can be made of combinations of wood and steel, stainless, bronze, or
aluminum. There are many ways to design and build
the boom gallows, as shown in Fig. 21-14. The boom gallows can also be used to suport a cockpit awning or to
secure lines, and it can even be designed to double as
a traveler.

SOURCES FOR SAILS

Cruising Sails

Thomas Clark & Co., Inc.
37 Pratt St.
Essex, CT 06426

Port Townsend Sails
315 Jackson St.
Port Townsend, WA 98368

Franz Schattauer
6010 Seaview Ave. N.W.
Seattle, WA

Nathaniel Wilson
P.O. Box 71, Lincoln St.
East Boothbay, ME 04544

Secondhand Sails

Bacon and Associates
528 Second St.
P.O. Box 3150
Annapolis, MD 21403

Fabric Manufacturers

Howe and Bainbridge
220 Commercial St.
Boston, MA 02109
or
14970 N.E. 31st Circle
Redmond, WA 98052

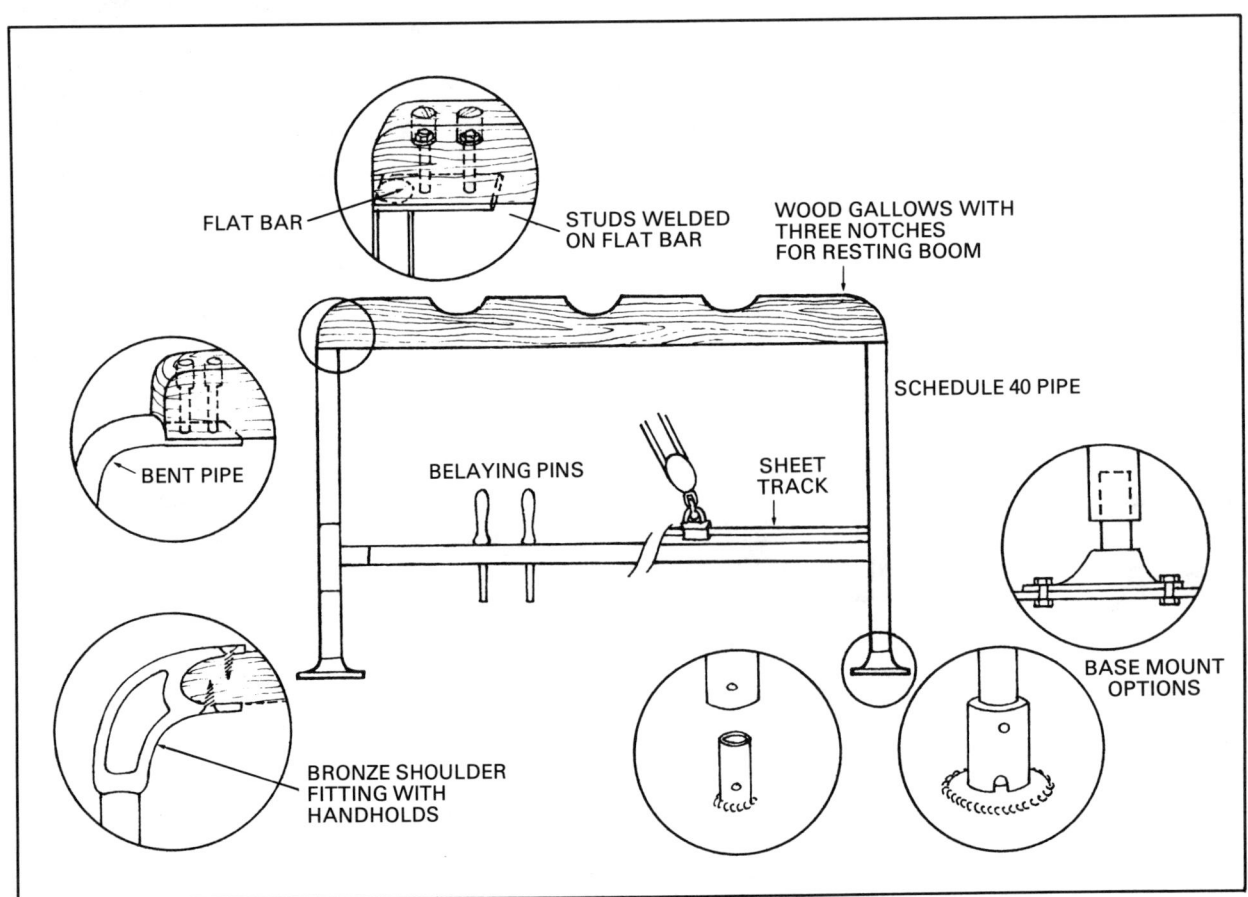

Fig. 21-14. *A boom gallows can be as simple or complex as the owner desires. Several different options are shown here for mounting removable legs and for attaching the wood gallows to the legs.*

Fig. 21-15.   *The pilothouse acts as a boom gallows on the 64' cutter* Ruby. *Note also the hefty steel railing.*

Courtesy of Coast Marine

339

—Chapter 22———————

Safety at Sea

Most accidents happen at home. And when your home is on the sea, a "minor mishap" can take on disastrous proportions. A steel boat itself is basically very safe, but certain precautions are needed to keep the crew out of harm's way.

Safety equipment should always be on standby and ready to use, either secured to the boat or welded integrally with the hull. The choice of exactly what you take along is governed partly by Coast Guard regulations and partly by personal preference and past experience, but common sense will usually prevail.

GENERAL SAFETY EQUIPMENT

"Man overboard" is the last thing that anyone wants to hear; it's the beginning of what could be the ultimate disaster for a member of the crew. Sturdy pulpits, stanchions, and life lines are perhaps the most important pieces of safety equipment, since they allow the crew to carry out necessary work without worrying about staying onboard. These safety features are even more important if there are children along on the cruise.

A stanchion is only as sturdy as its mount, and most of the stainless steel production stanchions and pulpits, which are designed to be through-bolted to a wood or fiberglass deck, wobble once they're mounted. But if you fabricate your own stanchions, you can design them so that the stanchion or mount is welded directly to the steel deck. This also does away with the leaks to which through-bolted stanchions are susceptible.

Whether it's the stanchion or mount that is welded to the deck depends on the mount design and which material you choose for the stanchions. Both steel and stainless steel can be used successfully, depending on the qualities you desire from the stanchion. Steel stanchions are inexpensive and can be repaired in place, so they are usually welded integrally; they are commonly fabricated of pipe, and are very stiff. Stainless stanchions, on the other hand, are stronger and more resistant to chafe than steel, but they must be removed in order to be repaired easily; they are usually designed with separate mounts that are welded to the deck.

Stanchions are generally fabricated of tubing or pipe whose outer diameter varies between $\frac{7}{8}$–$1\frac{1}{4}$", and are placed between 4' and 6' apart. Integral mounts can be designed with studs, rods, or sockets where the base of the stanchion is inserted into the mount. For added stiffness, the mount can be braced to the steel bulwarks or to the tabs welded on for attaching the wood bulwarks or rail (see illustration in Chapter 15).

The stanchions themselves should be designed to minimize any chance of corrosion. The top of the tubing or pipe should be welded shut so that water cannot get inside where it will be trapped at the base and cause corrosion. The eyes for life lines can be welded to the outside of the stanchion, or stainless sleeves can instead be inserted through the tubing and welded in place. When galvanized pipe is used for stanchions, adding stainless eyes or sleeves will help to control the chafe that can cause corrosion.

A minimum of two life lines (in some cases, these "lines" are actually pipe) at two different heights should run by or through each stanchion. The top line must be low enough so that it can be climbed over when necessary, but high enough so that it can effectively contain flying people or objects. Many production stanchions run the highest line between 26" and 28" above the deck, which hits most people mid-thigh or lower, with the bulk of their weight above the line. A line designed to reach to the hip (about 32" high) is safer. If children are onboard, netting can be laced between the life lines to keep them from slipping under the lowest one, and this netting will also keep doused headsails and other objects from sliding overboard.

The life lines themselves must be strong enough to withstand a heavy weight being hurled at them. Plastic-coated ⅛" or ³⁄₁₆" 7/7 stainless wire is commonly used,

with nicropress or swage terminals at the wire ends. However, instead of this small-diameter wire, which can develop stress cracks from chafing and can be hard on the hands, three-strand Dacron line can be stretched tightly through the stanchions. This soft, large-diameter line is easy to handle, and will not cause injuries if someone is thrown against the life lines. The Dacron line can be easily spliced, and a turnbuckle or rolling hitch at the ends can be used to adjust the tension. Of course, you will have to watch knives and sharp objects around the lines, but any fraying of the line due to chafe should be fairly obvious. No matter what the material, the lines or wires should be fitted with pelican hooks at the gate.

The major difference between pulpits and stanchions is that pulpits are bent to the shape of the bow (or stern) of the boat. Pulpits and the pushpits installed at the stern are usually made of stainless steel tubing or pipe, because chafe is prevalent in these areas. The ease with which the pulpit can be bent depends on the material; thin-walled tubing is harder to bend than pipe because it tends to buckle. Cold bending with a manual or hydraulic scroll or pipe bender is usually successful, although sometimes the stainless tubing must be heated to create a fair curve. A home fabricator can also make

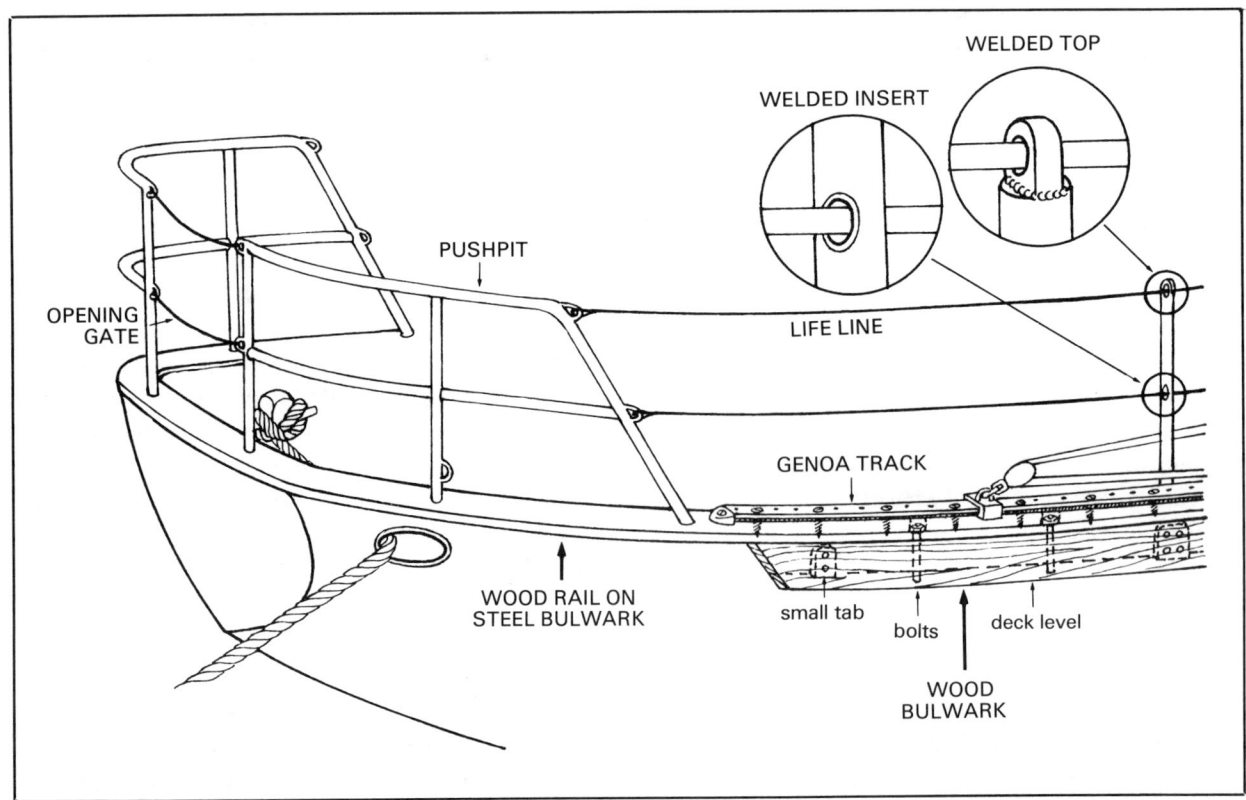

Fig. 22-1. *Both safety gear and sail-handling equipment are integrated in the stern. A life ring could also be attached to the pushpit.*

Fig. 22-2. *Everything is integral on this bow, including the figurehead. A platform made with flat bar is supported by the bowsprit, and an anchor roller and pipe pulpit are also incorporated. A rod bobstay holds the whole assembly down.*

a bending jig on the floor with a guide and tackle. Any joints should be welded together, rather than secured with set screws.

Pulpits are fabricated of tubing or pipe with a diameter at least as large as that used for the stanchions, and perhaps a bit larger. They must be designed and located so that they do not interfere with the headsails. An access gate should be installed on the stern pushpit for servicing the wind vane or exhaust, and it will also come in handy when someone is climbing aboard the stern. The stern anchoring required in many European ports is much easier with an access gate.

Large-diameter (1½–3″) stainless tubing or galvanized pipe can also be bent into guards in other areas, such as near the mast, over cowl ventilators, and around the pedestal. Many of the hand holds placed low on the deck, in the galley, and by companionways can be fabricated of tubing or a nice hardwood.

Although stanchions, life lines, and pulpits are definitely basic to safety, there are many other items that also lessen the chance of an "unpleasant incident" turning into a disaster. The U.S. Coast Guard certainly regards life jackets, fire extinguishers, and flares as basic, since they require all boats to carry them onboard. The bright orange Type I personal flotation devices are far superior to the inventory of flotation cushions and other

third-rate gear that some people drag along instead of laying out the money for the right equipment. There should always be one for each person aboard, and everyone should know how to put them on correctly.

As for fire extinguishers, the number required by the Coast Guard depends on the size of the boat. The Underwriters Laboratory recognizes three types of fires: Class A (paper, wood, cloth), Class B (gasoline, oil, paint), and Class C (live electrical equipment). The Coast Guard requires that you carry either CO_2, dry chemical, or Halon fire extinguishers (each of which will put out the three classes of fires) in a combination of sizes, depending on the length of the boat. They should be mounted in accessible spots, and every crew member should know where they are located and how to operate them.

A good radar reflector, either on a fixed mount high up a mast or hoisted on a pennant, is also a must, even though steel boats bounce back a better radar signal than fiberglass ones. But since small sailboats often don't show up well on a radar screen, a radio to contact a converging freighter (or to confirm your position after 6 days of clouds) will add to security.

A man-overboard kit is critical on a cruising yacht—it can help to save someone's life. The basic kit should be mounted in the stern and stowed so that it can be removed and thrown quickly and easily. This kit can include: a horseshoe life ring, flag pole, reflector tape, whistle, 50' of line, and a flashlight; a good strobe light would also be helpful. Seconds count when this situation occurs, and the crew should practice heaving the kit accurately at passing targets.

Once the person in the water has been recovered, the problem becomes getting him or her back onboard. Special slings are now available that are particularly helpful in getting an injured person back on the deck, and can be especially useful when the crew is small. Steps welded onto the transom can also serve this purpose, as well as provide a good way to return from any voluntary swims or outings.

When a man-overboard emergency or any questionable situation occurs at night, light may make the difference. A good collection of flashlights and the batteries to power them should be available at all times, and the boat can be fitted with a plug for a DC searchlight, which can also scan the water or illuminate the sails to point out the boat to a freighter.

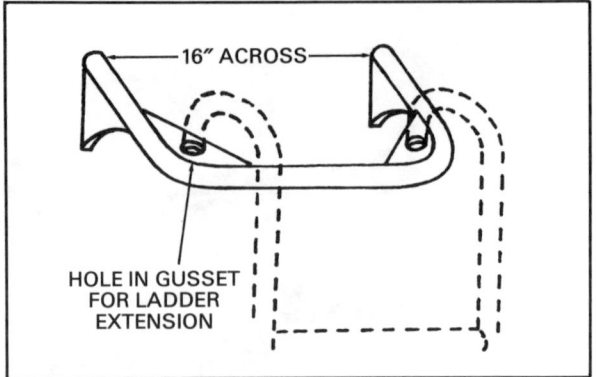

Fig. 22-4.   *A stern step ladder, fabricated of stainless steel tubing.*

A little time spent padding sharp corners like hatch edges with rubber or leather will pay off in fewer cuts and bruises. Turk's heads and macrame rope work can help to soften up small protruding bumps and knobs, as well as provide a decorative touch. The same rope or leather can be used to bind stainless steering wheels

Fig. 22-3.   *Steps are designed into the stern of this Grahame Shannon-designed* Amazon, *built by SP Metal Craft, and a stern ladder is ready to be lowered when needed.*

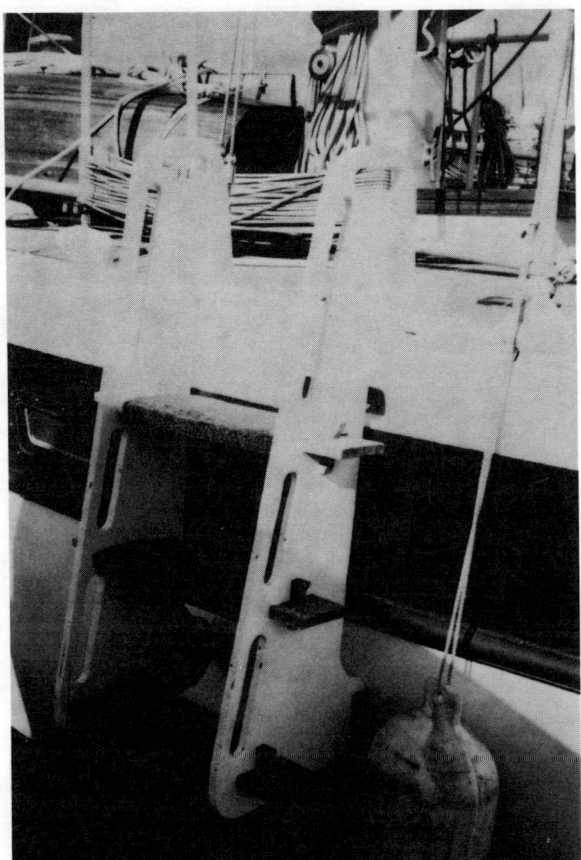

Fig. 22-5. *This wood ladder is sturdy and attractive when mounted, but it takes up a large amount of storage space when underway.*

so that they don't slip through the hands of the person at the helm. Non-skid sheathing on the deck and plastic or rubber mats for shower stalls and other wet areas will cut down the number of slips and falls. All crew members should keep an eye out for areas of the boat that are potentially dangerous.

The final component of basic safety equipment is the repair and maintenance kits for each of the boat systems—a well-maintained ship is a safe ship. The contents of these kits have already been described in the appropriate chapters on the engine, plumbing, electrics, standing rigging, sails, deck gear and fittings, steering, navigation, woodworking, paints, and metal work. In this chapter we will add two more: the emergency repair kit and the survival kit, neither of which should be omitted, though rarely used.

Guns are not safety equipment, although it may be tempting to carry one along to protect yourself from pirates and thieves. But unless you are trained to use a firearm and are positive the gun won't be turned on you, it might be wiser to try to scare the intruder off with

a flare gun, mace, or some other kind of spray. You could even carry a can of tacks, like Slocum did. Your best defense is to know those areas that might be dangerous and to keep a sharp lookout so that you have plenty of time to practice avoidance. Most cruisers hear about the bad places through the grapevine, and the Seven Seas Cruising Association (SSCA) puts out a helpful monthly publication in which members report on conditions in many areas of the world.

STORM SAFETY

When the storm winds are howling through the rigging, work on deck can become hazardous to life and limb. Sometimes a strong safety harness is the only thing that keeps a sailor with the ship, and there should be one onboard for each crew member. The harness should be made of good-quality nylon webbing, at least 2″ wide, with stainless steel clips or D rings; one comfortable design includes the harness as part of a strong, padded vest. The tether rope should be long enough so that movement is not hampered, and it should be inspected constantly for signs of chafe.

Stainless steel eyes can be welded to various strategic points in the cockpit, on the deck, and just outside the companionway so that clipping-on is always convenient. Eyes can also be incorporated into pedestal or mast guards. Another good practice is to stretch strong Dacron line fore and aft over the centerline of the boat; this way you can be secured the whole time you are moving along the length of the boat.

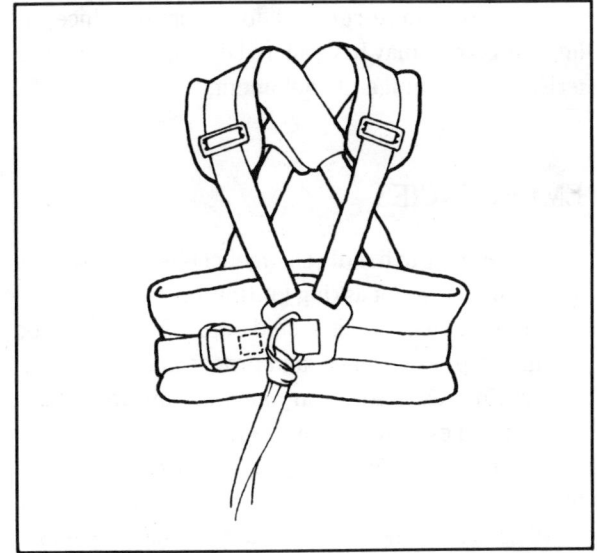

Fig. 22-6. *A soft, padded safety harness is more comfortable to wear than one made only of webbing.*

Foul-weather gear is also necessary during stormy weather, and in northern latitudes an insulated float coat or jump suit will also help to keep crew members warm and dry. Foul-weather food, like canned soup, that can be heated up quickly will come in handy when conditions are too rough for anyone to cook a good, hot meal.

The boat, too, must be ready to meet the gales, so that she can take care of you if necessary. A good set of storm sails (discussed in Chapter 21) will allow you to maintain steering control, and a well-designed sea anchor is a necessity when conditions require it. In addition, you should carry some large (minimum diameter of ¾″) hemp, nylon, or polypropylene warp line. A piece of automobile tire with a line secured to either end can also be turned into a good warp.

Lightning, whether associated with a storm or flashing down on its own, can be a frightening event on a sailboat, especially when you consider that your mast is the highest object around for many, many miles. The consensus of opinion about lighting protection is to provide a direct path for grounding so that damage is held to a minimum. Therefore, steel is the safest hull material during a lightning strike, since the entire boat is grounded. The best protection comes when an aluminum mast is used, since it acts as a giant lightning rod, but with a wood spar the stays will ground the currrent to the hull. A solid metal rod extending above all antennas and connected to the stays will assure that this is the path the lightning will take, although some masthead antennas can also serve as initial strike points.

Even if no visible harm has been done to the boat or crew when struck by lightning, you may need to swing the compass and re-correct it for deviation, since the lightning strike may have altered the magnetic characteristics of the hull and equipment.

EMERGENCIES

The best way to handle emergencies is to plan ahead for them; this is not asking for trouble, but being prepared to deal with it if it should occur. Although good seamanship, experience, and proper maintenance of the boat increase the odds in your favor, the unexpected can happen even to the best sailor.

Disasters can basically be grouped into two categories: major and minor. Minor failures include breakdown of small parts that render a system temporarily inoperable. But, depending on the situation, a minor breakdown can turn into a major disaster. For example, if the engine

Fig. 22-7. *Emergencies at sea can take many different forms. A piece of rope serves as her survival gear.*

fails to start in the open sea, not much harm is done. You only need to trace down the problem and fix it. (Of course, it's never as easy as it sounds!) However, if the failure occurs while motoring through a channel with a strong current, the boat could be driven ashore or go aground before the fault is cured. Split-second timing can make the difference, and that's where planning ahead pays off. Crew members should be involved in planning and practicing for emergencies so that everyone is thinking and acting together.

The problems that might have to be dealt with on a cruising sailboat are numerous, though rare, and they can include: man overboard, hull rupture, steering malfunctions, broken tiller, losing the rudder, fouling or losing the propeller, dragging anchor, injury to a crew member, dismasting, parting of a shroud, engine failure, fire, contaminated fuel or water, broken seacocks, collisions, sinking, and survival in a life raft. Of course, with a good steel hull some of these may never happen, but a plan of action for each must be ready to go.

The art of jury rigging may need to be practiced at unexpected moments, and success depends primarily on having a good selection of parts and materials with which to work. The trick is to select materials that can be used in several different ways, since there is a practical limit to the amount that can be carried. For example, if the rudder is lost, a makeshift rudder can be improvised using a whiskerpole and some scrap plywood. That same whiskerpole can turn into a boom or spar, and the plywood might be used to seal off a broken porthole or hatch cover. If the steering system fails, the rudder can be controlled by connecting the line or wire carried in the rigging repair kit to eyes previously welded to the rudder.

When the emergency is a collision or grounding that ruptures the hull, quick action with an emergency repair kit must be taken if the boat is not to sink. The contents of such a kit are listed in Table 22-1. In these situations, a good flare kit with handheld, parachute or rocket flares and a flare gun might be necessary to signal for some assistance.

Table 22-1. EMERGENCY HULL REPAIR KIT
Asphalt and tar
Quick-set epoxy
Underwater epoxy (e.g., Titan and Tarthan Technics)
Scrap pieces of 10–12 gauge plate
Scrap framing stock
Scrap plywood of various sizes
Nails and fasteners
Hammers and mallets of various sizes
Pieces of canvas
Small bag of cement
Umbrella repair assembly for holes
Dogging and clamping devices for removing dents and sealing leaks
General tool kit
Bilge pump
Auxiliary diesel welder (optional)

And then there is the ultimate emergency—sinking. Let's hope it never happens, but if it does, the supplies and equipment must be there to allow the crew to survive away from the boat. A 4–6-person life raft is first on the list. An inflatable dinghy might do the job in a pinch, but a life raft that is specially designed to protect survivors from the sun and the elements is better. When choosing the brand of life raft, consider the availability of servicing, since this will have to be done every few years to make sure that the raft is in tip-top condition. If you're in Hawaii and the only service center for your inexpensive but exotic raft is in England, you may have a problem.

A good survival kit should either be packed with the life raft or secured close to it, and the contents should be posted on the outside on waterproof or sealed paper. This kit should include water, up-to-date flares, a signal mirror, flashlights, whistle, fishing gear, line, canned food, a can opener, a knife, dried fruit, and plastic bags. A simple solar still may be a life-saver if you're adrift for a long time. An EPIRB (emergency position indicating radio beacon) will help the rescue operation by allowing your position to be tracked. In northern water, a survival suit may make a crucial difference, and even in warm water a dry suit or wet suit can make the wait more comfortable.

Since you may not have an opportunity to grab the ship's medicine chest before you have to abandon ship, an emergency first aid kit should also be part of the survival gear. The basic supplies should include sunburn lotion, eye ointment, petroleum jelly, antibiotics, pain

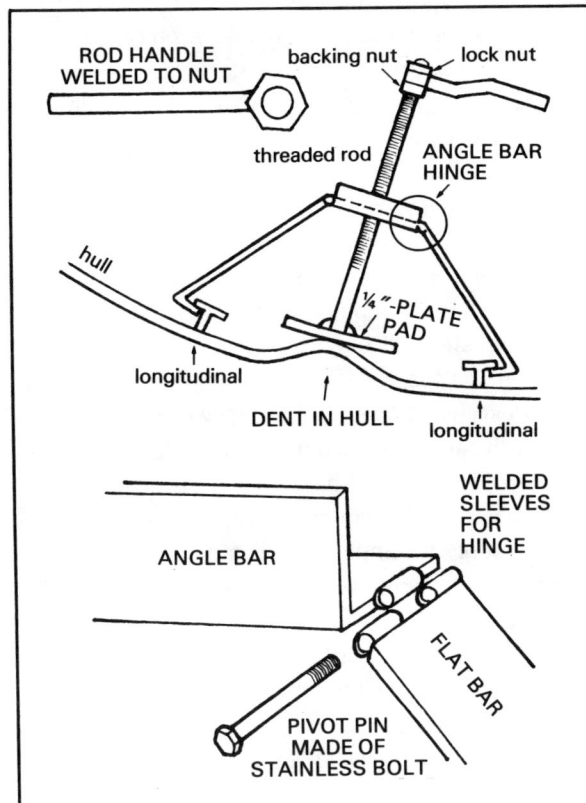

Fig. 22-8. *Although the tool pictured is designed to push out dents in the hull caused by collisions or groundings, it can also be used to plug leaks by fitting a sheet of rubber under the plate pad.*

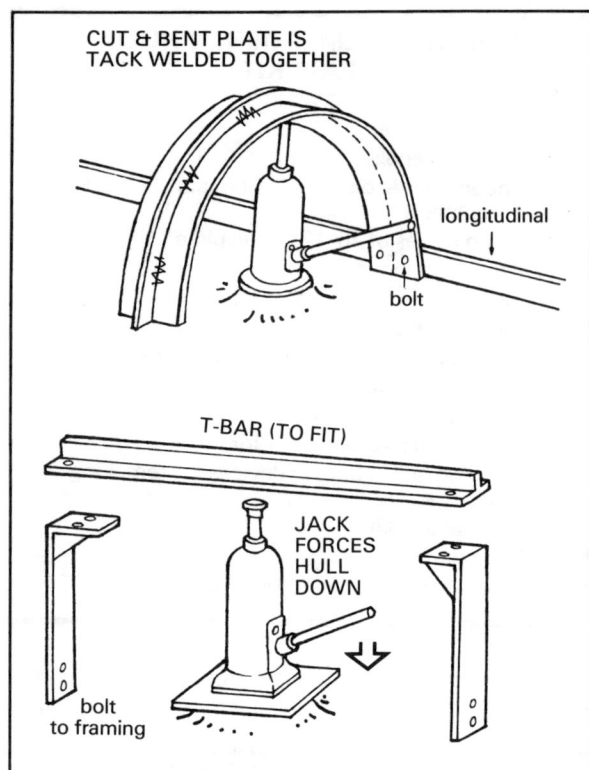

CUT & BENT PLATE IS
TACK WELDED TOGETHER

longitudinal

bolt

T-BAR (TO FIT)

JACK
FORCES
HULL
DOWN

bolt
to framing

Fig. 22-9. *A jack and some pieces of steel can form a tool to push out dents in the hull. In both cases, the steel can be bolted or tack-welded to the longitudinals and the assembly put together in place.*

relievers, medicine for diarrhea and seasickness, scissors, adhesive tape, gauze, and safety pins.

If plans are made and survival equipment is accessible and complete, the ultimate emergency won't turn into the ultimate disaster. You may lose the boat, but not your life or the lives that crew members have entrusted to you.

SEA LIFE

The active life of the ocean traveler demands good-quality equipment—equipment that will allow the crew to safely enjoy all the pasttimes that improve health and morale. With the proper gear, you can explore the water you live on and the distant lands you travel to, which makes the adventure more complete.

Dinghies are a cruiser's link to shore, and they can also be employed for jobs like kedging off a sand bank. If the dinghy can be sailed as well as rowed, you will be able to explore an anchorage with much less effort. The basic inventory of equipment for the dinghy includes:

a polypropylene painter line with a small "comb lock" chain; a double set of oarlock sockets; oarlocks with string or wire stoppers; spruce, ash, or fir oars with hardwood or copper tips and a leather oarlock band; a sailing rig complete with rudder, centerboard, spar, lines, sail, and hardware; a small 10–20 lb. grapnel or mushroom anchor; and possibly some foam flotation.

Although dinghy davits are handy, a small dinghy can also be loaded and unloaded using a whisker pole. Good wood or plastic deck pads below where the dinghy is stored will save unnecessary chafe when the dinghy is secured.

Inflatables are good to have along as back-up dinghies, and can be used as primary shore boats in sloppy conditions, since they are stable and won't sink if they capsize. But they are harder to row or sail, and can be damaged or punctured by coral and rocks. Inflatables can be powered quite easily with a 3–5 h.p. outboard.

Activities like swimming, diving, fishing, and camping on land are a natural part of the sailor's life. Many of these activities take place while at anchor in some remote lagoon or tropical atoll, and the proper gear must be onboard from the beginning of the cruise. Besides the basic deck shoes and boots, sweaters, long johns, heavy pants, shorts, and sunglasses necessary for different weather conditions, each crew member should bring along a swim suit, diving mask, snorkle, fins, diving knife, and nets. Those with the proper experience may also want diving gear like tanks. If you prefer to just float along, pack an inflatable mat and a bicycle pump. Sailboards and surfboards offer other variations on water sports, and they aren't that difficult to secure on deck. The limits are really only your preferences and the available storage space.

A good collection of fishing gear will always come in handy. It can include trolling reels with 300′ of 80-lb. filament, mounted on the stern of the boat; fishing nets; folding traps, fishing rods and reels; spear guns and Hawaiian slings for underwater fishing; and a tackle box with lures, leaders, weights, swivels, feathers, hooks, bait, and line.

A few items are worth carrying to make it easier to travel about on land, whether the land is an island or a city. Net bags are handy to carry both laundry and food, and tents are useful if you want to sleep ashore. Folding bicycles are a popular transportation supplement, but they have to be carefully stowed so that they don't rust. A small motor scooter makes exploring even quicker, if you have the room to store it. And for those jungle areas, hammocks, rain tarps, machetes, mosqui-

Fig. 22-10. *This steel boat sails on a mission of peace and understanding.* Courtesy of the Pacific Peacemaker

to netting, and insect repellant will help to make your stay safer.

Incidental equipment on the boat depends on your interests. Some people travel for the sake of travel, while others are interested in hobbies, trade, research, or cultural exchange. If your purpose is photographic, you may want a small darkroom; if cargo is to be carried, you will need a good-sized hold.

Also onboard should be all of the documentation that will be required by the various officials you will meet. This will include the boat's registration or documentation, builder's certificate, crew lists, crew passports and visas, bonded stores list, ship's log, and insurance pa-

pers. Courtesy flags and signal flags (especially a Q flag) are also standard equipment, and making the flags is a pleasant way to occupy yourself while stranded in the doldrums.

All things considered, the cruising life is a healthy one, and if the boat and crew are properly equipped, it should be a safe life, too.

SOURCES

Seven Seas Cruising Association
P.O. Box 2190
Covington, LA 70434

—Epilogue

In retrospect, it's easy to see the shortcomings in anything—a book, a boat, a life lived without adventure. Understanding and skill continue to grow faster than can be put down on paper. However, each new voyage of discovery and each risk taken add to the body of knowledge that we all use and share.

One final word about dreamboats. After reading this book and others like it, and hearing sailors talk about how they are sinking all their life earnings into a dream while eating peanut butter sandwiches in their humble dwellings, a prospective boat owner can easily be scared away by the cost and sacrifice required by this under-taking. But compare a nice floating home to that of a house on land, tucked in among the rows of neighbors and hemmed in by neatly platted streets. Not much difference in cost. But what a difference in outlook. The sailor has a constantly changing front lawn, and a heart and spirit that are strengthened by living on the edge. The crystal depths of the oceans and the singing of the winds beckon us on to the true adventure of life: seeking the unknown.

This book is about steel boats, but we also hope that it brings the smell of salt air to your nose. The opportunity to STEEL AWAY is here and now. The choice is yours.

─Appendix───────────

Material Costs

Yes, it's true. Boats eat money; in fact, they gobble it up as quickly as you can earn it. After you have made the final payment on your bare-hull assembly or have bought the steel and tools and built your own, you're still faced with the cost of finishing out the hull and outfitting it for cruising. This phase will more than double your investment in the boat, but if you give yourself enough time to search out the best deals, you can find many ways to save.

The list of things you will need to purchase is long and disparate—from a box of stainless screws to a suit of sails. We all tend to budget ahead for the major expenditures, but let the minor ones add up until, all of a sudden, there's nothing left in the kitty for that last tube of bedding compound. As Table A-1 shows, of the 60 most expensive items needed, only 12 cost more than $1,000, while over 30 require a relatively "minor" expenditure of between $150 and $300. It should be no surprise to anyone who has read through to this point, that we advocate planning ahead so that there are no financial crises as the boat nears completion.

In an attempt to demonstrate the form that the planning can take, this appendix begins at the end of the bare-hull stage and lists in detail the equipment and materials that will be needed to finish out each system of an average 40' ketch. As you page through the lists, you will notice that prices have been given in three categories: low, middle, and high. These classifications take into account the fact that the figures quoted by an eager salesman at the local chandlery may not be the best price you can get. "Low" prices are the best buys: the stainless tubing discovered in the corner of a junk yard, the propeller you traded for at a swap meet, the wooden hatch cover that you made yourself. "Middle"

prices represent fair discounts; you may be able to get a great deal on a case of bedding compound at a boat show, or knock something off the price by ordering through a builder who is willing to pass part of the discount along to you. The "high" prices are generally average retail prices. However, the different sizes and models available for some can also affect the classification; you pay more for a large inflatable than for a small one. In general, the prices given are the result of extensive, but not exhaustive, research. Another person pricing out all the boat systems might come out with different results. Brand names are occasionally listed, but only to give you an idea of where to begin looking for good quality at a reasonable cost; there are many other brands of equipment worth considering and evaluating.

Prices seem to be changing so rapidly that this appendix can only hope to serve as a comparative guide. You could probably safely add 5–10% to the figures each year, although the cost of some of the more sophisticated electronic equipment continues to fall as the manufacturing technology improves. Maybe in 10 or 15 years, people will be marveling at the incredibly high prices we had to pay before inflation was brought under control. Well, we can hope.

The cost of outfitting the boat remains about the same whether you build the hull yourself or have it professionally done. However, the total price tag on a boat increases dramatically when it is finished out by a professional yard. These final figures will certainly have an influence on your decision to build or buy.

As a rough approximation, a professionally built hull-deck assembly for a 40' chine boat can cost an average of $1.25 per pound of displacement, blasted and primed; a round hull will run about $1.40 per pound of displace-

Table A-1.   THE 60 MOST EXPENSIVE ITEMS USED ON A CRUISING SAILBOAT

	Cost			Cost
1. Basic sails	$6,500		31. Fo'c's'le hatch	$300
2. Engine	5,800		32. Dinghy	300
3. Wood	4,300		33. Dinghy outboard	300
4. Ballast	3,000		34. Sextant	300
5. Coating system	2,200		35. Plumbing fittings	260
6. All winches	2,150		36. Foam mattresses for bunks	250
7. Ham radio	1,800		37. Two toilets	240
8. Spar fittings	1,700		38. Aft hatch	230
9. All line	1,500		39. Lazarette hatch	230
10. All fasteners	1,430		40. 45-lb. CQR anchor	220
11. Life raft	$1,200		41. Emergency survival kit	$200
12. Charts (200)	1,000		42. Binoculars	200
13. All blocks	900		43. EPIRB	200
14. Anchor windlass	900		44. Flash water heater	200
15. Stainless rigging wire	900		45. Batteries	200
16. Wheel assembly	855		46. Wind generator	200
17. Loran-C	750		47. 33-lb. Bruce anchor	200
18. Inflatable Avon dinghy	700		48. Electric repair kit	200
19. Turnbuckles	650		49. Sail repair kit	200
20. Insulation	600		50. Sail repair parts	200
21. Awning fabrics	$ 540		51. Cabin heater	$180
22. Cook stove	500		52. Rigging tools	180
23. Non-integral tanks	500		53. Dorade ventilator cowls	180
24. Wire terminals	400		54. Speed log	180
25. Non-skid decking	400		55. 75-lb. Yachtsman anchor	180
26. Anchor chain	400		56. Epoxy	180
27. Portholes	400		57. VHF radio	170
28. All lights	400		58. 35-lb. Danforth anchor	170
29. 60-lb. CQR anchor	300		59. Seacocks	160
30. Solar panels	300		60. Stainless steel pulpit tubing	160

NOTE: Prices are based on minimum discounts.

Table A-2.   COST COMPARISON BETWEEN BUILDING AND BUYING A STEEL SAILBOAT

Size	Owner Built			Owner Finished			Professionally Built	
	Hull*	Other Systems	Total	Professionally built bare hull	Other Systems	Total	Basic	Custom
Average 30'	$10,000	$25,000	$35,000	$20,000	$25,000	$ 45,000	$ 60,000	$ 80,000
Average 35'	$14,000	$30,000	$44,000	$24,000	$30,000	$ 54,000	$ 72,000	$100,000
Average 40'	$18,000	$35,000	$53,000	$31,000	$35,000	$ 66,000	$ 85,000	$125,000
Average 45'	$23,000	$40,000	$63,000	$42,000	$40,000	$ 82,000	$110,000	$160,000
Average 50'	$30,000	$45,000	$75,000	$55,000	$45,000	$100,000	$140,000	$200,000

* Includes setup costs, overhead, tools, and materials.

Discount 5–10% for chine hulls.

Table A-3. THE COST OF MATERIALS FOR THE BOAT SYSTEMS OF AN AVERAGE 40′ KETCH

System	Cost	Approx. % of Total	Comments
Basic Sails	$ 6,500	12%	With only 5 working sails
Engine & Accessories	5,800	10%	Could be less with rebuilt engine
Navigation Equipment	5,500	9%	Includes Loran, ham radio, and some charts
Running Rigging	5,000	8%	Includes all line, winches, and deck gear
All wood	4,300	7.5%	Includes spure for spars
Mooring & Anchoring	4,200	7.5%	Includes dinghy and avon
Ballast	3,000	6%	Lead
Other Materials	2,700	5.5%	For construction only
Safety & Emergency	2,700	5.5%	Includes small life raft
Standing Rigging	2,500	5%	Stainless wire and bronze turnbuckles
Accommodations	2,200	4%	Includes galley and head fixtures and appliances
Coatings	2,200	4%	Epoxy and urethane system after blasting
Plumbing	2,000	3%	Integral tanks not included
Steering	1,800	3%	Includes inexpensive wind vane
Electrics	1,800	2.5%	Nothing fancy
Spar Fittings	1,700	2.5%	Mostly cast bronze
Hatches and Openings	1,600	2.5%	Wood used for most hatches
Alternative Power	800	1.5%	Solar and wind only
Insulation	620	1%	Minimum thickness

NOTE: Costs are based on average minimum cost, rounded off to nearest $100.

---

ment. These figures translate to an average cost of just under $750 per foot ($30,000) for a chine hull and $900 per foot ($36,000) for a round hull. A home-built hull of the same dimensions can require expenditures between $9,000 and $28,000, depending on the price classification used (see Table A-4).

The final planning element is the amount of time it will take you to finish out the boat. A professionally built hull-deck assembly of a custom design will probably be delivered in 7–8 months; when a builder is familiar with the design, the hull can be delivered in 5–6 months. If the owner requests metal work beyond the basic hull-deck assembly, extra time (and money) will be required to complete the boat. It's almost impossible to estimate the amount of time a home builder would spend, because it will depend on the free time available for building. As Table A-5 shows, the boat *could* be finished 65 weeks after you take delivery. However, this figure is based on one person, who knows how to do the work, devoting a minimum of 40 hours a week to installing the systems on a 40′ boat. Naturally, these figures will change with the amount of time available, the skill level

of the builder, and the size of the boat. Some of the work will probably be contracted out to professionals, and some will inevitably take longer than expected. But the motivation grows stronger as the hoped-for launching day approaches and the builder yearns to be a sailor again.

Table A-4. TYPICAL COST OF HULL ASSEMBLY FOR THE HOME BUILDER

Item	Low	Middle	High
Set-up equipment	$1,000	$ 3,000	$ 5,000
Basic tools	2,000	4,000	8,000
Materials (steel and stainless)	3,000	5,000	7,000
Disposables (electrodes, gas, electricity, etc.	2,000	3,000	4,000
Contracted work (blasting, rolling)	1,000	2,000	4,000
TOTALS	$9,000	$18,000	$28,000

Table A-5. TIME TABLE FOR COMPLETING THE INSTALLATION OF ALL BOAT SYSTEMS

		Weeks
1. Ballast	★	1
2. Blasting and coating (except anti-foulant)	★ ★ ★ ★ ★ ☆ ☆	7
3. Insulation (allow for cleanup)	☆	1
4. Other materials installed	★ ★ ★	4
5. Plumbing (non-integral tanks)	★ ★	2
6. Openings (ports, vents, hatches)	★ ★ ★ ★	5
7. Wood joinery (inside and outside)	★ ★ ★ ★ ★ ★ ★ ★ ★ ★ ★ ☆	12
8. Electrics installation	★ ★ ☆	3
9. Installing engine mount, engine, shaft, and accessories	★ ★ ☆	3
10. Steering and wind vane	★	1
11. Mooring and anchoring system	★	1
12. Accommodations and decorative touches	★ ★ ★ ★ ★ ★ ★ ★	8
13. Spars (wood construction)	★ ★ ☆ ☆	4
14. Install rigging and fittings	★ ★	2
15. Sailmaking (owner does hand work)	☆ ☆ ☆ ☆ ☆ ★ ★	7
16. Installing navigation equipment, safety gear, and extras	★ ★ ★	3
	TOTALS	65

★ = Owner   ☆ = Contracted out

BALLAST

ITEM	QUAN-TITY	LOW	MIDDLE	HIGH	YOUR PRICE
Lead ballast—scrap or pure (iron mix would cost about half this amount).	5 tons	$3,000	$4,000	$5,000	
Ballast cover—steel, cement coating, etc.	1	40	100	200	
TOTALS		**$3,040**	**$4,100**	**$5,200**	

COATINGS

ITEM	QUAN-TITY	LOW	MIDDLE	HIGH	YOUR PRICE
Primer coats for inside and out, 2 coats	8 gal.	$ 320	$ 450	$ 640	
Barrier or intermediate fairing coats, inside and out, 2 coats minimum	8 gal.	360	490	720	
Top coats					
Interior, 1 coat	3 gal.	90	120	180	
Deck and cabin, 3 coats	6 gal.	240	360	480	
Topsides, 4 coats	7 gal.	350	500	800	
Anti-fouling (cupro-nickel or organo tin), 2 coats	3 gal.	300	400	600	
Paint or varnish for interior woodwork	5 gal.	100	150	200	
Utensils and tools for application and repair					
Paint solvents	4 gal.	70	100	140	
Acetone	2 gal.	35	50	70	
Mineral spirits	2 gal.	30	45	60	
Sandpaper, all in boxes of 100					
80 grit	4	40	60	80	
100 grit	2	20	30	40	
120 grit	8	80	120	160	
220 grit	2	20	30	40	
40 and 60 coarse grit	2	20	30	40	
Brushes of various sizes	10	40	60	80	
Strainers, stirrers, containers, and sanding blocks	—	10	20	30	
OPTIONAL: Spray gun and canister, rollers and pans, and compressor unit.					
TOTALS		**$2,125**	**$3,015**	**$4,360**	

INSULATION

ITEM	QUAN-TITY	LOW	MIDDLE	HIGH	YOUR PRICE
Close-cell, moisture-resistant foam (placed or sprayed type). Typical need, 640 sq. ft. with average thickness of 1 to 2″					
Polyethylene foam, placed	—	$260	$320	$ 400	
Polystyrene foam or styrofoam, placed (cost is about half of polyethylene					
Contact glue for placed foam	4 gal.	120	150	180	
Polyurethane foam, sprayed (640 sq. ft.). Professional applicators charge and average of $1.20 per sq. ft. for each inch of thickness. If owner does own work with rented safety equipment, the total cost may equal that of placed polyethylene	—	640	770	900	
Fire-resistant coating, 1 coat	5 gal.	100	150	200	
OPTIONAL: Insulation for exhaust and engine room					
TOTALS		**$480**	**$620**	**$1,100**	

OTHER MATERIALS

ITEM	QUAN-TITY	LOW	MIDDLE	HIGH	YOUR PRICE
Fasteners for wood joinery (box of 100)					
Stainless steel screws, #8, 1″	2	$ 20	$ 30	$ 40	
Stainless steel screws, #8, 1½″	2	30	45	60	
Stainless steel screws, #10, 1½″	4	80	120	160	
Stainless steel screws, #10, 1¾″	10	220	330	440	
Stainless steel screws, #10, 2″	2	50	75	100	
Stainless steel screws, #12, 1¾″	4	120	180	240	
Stainless steel screws, #12, 2″	2	70	110	140	
Bolts, galvanized or stainless lag, ¼″	2	80	120	160	
Bolts, galvanized or stainless lag, ⅜″	1	50	75	100	
Bolts, galvanized carriage, ¼″	1	70	110	140	
Fasteners for wood-to-metal or metal-to-metal joinery (Box of 100)					
Machine screws (bolts)					
¼″ × 2″	2	30	45	60	
¼″ × 3″	2	70	110	140	
⅜″ × 1½″	1	25	40	50	
Machine hex cap bolts					
¼″ × 2″	1	20	30	40	
⁵⁄₁₆″ × 2″	3	75	120	150	
⅜″ × 1½″	2	60	90	120	
⅜″ × 2½″	1	35	50	70	
Studs (stainless bolt or rod), ¼″ to ½″ sizes, various lengths	60	50	75	100	
Various nuts and washers (hex, cap, wing, and Nylock) for all the bolts	1,500	200	300	400	

continued

OTHER MATERIALS (continued)

ITEM	QUAN-TITY	LOW	MIDDLE	HIGH	YOUR PRICE
Miscellaneous fasteners: pipe plugs, stainless steel rod, threaded bronze nails, set screws, self-tapping screws, sheet metal screws, rivets, cotter pins		75	120	150	
Adhesives					
Resorcinol	1 gal.	20	25	30	
Plastic resin	1 gal.	20	30	40	
Polyester resin	1 gal.	25	25	30	
Epoxy resin	5 gal.	180	230	300	
Optional: underwater repair epoxy (2 qt. package)					
Insulators, gaskets, and bedding compounds					
Bedding compound (SikaFlex, 5200), cases	2	100	150	200	
Anti-fungal bedding (Dolphinite)	1 qt.	10	15	20	
Neoprene gasket material, sheets of different thicknesses	—	100	200	300	
Plastic insulating pads and sleeves	—	30	60	90	
High-impact plastic (e.g., Monocast)	—	80	120	160	
Coverings and sheathings					
Rubber, cork, and plastic non-slid deck coverings (e.g., Treadmaster, Vetus, Polygrip), usually available in sheets 39″ × 78″	—	400	700	900	
Heat-resistant sheathing for stove, heaters, etc. (e.g., sheet metal, asbestos, Pyrodur, ceramic)	—	40	60	80	
Water-resistant decorative coverings (e.g., tile, formica)	—	100	150	200	
Nondecorative water-resistant covering (e.g., Nexus cloth or other polyester mat)	—	30	40	50	
Preservatives, oils, solvents, cleansers, and other chemicals	—	80	160	240	
Application tools	—	50	100	200	
TOTALS		**$2,695**	**$4,240**	**$5,700**	

OPENINGS

ITEM	QUAN-TITY	LOW	MIDDLE	HIGH	YOUR PRICE
Hatches—can be homemade wood or steel or production cast aluminum (e.g., Bowmar, Lewmar, Atkin-Hoyle). Low figures are for homemade wood hatches.					
Main companionway hatch, sliding type, 27″ × 29″	1	$ 30	$ 400	$ 800	
Turtle top (aluminum, fiberglass or wood)	1	50	150	300	
Aft-cabin hatch, lifting type, 21″ × 21″	1	230	300	340	
Lazarette hatch, lifting type, 24″ × 24″	1	230	300	340	
Fo'c's'le hatch, lifting type, 24″ × ″	1	300	350	400	
Skylight, 19″ × 19″	1	40	200	300	

continued

OPENINGS (continued)

ITEM	QUAN-TITY	LOW	MIDDLE	HIGH	YOUR PRICE
Engine access panel (aluminum or steel with neoprene gasket)	1	25	200	400	
Portholes, either fixed or opening, 5″× 12″ or 7″× 14″	14	400	1,000	3,000	
Lexan, Tuffak, or Plexiglas for ports, deadlights, and windows	—	40	90	150	
Wood dorade vents with plastic or metal cowls and PVC deck spools, 4″ diameter	6	180	300	600	
Engine vents (stainless steel, plastic, or steel)	4	—	50	200	
Galley stove vent (steel, plastic, or stainless steel)	1	20	40	60	
Heater stack (charlie noble) (integral steel, galvanized or stainless)	1	30	50	70	
Prisms, 3″× 10″	2	40	100	180	
OPTIONAL: parts like hinges, latches, shutters, and holding tank vents					
TOTALS		**$1,615**	**$3,530**	**$7,140**	

WOODWORK

ITEM	QUAN-TITY	LOW	MIDDLE	HIGH	YOUR PRICE
Lumber costs are based on board feet (bf) within price range listed.					
Plywood for bulkheads, panels, semi-bulkheads, etc.	900 bf	$ 966	$1,500	$ 2,000	
Sitka spruce for spars. $2–6/bf	600 bf	1,200	2,400	3,600	
Fir or pine for cleating, liners, posts, etc. 80¢–$2/bf	400 bf	400	600	1,000	
Yellow cedar for ceilings, lockers, and partitions. $1.30–2.30/bf	200 bf	240	360	460	
Mahogany (Honduran) for trim and exterior woodwork $1.80–3.50/bf	550 bf	1,100	1,375	1,925	
Hardwoods like oak, balou, or teak for mounting pads, rub rails, and miscellaneous uses. $2.50–7.00/bf	100	250	400	700	
Stainless steel fittings	—	30	50	90	
Hardware for cabinets, doors, drawers, hasps, etc.	—	80	200	500	
TOTALS		**$4,266**	**$6,885**	**$10,275**	

PLUMBING

ITEM	QUAN-TITY	LOW	MIDDLE	HIGH	YOUR PRICE
Seacocks (stainless steel, bronze, or plastic)	7	$ 160	$ 300	$ 500	
Cedar wood plugs for emergencies	3	0	5	10	
Filters, strainers, and screens for intake lines	4	40	90	160	
Plastic deck filler plates for water and fuel tanks	2	30	50	70	
Non-integral tanks for fuel, water, kerosene, etc. (steel or stainless). $2–5/gal. is typical charge. 250 gallons in all tanks.	3	500	800	1,200	
Holding tanks (polyethylene or PVC)	2	100	150	200	
Clear plastic tank breather lines	4	20	30	40	
Tank shut-off valves (bronze, stainless, or plastic)	6	60	80	120	
Y-valves (PVC)	2	30	60	80	
Head elbow vent loops (PVC)	2	20	40	60	
T-fittings (PVC or other plastic)	4	30	50	70	
Bend fittings, 45º or 90º (PVC or other plastic)	6	30	50	70	
Other joints and hose cuffs (mostly plastic)	10	50	70	90	
Adaptors for hoses (mostly plastic)	10	60	80	100	
Hose clamps, box of various sizes in stainless steel	50	30	40	50	
Hose mounting brackets (galvanized or plastic)	30	10	15	20	
Hoses of various sizes and makes					
Raw intake (at sea chest in hull kit assembly)					
Engine water (reinforced neoprene)	10 ft.	20	35	50	
Galley (polyester, corrugated or reinforced polyethylene)	6 ft.	5	8	12	
Head water (reinforced neoprene or corrugated polyethylene)	8 ft.	6	10	14	
Clean intake					
Water deck fill line (vinyl)	12 ft.	3	6	9	
Diesel fill line (polypropylene or neoprene)	8 ft.	16	30	40	
Leading lines					
Fuel tank to engine (neoprene or copper tubing)	6 ft.	3	5	6	
Water tank to sink (vinyl)	30 ft.	6	12	18	
Hot water lines, if any (reinforced vinyl or PVC)	3 ft.	1	2	3	
Drains for black and grey water (head to holding and out, sink to holding and out, shower to holding and out) (reinforced or corrugated polyethylene)	25 ft.	20	30	40	
Bilge pump hose (reinforced vinyl or corrugated polyethylene)	10 ft.	6	9	12	
Cockpit scupper hose (PVC, reinforced neoprene or steel)	20 ft.	6	10	12	
Engine exhaust (steel, stainless or reinforced neoprene)	12 ft.	30	45	60	
Pumps					
Bilge sump pump (plastic and rubber)	1	30	50	70	
Holding tank pump, manual or electric	1	20	30	40	
Heavy-duty bilge pump	1	50	100	200	
Small engine oil pump	1	10	20	30	
Small hand pump for cleaning out lockers	1	20	30	50	
Pump repair kit with spare parts for each pump	3	20	40	60	

continued

PLUMBING (continued)

ITEM	QUAN-TITY	LOW	MIDDLE	HIGH	YOUR PRICE
Extra 5–10 gallon plastic jugs for water, fuel, and kerosene	5	30	50	70	
Drinking water foot pumps for all sinks	3	75	150	240	
Faucets (stainless steel or plastic)	3	45	90	150	
Faucet filters (strainer with charcoal)	2	20	30	40	
Sinks					
Galley: stainless steel double sink	1	80	110	160	
Head: stainless steel or plastic	2	60	90	120	
Water heater, propane in-line flash type (e.g., Paloma)	1	200	250	300	
Plumbing kits with tools like pliers, hacksaw, nippers, hose glue, tape, etc. Spare parts like hoses, conduit, and clamps. Items like buckets, mop, disinfectants, tank dip stick, and gloves)	1	60	100	150	
OPTIONAL: engine PTO clutch, electric bilge and pressurized-water pumps, electric hot water heater, electric holding tank pump, hot tub					
TOTALS		**$2,012**	**$3,252**	**$4,796**	

ELECTRICS

ITEM	QUAN-TITY	LOW	MIDDLE	HIGH	YOUR PRICE
Batteries, 12 volt bank with regular and/or heavy-duty type	4	$ 200	$ 350	$ 500	
Battery box—used plywood, fasteners, and epoxy listed in other sections					
Master battery switch (e.g., Guest)	1	20	35	50	
Battery cables, 2 or 4 gauge	1	20	40	60	
Cable terminals	10	10	15	20	
Electric panel with switches, wire, terminals, fuses or or circuit breakers, bus bar, and cover	1	50	150	260	
Ground cable, 2 to 8 gauge	1	30	60	90	
Voltage regulator	1	30	50	80	
Wire (insulated, parallel, two-way type)					
10 gauge	50 ft.	20	30	40	
12 gauge	50 ft.	10	20	30	
14 gauge (includes lights on mast)	200 ft.	40	60	80	
16 gauge, throughout interior	300 ft.	50	70	90	
18 gauge	100 ft.	10	20	30	
Other switches	6	30	45	60	

continued

ELECTRICS (continued)

ITEM	QUAN-TITY	LOW	MIDDLE	HIGH	YOUR PRICE
Junctions	5	20	30	40	
Lights for interior (brass-rimmed or stainless)					
Regular interior	10	80	120	160	
Flexible navigation lights	2	20	40	60	
Small night lights	3	10	20	30	
Small locker lights	2	20	40	60	
Fluorescent lights for shop and engine room (e.g. Schaefer)	2	40	70	140	
Lights for exterior with brackets (e.g., Aqua Signal)					
Running lights	2	25	60	120	
Masthead	1	20	45	60	
Bow light/anchor light	1	20	30	60	
Stern light	1	20	30	50	
Cockpit light	1	10	20	30	
Spreader lights	2	20	40	60	
Plug-in spotlight	1	25	50	100	
Emergency strobe light	1	40	80	120	
Emergency back-up kerosene lanterns for exterior use	2	40	80	170	
Gimballed kerosene lanterns for interior	6	120	300	600	
Kerosene tank with spigot (2–10 gal.)	1	50	100	150	
Portable flashlights					
Large	1	20	30	40	
Small	6	40	80	120	
Underwater light	1	30	50	80	
Battery charger, float type, 20–40 amps	1	140	300	500	
Portable battery charger, 10–20 amps	1	30	50	80	
AC plug-in sockets	2	20	40	60	
AC circuit wiring	30 ft.	20	30	40	
AC dockside power cord with 30-amp plug, 50 ft.	1	40	70	100	
Stray current monitor	1	40	60	80	
Corrosion control monitor, throughhull or portable	1	100	200	300	
Ventilation fan (mechanical, 12 volt, or solar)	1	15	30	50	
Electrical parts and tool kit for installation, maintenance and repair including volt meter, soldering gun, wire cutters, needle-nosed pliers, silicon seal, tape, glue, heat-shrink tubing, crimp connectors, distilled water, circuit tester, battery tester. Spare parts such as straps, terminals, fuses, switches, kerosene wicks and chimneys, etc.	—	200	300	500	
OPTIONAL: DC to AC inverter, battery isolator, and alternator controller					
TOTALS		**$1,795**	**$3,340**	**$5,350**	

ENGINE AND ACCESSORIES

ITEM	QUAN-TITY	LOW	MIDDLE	HIGH	YOUR PRICE
Diesel engine with 30–70 continuous horsepower rating	1	$3,000	$5,000	$7,000	
Shaft with key way and lock nut, average 6 ft. length, 1¼" to 1½" diameter	1	100	200	300	
Propeller (specified diameter and pitch)	1	200	400	700	
Coupling, flexible type	1	20	40	60	
Engine mounts, flexible	4	40	60	100	
Fuel filters (e.g., Dahl)	2	100	300	500	
Bearings for shaft—see listing under "Other Materials"					
Stuffing box (bronze) with hose and clamps	1	30	40	50	
Control levers and cable for shift and throttle	2	80	120	160	
Monitor panel with gauges for oil pressure, engine temperature, rpm's, and amperage with fuses, terminals, and ignition	1	80	160	280	
Exhaust pipe (galvanized, neoprene, or stainless)	1	20	30	40	
Muffler, water-trap type	1	70	150	240	
Spare parts kit with filters, oil, etc.	—	100	300	500	
OPTIONAL: power take-off (PTO), shaft lock					
TOTALS		**$3,840**	**$6,800**	**$9,930**	

ALTERNATIVE POWER SOURCES

ITEM	QUAN-TITY	LOW	MIDDLE	HIGH	YOUR PRICE
Solar power, fixed or movable panels	2	$ 300	$ 500	$ 800	
Wind generator	1	200	400	600	
Portable gas-driven generator (e.g., Honda, Sears)	1	150	300	500	
Engine power take-off with clutch and belt	1	100	300	700	
OPTIONAL: portable diesel AC welder-generator, hydraulics, auxiliary propeller, shaft PTO, large auxiliary generator					
TOTALS		**$ 750**	**1,500**	**$2,600**	

STEERING AND SELF-STEERING

ITEM	QUAN-TITY	LOW	MIDDLE	HIGH	YOUR PRICE
Steering wheel (wood, aluminum, or stainless steel), 30–32″ diameter	1	$ 100	$ 400	$1,200	
Pedestal with brake (e.g., Edson, Merriman), 28″ height	1	200	300	400	
Guard for pedestal and binnacle (narrow stainless steel tubing)	1	80	120	150	
Chain and wire cable (¼″ stainless steel)	60 ft.	50	100	200	
Pulleys					
Parallel "D" idler	1	60	90	120	
Double wire rope sheave	1	50	80	110	
Single wire rope sheaves	4	130	200	260	
Small parts: terminals, eyes, Teflon lube, toggles, and clips	—	50	75	100	
Quadrant (bronze), proper size with separate stops	1	110	150	200	
Conduit (PVC)	10 ft.	25	40	55	
Emergency tiller extension pipe with deck plate (galvanized)	1	10	20	30	
Emergency tiller	1	10	20	30	
Self-steering wind vane, servo-pendulum type (e.g., Aries, Monitor, Navik, RVG, Fleming)	1	900	1,400	2,000	
Drum for hooking up wind vane to wheel	1	20	70	140	
For rudder post bearing see listing in "Other Materials"					
Rudder post stuffing box (for internal rudder only)	1	20	40	60	
OPTIONAL: steering gloves, hydraulic steering, electric auto pilot					
TOTALS		**$1,815**	**$3,105**	**$5,055**	

ANCHORING AND MOORING

ITEM	QUAN-TITY	LOW	MIDDLE	HIGH	YOUR PRICE
Anchors					
60-lb. CQR	1	$ 300	$ 360	$ 470	
45-lb. CQR	1	220	300	400	
35-lb. Danforth	1	170	210	250	
33-lb. Bruce	1	200	250	300	
75–90 lbs. Yachtsman or similar type	1	180	270	360	
Small grapnel and dinghy anchor	2	50	80	120	
Swivels, various sizes for each anchor	6	60	90	120	
Shackles, various sizes	20	100	200	300	
Shackle tie wire, small reel of stainless steel wire	1	10	20	30	
Anchor chain, 3/8″ proof coil or BBB, 400 ft. drum	1	400	800	1,200	

continued

ANCHORING AND MOORING (continued)

ITEM	QUAN-TITY	LOW	MIDDLE	HIGH	YOUR PRICE
Nylon anchor and mooring line—see listing under "Sails"					
Stainless steel pin and plastic or rubber rollers	2	25	50	75	
Chain dog	1	10	20	30	
Windlass, manual, electric, hydraulic, or combinations; vertical or horizontal mount (e.g., Nilson, Keefe, Dickinson, Lofrans)	1	900	1,800	2,700	
Spare parts	—	20	30	40	
Fenders of different sizes	6	110	180	240	
Boat hook	2	15	25	55	
Mooring buoy	1	60	100	150	
Dinghy, approx. 8′ long plywood or fiberglass with parts	1	300	500	700	
Inflatable, 10′ long (e.g., Avon, Zodiac, Nova, Zed)	1	700	1,500	2,000	
Extra dinghy parts: oars, sail rigs, etc.	—	40	80	180	
Outboard engine, 3-5 hp (e.g., Honda, Johnson, Evinrude)	1	300	700	1,000	
TOTALS		**$4,170**	**7,565**	**$10,720**	

ACCOMMODATIONS

ITEM	QUAN-TITY	LOW	MIDDLE	HIGH	YOUR PRICE
Anchor locker					
Floor sealant (asphalt, plywood, or plastic container)	—	$ 20	$ 40	$ 60	
Fo'c's'le					
Foam for all cushions and berths: 2 doubles, 2 singles, salon settees, navigation seat, aft cabin seat, 3″ thick	—	250	350	500	
Mattress covers (cotton, canvas, or synthetic)	—	100	220	450	
Blankets, sheets, pillows, duffel bags, etc.	—	10	20	30	
OPTIONAL: carpet covering (nylon, acrylic, polyester)					
Head					
Toilet with manual pump (e.g., Raritan)	2	240	700	1,600	
Head repair kit	1	30	40	50	
OPTIONAL: electric toilet with pump and vaccuum sensor					
Mirror on cabinet	2	20	30	50	
Shower curtain	2	25	35	50	
Portable sun shower with plastic sack	1	20	30	40	
First aid kit	1	30	50	70	
Medicine kit	1	40	100	180	
Chemical treatment for toilet (e.g., DX)	1 gal.	10	15	20	

continued

ACCOMMODATIONS (continued)

ITEM	QUAN-TITY	LOW	MIDDLE	HIGH	YOUR PRICE
Lockers					
Air fresheners	2	10	20	30	
Bamboo strapping for ventilation	—	10	15	20	
Main salon and settee area					
Decorations like curtains	—	20	40	60	
Cabin heater, minimum 9,000 BTU's	1	180	400	900	
Main salon table legs, 30″ galvanized pipe with flanges	2	20	30	50	
OPTIONAL: TV, tape deck, video, speakers, etc.					
Galley					
Cook stove (kerosene or propane), 3 burner with oven, gimballed (e.g., Kenyon, Force 10 Dickinson, Seaward)	1	500	900	1,800	
Webbing strap with snap hooks	1	10	15	20	
Stainless steel stove guard rail	1	10	20	30	
Propane assembly parts, including propane leak detector with light, solenoids, vapor alarm, neoprene tubing, regulator, pressure gauge, level gauge, and two 2.5 gal. or 10 lb. propane tanks, 11″×17″ each, in exterior locker	—	260	410	610	
Refrigerator/ice chest	1	100	400	1,000	
Electric 12-volt ice-box conversion unit (e.g., Cold Machine)	1	140	300	600	
Small portable cooler in cockpit locker	1	30	60	90	
Cleaning locker with cleansers, bilge cleaner, soaps, wax, polish, sealants, oils, chemicals, fresheners	1	30	50	70	
Navigation station—see listing under "Electrics"					
TOTALS		**$2,115**	**$4,290**	**$8,380**	

SPARS AND THEIR FITTINGS

ITEM	QUAN-TITY	LOW	MIDDLE	HIGH	YOUR PRICE

Note: The prices in this section are based on home-built wooden spars for a split rig like a ketch or a yawl. The actual cost of the materials is included in the section on "Woodwork." The following spars are included:

Main mast, 56′ length, 6×9″	*1*				
Main boom, 18′ length, 3×5″	*1*				
Mizzen mast, 40′ length, 5×6″	*1*				
Mizzen boom, 10′ length, 3×4″	*1*				
Stays'l club boom, 12′ length, 2×3″	*1*				
Spreader, 4′ average	*3 sets*				
All spars built professionally of aluminum (low price is spar kit, while high price is complete with all fitting)		*$5,000*	*$7,000*	*$9,000*	
If spars built professionally of wood		*$3,000*	*$5,000*	*$10,000*	

Prices for spar fittings are based on the use of either manganese bronze or stainless steel. Galvanized steel or aluminum spar fittings can also be used.

continued

SPARS AND THEIR FITTINGS (continued)

ITEM	QUAN-TITY	LOW	MIDDLE	HIGH	YOUR PRICE
Whisker or genoa poles, 10-22', extending aluminum	2	$ 150	$ 260	$ 500	
Masthead band with brackets and tangs	2	130	400	700	
Masthead halyard sheaves	2	100	300	500	
Tangs for all shrouds, stays, and halyards	11	200	290	380	
Spreader connectors (flexible)	3	150	220	300	
Spreader tips	6	70	140	220	
Gooseneck assembly with band	2	100	150	200	
Mast and boom sail track, ⅞" stainless steel	98 ft.	140	210	270	
Storm sail track with switch, 6' long	1	30	50	100	
Track slide stoppers	2	20	30	40	
Main mast whiskerpole track assembly	2	80	160	300	
Boom bail	2	80	120	160	
Boom vang band	2	70	110	150	
Outhaul track and car assembly	2	60	90	140	
Outhaul cleats	2	10	20	30	
Halyard cleats	5	40	70	100	
Winch mount pads	5	30	80	140	
Other cleats for topping lift, cunningham, lanyard, jiffy reefing, downhauls, spinnaker, etc.	18	160	240	380	
Jiffy reef cheek blocks	4	30	40	50	
Mechanical masthead wind indicator (electric optional)	1	10	15	20	
Mast boot collar (plastic, rubber, or canvas) and wood shims	2	25	40	60	
OPTIONAL: spar steps, lanyard pulleys, gooseneck and boom bail for club jib boom					
TOTALS Without spars		**$1,685**	**$3,035**	**$4,740**	

STANDING RIGGING AND FITTINGS

ITEM	QUAN-TITY	LOW	MIDDLE	HIGH	YOUR PRICE
NOTE: Prices for rigging based on 40' split rig.					

Stainless steel rigging wire, 1/19 (if galvanized wire is used, the cost is about ⅓). The extra lengths of wire given are for emergency uses.
   422' of ¼" plus extra 78'. Total 500'.
   304' of 5⁄16" plus extra 96'. Total 400'.
   56' of ⅜" plus extra 44'. Total 100'.
	1,000'	$ 900	$1,600	$2,200	

Stainless steel wire terminals (galvanized are much less expensive). Cost varies mostly in terms of type (prices are based on combination of socket and mechanical).	44	400	850	1,200	

continued

STANDING RIGGING AND FITTINGS (continued)

ITEM	QUAN-TITY	LOW	MIDDLE	HIGH	YOUR PRICE
Thimbles (only for nicropress terminals)	16	30	45	60	
Shackles (stainless steel and some galvanized)	112	25	40	60	
Turnbuckles with doubled-ended toggles (e.g., Navtec), bronze, three different sizes to match wire	22	650	950	1,200	
Antenna backstay insulator	2	40	60	80	
Bobstay (galvanized chain, stainless steel wire, or stainless steel rod)	1	20	40	60	
Bobstay turnbuckle (galvanized or stainless)	1	30	50	80	
Pedestal for staysail boom (steel or stainless steel)	1	60	100	150	
Anti-chafe items: turnbuckle booties, spreader rollers, baggywrinkles, etc.	—	40	80	120	
Ratlins—for material see "Woodwork"					
Spare parts for maintenance and repair kit: terminals, cable sleeves, seizing wire, turnbuckles, toggles, shackles, cotter pins, tape, bulldog clips, serving cord, and appropriate gear for optional galvanized system	—	100	200	300	
Tools specific to rigging work: nicropress, cable cutters, rigger's vise, bolt cutters, and marlinspike	—	180	250	300	
OPTIONAL: Roller reefing for headsails, rod rigging, backstay adjusters, etc.					
TOTALS		**$2,475**	**$4,265**	**$5,810**	

SAILS AND OTHER FABRICS

ITEM	QUAN-TITY	LOW	MIDDLE	HIGH	YOUR PRICE
Sails (dacron), typical basic set of sailing for average 40′ cruising ketch. The cost, of course, will be lower for a sloop or cutter. Cost includes labor of sailmaker.					
Mainsail, 340 sq. ft., 8.2-oz. cloth	1	$1,500	$1,700	$1,900	
Mizzen, 135 sq. ft., 8.2-oz. cloth	1	500	650	800	
Staysail, 178 sq. ft., 8.2-oz. cloth	1	600	700	800	
Jib, 435 sq. ft., 7.2-oz. cloth	1	1,000	1,200	1,400	
Genoa jib, 650 sq. ft., 6.5-oz. cloth	1	1,400	1,600	1,800	
TOTAL OF BASIC SUIT	5	5,000	5,850	6,700	
Other sails for light and heavy weather					
Mizzen staysail, 275 sq. ft., 1.5-oz. nylon	*1*	*350*	*450*	*550*	
Cruising spinnaker (160%), 1,280 sq. ft., 1.5-oz. nylon	*1*	*1,200*	*1,400*	*1,600*	
Storm main trysail, 112 sq. ft., 9-oz. cloth	*1*	*500*	*600*	*700*	
Storm jib, 134 sq. ft., 9-oz. cloth	*1*	*500*	*600*	*700*	

continued

SAILS AND OTHER FABRICS (continued)

ITEM	QUAN-TITY	LOW	MIDDLE	HIGH	YOUR PRICE
Sail bags (commonly come with sails)					
Sail bags (canvas)	3	80	160	300	
OPTIONAL: insignia on sails					
Other fabrics:					
Canvas for deck awnings, cockpit covers, etc.	—	120	240	400	
Acrylic or vinyl-coated nylon for awnings, spray shield, wind scoop, etc.	—	300	500	800	
Polyethylene for water catcher, cheap tarps, and equipment covers	—	40	60	80	
Sailmaking parts: slides, plastic inserts, grommets, cringles, rings, sail rivets, hanks, sail slide shackles, wire, clevis pins, thimbles, D rings, sail headboard, sewing punch	—	200	300	400	
Sewing machine (e.g., Pfaff 130/6)	1	500	550	600	
Sail repair kit: grommet kit, grommet die, sail palm, canvas pliers, hole cutter, canvas bucket, bosun's chair, sail repair tape, polyester twine, tarred marline, seizing wire, Teflon gel, automatic awl, nicropress hand tool, ditty bag, rigger's knife, wire cutters, revolving punch, wire fid, other fids, mallets, rawhide, swivel bench hook, sail cleanser, needle set, beeswax, chafe-guard tape, pine tar, pricker (awl), scissors, fid for braided line, battens, burner tool	—	200	400	600	
TOTALS Excluding italized items		**$6,440**	**$8,060**	**$9,880**	

RUNNING RIGGING

ITEM	QUAN-TITY	LOW	MIDDLE	HIGH	YOUR PRICE
Blocks					
Singles	10	$ 150	$ 250	$ 400	
Doubles	2	40	60	80	
Single beckets	3	60	80	100	
Double beckets	2	50	75	100	
Single swivels	4	110	180	240	
Double swivels	2	120	200	260	
Snatch blocks	2	90	120	200	
Shackles	24	80	120	160	
Swivels	4	40	60	80	
Snap hooks	6	20	30	40	
Main boom vang tackle	1	60	100	200	
Mizzen vang tackle	1	50	90	180	

continued

RUNNING RIGGING (continued)

ITEM	QUAN-TITY	LOW	MIDDLE	HIGH	YOUR PRICE
Cleats, conventional or jam type	10	60	100	160	
Running line (e.g., Samson, Yale, Puritan, New England). Lengths include extra line so that spools can be purchased for a cost savings.					
Manila and polypropylene or polyethylene for dinghy, life raft, etc.	300 ft.	20	30	40	
Small working line for sails and pennants					
3/16" dacron, 3-strand	100 ft.	10	15	20	
3/8" dacron, 3-strand	600 ft.	100	150	200	
Dacron braided line for sheets, halyards, reefing, etc.					
3/16"	600 ft.	60	90	120	
1/4"	600ft.	80	120	160	
1/2"	600 ft.	240	360	470	
5/8"	600 ft.	370	550	740	
Nylon stranded line for docking, anchoring, and emergencies					
1/2"	600 ft.	130	200	270	
5/8"	600 ft.	210	320	430	
3/4"	600 ft.	290	440	580	
Winches (e.g., Barient, Barlow, Lewmar, Maxwell)					
Mizzen halyard winch, standard single-speed	1	50	70	90	
Mizzen sheet winch, standard single-speed	1	60	80	100	
Staysail halyard winch, standard single-speed	1	50	70	90	
Staysail sheet winch, standard single-speed	1	60	80	100	
OPTIONAL: jib halyard and sheet winches (can use genoa winches instead)					
Main halyard winch, two-speed	1	180	250	340	
Main sheet winch, two-speed, self-tailing	1	180	250	360	
Genoa halyard winch, two-speed, self-tailing	1	170	250	360	
Genoa sheet winch, two-speed, self-tailing	2	1,400	2,000	3,000	
Winch handles	9	90	180	270	
Sheet tracks (travelers) for main, mizzen, and stay-sail, various types in stainless, aluminum, or bronze	3	50	150	300	
Genoa jib sheet tracks, various lengths	2	60	120	260	
Running backstay levers for main mast	2	100	200	300	
Boom gallows hardware	—	20	30	40	
OPTIONAL: extra fairlead and turning blocks for self-tending capabilities, running backstay and spinnaker pole winches					
TOTALS		**$4,910**	**$7,470**	**$10,840**	

NAVIGATION EQUIPMENT

ITEM	QUAN-TITY	LOW	MIDDLE	HIGH	YOUR PRICE
Compass (e.g., Aquameter) with 30° card	1	$ 130	$ 350	$ 500	
Handbearing compass (e.g., Silva, Mini)	1	75	100	140	
Telltale compass	1	60	100	150	
Barometer	1	100	200	400	
Ship's clock	1	70	300	500	
Chronometer (e.g., Casio wristwatch)	1	25	50	75	
Ship's bell	1	20	30	40	
Horn, manual or butane with extra canisters	1	15	25	50	
Binoculars (7 × 50)	1	200	400	600	
Radio direction finder (RDF) (e.g., Aquameter, Ray Jefferson) OPTIONAL: handheld RDF (e.g., Vecta)	1	150	400	600	
VHF radio with 24 to 55 channels (e.g., Icom, Inmar, Ray Jefferson)	1	170	400	700	
Handheld VHF with weather alert channel for excursions	1	30	75	150	
Antenna for VHF, 3 dB, plus 60 feet of extra cable	1	50	100	150	
Short emergency VHF antenna	1	10	20	30	
Depth sounder with transducer (e.g., Coastal Navigator)	1	130	400	600	
Sounding lead with 12-fathom line (knotted)	1	10	20	30	
Sextant, good metal type	1	300	600	1,000	
Inexpensive plastic back-up sextant (e.g., Davis)	1	30	70	120	
Taffrail log, speedometer or electric knotmeter	1	180	400	600	
Wind anemometer/wind direction indicator with wiring	1	70	280	450	
Shortwave radio receiver (could be included in RDF)	1	—	250	400	
Loran-C with antenna (e.g. Raytheon Micrologic, Sitex)	1	750	2,000	4,000	
Ham radio (e.g., Icom)	1	1,800	3,000	6,000	
Charts (presently cost about $5.00 each)		1,000	2,000	3,000	
Navigation tools and books: parallel rulers, dividers, protractor, log books, guide books, pencils, pilots, sailing directions, celestial navigation tables, nautical almanac, calculator, light list, navigation instruction books, etc.	—	110	190	370	
EXPENSIVE OPTIONALS: Radar, SatNav, Omega, barograph, bottom graph recorder, weather plotter, gyro compass, single-sideband radio (SSB), hailer, clinometer, portable computer					
TOTALS		**$5,485**	**$11,760**	**$20,655**	

SAFETY AND EMERGENCY EQUIPMENT

ITEM	QUAN-TITY	LOW	MIDDLE	HIGH	YOUR PRICE
Basic safety equipment					
Stanchions (steel or stainless steel)	14	$ 40	$ 100	$ 300	
Lifelines, vinyl-covered 7/7 1/8″ stainless steel or dacron line	—	15	45	60	
Small turnbuckle for each line	4	30	45	60	
Pelican hooks for opening sections	4	10	20	30	
Bow pulpit, 1″ O.D. stainless steel tubing	1	80	160	240	
Stern pulpit, ⅞″ O.D. stainless steel tubing	1	70	140	210	
Life jackets, USCG approved commercial type	6	140	180	220	
Fire extinguishers, type A,B,C, 20 lb.	3	140	300	450	
Radar reflector, metal or wood with foil cover	1	20	30	40	
Life ring (orange) with line, flag, whistle, and strobe light	1	70	140	160	
Basic storm equipment					
Safety harness for each crew member	6	120	240	350	
Foul weather jumpsuit or rain gear	1	100	180	260	
Canvas message slingshot	1	20	30	40	
Flares, hand-held type	6	20	30	40	
Flare gun with pack of rocket flares	1	60	90	120	
Signal flags	—	30	80	150	
General maintenance and emergency repair kit for the hull and various boat systems	1	100	200	300	
Special emergency equipment					
EPIRB (e.g., Guest)	1	200	300	500	
Gale/survival kit with first aid supplies, medicine, food, line, fish hooks, knives, plastic bags, water, lights, flares, etc. All in container with life raft.	1	200	300	500	
Inflatable life raft (4–6 person) (e.g., Gibbons)	1	1,200	2,400	5,000	
OPTIONAL: radar detector alarm, sea anchor, exposure survival suit (e.g., Bailey, Stearns, Harvey), burglar alarm, float vest					
TOTALS		**$2,665**	**$5,010**	**$9,030**	

GRAND TOTALS FOR ALL SYSTEMS	**$54,378**	**$91,842**	**$141,561**

—Recommended Reading——

Almeida, Oscar. *Metal Working*. New York: Drake Publishers, 1976.

American Bureau of Shipping. *Approved Welding Electrodes, Wire-Flux, and Wire-Gas Combinations*. New York: American Bureau of Shipping, 1982.

——. *Rules for Building and Classing Aluminum Vessels*. New York: American Bureau of Shipping, 1975.

——. *Rules for Building and Classing Steel Vessels*. New York: American Bureau of Shipping, 1978.

——. *Rules for Building and Classing Steel Vessels under 61 Meters (200 Feet) in Length*. New York: American Bureau of Shipping, 1973.

——. *Rules for Nondestructive Inspection of Hull Welds*. New York: American Bureau of Shipping, 1975.

American Institute of Steel Construction. *Manual of Steel Construction*. 8th ed. Chicago: American Institute of Steel Construction, 1980.

American Technical Society. *Study Guide for Welding Skills and Practices*. 4th ed. Chicago: American Technical Society, 1971.

American Welding Society. *Corrosion Tests of Flame-Sprayed Coated Steel—19 Year Report*. AWS C2.14-74. Miami: American Welding Society, 1974.

——. *Guide for Steel Hull Welding*. AWS D3.5-76. Miami: American Welding Society, 1976.

Badham, Philip G. *Steel Boats*. Trenton, Ontario: Murray Boats (RR4, Trenton, Ontario, Canada K8V 5P7).

Bainbridge, C.G. *Welding*. 3d ed. A Teach Yourself Book. Sevenoaks, Kent, England: Hodder and Stoughton, 1977.

Bardes, Bruce P., ed. *Metals Handbook*. Vol. 1, *Properties and Selection: Iron and Steel*. 9th ed. Metals Park, Ohio: American Society for Metals, 1978.

Belcher, Bill. *Wind-Vane Self-Steering: How to Plan and Make Your Own*. Camden: International Marine, 1982.

Bingham, Fred P. *Practical Yacht Joinery*. Camden, Maine: International Marine, 1983.

Black, Perry O. *Diesel Engine Manual*. 3d ed. Indianapolis, Indiana: Howard W. Sams & Co., 1978.

Blandford, Percy W. *Modern Sailmaking*. Blue Ridge Summit, Pennsylvania: Tab Books, 1979.

Boatbuilder Magazine, 11 East Putnam Ave., Riverside, CT 06878.

Brewer, Edward S. and Jim Betts. *Understanding Boat Design*. Camden, Maine: International Marine, 1977.

Brown, Donald V. *Metallurgy Basics*. New York: Van Nostrand Reinhold, 1983.

Colvin, Thomas E. *Cruising As a Way of Life*. New York: Seven Seas, 1979.

——. *Cruising Designs*. Newport, Rhode Island: Seven Seas, 1977.

——. *Steel Boat Building*. Vol. 1, *From Plans to Bare Hull*. Camden, Maine: International Marine, 1985.

D'Arcangelo, Amelio M. *A Guide to Sound Ship Structures*. Cambridge, Maryland: Cornell Maritime Press, 1964.

Dashew, Steve and Linda. *The Circumnavigator's Handbook*. New York: W.W. Norton & Co., 1983.

Etsell, Richard W. "CAD/CAM at Tacoma Boatbuilding, Co." Report to Tacoma Boatbuilding Co., 1985.

Gardner, Joy. *Healing Yourself*. RR1, Winlaw, B.C., Canada V0G2J0.

Giachino, J.W., William Weeks, and Elmer Brune. *Welding Skills and Practices*. 4th ed. Chicago: American Technical Society, 1971.

Griffith, Bob. *Blue Water*. Boston: Sail Books, 1982.

Hiscock, Eric. *Sou'West in Wanderer IV*. Toronto and New York: Oxford Univ. Press, 1974.

Hobart School of Welding Technology. *Hobart Welding Guide*. EW-385. Troy, New York: Hobart Brothers Company, 1980.

Howard-Williams, Jeremy. *Sails*. 5th ed. Clinton Corners, New York: John de Graff, 1983.

International Association of Amateur Boat Builders (IAABB). "The Amateur Boatbuilder Quarterly."

Kinney, Francis S. *Skene's Elements of Yacht Design*. 8th ed. New York: Dodd, Mead & Company, 1973.

Klingel, Gilbert C. *Boatbuilding with Steel*. Camden, Maine: International Marine, 1973.

Lewis, David. *Ice Bird*. New York: W.W. Norton & Co., 1976.

Lloyd's Register of Shipping. *Rules for the Hull Construction of Steel Yachts*. West Sussex, England: Lloyd's Register of Shipping, 1974.

———. *Rules and Regulations for the Classification of Yachts and Small Craft*. Notice No. 2. West Sussex, England: Lloyd's Register of Shipping, 1983.

Materials Engineering. "1983 Materials Selector." Cleveland: Penton/IPC Publ., 1983.

McDonnell, Leo P. *The Use of Hand Woodworking Tools*. New York: Van Nostrand Reinhold, 1978.

Miller, Conrad, and E.S. Maloney. *Your Boat's Electrical System*. New York: Hearst Books, 1981.

Moitessier, Bernard. *The Long Way*. London: Granada Publ., 1977.

Monk, Edwin. *Modern Boat Building*. Rev. ed. New York: Charles Scribner & Sons, 1973.

Nicolson, Ian. *Small Steel Craft—Design, Construction, and Maintenance*. New York: Granada Publ., 1978.

———. *Surveying Small Craft*. 2nd ed. Camden, Maine: International Marine, 1984.

Norgrove, Ross. *Cruising Rigs and Rigging*. Camden, Maine: International Marine, 1982.

Perkins Engines, Inc. *Marine Engine Installation Know-How*. Wayne, Michigan: Perkins Engines, Inc., 1979.

Phillips-Birt, Douglas. *Sailing Yacht Design*. 3rd ed. London: Adlard Coles, 1976.

Pratt, Mike. *Own a Steel Boat*. Camden, Maine: International Marine, 1979.

Pretzer, Roger. *Marine Metals Manual: A Handbook for Boatmen, Builders, and Dealers*. Camden, Maine: International Marine, 1975.

Rabl, S.S. *Ship and Aircraft Fairing and Development*. Cambridge, Maryland: Cornell Maritime Press, 1941.

Roberts, Bruce. *Boat Building for the Amateur*. Tonawanda, New York: Clark Craft Boat Co.

———. *Build for Less*. Newport Beach, Calif.: Bruce Roberts International.

Robertson, Laurel, Carol Flinders, and Bronwen Godfrey. *Laurel's Kitchen.* Petaluma, Calif.: Nilgiri Press, 1976.

Saunders, Mike. *Yacht Joinery and Fitting.* Camden, Maine: International Marine, 1981.

Slade, K.A. *Steel Boat Construction.* Newnes Technical Books. Woburn, Mass.: Butterworth Publishers, 1979.

Teale, John. *Designing Small Craft.* New York: David McKay Co., 1977.

U.S. Code of Federal Regulations, No. 46, Part 1–40. Washington, D.C.: U.S. Government Printing Office, 1984.

U.S. Code of Federal Regulations, No. 46, Part 166–199. Washington, D.C.: U.S. Government Printing Office, 1984.

U.S. Department of Agriculture. *Wood Handbook: Wood as an Engineering Material.* Agricultural Handbook No. 72, Forest Products Laboratory, U.S. Forest Service. Washington, D.C.: Government Printing Office, 1974.

Van de Stadt Design, "Building Manual—Steel Frameless Fairing System." Manual. Wormeveer, Holland.

Verney, Michael. *Complete Amateur Boatbuilding.* Camden, Maine: International Marine, 1979.

Walker, John R. *Modern Metalworking—Materials, Tools, and Procedures.* South Holland, Illinois: Goodheart-Willcox Co., 1976.

Wallace, Ross. *Sail Power.* New York: Alfred A. Knopf, 1984.

Warren, Nigel. *Metal Corrosion in Boats.* Camden, Maine: International Marine, 1980.

Weismantel, Guy. *Paint Handbook.* New York: McGraw-Hill, 1981.

Wood, Charles E. *Building Your Dream Boat.* Centreville, Maryland: Cornell Maritime Press, 1981.

Wright, Dermot. *Marine Engines and Boating Mechanics.* Devon: David & Charles, 1979.

Zadig, Ernest A. *The Complete Book of Pleasure Boat Engines.* Englewood Cliffs, New Jersey: Prentice-Hall, 1980.

Directory of Designers and Builders Working in Steel

Directories of anything are notoriously hard to put together and even harder to keep up to date. Why then are they so popular? Most people don't have the time or the inclination to do the research; they want a "yellow pages" specializing in their field of interest. That's what we wanted when we first became interested in having a steel sailboat designed and built, but it wasn't available. So we began saving ads from all the yachting magazines we could find.

As you can imagine, once we started looking for information, it came in all forms, from a classy ad in *Cruising World,* to a suggestion from a friend about a brother-in-law's partner who once welded up a hull. It became important to define who was going to be included in such a directory.

Obviously the two key words are *steel* and *sailing,* since this is a directory of steel sailing vessels. There are many fine designers who have simply never worked with steel. Excellent steel power boats are turned out by yards that have never attempted a sailing hull. These folks, however reputable, have not been included.

This directory includes professional designers and builders of steel sailboats from 20' on up, whether they are destined for commercial use or for pleasure. The main focus is on cruising designs, although large charter vessels or fishing schooners can also be found here. Many of the people listed also have designed or built steel power craft or aluminum hulls, and they would be happy to provide more information on these boats.

Next it was time to wrestle with the word "professional." The directory couldn't include everyone who has ever dreamed up or patched together a steel hull.

The success of a designer is best judged by the outcome of his or her work. The title, "Naval Architect," is an exclamation point after the title "designer," showing that the person has a specific type of education and probably has performed some commercial work. Each designer has a particular style and way of blending artistry and mathematical formulas, and a good designer combines customer requests with what works for the hull material. Many designers are very capable of working with a variety of materials, but we've chosen to focus on those who are actively designing in steel.

Included in the directory are only those builders who are knowledgeable about metal working, have built more than one steel hull, and who plan to continue making their living building steel hulls. In other words, people who depend on a reputation for craftsmanship. Amateurs, on the other hand, generally build only for themselves, and frequently only build one boat, which is often a work of art, but occasionally an ugly tub.

The folder of clippings and notes began to bulge, and we wanted to get more information about each designer and builder. We tried to contact each person on our first list by letter. Many replied. From those replies, we narrowed the list down according to the criteria discussed above. Then we sent off a questionnaire to each person to get more detailed information about their experience, skills, facilities, and "philosophy."

In the summer of 1984, we had the opportunity to travel around the U.S. and visit many of the designers and yards with whom we had corresponded. Some of the information included in the directory came from these personal visits. Seeing the number of steel boats being built and the quality of the work being done was quite an inspiration.

Since we have a definite preference for round hulls, we asked designers and builders if they had experience with this hull shape, and we have tried to include the hull shape for each boat attributed to a designer or builder. Builder's responses showed that the increase in cost to build a round hull ranges from 0% to 50%, with an average increase of 15%. The lower figures came from yards that produce mostly round hulls, while yards that do not have as much practice quoted steeper price increases. Happily, the number of builders with experience in round-hull construction is increasing, as knowledge of fabrication methods and required skills spreads.

In several cases, we ran into people who designed *and* built steel boats, sometimes building their own designs exclusively. Are they builders or designers? Generally, if other people also built their designs, we listed them as designers. If design is an offshoot of their building experience, we listed them as builders. Nobody made it into both lists, although there were some very close decisions.

Every directory has its limitations, and this one has two major weaknesses. We hope that inaccuracy is not a third.

First, the listings are somewhat dependant on replies to letters sent out to designers or builders. Some did not reply or their addresses were incorrect. We often tried mailing another letter or checking with another source, with no success. We know that some people who should be included have been left out. In some cases there is not much information on a particular designer or builder. This is not a reflection on their abilities; the details were not available. Some chose not to be listed.

The second limitation, as with any directory, is how up-to-date the information is. There are probably already mistakes in the listings. Boatbuilding is usually a small-business operation, and with today's economy, the demise of a business is all too frequent. Ten yards that were on the original list are no longer in business. On the other hand, 30 new ones have sprung up. Some designers or builders with whom we've talking were thinking about getting into steel. Although they may now "qualify" for inclusion, they aren't yet listed in this edition of the directory.

We're going to keep saving ads and pestering people with letters. And when we get enough new information, we plan to put out a second, updated, more-detailed edition of this direction. Steel boats and steel boatbuilding are just starting to ride up the crest of the wave, and many more people are trying out the water.

TO THE READER:

This directory, like the rest of *Steel Away,* is intended to be a guide that offers the reader as many bases for comparison as possible. In that spirit, boat descriptions and prices are included. Many builders and designers asked us not to include their prices since, unfortunately, they are changing rapidly. **PRICES LISTED ARE ONLY FOR COMPARISON.** Whatever you do, don't wave a copy of this directory under people's noses if they quote a different price than is listed here.

TO BUILDERS AND DESIGNERS:

We tried. Oh, did we try hard to make the listings as accurate as possible. If we have erred, we apologize and will be glad to correct the information in the next edition. Designers and builders who would like to be included should contact us so that we can get the necessary information. In many ways, this directory is an affirmation of the health and vigor of steel boatbuilding.

Directory of Designers

The listing of designers is worldwide, and is arranged alphabetically by last name. The designs are listed in order of length on deck to the nearest foot, and include the design name, title or number, when known; basic hull shape; displacement; some layout options; cost for study plans and complete stock plans; and, in some cases, the builders who have constructed the particular hull. Many designs have different rig options; the ones mentioned are those usually advertised with the design.

When available, other information is also included, such as the designer's background in design and, specifically, in steel. We've also noted when a designer is also a builder or has building experience, since we feel this reflects a better understanding of steel construction. If the designer has a specialty (for example, commercial, round hulls, windjammers) or is responsible for any innovations, these facts are included.

At present, there is a fairly large selection of stock designs available, especially if designers working outside the U.S. are included. Over 800 stock and custom plans are listed here.

Stock plans for steel yachts cost between $10 and $100 per foot, depending on the particulars of the design. Based on the responses of the designers, average prices are as follows:

30' boat	$10/ft. or $300
40' boat	$15/ft. or $600
50' boat	$20/ft. or $1,000
60' boat	$35/ft. or $2,100
70' boat	$50/ft. or $3,500

Custom plans run between 3 and 5 times this amount—in other words, 3–10 % of the total cost of the boat. But it is money well spent if you have specific requirements for your dreamboat.

ABBREVIATIONS USED IN THE DIRECTORY LISTINGS

HULL SHAPES:

SC	Single chine (hard or soft), V-bottom
DC	Double chine, strip chine
MC	Multi-chine, lapstrake
R	True round, fully developed molded-radius, wineglass

PRICE LISTS:

SP	Study plans
CP	Construction plans
BH	Bare-hull assembly (hull, deck, cabin)
Comp	Completed vessel

ADAMS YACHT DESIGN PTY. LTD. / Office 6, Pittwater Center
Cnr. Beaconsfield & Kalinya Sts. / Newport, N.S.W. / Australia 2106
Tel. (02) 997-2749

With over 15 years of experience, the Adams design group has many designs in all materials to their credit. Most of their steel stock designs are appropriate for home builders; much of their work focuses on performance cruising boats. The Adams 40 is the most popular design, and over 120 have been built. The stock plans, with different rig and keel options, are listed in a booklet available for $8 U.S. Adams also supplies drawings of a "wheeling machine" for home builders working on a round hull.

30' MC motorsailor sloop, 7 tons	$550 AUS
33' R or MC center-cockpit cutter, 6 tons	650
35' R or MC aft-cockpit cutter, 6 tons	650
36' DC motorsailor sloop, 11 tons	650
40' R or MC aft-cockpit cutter or ketch, 10 tons	650
40' R or MC shallow-draft cutter or ketch, 10 tons	650
45' R or MC center-cockpit cutter or ketch, 14 tons	650
45' R or MC aft-cockpit cutter or ketch, 14 tons	650
54' R or MC center-cockpit cutter, 21.3 tons	650
60' R or MC center-cockpit cutter, 22.8 tons	650
98' schooner (not complete)	

AMSTERDAM NAVAL ARCHITECTURE / 2 Herman Heyermans Weg
1077 JH Amsterdam / Holland

Good round-hulled steel yachts of various sizes.

ATKIN & CO. / P.O. Box 3005 / Noroton, CN 06820

Atkin & Co. has been designing boats in wood since 1906 and in steel as early as 1930. William Atkin is known for his carry-over and development of Scandinavian designs, for example, the Atkin Ingrid 38 double ender done in the manner of Colin Archer. Today John Atkin carries on with designs in various materials, including steel. A complete set of plans usually has 8–10 drawings. Atkin feels that laying plate on a diagonal makes plating a round hull easier. He has written four enjoyable books.

19' MC V-bottom knockabout, *Lizza Jane*	$ 40
30' SC V-bottom schooner, *Maid of Kent*	200
36' SC V-bottom schooner, *Island Princess*	300
55' MC schooner, *Metcalf*	700

WALTER C. BECKMANN, LIMITED / 93 Harbor Island Rd. / Narragansett, RI 02882
Tel. (401) 783-1859

Mr. Beckmann has some 26 years experience with steel and aluminum. With Rhode Island Marine Services, he has designed and built various sailing vessels in steel, as well as designing tugs and launches. He has experience in round hulls, although most of his designs are chine. The yard has been active in construction and repair of all hull materials in Snug Harbor since 1956. Charges for custom designs range from $100 to $3000 per sheet with 7 sheets generally included. Stock plans can occasionally be found on sale, and there may be no charge for the design if the Rhode Island Yard builds the boat for you.

35' *Debbie*, cruising sloop	$ 597
37' *Block Island*, cruising ketch	897
38' *Classic*, cruising sloop	597
40' *Spray*, replica of Slocum's boat	897
44' *Ocean*, cruising ketch, 17 ton	1198
47' *Nicole*, schooner	1497
50' *Classic*, aft cabin ketch	1797
50' *World*, schooner	2097
60' *Atlantis*, schooner	2697
81' *Tamaris*, luxury ketch	5394

JAY BENFORD / 758 Trenton Ave. / Severna Park, MD 21146
Tel. (301) 544-5077

Mr. Benford is a naval architect who has been working in a variety of hull materials, including steel, for over 20 years. Most of his steel hulls are chine, although he will design round bottom boats. All custom design work is done on an hourly basis rather than on a percentage of the boat's cost. He will work with any builder.

	SP
30' MC, many rig variations, 11,000 lbs.	$11
33' DC lug schooner, 18,980 lbs.	7
35' Colin Archer *Mercedes*, R cutter/ketch, 23,240 lbs.	18.50
36' DC ketch, 25,876 lbs.	9
37' *Corcovado*, SC pilothouse ketch or cutter, 28,450 lbs.	22
40' MC brigantine, 37,100 lbs.	7
40' SC skipjack ketch or schooner, 26,000 lbs.	15
42' MC schooner, rig variations, 36,000	22
42'/43' MC motorsailor, topsail ketch, 33,000	22
45' *Argonaut*, R or DC cutter, 29,400 lbs.	15
45' *Boundary Bay,* DC cat ketch, 30,420 lbs.	7
45' *Inscrutable,* DC lug schooner or cutter, 35,200 lbs.	15

FRED BINGHAM YACHT DESIGN / 516 E. Arrellaga No. 5 / Santa Barbara, CA 93103
Tel. (805) 966-2015

Mr. Bingham is well known for his excellent boatbuilding books. He designs in a variety of hull materials, including steel.

	SP	CP
29' *Isabella*, DC cutter or ketch, 17,180 lbs.	$12.50	$305
31' *Mark II*, cutter; hull kit reportedly built for $10,000		

BODEN BOAT PLANS / P.O. Box 316 / Cremorne 2090 / Australia
Tel. (02) 906152

Cecil Boden, B.E., F.R.I.N.A., the executive of Boden Boat Plans, was one of the first designers of steel cruising yachts in Australia. His craft tend to be traditional with long keels and classic lines, except for the 39' steel cruising catamaran, *Catrina,* and the 39' multi-chine ketch, *South Sea.* Full-size patterns are available for many of his designs, all of which are illustrated in the 112-page publication *Boden's Boat Designs and Boatbuilding,* which is $12.00 (U.S.). Brian Poole is the present design director of Boden Boat Plans, which was established in 1956. He has been involved over the last 30 years with all aspects of boatbuilding. He also oversees introduction of designs by other leading Australia designers through Boden Boat Plans. Bill Bollard, senior partner of W. Bollard and Partners Pty. Ltd. has been associated with the boating industry for 25 years, and is a designer of fast steel cruising and racing yachts. His designs are available through Boden Boat Plans.

A selection from the 100 + designs of Mr. Boden. Study plans are available for $30 U.S., air mail postage.

36' *Helena,* MC cutter ketch, 8 tons	$ 359 AUS
36' *Germaine,* R cutter or ketch, 8 tons	359
36' *Christine,* MC shoal-draft cutter	375
36' *Daru,* MC ketch	375
36' *Catrina,* DC catamaran	875
37' *Bass Strait Clipper,* SC center cockpit ketch, 8.2 tons	900
39' *South Sea,* MC pilothouse ketch	575
40' *Elizabeth,* MC shoal-draft ketch, 9.6 tons	395
41' *Kiama,* MC motorsailor ketch	500
41' *Trade Winds,* DC ketch for charter/cruise	780
42' *Sea Mist,* SC clipper ketch	550
44' *Togari,* DC trawler, gaff ketch	1550
52' *Marion,* MC luxurious motorsailor ketch	995
52' *Reef Master,* DC commercial fishing ketch	1175

Bill Bollard has designed many sail and power craft in steel. The following are some of his sailing designs:

31' (9.5 m) DC sloop (Des. No. 102), 5.6 tons	$ 450 AUS
36' (11 m) MC sloop (Des. No. 142), 7.6 tons	575
36' (11 m) R sloop (Des. No. 143), 4.6 tons	600
37' DC sloop (Des. No. 117), 10 tons	475
46' (14 m) R cutter (Des. No. 116), 12.5 tons	800
46' (14.3 m) DC motorsailor (Des. No. 125), 16 tons	660
50' (15 m) R cutter (Des. No. 118), 15 tons	900
55' (17 m) R ketch (Des. No. 135), 32 tons	750

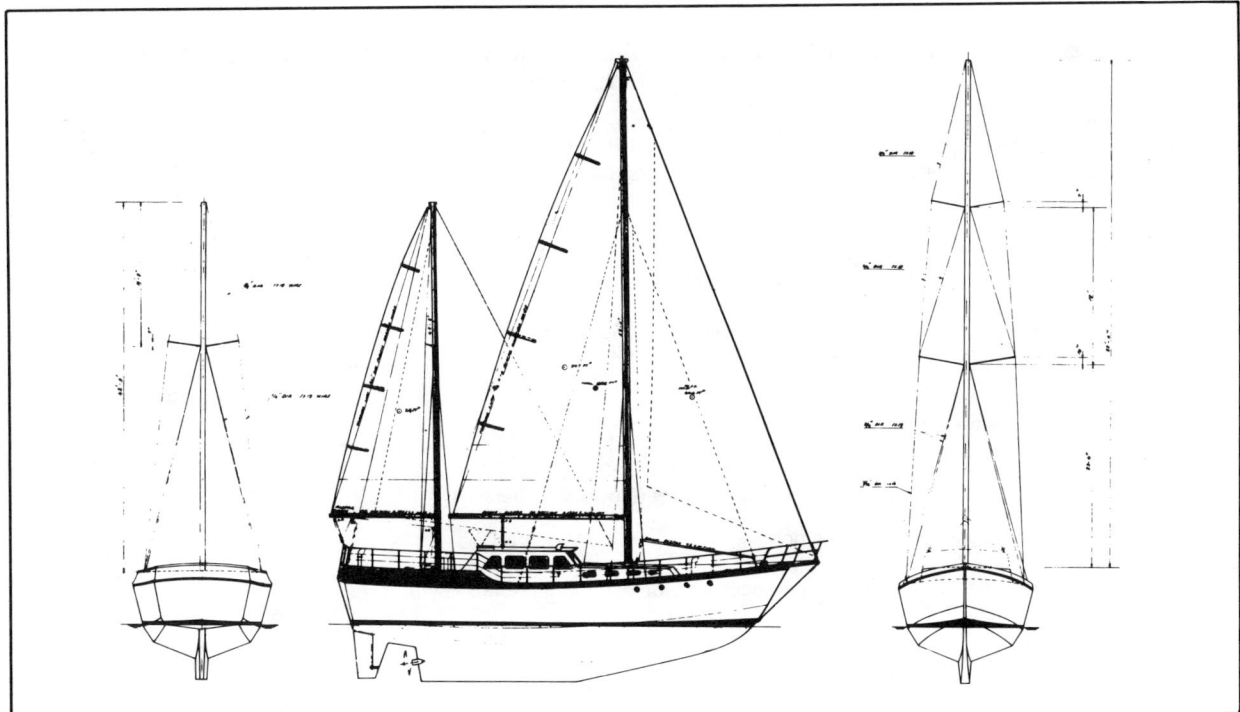

Marion III, *designed by Cecil E. Boden.*

PHILIP C. BOLGER / 250 Washington St. / Gloucester, MA 01930

Mr. Bolger, known for innovative designs and his publications on instant boatbuilding, is basically a designer of easy-to-build chine hulls. He has been working off and on with steel for 34 years, and Ron Barnes of St. Augustine, FL has built some Bolger *Solution 48* hulls.

48′ *Solution*, SC shoal draft.

JOHN BRANDLMAYR / c/o Shore Boatbuilders / 23511 Dyke Rd. / Vancouver, BC / Canada
Tel. (604) 524-1341

Mr. Brandlmayr designs both aluminum and steel yachts.

35′ SC sloop	$800
41′ ketch or schooner, 28,774 lbs.	800
47′ SC center-cockpit ketch, 42,000 lbs.	950

ROBERT BRASTED / 22 Southview Place / West Cliff, Bournemouth
Dorset / England BH2 5PN / Tel. Bournemouth 25213

Mr. Brasted has been designing in steel for 12 years, and most of his designs to date have been round hulls. Although most of his designs are long keeled, some of the larger ones, like the schooner *Spirit of Labrador*, have centerboards. Brasted is also working more and more with composites using the West System, and is involved in design and consultancy for third-world fisheries projects. Study plans are available for £35; design fees are by fixed quotation.

35′ R or MC sloop
43′ R schooner (Des. No. 43)
45′ MC or R round ketch (Des. No. 39), not complete
51′ MC or R cutter or ketch
55′ *Agapanthus*, R centerboard ketch (Des. No. 29)
57′ *Czarina*, R ketch (Des. No. 40)
67′ *Spirit of Labrador*, R centerboard schooner (Des. No. 25), built by Joyce Marine

---

TED BREWER YACHT DESIGN / 217 Edith Point Rd. / Anacortes, WA 98221
Tel. (206) 293-2282

Mr. Brewer has been designing boats in steel since 1963, and has over 20 steel sailing designs, most of them round. He worked with steel at the Luders yard for seven years, and with his high respect for the strength of steel, he has designed some of the lightest steel yachts around. Brewer helped popularize the molded-radius style of hull construction and also has designs for fully developed round hulls.

	SP	CP
30' *Bulldog,* R cutter, 12,000 lbs.	$ 50	$ 350
32' *Mistral,* R fin-keel cutter, 13,250 lbs.	50	400
32' *Tern,* SC ketch	35	250
33' *Murray,* R sloop (Murray exclusive) Plans sold only outside N. America		250
34' *Kaiulani,* R cutter (Kaiulani exclusive), 16,000 lbs.		
35' *Goderich,* (designed with Wallstrom) R cutter, 17,000 lbs.	50	550
37' *Goderich,* R ketch	50	550
38' *Kaiulani,* R cutter (Kaiulani exclusive)		
40' *Cape Sable,* fully developed	80	600
40' *Verity,* R fin-keel cutter (Kelly exclusive), 22,950 lbs.		
40' & 42' *Corten,* DC/R schooner or cutter (Mooney, Jefferson), 29,600 lbs.	60	600
43' *Alaska,* DC cutter, 35,000 lbs.	80	800
43' fully R yawl (not complete)		
44' & 46' *Cape Race,* center-cockpit motorsailor centerboard ketch, 40,200 lbs.	90	900
45' *Atlantic,* R ketch (Kanter exclusive), 36,000 lbs.		
45' *Kingsland,* R cutter, 40,000 lbs.	80	800
45' *Miami,* R flush-deck, doghouse ketch, 36,000 lbs.	80	800
46' *Cape Flattery,* R keel or centerboard ketch	90	1000
53' *Arielle,* R motorsailor	100	2500
56' *Pacific,* R ketch	100	3000

D.E. BROOKE / Ewbank, Brooke & Associates / Rooms 55–57, Ferry Building
Quay Street / C.P.O. Box 2560 / Auckland / New Zealand
Tel. 32383

Mr. Brooke designed his first steel yacht in 1973, after concentrating on competition racing craft. He also worked as a builder, pioneering the building of large luxury yachts for export from New Zealand, and has designed and built special plate formers and benders. Although Brooke designs all types of hulls, he prefers round bilges for steel. Design fees are approximately 3% of the estimated total building cost.

70' *Paulmarkson I,* ketch
72' *Summer Wine,* R ketch
72' *Paulmarkson II,* ketch
75' *Shangri La I,* ketch
77' *Aqua Vector,* R ketch - 54 T (built by McNiven Yachts)
78' R ketch
80' *Cavalier 80,* ketch
80' *Shangri La II,* ketch
82' *Ciao,* ketch
82' *Rushcutter,* ketch
84' *Chardonay,* ketch
92' *Pegasus II,* cutter
112' R workboat schooner
127' *Spirit of New Zealand,* R barkentine for sail training

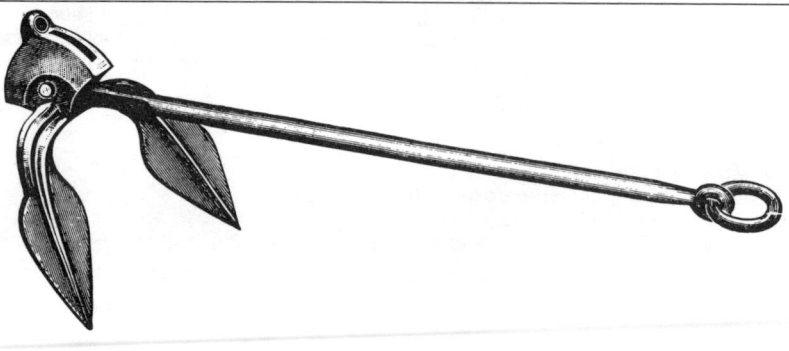

ALAN BUCHANAN & PARTNERS / LeBourg Slip, St. Clement
Jersey, Channel Islands / England
Tel. 0534-51370

Mr. Buchanan has over 40 steel designs to his credit from 28′ to 90′, and his firm has been working in this material for over 40 years. As well as round hulls, they have several chine and multi-chine hulls designed for both amateur and professional construction, using a conic system for flat plate. The daily design rate is about £250 per day, but most requirements can be met from their stock plans. Stock plans are available without modification or alteration for between £50 and £80, plus a keel fee of about 1% of the construction cost.

28′ round sloop (Amsterdam)	£50
34′ round sloop	60
35′ round sloop (Holland)	60
36′ round motorsailer ketch (two designs) (Holland)	75
37′ 6″ round ketch (Amsterdam)	60
39′ 9″ MC round ketch	85
42′ 8″ round yawl	75
45′ round, center-cockpit ketch	80
46′ round cutter (U.S.)	80

GEORGE BUEHLER / Box 966 / Freeland, WA 98249

Mr. Buehler has designed in steel for 6 years and in wood since 1970. His designs are aimed at amateur builders, and he also does custom design work. His stock plans range from 30′ to 67′ and are listed in his catalog, available for $6.50. His best-known design is a 43′ chine cutter or schooner.

FRANK F. CARIUS / 1471 Appin Rd. / North Vancouver, BC / Canada

45′ *Horizon*, SC center cockpit cutter (used to be built by Horizon Boats, now out of business)

CLARK CRAFT BOATS / 16-C Aqua Lane / Tonawanda, NY 14150

This firm designs primarily chine hulls that are good for home builders. They publish a booklet, "Boat Building for the Amateur," which includes study plans of the various designs, and is available for $2.00.

	SP	CP
20′ MC sloop		$189
23′ SC sloop		209
25′ SC twin-keel sloop, 5,620 lbs.	10	244
28′ *Serenade*, DC sloop	10	311
28′ DC motorsailer sloop	15	209
30′ *Starfire*, R or DC sloop, twin bilge keels	15	284
32′ *Soliloquy*, DC sloop,	15	395
35′ SC center-cockpit sloop	15	400
35′ *Morning Mist*, ketch or sloop	15	420
37′ *Windsong*, DC center-cockpit sloop or ketch	26	425
42′ *Windward*, R ketch	26	450
52′ *Crosswinds*, SC, DC, or R center-cockpit ketch, 44,500 lbs.	28	485

A George Buehler design, constructed by a talented home builder.

THOMAS E. COLVIN / Fiddler's Green / Miles, VA 23114

No directory of steel yacht designs would be complete without the name of Thomas E. Colvin, although he is now involved mostly in the design of commercial sailing vessels. Some of the most popular steel yacht designs are Colvin's: over 300 *Gazelles* and over 100 *Saugeen Witches* are sailing today. He has worked with steel for about 45 years, and will design any shape hull to suit the owner. However, most of his stock designs are chine. Mr. Colvin sails his own steel Chinese junk with a lug rig. Three of his books, *Cruising Designs, Cruising as a Way of Life,* and *Coastwise and Offshore Cruising Wrinkles* are available from Seven Seas Press. Mr. Colvin recently completed a two volume set called *Steel Boatbuilding.*

    Study plans for any of the designs listed below may be obtained from the designer for $25 per set; $30 outside the U.S.

25' *Hobo/Julia,* gaff ketch	$ 250
32' *Sans Souci,* sharpie, jib-headed or gaff ketch	125
33' *Lazy Lug,* sharpie	125
34' *Saugeen Witch,* SC, all rigs	400
34' *Tamarack,* gaff schooner	400
36' *Radian,* ketch	400
36' *Shaoing-Ch'au,* flat-bottomed junk	500
36' Bahamian cutter (large, SC *Saugeen Witch*)	
36' *Ying-Yang,* pinky schooner, lug or gaff rig	600
38' *Ola'Loa,* SC jib-headed ketch	800
38' *Doxy,* gaff or staysail schooner or junk	600
41' *Aderyn Mor,* gaff ketch or schooner	600
41' *Oothoon,* junk	600
42' *Gazelle,* SC lug schooner, gaff schooner, or gaff ketch	600
42' *Dunmowen,* pinky schooner	600
43' *Sea Wolf,* pinky, MC gaff schooner	600
44' *Dorothy C,* R ketch	1,000
45' *Alsanal Too,* R center-cockpit ketch	1,200
45' *Yankee Point,* gaff schooner, junk, ketch, or brigantine	800
48' *K'ung Fu-Tse,* junk	1,000
48' *Amphora,* pinky gaff schooner or junk	800
50' *Amphora,* ("Pipistrelle," "Memory"), lug schooner	800
52' *Sultana,* three-masted cargo schooner	1,000
53' *McAlister,* MC, three-masted pinky schooner	1,000
53' *Chief Aptakistic,* schooner	800
54' *Luk-Chin,* junk	1,000
58' *Phantom,* SC Bahamian centerboard schooner	1,200
66' *Gypsy,* SC three-masted, commercial schooner	1,200
78' *Irregardless,* three-masted sharpie schooner	

DUDLEY DIX / Box 285 / Tokai, 7966 / South Africa

Mr. Dix has worked in a variety of hull materials besides steel. His *Pratique 35* was drawn mainly with the skilled amateur builder in mind. He is currently working on a 38 of similar concept and construction to the 35. Plans are available directly from him, and completed *Pratiques* can be obtained from Mr. Howdy Bailey at Marine Metals in Norfolk, Virginia.

	SP	CP
35' *Pratique (Salty Dog II),* MC cutter	$10	$399
64' *Dix,* MC schooner with radiused top chine (Bailey), 36.6 tons		

EMSWORTH MARINE SALES / Thorney Road, Emsworth
Hampshire / England PO10 8BP / Tel. 02434-71744

36' *Sea Roamer,* SC motorsailor ketch, 9 tons. Cabin is composite fiberglass. Built by KCS Marine in England for £11,385 in 1980.

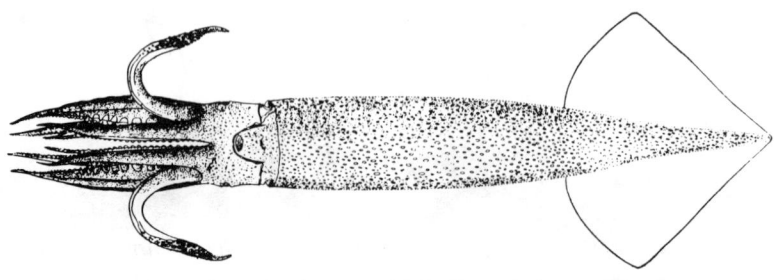

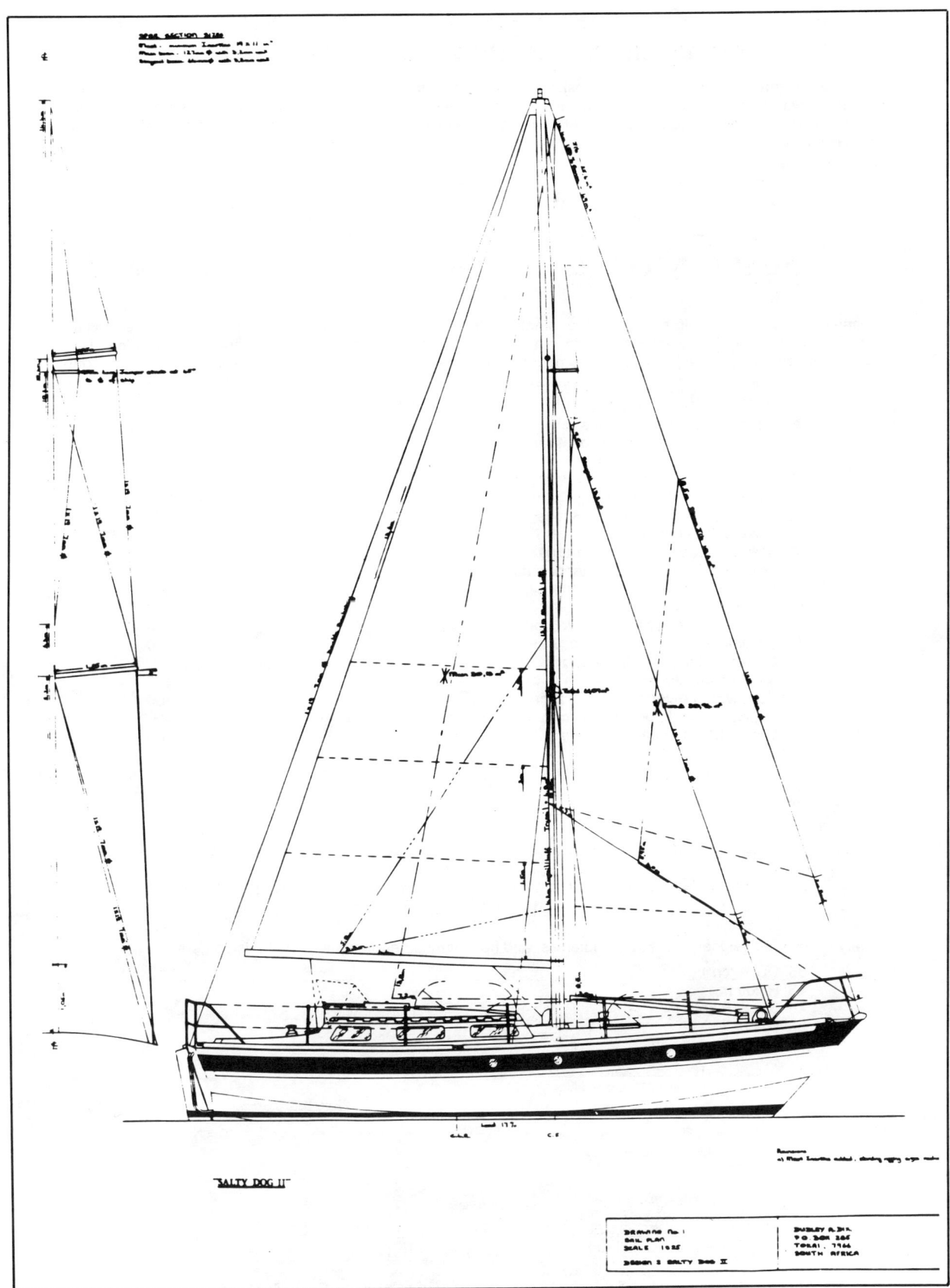

Salty Dog II, *one of the* Pratique *class boats designed by Dudley Dix.*

WESTON FARMER ASSOCIATES / 18970 Azure Rd. / Wayzata, MN 55391

Although Mr. Farmer is now deceased, the designs produced during his 60 years of work are still available through his son Wes. He was one of the most respected naval architects of his time, and is perhaps best known for his *Tahitiana* ketch, a steel version of John Hanna's Tahiti ketch. Many yards have built his designs, including Sierra Yachtwerks and Lund in England.

	SP
23' *Cherub,* SC, 5,000 lbs.	$69.50
31' 6" *Tahitiana,* MC ketch, 18,000 lbs.	69.50

DENIS H. GANLEY / P.O. Box 23 , Greenhithe / Auckland, 10 / New Zealand
Tel. Auckland 413.9868

Mr. Ganley has been designing steel yachts for amateur construction for 13 years, although many of his designs are also professionally built. He produces both round and soft chine boats. Reportedly the hull shapes have developed surfaces that are rounded so that the hull can be produced without plate rolling. Most of his 67 designs are either a rounded deep V or soft chine style, and range from 16' to 75'. In New Zealand his boats are built by WECO and Greenwood Boat Builders Ltd., and in the UK by FL Steel Craft Ltd. Study plans for any boat are available for $1.00 NZ.

25' *Hitch Hiker,* cutter, 4.5 tons	$250 NZ
26' *Snapper Cather,* motorsailor, 4 tons	150
29' *Greenhithe,* sloop, 6 tons	150
30' *Snowbird,* sloop or ketch, 6 tons	300
32' *September,* ketch or cutter, 6 tons	300
32' *Chevron,* ketch or cutter, 6.8 tons	400
33' *Cruising Spirit,* ketch or cutter, 8.7 tons	300
34' *Shadow,* sloop or cutter, 6.1 tons	500
34' *Pine Island Clipper,* schooner or cutter, 7.2 tons	500
36' *Pastime,* cutter or ketch, 9 tons	500
38' *Fiddler,* 8.7 tons	500
39' *Tara,* sloop, cutter or ketch, 7.7 tons	700
40' *Pacemaker,* flush-deck sloop, 9 tons	700
40' *Lucas,* cutter or ketch, 14.8 tons	600
42' *Solution,* center-cockpit ketch or cutter, 14.5 tons	400
43' *Salazar,* flush-deck cutter, 14 tons	800
46' *Gulf Trader,* schooner, Freedom style, centerboard, 18 tons	400
48' *Great Barrier,* ketch, 15.7 tons	800
49' *Outer Gulf,* ketch, 18 tons	800
54' *Lion Heart,* twin-centerboard ketch, 24.5 tons	P.O.A.
59' *Liamedos,* ketch, 27 tons	P.O.A.
75' schooner	

WILLIAM GARDEN / Toad's Landing, Canoe Bay / Sidney, B.C. / Canada
Tel. (604) 656-3761

This very reputable designer works in all materials, and has many other designs than are listed here.

- 36' DC ketch
- 43' R ketch
- 45' Spirit, R ketch
- 58' ketch
- 58' R motorsailor ketch

LAURENT GILES LTD. / Station Street / Lymington, Hampshire / England S04 9BA
Tel. 0590 73223/4

Laurent Giles have been designing boats since 1926, producing their first steel hull shortly after World War II. They design both round and multi-chine hulls, and will make recommendations about the facilities and experience needed to build a design. Laurent Giles have pioneered the use of heat-line bending techniques on smaller steel craft, and are currently building ten 70′ ketches with British Shipbuilders at Newcastle using this method. Design fees are based on hourly rates, which are between £17.50 and £20.00.

33′ *Keyhaven,* R or MC yawl, 13,000 lbs.
32′ *Alderney,* MC, 8,100 lbs.
33′ *Giles,* MC, 14,500 lbs.
38′ *Azores,* R, 23,350 lbs.
39′ *Aquamarine,* R ketch, 25,500 lbs.
46′ *Azores,* MC, 36,000 lbs.
50′ *Giles,* MC, 38,000 lbs.
70′ *Shipwright,* R, 84,000 lbs.
75′ *Greater Manchester Challenge,* MC, 85,000 lbs.

GIORGETTI & MAGRINI S.R.L. / via C.G. Merlo 1 / 20122 Milano / Italy
Tel. 02-791094/799561

Giorgetti & Magrini, who recently completed the design for *Italia* (Italy's next America's Cup challenger), was founded in 1970. They have been working with steel for 10 years, and generally use this material for boats over 60′. They design both round and chine hulls, but prefer round. Most of their boats are built with transverse framing. Giorgetti & Magrini hulls have been constructed by amateurs and professional yards all over Europe.

45′ *Ashanti,* R center-cockpit schooner, 14 tons
50′ *Ashanti,* R schooner
70′ *Ashanti,* R schooner
62′ *Uxmal,* R aft-cockpit schooner, 27 tons
74′ *Uxmal,* R schooner
100′ *Uxmal,* R aft-cockpit schooner, 125 tons

GLEN-L MARINE / 9152 Rosencrans / Bellflower, CA 90706

Glen-L Marine has been designing especially for amateur builders for 32 years, moving into steel in the last 8 years. Their hulls are chine and multi-chine designs, and they do not do any custom work. Glen-L also has design publications and catalogs. All plans include full size patterns and a copy of *Steel Boatbuilding Guide.* Prices are post paid in the U.S.

	SP	CP
31′ *Aurora,* MC cutter	$7	$200
35′ *Aquarian,* MC cutter or ketch	8	255
35′ *Steel Away,* MC cutter	8	250
39′ *Spirit,* MC cutter or ketch, 22,625 lbs.	8	275

DANNY GREENE / Colebrook Rd. / Little Compton, RI 02837

Mr. Greene is a relatively new designer who recently had the following design built. He has cruised extensively and lived aboard other boats.

| 34′ 6″ *Integrity,* DC cutter, ketch, 15,800 lbs. (Gladding-Hearn) | $20 | $500 |

MAURICE GRIFFITH / c/o Bruce Roberts (see entry)

| 33′ Levanter, DC cutter | £225 |
| 37′ Francis Drake, DC sloop | 225 |

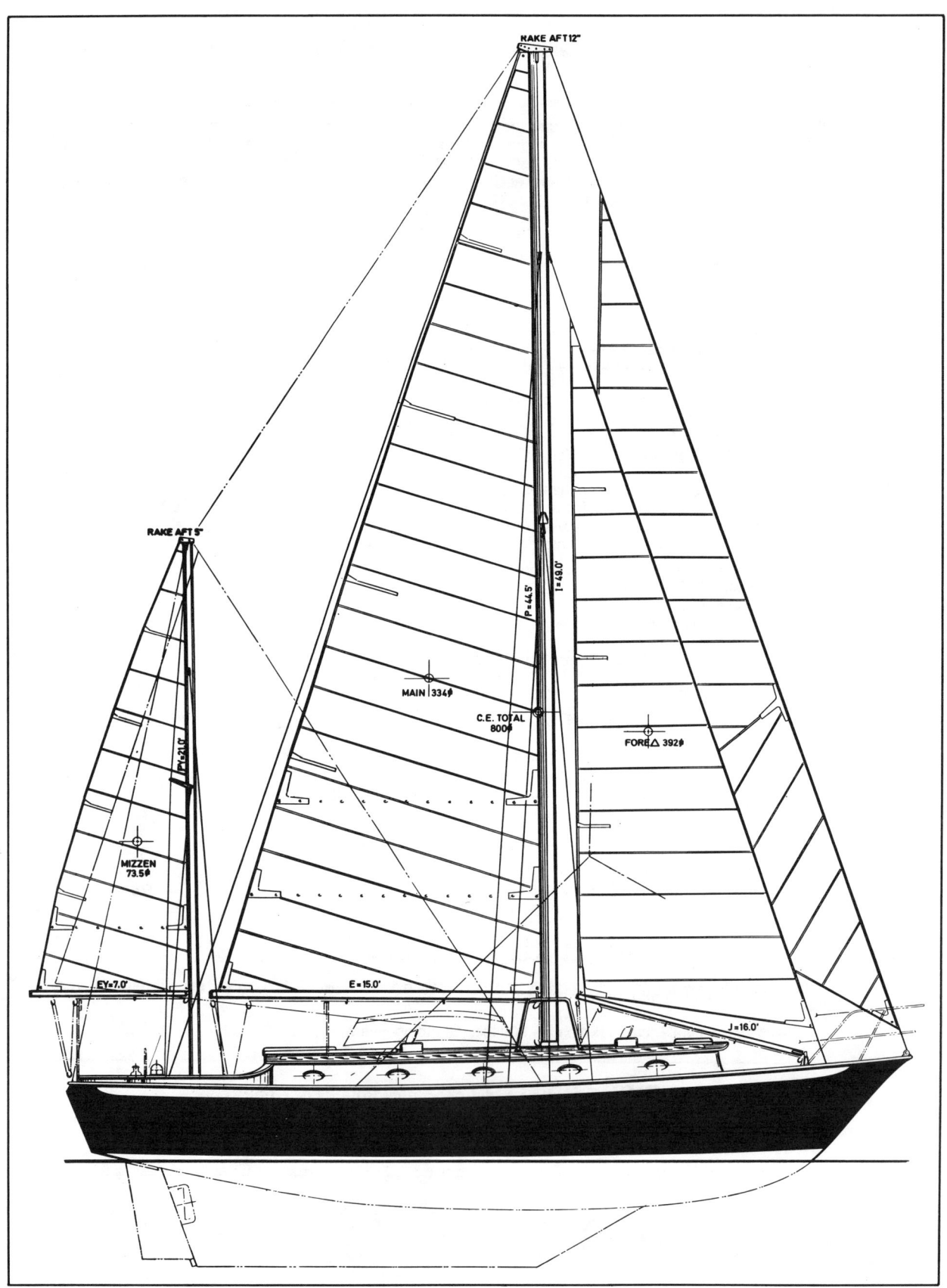

Spirit, *designed by Glen-L Marine.*

Courtesy of the designer

ERWIN HAAG / 78 West View Crescent / Whangarei / New Zealand
Tel. 61-394

Mr. Haag has been designing boats for 25 years, and has worked with steel for the past 15. He prefers round hulls, but finds that many customers want chine shapes for easier construction. Fees for custom designs are determined by multiplying the length times the beam times the depth times the hourly rate of the yard in which the boat will be built. Charges for stock plans are approximately half that of custom. Study plans are $5 NZ each.

31' DC, fin-keel, aft-cockpit sloop (Des. No. 144), 5.0 tons
33' MC fin-keel, aft-cockpit junk (Des. No. 162), 5.0 tons
33' DC full-keel, double-ended sloop (Des. No. 164), 11.5 tons
35' DC fin-keel, aft-cockpit sloop (Des. No. 148), 6.8 tons
35' SC fin-keel, aft-cockpit cutter (Des. No. 5), 7.3 tons
35' SC full-keel, aft-cockpit cutter (Des. No. 113), 9.5 tons
36' SC full-keel, aft-cockpit cutter (Des. No. 106), 11.4 tons
36' R full-keel, aft-cockpit sloop (Des. No. 118), 8.5 tons
37' R fin-keel, center-cockpit sloop (Des. No. 160), 9.5 tons
38' DC centerboard, aft-cockpit cutter (Des. No. 114), 9 tons
39' DC centerboard, aft-cockpit cutter (Des. No. 74), 10 tons
39' R long-keel, center-cockpit cutter (Des. No. 147), 14 tons
40' flat-bottomed, centerboard, aft-cockpit sloop (Des. No. 155), 14 tons
40' DC fin-keel, aft-cockpit sloop (Des. No. 137), 9.3 tons
40' R long-keel, aft-cockpit sloop (Des. No. 120), 10 tons
41' R short-keel, aft-cockpit sloop (Des. No. 1), 11.6 tons
41' R bilge-keel, center-cockpit sloop (Des. No. 168), 12 tons
41' DC full-keel, centerpcockpit ketch (Des. No. 15), 12 tons
41' SC fin-keel, aft-cockpit cutter (Des. No. 217), 10.4 tons
42' R full-keel, wheelhouse ketch (Des. No. 25), 16 tons
43' DC short-keel, aft-cockpit sloop (Des. No. 183), 13 tons
44' DC short-keel, aft-cockpit cutter (Des. No. 187), 14.3 tons
44' DC bilge-keel, center-cockpit ketch (Des. No. 83), 16.2 tons
45' DC short-keel, center-cockpit ketch (Des. No. 68), 15 tons
45' DC short-keel, center-cockpit ketch (Des. No. 115), 15 tons
45' R short-keel, center cockpit cutter (Des. No. 198), 15 tons
46' R short-keel, center-cockpit ketch (Des. No. 37), 15 tons
48' DC short-keel, center-cockpit ketch (Des. No. 109), 18 tons
49' SC bilge-keel, center-cockpit cutter (Des. No. 134), 17 tons
49' DC short-keel, center-cockpit ketch (Des. No. 116), 18 tons
50' SC fin-keel, center-cockpit cutter (Des. No. 209), 17 tons
51' SC centerboard, aft-cockpit ketch (Des. No. 156), 20 tons
53' R long-keel, center-cockpit ketch (Des. No. 62), 25 tons
53' R full-keel, wheelhouse ketch (Des. No. 49), 35 tons
53' R full-keel, wheelhouse ketch (Des. No. 136), 40 tons
54' R full-keel, center-cockpit ketch (Des. No. 14), 22 tons
54' DC short-keel, center-cockpit schooner (Des. No. 32), 17 tons
56' SC full-keel, wheelhouse schooner (Des. No. 151), 30 tons
57' R full-keel, wheelhouse ketch (Des. No. 4), 33 tons
67' R short-keel, center-cockpit ketch (Des. No. 30), 37 tons
78' R full-keel, wheelhouse ketch (Des. No. 6), 68 tons
89' R full-keel, center-cockpit schooner (Des. No. 226), 90 tons
98' R short-keel, center-cockpit ketch (Des. No. 64), 98 tons
118' R full-keel, wheelhouse brigantine, sail training ship (Des. No. 152), 260 tons
121' R full-hull cargo brigantine (Des. No. 153), 350 tons
164' sailing ship (Des. No. 197)
190' sailing ship (Des. No. 71)

ROBERT HARRIS, N.A. / 212-1656 Duranleau St. / Granville Island
Vancouver, B.C. / Canada V6H 3S4/ Tel. (604) 683-6321

Mr. Harris has been designing yachts for 25 years, working with both chine and round steel hulls. He prefers round hulls, and his have been built by Pheon Yachts in England and Waterline Yachts in Canada. He also designed the 61' round bilge *Angantyr* with Frank MacLear.

	SP	CP
38' *Pheon*, MC cutter, (Pheon Yachts), 12 tons	$50	$2000
38' *Vancouver*, R cutter, 11.5 tons		

J.P. HARTOG, N.A. / Holland Marine Designs
3510 Geary Blvd. / San Francisco, CA 94118 / Tel. (415) 387-3110

Mr. Hartog has been designing for 50 years, having learned his craft in Holland. He designs both round and V-bottom hulls, and introduced the idea of diagonal plating over longitudinal framing. He works closely with Coast Marine Construction in Cotati, CA, as well as several other yards. Fees for custom work are based on an hourly rate. His stock plans are quite inexpensive.

26' SC sloop (Des. No. SVST 8404), 5.1 tons	$ 85
28' SC sloop (Des. No. SMVST 8317), 5.9 tons	85
36' SC or DC ketch/sloop (Des. No. SVST 7803)	85
40' DC cutter (Des. No. SVST 7708), 15tons	90
40' SC motorsailor, gaff ketch (Des. No. SVST7908 V), 26 tons	95
46' R ketch (Des. No. SRST 7404), 16.4 tons	90
48' SC fishing motorsailor, sloop (Des. No. SMVSTC8004V), 30 tons	105
48' SC ketch (Des. No. SVST 8006), 28 tons	95
63' R ketch (commercial potential) (Des. No. SRST 7211), 40 tons	180
66' SC or DC fishing schooner (Des. No. SMVSTC8002), 54 tons	185

ROBERT HUNDY / Bay Class Yacht Designs / 3 Dome Hill Peak
Caterham, Surrey / England CR3 6EH / Tel. (0) 833-42261

Mr. Hundy has been working with steel since 1960 and designing in steel for 14 years. After service in the Royal Navy, he worked with and for Trewes International in Holland, designing and supervising the construction of steel vessels. After spending several years as a freelance designer, he joined forces with the Conyer Yard to produce the Bay Class yachts. All his designs are round, and some have clipper-style bows. Mr. Hundy now works exclusively with Conyer Marine Ltd. in England.

38' *Donegal Bay,* R cutter, 11.25 tons
40' *Table Bay,* R center or aft-cockpit ketch
42' *Tahitian Bay,* R ketch, 15 tons
47' *Seven Islands,* R clipper ketch or cutter, 18.7 tons
49' *Bantry Bay,* R clipper ketch, cutter or schooner, 22 tons
53' *San Francisco Bay,* R ketch
53' *Bay of Fundy,* R ketch, center-cockpit version

PETER IBOLD, N.A. / Palais de la Scala / Ave. Henri-Dunant
Monte Carlo / MC 98000 Monaco / Tel. (93) 50.39.44

Mr. Ibold has been in the yacht design business for 15 years and has been designing in steel from the beginning, although most of his steel designs are for power craft. To date he has only designed round hulls, and prefers them. He will work wth any competent builder, although several builders in Europe have produced his designs in considerable numbers. Custom design fees are based on a fixed quote, which is a percentage of the estimated value of the finished yacht.

35' *Endurance,* R cutter or ketch, 18,550 lbs.	$500 U.S.
44' *Endurance,* R ketch, 29,550 lbs.	800 U.S.

C. WILLIAM LAPWORTH / Box 1756 / Newport Beach, CA 92660 / Tel. (714) 673-6322

45' R center-cockpit cutter	$4000

NILS LUCANDER / 5307 N. Pearl St. / Tacoma, WA 98407 / Tel. (206) 752-4205

Mr. Lucander has designed in steel for 21 years and in other hull materials for over 50 years. He specializes in innovative power and sail boat designs and systems, and is a designer who often thinks contrary to the normal rules. All study sheets cost $5. His designs are inexpensive and also include wineglass and round designs.

28' *Snapper*, DC sloop, 10,500 lbs.	$ 195
36' *Swift*, SC sloop, 12,900 lbs.	695
41' *Navigator*, R center-cockpit ketch, 22,000 lbs.	395
43' *Navigator*, R center-cockpit ketch, 33,000 lbs.	450
48' *Albacore*, DC pilothouse sloop, 48,000 lbs.	975
58' *Albacore*, DC pilothouse ketch, 72,000 lbs.	1275
64' *Albacore*, DC pilothouse, staysail schooner, 85,000 lbs.	1950
66' *Navigator*, DC center-cockpit ketch, 87,000 lbs.	1475
68' *Albacore*, DC pilothouse ketch, 90,000 lbs.	1495
74' *Chartermaster*, DC center-cockpit ketch, 95,000 lbs.	9950

The *Albacore Clippers* are all also available as commercial boats with cargo holds. They are also available with so-called "Easy Sailer Rigs" which can be controlled from inside the pilothouse. In these designs the chines meet at a point aft for a double-ended underwater effect, while the lower chine disappears forward to gain a fine entry. The 74' *Chartermaster* ketch includes Coast Guard "Small Passenger Carrying" certification for 12 passengers.

LUNSTROO CUSTOM DESIGNS / Prins Hendrikkade 152 / 1011 AW Amsterdam
Holland / Tel. 020-2275 08

Lunstroo Custom Designs has been working on steel yacht designs for about 25 years; Mr. H. Lunstroo Jr. is a naval architect with 35 years of experience. They mainly design round-bilged yachts, but have done some multi-chine sailing hulls and single-chine power boats. They have worked out designs so that almost none of the steel plate is wasted. The firm works internationally with experienced builders.

26' SC traditional Dutch fishing boat (Des. No. 29)
29' R traditional Dutch fishing type (Des. No. 104)
30' *Skoit*, R schooner
33' SC skipjack cutter with centerboard
33' *Swift*, MC cutter
34' R lemmeraak ("most beautiful and reliable sea boat of the Dutch types"), (Des. No. 21.014)
34' R cutter, Norwegian double-ender, Corten hull, aluminum deck, cabin and cockpit (Des. No. 20.008)
34' *Gladys*, R cutter, long keel (Des. No. 21.026)
36' R ketch with clipper bow (Des. No. 24.095)
37' R motorsailor, sloop (Des. No. 77)
37' R motorsailor, ketch (Des. No. 126)
40' R lemmeraak (Des. No. 83)
40' R motorsailor, shoal-draft, centerboard, flush-deck ketch
43' R staysail schooner (Des. No. 24.098)
46' R lemmeraak (Des. No. 116)
48' R flush-deck, double-ended ketch (Des. No. 90)
49' R motorsailor, double-ended, flush-deck ketch
52' R ketch, charter version (Des. No. 119)
54' R lemmeraak (Des. No. 89)
54' R motorsailor, ketch (Des. No. 22.043)
55' R double-ended ketch (Des. No. 128)
56' R long-keel, staysail schooner (Des. No. 108)
57' R ketch, charter version (Des. No. 21.013)
59' R cutter, double-ended with raised wheelhouse (Des. No. 131)
66' R ketch, modern (Des. No. 124.088)
85' R gaff-rigged topsail schooner (Des. No. 95)
95' R gaff-rigged topsail schooner (Des. No. 24.090)

ROGER MARSHALL / 44 Fort Wetherill / Jamestown, RI 02835 / Tel. (401) 423-1400

Mr. Marshall has been designing steel hulls for 5 years, and has experience working with steel itself. He designs both round and chine hulls, and is another builder who uses conic sections with radius chines to achieve a round hull. He does not work with any particular builder, and adapts his designs for amateur building by providing much more detail.

49' R ketch, 40,907 lbs.

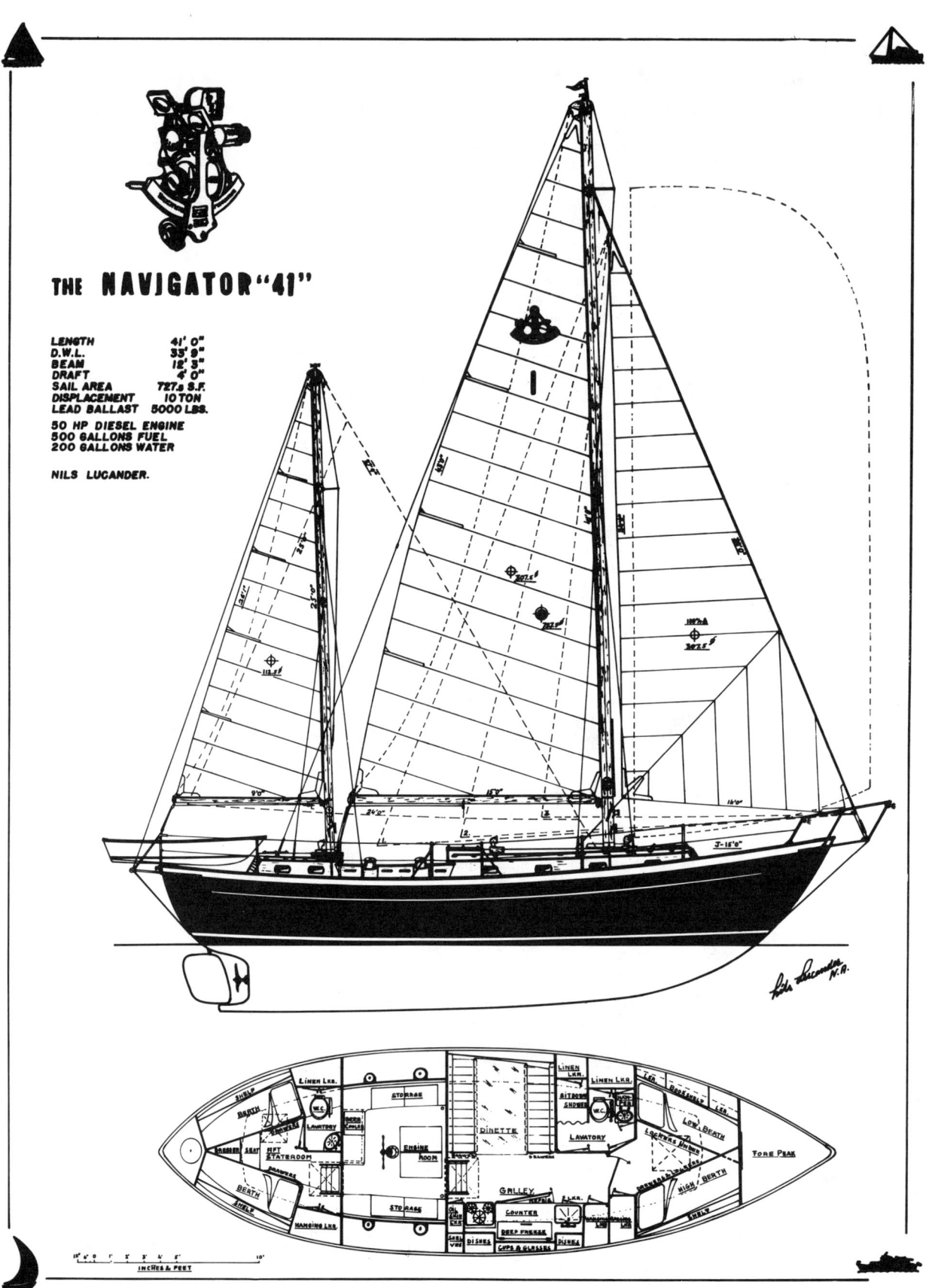

THE NAVIGATOR "41"

LENGTH   41' 0"
D.W.L.   33' 9"
BEAM   12' 3"
DRAFT   4' 0"
SAIL AREA   727.8 S.F.
DISPLACEMENT   10 TON
LEAD BALLAST   5000 LBS.

50 HP DIESEL ENGINE
500 GALLONS FUEL
200 GALLONS WATER

NILS LUCANDER.

Navigator 41, *designed by Nils Lucander.*

AL MASON / P.O. Box 3586 / Napa, CA 94558

Mr. Mason has over 50 years of design experience, mostly with the well-known offices of Sparkman and Stephens, Phillip Rhodes, John Alden, Tams, Inc., and the small-craft design section of the U.S. Navy. He also worked for a period of time with Steelcraft Boats. His designs range from 18′ naval harbor tanks to many sail and power craft, including 75′ and 100′ sailboats. Most of his steel yachts are double chine, and some have centerboards; a third reverse chine is used at the "garboard" of his 41. Many of his designs do not have study plans, and the construction plans drawn up for professional builders don't include the details an amateur might need. His small yacht designs have been built by T.D. Vinette, North Carolina Steel Builders, and Gladding-Hearn.

> 30′ *Intrepid,* MC sloop (over 35 built)
> 33′ MC cutter or ketch, 13,180 lbs.
> 40′ DC yawl (also centerboard version), 24,800 lbs.
> 41′ MC sloop or ketch, 23,500 lbs.
> 45′ *Cavu,* custom motorsailor ketch
> 45′ R semi-custom, centerboard ketch
> 48′ New design (not complete), will be built in New Zealand
> 50′ R centerboard sloop or ketch
> 53′ *Carolina,* R centerboard ketch

RUSSELL MC NAB / Box 225 / Warragul, Victoria 3820 / Australia

Most of his designs are single chine hulls. His *Caravel* schooner designs are quite unique.

	SP	CP
27′ *Caravel,* SC schooner, 3100 kg		
36′ *Caravel,* SC genoa schooner		$285 AUS
39′ *Starflash,* schooner	$20	585
47′ *Starflash,* SC schooner	20	
62′ Australian sailor schooner	26	

ALAN MUMMERY / Putiki Bay / Waiheke Island / New Zealand

With 16 years experience designing steel vessels, Mr. Mummery prefers round hulls, but recognizes that chine hulls are more practical for amateur builders. Approximately 75% of his designs are round, and many have been built by home builders. He does not work with any particular builder, and most of his work is either custom or semi-custom (modifying existing or stock designs), with charges being estimated following a firm inquiry.

> 39′ *Cape Three Nine,* R medium fin-keel, aft-cockpit sloop, 10 tons
> 39′ *Donato Polo,* R long fin-keel, aft-cockpit, flush-deck sloop or yawl, 12.5 tons
> 41′ *Heartbeat,* DC medium fin-keel, center-cockpit, flush-deck sloop or cutter, 12.5 tons
> 42′ *Polette,* R, long fin-keel, center-cockpit cutter, 13 tons
> 43′ *Te Matuku,* DC medium fin-keel, flush-deck sloop or cutter, 13.5 tons
> 46′ *Mandala,* R, medium fin-keel, center-cockpit cutter, 15 tons
> 50′ *Astral Rose,* R long fin-keel, center-cockpit, flush-deck ketch, sloop, or cutter, 22 tons
> 60′ *Quintessa,* R long-keel, center-cockpit, flush-deck ketch, 36 tons

MYLNE & CO. / Silverhills, Rosneath / Hellensburgh, Dunbartonshire
England G84 0RW / Tel. Clynder 043-683-257

Mylne & Co. have been designing boats since 1896. Ian Nicholson, author of *Small Steel Craft,* is associated with this design firm. They have a special interest in ketch designs and have recently designed a 55′ round steel ketch, charging 600 for prelims. The cost of preliminaries is deducted if the full design is done.

NELSON & MAREK / 2820 Canon St. / San Diego, CA 92106
Tel. (619) 224-6347

54′ chine cutter, 50,000 lbs.

ALAN PAPE / Haye, Courtenay Close / East Looe, Cornwall / England PL13 1JK
Tel. Looe 2150

Mr. Pape has had some 42 years of experience in yacht design, 39 of which includes steel design. He designs both round and chine hulls. There are currently five builders in the U.K. doing his stock designs, but many have been constructed as one-offs by amateurs and professionals.

30' *Petrel,* chine sloop, 6.23 tons (Oceancraft)	£200
30' MC cutter, 7.5 tons (Watercraft)	250
33' *Ebbtide,* MC cutter, 8.1 tons (Oceancraft exclusive)	
34' *Steelmaid,* MC cutter (CMC)	350
35' *Saga,* R cutter, 7.6 tons	350
36' *Ebbtide,* MC cutter, 11.69 tons (Oceancraft exclusive)	
38' *Steelmaid,* MC ketch, 11.5 tons (CMC)	400
39' MC cutter, 14.4 tons (Watercraft)	400
42' R or MC cutter, 13.71 tons (Watercraft)	400
45' *Steelmaid,* MC ketch, 17.00 tons (CMC)	400
48' R ketch, 20.5 tons	500
50' R ketch, 23.00 tons	600
57' R ketch, 35.00 tons	700

PENCE MARINE / Joe Pence, Jr. / 43300 Airport Road / P.O. Box 365
Little River, CA 95456 / Tel. (707) 937-5785

Mr. Pence is also a builder, whose yard is a natural outgrowth of his design work. He prefers to work with his own designs, although he will build from complete plans by reputable designers. He primarily does chine hulls, but can do round for extra expense. He also handles designs by Van de Stadt of Holland (see entry). He will build the following boats of his own design.

26' *Pony Express*
32' *Courier,* sloop, 14,755 lbs.
35' *Tradition*
39' *Courier*
56' *Frontier,* DC cutter

ROBERT PERRY YACHTS DESIGNERS, INC. / 6400 Seaview Ave. NW
Seattle, WA 98107 / Tel. (206) 789-7212

Mr. Perry is very active in design at present, and is known for designs with small wetted surface area but spacious interiors. The office has been in existence for the past ten years, and involved with steel for the past six years. Most of their designs for cruising boats are of a D/L ratio which allows for construction in steel, and they are happy to develop custom designs.

35' R sloop or cutter (Olympic Torque Tool)
48' SC, canoe-stern cutter
40' *Passport* type
42' double-molded-radius fin-keel cutter, 24,000 lbs.

S.L. PETCHUL / 1380 SW 57th Ave. / Ft. Lauderdale, FL 33317 / Tel. (305) 525-4991

For the past 15 + years, Mr. Petchul has been mainly doing commercial design work, but has recently moved into sailing design. He also has experience in construction of aluminum and steel round and chine hulls.

39' center-cockpit cutter	$950
47' center-cockpit ketch	950

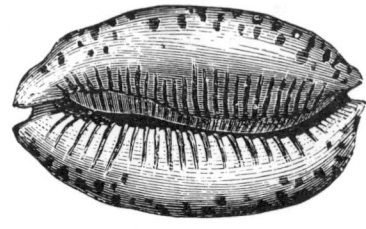

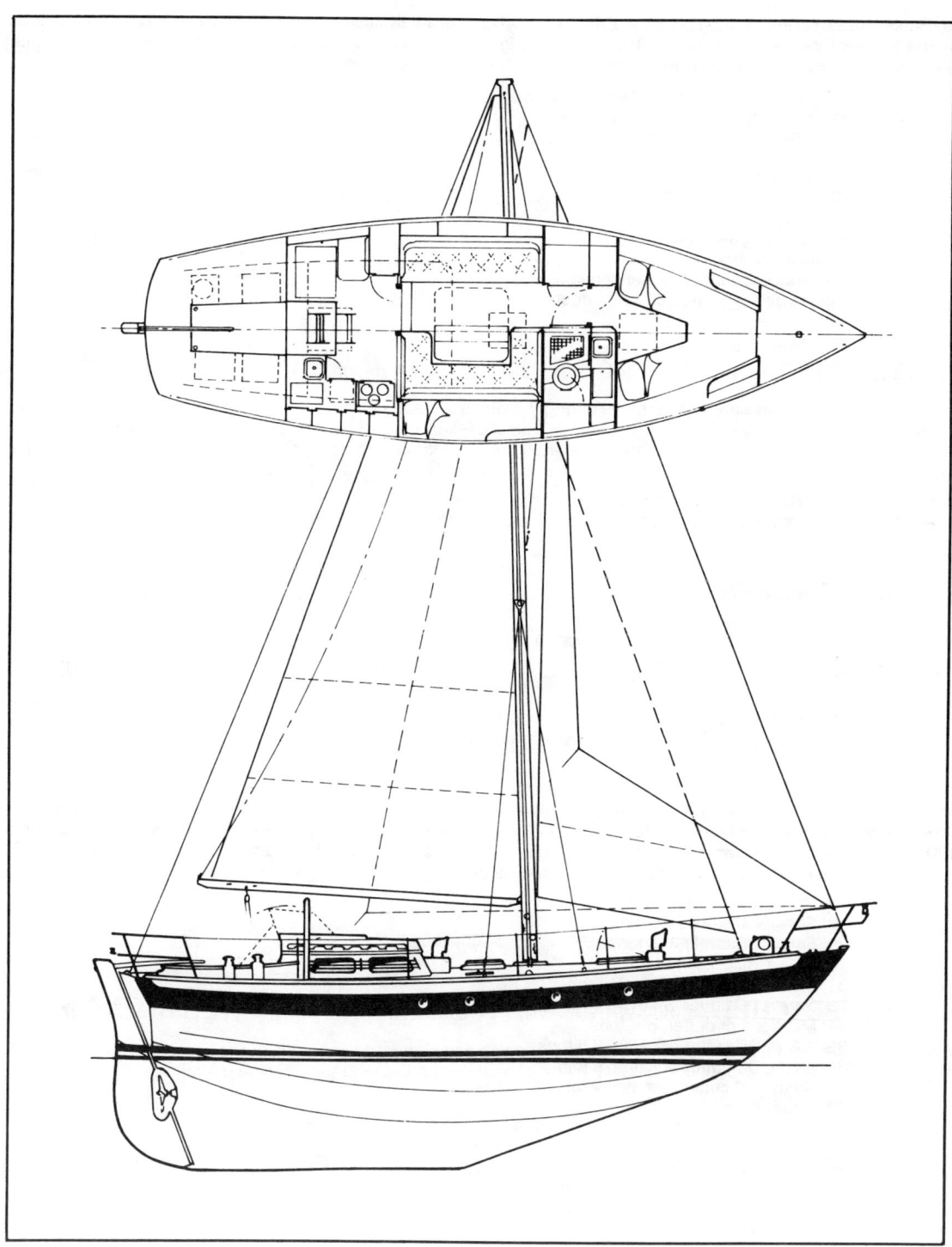

Ebb Tide 33, *designed by Alan Pape*

WILLIAM PRESTON / Marine Power Inc. / Box 549 / Gulf Breeze, FL 32561
Tel. (904) 932-7620

Mr. Preston has a large collection of designs, most of which are for steel construction. He has designed primarily various commercial vessels primarily of chine hull construction. Most of his sailing vessels have a clipper-type profile. T.D. Vinette in Michigan has built a number of his designs. A nice catalog of his designs is available.

30' *Boeier Jacht,* R lifeboat conversion
38' SC ketch
39' centerboard schooner
42' ketch
47' schooner
50' ketch
51' ketch
55' square rigger sailboat
62' fishing schooner
110' knockabout passenger schooner
115' topsail schooner, 30 passengers

RAYMOND RICHARDS / P.O. Box 3271 / Newport Beach, CA 92665 / Tel. (714) 675-3483

Mr. Richards has been designing steel boats during the whole of his 31-year career, but the bulk of his work has been either for commercial builders or custom designs. His steel designs range from a 16' flat-bottomed boom boat, through single chines, multi chines, and round bilges, to a 25,000-long-ton ocean-going chemical barge. He developed the hydroconic skeg used on a 102 ft. tug in 1955. All custom work is done on a fixed-fee basis.

65' MC, shoal-draft trading packet, gaff ketch with squaresails
221' *Frontier Challenger,* 3-masted research vessel (not complete)

BRUCE ROBERTS / 35 Belleview Dr. / Severna Park, MD 21146 / Tel. (301) 544-4311

AUSTRALIA
BRUCE ROBERTS INTERNATIONAL / Molle Rd. / Gumdale, QLD 4154 / Tel. 901150

CANADA
BRUCE ROBERTS INTERNATIONAL / 15081 Marine Dr. / Whiterock, B.C.
Tel. (604) 531-4122

Mr. Roberts has been designing steel boats since 1972, and is very well known for promoting amateur steel yacht construction, especially for the home builder. Over 2000 of his hulls have been built to date, and another 5000 are being built worldwide. He has also written a book on the subject, *Build for Less.* Most of his designs are double chine, and each have various versions of layout and rig. He can also arrange for construction by a number of builders.

	SP	CP
22' *Spray,* DC sloop, 1.5 tons		
28' *Spray,* DC cutter, 6.5 tons	$ 15	$365
28' DC ketch, 6.7 tons	15	485
31' DC sloop (custom 310), 5.7 tons	15	499
33' *Spray,* DC cutter or ketch, 11 tons	15	499
34' MC sloop or cutter, 6 + tons	575	
35' A & B, DC cutter or ketch, 6.5 tons		
36' A & B, DC cutter or ketch, 9 tons	15	509
36' *Spray,* DC cutter or motorsailor, 12 + tons		
37' sloop, 9.3 tons		
38' *Spray,* center-cockpit ketch, 14.5 tons	630	
38' *Offshore A & B,* DC cutter or ketch, 7.8 tons	15	548
39' DC sloop, 12.3 tons	15	550
40' DC, center-cockpit ketch or cutter	630	
40' *Spray,* DC gaff rig ketch, 17.8 tons		
43' *Mauritius,* DC center-cockpit ketch, 14 tons	15	560
43' R flush-deck ketch, 13.4 tons		
44' *Offshore A,* DC ketch or cutter, 13.4 tons	630	
53' DC cutter ketch, also available R, 21.4 tons	15	700
64' DC center cockpit cutter or ketch, 40 tons	15	950

ROSS & ASSOCIATES, N.A. / 21 Belmore St. / Burwood, New South Wales 2134
Australia / Tel. 869-1097/745-2969

Richard Ross has over 20 years of experience working with both steel and aluminum. He has primarily designed single-chine hulls. It is reported that he has various other designs than are listed here.

24' Cape Cod catboat yawl

SEATON & NEVILLE / Suite 206 / 320 N. Bayshore Rd. / Clearwater, FL 33519
Tel. (813) 725-5329

Seaton & Neville specialize in cruising power and sail designs, and are familiar with metal work through observation of builders. They have designed many round power yachts, and plan to design round sailing vessels in the future.

39' *Sandpiper,* cutter (not complete)
40' ketch (not complete)

GRAHAME SHANNON / F110-201 CW / Blaine, WA 98230
or
12891 116 Ave. / Surrey, B.C. / Canada V3R 2S6 / Tel. (604) 584-6118

Steel designs are over 60% of Mr. Shannon's work. He is an avid user of the computer for calculations of scantlings, weights, center of gravity, and developed hull shapes, and he is one of the few designers that supplies computer-faired full-scale plans on mylar. He has developed a double-chine style in which the upper chine is a molded radius and all hull plate is developed. He has also edited a collection of designs called *The Yacht Design Catalog,* which includes various steel designs for $3. Mr Shannon will also make design conversion of chine hulls into round.

24' *Tom Thumb,* DC sloop
28' *Opal,* cutter
29' *Amazon Pilot,* DC sloop
33' *Ruby,* cutter
35' R cutter in design stage
37' *Amazon,* DC sloop, radiused top chine
38' *Pearl,* ketch
39' *Radicon (Amazon),* DC sloop, radiused top chine. Hull kit only
41' *Amazon Pilot,* DC cutter, radiused top chine

JOHN SIMPSON, LTD. / 6551 Yeats Crescent / Richmond, B.C. / Canada V7E 4E1
Tel. (604) 277-7593

With a lifetime of boating experience, Mr. Simpson has been designing yachts for almost 20 years. After 8 years of work for five other naval architects in Vancouver and 5 years of boatbuilding and yard management, he formed his own design company. Steel boat designs have become an increasing percentage of his output since he began working with the material in 1972. He designs both pleasure and commercial craft in all hull materials, as well as consulting with builders, making design modifications, and surveying boats. Stock plans cost roughly ½% of the boat's value; custom plans range from 3–5% of the estimated value. His designs have been built by Folkes Marine, Horizon Steel Boats, T.D. Marine, Aqua-Marine, Waterline Yachts, Topper Hermanson, Mooney Marine, and Ivan Wilson.

33' DC cutter
36' DC cutter, 18,900 lbs.
37' DC lug-rig schooner, 19,000 lbs.
42' *Fidelity,* DC center-cockpit cutter, 30,000 lbs.
43' *Perelandra,* R cruising ketch, 34,000 lbs.
45' *La Briza,* DC ketch, 42,000 lbs.
50' DC center-cockpit ketch, 46,000 lbs.
64' DC ketch, 77,500 lbs.
70' *Black Eyes,* DC 2-masted staysail charter schooner, 29 berths

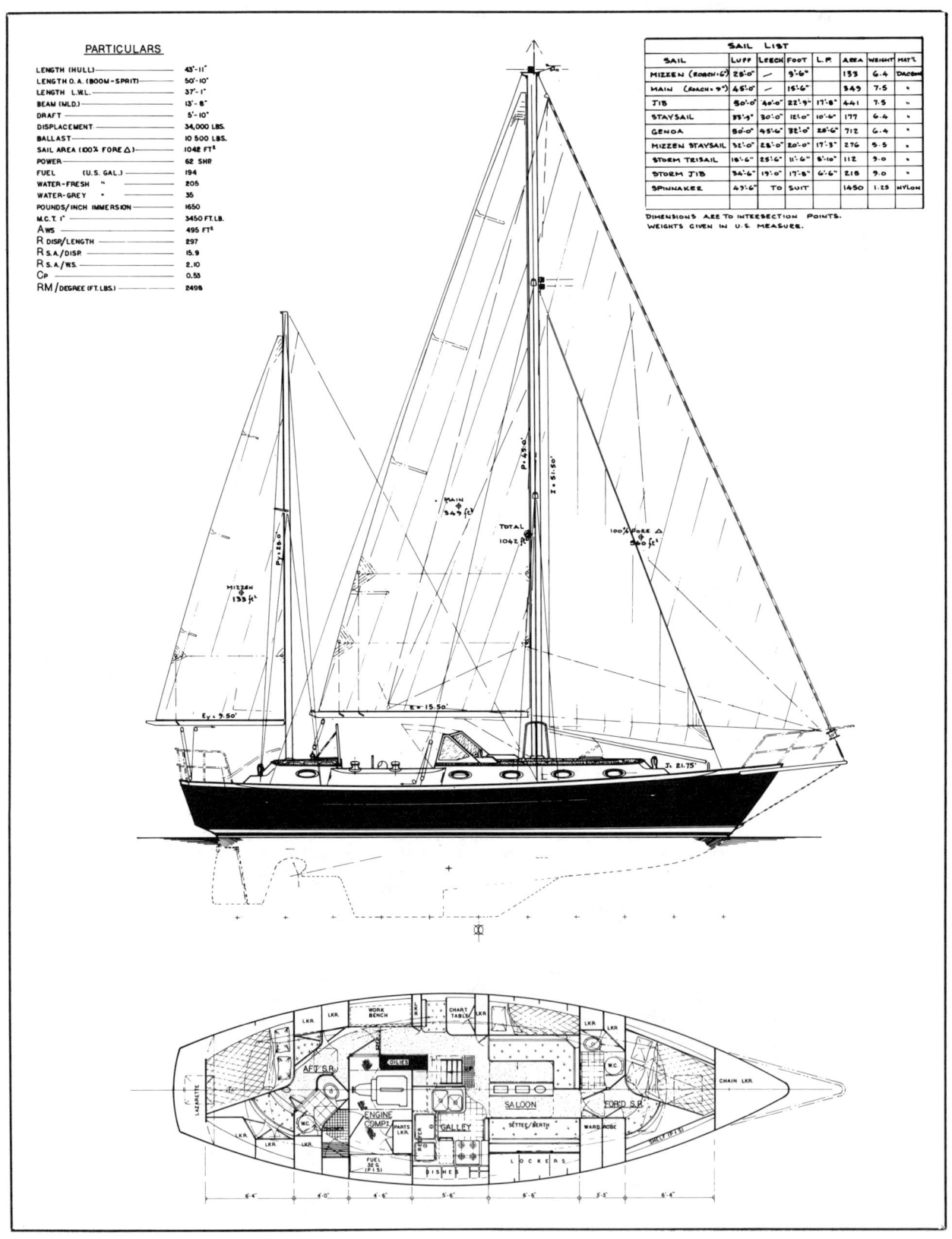

PARTICULARS

LENGTH (HULL)	43'-11"
LENGTH O.A. (BOOM-SPRIT)	50'-10"
LENGTH L.WL.	37'-1"
BEAM (MLD.)	13'-8"
DRAFT	5'-10"
DISPLACEMENT	34,000 LBS.
BALLAST	10,500 LBS.
SAIL AREA (100% FORE △)	1042 FT²
POWER	62 SHP
FUEL (U.S. GAL.)	194
WATER-FRESH "	205
WATER-GREY "	35
POUNDS/INCH IMMERSION	1650
M.C.T. I"	3450 FT.LB.
A WS	495 FT²
R DISP/LENGTH	297
R S.A./DISP.	15.9
R S.A./WS.	2.10
Cp	0.53
RM /DEGREE (FT.LBS.)	2498

SAIL LIST

SAIL	LUFF	LEECH	FOOT	L.P.	AREA	WEIGHT	MAT'L
MIZZEN (ROACH-6")	29'-0"	—	9'-6"		133	6.4	DACRON
MAIN (ROACH-9")	45'-0"		15'-6"		349	7.5	"
JIB	50'-0"	40'-0"	22'-9"	17'-8"	441	7.5	"
STAYSAIL	33'-3"	30'-0"	12'-0"	10'-6"	177	6.4	"
GENOA	50'-0"	45'-6"	32'-0"	28'-6"	712	6.4	"
MIZZEN STAYSAIL	32'-0"	28'-0"	20'-0"	17'-3"	276	5.5	"
STORM TRISAIL	18'-6"	25'-6"	11'-6"	8'-10"	112	9.0	"
STORM JIB	34'-6"	19'-0"	17'-8"	6'-6"	218	9.0	"
SPINNAKER	49'-6"		TO SUIT		1450	1.25	NYLON

DIMENSIONS ARE TO INTERSECTION POINTS.
WEIGHTS GIVEN IN U.S. MEASURE.

Perelandra 43, *designed by John Simpson.*

Courtesy of the designer

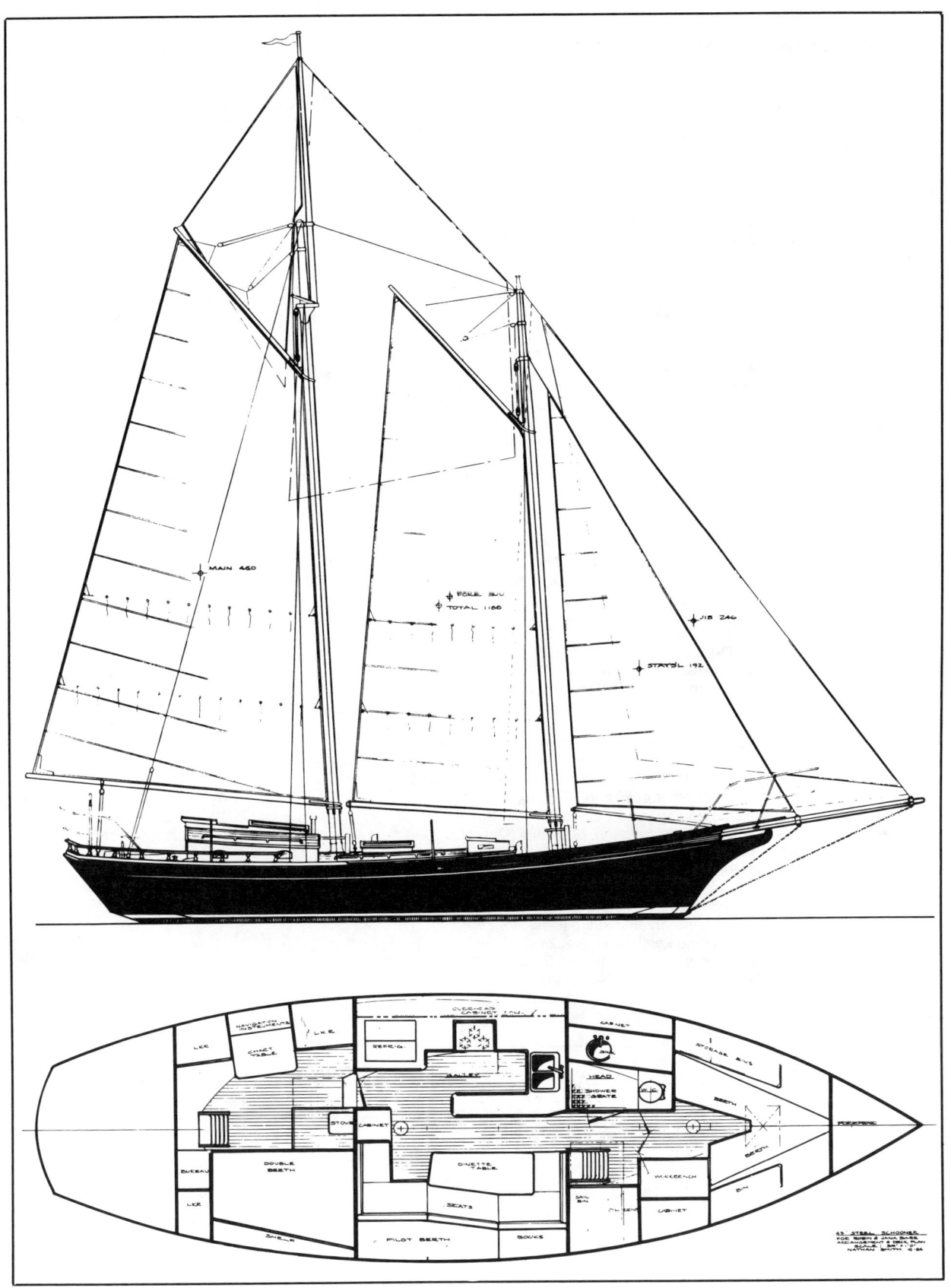

A 43' schooner designed by Nathan Smith.

Courtesy of the designer

NATHAN SMITH / 10897 N.E. Seaborn Rd. / P.O. Box 10542 / Bainbridge Island, WA 98110
Tel. (206) 842-5003

In addition to his design work, Mr. Smith has a small, well-equipped boatyard, and is active as a welder himself, specializing in marine hardware fabrication in all metals. He designs both round and multi chine hull for sail and power. His custom plans generally cost 2 to 3% of the value of the completed vessel, depending on the complexity and nature of the design. A design portfolio is available for $7.50.

	SP	CP
40' DC cutter (not complete)		
42' R cruising cutter, centerboard, 32,500 lbs.	$5	$500
43' DC coasting schooner, full- or fin-keel, gaff or staysail rig, 35,000 lbs.	5	400

SPARKMAN & STEPHENS / 79 Madison Ave. / New York, NY 10016 / Tel. (212) 689-3880

Sparkman and Stephens have been designing yachts for over 55 years and have done a few in steel, although their reputation for performance yachts has caused them to tend toward lighter building materials. All of their designs are round bottomed, and many have been built using Corten steel. Their larger designs are usually classed by ABS or Lloyds. They are in the business of providing designs for competent builders, not for backyard projects. Many of their designs have been built by European builders. Free information sheets are available for all their designs. Stock plans are available for approximately $100 per foot of overall length; custom designs will be quoted on after specifics are settled.

28' *Crusader Jr.,* motorsailor sloop (Des. No. 1329.1)
32' *Crusader,* motorsailor sloop, 9.7 tons (Des. No. 1329)
42' *Prospect of Whitby,* racing sloop, 12.3 tons (Des. No. 1985)
45' *Prospect of Whitby,* racing sloop, 12.5 tons (Des. No. 2957)
47' *TocToc,* motorsailor ketch, 24.9 tons
49' *Flair,* motorsailor ketch (Des. No. 1397)
50' *Yankee,* cruising ketch, twin centerboards (Irving Johnson's boat),
    31.2 tons (Des. No. 1278)
53' *Captiva,* cruising ketch, 26.8 tons (Des. No. 1925)
53' *Pavanne II,* motorsailor sloop, 26 tons (Des. No. 1428)
56' *David Schmidt,* cruising ketch (Des. No. 2100.1)
59' *Torea,* cruising ketch, 43 tons (Des. No. 1927)
60' *Sardini,* cruising ketch (Des. No. 2337)
61' *Northern Light,* racing yawl, 26.3 tons (Des. No. 2055)
62' *Big Blue,* motorsailor ketch, 38.5 tons (Des. No. 1884.1)
62' *Cordonazo,* motorsailor ketch, 43.4 tons (Des. No. 1265)
68' *Pandora IV,* cruising centerboard ketch, 50.5 tons (Des. No. 1255)
68' *Mai Tai I,* cruising ketch, 41.6 tons (Des. No. 1213)
70' *Vaer-Wel II,* motorsailor ketch (Des. No. 1229)
73' *Amazon,* racing yawl, 52.5 tons (Des. No. 2084)
76' *Mai Tai II,* cruising ketch, 66.3 tons (Des. No. 1598.1)
87' *Amazon,* cruising ketch (Des. No. 2363)
90' *Sea Star,* cruising ketch, 92.5 tons (Des. No. 1449)
94' *Wayfarer,* cruising ketch, 106 tons (Des. No. 1223)
116' *Tizianna,* cruising ketch, 78 tons (Des. No. 1663)
117' *Vagrant,* motorsailor ketch (Des. No. 380)
120' *S&S,* racing ketch (Des. No. 2412)
126' auxiliary schooner (Des. No. 2477)
157' 3-masted bark (Des. No. 2334)
170' cruising schooner (Des. No. 2434)
183' cruising schooner (Des. No. 2335)

SCOTT SPRAGUE / P.O. Box 10635 / Bainbridge Island, WA 98110 / Tel. (206) 842-5003

His custom designs generally cost between 1½ and 3% of the market value of the boat, depending on what is needed. Most of his designs employ an attractive, sweeping sheer.

37' DC cutter, 22,000 lbs.
38' DC motorsailor, junk style
39' DC cutter, 27,000 lbs.

Yankee, *designed by Sparkman & Stephens and sailed by Irving Johnson.*

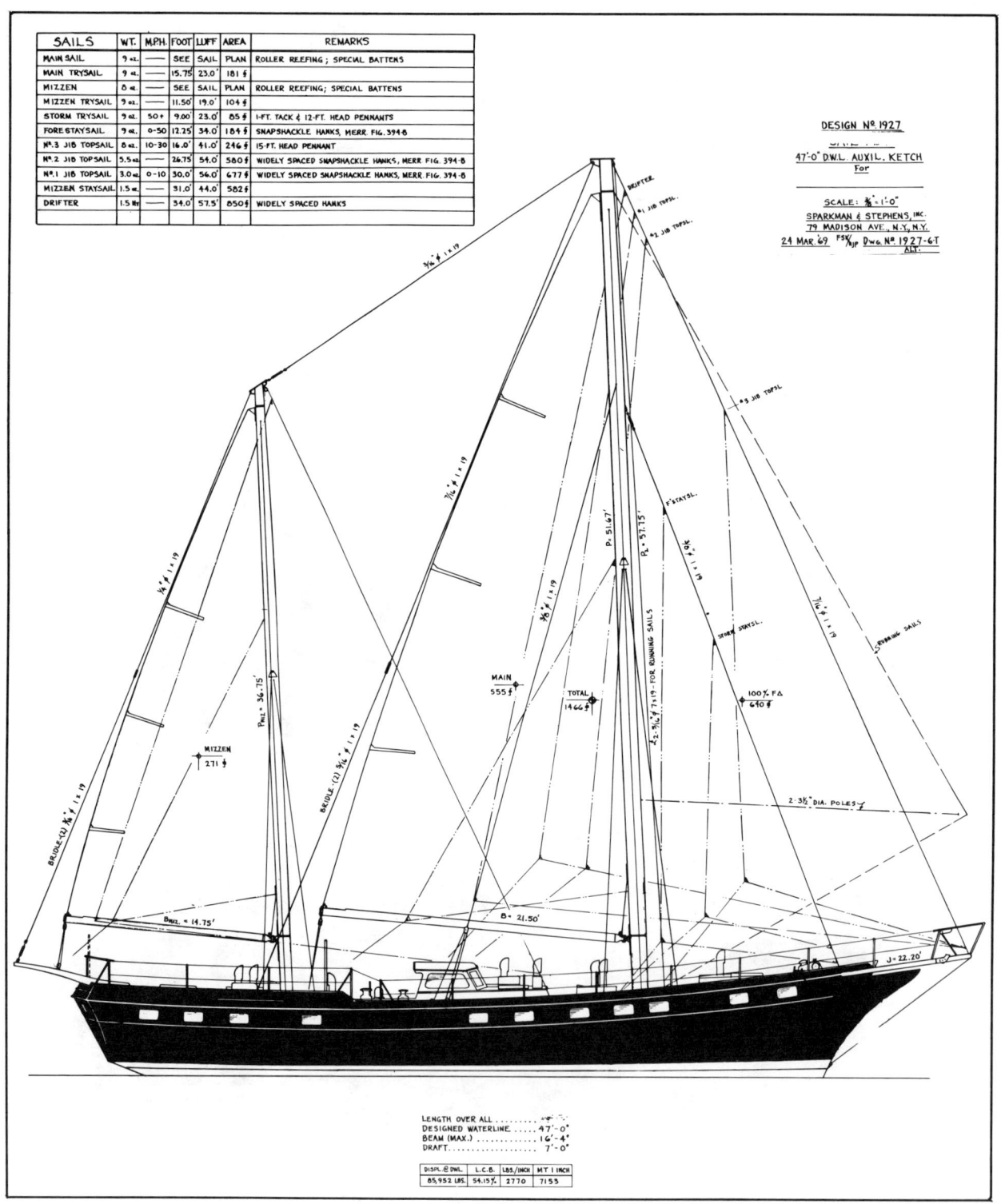

SAILS	WT.	M.P.H.	FOOT	LUFF	AREA	REMARKS
MAIN SAIL	9 oz.	—	SEE	SAIL	PLAN	ROLLER REEFING; SPECIAL BATTENS
MAIN TRYSAIL	9 oz.	—	15.75	23.0'	181 ƒ	
MIZZEN	8 oz.	—	SEE	SAIL	PLAN	ROLLER REEFING; SPECIAL BATTENS
MIZZEN TRYSAIL	9 oz.	—	11.50'	19.0'	104 ƒ	
STORM TRYSAIL	9 oz.	50+	9.00	23.0'	85 ƒ	1-FT. TACK & 12-FT. HEAD PENNANTS
FORE STAYSAIL	9 oz.	0-50	12.25	34.0'	184 ƒ	SNAPSHACKLE HANKS, MERR. FIG. 394-B
Nº 3 JIB TOPSAIL	8 oz.	10-30	16.0'	41.0'	246 ƒ	15-FT. HEAD PENNANT
Nº 2 JIB TOPSAIL	5.5 oz.	—	26.75	54.0'	580 ƒ	WIDELY SPACED SNAPSHACKLE HANKS, MERR. FIG. 394-B
Nº 1 JIB TOPSAIL	3.0 oz.	0-10	30.0'	56.0'	677 ƒ	WIDELY SPACED SNAPSHACKLE HANKS, MERR. FIG. 394-B
MIZZEN STAYSAIL	1.5 oz.	—	31.0'	44.0'	582 ƒ	
DRIFTER	1.5 lbs	—	34.0'	57.5'	850 ƒ	WIDELY SPACED HANKS

DESIGN Nº 1927

47'-0" D.W.L. AUXIL. KETCH

For

SCALE: ⅜" = 1'-0"

SPARKMAN & STEPHENS, INC.
79 MADISON AVE., N.Y., N.Y.

24 MAR. '69   Dwg. Nº 1927-6-T
ALT.

LENGTH OVER ALL ....
DESIGNED WATERLINE ...... 47'-0"
BEAM (MAX.) .... 16'-4"
DRAFT .... 7'-0"

DISPL. @ D.W.L.	L.C.B.	LBS./INCH	M.T. 1 INCH
85,952 LBS.	54.15%	2770	7155

Sparkman and Stephens Design No. 1927.

Courtesy of the designer

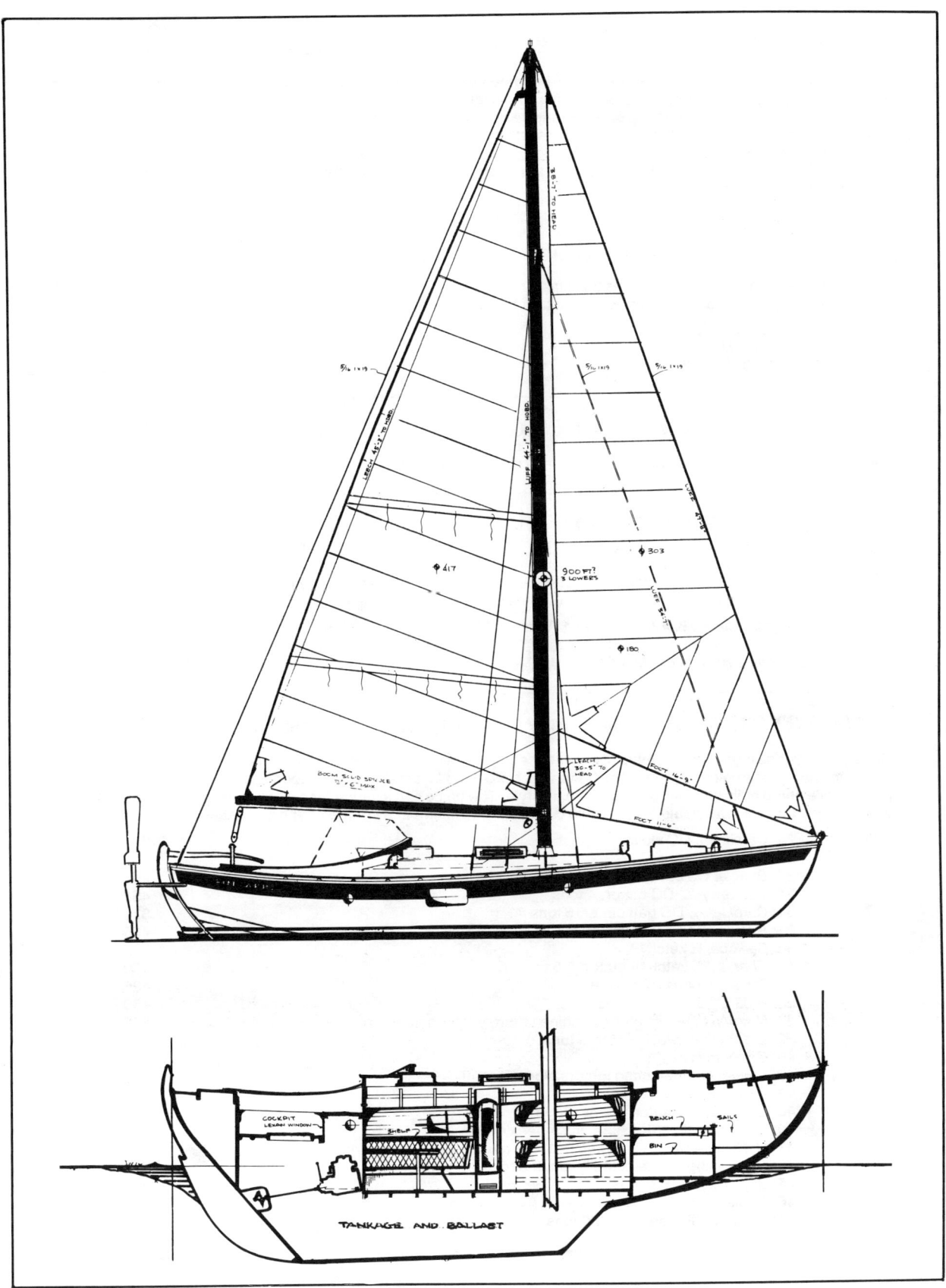

A 39' cutter designed by Scott B. Sprague.

GEORGE WM. SUTTON / Rt. 1, Box 144A / St. Augustine, FL 32084 / Tel. (904) 471-1745

George Sutton has been in the boat design and building business since 1938. He started working on steel vessels as a loftsman during World War II. As a result of his own building, he became an advocate of the dished sheel technique of plating and of longitudinal framing on both round and hard chine hulls. Sutton has designed and built steel sailing vessels from 26′ to 150′, as well as commercial vessels (from workskiffs to inter-island cargo vessels), and motor yachts. Presently he designs most of the vessels he builds. He has a long list of designs and is one of the most knowledgeable designer-builders in the U.S. Some of his designs are listed under Schreiber Schooners, who build some of his standard round hull sailing designs.

YVES-MARIE TANTON / Box 270 / Newport, RI / Tel. (401) 847-4112

Mr. Tanton's experience with steel goes back many years, and his boats have been built at the Maas yard in Holland. He charges roughly 7% of the construction cost for his plans.

22′ DC cat boat
27′ R cat boat
35′ DC schooner

TEKONA YACHT DESIGN / Box 4008 / S-131.04 Nacka / Sweden

Reported to have done various designs. Custom and stock plans are same price. Sorry, no data on plans available.

TREWES INTERNATIONAL, NV / c/o Holland Yachts, Inc. / 303 Riverside Avenue
Westport, CN 06880 / Tel. (203) 226-4474

Trewes International is a design organization headed by S.M. Van der Meer. They have been in operation since just after World War II, and have many round hull vessels to their credit, including Eric Hiscock's *Wanderer IV*.

Clipper Class 38, 42, 44, 50 & 61 (Van der Meer)
Privateer 38, 44, 50, 52, 56, 64
Ventura 70 (Van der Meer)

ROBERT TUCKER / Robert Tucker Designs, U.S.A. / 27 Dana St. / Cambridge, MA 02138

Robert Tucker has more than 25 years of experience in steel design, and his son Tony has joined him in the business. They are known for strip-chine, fin-keel designs, which are good for amateurs. Their round hulls are plated with diagonal plates while chine hulls are commonly strip chine style. The office can arrange for custom building at a variety of steel yards. Study plans are available for $3, while custom work is done at a charge of approximately $150 per sheet.

24′ *Cambrian*, DC sloop	$ 325
27′ *Calliope*, R sloop	
28′ *Beagle*, DC cutter, 4 tons	250
31′ *Cei Newydd*, DC cutter, 4 tons	450
31′ *Cordingley*, DC gaff cutter, 6 tons	375
31′ *R.W.*, cutter, 6.7 tons	425
34′ *Calliope*, R ketch	
35′ *Charybdis*, ketch or cutter, 5.5 tons	450
38′ *Ryton*, various rigs, 6 tons	425
38′ *R 383*, SC cutter, 6 tons	450
39′ *Norman Steel*, single-strip-chine ketch, 8.9 tons	575
39′ *Elizabethan Steel*, cutter, 9 tons	575
40′ *Calliope*, R ketch	
40′ *Kariba*, double-ended motorsailor, sloop, 8–9 tons	475
41′ *CA 41*, canoe-stern ketch	450
40′ *Saxon Steel*, cutter, 9 tons	575
40′ *Scylla*, single-strip-chine, flush-deck cutter	450
43′ *G 43*, R center-cockpit ketch, 11.25 tons	475
44′ *Scylla*, single-strip-chine ketch, 9.5 tons	550
45′ *Scylla*, ketch, 9.5 tons	600
46′ *Scylla*, ketch	
51′ *Turanna*, SC schooner, 20 tons	1190

E.G. VAN DE STADT & PARTNERS B.V. / Industrieweg 35, Postbus 193
1520 AD Wormerveer / Holland / Tel. (075) 21 65 81

PLANS IN U.S. / c/o Pence Marine / 43300 Airport Road / P.O. Box 619 / Little River, CA 95456

The van de Stadt organization has 50 years of experience in design and boatbuilding, including 35 years in steel. They built one of the first welded steel yachts in Holland, the yawl *Tulla*. The firm designs both round and chine hulls, and has introduced the frameless fairing method, outlined in a special building manual. They have a separate amateur boat-building department, and a catalog of suitable stock designs is available for $7.50. Charges for custom work are about 6–7% of the complete price of the yacht. The designs listed below are from their design catalog; they also have many designs up to 70′ available for professional construction.

29′ *Sea Dog,* MC sloop, 8,378 lbs. (Des. No. 267)
33′ *Orion,* R sloop, 11,905 lbs. (Des. No. 281)
34′ MC frameless sloop, 12,000 lbs. (Des. No. 391)
36′ *Seal,* R or MC sloop, 20,393 lbs. (Des. No. 260)
36′ *Falco,* MC motorsailor ketch, 21,605 lbs. (Des. No. 305)
44′ R or MC cutter or ketch, 37,073 lbs. (Des. No. 393)
49′ *Scorpion,* R cutter or ketch, 34,392 lbs. (Des. No. 206)
49′ *Pacific,* R or MC cutter or ketch, 40,124 lbs. (Des. No. 296)

GILBERT VIK / Vik Boat / 275 East Sunny Sands Rd. / Cathlamet, WA 98612
Tel. (206) 849-4440

Mr. Vik has been designing boats for 12 years, focusing on traditional wood construction, and using steel for larger boats. He designs both round and chine hulls, preferring gentle curves in both, and consults with builders on the construction details. Plans for home builders include detailed construction drawings. Charges for custom work are negotiable, either by the hour or on a contract. A design brochure containing study prints of his designs is available from Mr. Vik.

34′ SC sloop, 36,000 lbs. (Des. No. 45)	$ 350
40′ R ketch, 24,000 lbs. (Des. No. 18)	600
40′ SC ketch, 29,000 lbs. (Des. No. 11)	600
50′ R cutter, 42,000 lbs. (Des. No. 24)	1000
60′ SC ketch, 60,000 lbs. (Des. No. 16)	1500

WILLEM DE VRIES LENTSCH / Bureau voor Scheepsbouw B.V. / De Ryterkade 143
1101 AC Amsterdam / Holland / Tel. (020) 22 36 08

Mr. de Vries Lentsch is one of the foremost Dutch designers, and has been designing and working on steel sailboats for 45 years. He designs both round and chine hulls, conically developing hulls for home builders. He works with many builders in Europe, and charges 6–10% of the yard price for custom work.

Mr. de Vries Lentsch lists over 200 steel sailing designs, from a 25′ sloop to a 318′ 5-masted schooner (94 designs under 50′, 56 designs in the 50–70′ range, and 40 over 70′). Almost all of the larger designs are round hulls, while a fair number of the smaller ones are chine. The list is simply too long to include here.

RICHARD WALLACE / 71 Fairview Ave. / Stamford, CN 06902 / Tel. (203) 359-4126

42′ *Rise,* unusual SC cutter, 21,500 lbs.

WALLSTROM, WATKINS & ASSOC. / Blue Hills, ME 04614 / Tel. (207) 374-2218

The principals in this firm have designed in steel and aluminum since 1965 with various designs, pleasure and commercial, from a 20′ aluminum utility boat to a 270′ steel ship. They offer a wide array of commercial designs in steel, as well as several stock plans for yachts. The firm offers experience in designing to U.S.C.G. regulations and the ABS rules. Bob Wallstrom and Bob Watkins are also principals in YDI Schools, Blue Hills and Castine, Maine, which teach small-craft naval architecture in a wide range of programs from recreational to associate degree level by home study and in residence.

35′ R cutter (formerly *Huromic 35*), 17,000 lbs.
41′ R center-cockpit ketch/cutter (formerly *Huromic 41*), 23,600 lbs.
56′ MC schooner

MERRITT WALTER / Rover Marine Inc. / 1651 Bayville St. / Norfolk, VA 23503
Tel. (804) 583-1470

Merritt Walter has been designing since 1960, and is one of the few designers working exclusively in steel. All the Rover designs are single-, double-, or multi-chine hulls, and are easy-to-build types, with reportedly good sailing abilities. All hulls are computer-analyzed for stability and hydrostatics, and many are also computer-faired. His designs are reasonably priced, and custom designs are the same price as stock. Several of the plan sets are Coast Guard approved for carrying passengers for hire.

	SP	CP
32' *Tahiti Rover,* DC ketch, 18,411 lbs.	$15	$ 400
32' *Gypsy Rover,* DC cutter, 18,411 lbs.	15	400
33' *Irish Rover,* DC or R ketch, 17,786 lbs.	15	400
37' *Block Island Rover,* SC schooner, 21,000 lbs.	15	300
37' *English Rover,* DC or R ketch, 17,876 lbs.	15	500
38' *Tasmanian Rover,* SC ketch, 21,000 lbs.	15	400
38' *Wise Rover,* SC or R ketch, 29,292 lbs.	15	500
39' *Bermuda Rover,* SC cutter	15	600
39' *Tropic Rover,* SC schooner, 21,600 lbs.	15	400
44' *Merry Rover,* SC or R schooner, 30,460 lbs.	20	900
44' *Ocean Rover,* DC or R ketch, 39,000 lbs.	20	700
52' *Coast Rover,* SC ketch	20	1,000
53' *Bonny Rover,* MC or R schooner, 49,300 lbs.	20	1,200
55' *Steel Rover,* SC schooner, 66,500 lbs.	25	1,500
57' *Trade Rover,* SC schooner, 66,570 lbs.	25	1,500
63' *Seattle Rover,* SC schooner, 65,669 lbs.	25	6,000
96' *American Rover,* SC 3 mast schooner, 101 tons	25	20,000

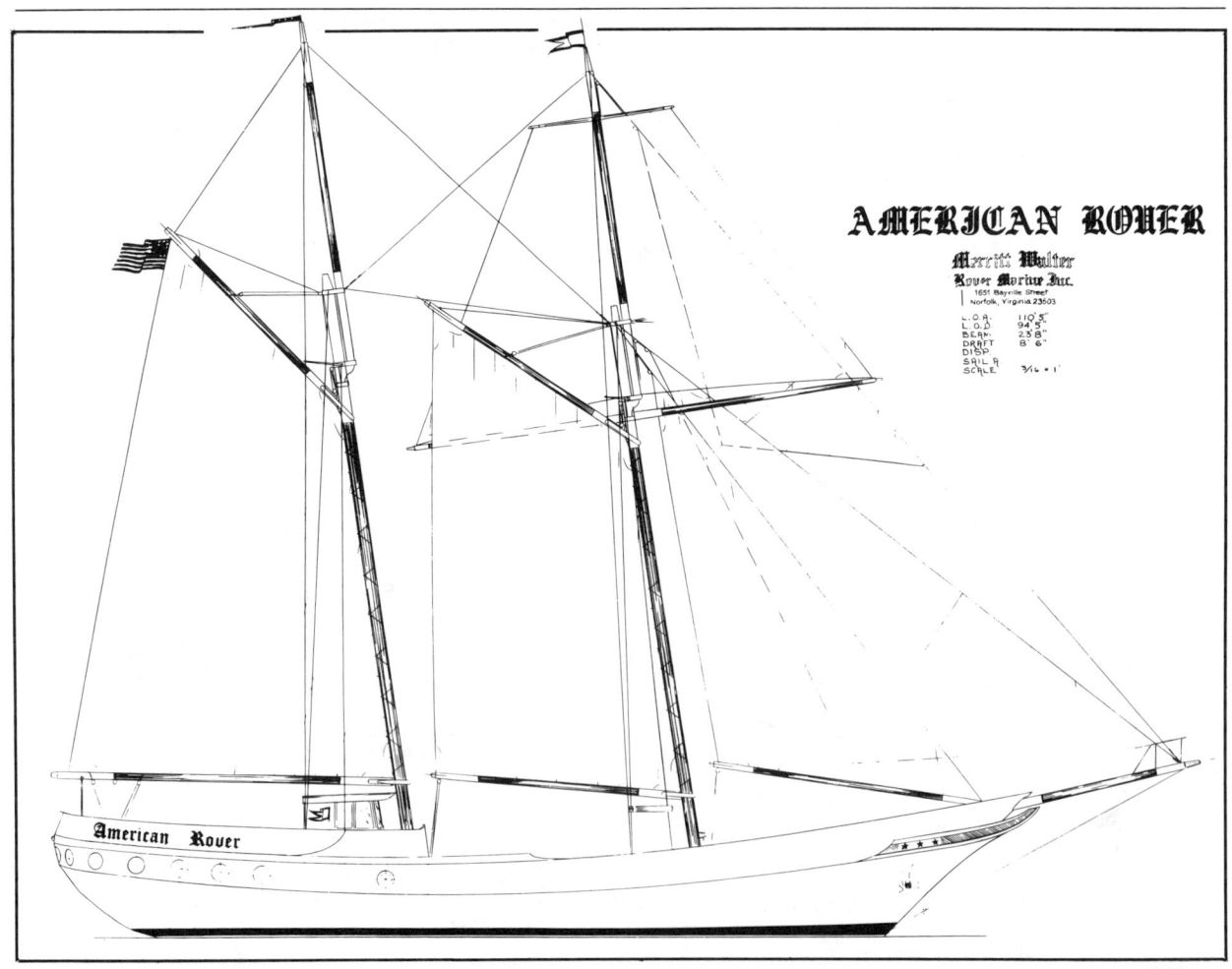

American Rover, *designed by Merritt Walter.*

ALAN WARWICK / The Loft / Te Kowhai Point, Doves Bay / RD 1 Kerikeri / New Zealand
Tel. 79469

Mr. Warwick has been active in the design field for the last 15 years, working quite frequently with steel. He only designs round hulls for sailing vessels, and has developed stainless steel tapered belting, retractable bow thrusters, and indented zinc blocks for use on his hulls. He works with several "nominated builders" and high-quality yards. Existing stock plans are generally sold between $3,000 and $10,000 New Zealand dollars, and custom work is based on 10% of the cost of the vessel.

47′ R center-cockpit cutter, 32,000 lbs.	$5,000 NZ
50′ R cutter, 35,919 lbs.	6,000
60′ R cutter with centerboard, 72,000 lbs.	
65′ R motorsailor cutter, 86,093 lbs.	
80′ R motorsailor cutter or ketch, 110,000 lbs.	
90′ R marconi schooner, 194,000 lbs.	
172′ R motorsailor schooner	

J. MURRAY WATTS

Designs are handled by Charles Wittholz (see entry)

37′ DC twin-keel ketch	
42′ R double-ended cutter (Hoskins-Perth)	
45′ *Victoria,* ketch	
50′ flush deck, double-ended, gaff rigged schooner, 14 tons	
60′ R cargo ketch with 10 ton hold, 36 tons	
85′ SC, V-bottom trading schooner	$3700

WESTLAWN ASSOCIATES / John Ammerman / Montville, NJ

	SP
Grey Dawn class, Dutch style	
16′ gaff cat sloop	20
22′ gaff schooner, cat sloop	30
29′ gaff ketch or sloop	40
37′ gaff ketch	100

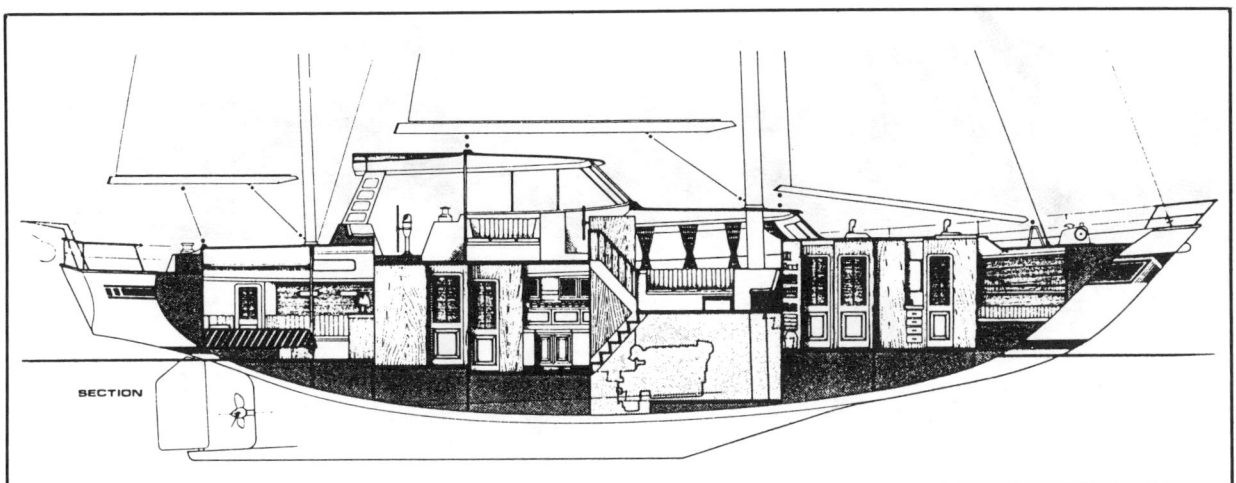

The Warwick 80, *a motor cutter designed by Alan Warwick.*   Courtesy of the designer

CHARLES W. WITTHOLZ / 100 Williamsburg Dr. / Silver Springs, MD 20901
Tel. (301) 593-7711

Mr. Wittholz has designed in steel for 30 plus years. Like many designers today, he is starting to use a computer as a time-saving tool. His study plans usually cost $10, and there are usually 6 to 10 drawings in his designs. His single chines are V-bottom style. Mr. Wittholz also handles Murray Watts' designs. Builders: Mooney, T.D. Vinette, and others.

22' aux. sloop, V-bottom, 5,000 lbs.	$ 100
27' V-bottom sloop, 5,800 lbs.	175
32' *Sailillo,* SC ketch or cutter, 6.1 tons	275
35' *Departure,* sloop or yawl (Mooney), 7.6 tons	300
39' *Presto,* SC ketch, cutter or schooner	350
39' SC centerboard ketch or cutter, 22,500 lbs.	375
39' SC motorsailor, 24,100 lbs.	400
42' R cutter	400
42' SC cutter or ketch, 24,500 lbs.	500
45' R ketch, full keel, 32,370 lbs.	650
48' DC ketch, 18 tons	900
50' SC double-ended schooner	1050
53' SC gaff-rigged charter schooner	1200
56' DC ketch with round stem	2000
60' *Romantic,* DC motorsailor ketch (R stern), 36 tons	2500
68' DC fishing ketch, good accommodations	
70' R ketch	
85' SC trading schooner	3700
85' *Mystic Clipper,* SC passenger schooner, built by Blount Marine, 277,760 lbs.	
90' *Pegasus,* R schooner (not complete)	

WOODIN & MAREAN / Russel M. Woodin, Parker E. Marean, III, Roger W. Long
4 Bridge St. / Box 697 / Boothbay Harbor, ME 04538 / Tel. (206) 633-3706

Woodin & Marean are primarily designers of commercial vessels, although they do some yacht work. Large, institutional sailing vessels, such as school ships and certified passenger vessels, are their major area of specialization for both design and consultation. Their fee structure and level of engineering are geared to this type of work and are probably beyond the reach of most home builders. They are presently designing a 105' brigantine for the Sea Education Association.

Directory of Builders

The listings include mostly builders in the U.S. or Canada, although some Europeans, Australians, New Zealanders, and one Taiwanese yard have been included; the list of builders from abroad is far from complete. Many of the large yards have commercial backgrounds and are only beginning to focus on smaller sailing yacht construction. Some builders specialize in only one boat; most, however, have good experience in metal-working and are willing to build new custom designs by reputable designers.

The builders are listed in alphabetical order, and varying amounts of information about their backgrounds, years of experience, and specialities (for example, round hulls, commercial, own designs) are discussed. As evidence of their experience, a list of the steel vessels they have built or would consider building on a regular basis is included. The list of boats shows the length on deck, the vessel's name and designer, the hull type, and the cost of a hull kit (unless otherwise specified). Also included is information about unusual tooling, the shop facilities, the number of working crew, standard hourly wages, time for construction, and the kind of work contracted out.

The number of steel boatbuilders is definitely increasing, but the size of the different shops continues to vary. Over 50% of the yards have a crew of 3 or under; 20% keep 3-20 people working; another 20% have 20-100 employees; and less than 10% hire more than 100 crew members. The largest steel boatbuilding operation has a working crew of about 450 people. The second-largest hires 150 people. But size doesn't necessary reflect quality, and an owner may get more personal attention from a smaller organization.

The number of boats being built in yards is naturally proportional to the size of the crew. One European yard (not listed in the directory) reportedly builds 30 medium-sized yachts a year. About 10% of those listed are capable of building over 10 boats a year. 15% of the yards construct between 6-10 vessels a year, and about 25% turn out 3-6 steel boats each year. The builders with fewer than 3 crew members finish between 1-3 boats in a year. Of course these figures change with the size of the boats being built and the stage of completion to which they are carried.

The size of the shop often dictates the number of boats that can be built at the same time. 50% only have room for one boat, while another 30% can handle two or three at once. 15% of the yards construct 3-8 boats simultaneously, and another 5% have over 8 boats in the shop at one time.

Of all the builders listed, 65% work stricly on barehull assemblies. The other 35% will build completed yachts. But these percentages seem to be changing rapidly, as more builders decide to complete the boats they begin. A few years ago, only 25% of the yards were willing to build round hulls; this figure has now risen to almost 50%.

Steel boatbuilding is definitely on the rise, especially in the U.S. Over 50% of the builders listed started doing business within the last 10 years. 20% began operations between 1960 and 1975, and another 20% have been building since shortly after World War II (1945-1960). Abeking & Rasmussen in Germany is the oldest yard listed; they began building steel boats in 1890.

When touring the country and visiting various builders, we found that most steel boats are custom creations, even though their builders may construct the same hull over and over again. The nature of the work and the skill required keep a steel "production" boat from ever looking mass-produced.

ABBREVIATIONS USED IN THE DIRECTORY LISTINGS

HULL SHAPES:

SC	Single chine (hard or soft), V-bottom
DC	Double chine, strip chine
MC	Multi-chine, lapstrake
R	True round, fully developed molded-radius, wineglass

PRICE LISTS:

SP	Study plans
CP	Construction plans
BH	Bare-hull assembly (hull, deck, cabin)
Comp	Completed vessel

ABEKING & RASMUSSEN GMBH & CO.
Postfach 11 60 / 2874 Lemwerder / Federal Republic of Germany / Tel. (04 21) 67 33-0

Abeking & Rasmussen have been building steel boats for 75 years and have turned out over 900 yachts to technical standards appropriate for the naval craft they also build. With a crew of 450, they can work on 8 vessels at a time with completion times between 3 and 15 months, depending on size. They build only complete yachts, acting as the prime contractor, and work from both their own designs and plans from other designers. The increase in cost for round hulls depends on the design.

ALU-STEEL BOAT CO. / Jack Farrell / 3301 N. 31st
Tacoma, WA 98407 / Tel. (206) 759-1272

Mr. Farrell builds both aluminum and steel commercial vessels and yachts, and specializes in chine hulls.

ANACORTES STEEL YACHTS / P.O. Box 1104 / Anacortes, WA 98221

This small yard is headed by a builder with 23 years of experience, and builds chine boats to any stage of completion. They are presenting finishing Ted Brewer's *Atlantic 43,* and will soon begin a *Roberts 53.* Flat bar framing is preferred, and the yard recommends the use of pre-primed plate.

ARAGOSA YACHTS / 2704-555 Sherbourne St. / Toronto, Ontario
Canada M4X 1W6 / Tel. (416) 962-0009

Aragosa has been building steel boats for 6 years, and, although they do not specialize in any particular designs, they prefer to build those of Ted Brewer. In addition to the boats listed below, they have also constructed Colvin's *Gazelle* and Dickerson's 43′ double-chine yawl. Round-hull construction averages a 30% higher cost than chine. With 2–3 workers, they can build two boats simultaneously to any stage of completion. Most of the work is done in their shop; only a few jobs are contracted out. Hull-deck assemblies take 4–6 months (longer for developed round hulls), and cost an average of $1.50 Canadian per pound of displacement. Arrangements can be made for the owner to finish out the hull locally. Prices listed below include lead ballast, sandblasting, and primer coat.

Bull Dog 30 (Brewer), R cutter	$24,000 CAN
Goderich 35 (Brewer/Wallstrom), R cutter	30,000
Endurance 35 (Ibold), R cutter	39,000
Goderich 41 (Brewer), R cutter or ketch	39,500
Endurance 44 (Ibold), cutter or ketch	49,000

BALEHI MARINE, INC. / Dennis Frantz / Box 600 / Lacombe, LA 70445
Tel. (504) 822-5221 or 552-5586

Balehi is primarily a commercial shipyard building in steel and aluminum. They do repair work on yachts and will consider building vessels in the 37′ to 45′ range. Labor charge is $23/man hour (1983) plus surcharges.

RON BARNES / Box 1951 / St. Augustine, FL 32084 / Tel. (904) 824-6643

The Barnes yard, with 12 years of experience, specializes in soft chine hulls, especially Colvin's *Gazelle,* but will build other designs. The 3–4 person crew builds about 6 or 7 hulls a year. In addition to bare hull assemblies, Barnes offers a special kit in which the hull is welded up completely, but the owner finishes the keel, rudder, bulwarks, deck and deck structures, engine bed, and mast steps.

Islander 32 (similar to Harry Pidgeon's)		$10,000
Tahitiana 32 (Farmer)		20,000
Radian 37 (Colvin)	($6,500 kit)	13,000
Gazelle 42 (Colvin)	($9,500 kit)	19,000
Solution 48 (Bolger)		18,000
Pipistrelle 51 (Colvin)		34,000
Memory 51 (cargo version of *Pipistrelle*)		34,000

BLOUNT MARINE CORP. / P.O. Box 368 / Warren, RI 02885
Tel. (401) 245-8300

Blount Marine has been operating since 1949 with 125 employees, building commercial work boats and large passenger vessels. They recently completed a 110' *Mystic Clipper* schooner. The yard builds 3–5 boats at a time with elaborate tooling. They prefer chine construction, although they will build round hulls, and 65' is the minimum size yacht they would consider building.

CMC (CRANDON MARINE CONSTRUCTION) / Unit 14A, Telford Road
Bicester, Oxon / England OX6 OTZ / Tel. Bicester (0869) 245353

CMC builds double-chine Alan Pape designs to any stage of completion from bare hull assembly to delivery. They use modern welding equipment, and finish their hulls with epoxy paints.

> *Steelmaid 35* (Pape)
> *Steelmaid 38* (Pape)
> *Steelmaid 45* (Pape)

COAST MARINE CONSTRUCTION / Millerick Bros.
P.O. Box 357 / Cotati, CA 94928 / Tel. (707) 829-2507

With 10 years of experience in boatbuilding and 20 years in fabrication and sheet metal work, Coast Marine builds any reputable design in steel or aluminum. Customers most often request bare hull assemblies, but they will work to any stage, subcontracting out work on boat systems, blasting, and insulation. The yard has worked with many designers, including Bruce Roberts, Hartog, K.J. Seymour, Monk, Groupe Finot, and Van de Stadt. There are usually 3 or 4 crew members working on 2 or 3 hulls at a time. They have done round hulls in aluminum but not in steel, although they would be glad to build round steel boats.

> 30' SC cutter
> 38' SC ketch
> 40' MC flush-deck sloop
> 64' SC cutter

CONYER MARINE LTD. / Conyer Quay / Teynham, Kent
England ME9 9HW / Tel. 0795-521276

This family-owned and -operated yard has been in business since the early 1960's, and specializes in round bilge hulls. They are so confident of their ability to prevent any corrosion in the interior that they offer a 15-year guarantee. Flat bar frames are hot-bent on a special table jig. They build both sailboats and motor yachts designed by Hundy, Griffiths, Pape, and Spears under the names of *Bay Class Yachts* and *Blue Water Yachts*. They will also build hulls by other designers. Every vessel is custom designed and built for the individual owner, using completed vessels as examples.

	£
Noontide 32 (Griffiths), SC cutter	36,000
Trinity Bay (Hundy)	53,000
Donegal Bay 38 (Hundy/Griffiths)	56,000
Willem Barentz 38 (Koopmans), cutter	60,000
Blue Water 38 (Spears), cutter	58,000
Blue Water 40 (Spears)	80,000
Tahitian Bay 42 (Hundy/Spears), ketch or cutter	89,000
Blue Water 42 (Spears), ketch	99,000
Bay of Island 44 (Hundy/Griffiths), ketch	105,000
Seven Island Bay 47 (Hundy/Spears), ketch	120,000
Bantry Bay 49 (Hundy/Spears)	130,000
Blue Water 53 (Spears), cutter	168,000
Bay of Fundy (Hundy/Spears)	185,000
San Francisco Bay 53 (Hundy/Spears), ketch	185,000
Delaware Bay 58 (Hundy/Spears), ketch	325,000
Chesapeake Bay 72 (Spears), ketch	490,000

CROFT MARINE PRODUCTIONS LTD. / Atherstone Airfield, Atherstone-on-Stour
Stratford on Avon, Warwickshire / England CV37 8NF / Tel. Alderminster (07987) 615

The Croft yard builds primarily steel and aluminum round hulls (both reverse-garboard and box-keel construction) up to 60' long to any stage of completion from any reputable design. In the past, they've built yachts by various designers, including Lawrent Giles, Jean Knocker, Alan Pape, Angus Primrose, and Robert Tucker. Hard chine hulls will only be constructed at the customer's specific request. The construction staff of 8–10 can handle all boat systems, although metal casting and sprayed insulation are contracted out. Three to four boats are built at a time using special round bilge plate-forming tools. The boats are metallized at the end of the 2–3 months completion time.

Calliope 34 (Tucker), sloop	(BH)	£13,250
35' shoal-draft, double-ended cutter (Pape)		
Calliope 36 (Tucker), sloop, cutter, or ketch	(BH)	14,200
	(Complete)	56,785
Callisto 38 (Bill Dixon), sloop, cutter, or ketch, various keels	(Complete)	63,400
Calliope 40 (Tucker), sloop, cutter or ketch with dog house	(BH)	16,400
	(Complete)	67,800
Callisto 43, cutter or ketch	(BH)	19,225
Calliope 44, cutter or ketch	(BH)	19,725
Callisto 48		

CUSTOM STEEL BOATS / Richard E. Flowers
P.O. Box 63 / Arapahoe, NC 28510 / Tel. (919) 633-4772

Custom Steel Boats has worked in steel construction for 35 years, with 75% of their experience in commercial vessels. Bruce Roberts considers the yard an "accredited builder," and they have been building Roberts' hulls up to 100' since 1981. Three boats are built at a time, all at various stages of completion, and it takes 3–4 months to finish a hull, using 3 workers per boat. Electrics, plumbing, and insulation are contracted out. Round hulls are available for a 33% increase in price. There is space for the owner to use to finish a boat out.

Spray 22 (Roberts), DC sloop	$ 3,795
Spray 28 (Roberts), DC cutter	19,600
Roberts 31, DC sloop	17,500
Spray 33 (Roberts), DC cutter or ketch	23,300
Roberts 34, MC cutter or sloop	18,650
Spray 36 (Roberts), DC motorsailor	25,900
Roberts 37	
Roberts 38, DC cutter or ketch	25,250
Spray 40 (Roberts), DC gaff-rigged ketch	31,900
Roberts 43, DC ketch	26,000
Offshore A 44 (Roberts), DC ketch	27,000
Roberts 53, DC cutter or ketch	44,000

FEADSHIP AMERICA / 801 Seabreeze Ave. / Box 3100, Bahia Mar
Ft. Lauderdale, FL 33316 / Tel. (305) 761-1830

Feadship built sailboats in the 1950's, but now basically works on large power yachts, 85-220'. They have built 62' and 77' motorsailors, and would build a 58' DeVries design.

GLADDING-HEARN SHIPBUILDING CORP.
1 Riverside Ave. / Box D / Somerset, MA 02726
Tel. (617) 676-8596

Gladding-Hearn have been building various types of steel vessels since 1955. Since 1980, they have been constructing 60–70' custom aluminum motor yachts. They are a well-equipped and well-established yard, and even have a furnace for hot-bending very accurate frames, rollers, shears, and plasma arc welding equipment. In 1966, they rebuilt the famous 65' *Pioneer,* an iron schooner built in 1885. Although Gladding-Hearn primarily builds large, specialty commercial vessels, they've done a few sailboats, including a Mason *Carolyn 55,* a Colvin pinky, and two 35' chine sloops designed by Danny Greene. They have a crew of over 50, and build 4–8 boats at one time. Round hulls are constructed for up to 50% extra cost.

GOUDY & STEVENS / East Boothbay, ME 04544
Tel. (207) 633-3521 or 633-3522

This yard has been in operation since 1920, primarily building fishing boats. They have a 40′ minimum size limit, and work in both round and chine. Goudy & Stevens built a 120′ sailing yacht for President Franklin D. Roosevelt and, in 1967, a replica of *America*.

HAGLUND BOAT WORKS / 64 Bulkhead Road, Reynolds Industrial Park
Box 1155 / Green Cove Springs, FL 32043 / Tel. (904) 284-1500 or 284-3332

Mr. Haglund is presently building his third schooner from a design by W.W. Bates, originally constructed in 1854. These are large, round schooners, 90′ and 152′ LOA. He has good facilities and works on only one boat at a time, taking about a year to finish a hull at a charge of $8 per hour. Only sailmaking is contracted out. There are arrangements for space for an owner to finish out a hull.

TOPPER HERMANSON BOATBUILDING / 1619 North 14th St.
Fernandina Beach, FL 32034 / Tel. (904) 261-2606

This yard has built over 20 boats in the last 8 years in steel, aluminum, and stainless steel, from designs by Colvin, Roberts, Simpson, Wittholz, Scott, Brewer, and Tanton. They also produce their own *Chance Christian* design, a round hull with developed radius plate. Four round-bilge yachts were recently completed at a yard rate of $16–18 per hour. They do their own rolling, and blasting and priming are included in the hull kit price. All stages of construction are available, from completed hull-deck assemblies to fully found yachts. The yard itself employs welders, carpenters, and painters. The prices below are subject to change.

22′ Cape Cod cat boat (Brewer)	$ 4,995
Chance Christian 25 (Wittholz), chine sloop, 7500 lbs.	5,995
27′ cat boat (Tanton), sloop, 8,557 lbs.	
Chance Christian 27 (Wittholz), SC	6,995
Chance Christian 33 (Hermanson), R cutter, 13,810 lbs.	18,500
Chance Christian 36 (Hermanson), R cutter, 17,500 lbs.	21,500

HIGH SEAS YACHT CORP. / Pierre Rothe / P.O. Box 164 / Nanaimo, B.C. / Canada

The yard was established in 1981 to build the racy, fin-keel, multi-chine Groupe Finot designs in Canada. All prices are 1983.

Reve d'Antilles 38, sloop, 19,800 lbs.	$38,500 CAN
Reve Des Seychelles 40, sloop, 26,000 lbs.	42,500
Reve des Tropiques 43, cutter, 28,600 lbs.	54,900

ISLAND STAR MARINE / Box 6622 / Gulfport, MS 39501
Tel. (601) 863-3488

Island Star constructs power and sail boats up to 75′, using their own designs and those of Bruce Roberts, as well as those produced by other designers. Steel and aluminum flame spraying is available.

JEFFERSON MARINE, INC. / 10685 Sunnyside Rd.
Jefferson, OR 97352 / Tel. (503) 363-0121

Jefferson Marine is not a boatbuilder in the normal sense, but rather produces steel kits for owner assembly. The plate is cut with a plasma arc cutter from computer-faired offsets. At present, they offer a kit for a multi-chine version of Ted Brewer's *Corten 42*, a gaff-rigged schooner or cutter. They can develop hull kits for any well-designed steel boat.

JACHTWERF JONGERT B.V. / Industrieweg 6
EW Medemblik / Holland / Tel. 02274-2544

JONGERT SALES OFFICE / Dahm International / Rathausufer 22
400 Dusseldorf / Federal Republic of Germany

This Dutch yard has been in operation for approximately 32 years, and builds primarily their own designs. They have constructed steel yachts ranging in size from 8 to 28 meters. With 110 workers, they build 5 or 6 vessels at a time. Jongert only builds complete yachts, taking approximately 4 months to finish one. All work except metal casting is done in the yard.

KAIULANI SAILING VESSELS / Box 2843 / South Portland, ME 04106
Tel. (207) 781-4231

This is a relatively new yard with an experienced crew of 5–6 men who build the developed molded-radius *Kaiulani 38*, designed by Ted Brewer. A complete hull kit, metallized and primed, is available for $51,600. They have just introduced the *Kaiulani 34*, similar to the 38 in underbody, profile, and construction. The yard has particularly developed the art of proper epoxy fairing, and has room for two hulls to be built simultaneously.

KANTER YACHTS CORP. / 9 Barrie Blvd. / St. Thomas, Ontario
Canada N5P 4B9 / Tel. (519) 633-1058

The Kanter yard builds round hull boats, specializing in Brewer's *Atlantic*, a fin-keel ketch with an aluminum pilothouse. They have also constructed the *Roberts 34* and *43*, and will build chine hulls if requested.

KELLY MARINE / Frank Kelly / Box 3879 / Redding, CA 96049
Tel. (916) 221-5129

Kelly Marine is a small boatbuilding yard with an ample pool of craftsmen on whom to call. They build hard chine and round bilged boats in either steel or aluminum to almost any size, including Brewer's *Verity 40*, a true round hull. This performance cruiser is one of the lightest steel designs for its size. Their boats are available either as a metallized and primed bare-hull assembly or as completed yachts. Prices are subject to change.

Gazelle (Colvin)	$20,000
Tanton 35 (Tanton), DC cat ketch with fin keel and skeg rudder	18,000
Verity 40 (Brewer), R cutter	40,000

LAND & SEA / Lin Heath / P.O. Box 1907 / La Plata, MD 20646

This yard builds various Bruce Roberts designs, including the *Spray 22*, to any stage.

DAVID LUND MARINE LTD. / Alvion Dockyard, Hanover Place / Bristol
England BS1 6UT / Tel. Bristol (0272) 25730

The yard has built 23 of Farmer's *Tahitiana* hulls, but at present are concentrating on general yard work.

MARINE ENGINEERS / Michael Kolesar / P.O. Box 9240
Panama City, FL 32407 / Tel. (904) 769-5583

Marine Engineers is a full-service steel boatbuilding company, founded in 1979, engaged in the construction of yachts, work boats, and barges. They build primarily double-chine hulls, and are presently completing their tenth vessel, a 96' schooner. The yard uses both gas and plasma cutting for the steel work. Zinc and aluminum flame spraying are also available. At present, they can build up to three boats with maximum 24' beams at a time, employing a work force of 7.

Squaw 27 (Tucker), DC
Tahiti Rover 32 (Walter), DC
Block Island Rover 38 (Walter), SC
Tropic Rover 38 (Walter), SC
American Rover 96 (Walter), SC

Kaiulanı 38, *built by Kaiulani Yachts from a design by Ted Brewer.* Picture by Stephen Davis, courtesy of the builder

MARINE METALS / Howdy Bailey / 4524 Dunning Rd.
Norfolk, VA 23518 / Tel. (804) 480-0058

This small yard has been working with metal for 20 years, and recently has completed four steel hulls, from 34' to 60'. The vessels are finished out to any stage, using plasma arc cutting equipment. They have built Merritt Walter designs and plan to do more with some new Dudley Dix designs. The yard will not build round hulls, preferring to work with multi-chine designs. A brochure is available for $3.

Irish Rover 33 (Walter)	$21,000
Dylan 34 (Dix)	21,000
Gypsy Rover 36 (Walter)	19,000
Roberts Custom 45	
Dix Custom 52, schooner	
Dix Custom 64	

MARS MACHINE WORKS / Box 190 / Gloucester Point, VA 23062
Tel. (804) 642-4760

This is a small yard that is also a machine shop. They have built an aluminum *Bolger 30* and will do steel. They have their own stock plans, but mainly build custom designs.

MC NIVEN YACHTS / P.O. BOX 32-103 / Devonport / Auckland, 9 / New Zealand

This yard builds designs by D.E. Brooke.

META SHIPYARDS / BP 109 / 69170 Tarare / France / Tel. (74) 63-13-58

The META yard is perhaps most famous for building Moitessier's *Joshua*. Since 1963, they have built 70 *Joshuas* and 35 *Damiens* as well as over 60 other boats from French designers in both steel and aluminum. The design team of Michel Joubert, Bernard Nivelt, and Joseph Fricaud develop their in-house designs. The yard uses a patented STRONGALL system for their aluminum boats, and plan to build almost exclusively with this system. Some of their hulls are especially suited for amateur construction: *Embrun, JNF 38, JNF 34.*

JNF 34 (Joubert/Nivelt/Fricaud)
Oreade 34 (Amiet), ketch, 19,842 lbs.
Sainte-Marthe 36 (Amiet), sloop motorsailor, 19,860 lbs.
JFN 38 (Joubert/Nivelt/Fricaud)
Ophelie 39 (Amiet), ketch, 30,865 lbs.
Joshua 40 (Knocker), R ketch, 30,860 lbs.
Damien 40 (Joubert), R cutter
Embrun 40 (Amiet), DC ketch
Damien II 46 (Joubert), R schooner, 29,762 lbs.
Pierre-Louis 49 (Knocker), 44,100 lbs.

METANAV, INC. / 210, Point-du-jour nord / L'Assomption, Quebec
Canada J0K 1GO / Tel. (514) 589-2345

Metanav has built 14 steel and aluminum boats since 1979, from 30' to 41'. The yard builds radiused chine hulls and has shop space for two 40' boats. It takes an average of 2–3 months to build a boat with 3 people working on it. Shop rate is $25 Canadian.

Sea Dog 29 (Van de Stadt), DC sloop	
Benford 30, SC trawler yacht	
Nautilus 33 (Van de Stadt), SC	
Van de Stadt 34, MC	$18,900 CAN
Triade 38 (Langevin), MC sloop	
Corten 40 (Brewer), R version, schooner	36,000
Benford 44, MC cat ketch	

MOONEY MARINE / P.O. Box 280 / Deltaville, VA 23043
Tel. (804) 776-6392

Although Mooney Marine have been building steel sail and power boats for over 9 years, they have decided to specialize in selling Wittholz's *Departure 35* building plans with full mylar plate and frame templates from proven building methods. These plans cost $600; study plans are $30. They have built Farmer's *Tahitiana 31*; Brewer's *32, Corten 40,* and *Cape Race 44;* a *Mason 40;* Wittholz's *Departure 35, 42,* and *56;* and Walter's *Bonny Rover 52.*

MURRAY BOATS / Phil Badham / RR#4 / Trenton, Ontario
Canada K8V 5P7 / Tel. (613) 392-7327

Mr. Badham has been building Ted Brewer's double-chine *Murray 33* for 8 years, after spending 10 years in steel fabrication and engineering work. He works alone, building one boat at a time, and will build other custom chine designs up to 37' for an additional 30%. Blasting and painting are contracted out. The exclusive *Murray 33* is available as a bare-hull assembly for $18,000 Canadian.

NORTH CAROLINA STEEL BUILDERS / Gavin Frost
Rt. 1, Box 400 / Bayboro, NC 28515 / Tel. (919) 745-5272

Mr. Frost has been associated with both Thomas Colvin and Ted Brewer. The yard will build round hulls, although they are much more expensive than their chine ones. The shop rate is $15 per hour, and space can be rented for $50 a month to finish out a boat. Their steel boatbuilding course was recently turned over to Seaward Bound in California.

Gazelle 42	$22,500
Spray 40	24,600

OCEANCRAFT / Malpas / Truro, Cornwall
England TR1 1QJ

This English yard builds full-keel ocean-cruising yachts. They work on one boat at a time with a crew of 10, and specialize in Alan Pape's *Ebb Tide* series.

30' DC long-coachroof sloop	£ 31,000
33' MC flush-deck cutter or sloop	41,800
36' MC flush-deck cutter or sloop	57,800
39' MC long-coachroof, center-cockpit ketch, cutter or schooner	68,000
42' MC or R flush-deck cutter or ketch	78,000
45' MC or R long-coachroof, center-cockpit or pilothouse cutter or ketch	97,000
48' R flush-deck cutter or ketch	156,000
50' R center-cockpit ketch	168,000

OLYMPIC TORQUE TOOL / Dave Smith / 516 Penguin Court S.E.
Olympia, WA 98503 / Tel. (206) 456-6311

Dave Smith has worked with steel for over 13 years, and likes to build round hulls. He has constructed a *Spray 33* and a *Perry 43* (Robert Perry's second steel design), which is a double-molded-radius cutter. The *Perry 43* bare-hull assembly, blasted, primed, and with tanks, costs $42,000. Dave also recently put together a fine steel yacht seminar.

OSSIM PLOCCO / via Fabi / Frosinone / Italy

This yards builds various round hull designs including those of designers Giorgetti & Magrini of Milan, Italy.

PHEON YACHTS, LTD. / Robinson Rd. / Newhaven, Sussex
England BN9 9BL / Tel. Newhaven (0273) 515828

Pheon fits out 34' to 50' steel ocean-cruising hulls from designs by Robert B. Harris, Tony Tucker (Rober Tucker Designs, Ltd.), Bill Dixon (Angus Primrose, Ltd.), and Alan Pape. With 18 employees, they can work on 5 vessels at a time. At a labor cost of £130 per 40-hour week, they take about 9 months from date of order to complete one of the specialty hulls. Their steel subcontractors have built steel vessels for many years and can construct top-quality round-bilge hulls for the same cost as chine. Pheon's boats are metallized with aluminum.

RHODE ISLAND MARINE SERVICES / 93 Harbor Island Road
Narragansett, RI 02982

This boatyard was established in 1956 and builds in steel, aluminum, cold-molded wood, and fiberglass. They have constructed sailing designs by Walter Beckmann, as well as those of Sparkman & Stephens and Rhodes. They operate with a crew of 3–12 and take 3–9 months per hull. The yard does all work but rigging, sails, engine, and casting at a shop rate of $19 per hour, and has a complete machine shop, mill, carpentry shop, and paint shop. They can work on 3–5 boats at a time. Almost all of the designs listed below are by Walter Beckmann, and there is no charge for the plans if they build the hull. The prices are as of 1984.

Debbie S35, sloop	$ 17,950
Block Island S35, ketch	18,950
Classic S38	22,950
Spray 40 (classic replica)	30,000
Ocean 44, ketch	34,950
Nicole S47, schooner	39,950
Classic S50, aft-cabin ketch	44,950
World S50, schooner	49,950
Atlantic S60, schooner	99,950
Tamaris S81, ketch	174,950

BRUCE ROBERTS (UK) LTD. / 125 Southland Road
Bromley, Kent / England BR2 9QT / Tel. 01-290 0427

The yard concentrated initially on the Roberts *Spray 38*, but also builds other Roberts designs and will gladly custom build any Bruce Roberts or Maurice Griffiths design for steel. They contract out everything but the building, but supervise very closely to guarantee quality end products. This firm is very strongly against metallizing steel hulls.

Roberts 28, MC cutter or ketch
Spray 28 (Roberts), MC cutter
Spray 33 (Roberts), MC cutter or ketch
Roberts 34, MC sloops
Roberts 35, MC cutter or ketch
Roberts 36, MC cutter or ketch
Spray 36 (Roberts), MC cutter
Roberts 38, MC cutter or ketch
Spray 38 (Roberts), MC ketch
Roberts 39, MC sloop or ketch
Spray 40 (Roberts), MC ketch, cutter, or schooner
Gulf Stream 42 (Griffiths), MC ketch
Roberts 43, MC cutter or ketch
Roberts 44, MC cutter or ketch
Roberts 53, MC cutter or ketch
Roberts 64, MC cutter or ketch

ROVER MARINE / 1651 Bayville St. / Norfolk, VA 23503
Tel. (804) 583-1470

This yard builds only Merritt Walter designs, and is under the direction of Merritt's son Shon. See the Walter entry in the Directory of Designers for choices.

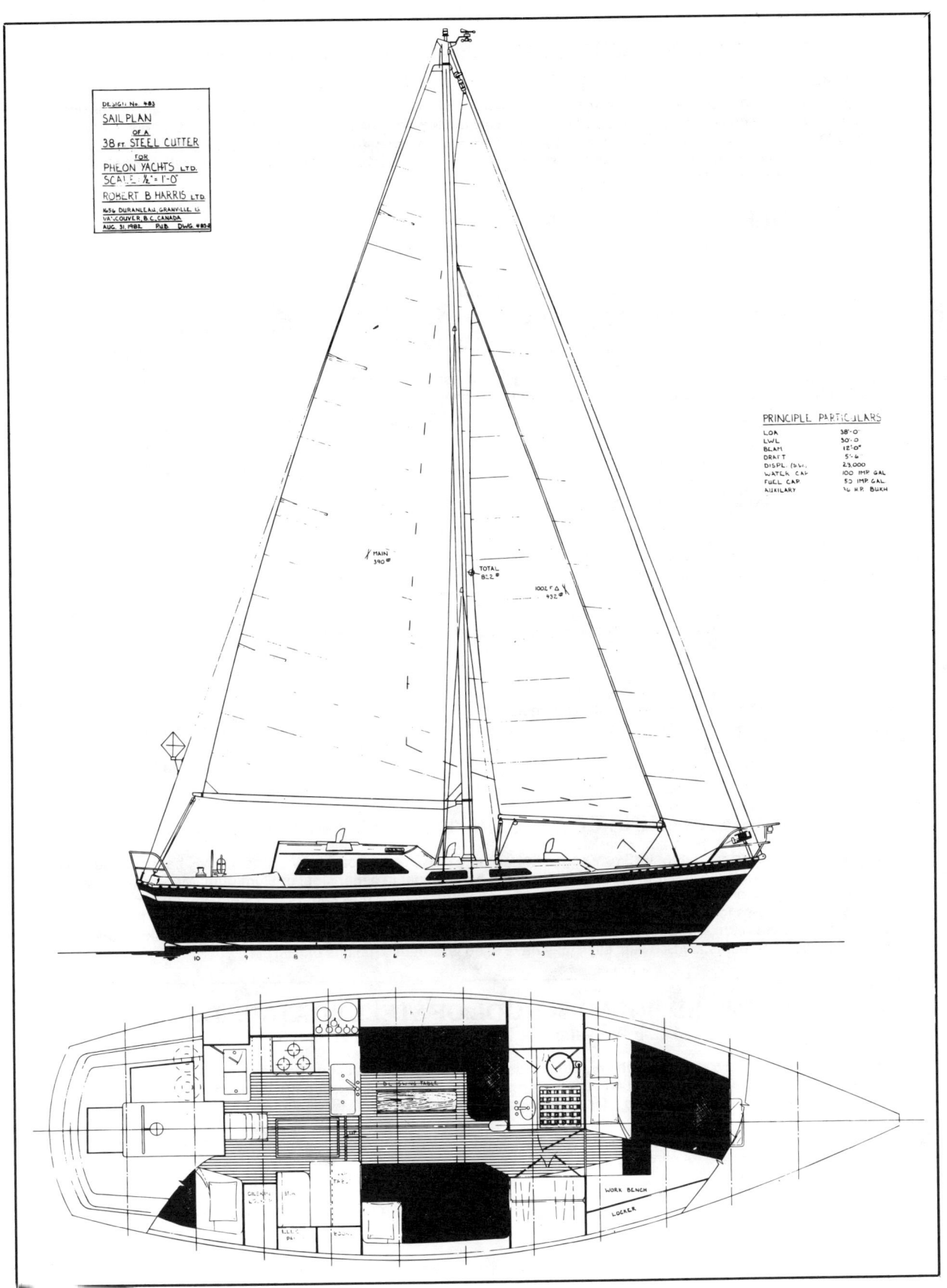

Pheon 38, *built by Pheon Yachts from a design by Robert Harris*

Courtesy of the builder

SANFORD-WOOD MARINE / 530 W. Cutting Blvd. / Richmond, CA 94804

Sanford-Wood is primarily a repair yard with complete haul-out facilities that has been in business for years. However, in the last 3 years, they've built three steel chine hulls, two by Hutton (one of which is a 49′ cutter). Last year, they donated space for Bernard Moitessier to have his new Hutton design built. They plan to be designing their own line soon, and will build from plans by other reputable designers. They have the facilities to build two boats at a time while they repair up to 30 boats. No work is contracted out, and Sanford-Wood will take a boat totally to completion with their own crew.

SCHEEPSBOUWBEDRIJF KUIJPER, B.V. / Schoorldam, Kanaalkade 35
1749 CN Warmenhuizen (N.H.) / Holland

U.S. REPRESENTATIVE:

D. STREET YACHT SERVICES / P.O. Box 642 / Newburyport, MA 01950
Tel. (617) 462-4605

Mr. Streeter imports hulls and complete boats from the Scheepsbouwbedrijf Kuijper yard. At this point, he is offering the *Breewijd 31*, but larger boats and custom building are available.

Breewijd 31, R sloop, semi-custom, with interior and accommodations	(Comp.)	$79,500
as requested by the owner.	(BH)	48,000

SCHREIBER BOATS / Rt. 7, Box 254-B / St. Augustine, FL 32084
Tel. (904) 824-6943

Dennis Schreiber has 7 years of experience building steel vessels, and specializes in the construction of round hull designs. He features the designs of George W. Sutton, who has been designing and building since 1938. Schreiber's work also includes designs by Colvin, Walter, Garden, Defever; quotes are given on the construction of hulls by other reputable designers. Schreiber Boats offers a steel package for hulls up to 55′. No interior work is done, but there are several local craftsmen who offer their services independently. In conjunction with his own hull construction, Schreiber offers space to do-it-yourself builders looking for a good climate and atmosphere in which to work. Basic living accommodations may be offered in the future.

Sutton 36, R cutter, ketch, or schooner	$19,500
Sutton 42, R or C cutter, ketch, or schooner	24,000
Sutton 46, R cutter, ketch, or schooner	28,500
Sutton 55, R cutter, ketch, or schooner	48,000

SCHWARZ MARINE CO., INC. / 1206–25th St. / Two Rivers, WI 54241-2307

Mr. Schwarz founded his company 40 years ago after working with Burger Boats in Wisconsin. They have built several hundred boats, both chine and round, and can build any type of boat in either steel or aluminum. Mr Schwarz began working with longitudinal framing on boats in 1950, a technique which is now standard in steel boatbuilding. He also uses pre-formed dies for round bilge boats, although this adds considerably to the cost of the hull, and he will build wineglass or double compound hulls. The yard employs up to 12 people, building 4 boats at a time. In all the years they have been building boats, Mr Schwarz says they have used less than 5 gallons of filler.

SEAWARD BOUND SCHOOL OF STEEL BOATBUILDING
722-F W. Betteravia Rd. / Santa Maria, CA 93455

In addition to operating a yard in which only steel hulls are built, this organization offers a home study course in steel boatbuilding that covers every operation from design selection through lofting, construction, and launching. They do not teach welding, however. They also offer the services of several specialists for engineering and design problems on a fee basis.

SIERRA YACHTWERKS / P.O. Box 426 / Bethel Island, CA 94511

In addition to operating a mobile metallizing business covering the West Coast, Doug Knight has been working with steel for 10 years and building steel boats for 4 years from designs by Farmer, Pence, and Van de Stadt. The yard is small, employing 1 or 2 people, and they do all their own machining. Three or four boats at a time can be accommodated, and a 35 ton travel lift is available. Boats are available at any stage of completion, including blasting, metallizing, and painting. An intensive hands-on workshop covering welding and all phases of construction is offered twice a year.

Custom sandblasting and metallizing are provided through Knight's Mobile Metal Spray, which also offers consultation on marine paint and corrosion control. For metallizing with zinc or aluminum, a flat rate per square foot of coverage is charged, which includes blasting and a single wash primer coating. The travel fee that is charged can be shared if there are several jobs in the same area. A bid sheet is available on request.

Cherub 23 (Farmer), SC sloop	$ 3,675
Seadog 29 (Van de Stadt), MC	
Tahitiana 31 (Farmer), MC cutter or ketch	
Alpenglo 34 (Van de Stadt), MC sloop	14,000
Seal 36 (Van de Stadt), MC or R	
Van de Stadt 44, MC or R	
Mason 65, MC schooner	

SP METAL CRAFT / F110-201 CW / Blaine, WA 98230
or
12891 116 Ave. / Surrey, B.C. / Canada V3R 2S6 / Tel. (604) 580-4241

SP Metal Craft has been in operation for only a few years, but within that time they've constructed over 10 yachts ranging from 24' to 44'. They've built mostly designs by Grahame Shannon, with whom they work closely; however, they will bid on other designs. With spacious facilities and 10 employees, they can work on 3–4 boats at a time, and have the capacity to finish off the boats to various stages. They also closely supervise the pre-priming of the plate, which is done nearby. The yard contracts out plate rolling and foam spraying. They build custom round hulls for a 15% increase in cost.

All designs are Shannon's
Tom Thumb 24
Opal 28
Amazon Pilot
Ruby 33
Amazon 37
Pearl 38
Amazon Pilot 41

TA CHIAO SHIP BUILDING CO., LTD. / 12-1 Su Tzu Toe
Pali Shiang, Taipei Hsien / Taiwan / Republic of China / Tel. (02) 610-3611-4

Ta Chiao has been building metal boats for four years, including the *Condor 164*, a 16.4-meter sailboat with a stainless hull (also available in steel and aluminum), and 22.9-meter yacht in aluminum. They will work from designs for round or chine hulls by any expert designer, and deliver only fully completed yachts. A team of 12 to 15 people build the hull, including 4 welders approved by Lloyd's. It takes less than 4 months to build a hull under 100'. All operations are carried out in the yard.

TREWORGY YACHTS, INC. / Mark Treworgy
Rt. 1, Box 139D / St. Augustine, FL 32086 / Tel. (904) 445-5878

Mr Treworgy has been building Sutton round steel designs for 7 years, and is presently specializing in tugs and round steel sailing yachts, with plans to expand into aluminum. He also builds his own designs. The good-sized shop with ample tooling can compete 2–3 bare-hull assemblies at a time in about 3 months for the 34' and 9 months for the 62'. The labor charge is $16 per hour, and rolling, fabrication, and foam insulation are contracted out. The yard builds to any stage of completion, and prefers Imron paint. Mr. Treworgy is presently working on new designs for radiused round hulls with a shape between soft chine and fully round.

33' motorsailor ketch (Roberts), DC	
Atlantis 34 (Treworgy), R motorsailor cutter	$19,000
39' cutter (Treworgy), R	
42' schooner (Treworgy)	
43' ketch (Treworgy)	
43' cutter (Treworgy), R	
44' (Walter), SC	
50' ketch (Treworgy), R	
62' ketch (Treworgy), R	

VAN DAM NORDIA SHIPYARD / Helling 49, Postbox 33
Aalsmeer / Holland / Tel. (0) 2977-24527/23466

Van Dam Nordia has been building steel and aluminum boats for over 60 years, and have completed about 200 vessels. They offer only complete yachts from their own custom designs. All boatbuilding operations are carried out in their shop.

> *Nordia 45*, R motorsailor ketch, 18 tons
> *Nordia 51*, motorsailor, 30 tons
> 54′ motorsailor, 32 tons
> *Nordia Cruiser 54*, R ketch, 32 tons
> *Nordia Cruiser 58*, R ketch, 33 tons
> 61′ R motorsailor ketch, 45 tons
> *Calculus 61*, R ketch, 45 tons
> *Nordia Cruiser 66*, R ketch, 52 tons
> 66′ R motorsailor ketch, 52 tons
> *Nordia Cruiser 83*, R ketch, 90 tons
> 83′ R motorsailor ketch, 90 tons

T.D. VINETTE & CO. / Box 416 / Port Escanaba, MI 49829
Tel. (906) 786-1884

Vinette & Co. has been an established custom yard since 1947, building both power and sailboats. They've constructed many commercial hulls, including tugs and ferry boats, as well as various round hull yachts designed by Lucander, Brewer, Mason, and Prescott. Their facilities are quite large, as is the crew, and they can handle up to 8 vessels at a time. They do their own rolling and forming, and are very capable with round hulls, for which they charge about 15% more. They also build some of their own designs.

> *Lucander 41* and *45*, ketches
> *Miami 45* (Brewer), R ketch
> *Mason 40*, DC cutter
> Numerous others

DE VRIES YACHT BUILDERS / Oosteinderweg 25 / Box 258
Aalsmeer / Holland / Tel. 02977-21551

The yard has been building mostly round steel hulls since 1929.

> 51′ R center-cockpit motorsailor ketch
> 58′ ketch
> 60′ *Jonathan Swift*, R cutter
> 66′ R motorsailor ketch
> 118′ R staysail schooner (de Vries Lentsch)

WASHBURN, DOUGHTY & ASSOC. / Enterprise St. / East Boothbay, ME
Tel. (207) 633-6517

Washburn & Doughty have been working with chine steel hulls for 8 years, and recently built the *Bay Lady II*, a 60′ multi-chine passenger schooner. They work from plans by Washburn and S. Jones, and deliver only completed yachts. With 30–50 employees, four boats are built at a time. They prefer not to build round hulls.

WATERCRAFT / The Boatyard, Common Road / Evesham, Worcs. / England

The yard has built some of Alan Pape's designs. Sorry, no other data.

426

WATERLINE YACHTS / 10223C McDonald Park Rd. / P.O. Box 2576
Sidney, B.C. / Canada V8L 4C1 / Tel. (604) 656-9331

The partners in Waterline Yachts have participated in the design and construction of over 20 metal boats, and each has a college education in metal boat design and construction. This combination allows them a high degree of flexibility in the modification of existing designs. They specialize in moderate-displacement, molded-radius, in-house designs, and offer construction of other designs, especially those of Robert Harris and John Simpson. They have developed a unique framing system which eliminates "hungy horse" ribs. A computer-controlled flame cutter has been developed in-house to pattern and cut heavier plating, while nibblers and a plasma arc cutter are used on lighter materials. Waterline can build either a hull-deck shell or a complete yacht with custom interior.

Waterline 333, R cutter, 14,000 lbs.	$19,700 CAN
Waterline 363, R cutter	25,700
Waterline 363 Pilothouse	26,300
Vancouver 38 (Robert Harris)	32,000
Waterline 424	32,000
Perelandra 43 (Simpson)	

WHANGEREI ENGINEERING & CONSTRUCTION LTD. (WECO)
P.O. Box 24 / Whangerei / New Zealand

WECO is a large operation that has been in business since 1963 building primarily commercial vessels such as tugs, fishing boats, dredgers, and naval craft. They have constructed some sailing yachts, principally in steel, although they also have the facilities to fabricate aluminum hulls and superstructures. A staff of approximately 150 can build yachts to any stage, and there are many outside contractors in the are who could finish out the boat if desired.

Pacemaker 40, fin keel
Warwick 60, full-keel cutter
78' R motorsailor ketch
130' replica of *HMAS Bounty*, R square-rigged brig

IVAN WILSON / #39-2665 Cape Horn Ave. / Coquitlan, B.C.
Canada V3K 6B8 / Tel. (604) 525-3927

Mr. Wilson has been involved in boatbuilding for 14 years, having learned the craft from his father. Most of his experience is with commercial vessels, both steel and aluminum, ranging in size from 30–75'. At present, however, is is focusing on steel yacht construction. Last year he completed a 51' steel yacht and a 33' aluminum boat, both double-chine designs of John Simpson's. Those vessels were bare-hull assemblies, but he will price and build to any stage with the help of other qualified contractors.

PAUL WINCH YACHT BUILDERS / Chambers Wharf, Abbey Road
Faversham, Kent / England ME13 7BT / Tel. Faversham (0795) 537056

This yard, located in a traditional shipbuilding town, specializes in shoal-draft craft, especially their gaff-rigged *Southcountryman* barge yawls, modeled after the Thames River barges. Steel is exploited to the full in these boats, which use heavy construction low down as ballast. The head of the yard has 27 years of experience in boatbuilding, principally with steel, and is also a naval architect who prefers single- and multi-chine designs. The *Southcountryman* barge is an exclusive with the yard, but they also have other designs available.

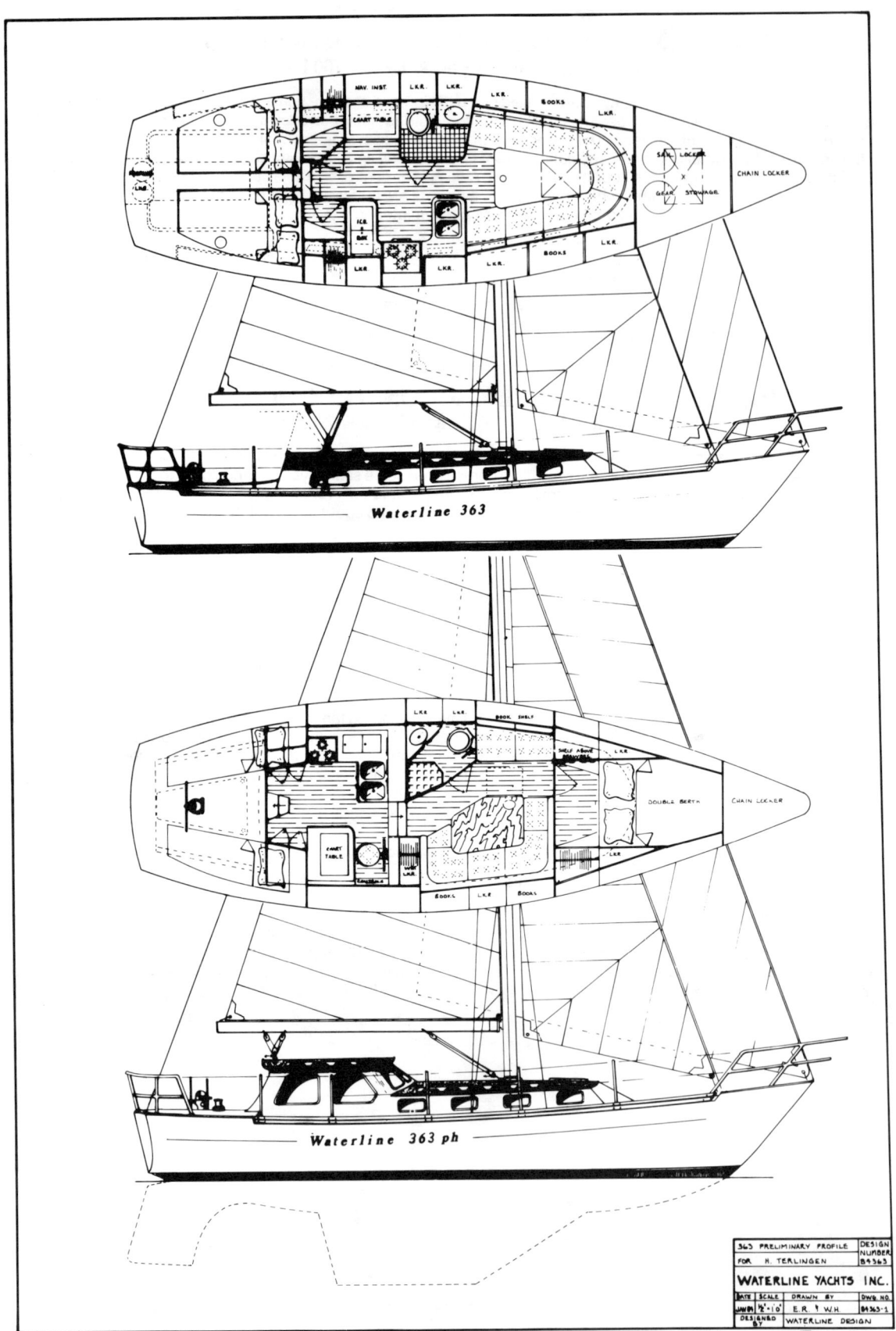

Waterline 363, *designed and built by Waterline Yachts.*

—Index—————————————

ABOUT THE AUTHORS

The first sounds that **LeCain Smith** remembers hearing are the bell buoys rocking on the ocean swells off the down-east coast of Maine, where he was born. As a Coast-Guard licensed captain, he has sailed over 50,000 miles on different boats in the Atlantic and Caribbean, completed various yacht deliveries, and taught sailing and navigation in Florida. The six-time harbormaster of Port Townsend's Wooden Boat festival has made an active career out of boat-building and repair, outfitting boats, marine surveying, and collecting file cases full of information. He is presently completing his own boat for world cruising while turning his attention to the production of sea videos. Look out for *Cats at Sea* and *Perelandra in Paradise*.

Sheila Moir is a waterfront lady from the shores of Lake Erie, now at the intermediate adventurer stage. She brings to the project a background in technical editing, writing, and typesetting. A woman of diverse interests, she is a retired social worker and a founding member of the Children's Workshop Theater of Port Townsend. She is in love with the English language.

Both are looking forward to cruising the world on their new steel sailboat, *Perelandra*. Row over and say hello.

Designed by Cindy Wacker

Text edited on an Epson QX-10 using the Spellbinder Word Processing program

Composed by Graphiti, Inc., Port Townsend, Washington, in ITC Cheltenham with display lines in Shamrock by Alan Withers

Printed by McNaughton & Gunn, Lithographers Ann Arbor, Michigan

Cover composition by Advertising Services, Inc. Seattle, Washington